Fodor's Features

MAPS

Chapter 1

EXPERIENCE PROVENCE AND THE FRENCH RIVIERA

20 ULTIMATE EXPERIENCES

Provence & the French Riviera offer terrific experiences that should be on every traveler's list. Here are Fodor's top picks for a memorable trip.

1 Pont du Gard

Rising 160 dramatic feet above the Gardon River, the triple-tiered Pont du Gard is France's highest and most beautifully preserved Roman bridge. *(Ch. 3)*

2 Carnival in Nice

Started in 1924, Carnaval de Nice is now the third largest Carnaval celebration in the world, with the Flower Battle parade its biggest event. *(Ch. 7)*

3 Aix-en-Provence

Spend an afternoon at a café on one of Aix-en-Provence's tree-shaded avenues and elegant streets lined with graceful old *hôtel particulières* (family mansions). *(Ch. 5)*

4 The Lavender Route

Join the lavender-happy crowds from June to mid-July and travel the Route de la Lavande, a 560-mile blue-purple swath that produces a third of the world's lavender. *(Ch. 4)*

5 Corniche d'Estérel

Bordered by rocky cliffs and impossibly turquoise waters, the Corniche d'Estérel is one of the most scenic drives along the Riviera, thanks to its breathtaking panoramas. *(Ch. 6)*

6 Èze

The expression "bird's-eye-view" takes on new meaning in Èze, a tiny medieval jewel soaring 1,400 feet above the Riviera. It's a standout for its eye-popping views. *(Ch. 7)*

7 Arles

Immortalized by Vincent van Gogh, who was enchanted with its clear light, ancient Arles is also filled with art museums, galleries, and festivals. *(Ch. 3)*

8 Art Museums

Provence has dozens of excellent art museums filled with the works of artists who fell in love with the region, including Matisse, Renoir, Picasso, Van Gogh, and more. *(Ch. 3–7)*

9 Cannes

Home to the world's most famous film festival, Cannes is an epicenter of French Riviera glamour and bling. *(Ch. 7)*

10 Grasse

The cradle of modern perfumery, Grasse is home to names like Fragonard, Galimard, and Molinardoffer, where you can take workshops to learn the industry's secrets and create your very own perfume. *(Ch. 7)*

11 The Camargue

At the southern reaches of Provence is the Camargue, where you'll feel you've come to the ends of the earth. The nature park is filled with French cowboys, bulls, and birds, including 50,000 flamingos. *(Ch. 3)*

12 Perched Villages

Provence's gravity-defying medieval perched villages, from Gordes to Lacoste, are little glimpses into another time. *(Ch. 3–7)*

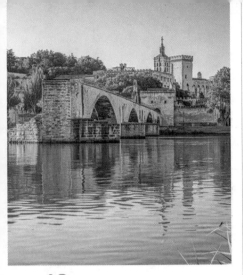

13 Avignon

Once the Holy Roman Empire's papal seat, today ancient Avignon holds some of the region's most important arts festivals, like the Avignon Festival and Le Festival OFF. (*Ch. 4*)

14 Wine-Tasting on the Côtes du Rhône

The celebrated appellations of the Côtes du Rhône are named for its villages and regions: Gigondas, Beaumes-de-Venise, Châteauneuf-du-Pape, Côtes du Luberon, and more. (*Ch. 4*)

15 Beaches in St-Tropez

When Bridget Bardot kicked up some sand on the Plage de Pampelonne, St-Tropez became an emblem of beachside glam and still beckons with its white sand beaches (a rarity on the Riviera). (*Ch. 6*)

16 Cap d'Antibes

The Riviera's most exclusive corner is filled with luxury hotels and Michelin-starred restaurants inviting you to live lavishly like Zelda and F. Scott Fitzgerald did, even for just one afternoon. (*Ch. 7*)

17 Gambling in Monte Carlo

This gilded playground in Monaco has captivated European royalty and the international elite since the Belle Époque years of the late 19th century. *(Ch. 8)*

18 Gorges du Verdon

The Gorges du Verdon's vertiginous limestone cliffs have earned the natural wonder the nickname of the Grand Canyon of Europe. *(Ch. 6)*

19 Antique Shopping in L'Isle-sur-la-Sorgue

Famed for its Sunday markets, L'Isle-sur-la-Sorgue is literally wall-to-wall with antique stores of every shape, size, and caliber. *(Ch. 4)*

20 Marseille

Marseille has always been France's quintessential melting pot. Nowadays, its cultural richness is reflected in everything from its museums to its cuisine. *(Ch. 5)*

WHAT'S WHERE

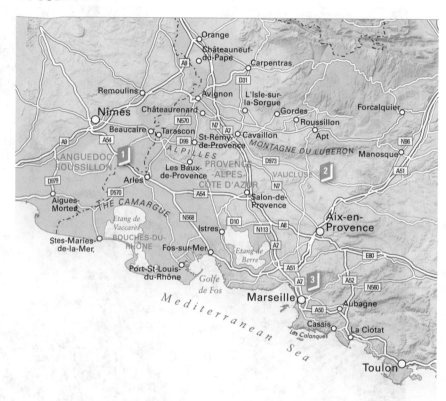

1 Nîmes and the Alpilles.
Between the Rhône River
delta and the hills of the
Alpilles, this region has been
a major crossroads since
Roman times. Haunting
natural beauty can be found
in the Camargue, but nearby
are the cosmopolitan centers
of the feisty Latin Nîmes,
chic St-Rémy, and Van Gogh's
golden Arles.

**2 Avignon and the
Vaucluse.** Anchored by the
medieval city stronghold of
Avignon, the Vaucluse
spreads luxuriantly north
into the Rhône vineyards of
Châteauneuf-du-Pape and
east along the Lavender
Route. Check out the Roman
theater in Orange, then head
to the Luberon—the quintessential Provençal
landscape—set with magical
hilltop towns like Gordes
and Roussillon.

**3 Aix, Marseille, and the
Central Coast.** Famous for
its boulevards, Aix-en-
Provence has a bevy of posh
cafés where you can enjoy
people-watching, just as
Cézanne used to do. South
lies Marseille, France's
second-largest city and a
Mediterranean melting pot.
Studded with the rocky
Calanques, the nearby coast
has pockets of natural
beauty.

4 The Western French Riviera. This is where the legend begins: palm trees, parasol pines, and the improbably blue sea, all framed against the red-rock Massif de l'Estérel. There's St-Tropez, with its white-sand beaches and its port bars thick with off-duty celebs plus *sportif* resorts like St-Raphaël. Inland, the woolly backcountry of Haute-Provence headlines the Gorges du Verdon.

5 Nice and the Eastern French Riviera. This is the heart of the Côte d'Azur. Nice has its Old Town's bonbon-color palaces while eastward lies Cannes, famed for its May film festival, and the zillion-dollar hotels of Cap d'Antibes. The sky may kiss the perched village of Èze, but the rainbow ends in the famous art villages: Renoir's Haut-de-Cagnes, Picasso's Antibes, and Matisse's St-Paul and Vence.

6 Monaco. Take the high-rises of Hong Kong, add the amusement-park feel of Disneyland, and mix in a royal touch, and there you have all 473 acres of Monaco, the playground of royalty, wealthy playboys, and glamorous film stars.

What to Eat and Drink in Provence and the French Riviera

BOUILLABAISSE

Originating from the fishing port of Marseille, this iconic dish consists of a broth of small fish, tomatoes, onion, garlic, fennel, olive oil, and saffron, served with a garlicky bread crumb sauce called rouille. Next, four to six larger fish are added to the soup and served as a second course.

PROVENÇAL ROSÉ WINE

Provence is the world's largest rosé producer, using Grenache, Cinsault, Mourvedre, and Syrah grapes, which help create that pale orange-tinted pink color. You'll find plenty of options to sample here, and you can even visit a few vineyards specializing in rosé production.

FOUGASSE

The Provençal answer to Italian focaccia, this soft flatbread is distinguished by holes that give it the appearance of a lacy leaf. It can be made savory—flavored with olives, anchovy, bacon, cheese, or anything else the baker has on hand—or sweet, enriched with olive oil and dusted with icing sugar.

SALADE NIÇOISE

Forget politics, nothing divides the residents of Nice more than the question of what goes in their beloved salade niçoise. Cooked vegetables are banned from the salad, that's the one rule. And contrary to popular belief, no green beans either. It's a simple recipe of tomatoes, cucumber, peppers, onions, and cooked eggs, with a few leaves of lettuce and tuna if you want to get fancy.

DAUBE DE BOEUF

To distinguish their prized beef stew from *boeuf bourguignon*, Provençal chefs make a point of not marinating the meat, instead cooking it very slowly in tannic red wine that is often flavored with orange zest. In the Camargue, daube is made with local *taureau* (bull's meat) and is considered a specialty of the region, while the Avignon variation uses lamb.

SOUPE AU PISTOU

The Provençal version of pesto, *pistou* consists of the simplest ingredients—garlic, olive oil, fresh basil, and Parmesan—ideally pounded together by hand in a stone mortar with an olive wood pestle. Most traditionally it delivers a potent kick to *soupe au pistou*, a kind of French minestrone made with green beans, white beans, potatoes, and zucchini.

PASTIS

What could be more Provençal than sitting at Les Deux Garçons in Aix-en-Provence sipping

Daube de Boeuf

a pastis? The French put back on average two liters a day of the chalky-light amber, anise-flavored spirit, which is served on ice with a carafe of cold water on the side. After the ban of the hallucinogenic absinthe in 1915, pastis appeared like an aniseed cousin to the green fairy. But not all pastis are created equal. Ricard (now Ricard Pernod) was the first to produce the silky beverage. Newcomer Pastis des Creissauds takes 18 months to make each bottle and aromatizes with notes of fennel, aniseed, and essential oils. Enjoy one as an aperitif, before or after your dinner.

L'ORANGERIE LIQUEUR

What else can you do with Monaco's 600 organic bitter orange trees but make a refreshing liqueur? Young food trader Philip Culazzo had the idea in 2017 to bottle the first premium bitter orange liqueur (30% alcohol) in his Monaco distillery. Try the Monaco Spritz, L'Orangerie, topped up with Prosecco and orange zest, or pick up a retro-designed three-miniature-gift-pack (50 ml) from the atelier as a souvenir.

CITRON PRESSÉ

You can't get fresher lemonade than if you picked the lemon from the tree yourself. Order a satisfying citron pressé in a café and you'll be served a tall glass filled with ice, the juice of a freshly squeezed lemon, a little pitcher of water, and a dish of sugar cubes so you can make it as sweet or as tart as you wish. It's the ultimate refreshing summer drink in France.

NIÇOIS SOCCA

Nice is known for socca, a sort of chickpea flour pancake that Chez Pipo has been making and serving since 1923. It takes a bit of time to get perfectly cooked, so order some of delicious *tartinades*, or local dips, while you wait.

What to Buy in Provence and the French Riviera

HERBS DE PROVENCE

This rock star of spice blends consists of the usual suspects of thyme, rosemary, and bay leaf, with other herbs like oregano, basil, tarragon, marjoram, savory, sage, fennel, and dill thrown in, all grown in the southeast of France.

CALISSON

There's a sweet tooth and then there's the Calissons d'Aix, a regal candy made from a paste of candied fruit and almonds topped with icing sugar; it was first served in 1473 at the second wedding of King René. In the 16th century, as almond trees started to grow around the Aix-en-Provence region, production of the diamond-shape morsel took off. The strict method of making Calissons has been protected in France since 1991, but by the time it took French manufacturers to file a global trademark bid at the Protected Geographical Indication, the trademark had already been snapped up by the Chinese. In 2017, the French Union of Calisson ultimately blocked the Chinese trademark registration, and the darling of Aix returned to its rightful owners. Today, you can find the candy in plenty of stores throughout Provence and discover the origins of Provence's favorite treat (with samples!) at Aix's Musée du Calisson-Confiserie du Roy Réné.

LAVENDER PRODUCTS

Driving through the lavender fields of Provence should be on everyone's bucket list. During the summer bloom, you'll see endless rows of vibrant purple lavandin, or French lavender, a hybrid created in 1920 for the French perfume industry. The less fragrant lavandin produces almost five times more essential oil than true lavender, with 1 ton producing 25 to 40 liters. That's plenty to scent the pretty soaps and candles that visitors shop for, along with the creams and aromatic sprays that can act as disinfectants or help with sunburned lips, dry skin, insect bites, and nausea. But remember: only the label "PDO (AOC or AOP) Lavender Essential Oil" tells you that a product has authentic lavender essential oils from Haute Provence.

OLIVE OIL

While the olive oil product in France doesn't quite match the likes of Italy, Spain, and Greece, the French choose to emphasize quality over quantity. Historically, the town of Roussillon has been the country's leading olive oil producer, creating high-quality, aromatic, and organic olive oils. Visit Domaine les Fonts for a tasting and an oil grove, too. French olive oil is also for sale in many stores and street markets.

PERFUME

Follow your nose to the microclimatic town of Grasse, north of Cannes. Here you'll find the perfume capital of the world, thanks to Jean de Galimard who first invented fashionable perfumed gloves to cover the nauseating smell of tanners (those who regularly tanned and skinned leather hides). Two-hundred-and-fifty years later, the $49.4 billion

Olive oil

global perfume market is booming like never before. But why choose from more than 8,000 perfumes on the market when you can create your own scent? Galimard, Fragonard, and Molinard all offer Make Your Own Perfume workshops, varying from 20 minutes to four hours (which includes a champagne break).

POTTERY

From the moment Picasso met Suzanne and Georges Ramié in 1946 at their ceramics factory in Vallauris in Provence, the pottery industry in France would never be the same. Picasso produced 633 original pieces over 23 years, and the Madoura workshop still attracts art enthusiasts eager to see his clay masterpieces. With the bonus of clay rich soil and hot sun, many villages in the region continue to pay tribute to the country's earthen cookery history, especially in Provence where you find the emblematic sunshine-yellow-color water jugs and two-part olive bowls.

PROVENÇAL FABRIC AND PLACE MATS

It's next to impossible to choose between the Provençal place mats or the matching tablecloth, so just buy both. Known as *les indiennes,* these colorful cottons date back to the 16th century when they were first imported from India to Marseille. The material was so popular with the high bourgeoisie that in 1686, French textile manufacturers in Lyon were so worried about going out of business, they ordered an import ban. This led to Armenian craftsmen coming to France to create similar patterns that you still see today on everything from tablecloths and napkins to clothing and ceramics.

SOCCA CHIPS

New on the gourmand circuit is the chickpea-based Socca Chip, created by Niçois chef Luc Salsedo in 2016. It may look like a nacho chip in shape, but these crunchy snacks are 100% natural (and gluten-free), made from chickpea flour, olive oil, salt, pepper, and sunflower oil. These are the same ingredients for making socca, Nice's version of a pancake. There are now lots of knockoffs, but Salsedo's Socca Chip is authentic and perfect for sampling rosé or any apèro. In March 2019, the chef launched the organic SoccApero, a liquid batter in a bottle that simply requires adding water to make your own socca at home.

Best Villages in Provence

CASSIS

No longer a true hidden gem, Cassis still offers a pleasant respite from Provence's more popular port cities with its dramatic seaside setting, framed by the imposing russet cliffs and the series of calanques (narrow inlets) tucked among them. Winemaking is now the primary activity in the region, but Cassis has maintained its idyllic fishing village vibe.

GORDES

Often listed as one of the most beautiful villages in France, Gordes is a charming mix of sleepy French hillside village and posh resort town. The area is a favorite among celebrities as a quiet summer retreat, but the atmosphere is still unpretentious.

MÉNERBES

This charming village, whose sand-color buildings seem to disappear into the leafy landscape, is dominated by the Protestant-built citadel, a remnant from Ménerbes' time as an important Protestant stronghold during the French Wars of Religion.

SAINT-RÉMY-DE-PROVENCE

If the rolling wheat fields and gnarled olive groves surrounding Saint-Rémy-de-Provence look familiar, don't be surprised; Van Gogh spent a year in a psychiatric hospital here during one of his more productive periods, during which he composed *Starry Night*.

PORQUEROLLES

The largest of the Îles d'Hyères, Porquerolles has some of the best beaches in all of Provence. Porquerolles' small village is brand-new compared to most of Provence; constructed in the 19th century, it has an atmosphere more akin to an Italian port town than a hillside Roman village.

L'ISLE-SUR-LA-SORGUE

Situated on the banks of the Sorgue River, this town is a shopper's paradise, only instead of shopping malls and boutiques, visitors are met with fabulous antiques stores and bustling weekend markets. Wake up early to stroll along the stalls at the famous Sunday market.

ROUSSILLON

At sunset, the village of Roussillon practically glows, its fiery red and orange buildings lighting up the surrounding landscape. Its unique color palette—most Provençal towns are a study in sandy beiges and creamy whites—is due to the large ocher clay deposits in the vicinity.

LACOSTE

Old stone houses made from ochre limestone are just the first pages of this storybook village. As you walk deeper through the streets, history unfolds to reveal medieval architecture and the town's famous 11th-century château that was home to the Marquis de Sade.

LE BARROUX

Few places in Provence feel further removed from the well-trod tourist path than Le Barroux. The tiny village is seemingly one giant looping street, with impossibly narrow alleyways punctuated by mint green and robin's egg blue shutters and window flower boxes hanging from the rugged stone facades.

VAISON-LA-ROMAINE

It wasn't the Romans but the Celts who were the first people to settle this picturesque hill in the Vaucluse department. Today, Vaison-la-Romaine is a charming mix of the old and new, with the steep medieval-era streets leading up to the Colline de Château on the south side of Ouvèze River.

Best Beaches in the French Riviera

Plage de la Salis, Antibes

PLAGE DE LA SALIS, ANTIBES

One of the coastline's more glamorous addresses, Antibes is lined with beaches both public and private. The Plage de la Salis has golden sands (don't dig too deep as there are pebbles underneath) and stunning views of the old town, mountains, and the Garoupe lighthouse.

PLAGE DE LA GAROUPE, CAP D'ANTIBES

A long, sandy beach on a sparkling bay favored by sailboats, Plage de la Garoupe is one of the loveliest in Cap d'Antibes. While several sections of the beach are private (it's the only beach in Cap d'Antibes with any private sands), there are designated public areas.

PORT DE CROUTON PLAGE, JUAN-LES-PINS

On the west side of Cap d'Antibes lies the charming village of Juan-les-Pins, well-known as the 1920s home of writer F. Scott Fitzgerald, his wife Zelda, and their daughter Scottie (their actual house is now the five-star Belles Rives Hotel). Port de Crouton is smaller than Juan-les-Pins's other main beaches and

The Calanques, Cassis

sheltered by stone jetties on either side.

THE CALANQUES, CASSIS

Like tiny pockets of paradise, more than a dozen azure blue Calanques can be found tucked away in the rocky cliffs between Marseille and Cassis, a charming fishing village that's now a favorite of European tourists.

PLAGE DES MARINIÈRES, VILLEFRANCHE-SUR-MER

A little ways east of Villefranche-sur-Mer city center, the Plage des Marinières curves around the bay for nearly a mile past the old town. Between steep cliffs and the glimmering sea, with excellent views of Villefranche, this narrow, coarse white sand beach is a stunner.

PLAGE DE PALOMA, ST-JEAN-CAP-FERRAT

Jutting into the sea between Nice and Monaco, St-Jean-Cap-Ferrat is one of the world's most fabulous addresses. You can also experience this haven of calm at the Plage de Paloma, one of the peninsula's five beaches and a top contender for St-Jean-Cap-Ferrat's most Instagrammable beach.

TAHITI BEACH, ST-TROPEZ

The famous Tahiti Beach can be found at the northernmost edge of Pampelonne Beach's 3-mile stretch of white sand—half in St-Tropez and half in Ramatuelle—that can be reached from Pampelonne. Head for the stand of pine trees and be prepared for bathers in various stages of undress, as this is the Riviera's legendary "clothing-optional" beach.

PLAGE DE LA RÉPUBLIQUE, FRÉJUS

A long, sprawling beach fronting the pleasant town of Fréjus, in the Var region of Provence, Plage de la République is the most central of Fréjus's four beaches. The beach's large expanse of fine-grained sand and calm waters attract serious swimmers while its proximity to the Fréjus Nautical Club makes it an ideal beach for water sports.

PLAGE BEAU-RIVAGE, ST-RAPHAEL

Set between the Veillat Beach and the Santa Lucia port, Plage Beau-Rivage is lined with a pretty promenade and a leafy park. The beach itself is a mix of sand and pebbles, with tranquil waters and wonderful views of the bay of St-Raphael and Lion de Mer Island.

Best Art Towns in Provence and the French Riviera

ARLES
This town's light, landscapes, and characters inspired Van Gogh's greatest masterpieces. The Fondation Vincent Van Gogh commemorates the artist while cultural center Luma Arles adds to the city's artistic allure.

HAUT-DE-CAGNES
Cagnes-sur-Mer may seem like nothing to write home about, but its hilltop old town is among the loveliest perched villages in Provence and particularly adored by artist Auguste Renoir. The town is home to Musée Renoir, the building where Renoir spent his last 12 years.

ST-PAUL-DE-VENCE
In St-Paul-de-Vence, you'll find the famed La Colombe d'Or Inn, where artists paid for their stays with artwork and today proudly displays art by the likes of Picasso, Matisse, and Miro. The town also is home to the Fondation Maeght, France's first art foundation and one of the largest modern art collections in Europe.

NICE
Henri Matisse's love affair with Nice lasted 37 years until the artist's death in 1954; he had a total of four dwelling places in the city, and the fourth and final is now the Musée Matisse. The city also has the Musée National Marc Chagall and the Musée des Arts Asiatiques.

ANTIBES
Several famous artists have fallen in love with the ancient city of Antibes over the years, including Monet, Cross, Boudin, and Harpignies, but Picasso left the biggest mark. On a cobbled street in the charming old town of Antibes, with beautiful views of the sea, the Musée Picasso is housed in the 17th-century Château Grimaldi, where Picasso worked in an attic studio for six happy months.

MARSEILLE
The cultural scene of Marseille was robust even before the city's resurgence, but since its year-long stint as a European Capital of Culture in 2013, the city has been unstoppable. Famed museums include the Musée des Civilisations de l'Europe et de la Méditerranée (or the Mucem, as it's commonly called), the Regards de Provence, the Musée d'Archéologie Méditerranéenne and the Musée d'Arts Africains, Océaniens et Amérindiens, and finally, Cité Radieuse, Le Corbusier's experiment in collective living.

Nice

AVIGNON

Avignon is an epicenter for the arts in Provence, starting with the Avignon Festival, and its offshoot, the more edgy Le Festival OFF, Europe's biggest contemporary performing arts festival and France's oldest. Museums also flourish here: the Musée du Petit Palais, the Musée Calvet, the Musée Angladon, and,

of course, the Collection Lambert, one of France's great modern and contemporary art collections.

VALLAURIS

Picasso's giant Riviera footprint extends 4 miles from Antibes and Juan-les-Pins to Vallauris, where he lived from 1948 until 1955, and where he married François Gilot in top secret

at the Vallauris town hall. An old pottery town, Vallauris was pivotal for Picasso, who began his fertile foray into ceramics and sculpture there.

VENCE

Among the many attractions in Vence are a charming old town, a top-notch morning market, and Henri Matisse's exquisite Chapelle du Rosaire, aka the Matisse Chapel. The immaculate white structure, a gift to the nuns who nursed him through an illness, is all the more moving for its purity and simplicity.

AIX-EN-PROVENCE

Famed Postimpressionist painter Paul Cezanne was born, raised, and died in Aix-en-Provence, and the city's gorgeous light and stunning colors are said to have inspired much of his work. Today, its famed art museums include Musée Granet, the Fondation Victor Vasarely, and Atelier Cézanne.

Provence Today

POLITICS

The local political climate can be summed up in one word: immigration. Neighboring Italy saw 23,000 migrants arriving by boat in 2018 (up from more than 18,000 in 2017), making it hard not to notice those who manage to get past the Ventimiglia border into Menton, France. Eritreans, Syrians, and Somalians are often living on the beach or camped out at train stations, especially in main towns like Nice, which can take them north to their probable destination: England via Calais. The Provence-Cote-d'Azur region, otherwise known as PACA, has always leaned heavily to the right politically, but between its 10.4% unemployment rate, ranking of the fourth poorest zone in France (17% of the population live off €990 a month), and a deeply divided growing migrant crisis, the extreme-right, antiimmigration, antigay Rassemblement National (the new name for the National Front, renamed in an effort to soften its racist image) has maintained its momentum in the south, despite President Macron's handy national win over Marine Le Pen in 2017. An unprecedented 14 FN party members were elected mayors throughout the 2010s, including David Rachline in Fréjus, who made headlines when he told local artists to give free workshops to schoolchildren or lose their subsidized studios. In Nice, Marion Maréchal-Le Pen, the granddaughter of the FN's founder Jean-Marie Le Pen, swept the first round of regional elections in December 2015, only to be slightly edged out in the second round by Nice Mayor Christian Estrosi, head of "Les Républicains" (Nicolas Sarkozy's rebranded right-wing party). Still, this was seen as a monumental victory for the girl wonder of the extreme-Right and her party gained even more momentum during the 2019 European Union elections, which saw Reassemblement National come in first with 24% of the vote. The next round of municipal elections will happen in 2020.

FOOD

The rule of thumb, according to locals, is that American trends come to Provence and the rest of France about 10 years later than the rest of the world. Take fast food: obesity rates in France have reached unprecedented heights, at 19.8% of the population (compared to 33% stateside), and the French are in fact the second biggest consumers of Big Macs outside of the United States and sales at fast-food chains now beat out traditional restaurants. These days the French spend less than 30 minutes eating the average meal (down from 1 hour and 20 minutes in 1975), and even daily bread consumption has fallen from a whole baguette per person 30 years ago to less than half that in 2018. Conversely, France's sales of gluten-free breads tripled over the last five years while trendy vegan cafés and organic shops keep popping up along the coast. Provence is now seeing the rise of nongluten haute cuisine, unheard of only a year or two ago. One thing you still won't see in the south of France is people eating on-the-go; civility still rules when it comes to sitting down for a meal, however quick.

LANGUAGE

For those who want to come across as a veritable native, ditch the touristy name "French Riviera" in favor of Côte d'Azur, a phrase coined by Stéphen Liégeard in 1887, as pronunciation en français is what truly distinguishes American visitors from other nationalities. For example, when Americans say Cannes, the city of the famous international film festival, it comes across as "Cans," but in French the "s" at the end of a word is silent. Ditto for Antibes, Picasso's adopted town east of Can-ne. For the most part you'll find most waiters and shopkeepers will grunt a few reassuring words in English, but if you want to buy a train ticket from a station machine there is no language option, so it's all in French. If all else fails, Google Translate or a free language app is just one touch away on your tablet or smartphone. Luckily, there are several local English-language media outlets available: Riviera Radio 106.5 from Monaco broadcasts news, weather, and traffic while the free *Riviera Reporter* magazine can be downloaded to your iPad or picked up at the three English-language bookstores in Antibes, Cannes, and Valbonne.

CAFÉS

Although many local traditions are falling by the wayside, café culture is very much alive in the south of France. You will not see the French sipping from an insulated mug in their car or on the bus. Most stop by their local haunt for an unhurried *café* (espresso), which they enjoy sitting or standing at the bar, sipping every last caffeinated drop. So what to order? Order a *petit café,* or *un express,* and a tiny shot of coffee will be placed before you. If you prefer to keep your eyes in their sockets, try a *café américain* (also known as a *café allongé*), which is that same espresso diluted with more water and put in a bigger cup. Sugar will always be served on your saucer, but you'll need to ask for milk. Coffee aficionados can relax, as the craft coffee craze has arrived from Paris to the south, with barista cafés springing up everywhere in Provence. Dairy options are still limited, but more cafés are offering low-fat milk. For the lactose intolerant, there are more and more places in Nice that serve soy milk, including Café Marché, Loving Hut in Menton, or Starbucks in Monaco. One last piece of coffee advice: it's only tourists who order their evening coffee at the same time as dessert—everyone else orders it afterward.

THE WEALTHY

If you want to be part of the Riviera in-crowd, you have to play by the rules. Don't bat an eyelash at spending €50 for a breakfast that consists of a croissant and coffee or €14 for a beer in a hotel, as this is how the richest 1% live. And €500 for a bottle of champagne to spray poolside at Nikki beach in St-Tropez? Order two! That said, it's absolutely worth splashing out extra for that upgraded sea-view suite or splurging on a Michelin meal with a Mediterranean view. The impeccable service and superstar treatment will make all the difference between a once-in-a-lifetime vacation and returning home with regrets. And not to worry, the only thing that separates you and the jet-setter at the next table is his Philippe Patek watch. But there is a price to pay for being loaded; in the eyes of would-be thieves any English-speaking tourist or expat here is considered rich.

COVID-19

A new novel coronavirus brought all travel to a virtual standstill in the first half of 2020. Although the illness is mild in most people, some experience severe and even life-threatening complications.

Older adults have a greater chance of having severe complications from COVID-19. The same is true for people with weaker immune systems or those with certain medical conditions. Two weeks before a trip, be on the lookout for some of the following symptoms: cough, fever, chills, trouble breathing, muscle pain, sore throat, new loss of smell or taste. If you experience any of these symptoms, do not travel.

To protect yourself during travel, wash your hands often with soap and water. Limit your time in public places, and, when you are out and about, wear a cloth face mask that covers your nose and mouth.

Bring extra supplies, such as disinfecting wipes, hand sanitizer (12-ounce bottles were allowed in carry-on luggage at this writing), and a first-aid kit with a thermometer.

What to Read and Watch Before You Go

A YEAR IN PROVENCE BY PETER MAYLE

For many years, the south of France was a mecca for British ex-pats, many of whom were inspired by this book by Peter Mayle about his attempts to live the good life in an exceptional corner of the world. Half-cautionary tale and half-amusing memoir, A Year in Provence gives great insight into how wonderful and frustrating living in France can be.

ESCAPE FROM AMERICA, EXILE IN PROVENCE BY JULES B. FARBER

After living in other cities in Europe, including Paris, the great American writer James Baldwin settled in St-Paul-de-Vence in a small house that would become a major epicenter for visiting French and American artists, writers, poets, and musicians. Driven by pervasive racism and homophobia to leave the United States, Baldwin found in Provence a haven where he could live and write in peace. In this book, writer Jules B. Farber explores these 17 years through interviews with various figures who knew Baldwin, including Toni Morrison, Maya Angelou, and Quincy Jones as well as local residents of St-Paul-de-Vence.

BONJOUR TRISTESSE BY FRANÇOISE SAGAN

While these days most teenagers might aspire to go viral, back in the day young writers like Françoise Sagan dreamt of literary accolades. Her first novel, published in 1954 when she was just 18, became an overnight sensation. The plot revolves around a bored young girl and her equally bored philandering father who both find themselves bereft of meaning and love while spending the summer on the French Riviera. Spoiler alert: there is no happy ending.

TWO TOWNS IN PROVENCE BY M.F.K. FISHER

Told in a vivid, literary style, this is the tale of two rival cities: Marseille and Aix-en-Provence—where Fisher lived for a year from 1954 to 1955. A friend of Julia Child, Richard Olney, and the group of trail-blazing food writers who put Provençal cooking on the map, Fisher made many journeys to Provence between the 1930s and the 1970s. In this story, alone in Aix with her two daughters aged 8 and 11, she describes a now-vanished Provence still reeling from World War II, through candid and insightful descriptions of the people she meets, from proud yet penniless aristocrats to her café waiter.

TENDER IS THE NIGHT BY F. SCOTT FITZGERALD

F. Scott Fitzgerald is the one who redefined the tourism industry for France in the early 20th century. In the 1920s, he was invited, along with his wife Zelda Fitzgerald, to the French Riviera to spend time with some friends near Antibes and his descriptions of the area changed the tourist season from winter to summer. Inspired by his lifestyle there, Fitzgerald wrote his fourth and final novel, which he considered his best work.

MARSEILLE

While the south of France is famous for scenic sea views, long hot summers, and endless rosé with every meal, it can also have a darker side. The Netflix television series Marseille explores the politics and culture of France's second largest city. The series stars Gerard Depardieu as the city's mayor of 20 years, who enters a war of succession with his political rival. It gives great insight into how local politics work, as well as showing you a part of France that is definitely not on the tourist map.

Chapter 2

TRAVEL SMART PROVENCE

Updated by
Nancy Heslin

ḯ POPULATION:
5 million

⌨ LANGUAGE:
French

$ CURRENCY:
Euro

☎ COUNTRY CODE:
33

⚠ EMERGENCIES:
112

🚗 DRIVING:
On the right

⚡ ELECTRICITY:
220v/50 cycles; electrical
plugs have two round prongs

🕐 TIME:
Six hours ahead of New York

🌐 WEB RESOURCES:
us.franceguide.com
www.paris.fr/english

What You Need to Know Before You Go

Provence is a large region, with several distinct cultures and landscapes, but no matter where you're going, here are a few tips that will help your trip go as smoothly as possible.

SUMMER IS A TOUGH TIME TO VISIT.

July and August can be stifling here, not only because of the intense heat but because of the crowds of tourists and vacationers (almost all of France goes on holiday the second half of July and all of August). Don't travel on or around July 14 (Bastille Day) or August 1, 15, and 31, when every French family is either driving to or from home. Free of midsummer crowds, June comes with balmy weather and long daylight hours, although cheaper prices and many warm days often lasting well into October make September equally as attractive. Watch out for May, riddled with church holidays—one per week— and the museum and store closings they entail, as well as reduced public transportation. Anytime between March and November will offer you a good chance to soak up the sun on the Côte d'Azur although usually April and October are the wettest months, but climate change plays its hand here, too, so expect the unexpected. After November 1, the whole region begins to shut down for winter, and main resort hotels don't

open until Easter. Still, off-season has its charms: the pétanque pitches are just the town folks' game, the most touristy hill towns are virtually abandoned, and when it's nice out you can bask in direct sun in the cafés. Although be aware that in winter (and sometimes spring), "le Mistral," a bone-chilling north wind phenomenon, brings 60-mph (100-kph) gusts, making the area most inhospitable.

KNOW WHEN PLACES MIGHT BE CLOSED.

With 11 national *jours feriés* (holidays) and five weeks of paid vacation, the French have their share of repose. Be sure to check Facebook feeds or check directly with museums, restaurants, and hotels in advance to make sure they will be open to avoid disappointment during these key dates. Holidays to keep in mind: January 1, New Year's Day; early to mid-April, Easter and Easter Monday; May 1, Labor Day; May 8, VE Day; mid- to late May, Ascension; late May–early June, Pentecost Monday; July 14, Bastille Day; August 15, Assumption; November 1, All Saints; November 11, Armistice; December 25,

Christmas. Tourist sites are nearly all closed on New Year's, Labor Day, and Christmas.

THE BEACHES MIGHT NOT BE WHAT YOU EXPECT.

With worldwide fame as the earth's most glamorous coastline, the beaches here often come as a shock to first-timers: much of the Côte d'Azur is lined with rock and pebble, and the beaches are narrow swaths backed by city streets or roaring highways. Some beaches are reviled for their famous *galets*, or round white stones the size of a fist, heaped along the shoreline, just where the sand should be. There are some natural-sand beaches on the southern French coast—especially between St-Tropez and Cannes—and beaches like La Garoupe on Cap d'Antibes enjoy legendary status. Provence's coastline—between the Camargue and St-Tropez— alternates sandy pockets with rocky inlets called *criques* and *calanques*, where you can perch on black rocks and ease yourself into the turquoise water.

In many of the resort towns along the coast you are charged a fee to use the restaurant/hotel beaches, which usually includes a sun-lounger and a parasol (you can often use many hotel beaches for free if you drink or dine on them). There are stretches of public beach where you'll need to bring your own parasol, sun chair, and towel. Be sure to arrive early in the summer, as all beaches are popular with locals.

A sign of the times: there are now 23 smoke-free beaches (*plage sans tabac*) along the Côte d'Azur and five beaches with jellyfish (*méduse*) nets. Both public and private beaches usually post warnings daily if there are jellies. And if you're on the fence about ditching that bikini top, according to a survey by the French Institute for Public Opinion published in July 2019, the number of French women who sunbathe topless dipped from 29% to 19% over the past three years (down from 43% in 1984).

BE ON THE LOOK-OUT FOR A PÉTANQUE GAME.

In every village from the Rhône Valley to the Italian border, under every deep-shaded plane tree, the theater of Provençal life plays itself out slowly, serenely, and sociably. The café is a way of life in Provence, a cool outdoor living room where friends gather like family and share the ritual of the long, slow drink, the discussion of the weather (hot), and an amble over to the *pétanque* (lawn-bowling) court. The players stand, somber and intense, hands folded behind backs, and watch the intricate play of heavy metal balls rolling and clicking. A knot of onlookers gathers, disperses, is reinforced. In this region of the animated debate, the waving gesture, the forefinger punching the chest, it is a surprisingly quiet pastime.

RENTING A CAR MIGHT BE THE WAY TO GO.

When not on strike, the SNCF train service is a scenic and time-efficient option to travel along the coast, but if you want to reach all those perched villages, driving is the only option. When it comes to car rentals, forget the SUV and go for a small car that's easy to maneuver along tiny village cobblestone streets or to parallel park. Check that the vehicle has GPS (and in English!) and be sure to enter the full name of your destination: for instance, use "St-Paul-de-Vence" and not just St-Paul. The downside of driving is that France's toll highways can add up quickly; Paris to Nice is nearly €77.10 one-way, so if you have the time, stick to the National (RN) or District (RD) roads.

BE PREPARED FOR SOME HIGH (LIKE, REALLY HIGH) PRICES IN CERTAIN TOWNS, BUT YOU CAN COME HERE WITHOUT BREAKING THE BANK.

Yes, you are visiting a place that is widely considered a playground for the rich and famous, and while it's true that you could easily spend a lifetime's fortune in just a weekend here at some hotels and restaurants, mere mortals can (and do) visit this area without going bankrupt. Many French tourism websites have a section that lists free stuff (concerts, Wi-Fi, exhibits, food, etc.) while "greeters" are locals who give free tours (tip recommended) and national museums are free the first Sunday of each month. Buy

tickets online when you can; most cultural centers, museums, and tour companies offer reduced ticket sales in advance, and the small service fee you'll pay might be worth the time saved waiting in admission lines. City tourism cards, like the French Riviera Pass, can save you money if you're planning on serious sightseeing (and can allow you to bypass the lines) and usually include public transport.

And remember, this is France, where nearly every town has a food market, so pack a picnic and stay hydrated. Take a water bottle with you and fill it up for free at one of the numerous *eau potable* fountains and, later in the day, look for happy hour drinks at reduced prices in many of the city's bars and café. There are free public restrooms in department stores, and many parks and cultural sites have toilets. And even if you end up spending €27 for a glass of water at Jimmy'z in Monaco or €150 on a piece of langouste you unknowingly ordered that is priced per 100/grams, remind yourself you're lucky to be experiencing a part of the world many others can only dream of—and think of the colorful story you'll be able to tell post-trip.

Getting Here and Around

The "Getting Here" sections listed under towns in the regional chapters of this book provide detailed information about bus and train routes; in many cases, prices, transport companies, and schedules to and from the towns are listed. It's possible to see the entire region just by taking the train: there are comprehensive connections all the way from Montpellier to Avignon to Marseille and on to the full length of the Italian coast. There are also good regional bus networks that connect out of train stations; they may not be the best thing for quick village-hopping and multistop sightseeing (their schedules rarely intersect with yours), but they can prove highly useful. When in doubt, check out tourist office websites or ask your hotel concierge for more information.

 ## Air

Flying time to Paris is 75 minutes from London, 7½ hours from New York, 8 hours 10 minutes from Chicago, and just under 11 hours from Los Angeles. A direct flight from New York to Nice is eight hours. Scheduled flying time between Paris to either Marseille or Nice is approximately 1½ hours. Given the possibility of strikes in France, it's a good idea to confirm your flight online the day before.

AIRPORTS
The major gateways to France are Paris's Orly and Charles de Gaulle airports. Nice, Marseille, and Montpellier's airports are also served by frequent flights from Paris and London, and daily connections from Paris arrive at the smaller airports in Avignon and Nîmes.

FLIGHTS
Most major airlines fly to Paris and have connecting flights to the south of France on domestic airlines. The one exception is Delta, which flies nonstop to Nice from New York. From the United Kingdom, EasyJet offers inexpensive nonstop service to Nice and Marseille; British Airways has direct flights to Nice and Marseille; low-cost Ryanair flies to Nîmes and Marseille.

Within France, Air France flies frequently from Paris to Marseille, Nice, Montpellier, and Toulon. EasyJet has flights from both Paris airports to Nice.

 ## Bus

Long-distance buses are rare; regional buses are found mainly where train service is spotty. The weakest rail links in the south lie in the Luberon region of the Vaucluse, in the Alpilles, and in the backcountry of the Haut Var, Haute-Provence, and the pre-Alpes behind Nice. To explore these regions, you must work closely with a bus schedule (available at most train stations and sometimes online through tourist offices) and plan connections carefully. Don't plan on too much multistop sightseeing if you're limited to bus connections, as they rarely dovetail with your plans. To visit the popular hill towns just behind the Côte d'Azur— Grasse, St-Paul, Vence, and Biot—you can catch a regional bus or watch for commercial bus excursions advertised in the bigger coastal resorts. Tourist offices and their websites provide information on accompanied excursions.

Buses from the United Kingdom generally depart from London, traveling via hovercraft or ferry from London to Paris. If you're planning to travel extensively throughout Europe, you may wish to purchase a Eurolines Europass, valid for unlimited bus travel between 49 European cities (London, Paris, and Marseille included) for up to 30 days.

Car

Car travel is the best way to see Provence, especially because buses go to the famous hilltop villages only once a day. However, a car may not be the fastest or most economical way to actually get to Provence: consider flying into Paris, connecting via a smaller airline to Nice or Marseille, and then renting a car in the south. Or purchase a rail-drive pass, available from the SNCF (French national rail company) or one of the larger car-rental companies. This will allow a few days' rail travel—say, from Paris to Nice—and a block of car-rental time. By using the train to cover the long distances, then exploring the region in depth by car, you can make the most of both modes of transit.

France's roads are classified into three types and prefixed *A, N,* or *D.* For the fastest roads between two points, look for roads marked *A* for *autoroutes.* A *péage* (toll) must be paid on most expressways: the rate varies but can be steep. Sample toll charges are €77.10 from Paris to Nice, €17.90 from Nice to Aix-en-Provence. At your first toll stop you will simply retrieve a ticket, and at the next toll you will pay. You may pay by credit card; Visa and American Express are accepted at most toll booths. The main toll roads through Provence are the A6 and A7, which connect Paris to Marseille via Lyon, Avignon, and Aix; and the east–west A8, which traverses the region from the Italian border to Aix via Nice.

The *N* (Route Nationale) roads, which are sometimes divided highways, are the route of choice for heavy freight trucks, and are often lined with industry and large chain stores. More scenic, though less trafficked than the Ns, are the *D* (Route Départementale) roads, often also wide and fast. Although routes are numbered, the French generally guide themselves from city to city and town to town by destination name.

Negotiating the back roads requires a careful mix of GPS navigation and sign reading, often at high speeds around suburban *giratoires* (rotaries, also known as roundabouts). But once you head out into the hills and the tiny roads, which are one of the best parts of Provence and the French Riviera, give yourself over to road signs and pure faith. Directions are indicated by village name only, with route numbers given as a small-print afterthought. Of course, this means you have to recognize the names of minor villages en route.

To leave Paris by car, figure out which of the *portes* (gates) corresponds to the direction you are going. Major highways connect to Paris at these points, and directions are indicated by major cities. For instance, heading south out of the city, look for Porte d'Orléans (direction Lyons and Bordeaux); after Lyons, follow Avignon, and after Avignon follow Nice and/or Marseille. It's best to steer clear of rush hours (7–9:30 am and 4:30–7:30 pm), although this is only a real concern between Aix and Marseille and around Nice.

GASOLINE

Gas is expensive, especially on expressways and in rural areas (if you recall, France's Yellow Vest movement in November 2018 was a protest against a tax on petrol and diesel). When possible, buy gas before you get on the expressway and keep an eye on pump prices as you go. These are roughly €1.51 per liter,

Getting Here and Around

or about $6 per gallon. The cheapest gas can be found at *hypermarchés* (very large supermarkets), but be ready for long lines. It is possible to go for many miles in the country without passing a gas station—don't let your tank get too low in rural areas. If you are worried about your budget, ask for a diesel car (€0.84/liter); diesel fuel at gas pumps can be labeled as *diesel, gasoil,* or *gazole.* Unleaded gas will be labeled as *sans plomb* (SP95 for regular unleaded and SP98 for super unleaded). Be careful, as some gas stations still sell leaded gas.

PARKING

Parking can be difficult in large towns; your best option (especially in a metropolis like Nice or Marseille) is to duck into the parking garage nearest the neighborhood you want to visit. Carry the ticket with you, and pay at the vending machine–style ticket dispenser before you go back to your car. On the street, ticket machines (pay and display) are common and you'll need to put the receipt, which must be clearly visible to the meter patrol, on the dashboard on the inside of the front window on the passenger side. Be sure to check the signs before you park, as rules vary. You can pay with coins, credit card, or download the PayByPhone app, which can be used in most French cities.

Be careful when parking your car overnight, especially in towns and village squares; if your car is still there in the early morning on a market day, it will be towed. In smaller towns, parking may be permitted on one side of the street only—alternating every two weeks—so pay attention to signs.

The coastal area of Provence—especially the Camargue and the Calanques—as well as overlooks along the Riviera are extremely vulnerable to car break-ins. It's important that you never leave valuables

visible in the car, and think twice about leaving them in the trunk. Any theft should be reported formally to the police.

ROAD CONDITIONS

Road conditions in Provence are above average and potholes are rare, especially on highways. Check with the highway information website ⊕ *www.vinci-autoroutes.com/fr/autoroutes-temps-reel* or listen to FM107.7 (the traffic station) to find out whether there's anything you should know before setting off.

RULES OF THE ROAD

In France, you may use your own driver's license, but it must be accompanied by an official translation. You must also be able to prove you have third-party insurance. Drive on the right and yield to drivers coming from streets to the right. However, this rule does not necessarily apply at roundabouts, where you are obligated to yield to those already within (to your left)—but you should watch out for just about everyone. You must wear your seat belt, and children under 10 may not travel in the front seat. French speed limits vary depending on weather conditions, and are lower in rural areas. The limits in dry weather are 130 kph (80 mph) on freeways, 110 kph (70 mph) on divided highways, 90 kph (55 mph) on other roads, 50 kph (30 mph) in towns, and 30 kph (15 mph) in school zones. French drivers break these limits often, which is why road mortality shot up nearly 18% between February 2018 and 2019, but police also hand out hefty on-the-spot fines. The cops are also fast to fine when it comes to using a mobile phone while driving: €135 and 3 points—which applies also to foreign licenses.

RENTAL CARS

When you reserve a car, ask about cancellation penalties, taxes, drop-off charges (if you're planning to pick up the car in one city and leave it in another), and surcharges (for being under or over a certain age, for additional drivers, or for driving across state or country borders or beyond a specific distance from your point of rental). All these things can add substantially to your costs. Request car seats and extras such as GPS when you book.

Rates are sometimes—but not always—better if you book in advance or reserve through a rental agency's website. There are other reasons to book ahead, though: for popular destinations, during busy times of the year, or to ensure that you get certain types of cars (vans, SUVs, exotic sports cars).

■ TIP → **Make sure that a confirmed reservation guarantees you a car. Agencies sometimes overbook, particularly for busy weekends and holiday periods.**

Though renting a car in France is expensive—up to twice as much as in the United States—and the cost of gas is very high as well, it may pay off if you are traveling with two or more people. And, of course, renting a car gives you the freedom to move around at your own pace. Rates begin at about €35 per day and €240–€300 per week for an economy car with a manual transmission (an automatic transmission will cost more). These days there are often multiday packages or weekly rates including some number of kilometers. No one wants to pay the exorbitant insurance rates, but do yourself a favor and opt for the all-inclusive; this is France and almost every time you park on the street, you'll be bumped by another car parking. Be careful to check whether the price includes the 20% V.A.T. tax or, if you pick it up from the airport, the airport tax.

Also, price local car-rental companies—whose prices may be lower still, although their service and maintenance may not be as good as those of major rental agencies—and research rates online. ADA, a French-owned rental company, has offices in towns, train stations, and airports throughout Provence. The Renault Eurodrive program lets non-EU citizens visiting between 21 days and 6 months lease cars short-term. Offices are at Paris CDG and in Marseille, Montpellier, and Nice.

In France your own driver's license is acceptable, provided you have a notarized translation. Most visitors don't actually have one, but in the event of a fender-bender that's not your fault, it will save hassle. You don't need an International Driver's Permit, unless you are planning on a long-term stay; you can get one from the American or Canadian automobile association, and, in the United Kingdom, from the Automobile Association or Royal Automobile Club.

Train

The SNCF is recognized as one of Europe's best national rail service: it's fast, punctual (when not on strike), comfortable, and comprehensive. You can get to Provence and the coast from all points west, north, and east, though lines out of Paris are by far the most direct. There are various options: local trains, overnight trains with sleeping accommodations, and the high-speed TGV (Trains à Grande Vitesse, or high-speed trains).

France is rightly proud of its TGV lines, which zoom along at 300 kph (186 mph). The LGV Méditerranée connects Paris to Avignon and Aix-en-Provence. With the hassles of airport check-in and transfer, you may find train travel the most efficient way to get from Paris to Provence.

All TGV trains to Provence leave from Paris's Gare de Lyon, and Ouigo trains—the

Getting Here and Around

low-cost service operated also by SNCF—leave from stations across the country. Travel time from Paris is 2 hours, 40 minutes to Avignon; between 3 to 3½ hours to Nîmes, Marseille, and Aix-en-Provence; 3¼ hours to Montpellier; 4 hours to Toulon; and 5½ hours to Nice.

Certain models of the TGV, called *train duplex,* offer luxurious comfort, with double-decker seating and panoramic views. When one of these passes along the coast—especially from Nice to Menton—it makes for a dramatic sightseeing excursion, though it pokes along at a local-train snail's pace. When you're connecting from one coastal city to another (Marseille–Toulon–Fréjus–Cannes–Nice–Menton), you're also likely to board a regional TER double-decker train.

Traveling first-class can cost about 50% more than second class, but, with the exception of wider seats, you won't get many more amenities and unless you're traveling internationally, you'll still need to buy your own food at the onboard café-bar. Many TGVs still don't offer Wi-Fi.

BOARDING THE TRAIN

Before boarding, you must punch your ticket (but not Eurail Pass or e-ticket) in one of the yellow machines at the entrance to the platforms, or else you risk a €10–€15 fine plus a processing fee, which has to be paid on the spot. If you board your train on the run and don't have time to punch it, look for a conductor (*contrôleur*) as soon as possible and get him to sign it.

It's a good rule of thumb to arrive at the station a half hour before departure.

RAIL PASSES

France is one of 31 countries in which you can use Eurail Passes, which provide unlimited first- and second-class rail travel, in all of the participating countries, for the duration of the pass. Select

between a one-country pass with up to eight days of travel within one month or a Global Pass: three, five, or seven days travel within one month; 10 or 15 days within two months; or chose unlimited travel over 15 or 22 days, or one to three months.

For two- to five adults traveling together, the France Rail Pass Saver allows three- to nine days of unlimited train travel (and a discount on Eurostar) in a one-month period. Prices begin at €212 each in second class, and €261 each in first class. For solo travelers, the France Rail Pass allows one to nine days of unlimited travel per month, starting at €140 for first class and €113 for second class for one day of travel. Additional days may be added for €35 per day in either class. Another option is the France Rail 'n Drive Pass, which combines the cost of rail travel and a rental car.

You need to book seats ahead even if you are using a rail pass. You must always make a seat reservation for the TGV—easily obtained at the ticket window or from an automatic machine. Seat reservations are reassuring but seldom necessary on other main-line French trains, except at busy holiday times (as in summer), particularly on popular routes. You will also need a reservation for sleeping accommodations.

SNCF offers a number of discount rail passes, which are available only for purchase in France. You can get a reduced fare if you are 60 or older with the SNCF's Carte Sénior, which costs €49 and entitles the bearer to deep discounts on rail and TGV travel for a year. There are also passes for young people (12 to 26), weekend passes (for ages 27 to 59), and passes for those traveling with small children.

Essentials

Lodging

Consider the kind of vacation you want to spend—going native in a country *gîte* (rental house), being pampered in a luxury penthouse overlooking the Mediterranean in Cannes, or getting to know the locals in a cozy B&B or a converted *mas* (farmhouse).

APARTMENT AND HOUSE RENTALS

Between Airbnb disrupting the national rental network (Paris mayor Anne Hidalgo is considering banning certain arrondissements from the service) and recent less-lenient tax legislation for property rentals, *gîtes* are struggling. The Fédération Nationale des Gîtes de France rents rural homes with regional flavor, often restored farmhouses or village row houses in pretty country settings, with owners on-site to greet you on your arrival. The system grew out of a subsidized movement to salvage wonderful old houses falling to ruin, but now less-regulated competition is steep.

BED-AND-BREAKFASTS

Airbnb has also affected France's bed-and-breakfasts, known here as *chambres d'hôtes,*. Check local tourist offices for details or contact Gîtes de France, an organization that lists thousands of B&Bs all over the country, from rustic options to luxurious châteaux. Often *table d'hôte* dinners (meals cooked by and eaten with the owners) can be arranged for an extra, fairly nominal fee. Note that in B&Bs, unlike hotels, it is more likely that the owners will speak only French, though in the south you'll find plenty of British-run B&Bs.

HOTELS

Hotels are classified by the French government from one-star to five-star deluxe. Rates must, by law, be posted at the hotel entrance and should include taxes and service; you are always charged per room, not per person. Remember that in France the first floor is one floor up (what Americans call the second floor), and the higher up you go, the quieter the street noise will be.

You should always check what bathroom facilities the price includes, if any. Because replumbing drains is often very expensive, if not impossible, old hotels may have added bathrooms—often with *douches* (showers), not *baignoires* (tubs)—to the guest rooms, but not toilets, although this is becoming a rarity. If you want a private bathroom, state your preference for shower or tub—the latter always costs more. Unless otherwise noted, lodging listings in this book include a private bathroom with a shower or tub.

When making your reservation, ask for a *grand lit* if you want a double bed. The quality of accommodations, particularly in older properties and even in luxury hotels, can vary greatly from room to room, as hotels are often renovated floor by floor; if you don't like the room you're given, ask to see another.

If you're counting on air-conditioning, you should make sure, in advance, that your hotel room is *climatisé* (air-conditioned). Air-conditioning is not a given, even at hotels in inland Provence, far from sea breezes. And when you throw open the windows, don't expect screens (*moustiquaires*). Nowhere in Europe are they standard, and the only exceptions are found occasionally in the Camargue marshlands, where mosquitoes are an issue.

Breakfast is not always included in the price, but you are sometimes expected to have it and are occasionally charged for it regardless, so be sure to inform the hotel if you are not going to be eating the

Essentials

pétit-déj there. In smaller rural hotels you may be expected to have your evening meal at the hotel, too.

Dining

The sooner you relax and go with the French flow, the more you'll enjoy your stay. Expect to spend at least an hour and a half for lunch in a restaurant, savoring three courses and talking over the wine; dinner lasts even longer. If you keep one eye on your watch and the other on the waiter, you'll miss the point and spoil your own fun.

You may benefit from a few pointers on French dining etiquette. Diners in France don't negotiate their orders much, so don't expect serene smiles when you ask for sauce on the side. Order your coffee after dessert, not with it. When you're ready for the check, ask for it. No professional waiter would dare put a bill on your table while you're still enjoying the last sip of coffee. And don't ask for a doggy bag; it's just not done.

Also a word on the great mineral-water war: the French usually drink wine or mineral water—not soda or coffee—with their food. You may ask for a carafe of tap water, *une carafe d'eau*. In general, diners order mineral water if they don't order wine. It's not that the tap water is unsafe; it's usually fine—just not as tasty as Evian or slightly fizzy Badoit. To order flat mineral water ask for *eau naturelle*; fizzy is *eau gazeuse*.

Restaurants along the coast are generally more expensive than those inland; basic, regional prix-fixe menus average €22–€32, though the high end of this figure represents the usual cost of seafood so often featured on restaurant menus. In high summer reserve ahead at popular restaurants, especially if you want a coveted outdoor table.

MEALS AND MEALTIMES

If you're antsy to get to the next museum, or if you plan to spend the evening dining in grand style, consider lunch in a brasserie, where quick, one-plate lunches and full salads are available. Cafés often serve *casse croûtes* (snacks), including sandwiches, which are simply baguettes lightly filled with ham or cheese; or *croques monsieurs*, grilled ham and cheese open-face sandwiches with a rich layer of béchamel. Bakeries and *traiteurs* (delis) often sell savory items like quiches, tiny pizzas, or pastries filled with pâté. On the Riviera, there's a wealth of street food, from the chickpea-based crêpes called *socca* to *pissaladière* (onion-olive pizza) and *pan bagnat* (a tuna-and-egg-stuffed pita-style bun).

You'll notice here more than anywhere in France that the lunch hour begins after 1; some places don't even open before that. If you don't mind being a gauche foreigner, eating at noon is one way to get into those sought-after restaurants that are actually open then. If you want to really do as the locals do, reserve a table for lunch at 1 or 1:30.

Breakfast is usually served 7:30–10:30; if you want it earlier, arrange a time the night before with your hotel. Dinner is usually eaten after 8, and most restaurants do not open for dinner before 7:30.

Unless otherwise noted, the restaurants listed in this guide are open daily for lunch and dinner.

✚ Safety

Car break-ins have become part of daily life in the south, especially in the isolated parking lots where hikers set off to explore for the day. Be especially careful around the marshes of the Camargue, the departure point for the Îles d'Hyères ferries, the rocky Esterel between Fréjus and Cannes, and the coastal path around St-Tropez: take valuables with you and, if possible, leave your luggage at your hotel.

Also beware of petty theft—purse and phone snatching and pickpocketing. Use common sense: avoid pulling out a lot of money in public, and wear a handbag with long straps that you can sling across your body, bandolier-style, with a zippered compartment for your money and passport. It's also a good idea to wear a money belt. Men should keep their wallets up front, as safely tucked away as possible. At airports and train stations, never leave your luggage trolley unattended even for a minute.

Although cities in Provence are relatively safe during the day, take caution at night, especially in port towns such as Marseille, Nice, and Toulon. Marseille is particularly known for its drug-related crime, although in general tourists are not targeted. Avignon also has a high crime rate, and tourists should be alert and walk purposefully through town at night. Ditto for Nice.

ⓢ Taxes

All taxes must be included in posted prices in France. The initials TTC (*toutes taxes comprises*—taxes included) sometimes appear on price lists but taxes are included whether they are or not. By law, restaurant and hotel prices must also include the tax, and hotels charge a daily habitation tax that can run from €0.80–€4.20 per day (depending on the size of the room you are in).

A number of shops participating in the Tax-Free Shopping program (you'll see a sticker in the shop window) offer V.A.T. refunds to foreign shoppers—under very limited circumstances. To qualify for the refund, you must be a national of a non-EU country, at least 15 years old at the time of purchase, and visiting France for less than six months. If you qualify, you are entitled to an export discount of up to 20%, depending on the item purchased, and only on purchases of at least €175 in a single store.

💷 Tipping

The French have a clear idea of when they should be tipped. Bills in bars and restaurants include a 15% service fee, but it is customary to round out your bill with some small change unless you're dissatisfied. The amount of this varies: anywhere from €0.10 if you've merely bought a beer, to €2–€5 after a meal. Tip taxi drivers and hairdressers about 5%. In some theaters and hotels, coat check attendants may expect nothing if there is a sign saying "*pourboire interdit*" (tips forbidden); otherwise give them €1. The same goes for washroom attendants, unless another sum is posted.

If you stay in a hotel for more than two or three days, it is customary to leave something for the housekeeper—about €1.50 per day. In expensive hotels you may well call on the services of a baggage porter, doorperson, and concierge. All expect a tip: plan on about €1.50 per item for the bellhop, but the other tips will depend on how much you've used their services—common sense must guide you here.

Train and airport porters get a fixed €1–€1.50 per bag, but you're better off getting your own baggage cart if you can.

On the Calendar

Spring

Antibes Art Fair. At this antique and modern art fair, held for two weeks mid-April–early May, some 25,000 people from all over the world come to view the treasures on display and pick up a little something for back home; it's one of the largest events of its kind in France. ✉ *Old Port, Antibes* ☎ *04–93–34–65–65* ⊕ *www.salon-antiquaires-antibes.com.*

Cannes International Film Festival. The Riviera's cultural calendar is splashy and star-studded, and never more so than during the Cannes International Film Festival in May. The film screenings are not open to the public, so unless you have a pass, your stargazing will be on the streets or in restaurants (though if you hang around the back exits of the big hotels around 7 pm, you may bump into a few celebs on their way to the red carpet). *Cinéma de la Plage* shows Cannes Classics and Out of Competition films free at Macé beach at 9:30 pm. In addition, Cannes Cinéphiles (⊕ *www.cannes-cinema.com*) gives 4,000 film buffs a chance to view Official Selections; you can apply online starting in February. ✉ *Cannes* ⊕ *www.festival-cannes.com.*

Fête de la Transhumance. Held on Pentecost Monday (the end of May), the famous Fête de la Transhumance celebrates the passage of the sheep from Provence into the Alps. Costumed shepherds lead some 4,000 sheep, goats, and donkeys through the streets. There's an antiques fair, sheepdog-training demonstration, and a cheese market in the ancient village, as well as other events throughout the day. ⊕ *www.saintremy-de-provence.com.*

Summer

Festival d'Aix-en-Provence. Every July, you can see world-class opera productions in the courtyard of the Palais de l'Archevêché. It is one of the most important opera festivals in Europe, attracting some 83,000 festivalgoers to the cutting-edge productions involving the best artists available. The repertoire is varied and often offbeat, featuring works like Britten's *Curlew River* and Bartók's *Bluebeard's Castle* as well as the usual Mozart, Puccini, and Verdi. Most of the singers are not celebrities, but rather an elite group of students who spend the summer with the Academie Européenne de Musique, training and performing under the tutelage of stars like Robert Tear and Yo-Yo Ma. Tickets can be purchased online beginning in January. ✉ *Palais de l'Ancien Archevêché, 28 pl. des Martyrs de la Résistance, Aix-en-Provence* ☎ *08–20–92–29–23* ⊕ *www.festival-aix.com.*

Festival d'Avignon. Held annually over three weeks in July, the Festival d'Avignon has brought the best of world theater to this ancient city since 1947. Avignon's version of fringe, the OFF Festival (*www.avignonleoff.com*), is staged at the same time. The two combined host more than 1,600 performances, with the main venue being the Palais des Papes. Tickets go on sale around mid-June and sell out quickly. ✉ *Avignon* ☎ *04–90–14–14–14 tickets and information* ⊕ *www.festival-avignon.com.*

Festival International Jazz à Juan. Every July the world-renowned Jazz à Juan festival stages a stellar lineup in a romantic venue under ancient pines. Launched in 1960, this festival hosted the European debut performances of such stars as Miles Davis and Ray Charles. More recently, it spawned the fringier Jazz

OFF, with 200 musicians and free street concerts, as well as the Jazz Club at Les Ambassadeurs beach, where you can enjoy a drink with live music (headliners have been known to pop in for impromptu concerts here). Book online or buy tickets directly from the tourist office in Antibes or Juan-les-Pins. ⊠ *Juan-les-Pins* ☎ *04–22–10–60–01 ticket information* ⊕ *www.jazzajuan.com.*

Grande Feria. The Grande Feria brings the Camargue to St-Rémy-de-Provence for this highly anticipated festival in mid-August. Bullfights (don't worry, they're not killed) and bull runs, peñas flamencas, DJs, parades, kids' races and plenty of food are all on offer during its four days. ⊕ *www.saintremy-de-provence.com.*

International Cannes Fireworks Festival. During this festival, which takes place over various nights in July and August, six countries compete in an amazing 25-minute musical fireworks display that lights up both the water and the sky. The fireworks are set off from barges 400 meters offshore from the Baie de Cannes; you can watch beachside for free among the masses of locals who come early. ⊠ *Cannes* ☎ *04–92–99–84–22 for info* ⊕ *www.festival-pyrotechnique-cannes. com.*

Les Rencontres d'Arles. In July the famed Rencontres d'Arles brings movers and shakers in international photography into the Théâtre Antique for five days of specialized colloquiums and other events. Ordinary folks can profit by attending the 35 exhibitions of mostly unpublished work. These are displayed at various heritage sites in Arles and are open to the public July–September. Tickets, which range from €6 for a single entry to €37 for a pass, can be purchased online or from various locations in Arles, including the festival office. ⊠ *Office, 34 rue du Docteur Fanton, Arles*

☎ *04–90–96–76–06* ⊕ *www.rencontres-arles.com.*

Voiles d'Antibes. The first week of June, check out the Voiles d'Antibes, a major meeting of beautiful old teak and brass sailing vessels, metric classes, and maxi-cruisers more than 20 meters long. The Match Race regatta sets sail across 23 km (14 miles) of coastline. The event marks the official opening of the classic yachting season, with other regattas in Cannes and St-Tropez in September. ⊠ *Old Port, Antibes* ☎ *04–93–34–42–47 for info* ⊕ *www.voilesdantibes.com.*

Winter

Menton Lemon Festival. Running 20 days from mid-February through the first week of March, the Fête du Citron is a full-blown lemon love-in, using 140 tons of the citrus fruit for floats in the daily parades and gardens, which are lit up at night as part of the Les Jardins de Lumières (tickets are needed for both). Think of this as France's answer to the Rose Bowl Parade. ⊠ *Menton* ☎ *04–92–41–76–95* ⊕ *www.fete-du-citron.com.*

Nice Carnaval. During the two weeks leading up to Mardi Gras and Lent, the Niçois let loose in disguise during this carnival, which attracts roughly 250,000 visitors. The parades in Place Masséna include €30,000 floats made up of some 80,000 flowers, dancers of varying levels of expertise and enthusiasm, more than 1,600 musicians, and face-painting stands for kids. For the best view, it's worth investing in tickets (book seats online, up to €26, standing-room €11). The main event now incorporates Lou Queernaval, the first Gay Carnival Parade in France (free). ⊠ *Nice* ⊕ *www.nicecarnaval.com.*

Helpful French Phrases

BASICS

Yes/no	wee/nohn	Oui/non
Please	seel voo play	S'il vous plaît
Thank you	mair- **see**	Merci
You're welcome	deh ree- **ehn**	De rien
Excuse me, sorry	pahr- **don**	Pardon
Good morning/ afternoon	bohn- **zhoor**	Bonjour
Good evening	bohn- **swahr**	Bonsoir
Good-bye	o ruh- **vwahr**	Au revoir
Mr. (Sir)	muh- **syuh**	Monsieur
Mrs. (Ma'am)	ma- **dam**	Madame
Miss	mad-mwa- **zel**	Mademoiselle
Pleased to meet you	ohn-shahn- **tay**	Enchanté(e)
How are you?	kuh-mahn-tahl-ay **voo**	Comment allez-vous?
Very well, thanks	tray bee-ehn, mair- **see**	Très bien, merci
And you?	ay voo?	Et vous?

NUMBERS

one	uhn	un
two	deuh	deux
three	twah	trois
four	**kaht**-ruh	quatre
five	sank	cinq
six	seess	six
seven	set	sept
eight	wheat	huit
nine	nuf	neuf
ten	deess	dix
eleven	ohnz	onze
twelve	dooz	douze
thirteen	trehz	treize
fourteen	kah- **torz**	quatorze
fifteen	kanz	quinze
sixteen	sez	seize
seventeen	deez- **set**	dix-sept
eighteen	deez- **wheat**	dix-huit
nineteen	deez- **nuf**	dix-neuf
twenty	vehn	vingt
twenty-one	vehnt-ay- **uhn**	vingt-et-un
thirty	trahnt	trente
forty	ka- **rahnt**	quarante
fifty	sang- **kahnt**	cinquante
sixty	swa- **sahnt**	soixante
seventy	swa-sahnt- **deess**	soixante-dix
eighty	kaht-ruh- **vehn**	quatre-vingts
ninety	kaht-ruh-vehn- **deess**	quatre-vingt-dix
one hundred	sahn	cent
one thousand	meel	mille

COLORS

black	nwahr	noir
blue	bleuh	bleu
brown	bruhn/mar- **rohn**	brun/marron
green	vair	vert
orange	o- **rahnj**	orange
pink	rose	rose
red	rouge	rouge
violet	vee-o- **let**	violette
white	blahnk	blanc
yellow	zhone	jaune

DAYS OF THE WEEK

Sunday	dee- **mahnsh**	dimanche
Monday	luhn- **dee**	lundi
Tuesday	mahr- **dee**	mardi
Wednesday	mair-kruh- **dee**	mercredi
Thursday	zhuh- **dee**	jeudi
Friday	vawn-druh- **dee**	vendredi
Saturday	sahm- **dee**	samedi

MONTHS

January	zhahn-vee- **ay**	janvier
February	feh-vree- **ay**	février
March	marce	mars
April	a- **vreel**	avril
May	meh	mai
June	zhwehn	juin
July	zhwee- **ay**	juillet
August	ah- **oo**	août
September	sep- **tahm**-bruh	septembre
October	awk- **to**-bruh	octobre
November	no- **vahm**-bruh	novembre
December	day- **sahm**-bruh	décembre

USEFUL PHRASES

Do you speak English?	par-lay **voo** ahn- **glay**	Parlez-vous anglais?
I don't speak ...	zhuh nuh parl pah ...	Je ne parle pas ...
French	frahn- **say**	français
I don't understand	zhuh nuh kohm- **prahn** pah	Je ne comprends pas
I understand	zhuh kohm- **prahn**	Je comprends
I don't know	zhuh nuh say pah	Je ne sais pas
I'm American/ British	zhuh sweez a-may-ree- **kehn** / ahn- **glay**	Je suis américain/ anglais
What's your name?	ko-mahn vooz a-pell-ay- **voo**	Comment vous appelez-vous?
My name is ...	zhuh ma- **pell** ...	Je m'appelle ...
What time is it?	kel air eh- **teel**	Quelle heure est-il?
How?	ko- **mahn**	Comment?
When?	kahn	Quand?
Yesterday	yair	Hier
Today	o-zhoor- **dwee**	Aujourd'hui

2

Tomorrow	duh-**mehn**	Demain
Tonight	suh **swahr**	Ce soir
What?	kwah	Quoi?
What is it?	kess-kuh-**say**	Qu'est-ce que c'est?
Why?	poor-**kwa**	Pourquoi?
Who?	kee	Qui?
Where is …	oo ay	Où est …
the train station?	la gar	la gare?
the subway station?	la sta-**syon** duh may-**tro**	la station de métro?
the bus stop?	la-ray duh booss	l'arrêt de bus?
the post office?	la post	la poste?
the bank?	la bahnk	la banque?
the … hotel?	lo-**tel**	l'hôtel …?
the store?	luh ma-ga-**zehn**	le magasin?
the cashier?	la **kess**	la caisse?
the … museum?	luh mew-**zay**	le musée …?
the hospital?	lo-pee-**tahl**	l'hôpital?
the elevator?	la-sahn-**seuhr**	l'ascenseur?
the telephone?	luh tay-lay-**phone**	le téléphone?
Where are the …	oo sohn lay	Où sont les …
restrooms?	twah-**let**	toilettes?
(men/women)	(oh-mm/ **fah**-mm)	(hommes/femmes)
Here/there	ee-**see** /la	Ici/là
Left/right	a goash/a draht	A gauche/à droite
Straight ahead	too drwah	Tout droit
Is it near/far?	say pray/lwehn	C'est près/loin?
I'd like …	zhuh voo-**dray**	Je voudrais …
a room	ewn **shahm**-bruh	une chambre
the key	la clay	la clé
a newspaper	uhn zhoor-**nahl**	un journal
a stamp	uhn **tam**-bruh	un timbre
I'd like to buy …	zhuh voo-**dray ahsh**-tay	Je voudrais acheter …
cigarettes	day see-ga-**ret**	des cigarettes
matches	days a-loo-**met**	des allumettes
soap	dew sah-**vohn**	du savon
city map	uhn plahn de **veel**	un plan de ville
road map	ewn cart roo-tee-**air**	une carte routière
magazine	ewn reh-**vu**	une revue
envelopes	dayz ahn-veh-**lope**	des enveloppes
writing paper	dew pa-pee-**ay** a **let**-ruh	du papier à lettres
postcard	ewn cart pos-**tal**	une carte postale
How much is it?	say comb-bee-**ehn**	C'est combien?
A little/a lot	uhn peuh/bo-**koo**	Un peu/beaucoup
More/less	plu/mwehn	Plus/moins
Enough/too (much)	a-say/tro	Assez/trop
I am ill/sick	zhuh swee ma-**lahd**	Je suis malade
Call a …	a-play uhn	Appelez un …
doctor	dohk-**tehr**	docteur
Help!	o suh-**koor**	Au secours!

Stop!	a-reh-**tay**	Arrêtez!
Fire!	o fuh	Au feu!
Caution!/Look out!	a-tahn-see-**ohn**	Attention!

DINING OUT

A bottle of …	ewn boo-**tay** duh	une bouteille de …
A cup of …	ewn tass duh	une tasse de …
A glass of …	uhn vair duh	un verre de …
Bill/check	la-dee-see-**ohn**	l'addition
Bread	dew panh	du pain
Breakfast	luh puh-**tee** day-zhuh-**nay**	le petit-déjeuner
Butter	dew burr	du beurre
Cheers!	ah **vo**-truh sahn-**tay**	A votre santé!
Cocktail/aperitif	uhn ah-pay-ree-**teef**	un apéritif
Dinner	luh dee-**nay**	le dîner
Dish of the day	luh plah dew **zhoor**	le plat du jour
Enjoy!	bohn a-pay-**tee**	Bon appétit!
Fixed-price menu	luh may-**new**	le menu
Fork	ewn four-**shet**	une fourchette
I am diabetic	zhuh swee dee-ah-bay-**teek**	Je suis diabétique
I am vegetarian	zhuh swee vay-zhay-ta-ree-**en**	Je suis végétarien(ne)
I cannot eat …	zhuh nuh puh pah mahn-**jay** deh	Je ne peux pas manger de …
I'd like to order	zhuh voo-**dray** ko-mahn-**day**	Je voudrais commander
Is service/the tip included?	ess kuh luh sair-**veess** ay comb-**pree**	Est-ce que le service est compris?
It's good/bad	say bohn/mo-**vay**	C'est bon/mauvais
It's hot/cold	say sho/frwah	C'est chaud/froid
Knife	uhn koo-**toe**	un couteau
Lunch	luh day-zhuh-**nay**	le déjeuner
Menu	la cart	la carte
Napkin	ewn sair-vee-**et**	une serviette
Pepper	dew **pwah**-vruh	du poivre
Plate	ewn a-see-**et**	une assiette
Please give me …	doe-nay-**mwah**	Donnez-moi …
Salt	dew sell	du sel
Spoon	ewn kwee-**air**	une cuillère
Sugar	dew **sook**-ruh	du sucre
Waiter!/Waitress!	muh-**syuh** / mad-mwa-**zel**	Monsieur!/ Mademoiselle!
Wine list	la cart day vehn	la carte des vins

Great Itineraries

Best of Provence

If you want to focus only on the best of Provence—its history, its architecture, its markets, and its cafés—devote your time to the "three As": Avignon, Aix, and Arles, as well as the area between them that anchors the heart of the region.

DAYS 1–2: AVIGNON

Nowadays the population of Avignon swells most during the extensive mid-summer Drama Festival that sees the gateway city to Provence at its liveliest. Yet this historic town, with its protective medieval ring of muscular towers, is seldom dull at any time of year. In the 14th century, this was the center of Christendom, when French-born Pope Clement V shifted the papacy from Rome to Avignon's magnificent Palais des Papes (Papal Palace). Spend your first day viewing the palace, the Pont St-Bénezet, and the Rocher des Doms Park, then escape into the cobblestone alleys to see the Avignonnais living their daily lives. Pop into the Musée Angladon to view Van Gogh's *Wagons de Chemin de Fer* and then head to the modern and contemporary museum, the Collection Lambert. The next morning, head to one of the city's food or flea markets or to the gorgeous indoor Marché des Halles with its 40 local vendors (open daily except Monday) and pick up a snack for an afternoon road trip 25 km (15 miles) west of Avignon to the three-tier stone spectacle that is the Pont du Gard, built in 19 BC as an aqueduct by the ancient Romans and known today as one of the wonders of the classical world.

DAY 3: ST-RÉMY

Escape to "the Hamptons of Provence," the picturesque town of St-Rémy-de-Provence, where mellow 18th-century mansions line the streets, the main ones leading to St-Paul-de-Mausolée, the ancient monastery where Vincent van Gogh spent some of his most productive months. From here, take a 90-minute guided tour "In the Footsteps of Vincent Van Gogh," or download a free map from the tourist office and make your own tour. Stop for lunch at the Café de Place before heading to the 6th-century archaeological site Glanum. You then might want to squeeze in Les Baux-de-Provence, one of the country's most spectacular perched villages.

DAYS 4–5: ARLES AND THE CAMARGUE

Head 33 km (21 miles) southwest to Arles, which competes with Nîmes for the title "Rome of France" thanks to its famous Roman theater, *arenès* (amphi-theater), Alyscamps, and Cryptoporticus. All the main sights are in the small *vieille ville* (Old Town), speckled with pockets where time seems to have stood still since 1888, the year Vincent van Gogh immortalized the town in his paintings. Study reproductions of the best canvas-es, which have come to define Provence as much as its herbs and traditional costumes, at Arles's Fondation Vincent van Gogh and see the places he painted along the town's Promenade Vincent van Gogh. Just off the Rond-Point des Arrènes, have your camera ready for a stroll up Rue Ernest Renan, the idyllic Provençal street. Over at the 15th-century priory, the Musée Réattu (the first fine art museum in the country to have a pho-tography section) has more Van Gogh, as well as a collection of Picasso drawings. Underneath Forum Square, wildly famous for Van Gogh's *Starry Night*, you'll dis-cover the Cryptoporticus du Forum, with foundations dating back to 1 BC.

DAY 5: CAMARGUE

At least a day is needed to take in the neighboring Camargue, famed for its pink flamingos, black bulls, white horses, and

gardens—one of the most unique natural preserves in France. Use Ste-Maries-sur-Mer, where gypsies from around the world pilgrimage to honor their patron saint Sarah, as your base and spend the morning riding the *chevals blancs* (white horses) along the spectacular sandy beaches. If you happen to arrive during one of the processions, horsefairs, or bullfights, you're in for a treat—but otherwise you can roam the cobblestone streets and climb the tower of the 9th-century church. Inquire at the tourist office about bus, bike, or walking tours of Camargue National Regional Park, a UNSECO World Heritage site.

DAYS 6–7: AIX-EN-PROVENCE

The museums and churches in Aix are overshadowed by the town itself, an enchanting beauty with elegant *hôtels particuliers* (mansions), luxurious fountains gracing every square, and an architectural layout that attests to Aix's prominent past as the 17th-century cultural and political capital of Provence. Walking is not only the easiest way to get around but also the best, as the center is a maze of narrow streets and lovely squares where people and café tables take up every available inch. The tree-lined Cours Mirabeau divides old Aix in half, with the Quartier Ancien's medieval streets to the north and the 18th-century mansions of the Quartier Mazarin to the south. Connecting most of the dots—including such sightseeing musts as the Musée Granet, the Cathédrale St-Sauveur, and the gorgeous Pavillon de Vendôme—is the Paul Cézanne Trail, which allows you to follow in the footsteps of Aix's most famous native son, from his studio and his Jas de Bouffan home to his favorite hangout, the Café-Brasserie Les Deux Garçons.

Great Itineraries

Best of the French Riviera

To hit the highlights of this sun-blessed region and get up close and personal with the tropical glamour of the Côte d'Azur, here's a weeklong itinerary that allows you to get a good feel for what makes the Riviera famous—and wonderful. Make like a movie star and follow the coastline from Antibes to St-Jean-Cap-Ferrat, hitting the best beaches, circling the emerald-green capes, perusing the markets, and making the requisite hill-town stop. Other than St-Paul-de-Vence, all destinations here are on the coast and linked by the wonderful coastal railway.

DAY 1: ANTIBES

Sitting on the western side of the Baie des Anges (Bay of Angels), Antibes is a heavenly place. While a bustling town, it also has a waterfront quarter that is so picturesque you'll be tempted to set up an easel just like Picasso, whose works are on view in the town's Château Grimaldi. The surrounding alleys are a maze of enchantment with the Cours Massena overflowing with charm and Le Safranier, an independent historic quarter of tiny cobblestone streets and flower box–filled windowsills. Then enjoy a day of tropical hedonism on the Cap d'Antibes, a rocky promontory (which juts out into the Bay of Millionaires) adorned with Gilded Age mansions, one of which, the Villa Eilenroc, is open to the public. Catch the sunset at Plage des Ondes, a sandy public beach frequented by locals.

DAY 2: ST-PAUL-DE-VENCE

Drive up to the pretty perched medieval village of St-Paul for a gorgeous panoramic selfie and work up an appetite by perusing the endless galleries before heading to lunch at the Picasso-blessed Colombe d'Or (the point of any trip to the Riviera—reservations absolutely essential). A digestive walk around the Fondation Maeght for a glance at the Giacometti courtyard comes highly recommended.

DAY 3: HAUT-DES-CAGNES

Could this be the most beautiful village in southern France? Part-time residents Renoir, Soutine, Modigliani, and Simone de Beauvoir are just a few who thought so. You will forever dream about this place after leaving: with its tiny medieval streets, array of 15th- and 17th-century houses, corkscrew alleys, and vaulted arches draped with bougainvillea, it is a lovely dip into the Middle Ages. Many of the pretty residences are like dollhouses (especially the hobbit houses on Rue Passebon) but looming over all is the medieval town castle, with a grand Renaissance courtyard and three quirky collections. Head back to Cagnes-sur-Mer for an afternoon beverage at one of the many beach cafés and a refreshing dip in the Mediterranean.

DAYS 4–5: NICE

Just 15 minutes from Haut-des-Cagnes by train, Nice is the big-city leg of your trip, so immerse yourself in culture: the Matisse and Chagall museums, set in the Cimiez suburb high over the city, or the cutting-edge modern art museum. Start the day, though, at the magnificent Cours Saleya Market, which shuts down by 1 pm—if you're up early enough, you can watch the chefs squabble over the best produce. Then stroll through the labyrinthine Old Town. A few steps away lies the shoreline, where you can spend an hour or two strolling the famed Promenade des Anglais bordering Nice's vast crescent of beach. Amble toward the port and you'll find La Promenade des 100 Antiquaires, which runs up to Place Garibaldi. You can spend a whole day here: rent a lounger and order a seaside lunch, enjoying the relaxing sea breeze and sunshine.

DAY 6: VILLEFRANCHE-SUR-MER AND ST-JEAN-CAP-FERRAT

Either of the pretty ports of Villefranche or St-Jean-Cap Ferrat will take you back to the days before the Riviera became the land of pink it is today. First, marvel at Villefranche's deep blue bay, study the hillside estates, and visit the town's Chapelle St-Pierre, decorated by Jean Cocteau. Then take the bus or walk over to Cap Ferrat, a favorite getaway of the sunglasses-and-sapphires set. Be sure to tour the art-charged rooms and expansive gardens of the Villa Ephrussi-Rothschild. Or set out to do a half-hour hike along the Promenade Maurice Rouvier (lots of movie stars do their power-walking here) to nearby Beaulieu-sur-Mer, home to the fabulous recreation of ancient Greece that is the Villa Kerylos.

DAY 7: ÈZE

Your final excursion should be to the sky-high village of Èze, an eagle's-nest wonder threaded by stone alleys that lead to the most spectacular vistas of the coast. One step higher and you will be, indeed, in paradise. Both Fragonard and Galimard perfumeries have boutiques here and offer free tours, but you also can take a perfume workshop guided by a professional nose (or for those who prefer the smell of burning rubber to lavender, you can test-drive a Lamborghini from outside Fragonard's factory with Liven Up). Take the free electric shuttle in summer back down to the coast and then the train to Nice to get back home.

Contacts

✈ Air Travel

AIRPORT INFORMATION
Avignon–Provence Airport.
✉ *100 rue Marise Bastié,
Montfavet* ☎ *04–90–81–
51–51* ⊕ *www.avignon.
aero.* **Charles de Gaulle.**
(*CDG*). ☎ *0033/1–70–36–
39–50 outside of France*
⊕ *www.adp.fr.* **Mar-
seille–Provence.** ☎ *08–
20–81–14–14* ⊕ *www.
marseille.aeroport.fr.*
Montpellier–Meditérranée.
☎ *08–25–83–00–03*
⊕ *www.montpellier.
aeroport.fr.* **Nice–Côte
d'Azur.** ☎ *08–20–42–33–33*
⊕ *www.nice.aeroport.
fr.* **Nîmes–Arles–Camar-
gue.** ☎ *04–66–70–49–49*
⊕ *www.nimes.aeroport.fr.*
Orly. ☎ *33/1–70–36–39–50
from outside France*
⊕ *www.parisaeroport.
fr.* **Toulon Hyères.** ☎ *08–
25–01–83–87* ⊕ *www.
toulon-hyeres.aeroport.fr.*

🚌 Bus Travel

**DISCOUNT PASSES Euro-
lines.** ☎ *08–92–89–12–00
(€0.35 per min), 01–41–
86–24–21 outside France*
⊕ *www.eurolines.fr.*

WITHIN FRANCE Le Pilote.
⊕ *www.lepilote.com.* **Nice
AirportXpress.** ⊕ *www.
niceairportxpress.com/
en.* **SNCF.** ☎ *3635* ⊕ *www.
sncf.com.*

🛏 Lodging Information

**LOCAL AGENTS Gîtes de
France.** ☎ *01–49–70–75–75*
⊕ *www.gites-de-france.
com.*

🚊 Train Travel

INFORMATION Eurail.
☎ *6–405–793–58
WhatsApp messaging
only* ⊕ *www.eurail.com.*
Eurostar. ☎ *01–70–70–60–
88* ⊕ *www.eurostar.com.*
Rail Europe. ☎ *800/622–
8600 in U.S. and Canada*
⊕ *www.raileurope.com.*
SNCF. ☎ *3635* ⊕ *www.oui.
sncf.*

📍 Visitor Information

**INFORMATION Côte d'Azur
Tourist Office.** ⊕ *www.
cotedazur-tourisme.com.*
France Tourism. ⊕ *us.
france.fr.* **Provence-Alpes-
Côte d'Azur Tourisme.**
(*CRT PACA*). ⊕ *www.
tourismepaca.fr.* **Provence
Tourist Office.** ⊕ *www.
visitprovence.com.*

Chapter 3

NÎMES AND THE ALPILLES

3

Updated by
Jennifer Ladonne

⊙ Sights	🍴 Restaurants	🛏 Hotels	🛍 Shopping	🍸 Nightlife
★★★☆☆	★★★☆☆	★★★☆☆	★★☆☆☆	★☆☆☆☆

WELCOME TO NÎMES AND THE ALPILLES

TOP REASONS TO GO

★ **Vincent van Gogh's Arles:** Ever since the fiery Dutchman immortalized Arles in all its chromatic drama, this town has had a starring role in museums around the world.

★ **Medieval history:** Wander the ghostly ruins of the Château des Baux in Les Baux-de-Provence—a tour de force of medieval ambience.

★ **Camargue Nature Park:** The famous lagoons of the Camargue will swamp you with their charms once you catch sight of their white horses, pink flamingos, and black bulls.

★ **St-Rémy-de-Provence:** Find inspired gourmet cooking, meditate quietly on Greco-Roman antiquity, or browse bustling markets, basket in hand, at this fashionable village enclave.

★ **The Pont du Gard:** This aqueduct of the ancient Roman era is also a spectacular work of art.

1 Nîmes. A classic Roman town turned lively modern city.

2 Uzés. A medieval and Renaissance jewel in an marvelous setting.

3 Pont du Gard. A famed Roman bridge.

4 Aigues-Mortes. A walled fortress-town.

5 Parc Régional de Camargue. One of France's most remarkable terrains.

6 Stes-Maries-de-la-Mer. A pilgrimage town located within the Camargue.

7 Arles. Splendid Roman ruins and contemporary art in the footsteps of Van Gogh.

8 Abbaye de Montmajour. Once Provence's spiritual center.

9 Tarascon. Home to a folk hero who slayed the mythical Tarasque monster.

10 Fontvieille. Hometown to writer Alphonse Daudet.

11 Les Baux-de-Provence. A lively tangle of medieval streets and views for miles.

12 St-Rémy-de-Provence. Van Gogh's famous refuge, now a ritzy retreat.

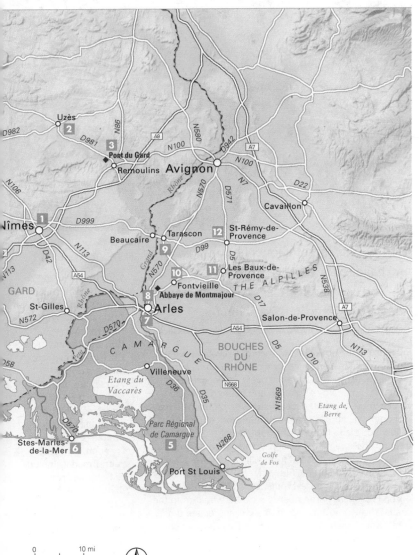

D982

Uzès **2**

D981

3

Pont du Gard

Remoulins   Avignon

N86

A9

N100

N580

D942

A7

N100

D22

Cavaillon

D571

N7

N570

Rhône

N106

Nîmes **1**

D999

D42

N113

Beaucaire   Tarascon **12**   St-Rémy-de-Provence

Grand

N570

9

D99

D5

10   **11**   Les Baux-de-Provence

N538

THE ALPILLES

Fontvieille

D17

8   Abbaye de Montmajour

GARD

St-Gilles

N572

A54

Rhône

7   Arles

Salon-de-Provence

A7

A54

CAMARGUE

BOUCHES DU RHÔNE

D5

D10

N113

258

Etang du Vaccarès

Villeneuve

D36

D35

N568

Etang de Berre

N15569

Parc Régional de Camargue

D570

5

N268

Golfe de Fos

Stes-Maries-de-la-Mer **6**

Port St Louis

0   10 mi

0   10 km

PROVENCE'S VILLAGE MARKETS

In Provence, forget about the supermarket and head to the marketplace—an integral part of French culture anywhere in France, but even more so in this region.

Provence is the equivalent of market heaven. Whether food, collectibles, antiques, or clothing, there is a (very often famous) street market in every Provençal town, each with an energy of its own and offering the best way to interact with the locals. So even though you may wonder if you should resist that tablecloth of pink-and-yellow Souleiado fabric, yield to the delight of puttering through a village market. Happily, they are a daily occurrence in Provence, passed from village to town—Sunday is for L'Isle-sur-la-Sorgue, Saturday for Arles, Wednesday for St-Rémy, and Tuesday, Thursday, and Saturday for Aix-en-Provence. Remember to pick the wheat from the chaff. Provence lovers back home will appreciate those sunflower coasters much more than Day-Glo versions of Van Gogh masterpieces.

FEATS OF CLAY

Top gifts include miniature figures called *santons*, or "little saints." When the French Revolution cracked down on Christmas reenactments, a crafty Marseillais decided to make terra-cotta figurines, which soon upstaged their human counterparts for good. Sold year-round, models include red-cheeked town drunks, lavender-cutters, and—wait, isn't that Gérard Depardieu and Carla Bruni Sarkozy?

AIX-EN-PROVENCE

Aix has some delightful street markets. Unlike some of the more traditional fare of other markets, Aix is more focused on food: you can find rare delicacies side by side with cured sausages bristling with Provençal spices; vats of olives, tapenade, and oils from the Pays d'Aix (Aix region); or bags of orange-spice shuttle-shape *navettes* (cookies). The food market takes place every day in Place Richelème.

ARLES AND THE CAMARGUE

Every Saturday morning, over 2 km (1 mile) along Boulevard des Lices hosts one of the richest and most varied markets in the area. Stands overflow with olives of every kind, fresh-pressed oils, herbs, cheeses, tapenade, and all the generous bounty of Provence. You can also find the famous *boutis* (cotton throws), textured fabrics, and an endless array of tablecloths, children's clothes, and Arlesian costumes. On the first Wednesday of every month, Boulevard Emile Combes converts into an antiques and collectibles market.

AVIGNON AND THE VAUCLUSE

Avignon has a great mix of French chains and youthful clothing shops, and Les Halles food stalls are a sight to see. Every Wednesday morning, St-Rémy-de-Provence hosts one of the most popular markets in France. Place de la République and the narrow town streets abound with fresh produce, olives, tapenade by the vat, and a variety of other delicacies. In the Vaucluse area, you can find anything made from lavender.

MARSEILLE

The main shopping drag lies between La Canebière and the Préfecture, but Marseille offers up a large selection of shops, boutiques, and stores all over the city. There is an assortment of street markets, from the daily fish market in the old port to the stamp market every Sunday morning in Cours Julien (which is also home to the Wednesday organic market). Probably the most famous item you'll find is the Savon de Marseille (Marseille soap).

THE SORGUE VALLEY

The best place to go trolling for time-burnished treasure is the famed antiques market held in the lovely Isle-sur-la-Sorgue every weekend. Twice a year, around Easter and mid-August, in addition to the town's 250 art and antiques dealers, some 200 antiques merchants set up shop over four days for the Grand Déballage, or "Great Unpacking."

Scoured by the mistral and leveled to prairie flatlands by aeons of earth deposits carried south by the Rhône, this region is Provence in its rawest form. At first glance it is endless space broken only by the occasional gully lined with wildflowers, yet after a few moments it starts to take form as one of the most beautiful and intriguing regions in France.

Mysterious, romantic, and colored with a kaleidoscope of lavenders, wheat-yellows, vibrant greens, and burnt reds. Only the giant rock outcrops of the Alpilles interrupt the horizon. Along the southern coast, the Camargue's wild landscape conceals exotic wildlife—rich-plumed egrets, rare black storks, clownish flamingos—as well as domestic oddities: dappled white horses and lyre-horned "taureau" bulls descended from ancient, indigenous species. In May and October, the Roma from all over Europe arrive for a procession to the sea honoring Sara, the patron saint of the Gypsies, as they have since the Middle Ages.

The scenery is surpassed only by the genuine warmth of the populace and the feisty energy of the cities. In-your-face Nîmes has a raffish urban lifestyle that surges obliviously through a gritty-chic Old Town and a plethora of Roman architectural marvels. Graceful, artsy Arles, harmonious in Van Gogh hues, also has a Colosseum-like Roman arena, and mixes serious culture with a healthy dose of late-night café street life. Chic, luxurious St-Rémy is a gracious retreat for cosmopolitan regulars, while outside the town are the ruins of Glanum, dating back to the Hellenist era of the 3rd century BC.

Rich in history and legends, the region is as varied as the people who inhabit it: precise and perfect miniature fortress towns, like Aigues Mortes and Les Baux-de-Provence or the wide-open marshlands of the Camargue. Add to these attractions Romanesque châteaux and abbeys, seaside fortresses that launched crusades, and sun-sharpened landscapes seen through the perceptive eyes of Van Gogh and Gauguin, and you have a region not only worth exploring in depth, but worth savoring every minute.

MAJOR REGIONS

Nîmes and Around. The westernmost edge of Provence is highlighted by Nîmes, which competes with Arles and Orange as "the Rome of France" and is home to the Maison Carrée, the best-preserved ancient temple in Provence. (Thomas Jefferson admired it so much he used it as a model for the Virginia state capitol.) To the north is the Pont du Gard, most awe-inspiring in the early morning light or lit up at nightfall.

The Camargue. A bus ride away from Arles and bracketed by the towns of Aigues-Mortes and Stes-Maries-de-la-Mer, the vast Camargue nature park is one of France's most fascinating areas. A land of haunting natural beauty, the Camargue was one of the forgotten areas of France only a few decades ago. Today, thousands of visitors come to discover its peculiar ecosystem and a wild, quirky culture that's just as unique. Ride horseback across its mysterious marshlands or discover its exceptional bird-watching, then enjoy home-style cooking at one of the exclusive *mas* hotels (converted farmhouse).

Arles and Around. Reigning over the austere but evocative landscape of the Camargue marshlands, the small city of Arles is fiercely Provençal, nurturing its heritage and parading its culture at every colorful opportunity. Although little is left of the town Van Gogh once painted, there are spots where you can still channel his spirit. Warming the wetlands with its atmosphere, animation, and culture, it is a patch of golden color in a sepia landscape—and an excellent home base for sorties into the raw natural beauty and eccentric villages of the Rhône delta.

The Alpilles. Whether approaching from the damp lowlands of Arles and the Camargue or the pebbled vineyards around Avignon, the countryside changes dramatically as you climb into the arid heights of the low mountain range called the Alpilles (pronounced "ahl- *pee*-yuh"). A rough-hewn, rocky landscape rises into nearly barren limestone hills, the fields silvered with ranks of twisted olive trees and alleys of gnarled *amandiers* (almond trees). These spiky mountains guard treasures like Les Baux-de-Provence—be bewitched by both its *ville morte* (dead town) and its luxurious L'Oustau de la Baumanière inn, the first restaurant in the region to gain a Michelin star

in 1947 (today it has two). Nearby is ritzy St-Rémy-de-Provence, Van Gogh's famous retreat.

Planning

Getting Oriented

Rugged and beautiful, the landscape here is different from everywhere else in the South. Nowhere else will you find the Camargue's hypnotic plane of marshland stretching out to the sea, or the rocky Alpilles that jut upward hiding medieval fortress towns. Yet urbanites find joy here, too, in Van Gogh's colorful Arles or in feisty, fiercely independent Nîmes. And if it all gets just a bit too dusty, there is a plethora of options for some pampered R&R.

When to Go

July and August are the high season, especially along the coast, and are best avoided if possible, both because of the crushing crowds and the grilling heat. In winter (November–February, even into March) you'll find many tourist services closed, including hotels and restaurants, and much of the terrace life driven indoors by rain and wind. Around Easter, the plane trees begin to leaf out and the café tables begin to sprout.

Planning Your Time

The best place to start your trip is either in Arles or Nîmes, because they both have direct train links to most major cities in France. Here you can start the process of slowing down; Provence is all about wiling away lazy afternoons. From either city you can easily plan trips into the countryside by bus or by car.

When mapping out your itinerary, remember that although Nîmes and lovely Uzès belong in spirit to the Languedoc, their proximity to the Camargue, Arles, and the Pont du Gard makes them a logical travel package. The Alpilles are a world apart, but easily accessible from Arles and environs. You can move from site to site, or choose a central base—say, Arles—and explore them all without driving more than an hour to any one attraction. A couple of days passing through the region allows you to see world-class antiquities; five days allows time to wander the Camargue; a week lets you see the principal sites, enjoy a nature tour, and take a break by the sea. And don't forget that the ravishing old city of Avignon is an hour's easy run up from Arles.

Festivals

Arles hosts its famous Fête des Gardiens ("cowboys") on May 1, when the Queen of Arles is crowned. In May, Nîmes celebrates Pentecost with its Spanish-accented féria, a festival of parades, bull races, and corridas (bullfights) in the town's Roman arena. In June, Arles also dusts off traditional costumes for its own féria, with bullfights, parades, and races in the town's famous Roman arena. In May, St-Rémy-de-Provence observes Pentecost with another beast—the sheep—through its Fête de la Transhumance, the great migration of the wooly herds; some 4,000 sheep trot through town guided by costumed shepherds. In early October, the Fêtes d'Aigues Mortes sees this Camargue fortress town go wild with bull races and dancing on Place St-Louis.

Getting Here and Around

Public transportation is well organized in the Alpilles, Arles, and the Camargue, with most towns accessible by train or bus. It's best to plan on combining the two: smaller Provençal towns often won't have their own train station, but a local bus connects to the train station at the nearest town. For instance, take a train to Nîmes or Arles and then bus to smaller towns like Les Baux or St-Rémy. Driving is perhaps the best option, since you can travel national or district roads or brave the speeding highways to go quickly from point to point. But be sure to get a good map—road signs can be confusing—and slow down to enjoy all the scenery.

AIR

Marseille (an hour drive from Arles) is served by frequent flights from Paris and London and a direct flight from New York.

Daily flights from Paris arrive at the smaller airport in Nîmes.

Air France flies direct from New York to Nice, 200 km (124 miles) from Arles.

BUS

A moderately good network of private bus services links places not served, or badly served, by trains. Arles is one of the largest hubs, serviced out of the gare routière (bus station) on Avenue Paulin-Talabot, opposite the train station. Within the city, bus stations are mainly on Boulevard G. Clémenceau.

You can travel from Arles to such stops as Nîmes (Edgard ligne 130, €1.50, 50 minutes, 11 daily) and Avignon (LER ligne 18, €7.10, one hour, 10 daily). Ten buses daily also head out to Aix-en-Provence (only two run on Sunday).

Popular destinations include the Camargue's Stes-Marie-de-la-Mer (Envia 20, €1, one hour, seven daily), Mas du Pont de Rousty, and Pont de Gau.

There are also stops in the Alpilles area, including Les Baux-des-Provence and St-Rémy-de-Provence (neither have train stations). You can also reach the latter's bus station at Place de la République by frequent buses from Avignon.

From Nîmes's bus station on Rue Ste-Félicité, you can connect to Avignon and Arles, while Edgard runs you into the deep country. As for Pont du Gard, this is a 40-minute ride from Nîmes; you are dropped off at Auberge Blanche, 1 km (½ mile) from the bridge.

BUS INFORMATION Edgard. ☎ 08–10–33–42–73 ⊕ www.edgard-transport.fr. **Envia.** ⊕ www.tout-envia.com. **LER.** ☎ 08–09–40–04–15 ⊕ www.info-ler.fr.

CAR
The A6/A7 toll expressway (péage) channels all traffic from Paris toward the south. It's called the Autoroute du Soleil (Highway of the Sun) and leads directly to Provence. From Orange, A9 (La Languedocienne) heads southwest to Nîmes. Arles is a quick jaunt from Nîmes via A54.

With its swift autoroute network, it's a breeze traveling from city to city by car in this region. But some of the best of Provence is experienced on back roads and byways, including the isolated Camargue and the Alpilles.

Navigating the flatlands of the Camargue can feel unearthly, with roads sailing over terrain uninterrupted by hills or forests. Despite this, roads don't always run as the crow flies and can wander wide of a clean trajectory, so don't expect to make good time.

Rocky outcrops and switchbacks keep you a captive audience to the arid scenery in the Alpilles; to hurry—impossible as it is—would be a waste.

HORSE
The best way to tour the Camargue park is on horseback, although the wild glamour of the ancient breed of Camargue horses becomes downright pedestrian when the now-domesticated beauties are saddled en masse. Rent-a-horse stands proliferate along the highways, especially near the major towns. Much of this land is limited to walkers and riders, so a trip on horseback lets you experience this landscape without getting your feet wet—literally.

TRAIN
Two Arles-bound TGV (Trains à Grands Vitesses) trains arrive direct from Paris daily; from the Gare Centrale station (Av. Paulin Talabot) you can connect to Nîmes (30 minutes, €11.30), Marseille (one hour, €16.30), Avignon Center (20 minutes, €9.20), and Aix-en-Provence (1 hour 30 minutes with connection, €29.70).

The Gare Avignon TGV station is a few miles southwest of the city in the district of Courtine (a navette shuttle bus connects with the train station in town); other trains (and a few TGV) use the Gare Avignon Center station at 42 boulevard St-Roch, where you can find trains to destinations like Orange (20 minutes, €5.20) and Arles (20 minutes, €7.90).

To Nîmes, there are more than a dozen TGV trains daily on the three-hour trip from Paris; frequent trains connect with Avignon Center (30 minutes, €9.60) and Arles (22 minutes, €9.90). To reach the Vieille Ville from the station, walk north on Avenue Fauchères.

CONTACTS SNCF. ☎ 3635 ⊕ www.oui.sncf.

Restaurants

Culinary pleasures abound in this rugged corner of Provence, from the piquant tapenades made from the area's abundant green or black olives, crème d'ail (roasted garlic cream), and salty anchoiade from Camargue anchovies, to the most sophisticated fare at a Michelin-starred restaurant, all enhanced by the deliciously sun-kissed local wines. The region abounds with top-notch restaurants, both modest and exalted, but a half-hour wander through any of this bountiful region's picturesque town markets (particularly Arles's famous Saturday morning marché) is evidence enough that you've arrived at one of France's great gastronomic capitals.

Hotels

Although Arles, Les Baux, and St-Rémy have stylish, competitive hotels with all the requisite comforts and Provençal touches, from wrought iron to *folklorique* cottons, Nîmes doesn't attract—or much merit—the overnight crowds; thus, its hotels, with rare exception, have little in the way of charm. But throughout the region and well outside the towns you can find lovely converted *mas* (farmhouses), blending into the landscape as if they'd been there a thousand years—but offering modern pleasures, such as gardens, swimming pools, and sophisticated cooking.

Restaurant and hotel reviews have been shortened. For full information, visit Fodors.com.

What it Costs in Euros

	$	$$	$$$	$$$$
RESTAURANTS				
	under €18	€18–€24	€25–€32	over €32
HOTELS				
	under €125	€125–€225	€226–€350	over €350

Visitor Information

Regional tourist offices often charge for a phone call (numbers begin with 08, €0.34 per minute) while written inquiries are free. If you prefer calling, be aware there may be an additional charge. The Comité Régional du Tourisme du Languedoc-Roussillon provides information on all towns west of the Rhône. The remainder of towns covered in this chapter are handled by the Comité Regional du Tourisme de Provence-Alpes-Côte d'Azur.

For information on the area around Arles and St-Rémy, contact the Comité Départemental du Tourisme des Bouches-du-Rhône.

CONTACTS Comité Départemental du Tourisme des Bouches-du-Rhône. ⊠ *13 rue de Brignoles, Marseille* ☎ *04–91–13–84–13* ⊕ *www.myprovence.fr.* **Comité Regional du Tourisme de Provence-Alpes-Côte d'Azur.** ⊠ *62–64 La Canebière, Marseille* ☎ *04–91–56–47–00* ⊕ *www.tourismepaca.fr* Ⓜ *Noailles.* **Comité Régional du Tourisme Occitanie - Montpellier.** ⊠ *417 rue Samuel Morse, Montpellier* ☎ *04–67–22–98–09* ⊕ *www.tourisme-occitanie.com.*

Tours

Arles Guided Visits

GUIDED TOURS | The Arles tourist office offers a wide variety of guided tours in English in all seasons, including tours of the antiquities and monuments, museums, the city's notable houses, and the Camargue. Tour descriptions and prices are readily available on the website and listed according to date. You can also hire a private English-speaking guide to escort you through the major sites or tailor a tour according to your interests. ⊠ *Bd. des Lices, Arles* ☎ *04–90–18–41–20* ⊕ *www.arlestourisme.com* ✉ *From €75.*

Tram

DRIVING TOURS | This taxi company specializes in tours around Nîmes and the area. You can tour the town in a taxi for an hour; when you stop in front of a monument, the driver plays commentary in the language of your choice. Taxis can also take you on a round-trip ride from Nîmes to the Pont du Gard. Ask the taxi to wait while you explore (about two hours). ⊠ *2 bd. Sergent Triaire, Nîmes* ☎ *04–66–29–40–11* ⊕ *www.taxisg7.fr* ✉ *From €60.*

Nîmes

24 km (15 miles) southwest of Pont du Gard; 29 km (18 miles) northwest of Arles.

If you have come to the south to seek out Roman treasures, you need look no farther than Nîmes (pronounced *neem*), for its Arènes and Maison Carrée are among Continental Europe's best-preserved antiquities. This proud, lively city is a model of versatility, where the ancient and the modern complement each other in dazzling juxtaposition. Its compact medieval Old Town has all the grace of Arles or St-Rémy without the tourist congestion or snobbiness. Its rumpled and rebellious side traces directly back to its Roman incarnation, when its population swelled with soldiers, arrogant and newly victorious after their conquest of Egypt in 31 BC. A 24,000-seat coliseum, a thriving forum with a magnificent temple patterned after Rome's temple of Apollo, and a public water network fed by the Pont du Gard attest to its classical prosperity.

Nîmes and its famous aqueduct hold forth in Gard, considered more a part of the Languedoc culture than that of Provence. Yet because of its proximity to the heart of Provence and its similar climate, terrain, and architecture, it is included as a kindred southern spirit. Center of gaily printed *indienne* cottons, Camargue-style bullfights, and spectacular Roman ruins, it cannot be isolated from its Provençal neighbors. After all, the *langue d'oc* (language of "oc") refers to the ancient southern language Occitane, which evolved from Latin; northern parts developed their own *langue d'oïl*. Their names derive from their manner of saying yes: *oc* in the south and *oïl* in the north. By an edict from Paris, the *oïl*s had it in the 16th century, and *oui* and its northern dialect became standard French. Languedocien and Provençal merely went underground, however, and still crop up in gesticulating disputes at farmers' markets today.

In a bid to win UNESCO Heritage status, Nîmes has opted against becoming a lazy, atmospheric Provençal market town and has invested in progressive modern architecture. Smack-dab across from the Maison Carrée stands the city's contemporary answer to it, Sir Norman Foster's impressive modern-art museum and municipal library dubbed the Carrée d'Art (Art Square) after its modernist four-square form—a pillared, symmetrical glass reflection of its ancient twin. Across from the Arènes, the Musée de la Romanité's rippling glass facade recalls a toga and offers some wonderful vistas of the ancient amphitheater and the clay-tiled rooftops of Nîmes from its green rooftop and restaurant. Other investments in contemporary art and architecture confirm Nîmes's commitment to modern ways. ■ TIP→ **If you want to see as much as possible in Nîmes, the Citypass is a good value: it costs €29, is valid for two days (€37 for four days), and can be purchased at most local monuments and sites.**

GETTING HERE AND AROUND

On the Paris–Avignon–Montpellier train line, Nîmes has a direct link to and from Paris (about a three-hour ride). The Nîmes *gare routière* (bus station) is just behind the train station. Edgard runs several buses to and from Arles (11 daily Monday–Saturday, two on Sunday); STD Gard has several buses (Monday–Saturday) between Avignon and Nîmes and Uzès and Nîmes. Some Uzès buses stop at Remoulins for the Pont du Gard and a few continue on to St-Quentin-la-Poterie. Note that although all the sites in Nîmes are walkable, the useful Tango bus runs a good loop from the station and passes by many of the principal sites along the way for €1.60.

Nîmes is a city ideal for walking. For a lovely tour on foot, start at the Jardin de la Fontaine, which is worth at least an hour's exploration around the bath and temple ruins and the wooded gardens above. Follow the canal down the graceful Quai de la Fontaine, an elegant neighborhood that recalls Aix-en-Provence. In ten minutes you'll reach the Maison Carré and the Carré d'Art. The Arène and Musée de la Romanité are a few minutes from here. The mazelike old town, a stone's throw away, is a joy to wander for its many local boutiques, cafés, and épiceries selling all the specialties of Nîmes.

VISITOR INFORMATION

CONTACTS Nîmes Tourist Office. ⊠ 6 rue Auguste ☎ 04–66–58–38–00 ⊕ www. nimes-tourisme.com.

 Sights

⭐ Arènes

ARCHAEOLOGICAL SITE | The best-preserved Roman amphitheater in the world is a miniature of the Colosseum in Rome (note the small carvings of Romulus and Remus, the wrestling gladiators, on the exterior and the intricate bulls' heads etched into the stone over the entrance on the north side). More than 435 feet long and 330 feet wide, it had a seating capacity of 24,000 in its day. Bloody gladiator battles, criminals being thrown to animals, and theatrical wild-boar chases drew crowds to its bleachers. Nowadays the corrida transforms the arena (and all of Nîmes) into a sangria-flushed homage to Spain. Concerts are held here year-round, thanks to a high-tech glass-and-steel structure that covers the arena for winter use. ⊠ Bd. des Arènes ☎ 04–66–21–82–56, 04–66–02–80–80 for féria box office ⊕ www.arenes-nimes. com ⊠ €10.

Carrée d'Art

MUSEUM | Directly opposite the Maison Carrée and looking like an airport terminal, the glass-fronted Carrée d'Art was designed by British architect Sir Norman Foster as its neighbor's stark contemporary mirror. It literally reflects the Maison Carrée's creamy symmetry and figuratively answers it with a featherlight deconstructed colonnade. It contains a library, archives, and the **Musée d'Art Contemporain** (Contemporary Art Museum). The permanent collection falls into three categories: French painting and sculpture; English, American, and German works; and Mediterranean styles—all dating from 1960 onward. There are often temporary exhibits of new work, too. ■ TIP→ **Atop the museum, you can enjoy spectacular views of the city and top-quality local dishes at lunchtime at the Ciel de Nîmes. It's also an excellent spot for a drink or afternoon tea.** ⊠ Pl. de la Maison Carrée ☎ 04–66–76–35–70 ⊕ www. carreartmusee.com ⊠ €5.

Cathédrale Notre-Dame et St-Castor (Nîmes Cathedral)

RELIGIOUS SITE | Destroyed and rebuilt in several stages, Nîmes Cathedral was damaged by Protestants during the 16th-century Wars of Religion but still shows traces of its original construction in 1096. A remarkably preserved Romanesque frieze portrays Adam and Eve cowering in shame, the gory slaughter of Abel, and a flood-wearied Noah. Inside, look for the 4th-century sarcophagus (third chapel on the right) and a magnificent 17th-century chapel in the apse. ⊠ Pl. aux Herbes ☎ 04–66–67–27–72 ⊠ Free.

Jardins de la Fontaine (Fountain Garden)

GARDEN | The Jardins de la Fontaine, an elaborate formal garden, was landscaped on the site of the Roman baths in the 18th century, when the Source de Nemausus, a once-sacred spring, was channeled into pools and a canal. It's a shady haven of mature trees and graceful stonework, and a testimony to the taste of the Age of Reason. It makes for a lovely approach to the Temple de Diane and the Tour Magne. ⊠ Corner of Quai de la Fontaine and Av. Jean-Jaurès ☎ 04–66–58–38–00 ⊠ Free.

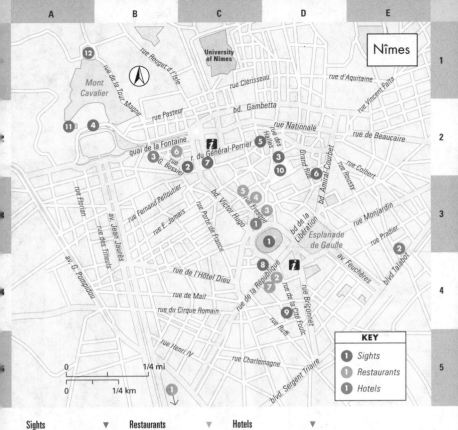

Nîmes

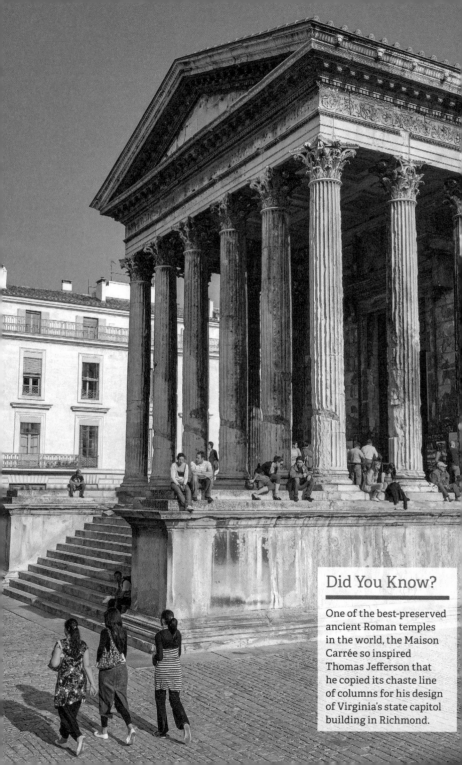

Did You Know?

One of the best-preserved ancient Roman temples in the world, the Maison Carrée so inspired Thomas Jefferson that he copied its chaste line of columns for his design of Virginia's state capitol building in Richmond.

★ Les Halles de Nîmes

MARKET | Nîmes's central covered market is an excellent spot to stock up on all the gastronomic specialties of the area at its more than 100 stalls: crisp PDO (Protected Designation of Origin) picholine olives and olive oil; anchoïade, a heady mix of anchovys crushed with garlic and olive oil; Pélardons goat cheeses from the Cévennes; and Costières de Nîmes wines (Clairette de Bellegarde, Tavel rosé, and Côtes du Rhône Gardoises, among others). This is also one of the best places in Nîmes to grab a bite at lunchtime. ■ **TIP→ For deeply satisfying regional cuisine— think brandade de morue or taureau with camargue rice—and the convivial company of locals head to Halles Auberge, open every day at lunch.** ⊠ *5 rue des Halles* ☎ *04–66–21–52–49* ⊕ *www. leshallesdenimes.com.*

Maison Carrée (*Square House*)

ARCHAEOLOGICAL SITE | Lovely and forlorn in the middle of a busy downtown square, this exquisitely preserved temple strikes a timeless balance between symmetry and whimsy, purity of line and richness of decoration. Modeled on the Temple to Apollo in Rome, adorned with magnificent marble columns and elegant pediment, the Maison Carrée remains one of the most noble surviving structures of ancient Roman civilization anywhere. Built around 5 BC and dedicated to Gaius Caesar and his brother Lucius, the temple has survived subsequent use as a medieval meeting hall, an Augustine church, a storehouse for Revolutionary archives, and a horse shed. Temporary art and photo exhibitions are held here, and among a permanent display of photos and drawings of ongoing archaeological work is a splendid ancient Roman fresco of Cassandra (being dragged by her hair by a hunter) that was discovered in 1992 and carefully restored. There's even a fun 3-D projection of the heroes of Nîmes. ⊠ *Pl. de la Maison Carrée* ☎ *04–66–21–82–56* ⊕ *www.arenes-nimes.com* 🎫 *From €6.*

Musée Archéologique et d'Histoire Naturelle (*Museum of Archaeology and Natural History*)

MUSEUM | **FAMILY** | This old Jesuit college houses a wonderful collection of local archaeological finds, including sarcophagi, beautiful pieces of Roman glass, statues, busts, friezes, tools, coins, and pottery. Among the highlights are a rare pre-Roman statue called *The Warrior of Grezan* and the Marbacum Torso, which was dug up at the foot of the Tour Magne. ⊠ *13 bd. Amiral Courbet* ☎ *04–66–76–74–80* 🎫 *€5* ⊙ *Closed Mon.*

★ Musée de la Romanité

MUSEUM | **FAMILY** | The newest museum in Nîmes is impossible to miss: first for its location just opposite the Arènes and second for its exterior—a gleaming translucent facade meant to evoke a Roman toga. This luminous edifice finally gives Roman Nîmes its due, highlighting the evolution of the town's Roman past with more than 5,000 artifacts. The museum's high-tech scenography includes touch screens, interactive displays, scale models of Nîme's Roman sites, and other state-of the art features that will delight both adults and kids. Highlights include intact mosaics discovered in Nîmes during recent excavations, a model of a *domus* (Roman house), and a green roof with panoramic views of the amphitheater and all the city's major sites. The sidewalk café is great for a quick lunch or drink, but the restaurant upstairs—with impressive views—is a sit-down affair. ⊠ *16 bd. des Arènes* ☎ *04–48–21–02–10* ⊕ *www.museedelaromanite.fr* 🎫 *€12* ⊙ *Closed Tues.*

★ Musée des Beaux-Arts (*Fine Arts Museum*)

MUSEUM | The centerpiece of this early-20th-century building, stunningly refurbished by architect Jean-Michel Wilmotte, is a vast ancient mosaic depicting a marriage ceremony that provides intriguing insights into the lifestyle of Roman aristocrats. Also in the varied collection are seven paintings devoted to Cleopatra by 18th-century Nîmes-born painter Natoire Italian, plus some fine Flemish, Dutch, and French works (notably Rubens's *Portrait of a Monk* and Giambono's *The Mystic Marriage of St. Catherine*). ⊠ *23 rue de la Cite Foulc* ☎ *04–66–28–18–32* ⊕ *www.nimes.fr* 🎫 *€5* ⊗ *Closed Mon.*

Musée du Vieux Nîmes (*Museum of Old Nîmes*)

MUSEUM | Housed in the 17th-century bishop's palace opposite the cathedral, this museum shows off garments embroidered in the exotic and vibrant style for which Nîmes was once famous. Look for the 14th-century jacket made of blue *serge de Nîmes,* the famous fabric—now simply called denim—from which Levi Strauss first fashioned blue jeans. ⊠ *Pl. aux Herbes* ☎ *04–66–76–73–70* ⊕ *www.nimes.fr* 🎫 *€5* ⊗ *Closed Mon.*

Temple de Diane (*Temple of Diana*)

ARCHAEOLOGICAL SITE | This shattered Roman ruin dates to the 2nd century BC. The temple's function is unknown, though it's thought to have been part of a larger Roman complex that is still unexcavated. In the Middle Ages Benedictine nuns occupied the building before it was converted into a church. Destruction came during the Wars of Religion. ⊠ *Jardins de la Fontaine.*

Tour Magne (*Magne Tower*)

ARCHAEOLOGICAL SITE | At the far end of the Jardins de la Fontaine are the remains of a tower the emperor Augustus had built on Gallic foundations; it was probably used as a lookout post. Despite losing 30 feet in height over the course of time, the tower still provides fine views of Nîmes for anyone energetic enough to climb the 140 steps. ⊠ *Jardins de la Fontaine , Pl. Guillaume-Apollinaire* ☎ *04–66–21–82–56* 🎫 *From €4.*

🍴 Restaurants

★ Alexandre

$$$$ | MODERN FRENCH | Michelin-starred chef Michel Kayser adds a personal touch both to the gradual transformation of the restaurant's modern interior—the restoration of the dining room, a library sitting room—and to local specialties and seasonal menus. Marinated rabbit traditionally cooked with a mustard dressing followed by a rich bull steak with pan-roasted Cantal potatoes and black olives served with a celery, caper, and anchovy "chausson" pastry, all drizzled in Camargue sauce, may not leave room for dessert. **Known for:** top-notch tasting menus; lovely garden terrace; seasonal, regional products. $ *Average main: €61* ⊠ *2 rue Xavier Tronc, Rte. de l'Aeroport* ☎ *04–66–70–08–99* ⊕ *www.michelkayser.com* ⊗ *Closed Mon. and Tues. Sept.–June, Sun. and Mon. in July and Aug., 3 wks in mid-Feb., and 2 wks in late Aug. No dinner Sun.*

★ Bistrot Le République

$$ | FRENCH | This quintessential locals' hangout is packed for lunch pretty much all year-round thanks to that dishes that are deeply French and deeply satisfying. The traditional bistro decor—long bar, leatherette banquettes, large mirrors, and brass railings—has something to do with the appeal of this marvelous restaurant that's casual in every sense except when it comes to food and wine. **Known for:** exceptional service; unpretentious atmosphere; bistro lunch classics. $ *Average main: €18* ⊠ *3 rue de la République* ☎ *04–66–64–26–17* ⊗ *Closed weekends. No dinner.*

★ Gard Ô Vin

$ | WINE BAR | This convivial wine bar, tucked in a corner near a pretty square in the Old Town, is the best place for tasting local wines. The selection of excellent value wines by the glass allows you to take in (literally) the vast wealth of the Côtes du Rhône, deliciously accompanied

Provence's Tasty Treats 🍴

If eating is the national pastime in France, it is a true vocation in Provence. And the pleasure of relaxing in a shady square over a pitcher of local rosé, a bowl of olives, and a regional *plat du jour* is only enhanced in western Provence by quirky local specialties. Consider nibbling tiny *tellines*, salty clams the size of your thumbnail, fresh from the Camargue coast. Or try a crockery bowl of steaming bull stew (*gardianne*), a sinewy daube of lean-and-mean beef from the harsh Camargue prairies, ladled over a scoop of chewy red Camargue rice. The mouthwatering oddity called *brandade* (salt cod pestled with olive oil and milk into a creamy spread) has a peculiar history: cod isn't even native to Nîmes, but was traded, in its leathery salt-dried form, by medieval Breton fishermen in exchange for south-coast salt. The Nîmois mixed in local olive oil and created a regional staple.

It's true that every meal is a culinary event here, but in summer the local cafés and hotels make a special effort to make breakfast memorable. In turn, breakfast is one of the loveliest meals of the day. It's coolest in the morning—the birds chirp, the air is crisp, and the smell of freshly baked croissants is in the air. Stroll to the nearest square to sit under shady plane trees and listen to the relaxing bustle of Provence waking up. Tables are adroitly nestled in gardens or sprawled across freshly swept cobblestones, wrapped in flower-print tablecloths, and sprinkled with nosegays of local flowers. Waiters bustle to and fro calling out friendly greetings while the first gilt-edged cups of espresso are prepared. "Early morning" can be misleading: it could well be 10 or 11 am, but another example of southern charm is the option of a late breakfast.

by local cheeses, charcuterie, or salad plates. **Known for:** friendly and fun atmosphere; top-quality food; wine-lover's paradise. [$] *Average main: €12* ✉ *3 pl. du Marché* ☎ *09–52–15–79–74* 🌐 *www.lafourchette.com/restaurant/gard-o-vin/67216* 🕒 *Closed Sun. and Mon. No lunch Tues. and Wed.*

Le Passage de Virginie

$$ | **BISTRO** | It may be a postage stamp–size dining room with an even smaller terrace on a miniscule street, but this typically southern bistro offers oversize pleasures in the form of fresh, well-prepared, and unpretentious cuisine served in a warm and inviting, if slightly funky, atmosphere. Dishes like tiny mussels with spicy aïoli and melting lamb shoulder with sweet onion confit enhanced by hearty regional wines—all at a reasonable price (especially the two-course €17 lunch menu)—keep devoted locals coming back. **Known for:** tiny hidden gem; fresh, light, healthy choices; warm and accommodating atmosphere. [$] *Average main: €19* ✉ *15 impasse Fresque* ☎ *04–66–38–29–26* 🕒 *Closed Sun. and Mon.*

Le Vintage

$ | **FRENCH** | This popular Old Town wine bar draws a loyal crowd of oenophiles for serious tastings and simple foods—cod stew, hot lentil salad with smoked haddock, beef stewed with capers and pickles, and a pressed goat-cheese terrine. The bar still dominates—all the better for bellying up to a glass of Costières de Nîmes—but the dining room has expanded to embrace the neighboring building. **Known for:** good-value fixed-price menu;

idyllic terrace dining; family-friendly vibe. [$] *Average main: €16* ✉ *7 rue de Bernis* ☎ *04–66–21–04–45* 🌐 *www.restaurant-levintage-nimes.com* 🕒 *Closed Sun. and Mon.*

L'Imprevu

$$ | BISTRO | FAMILY | This warm and convivial contemporary dining room—well located near the Musée d'Art Contemporain and the Old Town—has become a favorite haunt of locals seeking gourmet dining on a budget. Chef Laurent Brémond's market-driven cuisine emphasizes local bounty with a Mediterranean flair. **Known for:** modern takes on French classics; excellent wine list; charming outdoor terrace. [$] *Average main: €22* ✉ *6 pl. d'Assas* ☎ *04–66–38–99–59* 🌐 *www.l-imprevu.com* 🕒 *Closed Tues. and Wed.*

★ Skab

$$$$ | FRENCH | Don't be put off by the name—a blend of the initials of owners Sébastien Kieffer and Alban Barbette—because this restaurant has an enchanting shaded garden terrace and a seasonal menu by chef Damien Sanchez that will not disappoint. Crispy Provençal lamb with seasonal vegetables makes for a great main dish, and for dessert there's poached apple sections on a crispy pastry with apple jelly, nougat, heavy cream, and gingerbread ice cream. **Known for:** outstanding wine list; pretty outdoor courtyard for dining; vegetarian and gluten-free options. [$] *Average main: €50* ✉ *7 rue de la République* ☎ *04–66–21–94–30* 🌐 *www.restaurant-skab.fr* 🕒 *Closed Sun. and Mon., and last 2 wks in Apr.*

Hotels

Hôtel de l'Amphithéâtre

$ | HOTEL | This old private home has fortunately fallen into the hands of a loving and very hospitable owner, who has refinished 18th-century double doors and fitted rooms with restored-wood details, white-tiled bathrooms, and antique bedroom sets. **Pros:** ideally located; good value; friendly hosts. **Cons:** underground parking is a few blocks away; amenities are limited; no elevator. [$] *Rooms from: €90* ✉ *4 rue des Arènes* ☎ *04–66–67–28–51* 🌐 *www.hoteldelamphitheatre.com* 🛏 *14 rooms* 🍴 *No meals.*

La Maison de Sophie

$$$ | B&B/INN | Far from the hustle of town and yet just five minutes from the arena, this luxurious hôtel particulier has all the charm—especially in its elegant and tranquil guest rooms—that the city itself often lacks. **Pros:** big-city elegance mixes nicely with country charm and quiet nights; warm welcome; easy walk from city center and train station. **Cons:** often fully booked long in advance; pool is quite small; breakfast, though very good, is expensive. [$] *Rooms from: €240* ✉ *31 av. Carnot* ☎ *04–66–70–96–10* 🌐 *www.hotel-nimes-gard.com* 🛏 *7 rooms* 🍴 *Free breakfast.*

★ L'Imperator

$$$ | HOTEL | FAMILY | After a several-year, top-to-toe renovation, this local grande dame in a lovely neighborhood near the canal and Jardins de la Fontaine has emerged as a gorgeous contemporary hotel, complete with indoor and outdoor pools, a bistro, and a gastronomic restaurant overseen by superstar chef Pierre Gagnaire. **Pros:** richly atmospheric; excellent location; meticulous attention to detail. **Cons:** pricey; some rooms have better views than others; books up quickly in June around féria time. [$] *Rooms from: €350* ✉ *15 rue Gaston Boissier, off Quai de la Fontaine* ☎ *04–66–21–90–30* 🌐 *www.maison-albar-hotels-l-imperator.com* 🛏 *57 rooms, 8 private villas* 🍴 *No meals.*

Activities

The *corrida* (bull-fight) is a quintessential Nîmes experience, taking place as it does in the ancient Roman Arena. There are

Nîmes is often at its prettiest when bathed in Provence's extraordinary light.

usually three bullfighting times a year, always during the carnival-like citywide férias: in early spring (mid-February), at Pentecost (end of May), and during the wine harvest (end of September). These include parades, a running of the bulls, and gentle Camargue-style bullfights (where competitors pluck a ring from the bull's horns). But the focal point, unfortunately, is a twice-daily Spanish-style bullfight, complete with *l'estocade* (the final killing) and the traditional cutting of the ear. The practice is frequently criticized today and those who are squeamish or value animal rights should do their best to avoid the férias, but this is nonetheless a longstanding tradition in the region.

🛍 Shopping

In Nîmes's Old Town you'll find the expected rash of chain stores mixed with fabulous interior-design boutiques and fabric shops selling the Provençal cottons that used to be produced here en masse

(Les Indiennes de Nîmes, Les Olivades, Souleiado). Antiques and collectibles are found in tiny shops throughout the city's backstreets, but there is a concentration of them in the Old Town.

★ Atelier de Nîmes

CLOTHING | Where else should you buy blue jeans but in the birthplace of denim? Guillaume Sagot's hand-cut jeans for men and women, sold out of his chic boutique-atelier, draw fashionistas from near and far. ⊠ *2 rue Auguste Pellet* ☏ *09–53–40–15–89* ⊕ *www.ateliersden-imes.com.*

Maison Villaret

FOOD/CANDY | The longtime local favorite boulangerie-patisserie Villaret is the best place to buy Nîmes's other specialty: jaw-breaking *croquants* (roasted almonds in caramelized sugar). ⊠ *13 rue de la Madeleine* ☏ *04–66–67–41–79* ⊕ *www. maison-villaret.com.*

Pont du Gard

24 km (15 miles) northeast of Nîmes.

No other ancient Roman sight in Provence rivals the Pont du Gard, a mighty, three-tiered aqueduct midway between Nîmes and Avignon—the highest bridge the Romans ever built. Erected some 2,000 years ago as part of a 48-km (30-mile) canal supplying water to Roman Nîmes, it is astonishingly well preserved. You can't walk across it anymore, but you can get close enough to see the amazing gigantic square blocks of stone (some weighing up to 6 tons) by traversing the 18th-century bridge built alongside it.

GETTING HERE AND AROUND

The best way to get to Pont du Gard is via Nîmes, which is on the direct TGV line from Paris and takes about three hours. The Nîmes bus station is right behind the train station, and Edgard runs several buses daily except Sunday between Nîmes and Pont du Gard (about one hour, €1.50 one-way). If you are coming by car, take the A9 to Nîmes, Exit 50; then take the D979, direction Uzès. Pont du Gard is 14 km (9 miles) southeast of Uzès on the D981.

The Birthplace of Denim

Blue jeans were first created in Nîmes: the word "denim" is derived from the phrase "de Nîmes" ("from Nîmes"). Originally used by local farmers to make wagon covers and work clothes, denim soon made its way to San Francisco, thanks to Bavarian merchant Levi Strauss. Strauss's durable denim work pants, or jeans (which, incidentally, comes from the American mispronunciation of Gênes, the French name for the Italian port of Genova, from which the fabric was originally shipped), became an instant success with gold miners.

Sights

★ Pont du Gard

ARCHAEOLOGICAL SITE | The ancient Roman aqueduct is shockingly noble in its symmetry. The rhythmic repetition of arches resonate with strength, a testimony to an engineering concept that was relatively new in the 1st century AD, when the structure was built under Emperor Claudius. And, unsullied by tourists or by the vendors of postcards and Popsicles that dominate the site later in the day, nature is just as resonant, with the river flowing through its rocky gorge unperturbed by the work of master engineering that straddles it. You can approach the aqueduct from either side of the Gardon River. If you choose the south side (Rive Droite), the walk to the *pont* (bridge) is shorter and the views arguably better. Although the spectacular walkway along the top of the aqueduct is now off-limits, the sight of the bridge is still breathtaking. The nearby Espaces Culturels details the history of the bridge and includes an interactive area for kids. ✉ *400 rte. du Pont du Gard, Vers-Pont-du-Gard* ☎ *04-66-37-50-99* 🌐 *www.pontdugard.fr* 🎟 *€10, includes Espaces Culturels.*

Hotels

La Bégude Saint Pierre

$$ | **HOTEL** | A mere 2 km (1 mile) from Pont du Gard, a 17th-century coach house on 30 acres of greenery has been lovingly converted into this boutique hotel and gourmet restaurant. **Pros:** practical location; friendly staff; lovely pool. **Cons:** street-facing rooms can be noisy; can be difficult to find; vintage atmosphere not for everyone. [$] *Rooms* *from: €198 ✉ 295 chemin des Bégudes, Vers-Pont-du-Gard ☎ 04–66–02–63–60 🌐 www.hotel-begude-saint-pierre.com 🛏 26 rooms 🍴 No meals.*

★ **Le Vieux Castillon**

$$ | **HOTEL** | A five-minute drive from the Pont du Gard, this one-time residence of the Bishop of Uzès is an excellent choice for rest and relaxation in a charming village setting with panoramic views over vineyards and olive groves. **Pros:** exquisite setting; lovely location near Uzès and charming villages of Provence; excellent price-to-quality ratio. **Cons:** not open year-round; pool on the smallish side; some rooms lack views. [$] *Rooms from: €130 ✉ 10 rue Turion Sabatier, Castillon-du-Gard ☎ 04–66–37–61–61 🌐 www.vieuxcastillon.com ⏲ Closed Nov.–Mar. 🛏 34 rooms 🍴 No meals.*

Uzès

14 km (8½ miles) northwest of Pont du Gard; 24 km (15 miles) north of Nîmes.

The picture-perfect village of Uzès (pronounced "ou- *zes*") is a tiny Renaissance gem polished to a mellow shine. In the 1950s the village was falling to ruin, and then saved, as were many villages in France, by André Malraux, the French minister of culture from 1959 to 1969, who designated funds to safeguard France's heritage. As one of the prettiest villages in the region, Uzès caught the eye of wealthy investors from all over Europe and the United States, who sped its recovery by investing in second homes here. Now Uzès is a handsome upscale destination, full of stately Renaissance architecture, lovely boutiques, and a leafy market square (Place du Marché aux Herbes) whose pretty arcades are in full charm during the Saturday and Wednesday morning markets.

GETTING HERE AND AROUND

The nearest TGV station is in Avignon; four buses a day make the trip from Avignon Station to Uzès (No. 115). The direct trip takes about 48 minutes and costs €4 each way. By car, take the N100 to D981, which takes about 41 minutes.

VISITOR INFORMATION

CONTACTS Uzès Tourist Office. ✉ *Chapelle des Capucins, Pl. Albert 1er, Uzès ☎ 04–66–22–68–88 🌐 www.destination-pupg.com.*

Sights

Cathédrale Saint-Théodont

RELIGIOUS SITE | The one-time home of the Bishops of Uzès, the original Saint-Théodont was built in 1090 on the site of a Roman temple, but was demolished during the ensuing religious wars. Though the impressive Fenestrelle Tower—a ringer for the Tower of Pisa minus the tilt—remains, it is too delicate to actually visit. The 19th-century neo-Romanesque facade shelters a pared down interior and one of the oldest pipe organs in France. There are lovely views to be had from the cathedral grounds. ✉ *Rue du Portalet, Uzès ☎ 04–66–22–68–88.*

Ducal Palace

CASTLE/PALACE | The Middle Ages, the Renaissance, and the 17th century are on display at the 1,000-year-and-counting residence of the Dukes of Uzès (when the blue flag is flying you know the Duke is at home). Tours (in French) from the cellars to the Bermonde tower narrate the history of the castle (which is also basically the history of France), including one of its most colorful residents, Anne de Mortemart, wife of the 12th duke; she was the first woman in France to earn a driver's license and also the first to get a speeding ticket. ✉ *Pl. du Duché, Uzès ☎ 04–66–22–18–96 🌐 www.uzes.com/en/chateau/histoire.php 🎟 €13, €20 with guided tour.*

Jardin Médiévale

GARDEN | This lovely compact garden on a 12th-century site re-creates a typical botanical garden with plants commonly used in medieval medicines. It's well worth the steep 100-step climb up the King's tower for the eye-popping views of the town. Afterward, you'll be served a refreshing *tisane* made from the garden herbs. There's also a fascinating 19th-century jail and several art galleries showing local artists. ✉ *BP Hôtel de Ville, Rue Port Royal, Uzès* ☎ *04–66–22–38–21* 🌐 *www.jardinmedievaluzes.com/info-2* 🎫 *€6.*

🍴 Restaurants

La Table d'Uzès

$$ | **FRENCH** | Uzès's only Michelin-starred restaurant comes with a stately but cozy dining room that sets the stage for a memorable meal from start to finish. Give yourself time to fully appreciate the dishes of chef Christophe Ducros, whose magic lies in the seasonal pairings of the freshest ingredients from both the countryside (like lamb served three ways) and coast (coquilles Saint-Jacques with butternut squash, yuzu, and trompette mushrooms) with complementary local wines. **Known for:** location in the town's most elegant hotel; Michelin-star dining; good price-to-quality ratio. [$] *Average main: €22* ✉ *18 rue du Dr Blanchard, Uzès* ☎ *04–66–20–07–00* 🌐 *www.lamaisonduzes.fr/restaurant* 🕓 *Closed Mon. and Tues. year-round. Closed Wed. mid-Oct.–Apr.*

🛏 Hotels

★ **La Maison d'Uzès**

$$$ | **HOTEL** | Each of the nine rooms in this exquisite 17th-century mansion hotel is unique, but what they do have in common is beautiful decor, including high ceilings (many beamed), enormous baths, modern amenities, and typical Uzès charm. **Pros:** spacious rooms all with exquisite decor; easy walk to all of the town's major sights; Michelin-starred restaurant on-site. **Cons:** only one of the three buildings has an elevator; books up quickly in summer; not ideal for kids. [$] *Rooms from: €280* ✉ *18 rue du Dr Blanchard, Uzès* ☎ *04–66–20–07–00* 🌐 *www.lamaisonduzes.fr* 🛏 *9 rooms* 🍽 *Free breakfast.*

★ **l'Albiousse**

$$ | **B&B/INN** | Guests are immediately put at ease by the two charming hosts of this quietly refined bed-and-breakfast central to all the old town's major sights. **Pros:** beautiful decor; central location; resident golden retriever. **Cons:** only five rooms so it books up fast; interior perfume may bother sensitive noses; resident golden retriever. [$] *Rooms from: €187* ✉ *17 rue du Dr Blanchard, Uzès* ☎ *04–66–59–15–74* 🌐 *www.albiousse.com/luxury-bed-rooms-albiousse* 🛏 *5 rooms* 🍽 *Free breakfast.*

Aigues-Mortes

39 km (24 miles) south of Nîmes; 45 km (28 miles) southwest of Arles.

Like a tiny illumination in a medieval manuscript, Aigues-Mortes (pronounced "ay-guh- *mort*-uh") is a precise and perfect miniature fortress-town, contained within perfectly symmetrical castellated walls, with streets laid out in geometric grids. Now awash in a flat wasteland of sand, salt, and monotonous marsh, it once was a major port town from whence no less than St-Louis himself (Louis IX) set sail to conquer Jerusalem in the 13th century. In 1248 some 35,000 zealous men launched 1,500 ships for Cyprus, engaging the enemy on his own turf and suffering swift defeat; Louis himself was briefly taken prisoner. A second launching in 1270 led to more crushing losses, after which Louis finally succumbed to typhus in Tunis.

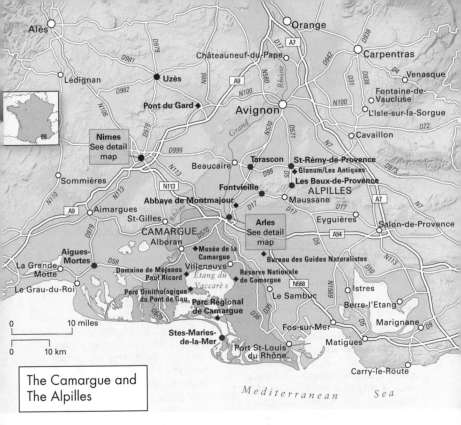

The Camargue and The Alpilles

Several trains a day run to Aigues-Mortes from Nîmes. The trip takes 45 minutes to an hour and costs €8.30. Edgard Transport's C32 bus runs every two hours from Nîmes to Aigues-Mortes. The trip takes an hour and costs €1.50 each way. By car, take the A9 to exit Gallargues (direction Aimargues–St-Laurent-d'Aigouze) and take the D979 directly to Aigues-Mortes.

VISITOR INFORMATION
CONTACTS Aigues-Mortes Tourist Office.
⊠ *Pl. St. Louis* ☎ *04–66–53–73–00*
⊕ *www.ot-aiguesmortes.fr.*

 Sights

Place St-Louis
PLAZA | A 19th-century statue of the father of the fleur-de-lis reigns under shady pollards on this square with a mellow village feel, a welcome retreat from the clutter of souvenir shops on surrounding lanes. The pretty, bare-bones Église Notre-Dame des Sablons, on one corner of the square, has a timeless air (the church dates from the 13th century, but the stained glass is modern), and the spectacular Chapelle des Pénitents Blancs and Chapelle des Pénitents Gris are Baroque-era marvels.
⊠ *Aigues-Mortes.*

Tour et Remparts d'Aigues Mortes
CASTLE/PALACE | The walls and towers of this Gothic fortress, once a state-of-the-art marvel, are astonishingly well preserved. The stout ramparts now contain the tourist-filled village of Aigues-Mortes, but the visit is more than justified by the impressive scale of the original structure, and the vistas of the surrounding

Camargue are stunning. Temporary exhibitions along the ramparts are held in summer, as well as a permanent exhibition on history of Protestantism in the region. ✉ *Pl. Anatole France, Porte de la Gardette* ☎ *04–66–53–61–55* 🌐 *www.aigues-mortes-monument.fr* 🎫 *€8.*

🍴 Restaurants

Chez Bob

$$$ | **FRENCH** | In a smoky, isolated stone farmhouse filled with old posters, you'll taste Camargue cooking at its rustic best. There's only the daily four-course menu (€45), which can include anything from *anchoïade* (crudités with hard-cooked egg—still in the shell—and anchovy vinaigrette) to homemade duck pâté thick with peppercorns, and often features the pièce de résistance: a thick, sizzling slab of bull steak grilled in the roaring fireplace. **Known for:** famous Sunday lunch with live music; meat-heavy menu; family-friendly atmosphere. [$] *Average main: €25* ✉ *Mas Petite Antonelle, D37, Rte. du Sambuc, Villeneuve-Gageron* ☎ *04–90–97–00–29* 🌐 *www.restaurant-bob.fr* 🕑 *Closed Mon. and Tues.*

L'Atelier de Nicolas

$$$ | **BISTRO** | Laid-back and unpretentious as this space may be, when it comes to the food, chef Nicolas Epiard is on his toes, serving up traditional local cuisine with a flair and exuberance that makes the unassuming restaurant one of the best choices in town. Modern style, an open kitchen, and a chalkboard menu—and a bright outdoor terrace—add to the casual feel, while the warm and friendly service enhances the dining experience, but it's the freshness of the food that really shines. **Known for:** sophisticated dining in a friendly, casual atmosphere; wine list with lots of local options; excellent taureau (slow-cooked bull), a local specialty. [$] *Average main: €25* ✉ *28 rue A. Lorraine* ☎ *04–34–28–04–84* 🕑 *Closed Wed., and Thurs. Sept.–June.*

🛏 Hotels

Les Arcades

$ | **B&B/INN** | This beautifully preserved 16th-century house has large, airy guest accommodations, some with tall windows overlooking a green courtyard. **Pros:** rooms overlook a lovely courtyard; free parking card provided at check-in; air-conditioning. **Cons:** not much English spoken at hotel; decor a bit dated; bathrooms are on the small side. [$] *Rooms from: €120* ✉ *23 bd. Gambetta* ☎ *04–66–53–81–13* 🌐 *www.les-arcades.fr* 💳 *No credit cards* 🛏 *9 rooms* 🍽 *No meals.*

Les Templiers

$$ | **HOTEL** | In a 17th-century residence within the ramparts, this delightful hotel sets the stage with stone, stucco, and terra-cotta floors. **Pros:** wonderfully warm welcome; charmingly intimate space; delightful restaurant with home cooking. **Cons:** some rooms are small; amenities are lacking (no minibars); simple decor. [$] *Rooms from: €140* ✉ *23 rue de la République* ☎ *04–66–53–66–56* 🌐 *hotell-estempliers.ellohaweb.com* 🛏 *14 rooms* 🍽 *No meals.*

Villa Mazarin

$$ | **HOTEL** | Despite being in the center of town, you may find it difficult to sleep because it's so quiet at the lovely Villa Mazarin. **Pros:** indoor heated swimming pool; lots of amenities; Clarins products in bathroom. **Cons:** restaurant on the pricey side; books up quickly; inconsistent service. [$] *Rooms from: €165* ✉ *35 bd. Gambetta* ☎ *04–66–73–90–48* 🌐 *www.villamazarin.com* 🛏 *23 rooms* 🍽 *No meals.*

A striking landmark of Aigues-Mortes, the Tour de Constance presides over Louis IX's spectacular fortress-port, erected during the age of the Crusades.

Parc Régional de Camargue

57 km (35 miles) south of Nîmes; 28 km (17 miles) southwest of Arles.

For 1,500 square km (580 square miles), the vast alluvial delta of the Rhône River known as the Camargue stretches to the horizon, an austere marshland unrelievedly flat, scoured by the mistral, swarmed over by mosquitoes. Between the endless flow of sediment from the Rhône and the erosive force of the sea, its shape is constantly changing. Yet its harsh landscape harbors a concentration of exotic wildlife unique in Europe, and its isolation has given birth to an ascetic and ancient way of life that transcends national stereotype. It is a strange region, one worth discovering slowly, either on foot or on horseback—especially as its wildest reaches are inaccessible by car. If people find the Camargue interesting, birds find it irresistible. Its protected

marshes lure some 400 species, including more than 160 in migration—little egrets, gray herons, spoonbills, bitterns, cormorants, redshanks, and grebes, and the famous flamingos. All this nature surrounds a few far-flung villages, rich in the region's odd history and all good launching points for forays into the marshlands.

A land of haunting natural beauty, the Camargue was one of the forgotten areas of France only a few decades ago. Today, thousands of visitors come to discover its peculiar ecosystem and a wild, quirky culture that's just as unique.

GETTING HERE AND AROUND

The best way to explore the park is by car. Roads around and throughout the park have parking areas from which you can set out on foot. You can also explore by bicycle, boat, on horseback, or guided tour. Detailed information on trails and rentals can be found at the tourist offices of both Aigues-Mortes and Stes-Maries-de-la-Mer—the park's major points of entry—and through the Camargue's main

Centre d'Information Parc Naturel Camargue at La Capelière (on the D36b road, 25 km [15½ miles] from Arles).

VISITOR INFORMATION

Centre d'Information de la Réserve Nationale de Camargue

INFO CENTER | At the easternmost point of the Etang du Vaccarès, La Capelière has a good visitor center with maps as well as exhibits on wildlife. There are three *sentiers de découverte* (discovery trails) radiating from its pond-side position, each leading to a small observatory. ⊠ *5 km (3 miles) south of Villeneuve/Romieu, off D37* ☎ *04–90–97–10–82* ⊕ *www.parc-camargue.fr.*

Centre d'Information du Parc Naturel Régional de Camargue

INFO CENTER | Pick up maps, information, and a permit (required for visitors to the reserve) at the center, just up the D570 from the Parc Ornithologique at Pont de Gau. To explore this area, you'll have to strike out on foot, bicycle, or horseback (the park's website has a downloadable English-language brochure with stables clearly marked on a map). Note that you are not allowed to diverge from marked trails. ⊠ *D570, Saintes-Maries-de-la-Mer* ☎ *04–90–97–10–40* ⊕ *www.parc-camargue.fr.*

Sights

★ Bureau des Guides Naturalistes

ECOTOURISM | Covering nearly 1,000 square miles, the triangle between the Camargue, Crau, and the Alpilles (known by naturalists as the *triangle d'or de la biodiversité*) is France's—and one of the world's—most biodiverse regions, home to myriad plant and wildlife species, many rare or endangered. Frédéric Bouvet, an ornithologist who studied extensively in England, is one of four naturalists who offer tours of this exceptional area. The only English-speaking guide of the bunch, Bouvet organizes small, personalized outings focusing on birdlife

Flamingos in the Camargue

In the Camargue, ivory-pink flamingos are as common as pigeons on a city square. Their gangly height, dodolike bill, and stilty legs give them a cartoonish air, and their flight style seems comic up close. But the sight of a few thousand of these creatures taking flight in unison is one you won't forget.

in any part of the region conducted year-round. Tours are customized to your interests, last either a half day or a full day (or up to several days if desired), and can start anywhere in or near the area, depending on the tour and where you are located. For example, his tour in search of the eagle owl, the world's largest nocturnal bird, begins at nightfall. A natural raconteur, Bouvet's passion, enthusiasm, and exceptional knowledge assure an experience—and sights—you will not soon forget. ⊠ *Arles* ☎ *06–20–70–09–61* ⊕ *www.guide-nature.fr* 🖃 *€200 half-day, €300 full-day.*

Domaine de Méjanes Paul Ricard

LOCAL INTEREST | Near the northern shore of the Etang de Vaccarès, one of the larger ranches in the Camargue has now been turned into a showplace for all things taurine. Bullfights, *ferrades,* horse rides, and *spectacles taurine* (bull-baiting) are just some of the activities offered at the Domaine de Méjanes Paul Ricard, 4 km (2½ miles) north of Albaron on D37. Funded by the Ricard pastis family, this unique cultural center allows you to see and meet *gardiens* (French cowboys). You'll learn about the history of the *toro,* or bull, virtually a totemic animal in these parts. The regional spectacle is the *cours camarguaise,* in which bulls are not killed in the arena, simply taunted by *raseteurs* (runners) who try to pluck

Gardians are a type of open-range cowboy you might see herding horses in the Camargue.

off a red cockade and two white tassels mounted on the bull's horns. There is no *mise à mort* (as in the bloody and cruel Spanish corrida); bulls live to enter the arena again and again, and some become such celebrities they make the covers of French magazines. At the Domaine, you can also ride a petit train for a 20-minute tour of the marshlands. ⊠ *D37, on edge of Etage de Vacarrès* ☎ *04–90–97–10–10* ⊕ *www.mejanes.camargue.fr.*

Musée de la Camargue
MUSEUM | North of the village of Albaron, between Arles and Stes-Maries-de-la-Mer, this former sheep ranch is now a museum devoted to the region's history, produce, and people, including the *gardians*. It's also a good place to pick up information about nature trails. ⊠ *Mas de Pont de Rousty, D570, Albaron* ☎ *04–90–97–10–82* ⊕ *www.museedelacamargue. com* ⊠ *€7.*

Parc Ornithologique du Pont de Gau (*Pont du Gau Ornithological Park*)
NATURE PRESERVE | FAMILY | The easiest place to view birdlife is the Parc Ornithologique du Pont de Gau. On some 150 acres of marsh and salt lands, birds are welcomed and protected (but in no way confined); injured birds are treated and kept in large pens, to be released if and when able to survive. A series of boardwalks (including a short, child-friendly inner loop) snakes over the wetlands, the longest leading to an observation blind, where a half hour of silence, binoculars in hand, can reveal unsuspected satisfactions. ⊠ *D570, 5 km (3 miles) north of Stes-Maries-de-la-Mer, Saintes-Maries-de-la-Mer* ☎ *04–90–97–82–62* ⊕ *www.parcornithologique.com* ⊠ *€8.*

Parc Régional de Camargue
NATIONAL/STATE PARK | As you drive the few roads that crisscross the Camargue, you'll usually be within the boundaries of the Parc Régional de Camargue. Unlike state and national parks in the United States, this area is privately owned and utilized within rules imposed by the state. The principal owners, the famous *manadiers* (the Camargue equivalent of

a small-scale rancher), with the help of their *gardians,* keep it for grazing their wide-horned bulls and their broad-bellied, white-dappled horses. It is thought that these beasts are the descendents of ancient, indigenous wild animals, and though they're positively bovine in their placidity today, they still bear the noble marks of their ancestors. The strong, heavy-tailed Camargue horse has been traced to the Paleolithic period (though some claim the Moors imported an Arab strain) and is prized for its stolid endurance and tough hooves. The curved-horned *taureau* (bull), if not indigenous, may have been imported by Attila the Hun.

When it's not participating in a bloodless bullfight (mounted players try to hook a ribbon from the base of its horns), a bull may well end up in the wine-rich regional stew called *gardianne de taureau.* Riding through the marshlands in leather pants and wide-rimmed black hats and wielding long prongs to prod their cattle, the gardians themselves are as fascinating as the wildlife. Their homes—tiny, whitewashed, cane-thatched huts with the north end raked and curved apselike against the vicious mistral—dot the countryside. The signature wrought-iron crosses at the gable invoke holy protection, and if God isn't watching over this treeless plain, they ground lightning. 🌐 *www.parc-camargue.fr.*

Réserve Nationale de Camargue
NATURE PRESERVE | If you're an even more committed nature lover, venture into this inner sanctum of the Camargue, an intensely protected area that contains the central pond called Le Vaccarès, mostly used for approved scientific research. The wildlife (birds, nutria, fish) is virtually undisturbed here, but you won't come across the cabins and herds of bulls and horses that most people expect from the Camargue.

Hotels

★ Mas de Peint
$$$ | HOTEL | Sitting on roughly 1,250 acres of Camargue ranch land, this exquisite 17th-century farmhouse may just offer the ultimate mas experience. **Pros:** isolated setting makes for a romantic getaway; on-site pool and lots of activities offered; no detail is missed in service or style. **Cons:** not all rooms have showers; a bit rustic, including lots of mosquitoes; not much to do once sun goes down, which some appreciate. [$] *Rooms from: €300* ✉ *D36, 20 km (12 miles) south of Arles, Le Sambuc* ☎ *04–90–97–20–62* 🌐 *www.masdepeint.com* 🕓 *Closed mid-Nov.–Mar.* 🛏 *13 rooms* 🍴 *No meals.*

Stes-Maries-de-la-Mer

31 km (19 miles) southeast of Aigues-Mortes; 40 km (25 miles) southwest of Arles.

The principal town within the confines of the Parc Régional de Camargue, Stes-Maries became a pilgrimage town due to its fascinating history. Provençal legend has it that around AD 45 a band of the first Christians was rounded up and set adrift at sea in a boat without a sail and without provisions. Their stellar ranks included Mary Magdalene, Martha, and Mary Salome, mother of apostles James and John; Mary Jacoby, sister of the Virgin; and Lazarus, risen from the dead (or another Lazarus, depending on whom you ask). Joining them in their fate: a dark-skinned servant girl named Sarah. Miraculously, their boat washed ashore at this ancient site, and the grateful Marys built a chapel in thanks. Martha moved on to Tarascon to tackle dragons, and Lazarus founded the church in Marseille. But Mary Jacoby and Mary Salome remained in their old age, and Sarah stayed with them, begging in the streets to support them in their ministry. The three women died at the same time and were buried together at the site of their chapel.

A cult grew up around this legendary spot, and a church was built around it. When in the 15th century a stone memorial and two female bodies were found under the original chapel, the miracle was for all practical purposes confirmed, and the Romanesque church expanded to receive a new influx of pilgrims. But the pilgrims attracted to Stes-Maries aren't all lighting candles to the two St. Marys: the servant girl Sarah has been adopted as an honorary saint by the Roma of the world, who blacken the crypt's domed ceiling with the soot of their votive candles lighted in her honor.

To honor the presiding spirits of Stes-Maries-de-la-Mer, two extraordinary festivals take place every year in Stes-Maries, one May 24–25 and the other on the Sunday nearest to October 22. On May 24 Roma pilgrims gather from across Europe and carry the wooden statue of Sarah from her crypt, through the streets of the village, and down to the sea to be washed. The next day they carry a wooden statue of the two St. Marys, kneeling in their wooden boat, to the sea for their own holy bath. The same ritual is repeated by a less colorful crowd of non-Roma pilgrims on October 22, who carry the two Marys back to the sea.

GETTING HERE AND AROUND
The nearest train station with bus connections to Stes-Maries-de-la-Mer is in Arles. Several buses a day run from Arles to Stes-Maries-de-la-Mer. The company serving this area is Envia, which runs buses up to seven times a day (line 20), depending on the season. The trip takes about one hour and costs €1 one-way. By car—your best bet by far—take the A54 and at exit 4 take the D570 directly to Stes-Maries-de-la-Mer.

VISITOR INFORMATION
CONTACTS Stes-Maries-de-la-Mer Tourist Office. ⊠ *5 av. Van Gogh, Saintes-Maries-de-la-Mer* ☎ *04–90–97–82–55* ⊕ *www. saintesmaries.com.*

 # Sights

As you enter this town's mammoth and medieval cathedral, the Église des Stes-Maries, you'll notice an oddity that wrenches you back to this century: a sign on the door forbids visitors to come *torse nu* (topless). For outside its otherworldly role as the pilgrimage center hallowed as the European landfall of the Virgin Mary, Stes-Maries is first and foremost a beach resort, dead-flat, whitewashed, and more than a little tacky. Unless you've made a pilgrimage to the sun and sand, you probably won't want to spend much time in the town center. And if you've chosen Stes-Maries as a base for viewing the Camargue, consider one of the discreet country inns outside the city limits.

Église des Stes-Maries
RELIGIOUS SITE | What is most striking to a visitor entering the damp, dark, and forbidding fortress-church Église des Stes-Maries is its novel character. Almost devoid of windows, its tall, barren single nave is cluttered with florid and sentimental ex-votos (tokens of blessings, prayers, and thanks) and primitive artworks depicting the famous trio. For €3 you can climb up to the terrace for a panoramic view of the Camargue (hours vary depending on the season). ⊠ *Saintes-Maries-de-la-Mer* ⊕ *www.sanctuaire-des-saintesmaries.fr.*

 # Hotels

★ Cacharel Hôtel
$$ | B&B/INN | FAMILY | A haven for nature lovers, this quiet, laid-back retreat is nestled in the middle of 170 acres of private marshland. **Pros:** can view flamingoes from your window; scintillating taste of the real Camargue in a beautiful wild

setting; fabulous pool. **Cons:** rooms are very sparse, almost monastic; not much to do in the way of socializing; a drive into town. $ *Rooms from: €151* ✉ *Rte. de Cacharel, 4 km (2½ miles) north of town on D85, Saintes-Maries-de-la-Mer* ☎ *04–90–97–95–44* ⊕ *www.hotel-cacharel.com* ⊋ *16 rooms* ⊖⦿ *No meals.*

Mas de la Fouque
$$$ | **HOTEL** | With stylish rooms and luxurious balconies that look out over a beautiful lagoon, this upscale converted farmhouse, just 2 km (1 mile) from deserted beaches, is a perfect escape from the rigors of horseback riding and bird-watching. **Pros:** excellent spa; in the heart of nature, with all the wildlife to prove it; eco-friendly ethos. **Cons:** no nightlife for those who need to be entertained; expensive (but worth it); breakfast not included in rate. $ *Rooms from: €320* ✉ *Rte. du Petit Rhone, Saintes-Maries-de-la-Mer* ☎ *04–90–97–81–02* ⊕ *www.masdelafouque.com* ⊗ *Closed Jan.* ⊋ *26 rooms* ⊖⦿ *No meals.*

Arles

31 km (19 miles) southeast of Nîmes; 40 km (25 miles) northwest of Stes-Maries.

If you were obliged to choose just one city to visit in Provence, lovely little Arles would give Avignon and Aix a run for their money. It's too charming to become museumlike, yet has a wealth of beautifully preserved classical antiquities and Romanesque stonework; quarried-stone edifices and shuttered town houses shading graceful Old Town streets and squares; and pageantry, festivals, and cutting-edge arts events. Its atmospheric restaurants and picturesque small hotels make it the ideal headquarters for forays into the Alpilles and the Camargue.

It wasn't always such a mellow site. A Greek colony since the 6th century BC, little Arles took a giant step forward when Julius Caesar defeated Marseille

in the 1st century BC, transforming it into a formidable civilization—by some accounts, the Rome of the north. Fed by aqueducts, canals, and solid roads, it profited from all the Romans' modern conveniences: straight paved streets and sidewalks, sewers and latrines, thermal baths, a forum, a hippodrome, a theater, and an arena. It became an international crossroads by sea and land and a market to the world. The emperor Constantine himself moved to Arles and brought with him Christianity.

The remains of this golden age are reason enough to visit Arles today. Yet its character nowadays is as gracious and low-key as it once was cutting-edge. If you plan to visit many of the monuments and museums in Arles, purchase a *visite générale* ticket for €16, which covers admission to all of them.

GETTING HERE AND AROUND
If you're arriving by plane, note that Arles is roughly 20 km (12 miles) from the Nîmes-Arles-Camargue airport. The easiest way from the landing strip to Arles is by taxi (about €35). Buses run between Nîmes and Arles 11 times daily on weekdays and four times on Saturday (not at all on Sunday). Four buses run weekdays between Arles and Stes-Maries-de-la-Mer, through Cartreize. The SNCF runs three buses Monday–Saturday from Avignon to Arles. Arles is along the main coastal train route, and you can take the TGV (Trains à Grands Vitesses) to Avignon from Paris and jump on the local connection to Arles. You can also reach Arles directly by train from Marseille. Once there, its monuments and pretty old neighborhoods are conveniently concentrated between the main artery Boulevard des Lices and the broad, meandering Rhône.

VISITOR INFORMATION
CONTACTS Arles Tourist Office. ✉ *Bd. des Lices* ☎ *04–90–18–41–20* ⊕ *www.arlestourisme.com.*

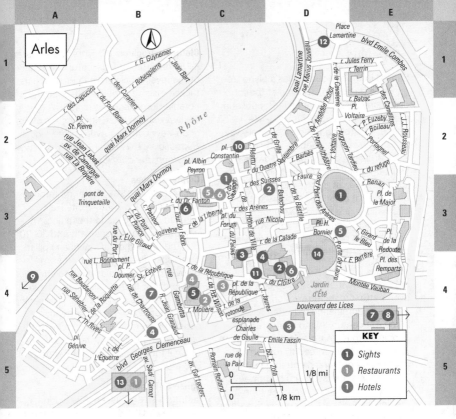

Arles

KEY

1	Sights
1	Restaurants
1	Hotels

⊙ Sights

Seated in the shade of Arles's plane trees on Place du Forum, sunning at the foot of the obelisk on Place de la République, meditating in the cloister of St-Trophime, or strolling the rampart walkway along the sparkling Rhône, you can see what enchanted Gauguin and drove Van Gogh mad with inspiration. It's the light: intense, vivid, crystalline, setting off planes of color and shadow with prismatic concentration. As a foil to this famous light, multihue Arles—with its red-and-gold ocher, cool gray stone, and blue-black shade—is unsurpassed.

★ Arènes (*Arena*)
ARCHAEOLOGICAL SITE | Rivaled only by the even better-preserved version in Nîmes, the arena dominating old Arles was built in the 1st century AD to seat 21,000 people, with large tunnels through which wild beasts were forced to run into the center. Before being plundered in the Middle Ages, the structure had three stories of 60 arcades each; the four medieval towers are testimony to a trans-formation from classical sports arena to feudal fortification. Complete restora-tion of the arena began in 1825. Today it's primarily a venue for the traditional spectacle of the corridas, which take place annually during the *féria pascale,* or Easter festival. The less bloodthirsty local variant Course Carmarguaise (in which the bull is not killed) also takes place here. Festivities start with the Fête des Gardians on May 1, when the Queen of Arles is crowned, and culminate in early July with the award of the Cocarde d'Or (Golden Rosette) to the most successful *raseteur.* Tickets are usually available, but be sure to book ahead. ⊠ *24 bis, Rond Point des Arènes* ☎ *04–90–18–41–20 for arena info, 08–91–70–03–70 for Courses Carmarguaise info* ⊕ *www.arlestourisme. com* 🎫 *€9, includes admission to Théâtre Antique.*

Cloître St-Trophime (*St. Trophime Cloister*)
RELIGIOUS SITE | This peaceful haven, one of the loveliest cloisters in Provence, is tucked discreetly behind St-Trophime, the notable Romanesque treasure. A sturdy walkway above the Gothic arches offers good views of the town. ⊠ *Off Pl. de la République* ☎ *04–90–18–41–20* ⊕ *www. arlestourisme.com* 🎫 *€6.*

Cryptoportiques
ARCHAEOLOGICAL SITE | Entering through the elegant 17th-century City Hall, you can gain access to these ancient underground passages dating to 30–20 BC. The horseshoe of vaults and pillars buttressed the ancient forum from belowground. Used as a bomb shelter in World War II, the galleries still have a rather ominous atmosphere. Yet openings let in natural daylight and artworks of considerable merit have been unearthed here, adding to the mystery of the site's original function. ⊠ *Pl. de la République* ☎ *04–90–18–41–20* 🎫 *€5.*

Église St-Trophime
RELIGIOUS SITE | Classed as a world treasure by UNESCO, this extraordinary Romanesque church alone would justify a visit to Arles. The side aisles date to the 11th century and the nave to the 12th; the church's austere symmetry and ancient artworks (including a stunning early Christian sarcophagus) are fasci-nating. But it's the church's superbly preserved Romanesque sculpture on the 12th-century **portal,** the renovated entry facade, that earns international respect. Particularly remarkable is the frieze of the Last Judgment, with souls being dragged off to Hell in chains or, on the contrary, being lovingly delivered into the hands of the saints. Christ is flanked by his chron-iclers, the evangelists: the eagle (John), the bull (Luke), the angel (Matthew), and the lion (Mark). ⊠ *Pl. de la République* ⊕ *www.arlestourisme.com* 🎫 *Free.*

Van Gogh immortalized the courtyard of this former hospital—now the Espace Van Gogh, a center devoted to his works—in several masterpieces.

★ Espace Van Gogh

GARDEN | A strikingly resonant site, this was the hospital to which the tortured artist repaired after cutting off his earlobe. Its courtyard has been impeccably restored and landscaped to match one of Van Gogh's paintings. The cloistered grounds have become something of a shrine for visitors, and there is a photo plaque comparing the renovation to some of the master's paintings, including *Le Jardin de la Maison de Santé*. The exhibition hall is open for temporary exhibitions; the garden is always on view. ⊠ *Pl. Dr. Félix Rey* ☎ *04–90–18–41–20* 🖾 *Free.*

Fondation Vincent Van Gogh

MUSEUM | Van Gogh's 15-month stay in Arles represents a climax in the artist's career. Enchanted with Arles's limpid light, vibrant landscape, and scenic monuments, Van Gogh experienced here what was to be his greatest blossoming in a decade as a painter. The Fondation Vincent Van Gogh, originally conceived in the mid-1980s in response to the 100th anniversary of the artist's arrival in Arles, pays homage to Van Gogh's legacy and monumental influence via an impressive range of artworks contributed by 90 contemporary artists. Opened in 2014 in the beautifully restored 15th-century Hôtel Léautaud de Donines, the Fondation houses a superb collection of contemporary art and provides a vital addition to Arles's cultural life with a revolving series of temporary art exhibitions, performance art, concerts, and other events. ⊠ *35 rue du Docteur Fanton* ☎ *04–90–93–08–08* ⊕ *www.fondation-vincentvangogh-arles. org* 🖾 *From €9.*

Les Alyscamps

CEMETERY | Although the romantically melancholic Roman cemetery lies 1 km (½ mile) southeast of the Vieille Ville, it's worth the hike—certainly Van Gogh thought so, as several of his famous canvases prove. This long necropolis amassed the remains of the dead from antiquity to the Middle Ages. Greek, Roman, and Christian tombs line the shady road that was once the main entry

A Good Walk in Arles

The best of Arles is enclosed in the inner maze of streets and alleyways known as the Old Town, nestled along the Rhône, where you can find noble 18th-century architecture cheek-by-jowl with antiquities. Only Les Alyscamps necropolis lies outside the city center, but it's still within walking distance.

Though it's a hike from the center, a good place to set the tone and context for your exploration of Arles is at the state-of-the-art **Musée Départemental Arles Antiques.** From here, take advantage of the free museum shuttle; there's an adjacent parking lot if you're day-tripping by car. Get off at the Boulevard Clémenceau and arm yourself with literature at the tourist information center just up the road, on Boulevard des Lices. Then walk up Rue du President Wilson, and left to the **Espace Van Gogh**, the hospital where Van Gogh was taken after he severed his ear. Continue

up Rue du President Wilson to the Rue de la République and the broad **Place de la République**, where you can study the Roman obelisk and the extraordinary Romanesque facade of the **Église St-Trophime.** Next door, enter the hidden oasis of the **Cloître St-Trophime.** Continue up Rue du Cloître to the **Théâtre Antique**, now in Byronesque ruins. Just above rears the **Arènes**, site of gladiator battles and modern bullfights.

Now wander down evocative back streets to the river and the **Thermes Constantin**, the ruins of Roman baths. On Rue du Grand Prieuré, stop into the **Musée Réattu**, which glorifies native-son painter Jacques Réattu and 20th-century peers. Not Van Gogh, alas. Pay homage to that painter by walking up Rue du Quatre Septembre and Rue Amédée Pichot to **Place Lamartine**, where the star-crossed artist lived in his famous Maison Jaune, destroyed in World War II.

to Arles, the Aurelian Way. The finest of the stone coffins have been plundered over the centuries, thus no single work of surpassing beauty remains here (they're in the Musée Départmental Arles Antiques). Next to the ruins rise the Romanesque tower and ruined church of St-Honorat, where (legend has it) St-Trophime fell to his knees when God spoke to him. ⊠ *Allée des Sarcophages* ☎ *04–90–49–38–20* ⊕ *www.arlestourisme.com* ⊠ *€5.*

★ Luma Arles
MUSEUM | The Luma artistic center focuses on the pioneers of contemporary art and culture, bringing together sculpture, painting, dance, philosophy, literature, gastronomy, sustainability, and design. Luma's several spaces house a rotating

series of cutting-edge exhibitions and workshops geared toward art lovers and the curious of all ages, and the Frank Gehry building, a twisting silo sheathed in glittering silver scales that shimmers on the Arles skyline, is spectacular. ⊠ *45 ch. des Minimes* ⊕ *www.luma-arles.org.*

Musée Départemental Arles Antiques
(*Museum of Ancient Arles*)
MUSEUM | Although it's a hike from the center, this state-of-the-art museum is a good place to set the tone and context for your exploration of Arles. You can learn all about the city in its Roman heyday, from the development of its monuments to details of daily life. The bold, modern triangular structure (designed by Henri Ciriani) lies on the site of an enormous Roman *cirque* (chariot-racing stadium),

and the permanent collection includes jewelry, mosaics, town plans, and carved 4th-century sarcophagi. ■TIP→ **One wing of the museum features a rare intact barge dating to AD 50 and a fascinating display illustrating how the boat was meticulously dredged from the nearby Rhône.** The quantity of these treasures gives an idea of the extent of Arles's importance. Seven superb floor mosaics can be viewed from an elevated platform, and you exit via a hall packed tight with magnificently detailed paleo-Christian sarcophagi. As you leave you will see the belt of St-Césaire, the last bishop of Arles, who died in AD 542 when the countryside was overwhelmed by the Franks and the Roman era met its end. Ask for an English-language guidebook. ⊠ *Av. de la 1ère Division Française Libre, Presqu'île du Cirque Romain* ☎ *04–13–31–51–03* ⊕ *www.arlestourisme.com* ⊠ *€8 (free 1st Sun. of month)* ☉ *Closed Tues.*

Musée Réattu
MUSEUM | Three rooms of this museum, housed in a Knights of Malta priory dating to the 15th century, are dedicated to local painter Jacques Réattu. But the standouts are works by Dufy, Gauguin, and 57 drawings (and two paintings) done by Picasso in 1971—including one delightfully tongue-in-cheek depiction of noted muse and writer Lee Miller in full Arles dress. They were donated to Arles by Picasso himself, to thank the town for amusing him with bullfights. ⊠ *10 rue Grand Prieuré* ☎ *04–90–49–37–58* ⊕ *www.museereattu.arles.fr* ⊠ *€6 (free 1st Sun. of month)* ☉ *Closed Mon.*

Place de la République
PLAZA | The slender, expressive saints of St-Trophime overlook the wide steps that attract sunners and foot-weary travelers who enjoy the modern perspective over this broad urban square, flanked by the classical symmetry of the 17th-century Hôtel de Ville. This noble Italianate landmark is the work of the great 17th-century Parisian architect François Mansart (as in mansard roofs); a passageway allows you to cut through its graceful vestibule from Rue Balze. The obelisk, of Turkish marble, used to stand in the Gallo-Roman cirque and was hauled here in the 18th century. ⊠ *Arles.*

Place Lamartine
PLAZA | Stand on the site of Van Gogh's residence in Arles—the now-famous Maison Jaune (Yellow House), destroyed by bombs in 1944. The artist may have set up his easel on the Quais du Rhône, just off Place Lamartine, to capture the view that he transformed into his legendary *Starry Night*. Eight other sites are included on the city's "Arles and Vincent van Gogh" tour (⊕ *www.arlestourisme.com*), including Place du Forum, the Trinquetaille bridge, Rue Mireille, the Summer Garden on Boulevard des Lices, and the road along the Arles à Bouc canal—each of which features in one canvas or another. ⊠ *Arles.*

Pont Van Gogh (*Langlois Bridge*)
BRIDGE/TUNNEL | He immortalized many everyday objects and captured views still seen today, but Van Gogh's famous painting of the Langlois Bridge over the Canal d'Arles à Bouc—on the southern outskirts of Arles, about 3 km (2 miles) from the old city—seems to strike a particular chord among locals. Bombed in World War II, the bridge has been restored to its former glory. ⊠ *Rte. de Port St-Louis.*

Théâtre Antique (*Ancient Theater*)
ARCHAEOLOGICAL SITE | Directly up Rue de la Calade from Place de la République, are these ruins of a theater built by the Romans under Augustus in the 1st century BC. It's here that the noted Venus of Arles statue, now in the Louvre, was dug up and identified. The theater was once an entertainment venue that held 10,000 people, and is now a pleasant, parklike retreat. Only two columns of the amphitheater's stage walls and one row of arches remain; the fine local stone was used to build early Christian churches. Only a few vestiges of the original

Van Gogh in Arles and St-Rémy

It was the light that drew Vincent van Gogh to Arles. For a man raised under the iron-gray skies of the Netherlands and the city lights of Paris, Provence's clean, clear sun was a revelation. In his last years he turned his frenzied efforts to capture the town's magic.

Arles, however, was not drawn to Van Gogh. Although it makes every effort today to make up for its misjudgment, Arles treated the artist badly during the time he passed here near the end of his life—a time when his creativity, productivity, and madness all reached a climax. It was 1888 when he settled in to work in Arles with an intensity and tempestuousness that first drew, then drove away, his companion Paul Gauguin, with whom he had dreamed of founding an artists' colony.

Frenziedly productive—he applied a pigment-loaded palette knife to some 200 canvases in that year alone—he nonetheless lived in intense isolation, counting his *sous*, and writing his visions in lengthy letters to his long-suffering, infinitely patient brother Theo. Often drinking heavily, occasionally whoring, Vincent alienated his neighbors, goading them to action. In 1889 the people of Arles circulated a petition to have him evicted, a shock that left him less and less able to cope with life and led to his eventual self-commitment to an asylum in nearby St-Rémy. The houses he lived in are no longer standing, though many of his subjects remain as he saw them. The paintings he daubed and splashed with such passion have been auctioned elsewhere.

Thus you have to go to Amsterdam or Paris to view Van Gogh's work.

But with a little imagination, you can glean something of Van Gogh's Arles from a tour of the modern town. In fact, the city has provided helpful markers and a numbered itinerary to guide you between landmarks. You can stand on Place Lamartine, where his famous Maison Jaune stood until it was destroyed by World War II bombs. *Starry Night* may have been painted from the Quai du Rhône just off Place Lamartine, though another was completed at St-Rémy.

The Café La Nuit on Place Forum is an exact match for the terrace platform, scattered with tables and bathed in gaslight under the stars, from the painting *Terrasse de café le soir*; Gauguin and Van Gogh used to drink here. (Current owners have determinedly maintained the Fauve color scheme to keep the atmosphere, but that's about all.) Both the Arènes and Les Alyscamps were featured in paintings, and the hospital where he came after he broke down and cut off his earlobe is now a kind of shrine, its garden reconstructed exactly as it figured in *Le jardin de l'Hôtel-Dieu*.

About 25 km (15½ miles) away is St-Rémy-de-Provence, where Van Gogh retreated to the asylum St-Paul-de-Mausolée. Here he spent hours in silence, painting the cloisters. On his ventures into town, he painted the dappled lime trees at the intersection of Boulevard Mirabeau and Boulevard Gambetta. Between Arles and St-Rémy-de-Provence are the orchards whose spring blooms ignited his joyous explosions of yellow, green, and pink.

stone benches are left, along with the two great Corinthian columns. Today the ruins are a stage for the Festival d'Arles, in July and August, and site of Les Recontres d'Arles (Photography Festival) from early July to mid-September. During these festivals, check for early closing hours. ✉ *Rue de la Calade* ☎ *04–90–49–38–20* 🌐 *www.arlestourisme.com* 🎫 *€9, includes admission to Arènes.*

🍴 Restaurants

★ La Chassagnette

$$$$ | **FRENCH** | Reputedly the original registered "organic" restaurant in Provence, this sophisticated yet comfortable spot, 12 km (7½ miles) south of Arles at the entrance of the Camargue, is fetchingly designed and has a dining area that extends outdoors, where large family-style picnic tables await under a wooden-slate canopy overlooking the extensive gardens. Using ingredients that are grown right on the property, innovative master chef Armand Arnal serves only prix-fixe menus that are a refreshing, though not inexpensive, mix of modern and classic French country cuisine. **Known for:** bucolic setting; outdoor dining; local, seasonal products. [$] *Average main: €37* ✉ *Rte. du Sambuc, D36* ☎ *04–90–97–26–96* 🌐 *www.chassagnette.fr* 🕒 *Closed 2 wks in Nov. and Christmas–early Jan. No dinner Sun.–Wed.*

L'Affenage

$$ | **FRENCH** | A vast smorgasbord of Provençal hors d'oeuvres draws loyal locals to this former fire-horse shed. They come here for heaping plates of fried eggplant, green tapenade, chickpeas in cumin, and a slab of ham carved off the bone—followed by roasted potatoes and lamb chops grilled in the great stone fireplace. **Known for:** copious dishes of local fare; terrace dining; reservations needed in summer. [$] *Average main: €18* ✉ *4 rue Molière* ☎ *04–90–96–07–67* 🕒 *Closed Sun. No lunch Mon.*

L'Atelier de Jean-Luc Rabanel

$$$$ | **MODERN FRENCH** | Jean-Luc Rabanel is the culinary success story of the region, famous for fresh garden-inspired cuisine that he features in this stylish restaurant and cooking school—one of the first among a growing list of organic eateries in France to merit two Michelin stars. Menus are prix-fixe only; the seven-dish tapas-style lunch (€65) is a treat not to be missed, and the "Emotion" dinner menu (€145) is unforgettable. **Known for:** dedication to local and organic cuisine; veggie-centric menu; sophisticated presentation and pairings. [$] *Average main: €125* ✉ *7 rue des Carmes* ☎ *04–90–91–07–69* 🌐 *www.rabanel.com* 🕒 *Closed Mon. and Tues.*

L'Autruche

$$ | **BISTRO** | This small contemporary bistro in central Arles provides friendly service and innovative, affordable cuisine with modern leanings. The menu changes frequently, depending on what's available in the market, but sumptuous dishes that are typical of this inventive chef's repertoire include fillet of cod with golden turnips, pumpkin puree, and wild mushrooms sprinkled with fresh chervil; and creamy risotto with beef bouillon and cheese crisps sprinkled with hazelnuts. **Known for:** a welcome respite from typical tourist fare; highlighting local products; sidewalk dining on quiet street. [$] *Average main: €23* ✉ *5 rue Dulau* ☎ *04–90–49–73–63* 🕒 *Closed Sun. and Mon.*

★ Le Galoubet

$$ | **MODERN FRENCH** | Tucked away under a canopy of green, this cozy and popular-with-locals bistro with a spacious and pretty outdoor terrace serves contemporary French fare far above the usual. Relax in a vintage armchair over an appetizer of creamy burrata cheese with perfectly ripe heirloom tomatoes, or grilled sardines with arugula and olives, followed by succulent guinea fowl or steak smothered in fresh morels with golden frites on the side. **Known for:**

excellent seafood dishes; terrific natural wines; bistro vibe. $ *Average main: €19* ✉ *18 rue du Dr. Fanton* ☎ *04–90–93–18–11* ⊘ *Closed Sun. and Mon.*

Les Filles du 16

$ | **FRENCH** | **FAMILY** | Locals and regulars swear by this laid-back, unpretentious bistro with a charming terrace, specializing in the tastes of the Camargue. The chalkboard menu lists the specials of the day, like a hearty house-made pork terrine, served with mustard and cornichons, followed by tried-and-true dishes like the famously succulent local bull meat stewed with olives or tender duck sweetened with Provençal honey. **Known for:** neighborhood vibe; accommodations for food allergies; excellent wine list. $ *Average main: €16* ✉ *16 rue du Dr. Fanton* ☎ *04–90–93–77–36* ⊕ *www.restaurantlesfillesdu16.fr* ⊘ *Closed weekends.*

Hotels

★ Hôtel d'Arlatan

$$$ | **HOTEL** | Once home to the counts of Arlatan, this ideally located 15th-century stone house, close to the Fondation Vincent Van Gogh, stands on the site of a 4th-century basilica, and a glass floor reveals the excavated vestiges under the lobby. **Pros:** whimsical decor with a cool history; lively atmosphere in the bar and restaurant; exceptional value. **Cons:** heated pool is small; rooms range dramatically in price; mad color schemes may prove distracting to some. $ *Rooms from: €299* ✉ *26 rue du Sauvage* ☎ *04–90–93–56–66* ⊕ *www.arlatan.com* ⊘ *Closed Jan.* ⇥ *45 rooms* ⊙ *No meals.*

Hotel de la Muette

$ | **HOTEL** | This prosaic Old Town option has 12th-century exposed stone walls, a 15th-century spiral staircase, and weathered wood everywhere. **Pros:** good value; convenient to all landmarks; generous buffet breakfast included in price. **Cons:** some rooms can be noisy, especially in summer; Wi-Fi can be spotty; no elevator. $ *Rooms from: €111* ✉ *15 rue des Suisses* ☎ *04–90–96–15–39* ⊕ *www.hotel-muette.com* ⊘ *Closed Jan. and Feb.* ⇥ *18 rooms* ⊙ *Free breakfast.*

Jules César

$$ | **HOTEL** | This 17th-century Carmelite convent makes a picturesque setting for Christian Lacroix's *fantaisie* interiors, featuring all of the fashion designer's signature flourishes: ultramodern color schemes, large (sometimes jarring) motifs, and a jumble of periods and styles. **Pros:** central location; lovely spa and pool; beautiful gardens. **Cons:** indifferent staff; parking not included in price; mod-Baroque decor can be distracting. $ *Rooms from: €190* ✉ *Bd. des Lices* ☎ *04–90–52–52–52* ⊕ *www.hotel-julescesar.fr* ⇥ *52 rooms* ⊙ *No meals.*

La Maison Molière

$$$ | **B&B/INN** | In the heart of Arles, resident *chineur* (that's fancy for "antiques hunter") Michel Montagne decorated his 18th-century home with vintage furniture and paintings from the following century. **Pros:** quiet and central; a little-known gem; breakfast and Wi-Fi included. **Cons:** on the expensive side; limited parking; can be hard to book in summer. $ *Rooms from: €230* ✉ *37 rue Molière* ☎ *06–87–73–39–59* ⊕ *lamaisonmoliere.fr* ⇥ *5 rooms* ⊙ *Free breakfast.*

Le Calendal

$$ | **HOTEL** | In a prime location in Arles's Old Town just steps from the Théâtre Antique, this quaint hotel lacks nothing in the way of charm or service—a more welcoming staff could hardly be imagined. **Pros:** extremely central; some rooms have stunning views of the arena; discounted parking for guests. **Cons:** rooms can be dark; breakfasts plentiful but standard issue; strict no-food policy in rooms. $ *Rooms from: €149* ✉ *5 rue Porte de Laure* ☎ *04–90–96–11–89* ⊕ *www.lecalendal.com* ⇥ *38 rooms* ⊙ *No meals.*

Le Cloître

$$ | HOTEL | Built as the private home for the provost of the Cloisters, this grand old medieval building has luckily fallen into the hands of a friendly, multilingual couple devoted to making the most of its historic details—with their own hands. **Pros:** lovely architecture enhanced by clever use of color; top-notch service from friendly owners; excellent location. **Cons:** no elevator; single rooms quite small; no safe or kettle in room (but available at front desk). $ *Rooms from: €139* ✉ *18 rue du Cloître* ☏ *04–90–96–29–50* ⊕ *www.hotelducloitre.com* ⇴ *19 rooms* ⦿ *No meals.*

★ L'Hôtel Particulier

$$$$ | HOTEL | Once owned by the Baron de Chartrouse, this extraordinary 18th-century *hôtel particulier* is delightfully intimate and decorated in sophisticated yet charming style, with gold-framed mirrors, white-brocade chairs, marble writing desks, artfully hung curtains, and hand-painted wallpaper. **Pros:** combines historical style with high-tech conveniences; quiet and secluded; only a five-minute walk to town center. **Cons:** nonrefundable deposit required when booking; small swimming pool; expensive breakfast (€26). $ *Rooms from: €389* ✉ *4 rue de la Monnaie* ☏ *04–90–52–51–40* ⊕ *www.hotel-particulier.com* ⊗ *Closed Jan.–mid-Mar.* ⇴ *18 rooms* ⦿ *No meals.*

🍸 Nightlife

To find out what's happening in and around Arles (even as far away as Nîmes and Avignon), free weekly *Le César* lists films, plays, cabaret, jazz, and rock events. It's distributed at the tourist office, in bars, clubs, and movie theaters. For information on what's happening locally in Arles and the towns of Provence, including festivals, exhibitions, and leisure activities, the online journal *Ferandole* is an excellent resource.

Patio de Camargue

BARS/PUBS | Although Arles seems like one big sidewalk café in warm weather, the best place to drink is at the hip bar-restaurant Patio de Camargue, with its great location on the banks of the Rhône. It serves terrific tapas, and you can hear guitar music and watch traditional dance from Chico and Los Gypsies, led by a founding member of the Gypsy Kings. Reservations are a good idea in high season. ✉ *49 ch. de Barriol* ☏ *04–90–49–51–76* ⊕ *www.patiodecamargue.com.*

🎭 Performing Arts

Association du Méjan

ARTS CENTERS | Founded in partnership with Actes Sud and housed in the beautiful Chapelle St-Martin du Méjan, this arts organization hosts a year-round program of classical and sacred music; a revolving series of exhibitions featuring painting, sculpture, and photography; and the superb Arles Jazz Festival, held every year in May. ✉ *Pl. Nina Berberova* ☏ *04–90–49–56–78* ⊕ *www.lemejan.com.*

Cinémas Actes Sud

ARTS CENTERS | Run by a large publishing house, this arts complex has a first-rate movie theater. ✉ *Pl. Nina Berberova* ☏ *04–90–99–53–52* ⊕ *www.actes-sud.fr/cinemas-actes-sud.*

🛍 Shopping

Despite being chic and popular, Arles hasn't sprouted the rows of designer shops found in Aix-en-Provence and St-Rémy. Its stores remain small and eccentric and contain an overwhelming variety of Provençal goods.

Arles's colorful markets, with produce, regional products, clothes, fabrics, wallets, frying pans, and other miscellaneous items, take place every Saturday

One of the centers of Provençal folklore, Arles is host to a bevy of parades featuring locals dressed in regional costume.

morning along **Boulevard des Lices,** which flows into Boulevard Clemenceau.

Antiquités Dervieux

ANTIQUES/COLLECTIBLES | Since 1886, the Dervieux family has specialized in antique Provençal furniture. Learn how the smallest of details can distinguish a *panetieres* (bread box) made in Arles from the rest of the country. ✉ *5 rue Vernon* ☎ *04–90–96–02–39.*

Christian Lacroix

CLOTHING | This shop has fabulous picks for women—exuberant scarves, accessories, and colorful sunglasses (Jackie O herself once bought a pair here), as well as a vibrant selection of scented candles, stationery, and glassware in a range of gorgeous jewel tones. There are also some vintage items. ✉ *52 rue de la République* ☎ *04–90–96–11–16* ⊕ *www. christian-lacroix.com.*

★ La Botte Gardiane

SHOES/LUGGAGE/LEATHER GOODS | A family enterprise since 1957, this boot-making company earned the coveted status of

Entreprise du Patrimoine Vivant (living heritage company) as the last shoemaker offering authentic boots for the famous Camargue cowboys, *les Gardians.* Aside from some chic cowboy-esque models, there are stylish and durable full-length fashion boots and booties, suede and leather chukka boots, supersoft espadrilles, and strappy sandals, all made from supple vegetable-tanned calf from the same tanner that supplies Hermès. ✉ *ZA Lallemande, RN 113 296, Aigues-Mortes* ☎ *04–66–73–20–85* ⊕ *labotte-gardiane.com.*

★ La Parfumerie Arlésienne

PERFUME/COSMETICS | Maire Duchêne, an independent perfumer trained in Grasse, the world capital of perfumes, dreamed of creating fragrances that would capture the essence of Arles and its beautiful surroundings. In 2012 her dream came true in this jewel of a boutique where her five sensuous perfumes evoke the spirit of Arles in a mix of citrus and pink peppercorn, the Camargue in notes of vetiver and amber, and Les Baux in lemon and white flowers. Her sublime smelling soaps and candles make for heady mementos of Provence. ⊠ *26 rue de la Liberté* ☎ *04–90–97–02–07* ⊕ *www. la-parfumerie-arlesienne.com.*

Le Château du Bois

PERFUME/COSMETICS | This boutique specializes in a huge range of pure, plant-based cosmetics from Le Château du Bois, one of Provence's oldest and most venerable producers of fine lavender oil. The range includes face creams, hand and body lotions, toning gels, massage oil, bath milk, hydrosol, and much more, all made with the purest essential oils produced nearby. ⊠ *42 rue de la République* ☎ *04–90–52–01–35* ⊕ *www. lavandeandco.fr.*

Les Olivades

TEXTILES/SEWING | Regional fabric is available at every turn, including in this home design boutique, with its tastefully designed drapes, throw pillows, table linens, and a range of their famously luxe upholstery fabrics. ⊠ *4 bd. des Lices* ☎ *04–90–96–37–55* ⊕ *www.lesolivades. fr.*

L'Occitane

LOCAL SPECIALTIES | Having put Provence on the worldwide fragrance map, the scents from this region flourish at this shop close to where it all began. The products here are still made in nearby Manosque using regional ingredients. Make sure to sniff Jasmine Immortelle Neroli, the newest women's fragrance, and Arlésienne, a floral tribute to the women of the South of France. ⊠ *58 rue de la République* ☎ *04–90–96–93–62* ⊕ *www.loccitane.com.*

Souleiado

CLOTHING | This well-stocked boutique has a good selection of fabrics, linens for the table, and clothes for men and women. ⊠ *10 bd. des Lices* ☎ *04–90–18–25–91* ⊕ *provence.souleiado.com.*

Abbaye de Montmajour

6 km (4 miles) north of Arles.

Once the spiritual center of the region and a major 12th-century pilgrimage site (it contained a small relic of the true cross), the haunting ruins of the Abbaye de Montmajour still dominate this romantic windswept landscape.

GETTING HERE AND AROUND

From Arles by car, take the D17 in the direction of Fontvieille and follow the signs to the Abbaye. Cartreize Bus No. 29 runs from Arles 10 times per day weekdays and twice per day on weekends (€2).

Sights

★ Abbaye de Montmajour

RELIGIOUS SITE | This magnificent Romanesque abbey looming over the marshlands north of Arles stands in partial ruin. Begun in the 10th century by a handful of Benedictine monks, the abbey grew according to an ambitious plan of church, crypt, and cloister and, under the management of worldly lay monks in the 17th century, became more sumptuous. When the Catholic church ejected those monks, they sacked the place, and what remained was eventually sold off as scrap. A 19th-century medieval revival spurred a partial restoration, but portions are still in ruins; what remains is a spare and beautiful piece of Romanesque architecture. The cloister rivals that of St-Trophime in Arles for its balance, elegance, and air of mystical peace: Van Gogh, drawn to its isolation, came often to the abbey to reflect, but the strong mistral winds kept him from painting there. The interior, renovated by contemporary architect Rudy Ricciotti, is used for world-class contemporary art exhibitions. ⊠ *D17* ☎ *04–90–54–64–17* ⊕ *www.abbaye-montmajour.fr* 🎫 *€6* ⊙ *Closed Mon. Oct.–Mar.*

Provençal Cottons

Vivid medallion prints, soft floral sprigs, assertive paisley borders—they've come to define the Provençal experience, with their sunny colors, naive prints, and country themes redolent of sunflowers and olive groves. These ubiquitous cottons are actually Indian prints (*indiennes*), first shipped into the ports of Marseille from exotic trade routes in the 16th century. Ancient Chinese wax-dyeing techniques—indigo dyes taking hold where the wax wasn't applied—evolved into wood-block stamps, their surfaces painted with mixed colors, then pressed carefully onto bare cotton. The colors were richer, the patterns more varied than any fabrics then available—and, what's more, they were easily reproduced. They caught on like a wildfire in a mistral, and soon mills in Provence were creating local versions en masse. Too well, it seems: by the end of the 17th century, the popular cottons were competing with royal textile manufacturers, and in 1686, under Louis XIV, the manufacture and marketing of Provençal cottons was banned.

All the ban did was confine the industry to Provence, where it developed in Marseille (franchised for local production despite the ban) and in Avignon, where papal possessions were above royal law. Their rarity and their prohibition made them all the sexier, and fashionable Parisians—even insiders in the Versailles court—flaunted the coveted contraband. By 1734, Louis XV cracked down on the hypocrisy, and the ban was sustained across France. The people protested: the cottons were affordable, practical, and brought a glimmer of color into the commoners' daily life. The king relented in 1758, and peasants were free to swath their windows, tables, and hips with a limitless variety of color and print.

But because of the 72-year ban and that brief burgeoning of the southern countermarket, the tight-printed style and vivid colors remained allied in the public consciousness with the name "Provence," and the region has embraced them as its own. Two franchises dominate the market and maintain high-visibility boutiques in all the best southern towns: Souleiado and Les Olivades. Fierce rivals, each claims exclusive authenticity—regional production, original techniques. Yet every tourist thoroughfare presents a hallucinatory array of goods, sewn into every saleable form from lavender sachets to place mats to swirling skirts and bolero jackets.

Tarascon

18 km (11 miles) north of Arles; 16 km (10 miles) west of St-Rémy.

Tarascon's claim to fame is the mythical Tarasque, a monster said to emerge from the Rhône to gobble up children and cattle. Luckily, Saint Martha (Ste-Marthe), who washed up at Stes-Maries-de-la-Mer, tamed the beast with a sprinkle of holy water, after which the natives slashed it to pieces. This dramatic event is celebrated on the last weekend in June with a parade and was immortalized by Alphonse Daudet, who lived in nearby Fontvieille, in his tales of a folk hero known to all French schoolchildren as *Tartarin de Tarascon*. Unfortunately, a saint has not yet been born who can vanquish the fumes that emanate from

Tarascon's enormous paper mill, and the hotel industry is suffering for it.

GETTING HERE AND AROUND
By car, take the D999 (which turns into the D99) from Nîmes or the N570 from Arles. Local trains also stop at Tarascon on the Avignon–Centre–Arles line. Cartreize is an umbrella organization of buses shuttling between Arles and Tarascon (three buses Monday–Saturday, €2.80, 30 minutes). Edgard buses also run from Nîmes (€1.50), although this is a longer journey (1¼ hours).

VISITOR INFORMATION
CONTACTS Tarascon Tourist Office. ⊠ 62 rue des Halles ☎ 04–90–91–03–52 ⊕ www.tarascon.org.

 Sights

Château
CASTLE/PALACE | Despite Tarascon's modern-day drawbacks, with the walls of its formidable château plunging straight into the roaring Rhône, this ancient city on the river presents a daunting challenge to Beaucaire, its traditional enemy across the water. Begun in the 15th century by the noble Anjou family on the site of a Roman *castellum*, the castle grew through the generations into a splendid structure, crowned with both round and square towers and elegantly furnished. René the Good (1409–80) held court here, entertaining luminaries of the age. Nowadays the castle owes its superb preservation to its use, through the ensuing centuries, as a prison. It first served as such in the 17th century, and released its last prisoner in 1926. Complete with a moat, a drawbridge, and a lovely faceted spiral staircase, it retains its beautiful decorative Renaissance stonework and original cross-mullioned windows. ⊠ Bd. du Roi René ☎ 04–90–91–01–93 ⊕ chateau.tarascon.fr ⊠ €8 ⊙ Closed Mon. Oct.–Mar.

Fontvieille

19 km (12 miles) northeast of Arles; 20 km (12½ miles) southeast of Tarascon.

The village of Fontvieille (pronounced "fohn- vyay-uh"), set among the limestone hills, is best known as the home of 19th-century writer Alphonse Daudet.

GETTING HERE AND AROUND
The nearest train station is in Arles, and from here Cartreize bus line runs several buses a day to Fontvieille (No. 29). The direct trip takes about 30 minutes and costs €1.50 each way. By car, take the A54 to RN113, then RN568, direction Fontvieille.

 Sights

Château de Montauban
HISTORIC SITE | Summering in the Château de Montauban brought French journalist and author Alphonse Daudet a peace he missed in literary Paris. Daudet frequently climbed the windswept, pine-studded hilltop to the rustic old windmill that ground the local grain from 1814 to 1915—the inspiration for his famous folkloric short stories *Lettres de mon moulin*. The windmill is now closed to the public, but the graceful château houses a museum devoted to Daudet's writings, and you can freely stroll the grounds to enjoy the peace and sweeping views of the Rhône valley and the Alpilles from the windmill that so inspired him. ⊠ Ch. Montauban ⊕ www.fontvieille-provence. fr ⊠ €5 ⊙ Closed Oct.–Mar.

Les Baux-de-Provence

9 km (5½ miles) east of Fontvieille; 19 km (12 miles) northeast of Arles.

When you first search the craggy hilltops for signs of Les Baux-de-Provence (pronounced "boh"), you may not quite be able to distinguish between bedrock and

Rising up from a calcareous rock valley, the Château des Baux is the most extraordinary landmark of the "dead city" of Les-Baux-de-Provence.

building, so naturally does the ragged skyline of towers and crenellation blend into the sawtooth jags of stone.

It was from this intimidating vantage point that the lords of Baux ruled throughout the 11th and 12th centuries over one of the largest fiefdoms in the south, commanding some 80 towns and villages. Their virtually unchallenged power led to the flourishing of a rich medieval culture: courtly love, troubadour songs, and knightly gallantry; but by the 13th century the lords of Baux had fallen from power, their stronghold destroyed.

Today Les Baux offers two faces to the world: the ghostly ruins of its fortress, once referred to as the *ville morte* (dead town), and its beautifully preserved Renaissance village. As dramatic in its perched isolation as Mont-St-Michel, in Brittany, and St-Paul-de-Vence, this tiny château-village ranks as one of the most visited tourist sites in France, yet has somehow escaped the usual tourist-trap tawdriness. Lovely 16th-century stone houses, even their window frames still intact, shelter elegant shops, cafés, and galleries that line its car-free main street, overwhelmed by day with the smell of lavender-scented souvenirs. But don't deprive yourself for fear of crowds: stay late in the day, after the tour buses leave; spend the night in one of its modest hotels (or at one of its two splendid domaine hotels); or come off-season, and you can experience its spectacular character—a tour-de-force blend of medieval color and astonishing natural beauty.

GETTING HERE AND AROUND

The easiest way to get to Les Baux is by car. Take the A7 until you reach Exit 25, then the D99 between Tarascon and Cavaillon. Les Baux is 8 km (5 miles) south of St-Rémy by the D5 and the D27. Otherwise, Cartreize runs a bus between Arles and Les Baux (summer only, €2.30). Local trains stop at Tarascon; from here in summer you can take a Cartreize bus to St-Rémy and Les Baux (20 minutes, €1).

VISITOR INFORMATION
CONTACTS Les Baux-de-Provence Tourist Office. ⊠ *Maison du Roy, Rue Porte Mage* ☎ *04–90–54–34–39* ⊕ *www.lesbaux-provence.com.*

 # Sights

Carrières de Lumières
ARTS VENUE | This vast old bauxite quarry has 66-foot-high stone walls that make a dramatic setting for a multimedia show in which thousands of images are projected onto the walls. Exhibitions change periodically, but recent showings have showcased the life and work of Van Gogh and Picasso and the Spanish Masters. ⊠ *Petite rte. de Mailliane, D27* ☎ *04–90–54–47–37* ⊕ *www.carrieres-lumieres. com* 🎫 *From €13.*

Château des Baux
ARCHAEOLOGICAL SITE | FAMILY | High above the Val d'Enfer, the 17-acre cliff-top sprawl of ruins is contained under the Château des Baux umbrella. At the entrance, the Tour du Brau contains the **Musée d'Histoire des Baux,** a small collection of relics and models that shelters a permanent music-and-slide show called *Van Gogh, Gauguin, Cézanne au Pays de l'Olivier,* featuring artworks depicting olive orchards in their infinite variety. From April through September there are fascinating medieval exhibitions: people dressed up in authentic costumes, displays of medieval crafts, and even a few jousting tournaments with handsome knights carrying fluttering silk tokens of their beloved ladies. Fire the catapult or try the crossbow: it's up to medieval you. The exit gives access to the wide and varied grounds, where the tiny **Chapelle St-Blaise** and towers mingle with skeletal ruins. ⊠ *Rue du Trencat* ☎ *04–90–54–55–56* ⊕ *www.chateau-baux-provence.com* 🎫 *From €8.*

Hôtel de Manville
GOVERNMENT BUILDING | Vestiges of the Renaissance remain in Les Baux, including the pretty Hôtel de Manville, built at the end of the 16th century by a wealthy Protestant family. Step into its inner court to admire the mullioned windows, Renaissance-style stained glass, and vaulted arcades. Today it serves as the *mairie* (town hall). Up and across the street, the striking remains of the 16th-century Protestant temple still bear a quote from Jean Calvin: "post tenebras lux" (after the shadows, light). ⊠ *Grand rue Frédéric Mistral.*

Musée Yves-Brayer (*Yves Brayer Museum*)
MUSEUM | In the Hôtel des Porcelet, which dates to the 16th century, the Musée Yves-Brayer shelters this local 20th-century artist's works. Figurative and accessible to the point of näiveté, his paintings highlight Italy, Spain, even Asia, but demonstrate most of all his love of Provence. Brayer's grave lies in the château cemetery. The house at No. 4 on Place de l'Eglise is also decorated with frescoes by the artist. ⊠ *Pl. François Hérain* ☎ *04–90–54–34–39* ⊕ *www. yvesbrayer.com* 🎫 *€8* ☉ *Closed Tues. Oct.–Apr.*

Restaurants

★ Le Bistro du Paradou
$$$ | FRENCH | FAMILY | This spot has seen its share of famous diners, from French movie stars to politicians, but you'd never know it from the friendly and laid-back atmosphere cultivated by the long-time chef and his loyal staff who loudly greet their friends—meaning everyone. From the apéritif until the bill comes (which could be awhile, as you'll want to take your time here), you're drawn into the rhythm of bistro dining in Provence, with a bottle of the house red wine ready at your table and a stellar cheese platter all to yourself. **Known for:** exceptional atmosphere; stellar quality ingredients; set menus with choice between two starters, two mains, and six desserts. $ *Average main: €28* ⊠ *57 av. de la Vallée*

des Baux ☎ 04–90–54–32–70 ⏲ Closed Sun. and Mon.

★ Les Baux Jus

$ | **VEGETARIAN** | Who would have thought to find this caliber of 100% organic, raw, gluten-free, and vegan restaurant in the heart of Provence? Like foodie heaven to those with restricted diets, Les Baux Jus offers a tantalizing range of cold-pressed juices, salads, pastries, and smoothies—the food is so good that even carnivores will appreciate its innovation and freshness. **Known for:** vegan and gluten-free dishes; 100% organic ingredients; friendly atmosphere. [$] *Average main: €16* ✉ *Passage de la Calade* ⏲ *Closed Tues.*

★ L'Oustau de Baumanière

$$$$ | **FRENCH** | This temple to haute-cuisine is an institution in Provence, where diners return year after year for updated versions of dishes they may have first experienced three decades ago. This was the first restaurant outside of the Riviera to earn three Michelin stars, and under chef Raymond Thuillier, a legend in Provence, it rose from the dining room of a small country inn to a table whose guest list included leading artists, movie stars, and heads of state (Picasso, Queen Elizabeth, Churchill, and Harry Truman all dined here). **Known for:** gorgeous setting in a five-star country hotel; refined Provençal cuisine made with fresh ingredients from the hotel garden; Provence's most respected wine list and wines from the hotel domaine. [$] *Average main: €85* ✉ *Mas de Baumanière* ☎ *04–90–54–33–07* 🌐 *www.baumaniere.com/en.*

Hotels

★ Baumanière Les Baux de Provence

$$$$ | **HOTEL** | Spread over five historic buildings just outside the village of Les Baux, guest rooms at this fabled hotel—sheltered by rocky cliffs and set amid formal landscaped terraces and gardens—are the last word in Provençal chic: breezy, private, and beautifully furnished. **Pros:** two of the great restaurants of Provence; full-service spa; three pools. **Cons:** get ready for some snob action; service hit-or-miss; expensive. [$] *Rooms from: €375* ✉ *Val d'Enfer* ☎ *04–90–54–33–07* 🌐 *www.baumaniere.com/en* ⏲ *Closed Mon. and Tues. early Jan.–early Mar. Restaurant closed Jan. and Feb., and Mon. and Tues. in Mar.* 🛏 *54 rooms* 🍴 *No meals.*

★ Domaine de Manville

$$$$ | **HOTEL** | With so much to recommend it—lovely decor, an idyllic setting, impeccable service, a spa, and a golf course—the Domaine de Manville is an ideal spot to relax in a charming location. **Pros:** full-service spa; superb gastronomic restaurant; well-equipped golf center and boutique. **Cons:** expensive; not lacking in snob appeal; some rooms need touching up. [$] *Rooms from: €500* ✉ *Les Baux-de-Provence* ☎ *04–90–54–40–20* 🌐 *www.domainedemanville.fr* 🛏 *38 rooms* 🍴 *No meals.*

La Benvengudo

$$$ | **HOTEL** | **FAMILY** | With manicured grounds shaded by tall pines, this graceful shuttered mas feels centuries old but was built to look that way some 30 years ago. **Pros:** quiet and secluded; lovely pool; excellent restaurant on the premises. **Cons:** set on a main road; strict dining hours observed; need to reserve meals in advance in high season to be sure to get a table. [$] *Rooms from: €250* ✉ *Les Baux-de-Provence* ☎ *04–90–54–32–54* 🌐 *www.benvengudo.com* ⏲ *Closed Nov.–Mar.* 🛏 *25 rooms, 3 apartments* 🍴 *No meals.*

La Reine Jeanne

$ | **B&B/INN** | Churchill and Jacques Brel, Sartre and de Beauvoir (who had separate rooms but a shared balcony) were all happy guests at this modest but majestically placed inn, nicely situated to provide rugged views of the château up the street. **Pros:** views are lovely; a family room sleeps four; charming restaurant. **Cons:** some rooms are tiny; only two rooms have (small) balconies; simple decor. $ Rooms from: €70 ⊠ Grande Rue ☎ 04–90–54–32–06 ⊕ www.la-reine-jeanne.com ⊗ Closed Jan. ⊷ 7 rooms, 1 apartment ❙⊙❙ No meals.

🛍 Shopping

⭐ Mas de la Dame

WINE/SPIRITS | What better place to taste and buy these award-winning wines than at the source? Some of Les Baux's most highly regarded wines, this fourth-generation winemaker's organic reds, whites, and rosés are severed in gastronomic restaurants countrywide. How are they able to reproduce a Van Gogh painting on their labels? Why, that's the family mas in the picture. ⊠ Chemin Départemental 5 ☎ 04–90–54–32–24 ⊕ www.masdeladame.com.

⭐ Moulin Castelas

FOOD/CANDY | This producer of fine local olive oils is an excellent place to learn how top-quality AOC (controlled origin) olive oils are made, from picking and pressing to blending and bottling. Free tours and tastings (in English) are a must when in this olive oil-rich region, and this is the best place to get a feel for why its renowned oils—some made from fermented black olives while most oils are made with only green olives—end up at the tables of some of the best restaurants in France. ⊠ Mas de l'Olivier ☎ 04–90–54–50–86 ⊕ www.castelas.com/huile-olive-baux-provence/en/visit-us.

St-Rémy-de-Provence

11 km (7 miles) northeast of Les Baux; 25 km (15½ miles) northeast of Arles; 24 km (15 miles) south of Avignon.

There are other towns as pretty as St-Rémy-de-Provence, and others in more dramatic or more picturesque settings. Ruins can be found throughout the south, and so can authentic village life.

Yet something felicitous has happened in this market town in the heart of the Alpilles—a steady infusion of style, of art, of imagination—all brought by people with a respect for local traditions and a love of Provençal ways. Here, more than anywhere, you can meditate quietly on antiquity, browse aromatic markets with basket in hand, peer down the very row of plane trees you remember from a Van Gogh, and also enjoy urbane galleries, cosmopolitan shops, and specialty food boutiques. An abundance of chic choices in restaurants, mas, and even châteaux awaits you; the almond and olive groves conceal dozens of stone-and-terra-cotta gîtes, many with pools. In short, St-Rémy has been gentrified through and through, and is now a sort of arid, southern Martha's Vineyard or, perhaps, "the Hamptons of Provence."

St-Rémy has always attracted the right sort of people. First established by an indigenous Celtic-Ligurian people who worshipped the god Glan, the village Glanum was adopted by the Greeks of Marseille in the 2nd and 3rd centuries BC, who brought in sophisticated building techniques. Rome moved in to help ward off Hannibal, and by the 1st century BC Caesar had taken full control. The Romans eventually fell, but the town that grew up next to their ruins came to be an important market town, and wealthy families built fine hôtels (mansions) in its center—among them the family De Sade (whose distant black-sheep relation held forth in the Lubéron at Lacoste). Another famous native son, the eccentric doctor, scholar, and astrologer Michel Nostradamus (1503–66), is credited by some as having predicted much of the modern age.

Perhaps the best known of St-Rémy's visitors was the ill-fated Vincent van Gogh. Shipped unceremoniously out of Arles at the height of his madness (and creativity), he had himself committed to the asylum St-Paul-de-Mausolé and

Did You Know?

No matter that St-Rémy-de-Provence is called "the Hamptons of Provence" (due to its chic shops and restaurants), the town has succeeded in remaining true to its Provençal roots.

wandered through the ruins of Glanum during the last year of his life.

GETTING HERE AND AROUND

Like Les Baux-de-Provence, the easiest way to get to St-Rémy is by car. Take the A7 until you reach exit 25, then the D99 between Tarascon and Cavaillon, direction St-Rémy on the D5. Otherwise, in summer Cartreize runs an Arles–St-Rémy–Les Baux bus service (Monday–Saturday, €2.30). Local trains stop at nearby Tarascon, and from here you can take a Cartrieze bus to St-Rémy (20 minutes, €1).

VISITOR INFORMATION

CONTACTS St-Rémy Tourist Office. ⊠ Pl. Jean-Jaurès ☎ 04–90–92–05–22 ⊕ www. saintremy-de-provence.com.

Sights

Collégiale St-Martin

RELIGIOUS SITE | St-Rémy is wrapped by a lively commercial boulevard, lined with shops and cafés and anchored by its 19th-century church Collégiale St-Martin. Step inside—if the main door is locked, the side door is always open—to see the magnificent 5,000-pipe modern organ, one of the loveliest in Europe. Rebuilt to 18th-century specifications in the early 1980s, it has the flexibility to interpret new and old music with pure French panache; you can listen for free on weekends mid-April–September. ⊠ Pl. de la République ⊠ Free.

Glanum

ARCHAEOLOGICAL SITE | FAMILY | A slick visitor center prepares you for entry into the ancient village of Glanum, with scale models of the site in its various heydays. A good map and an English brochure guide you stone by stone through the maze of foundations, walls, towers, and columns that spread across a broad field; helpfully, Greek sites are denoted by numbers, Roman ones by letters. Glanum is across the street from Les Antiques and set back from the D5, and

the only parking is in a dusty roadside lot on the D5 south of town (in the direction of Les Baux). Hours vary, so check ahead. ⊠ Rte. des Baux de Provence, off D5, direction Les Baux ☎ 04–90–92–23–79 ⊕ www.site-glanum.fr ⊠ €8 ⊗ Closed Mon. Oct.–Mar.

Hôtel de Sade

HOUSE | Make your way to the Hôtel de Sade, a 15th- and 16th-century private manor now housing the treasures unearthed from the ruins of Glanum. The de Sade family built the house around remains of fourth-century baths and a fifth-century baptistery, now nestled in its courtyard. ⊠ Rue du Parage ☎ 04–90–92–64–04 ⊕ www.hotel-de-sade.fr ⊠ €4 ⊗ Closed mid-Sept.–May.

Les Antiques

ARCHAEOLOGICAL SITE | Two of the most miraculously preserved classical monuments in France are simply called Les Antiques. Dating to 30 BC, the **Mausolée** (mausoleum), a wedding-cake stack of arches and columns, lacks nothing but a finial on top, and is dedicated to a Julian, probably Caesar Augustus. A few yards away stands another marvel: the **Arc Triomphal**, dating to AD 20. A lovely spot for a stroll—and within easy walking distance from the city center—the site is open during the day and at night (when handsomely illuminated). ⊠ Av. Vincent Van Gogh.

Musée Estrine Présence Van Gogh

MUSEUM | The 18th-century Hôtel Estrine now houses this museum and has many reproductions of the artist's work, along with letters to his brother Theo and exhibitions of contemporary art, much of it inspired by Vincent. It also contains a permanent collection dedicated to the father of Cubism, Albert Gleizes, who lived in St-Rémy for the last 15 years of his life, and hosts temporary exhibitions. ⊠ Hôtel Estrine, 8 rue Lucien Estrine ☎ 04–90–92–34–72 ⊕ www.musee-estrine.fr ⊠ €7 ⊗ Closed Mon.

St-Paul-de-Mausolé

HOSPITAL—SIGHT | This is the isolated asylum where Van Gogh spent the last year of his life (1889–90). Enter quietly: the hospital shelters psychiatric patients to this day, all of them women. You're free to walk up the beautifully manicured garden path to the church and its jewel-box Romanesque **cloister,** where the artist found womblike peace. ✉ *Chemin St-Paul* ☎ *04–90–92–77–00* 🌐 *www.saint-pauldemausole.fr* 🎫 *€6* 🕓 *Closed Jan.*

Vieille Ville

NEIGHBORHOOD | Within St-Rémy's fast-moving traffic loop, a labyrinth of narrow streets leads you away from the action and into the slow-moving inner sanctum of the Vieille Ville. Here trendy, high-end shops mingle pleasantly with local life, and the buildings, if gentrified, blend in unobtrusively. ✉ *St-Rémy-de-Provence.*

🍴 Restaurants

Bistrot Découverte

$$$ | **BISTRO** | Claude and Dana Douard were happy to collaborate with some of the greatest chefs of our time before getting away from the big city lights to open this bistro–wine bar hot spot in the center of St-Rémy. The wine selection is magnificent, and so is the simple food based on top-notch local ingredients. **Known for:** grilled sea bass; vegetarian-friendly options; terrace dining. $ *Average main: €25* ✉ *19 bd. Victor Hugo* ☎ *04–90–92–34–49* 🌐 *www.bistrotdecouverte.fr.*

★ **Chez Tata Simone**

$$ | **FRENCH** | **FAMILY** | Set in an 18th-century Provençal mas once owned by the *grandmère* of one of the owners, this countrified restaurant is a short drive outside the city but well worth the small effort. Sit inside at wooden tables or out under towering plane trees to enjoy delicious dishes made with locally sourced ingredients that mix classic recipes (yes, from Tata Simone) with a modern touch. **Known for:** country atmosphere; welcoming service; hearty home-cooked dishes. $ *Average main: €18* ✉ *Chemin du Mas de Jacquet* ☎ *04–90–99–65–12* 🌐 *chez-ta-ta-simone.business.site* 🕓 *Closed Mon. and Tues.*

★ **Comptoir 36**

$ | **FRENCH** | **FAMILY** | This stylish modern crêperie set squarely in the center of town is deservedly popular for its all-organic crêpes. All of the ingredients in their salads and delectable crêpes (which can be sampled together in a well-priced combo plate) focus on local, fresh, and artisanal products and are a great accompaniment with a pressed juice or fruit smoothie. **Known for:** chic setting; healthy foods; no alcohol but can BYO for a small corkage fee. $ *Average main: €17* ✉ *36 av. Marechal Juin* ☎ *04–90–94–41–12* 🌐 *www.comptoir36.com* 🕓 *Closed Sun. No lunch Sat.*

L'Aile ou la Cuisse

$$ | **BISTRO** | A popular place for lunch or dinner, this modern bistro and terrace in the heart of the Vieille Ville draws a lively mix of locals, expats, and tourists looking for authentic market-driven meals. A small but satisfying menu is generously laced with local delicacies—savory ragoût of wild boar, cod with pureed local vegetables and tapenade-laden croutons, and poached-egg cocotte with foie gras cream and tumeric-balsamic toasts. **Known for:** long wine list with local options; classic French bistro cuisine; fantastic desserts. $ *Average main: €24* ✉ *5 rue de la Commune* ☎ *04–32–62–00–25* 🌐 *www.laile-ou-la-cuisse-restaurant-saint-remy-de-provence.com* 🕓 *Closed Mon. and Tues. No dinner Sun. Nov.–Mar.*

★ **Restaurant Fanny Rey et Jonathan Wahid**

$$$$ | **FRENCH** | Named for its illustrious chef and pastry chef, the restaurant of the L'Auberge de Saint-Remy hotel draws foodies from near and far. Inventive, earthy, and refined, Rey's cuisine doesn't so much redefine Provençal cooking as expand it: with a laser focus on local, sustainable ingredients, she echews all animal fats, salt, and other staples of French gastronomy in favor of rich, slow-cooked fish and vegetable broths steeped with herbs and seaweeds, olive oil, pepper, and edible leaves and flowers to complement fish and meat. **Known for:** refined and healthy cuisine; famous chef and pastry chef; glassed-in kitchen to see the culinary team at work. $ *Average main: €55* ⊠ *12 bd. Mirabeau* ☎ *04–90–92–15–33* ⊕ *www.aubergesaintremy.com* ⊘ *Closed Wed. No lunch Thurs. and Fri.*

Hotels

Château de Roussan

$$$ | **B&B/INN** | Philippe Roussel, a descendant of the 17th-century owners, has filled his château with lovingly polished antique family furniture, buffed the red clay floors to their original shine, and ensured that guest rooms are light and airy and the bathrooms equipped with all the modern trinkets. **Pros:** eager-to-please, house-proud staff are happy to recount the hotel's history; rooms are very quiet; great restaurant. **Cons:** some rooms are small; elevator doesn't provide access to all rooms; on the pricier side. $ *Rooms from: €300* ⊠ *Rte. de Tarascon, D99* ☎ *04–90–90–79–00* ⊕ *www.chateauderoussan.com* ⇆ *20 rooms* ⧈ *Free breakfast.*

★ Château des Alpilles

$$$$ | **HOTEL** | Reached via a lane of majestic plane trees and set on 8 acres of luxuriant parkland, this gracious five-star manor (it's not exactly a château) dates back to medieval times, and it's one of St-Rémy's dreamiest spots—and that's saying a lot in this château-saturated territory. **Pros:** service that anticipates your every need; top-notch—and reasonably priced—dining on the premises; spectacular grounds in the country only a 5-minute drive from St-Rémy. **Cons:** expensive; not a lot to do after dark; if you prefer contemporary design it isn't

for you. $ *Rooms from: €350* ⊠ *Rte. de Rougadou* ☎ *04–90–92–03–33* ⊕ *www.chateaudesalpilles.com* ⊘ *Closed Jan.–mid-Mar.* ⇆ *21 rooms* ⧈ *No meals.*

★ Hotel de Tourrel

$$$$ | **HOTEL** | Rarely does a hotel aspire to, let alone achieve, such level of craft and elegance down to the finest details. **Pros:** St-Rémy's most beautiful hotel; Michelin-star dining and delicious breakfasts; in the center of town. **Cons:** not cheap; breakfast not included in price; only nine rooms. $ *Rooms from: €350* ⊠ *5 rue Carnot* ☎ *04–84–35–07–20* ⊕ *www.detourrel.com* ⇆ *9 rooms* ⧈ *No meals.*

 Performing Arts

Festival A-Part

ARTS FESTIVALS | For nearly two months of the summer, this Alpilles-wide contemporary arts festival fills nearly 15 venues in several towns, most prominently in St-Rémy. It aims to promote a diversity of disciplines and encourages exchange between artists and audience. ⊠ *St-Rémy-de-Provence* ⊕ *www.festival-apart.org.*

Shopping

Every Wednesday morning St-Rémy hosts one of the most popular and picturesque markets in Provence, during which Place de la République and narrow Vieille Ville streets overflow with herbs and spices, olive oil by the vat, and tapenade by the scoop, as well as fabrics and *brocante* (collectibles). There's a smaller version Saturday morning.

Calanquet

FOOD/CANDY | Olive oil producers for five generations, the family-run mill is known in the gastronomic temples of France for producing one of the country's finest oils. You can buy several varieties at the centrally located boutique—along with a tantalizing array of tapenades, sauces, condiments, conserves, and jams—or visit the mill a mile out of town to see firsthand how the oil is made. ⊠ *8 rue de la Commune* ⊕ *www.moulinducalanquet. fr.*

Christallerie Alban Gaillard

CERAMICS/GLASSWARE | Colorful, whimsical, elegant—these sculptural creations of handblown glass range from exquisite perfume flacons and decorative paperweights to everything you need to impress at the dining table. ⊠ *1405 rte. de Maillane* ☎ *04–32–60–10–28* ⊕ *www. cristalleriedart.com.*

★ Florame

PERFUME/COSMETICS | For fine French beauty products using top-quality organic essential oils distilled in Provence, the beautiful boutique of this Saint-Rémy based company is an excellent place to stock up on soaps, shampoo, body lotions, and everything else to beautify the face and body. ⊠ *6 av. de la Résistance* ☎ *04–32–60–05–18* ⊕ *fr. florame.com.*

Joël Durand Chocolatier

FOOD/CANDY | Known for his creamy ganaches, Joël Durand carries a range of gourmet chocolates, nut creams, toffee, and marmalades made in Provence from tree-ripened fruit. ⊠ *3 bd. Victor Hugo* ☎ *04–90–92–38–25* ⊕ *www.joel-durand-chocolatier.fr.*

★ Lilamand Confiseur

FOOD/CANDY | Much more than just a sweets shop, this historical *confiseur* dates back to 1866 and is in its fifth generation of family ownership on the same St-Rémy premises. Makers of the famous Provençal *calisson,* an almond-shape marzipan confection, as well as a gorgeous array of candied fruits—including everything from cherries and strawberries to kiwis, fennel, and even whole pumpkins—from a recipe credited to Nostradamus (a native son). There are also fruit syrups, jams, chocolates, and regional honey. A tour of the factory and a stop in the beautiful boutique make for a highly pleasurable hour or two. ⊠ *5 av. Albert Schweitzer* ☎ *04–90–92–11–08* ⊕ *www.confiserie-lilamand.com.*

Chapter 4

AVIGNON AND THE VAUCLUSE

4

Updated by
Jennifer Ladonne

◉ Sights	🍴 Restaurants	🛏 Hotels	🛍 Shopping	🍸 Nightlife
★★★☆☆	★★★☆☆	★★★☆☆	★★★☆☆	★☆☆☆☆

WELCOME TO
AVIGNON AND THE VAUCLUSE

TOP REASONS
TO GO

★ **Avignon:** While most exciting during the theater festival at the Palais des Papes (Pope's Palace) in July, Avignon is surprisingly youthful and vibrant year-round.

★ **Châteauneuf-du-Pape:** Probably the most evocative Rhône appellation, this village is just one of many in this area where you can sample exceptional wines.

★ **The Lavender Route:** Get hip-deep in purple by touring the Lavender Route between the Abbaye de Senanque and the historic towns of Sault and Forcalquier.

★ **Perched villages:** Experience the many perched villages of the region, including Gordes and Bonnieux, in a patchwork landscape right out of a medieval Book of Hours.

★ **Roussillon:** With its ocher cliffs that change tones—copper, pink, rust—depending on the time of day, this town is a gigantic ruby embedded in the Vaucluse bedrock.

1 Avignon.

2 Villeneuve-lez-Avignon.

3 Châteauneuf-du-Pape.

4 Orange.

5 Beaumes-de-Venise.

6 Gigondas.

7 Séguret.

8 Vaison-la-Romaine.

9 Crestet.

10 Le Barroux.

11 Mont Ventoux.

12 Crillon-le-Brave.

13 Sault.

14 Forcalquier.

15 L'Isle-sur-la-Sorgue.

16 Fontaine-de-Vaucluse.

17 Gordes.

18 Roussillon.

19 Ménerbes.

20 Lacoste.

21 Bonnieux.

22 Buoux.

23 Saignon.

24 Apt.

25 Lourmarin.

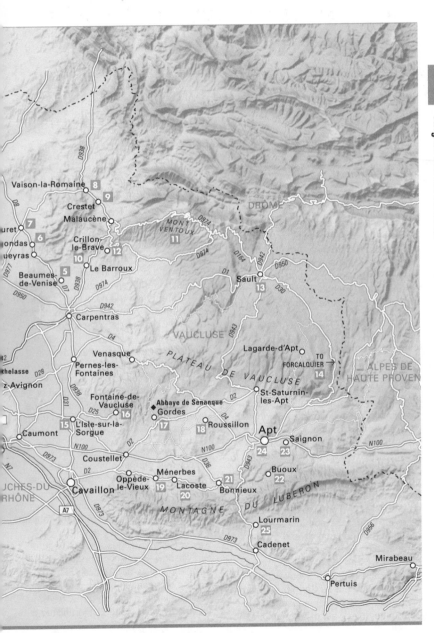

For many, the Vaucluse is the only true Provence—one vast Cézanne masterpiece, where sun-bleached hills and fields are tapestries of green-and-black grapevines and silver-gray olives, and rolling rows of lavender harmonize with mountains looming purple against an indigo sky.

It is here, in his beloved Luberon, that British author Peter Mayle discovered and described the simple pleasures of breakfasting on melons still warm from the sun, buying fresh-dug truffles from furtive farmers in smoke-filled bars, and life without socks. The world shared his epiphany, and vacationers now flock here in search of the same sensual way of life.

Anchored by the magnificent papal stronghold of Avignon, the glories of the Vaucluse region spread luxuriantly eastward of the Rhône. Its famous vineyards seduce connoisseurs, and its Roman ruins in Orange and Vaison-la-Romaine draw scholars, arts lovers, and history buffs. Plains dotted with orchards of olives, almonds, and cherries give way, around formidable Mont Ventoux, to a rich and wild mountainous terrain, then flow into the primeval Luberon. The antiques market in L'Isle-sur-la-Sorgue makes for a terrific Sunday excursion, as does the nearby Fontaine-de-Vaucluse, a dramatic spring cascade (outside drought season). But the Luberon and its villages perched high up in the hills are a world of their own and worth allowing time for—perhaps even your whole vacation. Note that the Pont du Gard, the superbly preserved Gallo-Roman aqueduct, is a 30-minute drive west of Avignon, and

that Arles, Nîmes, and the windswept Camargue are a stone's throw to the south and west.

Just north lies a wine-lover's paradise, as the Côtes du Rhône produce some of the world's most muscular vintages: Châteauneuf-du-Pape and Beaumes-de-Venise are two of the best-known villages, though the names Vacqueyras, Gigondas, and Cairanne also give wine buffs goosebumps. Despite their renown, this area feels off the beaten track even in midsummer, when it's favored by the French rather than foreign tourists. A brisk wind cools things off in summer, as do the broad-leaf plane trees that shade the sidewalk tables at village restaurants and cafés.

East of here, the countryside grows increasingly dramatic, first with the jagged Dentelles de Montmirail, whose landscape is softened by olive groves and orchards, then the surprisingly lush Mont Ventoux, best known as the Tour de France's most difficult stage. Along the way, you'll find villages such as Séguret and Vaison-la-Romaine, where you can sample the slow-paced local lifestyle over a game of pétanque or a lingering apéro. And all this lies a stone's throw from thriving Avignon, its feudal fortifications sheltering a lively arts scene and a culture determinedly young.

MAJOR REGIONS

Avignon. Avignon's most famous bridge—the subject of a French children's song—now stretches only halfway across the river, so don't make the mistake of trying to drive across it. Take the next bridge to L'Île de la Barthelasse, an amazingly rural setting minutes from the city where you can ride a bike through orchards and overnight in lovely auberges. Lorded over by the Palais des Papes, home of the medieval French popes, this fortified city is still encircled by beautifully preserved ramparts. During the world-famous Avignon Festival in July, theater lovers can choose from more than 1,500 performances a day.

Haut Vaucluse. To the north and northeast of Avignon, this land of rolling orchards and vineyards spreads lazily at the foot of Mont Ventoux (Provence's highest peak), redolent of truffles, lavender, and fine wine. Perhaps that's why the Romans so firmly established themselves here, erecting grand arenas and luxurious villas that still in part remain. From Avignon head north into the vineyards, making a brief tour of Châteauneuf-du-Pape, even if you don't stop to drink and buy wine. Orange is just up the highway; although the town isn't the most picturesque, its Roman theater is a must-see. Between Orange and Mont Ventoux are wine centers (Beaumes-de-Venise, Gigondas, Vacqueyras) and picturesque villages such as Crestet, Séguret, Le Barroux, and Malaucène, which the first French pope preferred to Avignon. Visit Vaison-la-Romaine for a strong concentration of Roman ruins.

The Sorgue Valley. This gentle, rolling valley east of Avignon follows the course of the River Sorgue, which wells up from caverns below the arid hills of the Vaucluse plateau, gushes to the surface at Fontaine-de-Vaucluse, and rolls down to turn the mossy waterwheels in picturesque L'Isle-sur-la-Sorgue. If you're fond of antiques, plan to join the festive hordes trawling for treasure at the famous Sunday flea market there. After exploring the fancier *antiquaires* (antiques stores) in town, enjoy an idyllic lunch by one of the town watermills, then track down the "source" of the River Sorgue in the famous spring of Fontaine-de-Vaucluse—the fifth largest in the world. It is a region of transition between the urban outskirts of Avignon and the wilds of the Luberon to the east.

The Luberon. The broad mountain called the Luberon is protected nowadays by the Parc Naturel Régional du Luberon, but that doesn't mean you should expect rangers, campsites, and his-and-her outhouses. It has always been and remains private land, though building and forestry are allowed in moderation and hiking trails have been cleared. The D10, anchored to the west by the market town of Cavaillon and to the east by bustling Apt, parallels the long, looming north face of the Luberon, and from it you can explore the hill towns and valley villages on either side. To its north, the red-ocher terrain around Roussillon, the Romanesque symmetry of the Abbaye de Sénanque, and the fashionable charms of Gordes punctuate a rugged countryside peppered with ancient stone *bories* (drystone huts). To its south lie Oppède-le-Vieux, Ménerbes, Lacoste, and pretty perched Bonnieux. From Bonnieux you can drive over the rugged crest through Lourmarin and explore the less gentrified south flank of the mountain. If you're a nature lover, you may want to venture into the wilder Grand Luberon, especially to the summit called Mourre Nègre.

Planning

When to Go

High heat and high season hit in July and August with a wallop: this lovely region is anything but undiscovered. Not only the French, but tourists from the four corners of Europe and beyond flock to the area for its legendary *savoir-vivre*. You'll miss the lavender if you go in the spring (April, May, and early June) or in September or October, but the vines are golden, the crowds are bearable, and the weather is mild. Crowds or no crowds, it's still an unparalleled corner of the world.

Low season falls between mid-November and mid-March, when many restaurants and hotels take two or three months off. That leaves spring and fall: if you arrive after Easter, the flowers are in full bloom, the air cool, and the sun warm, and you'll still be able to book a table on the terrace. The same goes for October and early November, when the hills of the Luberon turn rust and gold, and game and wild mushrooms figure in every menu.

Planning Your Time

The Vaucluse is more refined than its flashy counterpart, the Côte d'Azur, so take advantage of its gastronomic blessings and sign up for a wine tasting or a cooking course. Hôtel de la Mirande in Avignon offers a superb roster for 6–12 people, in English, including courses around truffles, pastry, cheese, and wine. Or at La Maison sur la Sorgue, the owners will arrange visits (and be the designated drivers) to several of the local vineyards for a dose of viticulture and tasting. While you're in L'Isle-sur-la-Sorgue, arrange to stay over on a Saturday and wake up to the chatter and clatter of the Sunday antiques vendors. Avignon is almost a never-ending festival:

Les Hivernales dance festival (February); Jazz Festival (July and August); Theater Festival (July); Le Off Festival (also July); and the Gastronomy Festival (September). On another musical note for July: Lacoste has a successful arts festival; Orange takes on opera; and noted dance troops take part in Vaison-la-Romaine's Dance Festival, held at the town's Roman theater. But if you want to tiptoe through the best lavender, you'll want to drive through the Luberon between late June and early August to take in endless rows of glorious lavender before it's too late.

Getting Here and Around

If arriving in Avignon by TGV train (Paris–Avignon, 2 hours 40 minutes; Nice–Avignon, 3 hours 15 minutes), arrange for a rental car prior to arrival. Driving is the best choice, allowing you to control your schedule and not fall slave to a public system that isn't on par with that of the Alpes–Maritimes.

Even anxious drivers can find roads linking one village to the next rather easy (pleasant even!) to handle—the only downside is that the driver won't be able to take in all those breathtaking views, like the descent from Le Barroux into the Luberon. Note that country roads, especially over the mountain ranges, can be quite twisty and narrow—and French drivers are unnervingly speedy— but just take it slow and you'll be fine.

Traveling by train in the region can be done from Avignon to L'Isle-sur-la-Sorgue, Cavaillon, Aix, Arles, Orange, and Carpentras. Vaucluse regional buses are few and far between with infrequent schedules, though service has improved from the main towns; consult ⊕ *www.tcra.fr* or ⊕ *www.beyond.fr* for up-to-the-minute listings and fares for Avignon, Orange, Vaison, Manosque, Castellane, and other bus routes.

AIR

Marseille's Marseille Provence, or MP, airport—commonly known as Marignane (which appears on all local signage)—is served by frequent flights from British cities in season; it's about an hour's drive from Avignon.

The smaller Avignon Caumont airport has several daily flights from Paris and Clermont Ferrand and weekly flights from Southampton and Birmingham late May through late September.

CONTACTS Avignon–Provence Airport. ⊠ *100 rue Marise Bastié, Montfavet* ☎ *04–90–81–51–51* ⊕ *www.avignon. aero.* **Marseille Provence airport.** (*Marignane*) ☎ *08–20–81–14–14* ⊕ *www. marseille.aeroport.fr.*

BUS

Major bus companies transport travelers from surrounding cities into towns not accessible by rail; bus and rail services usually dovetail. Avignon's *gare routière* (bus station) has the heaviest interregional traffic.

A reasonable network of private bus services (called, confusingly enough, *cars*) links places not served or poorly served by trains. Ask for bus schedules at train stations and tourist offices. Avignon has a sizable station, with posted schedules.

TransVaucluse has a booth just outside the Avignon train station, offering daily bus excursions into different regions—for instance, the Luberon, Vaison, and the Alpilles. The main destinations serviced to/from the Avignon bus station (10–20 buses daily) are Orange (€3, 45–60 minutes) and Carpentras (€2, 45 minutes). Five or fewer buses daily connect with: Aix-en-Provence (€7.60, 1½ hours), Apt (€5, 1½ hours), Arles (€6.60, 1½ hours), Cavaillon (€2, 1 hour), Nîmes (€1.50, 1½ hours), and Pont du Gard (€1.50, 1 hour).

Bus companies serving the Vaucluse have essentially all merged into Trans-Vaucluse to provide more routes, easier schedules, and cheaper fares. You can access the Luberon villages, Cavaillon, L'Isle-sur-la-Sorge, Aix-en-Provence, and some of the hard-to-reach hilltop villages like Bonnieux from the main Avignon bus station on Avenue Monclar with TransVaucluse buses. Some destinations need a transfer.

CONTACTS Gare Routière. ⊠ *5 av. Monclar at Bd. St-Roch, Avignon* ☎ *04–90–82–07–35.* **Zou.** ☎ *0809/400–415* ⊕ *www.info-ler. fr/449-Votre-reseau-ZOU21.html.*

CAR

The A6/A7 toll expressway channels all traffic from Paris to the south. Orange A7 splits to the southeast and leads directly to Avignon and D10 (in the direction of Apt), which dives straight east into the Luberon. To reach Vaison and the Mont Ventoux region from Avignon, head northeast toward Carpentras on D942. D36 jags south from D10 and leads you on a gorgeous chase over the backbone of the Luberon, via Bonnieux and Lourmarin; from there it's a straight shot to Aix and Marseille or to the Côte d'Azur. Or you can head back west up D973 to Cavaillon and Avignon.

With spokes branching out in every direction from Avignon and A7, you'll have no problem accessing the Vaucluse. The main *routes nationales* (national routes, or secondary highways) offer fairly direct links via D942 toward Orange and Mont Ventoux and via D10 into the Luberon. Negotiating the roads to L'Isle-sur-la-Sorgue and Fontaine-de-Vaucluse requires a careful mix of map and sign reading, often at high speeds around suburban *giratoires* (rotaries). But by the time you strike out into the hills and the tiny roads—one of the best parts of the Vaucluse—give yourself over to road signs and pure faith. As is the case throughout France, directions are indicated by village name only, with route numbers given as a small-print afterthought. Of course, this means you have to recognize the minor villages en route.

If you have access to the Internet while traveling, Vinci Autoroutes is a good website to consult. It not only gives directions for highways and village roads in southern France, but it also indicates weather conditions and traffic problems; although it's in French, it's not difficult to follow. Keep in mind that *péages* are toll booths and *aires* are gas and rest stops.

CONTACTS Vinci Autoroutes. ☎ *No phone* ⊕ *www.vinci-autoroutes.com.*

TRAIN

Trains arrive in Marseille from many main cities, including Paris, Strasbourg, Nantes, and Bordeaux. Those from Paris and Strasbourg pass through Orange and Avignon. The quickest train connection remains the TGV *Méditerranée* line that arrives in Avignon after a 2-hour 40-minute trip from Paris. These TGV trains then connect with Nîmes (from €9.90, 18 minutes), Marseille (from €22.10, 35 minutes), and Nice (from €53, 3 hours). From Avignon's central station, the Gare Avignon Centre, connections include Orange (€6.60, 15 minutes), Arles (€8, 20 minutes), and L'Isle-sur-la-Sorgue. Another big rail nexus is the city of Orange, but note that the city center is a 10-minute walk from the train station. Ticket prices range according to time of day and season, so look online before speaking with an agent.

CONTACTS SNCF. ☎ *3635 within France, 33–184–94–36–35 outside France* ⊕ *www.sncf.com.* **TGV.** ☎ *3635* ⊕ *www. oui.sncf.*

Visitor Information

The VPA Vaucluse Tourisme is a good source of information for the region. For the complete scoop on the hundreds of sights to see in Haute-Provence and other lavender-intensive areas, contact Les Routes de la Lavande.

CONTACTS Les Routes de la Lavande. ✉ *2 av. de Venterol, Nyons*

☎ *04–75–26–65–91* ⊕ *www.routes-lavande.com.* **VPA Vaucluse Tourisme.** ✉ *12 rue Collège de la Croix, Avignon* ☎ *04–90–80–47–00* ⊕ *www.provence-guide.com.*

Restaurants

As the cultural capital of the Vaucluse, Avignon might logically be considered the culinary capital, too. Visit during the July theater festival, however, and you'll have the opposite impression. Sunny sidewalk tables spill out temptingly onto the streets, but nearly all serve the kind of food designed for people on tight schedules: salads, pizzas, and charcuterie plates, often of indifferent quality. For more generous and imaginative Provençal food, you will have to seek out Avignon's culinary gems or scour the countryside, where delightful meals can be had in roadside restaurants, renovated farmhouses, and restaurants with chefs whose talents are as stunning as the hilltop settings where they operate. Be sure to indulge in the sun-drenched local wines from the Luberon, the Ventoux, and the Côtes du Rhône (especially its lesser-known appellations), and if a full bottle seems too much for two people, order one of the 50 cl bottles now popular here (the equivalent of two-thirds of a regular bottle). It pays to do research—too many restaurants, especially in summer, are cashing in on the thriving tourist trade, and prices are generally high.

Hotels

One of the most popular vacation regions in France (after the seaside), the Vaucluse has a plethora of sleek and fashionable converted *mas* (farmhouses), landscaped in lavender, cypress, and oil jars full of vivid flowers, as well as luxurious inns which cater to people fleeing Avignon's summer crowds. There are budget accommodations, too, in the form of cheerful *chambres d'hôtes* and modest but well-run hotels, which often have good restaurants.

Given the crushing heat in high summer and the distance from the sea, the majority have swimming pools and, these days, air-conditioning, although it's wise to check ahead if you're counting on it (one alternative is to stay higher up in the mountains, where there is a refreshing breeze). Only a few lodgings provide *moustiquaires,* mosquito netting put over the bed or window screens to keep out troublesome flies. Reservations are essential most of the year, and many hotels close down altogether in winter.

Restaurant and hotel reviews have been shortened. For full information, visit Fodors.com.

What it costs in Euros			
$	$$	$$$	$$$$
RESTAURANTS			
under €18	€18–€24	€25–€32	over €32
HOTELS			
under €125	€125–€225	€226–€350	over €350

Markets

Browsing through Les Halles, the *marché couvert* (covered food market) in Avignon, is enough to make you renounce dining in the tempting local restaurants.

All the *fantastique* seafood, free-range poultry, olives, and produce cry out to be gathered in a basket and cooked in their purest form.

Village open-air markets are carefully scheduled to cover in turn all the days of the week, including in the yard of the old barracks at Caserne Chabran on Boulevard Limbert on Saturday and a flea market at Place des Carmes on Sunday.

Cruising the Rhône

Tired feet after too many rocky cobblestone paths? Head over to the Allées de l'Oulle and take a cruise along the Rhône. For €12, Le Mireio (⊕ *www.mireio.net*) runs a year-round 45-minute cruise from Avignon to the Isle of Bathelasse to Villeneuve-lez-Avignon. A lunch cruise around the Popes' Palace or the vineyards near Châteauneuf-du-Pape is also a more civilized way to take in the surrounding sights.

But food plays second fiddle at one of the most famous markets in Provence. L'Isle-sur-la-Sorgue draws crowds of bargain hunters and collectors to its Sunday antiques and *brocante* (collectibles) fair. See our special Spotlight section on this famous marketplace.

Wineries and Vineyards

The most serious wine center in the South of France is the southern portion of the Côtes du Rhône, home to the muscular reds of Gigondas, Vacqueyras, Rasteau, Cairanne, and of their more famous neighbor Châteauneuf-du-Pape.

Nearby Beaumes-de-Venise is famous for its sweet, light muscat. Not to be overlooked are the wines of the Côtes du Ventoux and the Côtes du Luberon.

You can visit many vineyards without an appointment. If you find touring vineyards slightly intimidating or impractical, you can still purchase wines from the region: most communes have a shop where local wines are sold at the producer's price, with no markup.

Avignon

44 km (28 miles) northeast of Nîmes;
70 km (43 miles) northwest of
Aix-en-Provence.

Of all the monuments in France—cathedrals, châteaux, fortresses—the ancient city of Avignon (pronounced "ah-veen-yonh") is one of the most dramatic. Wrapped in a crenellated wall punctuated by towers and Gothic slit windows, its historic center stands distinct from modern extensions, crowned by the Palais des Papes, a 14th-century fortress-castle that's nothing short of spectacular. Standing on the Place du Palais under the gaze of the gigantic Virgin that reigns from the cathedral tower, with the palace sprawling to one side, the bishops' Petit Palais to the other, and the long, low bridge of childhood-song fame stretching over the river ("Sur le pont d'Avignon / On y danse tous en rond …"), you can beam yourself briefly into the 14th century, so complete is the context, so evocative the setting.

Yet you'll soon be brought back to the present with a jolt by the skateboarders leaping over the smooth-paved square. Avignon is anything but a museum: it surges with modern ideas and energy, and thrives within its ramparts as it did in the heyday of the popes—like those radical church lords, sensual, cultivated, and cosmopolitan, with a taste for lay pleasures. For the French, Avignon is almost synonymous with its theater festival in July; thousands pack the city's hotels to bursting for the official festival and Le Festival OFF, the fringe festival with an incredible 1,500 performances each day. If your French isn't up to a radical take on Molière, look for English-language productions or try the circus and mime—there are plenty of shows for children, and street performers abound.

GETTING HERE AND AROUND

Avignon is a major rail crossroads and springboard for the Vaucluse and has plenty of car-rental agencies at the Gare Avignon TGV (best to reserve your car in advance). The quickest train link is the high-speed TGV (Trains à Grande Vitesse) *Méditerranée* line that connects Paris and Avignon (2 hours 40 minutes); Nice to Avignon on the TGV (3 hours) costs €58. Keep in mind that the Gare Avignon TGV is a few miles southwest of the city (a train shuttle bus connects with the train station in town every 15 minutes from early morning to late at night). Other trains, such as the Avignon–Orange line (€6.60, 35 minutes) use the Gare Avignon Centre station; other lines go to Arles, Nîmes, Orange, Toulon, and Carcassonne. Next door you'll find the bus terminal; buses run to and from Avignon, Arles (€7.10, 1 hour), Carpentras (€2, 45 minutes), Cavaillon (€2, 1 hour), Nîmes (€1.50, 1½ hours), and farther afield to Orange, Isle/Sorgue, Marseille, Nice, and Cannes. The Avignon–Orange bus runs several times during the day and takes less than an hour (€2 one-way). In addition, there are 27 city buses to get you around Avignon itself, run by TCRA.

BUS CONTACTS Avignon Bus Terminal. ✉ *5 av. Monclar* ☎ *04-90-82-07-35.* **TCRA.** ⊕ *www.tcra.fr.*

TRAIN CONTACTS Gare Avignon Centre. ✉ *42 bd. St.-Roch* ☎ *3665* ⊕ *www.gares-sncf.com/fr/gare/fraes/avignon-centre.* **Gare Avignon TGV.** ✉ *Ch. du Confluent – La Courtine* ⊕ *www.gares-sncf.com/fr/gare/fravg/avignon-tgv.*

TOURS

Le Petit Train d'Avignon

TRAIN TOURS | FAMILY | Resembling a children's party ride, this tourist train—a type of tram—travels the city streets for a 40-minute ride through the Rocher des Doms gardens, the historic city center, and by major monuments. It departs from the Popes' Palace Square daily 10–7, mid-March–October 30 (until 8 in July and August). ✉ *Pl. du Palais* 🚢 *From €9.*

Les Croisières Mireio

BOAT TOURS | Boat trips include excursions to Arles, Tarascon, and Châteauneuf-du-Pape and range from a 45-minute "promenade" to wine discoveries and dinner and dancing cruises. Riverboat cruises for two to four people (champagne optional) depart from the Pont d'Avignon. Days of the week and times vary according to season; check the website for a full listing. ✉ *Allées de L'Oulle* ☎ *04–90–85–62–25* ⊕ *www.mireio.net* 🚢 *From €12.*

VISITOR INFORMATION

CONTACTS Avignon Tourist Office. ✉ *41 cours Jean-Jaurès* ☎ *04–32–74–32–74* ⊕ *www.avignon-tourisme.com.*

Sights

Although it is merely the capital of the Vaucluse these days, Avignon's lively street life, active university, and colorful markets present a year-round spectacle far beyond the thousands of productions on view during the summer's world-renowned Festival d'Avignon. To add to the allure, many of the landmark buildings and churches have been enhanced with new lighting fixtures that literally light up the nights.

As a city, Avignon boasts one of the most fabled and time-stained histories in France. It was transformed into the "Vatican of the north" when political infighting in the Eternal City drove Pope Clement V to accept Philippe the Good's invitation to start afresh. In 1309 his entourage arrived, preferring digs in nearby priories and châteaux; in 1316 he was replaced by Pope John XXII, who moved into the bishop's palace (today the Petit Palais). It was his successor Pope Benedict XII who undertook construction of the magnificent palace that was to house a series of popes through the 14th century. During this holy reign Avignon evolved into a sophisticated, cosmopolitan capital, attracting artists and thinkers and stylish hangers-on. As the popes' wealth and power expanded, so did their formidable palace. And its sumptuous architecture was legendary, inspiring horror and disdain from the poet Petrarch, who wrote of "towers both useless and absurd that our pride may mount skyward, whence it is sure to fall in ruins." The abandoned Italians dubbed Avignon a "second Babylon." Additionally, the University of Avignon, which had been founded in 1303, burgeoned as thousands of the faithful from across Europe came to Avignon on pilgrimage.

After a dispute with the king, Pope Gregory XI packed up for Rome in 1376, but Avignon held its ground. While he was on his deathbed in 1378, the French elected their own pope, Clement VII, and the Western Schism divided the Christian world. Popes and antipopes abused, insulted, and excommunicated each other to no avail, though the real object of dispute was the vast power and wealth of the papacy. When the king himself turned on the last antipope, Avignon lost out to Rome and the extravagant court dispersed.

Cathédrale Notre-Dame-des-Doms

RELIGIOUS SITE | Built in a pure Provençal Romanesque style in the 12th century, this cathedral was soon dwarfed by the extravagant palace that rose beside it. The 14th century saw the addition of a cupola, which promptly collapsed. As rebuilt in 1425, the cathedral is a marvel of stacked arches with a strong Byzantine flavor and is topped with a gargantuan Virgin Mary lantern—a 19th-century afterthought—whose glow can be seen for miles around. ✉ *Pl. du Palais* ☎ *04–90–80–12–21* ⊕ *www.metropole.diocese-avignon.fr.*

★ Collection Lambert

MUSEUM | Known for the breadth of its collection as well as the scope of its exhibitions, the Lambert is a must-see for contemporary art lovers. Housed in two elegant 17th-century mansions, this impressive assembly of contemporary artworks came out of the private collection of Paris art dealer Yvon Lambert, who founded the museum in 2000 in honor of Avignon's designation as European Capital of Culture. Comprising more than 1,200 pieces dating from the 1960s to the present, the Lambert Collection also hosts an influential series of three to four major exhibitions per year, cultural events, lectures, and arts eduction programs independently or in conjunction with other arts institutions worldwide. The foundation closes three months out of the year between new exhibitions, so be sure to check before going. The impressive bookshop carries dozens of original, limited-edition works by artists represented in the collection, including prints by Cy Twombly, Sol LeWitt, and Jenny Holzer, and the breezy courtyard café offers gourmet snacks, beverages, and light lunches under the shade of sleepy plane trees. ⊠ *5 rue Violette* ☎ *04–90–16–56–20* ⊕ *www.collectionlambert.fr* 🖃 *€10* 🕙 *Closed Mon. Sept.–June.*

Espace Saint Louis

RELIGIOUS SITE | This graceful old 17th-century Jesuit cloister has been converted for office use by the well-known Avignon Festival—a performing arts event that lasts most of the month of July. The cloister's symmetrical arches (now partly enclosed as the sleek Hôtel Cloître Saint Louis) are shaded by ancient plane trees. You can wander around the courtyard after you've picked up your festival information. Occasional exhibits are held inside as well. ⊠ *20 rue du Portail Boquier* ☎ *04–90–27–66–50* ⊕ *www.festival-avignon.com.*

Les Halles

MARKET | By 6 every morning (except Monday), merchants and artisans have stacked their herbed cheeses and arranged their vine-ripened tomatoes with surgical precision in pyramids and designs that please the eye before they tease the salivary glands. This permanent covered market is as far from a farmers' market as you can get, each booth a designer boutique of *haute de gamme* (top-quality) goods, from jewel-like olives to silvery mackerel to racks of hanging hares worthy of a Flemish still life. Even if you don't have a kitchen to stock, consider enjoying a cup of coffee or a glass of (breakfast) wine while you take in the sights and smells. Tuck into a plate of freshly shucked oysters and a *pichet* of the crisp local white. ⊠ *Pl. Pie* ☎ *04–90–27–15–15* ⊕ *www.avignon-leshalles.com.*

Les Remparts (*The Ramparts*)

MILITARY SITE | More than 4 km (2½ miles) long, these protective crenellated walls and towers were built by the popes in the 14th century to keep out rampaging brigands and mercenary armies attracted by legends of papal wealth. It's extraordinarily well preserved, thanks in part to the efforts of architect Eugène-Emmanuel Viollet-le-Duc, who restored the southern portion in the 19th century. Modern-day Avignon roars around its impervious walls on a noisy ring road that replaced a former moat. ⊠ *Pl. du Palais.*

Musée Anglodon

MUSEUM | This superb collection of major 18th- to 20th-century paintings and furnishings was assembled by the famous Parisian couturier Jacques Doucet (1853–1929), who counted many of the major painters and writers of his day among his close circle and purchased—or funded—some of the great works of the 20th century (he was the original owner of Picasso's *Demoiselles d'Avignon*). With an unerring eye, this great appreciator of the arts created a collection that he then housed in this mansion, which he purchased toward the end of his life; it includes works by Degas, Van Gogh, Manet, Cézanne, Modigliani, and Picasso, along with important drawings, sculpture, photography, and furniture. The museum also hosts

Beautiful town squares form the hub of historic Avignon, as seen in this view from the roof of the famed Palais des Papes.

temporary exhibitions. ☒ *5 rue Laboureur* ☎ *04–90–82–29–03* ⊕ *www.angladon. fr* ☒ *€8* ⊗ *Closed late Dec.–Jan., Mon. year-round, and Sun. Nov.–Mar.*

Musée Calvet

MUSEUM | Worth a visit for the beauty and balance of its architecture alone, this fine old museum contains a rich collection of antiquities and classically inspired works. Acquisitions include neoclassical and Romantic pieces and are almost entirely French, including works by Manet, Daumier, and David. There's also a good modern section, with works by Bonnard, Duffy, and Camille Claudet (note Claudet's piece depicting her brother Paul, who incarcerated her in an insane asylum when her relationship with Rodin caused too much scandalous talk). The main building itself is a Palladian-style jewel in pale Gard stone dating to the 1740s; the garden is so lovely that it may distract you from the art. ☒ *65 rue Joseph-Vernet* ☎ *04–90–86–33–84* ⊕ *www.musee-cal-vet.org* ☒ *Permanent collections free* ⊗ *Closed Tues.*

Musée du Petit Palais

CASTLE/PALACE | This residence of bishops and cardinals before Pope Benedict XII built his majestic palace houses a large collection of old-master paintings, the majority of which are Italian works from the early Renaissance schools of Siena, Florence, and Venice—styles with which the Avignon popes would have been familiar. Later works here include Sandro Botticelli's *Virgin and Child,* and Venetian paintings by Vittore Carpaccio and Giovanni Bellini. The museum café and tearoom, with a picturesque outdoor terrace in the mansion's ancient courtyard, is a favorite spot for lunch, coffee, or teatime (open 10–7). ☒ *Pl. du Palais* ☎ *04–90–86–44–58* ⊕ *www.petit-palais.org* ☒ *Permanent collections free* ⊗ *Closed Tues.*

Musée Lapidaire

MUSEUM | Housed in a pretty little Jesuit chapel on the main shopping street, this collection of sculpture and stonework is primarily from Gallo-Roman times but also includes Greek and Etruscan works. There are several interesting

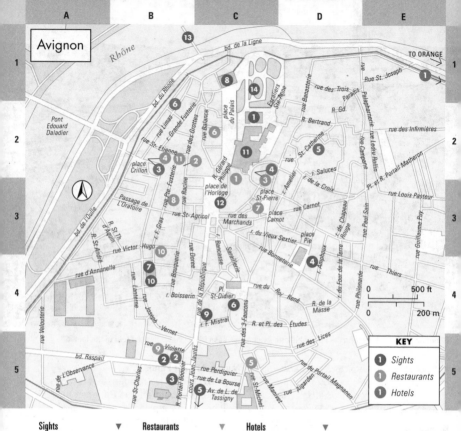

Avignon

inscribed slabs, a selection of *shabtis* (small statues buried with the dead to help them get to the afterlife), and a notable depiction of *Tarasque of Noves,* the man-eating monster immortalized by Alphonse Daudet. Most items, unfortunately, are haphazardly labeled and insouciantly scattered throughout the chapel, itself slightly crumbling yet awash with light. ⊠ *27 rue de la République* ☏ *04–90–85–75–38* ⊕ *www.musee-lap-idaire.org* ✉ *Permanent collections free, special exhibits €3* ☉ *Closed Mon.*

Musée Requien

MUSEUM | Don't bother to rush to this eccentric little natural history museum, but since it's next door to the Calvet Museum (and free) you might want to stop in and check out the petrified palm trunks, the dinosaur skeleton, the handful of local beetles and mammals, and the careful and evocative texts (French only) that accompany them. The museum is named for a local naturalist and functions as an entrance to the massive **library** of natural history upstairs. ⊠ *67 rue Joseph-Vernet* ☏ *04–90–82–43–51* ⊕ *www.museum-requien.org* ✉ *Free* ☉ *Closed Sun. and Mon.*

★ Palais des Papes

CASTLE/PALACE | This colossal palace creates a disconcertingly fortresslike impression, underlined by the austerity of its interior. Most of the original furnishings were returned to Rome with the papacy; others were lost during the French Revolution. Some imagination is required to picture the palace's medieval splendor, awash with color and with worldly clerics enjoying what the 14th-century Italian poet Petrarch called "licentious banquets." On close inspection, two different styles of building emerge at the palace: the severe **Palais Vieux** (Old Palace), built between 1334 and 1342 by Pope Benedict XII, a member of the Cistercian order, which frowned on frivolity, and the more decorative **Palais Nouveau** (New Palace), built in the following decade by the

The Avignon City Pass

One good investment is the *Avignon City Pass.* This prepaid card (24 hours, €21; 48 hours, €48) gives access to the following museums in Avignon and Villeneuve Lez Avignon: Palais des Papes, Le Pont d'Avignon, Collection Lambert, Musée Angladon, Musée Louis Vouland, Tour Philippe Le Bel, La Chartreuse, Jardins de l'Abbaye St André, Fort St André, and Musée Pierre de Luxembourg.

artsy, lavish-living Pope Clement VI. The Great Court, entryway to the complex, links the two.

The main rooms of the Palais Vieux are the **Consistory** (Council Hall), decorated with some excellent 14th-century frescoes by Simone Martini; the **Chapelle St-Jean,** with original frescoes by Matteo Giovanetti; the **Grand Tinel,** or Salle des Festins (Feast Hall), with a majestic vaulted roof and a series of 18th-century Gobelin tapestries; the **Chapelle St-Martial,** with more Giovanetti frescoes; and the **Chambre du Cerf,** with a richly decorated ceiling, murals featuring a stag hunt, and a delightful view of Avignon. The principal attractions of the Palais Nouveau are the **Grande Audience,** a magnificent two-nave hall on the ground floor and, upstairs, the **Chapelle Clémen-tine,** where the college of cardinals once gathered to elect the new pope. To get the most out of the experience, consider a €2 audio tour. ⊠ *6 rue Pente Rapide* ☏ *04–32–74–32–74* ⊕ *www.palais-des-pa-pes.com* ✉ *€12.*

Place de l'Horloge (*Clock Square*)
PLAZA | This square is the social nerve center of Avignon; the concentration of bistros, brasseries, cafés, and

restaurants draws swarms of locals to the shade of its plane trees. ⊠ *Avignon.*

Pont St-Bénézet (*St. Bénézet Bridge*)
BRIDGE/TUNNEL | "*Sur le pont d'Avignon / On y danse, on y danse …*" Unlike the London Bridge, this other subject of a childhood song (and UNESCO World Heritage Site) stretches its arches only partway across the river. After generations of war and flooding, only half the *pont* (bridge) remained by the 17th century. Its first stones allegedly laid with the miraculous strength granted St-Bénézet in the 12th century, it once reached all the way to Villeneuve. It's a bit narrow for dancing "*tous en rond*" (round and round), though the traditional place for dance and play was under the arches. You can climb along its high platform for broad views of the Old Town ramparts. The ticket price includes an audio guide or tablet, and the latter (for which you'll need to show your passport or drivers' license) illustrates how the bridge appeared in medieval times. ⊠ *Port du Rhône* ☎ *04–32–74–32–74* ⊕ *www.avignon-tourisme.com* ⊠ *€5.*

★ **Rocher des Doms** (*Rock of the Domes*)
GARDEN | Set on a bluff above town, this lush hilltop garden has grand Mediterranean pines, a man-made lake (complete with camera-ready swans), plus glorious views of the palace, the rooftops of Old Avignon, the Pont St-Bénézet, and formidable Villeneuve across the Rhône. On the horizon loom Mont Ventoux, the Luberon, and Les Alpilles. The garden has lots of history as well: often called the "cradle of Avignon," its rocky grottoes were among the first human habitations in the area. ⊠ *Montée du Moulin, off Pl. du Palais* ☎ *04–32–74–32–74* ⊕ *www. avignon-et-provence.com/sites-naturels/ rocher-doms-avignon.*

🍴 Restaurants

★ **Christian Étienne**
$$$$ | **FRENCH** | The stellar period interior of this renovated 12th-century mansion

makes for an impressive backdrop to innovative and delicious cuisine that has earned the chef a Michelin star. Try the pan-roasted veal medallion with dried porcini blinis and thinly sliced mushrooms with chervil, or splurge for the whole lobster sautéed in olive oil, muscat grapes, and beurre blanc with verjuice. **Known for:** meticulous sourcing and presentation; romantic setting with views of Papal Palace; one of Avignon's top chefs. $ *Average main: €36* ⊠ *10 rue de Mons* ☎ *04–90–86–16–50* ⊕ *www.christiane-tienne.fr* ⊗ *Closed Wed. and Thurs.*

La Fourchette
$$ | **FRENCH** | **FAMILY** | The food here is delicious, plentiful, and satisfying, as the bevy of locals clamoring to get in proves. Service is friendly, and you can dig in to heaping portions of escalope of salmon, chicken cilantro à l'orange, or what just might be the best Provençal daube (served with macaroni gratin) in France. **Known for:** cozy and elegant atmosphere; family-friendly vibes; reasonable prices, especially for fixed-price menus. $ *Average main: €21* ⊠ *17 rue Racine* ☎ *04–90–85–20–93* ⊕ *www.la-fourchette. net* ⊗ *Closed weekends and 1st 3 wks in Aug.*

★ **La Mirande**
$$$$ | **FRENCH** | Whether you dine under the 14th-century coffered ceilings, surrounded by exquisite paintings and Renaissance tapestries or in the intimate garden under the walls of the Palais des Papes, the restaurant of the luxurious Hôtel de la Mirande transports you to another time. Chef Florent Pietravalle, who won a Michelin star in 2019, offers authentic and original haute cuisine dishes with a focus on local products: wild cèpes with caviar and razor clams; line-caught dorade with roasted cucumber and a Granny Smith apple emulsion; and aged beef with Jerusalem artichokes and wild blackberries. **Known for:** Michelin-starred chef; unparalleled elegance; chef's table and wonderful workshops

Side-by-side with Avignon's gigantic Palais des Papes is the Byzantine-style Cathédrale Notre-Dame-des-Doms.

around food and wine. $ *Average main: €45* ⊠ *4 pl. de la Mirande* ☎ *04–90–85–93–93* ⊕ *www.la-mirande.fr* ⊗ *Closed Tues., Wed., and 3 wks in Jan.*

La Vieille Fontaine

$$$$ | FRENCH | Summer evening meals around the old fountain and box-wood-filled oil jars in the courtyard of the Hôtel d'Europe would be wonderful with *filet de boeuf* alone, but combine this romantic backdrop with top-notch southern French cuisine and you have a special event. Give yourself over to one of the great restaurants of the Vaucluse, complete with fine regional wines and an army of urbane servers—and hope for moonlight. **Known for:** beautiful setting; outdoor courtyard dining; exquisite presentation. $ *Average main: €36* ⊠ *12 pl. Crillon* ☎ *04–90–14–76–76* ⊕ *www.heurope.com* ⊗ *Closed Sun. and Mon.*

★ L'Agape

$$$ | MODERN FRENCH | An Avignon hot spot, this contemporary gastropub in the heart of the city aspires to something more akin to haute cuisine. Chef Julien Gleize applies a light, playful touch to a modern gastronomy steeped in the French tradition. **Known for:** devoted to freshest local ingredients; superb price-to-quality ratio; excellent wine list. $ *Average main: €29* ⊠ *21 pl. des Corps-Saints* ☎ *04–90–85–04–06* ⊕ *www.restaurant-agape-avignon.com* ⊗ *Closed Sun. and Mon. No lunch Sat.*

Le 46

$$ | MODERN FRENCH | A 200-plus wine list is a big highlight of this restaurant and *bar à vins,* yet the main focus is squarely on the food. Beautiful to behold and even better to eat, the choice menu of Mediterranean-inspired dishes flaunts the bounty of Provence in dishes like beef carpaccio, sliced razor thin and served with shaved Parmesan and crispy house frites, a tender zucchini tartlette with chèvre and herbes de Provence, or a copious salad of heirloom tomatoes, buffala mozzarella, Serrano ham and basil sorbet. **Known for:** loved by the locals; accommodating to different diets and food allergies; lovely outdoor terrace.

$ *Average main: €19* ⊠ *46 rue de la Balance* ☎ *04–90–85–24–83* ⊕ *www. le46avignon.com* ⊘ *No lunch weekends.*

L'Epicerie

$$ | FRENCH | This restaurant doesn't have great gastronomic pretensions, but the cheerful food, hip waiters, and perfect terrace in the quiet, cobblestone Place St-Pierre make it a local favorite. Order a steak with *vraies frites* (real chunky French fries) and soak up the atmosphere with the help of some well-chosen local wine. **Known for:** wonderful terrace on historic Square St-Pierre; charming interiors; reasonable prices. $ *Average main: €21* ⊠ *10 pl. St-Pierre* ☎ *04–90–82–74–22* ⊘ *Closed Jan. and Feb.*

L'Essentiel

$$$ | FRENCH | This chic hot spot, steps from the "Palais des Papes," is part of the "bistronomy" movement, which focuses on creative cooking, a casual atmosphere, and reasonable prices. The quaint terrace on a side street will lure in passersby, and the romantic 17th-century interior courtyard will keep them coming back. **Known for:** quality ingredients highlighting seafood; beautiful dining room; good-value lunch menu. $ *Average main: €25* ⊠ *2 rue Petite Fusterie* ☎ *04–90–85–87–12* ⊕ *www.restaurantlessentiel.com* ⊘ *Closed Sun., Mon., 2 wks in Nov., 2 wks in Feb., and 1 wk in Apr.*

★ Le Violette

$ | FRENCH | You could hardly beat the location of this (mostly outdoor) bistro sheltered in the shady, elegant courtyard of the Collection Lambert. Hearty lunches and dinners include a fish and meat choice with plenty of fresh local vegetables and salads on the side: salmon gravlax with an Asian-inflected cabbage salad, line-caught John Dory, or roasted lamb with bright steamed veggies. **Known for:** super fresh ingredients; unbeatable shaded terrace; organic wines by the glass. $ *Average main: €16* ⊠ *5 rue Violette* ☎ *04–90–85–36–42*

⊕ *www.collectionlambert.fr/46/le-violette.html* ⊘ *Closed Mon. and Tues. No dinner Sun.*

★ Pollen

$$ | FRENCH | This luminous, casual dining room is an absolute must on any foodie circuit of Provence. Chef Mathieu Desmarest's thoughtful approach to seasonal Provençal products and wild ingredients and exquisite attention to unusual flavor pairings make for a revelatory experience far beyond the usual gourmet cuisine. **Known for:** location on a charming street at the center of town; wild and sourced ingredients; casual setting for elegant dishes. $ *Average main: €22* ⊠ *3 bis rue Petite Calade* ☎ *04–86–34–93–74* ⊕ *pollen-restaurant.fr* ⊘ *Closed weekends.*

Simple Simon

$ | BRITISH | Since the 1970s, this quaint (there is no other word for it) English tearoom—dark wooden beams, teapots on shelves, a table laden with cakes and pies—has catered to homesick expats and locals, who are intrigued by the pieman's tempting wares and the properly brewed teas served in silver pots. Owned from the beginning by a Frenchwoman whose mother was English, Simple Simon is a real ode to British tradition, with Cornish salad, bacon and eggs, and hot dishes like shepherd's pie, cheese-and-onion crumble tart, or turkey hot pot at lunch. **Known for:** traditional English tearoom experience; excellent desserts; delicious scones. $ *Average main: €15* ⊠ *26 rue Petite Fusterie* ☎ *04–90–86–62–70* ⊘ *Closed Mon., Sun. May–Sept., and Aug. No dinner (except during festival).*

Hotels

★ Auberge de Cassagne

$$ | HOTEL | Once past the residential surroundings, an oasis of splendid gardens, indoor and outdoor pools, a full-service spa and fitness room, an excellent gastronomic restaurant, and an old-world welcome await. **Pros:** some rooms overlook gardens; exemplary service and fantastic restaurant; prices reasonable in most seasons. **Cons:** residential neighborhood doesn't appeal to everyone; 15-minute drive from Avignon; breakfast not included in room price. [$] *Rooms from: €220* ✉ *450 allée de Cassagne* ☎ *09–75–18–85–28* 🌐 *www.aubergedecassagne.com* 🛏 *42 rooms* 🍴 *No meals.*

Hôtel Boquier

$ | **HOTEL** | **FAMILY** | You might not guess that this friendly, family-run hotel, convenient to both the train station and the Palais des Papes, is a budget option. **Pros:** good continental breakfast; homey touches, like lavender on the pillows; air-conditioning. **Cons:** no elevator; some rooms dated; the resident cat might bother allergic guests. [$] *Rooms from: €69* ✉ *6 rue du Portail-Boquier* ☎ *04–90–82–34–43* 🌐 *www.hotel-boquier.com* 🛏 *12 rooms* 🍴 *No meals.*

Hôtel d'Europe

$$$$ | **HOTEL** | This classic, vine-covered 16th-century home once hosted Emperor Maximilian (as well as Victor Hugo and Napoléon Bonaparte), and some of its guest rooms are emperor size. **Pros:** authentic historical setting; romantic hideaway; close to everything. **Cons:** least expensive rooms are small and slightly shabby; high season can mean noisy evenings, especially from nearby bars; service could be better. [$] *Rooms from: €380* ✉ *12 pl. Crillon* ☎ *04–90–14–76–76* 🌐 *www.heurope.com* 🛏 *44 rooms* 🍴 *No meals.*

★ **Hôtel de la Mirande**

$$$$ | **HOTEL** | A romantic's dream of a hotel, this *petit palais* permits you to step into 18th-century Avignon—complete with painted coffered ceilings, precious antiques, extraordinary handmade wall coverings, and beautiful oriental rugs. **Pros:** a step back in time to a more gracious era; luxurious toiletries; beautiful courtyard garden. **Cons:** old-fashioned baths may not appeal to all; very pricey rooms and dining; breakfast not included in price. [$] *Rooms from: €485* ✉ *Pl. de la Mirande* ☎ *04–90–14–20–20* 🌐 *www.la-mirande.fr* 🛏 *27 rooms* 🍴 *No meals.*

★ **La Divine Comédie**

$$$$ | **HOTEL** | Divine is the word for this extraordinary property hidden away in the center of Avignon not far from the Palais des Papes. **Pros:** tranquil garden setting; Avignon's most beautiful interiors; delightful hosts. **Cons:** no restaurant; not ideal for young kids (but they're welcome); you'll have to leave sometime. [$] *Rooms from: €400* ✉ *16 Impasse Jean Pierre Gras* ☎ *06–77–06–85–40* 🌐 *www.la-divine-comedie.com* 🛏 *5 rooms* 🍴 *No meals.*

Le Limas

$$ | **B&B/INN** | Two minutes from the famous Avignon bridge, this contemporarily decorated B&B offers a rooftop terrace view of the palace but also tranquillity away from the noisy palace streets. **Pros:** rooftop terrace fridge stocked with rosé so you can enjoy evening refreshments with a view; very close to the bridge and Palais des Papes; air-conditioning. **Cons:** only one room can accommodate more than two people; limited parking; fills up quickly in high season. [$] *Rooms from: €160* ✉ *51 rue de Limas* ☎ *06–69–00–60–37* 🌐 *www.le-limas-avignon.com* 🛏 *4 rooms* 🍴 *Free breakfast.*

🍸 Nightlife

Within its fusty old medieval walls, Avignon teems with modern nightlife well into the wee hours.

★ **AJMI** (*Association Pour le Jazz et la Musique Improvisée*)

MUSIC CLUBS | At AJMI, in La Manutention, you can hear live jazz acts of some renown. ✉ *4 rue des Escaliers Sainte-Anne* ☎ *04–90–86–08–61* 🌐 *www.jazzalajmi.com.*

Did You Know?

While today it looks anything but heaven-sent—only four of the original 22 arches remain—legend has it that Avignon's famed Pont St-Bénezet was built in the 12th century by a shepherd boy acting on orders from heaven.

Bistrot d'Utopia

BARS/PUBS | Enjoy drinks in this dark, intimate space just outside the Utopia movie theater in La Manutention. ⊠ *4 rue des Escaliers Ste-Anne* ☎ *04–90–82–65–36.*

Le Delirium

MUSIC CLUBS | An ubercool hangout for live music, performance, and entertainment during the Avignon Festival and on weekends, Le Delirium covers its walls with ongoing exhibits to create a truly artsy atmosphere. ⊠ *23 rue de la République* ☎ *04–90–85–44–56* ⊕ *www.ledelirium.net.*

Le Rouge Gorge

CABARET | This is the venue for cabaret-style dinner shows, with singers and dancers; it also hosts jazz, blues, and rock concerts, theater performances, and special events. ⊠ *10 bis rue Peyrollerie* ☎ *04–90–14–02–54* ⊕ *www.lerouge-gorge.fr.*

Performing Arts

Small though Avignon is, its inspiring art museums, strong university, and 60-some years of saturation in world-class theater have made the city a second center for the arts, after Paris.

In July, Avignon is France's theater center, and many theaters operate throughout the year, though mostly in French. Your best bet for a year-round program of theater, ballet, opera, and classical music is the Opéra-Théâtre d'Avignon. La Manutention arts center is also a popular choice for an evening out. The center includes a movie theater screening a well-chosen program of art films plus first-run, mainstream movies in *v.o.* (*version originale,* meaning in the original language with French subtitles). There's also a café, restaurant, and jazz club and a lively vibe.

Cinéma Utopia–La Manutention

FILM | This theater shows hard-to-find international independent works. They have another location on rue Figuière. ⊠ *4 rue des Escaliers Ste-Anne* ☎ *04–90–82–65–36* ⊕ *www.cinemas-utopia.org/avignon* ⊠ *€7.*

FNAC

TICKETS | For information on events and tickets, stop at this massive book-and-record chain. ⊠ *19 rue de la République* ☎ *08–25–52–00–20* ⊕ *www.fnac.com.*

★ **La Manutention**

ARTS CENTERS | This hip cultural complex, on a picturesque cobbled street just behind the Palais des Papes, includes the Utopia–La Manutention movie theater, a well-regarded restaurant, La Manutention, the jazz club AJMI, and a relaxed bar that's popular even for those not here for a show or performance. Its location in front of the Avignon School of the Arts and its eclectic style—a mix of antique and contemporary touches—make it a big draw for the town's artsy crowd. ⊠ *4 rue des Escaliers Ste-Anne* ☎ *04–90–86–08–61 for jazz club, 04–90–86–86–77 for restaurant.*

Opéra-Théâtre d'Avignon

CONCERTS | This theater proves that culture and the arts are not limited to festival season, with a schedule that ranges from classical concerts, ballet, and opera to Broadway musicals. ⊠ *1 rue Racine* ☎ *04–90–14–26–40* ⊕ *www.operagrandavignon.fr/en.*

Shopping

Avignon is too residential to be full of tourist-aimed boutiques; instead, it has a cosmopolitan mix of French chains, youthful clothing shops (it's a college town), and a few plummy fashion streets. **Rue des Marchands,** off Place Carnot, is one shopping stretch, but **Rue de la République** is the main artery, the largest concentration of high-end clothing, jewelry, elegant thrift stores, and other fashion-forward shopping is along **Rue Joseph Vernet.** Shops are generally open Tuesday–Saturday, but chains will be open Monday, too. Shops often close at lunch, so don't be surprised to find a note on the door between noon and 3 pm.

Camili Books & Tea

BOOKS/STATIONERY | If you're hungry for books in English, this is your place. In addition to new and used books in English, it has a tearoom, café, and terrace. ⊠ 155 rue Carreterie ☎ 04–90–27–38–50 ⊕ www.camili-booksandtea.com.

★ CQFD

SPECIALTY STORES | Part charming café serving lunch, snacks, and coffee and part concept store, CQFD (Créations Éthiques Franco Décalées) is hands-down Avignon's chicest shopping destination. Its spacious rooms are brimming with a curated selection of whimsical fashion brands and jewelry, chic stationery, tableware, soaps, cosmetics, and handmade design items for the home (including eco-paints and handblocked wallpapers). Everything is eco-conscious and all of it is made in France. ⊠ 7 rue des Trois Faucons ☎ 04–90–01–70–64 ⊕ www.facebook.com/CQFDavignon.

Fusterie Quarter

SHOPPING NEIGHBORHOODS | If you're into Louis XVI, the Fusterie quarter caters to antique hunters and interior decorators. ⊠ Rue Petit Fusterie.

Joseph Vernet Quarter

SHOPPING NEIGHBORHOODS | The more luxurious shops along Rue Joseph-Vernet and St-Agricol in the Joseph Vernet quarter merit some lèche-vitrine (window licking, as the French say). ⊠ Avignon.

Les Délices du Luberon

FOOD/CANDY | For those with a taste for all things Provençal, this gourmet épicerie is a treasure trove of the many delicacies found in the best local markets, all neatly packaged and suitcase ready—if they make it that far. There's everything from olive oils, tapenades, herbs, sweet and savory preserves, bottled soups, fruit jams, honey, pastries, and lavender-based sweets and cosmetics to much more. ⊠ 20 pl. du Change ☎ 04–90–84–03–58 ⊕ www.delices-du-luberon.fr.

Mouret Chapelier

CLOTHING | This shop has a cornucopia of old-fashioned, old-world, and marvelously eccentric hats in a jewel-box setting. ⊠ 20 rue Marchands ☎ 04–90–85–39–38.

Pure Lavande

PERFUME/COSMETICS | For all things lavender—and not just any lavender—this shop has the best AOC essential oil (it must be from flowers that grow above 2,600 feet) from the famous Château de Bois, plus a range of top-quality soaps, body lotions, and other fine cosmetics made with lavender essential oil. ⊠ 61 rue Grand Fusterie ⊕ www.lavandeand-co.fr.

Souleïado

CLOTHING | All those famous, gorgeous Provençal fabrics can be found at Souleïado, made into elegantly tailored shirts, dresses, and skirts, along with a fine selection of leather boots, bags, and other accessories. You can also buy the fabrics by the meter. ⊠ 19 rue Joseph-Vernet ☎ 04–90–86–32–05 ⊕ www.souleiado.com.

Villeneuve-lez-Avignon

2 km (1 mile) west of Avignon.

Just across the Rhône from Avignon, this medieval town glowers at its powerful neighbor to the east. In the 14th century, Villeneuve benefited enormously from the migration of the popes into Avignon, as an accompanying flood of wealthy and influential cardinals poured over the river. No fewer than 15 of the status-seeking princes of the church built magnificent homes on this neighboring hilltop—in truth, some simply requisitioned mansions from other owners, giving these "freed" town palaces the unfortunate moniker livrées cardinalices. In addition, kings Philip the Fair and Louis VIII built up formidable defenses on the site to keep an eye on papal territories. Nowadays its abbey, fortress, and quiet streets offer a pleasant contrast to Avignon's bustle.

GETTING HERE AND AROUND

The No. 5 from the Avignon "center" train station runs every 20 minutes and costs €1.40 for the five-minute ride. To drive, it's 4 km (2½ miles) from Avignon; just follow the signs.

VISITOR INFORMATION

CONTACTS Villeneuve-lez-Avignon. ⊠ 1 pl. Charles-David, Villeneuve-lès-Avignon ☎ 04–90–25–61–33 ⊕ www.villeneuve-lezavignon.fr.

Sights

Abbaye St-André Gardens

GARDEN | Don't miss the formal Italianate gardens of Fort St-André, littered with remains of the abbey that preceded the fortifications. The gardens are now privately owned. ⊠ Rue Montée du Fort, Villeneuve-lès-Avignon ☎ 06–71–42–16–90 ⊕ www.abbayesaintandre.fr €7.

Chartreuse du Val-de-Bénédiction

RELIGIOUS SITE | The bounty and extravagant lifestyles of the cardinals nourished the abbey in Villeneuve-lez-Avignon. Inside the abbey—which translates, literally, as the Charterhouse of the Valley of Blessings—are spare cells with panels illuminating monastic life, the vast 14th-century **cloître du cimetière** (cemetery cloister), a smaller Romanesque cloister, and, within the remains of the abbey church, the Gothic tomb of Pope Innocent VI. Theatrical events are staged here during Avignon's annual theater festival. ⊠ 58 rue de la République, Villeneuve-lès-Avignon ☎ 04–90–15–24–24 ⊕ www.chartreuse.org €8.

Fort St-André

MILITARY SITE | At the top of the village is the Fort St-André, which once ostensibly protected the town of St-André, now absorbed into Villeneuve. The fortress's true importance was as a show of power for the kingdom of France in the face of the all-too-close Avignon popes. You can explore the fortress grounds and the bare ruined walls of inner chambers (there's a good view from the Notre Dame de Belvézet church within the fort walls), and you can also climb into the twin towers for broad views over Avignon, the Luberon, and Mont Ventoux. ⊠ Rue Montée du Fort, Villeneuve-lès-Avignon ☎ 04–90–25–45–35 ⊕ www.fort-saint-andre.fr Towers €6.

Musée Pierre de Luxembourg

MUSEUM | Below the abbey, the Musée Pierre de Luxembourg gives you access to one of the luxurious, 14th-century cardinals' manors, which contains a notable collection of art, including the spectacularly colorful and richly detailed Couronnement de la Vierge (Coronation of the Virgin), an altarpiece painted in 1453 by Enguerrand Quarton. One of the greatest paintings of the 15th century, it shows rows and rows of Avignonnais hieratically sitting around the figures of God the Father and God the Son. Depicted by Quarton—the leading painter of the Avignon School—as identical twins, they bless Mary and hover over a surreal landscape that places Montagne St-Victoire in between Heaven and Hell. ⊠ 2 rue de la République, Villeneuve-lès-Avignon ☎ 04–90–27–49–66 ⊕ www.villeneuve-lesavignon.fr €4 ⊗ Closed Jan. and Mon.

Hotels

Le Prieuré

$$$ | HOTEL | Heavenly peace is the theme at this charming five-star hotel set in a medieval convent among gardens and trees in postcard-perfect Villeneuve-lez-Avignon. **Pros:** a good base for Avignon and other scenic villages; private terraces with some rooms; Michelin-starred restaurant. **Cons:** some rooms on the dark side; expensive in high season; some buildings could use

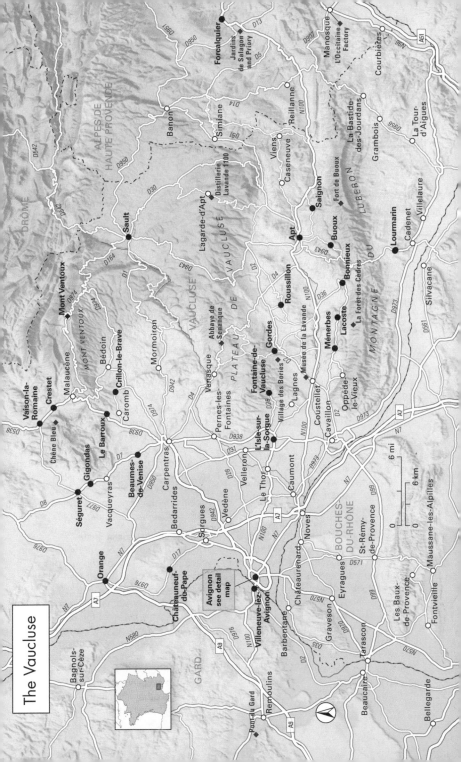

a spruce-up. $ *Rooms from: €280* ☒ *7 pl. du Chapitre, Villeneuve-lès-Avignon* ☎ *04–90–15–90–15* ⊕ *www.leprieure. com* ⊅ *39 rooms* ⎢⊙⎢ *No meals.*

Châteauneuf-du-Pape

17 km (10 miles) north of Avignon; 22 km (13½ miles) west of Carpentras.

A patchwork of rolling vineyards, of green-and-black furrows striping the landscape in endless, retreating perspective welcome you to one of France's great wine regions. Once the source of the table wine of the Avignon popes, who kept a fortified summer house here (hence the name of the town, which means "new castle of the pope"), these vineyards had the "good fortune" to be wiped out by phylloxera in the 19th century and re-grafted with resistant American root stock. The wine's revival as a muscular and resilient mix of up to 13 varieties with an almost portlike intensity (it can reach 15% alcohol content) moved it to the forefront of French wines. The whites, though less known, can also be sublime.

There are *caves de dégustation* (wine-tasting cellars) on nearly every street; get a free map from the tourist office. Also head to the discreet *vignobles* (vineyards) at the edge of town. Some of the top Châteauneufs (and the oldest) come from Château la Nerthe, Château de Vaudieu, and Château Fortia, and are priced accordingly. If you're not armed with the names of a few great houses, look for *medaille d'or* (gold medal) ratings from prestigious wine fairs; these are usually indicated by a gold sticker on the bottle. Better yet, for the best selection of wines in one place as well as expertise to match, go with Vinadea, the official *maison des vins* of Châteauneuf.

GETTING HERE AND AROUND

The Avignon bus (€2.10)—which is also the local school bus—runs once a day in the early evening and around noon on Wednesday and Saturday and takes 35 minutes. Going the other direction, however, from Châteauneuf-du-Pape to Avignon, the bus leaves in the morning (no buses on Sunday). To or from Orange, the 25-minute journey is €2.10 with several schedules throughout the day in both directions. It's better to drive, however: take the D225, the D907, and then the D17, direction Orange, and follow signs to Châteauneuf-du-Pape (about 30 minutes).

VISITOR INFORMATION

CONTACTS Châteauneuf-du-Pape Tourist Office. ☒ *3 rue de la République* ☎ *04–90–83–71–08* ⊕ *www.chateauneuf-du-pape-tourisme.fr.*

Sights

Château

CASTLE/PALACE | If you're disinclined to spend your holiday sniffing and sipping, climb the hill to the ruins of the château. Though it was destroyed in the Wars of Religion and its remaining *donjon* (keep) blasted by the Germans in World War II, it still commands a magnificent position. From this rise in the rolling vineyards, you can enjoy wraparound views of Avignon, the Luberon, and Mont Ventoux. ☒ *Châteauneuf-du-Pape.*

Musée du Vin Maison Brotte

MUSEUM | There's no better way to learn about the local wine production than to spend an hour at the Musée du Vin Maison Brotte. This private collection of winemaking equipment, displayed in the *caveau* (wine cellar) of the Brotte family, explains everything you need to know simply and enjoyably, including a tasting of Châteauneuf-du-Pape wines of your choice after your visit. Best of all, admission, an excellent audio guide in English (and five other languages), and the wine tasting are all free. ☒ *Av. St-Pierre* *de Luxembourg* ☎ *04–90–83–59–44* 🌐 *www.brotte.com* 🎫 *Free.*

Wine Appreciation Classes

LOCAL INTEREST | Held in the wine cellar of her "wine B&B" in the heart of Châteauneuf-du-Pape, Danièle Raulet-Reynaud's informative classes (in English) cover everything you'll need to know about this world-class appellation: tasting, buying, storing, serving, and pairing. A master sommelier of France, gastronomic cook, vice-president of the Women Vignerons of the Rhône, and a charming *raconteur,* Raulet-Reynaud has taught wine courses around the world for 40 years. Her wine-and-cheese tastings (€45) and popular Apèro Fun (€30) Friday workshops are a wonderful way to spend an hour or an afternoon learning about and tasting these magnificent wines. ✉ *20 av. Charles de Gaulle* 🌐 *www.chateauneuf-wine-bb.com* 🕒 *Closed Nov.–Mar.*

🍴 Restaurants

★ La Maisouneta

$ | **FRENCH** | **FAMILY** | This cozy restaurant with cheerful planters and homey lace curtains is run by a young husband-and-wife team and specializes in pasta dishes and regional French comfort food (from Savoie, Nice, and Provence). Although not exactly gastronomic, dishes like basil-and-cheese ravioli, stuffed peppers farci, and *crème anchoïade* (anchovy cream) are seasonal, well-prepared, and deeply satisfying. **Known for:** reliably excellent food; little-known Châteauneuf-du-Papes wines; lovely, but small, outdoor terrace. [$] *Average main: €17* ✉ *6 rue Joseph Ducos* ☎ *04–90–32–55–03* 🌐 *www.lamaisouneta.fr* 🕒 *Closed Jan. and Sun. No dinner Mon.–Wed.*

★ Le Pistou

$$ | **FRENCH** | Provençal specialties such as whole herb-roasted *dorade* (a small Mediterranean fish), lamb shank with Provençal herb sauce, or saffron crème brûlée are just some of your options here. The welcome is warm, the interior is filled with colorful tablecloths, fresh paint, and pictures, and set menus start cheap (€17–€24). **Known for:** small outdoor terraces; like dining at your French friend's house (who happens to be a great cook); stellar local wines. [$] *Average main: €19* ✉ *15 rue Joseph-Ducos* ☎ *04–90–83–71–75* 🌐 *lepistou-restaurant.e-monsite.com* 🕒 *Closed Mon. No dinner Sun. Apr.–mid-Oct.*

Le Verger des Papes

$$ | **FRENCH** | It's well worth the slog up the hill to the château simply to linger on the terrace of this long-established restaurant and savor the view over Mont Ventoux, Avignon, the Luberon, and the Rhône—and you can visit the restaurant's well-stocked wine cellar on your way to the top. The specialty here—tarte à la tomate confite with goat's cheese and iced white cheese—reveals a love for the region's cuisine. **Known for:** family-run for generations; fabulous views; excellent wine list. [$] *Average main: €20* ✉ *Rue Montée du Château* ☎ *04–90–83–50–40* 🌐 *www.vergerdespapes.com* 🕒 *Closed Mon. No dinner Sun.*

🛏 Hotels

★ Coucou Grands Cépages

$$$ | **RESORT** | **FAMILY** | On this sprawling property behind a locked gate, 15 contemporary "*eco-cabanes*" surround—or float on top of—a secluded emerald-green lake in the countryside five minutes from Châteauneuf-du-Pape center. **Pros:** total peace and privacy; beautifully designed cabins; food delivery and spa treatments available. **Cons:** must have a car to get here; no hot meals unless you go out to a restaurant; less delightful in cold or windy weather. [$] *Rooms from: €265* ✉ *2061 Chemin des Pompes* ☎ *04–88–95–87–58* 🌐 *www.cabanesdesgrandscepages.com* 🛏 *15 cabins* 🍴 *No meals.*

Châteauneuf-du-Pape is a beautiful hillside town, just a half-hour bus ride from Avignon, that lends its name to some of the world's most renowned wines.

Les Vignes

$ | **B&B/INN** | Rolling vineyards and a lovely view of the château make a nice backdrop from the infinity pool at this tranquil contemporary B&B minutes from the village center. **Pros:** tasteful interiors; good value; delightful hosts. **Cons:** books up fast; open only six months of the year; can't accommodate larger groups. [$] *Rooms from: €119* ✉ *23 rte. de Sel* ☎ *06–63–77–24–95* 🌐 *www.chambreles-vignes84.com* 🕒 *Closed Nov.–Apr.* 🛏 *1 room, 1 small house* 🍴 *Free breakfast* ☞ *No children allowed* 💳 *No credit cards.*

L'Espace de L'Hers

$$ | **B&B/INN** | The charming hosts of this serene and scenic country B&B set among vineyards and forest go to every length to assure that you enjoy a true Provençal experience, from organizing wine tastings and tours to offering cooking classes and allowing guests to assist in the kitchen. **Pros:** gourmet meals are served by advance reservation; price includes breakfast; free Wi-Fi. **Cons:** fills up quickly; no nightlife for miles around; no elevator. [$] *Rooms from: €150* ✉ *5 chemin de L'Hers* ☎ *06–22–65–41–18* 🌐 *www.espacedelhers.com* 💳 *No credit cards* 🛏 *5 rooms* 🍴 *Free breakfast.*

Shopping

Vinadea

WINE/SPIRITS | The official *maison des vins* of Châteauneuf-du-Pape, Vinadea has the town's best selection of wines, along with wine expertise if you have questions. Tastings are offered daily, and wines can be shipped internationally. Keep in mind that shipping rates are offset by the fact that you're getting "cellar door" prices with no markup. ✉ *8 rue Maréchal Foch* ☎ *04–90–83–70–69* 🌐 *www.vinadea.com.*

Orange

12 km (7 miles) north of Châteauneuf-du-Pape; 31 km (19 miles) north of Avignon.

Cradled in northern Provence in the land of Côtes du Rhône vineyards, Orange really isn't very big, but when compared with the sleepy wine villages that surround it, it's a thriving metropolis. In many ways, Orange captures the essence of the region: the Provençal accent here is quite thick, and savory food and wine can be had—for a price. Come to see its two ancient Roman monuments, the Théâtre Antique and the Arc de Triomphe, spectacular vestiges of history that seem transported from a different world.

GETTING HERE AND AROUND

The Paris TGV at 3 hours 20 minutes serves Orange twice daily, but from Nice to Orange by TGV is more complicated, involving a change of trains at Marseille; the fare is about €67, but with the stopover it takes about 5 hours 30 minutes. From Gare Avignon Centre to Orange, it costs €6.40 for the 20-minute train ride. Orange's center is a 10-minute walk from the train station (head from Avenue F. Mistral to Rue de la République, then follow signs). By bus from Avignon's *gare routière* (bus station) there are 10–20 buses daily at €2.60 one-way (45 minutes), arriving at the train station in Orange.

VISITOR INFORMATION

CONTACTS Orange Tourist Office. ⊠ 5 *cours Aristide Briand* ☎ 04–90–34–70–88 ⊕ *www.orange-tourisme.fr.*

◉ Sights

Arc de Triomphe

ARCHAEOLOGICAL SITE | North of the city center is the Arc de Triomphe, which once straddled the Via Agrippa between Lyon and Arles. Three arches support a heavy double attic (horizontal top) floridly decorated with battle scenes and marine symbols, references to Augustus's victories at Actium. The arch, which dates to about 20 BC, is superbly preserved—particularly the north side—but to view it on

foot, you'll have to cross a roundabout seething with traffic. ⊠ *Av. de l'Arc de Triomphe.*

Les Chorégies d'Orange

FESTIVAL | To witness the torches of *Nabucco* or *Aïda* flickering against the 2,000-year-old Roman wall of the Théâtre Antique and to hear the extraordinary sound play around its semicircle of ancient seats is one of the great summer festival experiences in Europe. Every July and first week in August, Les Chorégies d'Orange echo tradition and amass operatic and classical music spectacles under the summer stars in Orange. Be sure to book tickets well in advance; they go on sale in October. ⊠ *15 pl. Silvain* ☎ *04–90–34–24–24* ⊕ *www.choregies.fr.*

Musée d'Orange

MUSEUM | Across the street from the theater, this small museum displays antiquities unearthed around Orange, including fragments of three detailed marble *cadastres* (land survey maps) dating from the first century AD. Upstairs, a vivid series of 18th-century canvases shows local mills producing Provençal fabrics, each aspect illustrated in careful detail. There are also personal objects from local aristocrats and a collection of faience pharmacy jars. ⊠ *Rue Madeleine Roch* ☎ *04–90–51–17–60* ⊕ *www.thea-tre-antique.com* 🎫 *€10 combined ticket with Théâtre Antique.*

Théâtre Antique

ARCHAEOLOGICAL SITE | Even less touristy than Nîmes and just as eccentric, the city of Orange (pronounced "oh- *rawnzh*") nonetheless draws thousands every year to its spectacular Théâtre Antique, a colossal Roman theater built in the time of Caesar Augustus. The vast stone stage wall, bouncing sound off the facing hillside, climbs four stories high—a massive sandstone screen that Louis XIV once referred to as the "finest wall in my kingdom." The niche at center stage contains the original statue of Augustus, just as it reigned over centuries of productions of classical plays. Today the theater provides a backdrop for world-class theater and opera. ✉ *Pl. des Frères-Mounet* ☎ *04–90–51–17–60* 🌐 *www.theatre-antique.com* 🎟 *€10 combined ticket with the Musée d'Art et d'Histoire.*

Vieil Orange
NEIGHBORHOOD | This Old Town neighborhood, which you must cross to hike from one Roman monument to the other, carries on peacefully when there's not a blockbuster spectacle in the theater. Lining its broad squares, under heavy-leaved plane trees, are a handful of shops and a few sidewalk cafés. ✉ *Orange.*

🍴 Restaurants

Au Petit Patio
$$ | **BISTRO** | This ultrapopular eatery on the edge of Orange's Old Town consistently serves fresh, locally sourced cuisine with a price-to-quality ratio that keeps happy locals coming back. Imaginative dishes like the house foie gras with *teck*-fruit sauce, *pot au feu de coquilles Saint Jacques* (stewed scallops and vegetables), and mussels in saffron broth are ample and served with flair. **Known for:** cozy, romantic atmosphere; pretty garden terrace; top-notch service. [$] *Average main: €22* ✉ *58 cours Aristide-Briand* ☎ *04–90–29–69–27* 🕒 *Closed Sun. No dinner Wed. and Thurs.*

Le Mas des Aigras
$$ | **FRENCH** | This picturesque stone farmhouse restaurant recently updated its traditional dining room and its dishes, while still maintaining its high standards and charm. Set among vineyards just outside Orange, this gastronomic restaurant, one of the few in Orange, offers a sophisticated menu based on the French classics: salmon mousse, house-made foie gras, beef cheeks, and a fish of the day. **Known for:** pretty setting; attention to presentation; outdoor terrace. [$] *Average main: €20* ✉ *Chemin des Aigras* ☎ *04–90–34–81–01* 🌐 *www.masdesaigras.com/en-gb/home* 🕒 *Closed Oct.–Mar.*

🛏 Hotels

Château de Massillan
$$ | **HOTEL** | **FAMILY** | Ancient meets modern in a somewhat jarring juxtaposition at this 50-acre country wine estate and gardens 9 km (5½ miles) from Orange, where you can stay in an elegant beamed aerie in the crenelated 16th-century castle or a chic contemporary abode in the stylish addition. **Pros:** superb "bio" spa that includes a sensorial pool, sauna, whirlpool, and steam rooms; an all-organic credo, with an emphasis on nongluten foods; large luxurious bedrooms with all the amenities. **Cons:** some guests can't get past the ancient-modern thing; dining room lacks character; spa can get crowded. [$] *Rooms from: €140* ✉ *730 chemin de Massillan, Uchaux* ☎ *04–90–40–64–51* 🌐 *www.chateaudemassillan.fr* 🛏 *26 rooms* 🍽 *No meals.*

Hôtel Arene
$$ | **HOTEL** | On a quiet square in the old center, this comfortable hotel is a labyrinth of spacious guest rooms decorated in Provençal yellow and blue with Italian-style bathrooms and LCD TVs. **Pros:** relatively affordable; lots of in-room amenities; total peace and quiet. **Cons:** decor not to everyone's taste; very popular with groups; charming terrace on the small side. [$] *Rooms from: €140* ✉ *Pl. de Langes* ☎ *04–90–11–40–40* 🌐 *www.hotel-arene.fr* 🛏 *35 rooms* 🍽 *No meals.*

Hôtel Lou Cigaloun
$ | **HOTEL** | For price, location, and ambience this central budget hotel is hard to beat. **Pros:** comfortable beds; great location; secluded outdoor terrace. **Cons:** only two parking spots (for a fee); not the prettiest exterior; no elevator. [$] *Rooms from: €90* ✉ *4 rue Caristie* ☎ *04–90–34–10–07* 🌐 *www.hotel-loucigaloun.com* 🛏 *24 rooms* 🍽 *No meals.*

Beaumes-de-Venise

23 km (14 miles) east of Orange.

Just west of the great mass of Mont Ventoux, surrounded by farmland and vineyards, is Beaumes-de-Venise, where streets of shuttered bourgeois homes slope steeply into a market center. This is the renowned source of a delicately sweet muscat wine, but if you're tasting, don't overlook the local red wine. In the town center you can also buy fruity, unfiltered olive oil produced in the area; it's made in such small quantities that you're unlikely to see it anywhere else.

Beaumes lies at the foot of the Dentelles de Montmirail, a small range of rocky chalk cliffs eroded to lacy pinnacles—hence the name *dentelles* (lace). From tiny D21, east of town, you'll find dramatic views north to the ragged peaks and south over lush orchards and vineyards interspersed with olive groves, pine, and yew trees. It's a splendid drive, and if you love nature it would be well worth staying in this area—many of the stone houses have been converted into bed-and-breakfasts.

GETTING HERE AND AROUND

There is no direct bus service to Beaumes-de-Venise. You can take Bus No. 5.1 from Avignon to Carpentras, about 10 km (6 miles) away (€2.10, one hour), and take a taxi the rest of the way for about €20. The best way to get here is by car.

VISITOR INFORMATION

CONTACTS Beaumes-de-Venise Tourist Office. ⊠ *122 pl. du Marché* ☎ *04–90–62–94–39* ⊕ *www.ot-beaumesdevenise.com.*

 Sights

Domaine des Bernardins

WINERY/DISTILLERY | This vineyard has a tasting cave, where you can sample some of the wines, which include mostly whites but also reds from grapes such as grenache. ⊠ *138 av. Gambetta* ☎ *04–90–62–94–13* ⊕ *www.domaine-des-bernardins.com.*

Vacqueyras

TOWN | Smaller and more picturesque than Beaumes, with stone houses scattered along its gentle slopes, Vacqueyras gives its name to a robust, tannic red wine worthy of its more famous neighbors Châteauneuf-du-Pape and Gigondas. Wine domaines beckon from the outskirts of town, and the center strikes a mellow balance of plane trees and cascading wisteria, punctuated by discreet tasting shops. Thanks to its consistently rising quality, Vacqueyras is one of the latest of the Côtes du Rhônes to earn its own appellation—the right to put its village name on the bottle instead of the less prestigious, more generic Côtes du Rhône label. ⊠ *Vacqueyras.*

 Shopping

⭐ Rhonéa

WINE/SPIRITS | This elegant cooperative features the best of the legendary Beaumes-de-Venise wines, made exclusively from the Muscat grape, as well as the appellation's lesser-known but equally worthy reds, whites, and rosés; there's also options from the neighboring Gigondas and Vacqueyras. All can be tasted in the degustation room as can local olive oil, fruit juices, and more. Wines can be shipped worldwide. ⊠ *228 rte. de Carpentras* ☎ *04–90–12–41–00* ⊕ *www.rhonea.fr.*

Gigondas

3 km (2 miles) north of Vacqueyras.

The prettiest of all the Mont Ventoux Côtes-du-Rhône wine villages, Gigondas is little more than a cluster of stone houses stacked gracefully up a hillside overlooking the broad sweep of the valley below. At the top, a false-front

Baroque church anchors a ring of medieval ramparts; from here you can take in views as far as the Cévennes.

Its few residents share one vocation: the production of the vigorous grenache-based red that bears the village name. At the more than 60 caveaux scattered through the village and the surrounding countryside, you're welcome to visit, taste, and buy without ceremony. Pick up a contact list from the tourist office at the village entrance beside the town hall.

GETTING HERE AND AROUND

There is no direct bus service to Gigondas. The only way to get here is by car.

VISITOR INFORMATION

CONTACTS Gigondas Tourist Office. ✉ *5 rue du Portail* ☎ *04–90–65–85–46* 🌐 *www.ventouxprovence.fr.*

🍴 Restaurants

★ L'Oustalet

$$$ | **FRENCH** | Chef Laurent Deconinck won his first Michelin star in 2018, proving to the culinary mainstream what Provence gourmands have known all along: that this is one of the region's most coveted tables. In the elegant dining room, diners are assured of a stellar meal and superb wines (the sommelier is expert at pairing the local nectars, as the winemakers all flock here) in a convivial atmosphere. **Known for:** gourmet Provençal cuisine; beautiful setting in the heart of the village; excellent wines. [$] *Average main: €32* ✉ *5 pl. Gabrielle Andéol* ☎ *04–90–65–85–30* 🌐 *www.loustalet-gigondas.com.*

🛏 Hotels

Les Florêts

$$ | **HOTEL** | Winter or summer, Les Florêts makes a romantic hideaway with its full-on view of the Dentelles de Montmirail and a salon centered on a giant white fireplace and body-hugging red armchairs. **Pros:** breathtaking scenery from charming rooms; excellent dining; vast outdoor terrace with gorgeous views. **Cons:** mistrals could dampen outings; decor somewhat dated; a (pretty) 10-minute walk from Gigondas. [$] *Rooms from: €137* ✉ *1243 rte. des Florêts* ☎ *04–90–65–85–01* 🌐 *www.hotel-les-florets.com* 🕒 *Closed Jan. and 2 wks in Feb. during school vacations* 🔑 *15 rooms* 🍽 *No meals.*

🛍 Shopping

★ Maison du Gigondas

WINE/SPIRITS | Right on the town square, this is the best place to buy and sample 100 cuvées of this exceptionally drinkable wine and see for yourself why Gigondas is creating such a buzz in wine circles. ✉ *Pl. Gabrielle Andéol* ☎ *04–90–65–82–29* 🌐 *www.gigondas-vin.com/en/le-caveau-du-gigondas-en.*

Séguret

8 km (5 miles) northeast of Gigondas.

Nestled into the sharp rake of a rocky hillside and crowned with a ruined medieval castle, Séguret is a picture-book hill village that is only moderately commercialized. Its 14th-century clock tower, Romanesque Église St-Denis, and bubbling Renaissance fountain highlight steep little stone streets and lovely views of the Dentelles de Montmirail cliffs. Here, too, you can find peppery Côtes du Rhône for the tasting.

GETTING HERE AND AROUND

There is no direct bus service to Séguret. The only way to get here is by car.

🍴 Restaurants

Côté Terrasse

$$ | **BISTRO** | A modern restaurant with a pleasantly shaded terrace and a view describes dozens of restaurants in

Provence, including this one, but the real standouts here are the warm and welcoming service and the consistently good food. The menu features plenty of fresh and inventive salads, like wild salmon with shrimp, melon, and tomato confit—not always easy to find—alongside heartier dishes like cod with aïoli and grilled vegetables, Iberian pork with chestnuts and whipped potatoes, and a classic roasted duck breast. **Known for:** good prices for fixed menus (especially at lunch); very popular so be sure to book in advance; reliably good classic French food. $ *Average main: €18* ⊠ *Les Poternes* ☎ *04–90–28–03–48* ⊙ *Closed Nov.–Mar.*

Hotels

La Bastide Bleue
$ | **HOTEL** | Once an idyllic youth hostel, this old stone farmhouse with blue-shuttered windows is now an unpretentious but enchanting country inn set in a pine-shaded garden court. **Pros:** garden-lined pool; very good on-site restaurant with courtyard; recently updated rooms. **Cons:** proper and clean, but design nothing special; only seven rooms so books up quickly; breakfast not included. $ *Rooms from: €80* ⊠ *Rte. de Sablet, 1 km (½ mile) south of Séguret on D23* ☎ *04–90–46–83–43* ⊕ *www. bastidebleue.com* ⊙ *Closed Dec.–Feb.* ⊅ *7 rooms* ⎮○⎮ *No meals.*

Vaison-la-Romaine

10 km (6 miles) northeast of Séguret; 27 km (17 miles) northeast of Orange.

In a river valley green with orchards of almonds and apricots, this ancient town thrives as a modern market center. The Provençal market on Tuesday is a major tourist draw (there is also a smaller organic farmers' market on Thursday morning), as is the five-day food festival in early November. Yet it retains an irresistible Provençal charm, with medieval back streets, lively squares lined with cafés and, as its name implies, remains of its Roman past. Vaison's well-established Celtic colony joined forces with Rome in the 2nd century BC and grew to powerful status in the empire's glory days. No gargantuan monuments were raised, yet the luxurious villas surpassed those of Pompeii.

GETTING HERE AND AROUND
Bus No. 4 (€3; 40 minutes) runs throughout the day from the Orange SNCF station to Vaison, and Bus No. 11 runs from Carpentras (€2.10; 45 minutes). A taxi from Orange is €43; from Avignon, count on at least €85 on weekdays (weekend fares are 50% more).

VISITOR INFORMATION
CONTACTS Vaison-la-Romaine Tourist Office. ⊠ *Pl. Chanoine Sautel* ☎ *04–90– 36–02–11* ⊕ *www.vaison-ventoux-tourisme.com.*

Sights

Cathédrale Notre-Dame-de-Nazareth
RELIGIOUS SITE | The sober Romanesque cathedral was built from recycled fragments of a Gallo-Roman basilica. The **cloister** is surrounded by richly sculpted columns and arches. ⊠ *Av. Jules-Ferry.*

★ Patricia Wells's Cooking Classes
LOCAL INTEREST | While Vaison has centuries-old attractions, the most popular for Americans may well now be Patricia Wells's Cooking Classes. A living monument of Provence, the celebrated food critic first made her name known through posh food columns and *The Food Lover's Guide to France.* Firsthand, she now introduces people to the splendors of French cooking in her lovely farmhouse near Vaison through weeklong cooking seminars—luxe ($6,000 a student), 12 students only, and set over Madame Wells's own Chanteduc vineyards. The truffle workshop in January is usually sold out, so book early (online only).

✉ *Vaison-la-Romaine* 🌐 *www.patriciawells.com.*

Pont Romain (*Roman Bridge*)
ARCHAEOLOGICAL SITE | The remarkable single-arch Roman bridge, built in the first century, stands firm across the Ouvèze River. ✉ *Vaison-la-Romaine.*

Quartier de Puymin
ARCHAEOLOGICAL SITE | Like a tiny Roman forum, the Quartier de Puymin spreads over the field and hillside in the heart of town, visible in passing from the city streets. Its skeletal ruins of villas, landscaped gardens, and museum lie below the ancient theater, all of which are accessed by the booth across from the tourist office. Closest to the entrance, the foundations of the **Maison des Messii** (Messii House) retain the outlines of its sumptuous design, complete with a vast gentleman's library, reception rooms, an atrium with a rain-fed pool, a large kitchen (the enormous stone vats are still there), and baths with hot, cold, and warm water. It requires imagination to reconstruct the rooms in your mind (remember all those toga movies from the '50s), but a tiny detail is enough to trigger a vivid image—the thresholds still show the hinge holds and scrape marks of swinging doors. A formal garden echoes a similar landscape of the time; wander beneath its cypresses and flowering shrubs to the **Musée Archéologique Théo-Desplans.** In this streamlined venue, the accoutrements of Roman life have been amassed and displayed by theme: pottery, weapons, gods and goddesses, jewelry, and, of course, sculpture, including full portraits of the emperor Claudius (1st century) and a strikingly noble nude Hadrian (2nd century). Cross the park behind the museum to climb into the bleachers of the 1st-century **Theater,** smaller than the one in Orange but also used today for concerts and plays. Across the parking lot is the **Quartier de la Villasse,** where the remains of a lively market town evoke images of main-street shops, public gardens, and grand private homes, complete with floor mosaics. The most evocative image of all is in the *thermes* (baths): a neat row of marble-seat toilets lined up over a raked trough that rinsed waste instantly away. ✉ *Rue Burrus* ☎ *04–90–36–50–48* 🌐 *www.vaison-ventoux-tourisme.com* 🎫 *€9.*

🍴 Restaurants

La Belle Étoile
$$ | **FRENCH** | **FAMILY** | While not in the center of town, the relaxed, welcoming atmosphere and lovely country setting here are worth the short drive. The affable owner and cook presents an ever-changing market menu with an emphasis on what's fresh, local, and organic: salmon-and-sweet-onion tartlette nestled among a crisp mesclun salad makes a good starter, followed by chicken stuffed with local wild mushrooms. **Known for:** relaxed garden dining; fresh ingredients; beautiful outdoor terrace. [$] *Average main: €20* ✉ *1234 rte. des Princes d'Orange* ☎ *04–90–37–31–45* 🕓 *Closed Thurs. and mid-Feb.–mid-Mar.*

🛏 Hotels

★ **Bastide la Combe**
$$ | **B&B/INN** | A warm welcome awaits you at this picture-perfect country inn, set among vineyards with sweeping views of Mont Ventoux and the Dentelles mountains, just five minutes from town. **Pros:** abundant breakfast served in the garden; homemade gourmet meals available upon request; rooms are bright, airy, and tasteful. **Cons:** closed November through March; breakfast not included in price; only five rooms so fills up very quickly. [$] *Rooms from: €165* ✉ *1885 ch. de Sainte Croix* ☎ *04–90–28–76–33* 🌐 *www.bastide-lacombe.fr* 🕓 *Closed Nov.–Mar.* 🛏 *5 rooms* 🍽 *Free breakfast.*

Évêché

$ | **B&B/INN** | In the medieval part of town, this turreted 16th-century former bishop's palace has just four small rooms done with rustic charm—expect delicate fabrics, exposed beams, and wooden bedsteads. **Pros:** copious, complimentary breakfast is excellent; hosts are available to give advice; charming decor. **Cons:** some rooms are a little small so best to go for the suites; house can be cold in winter; books up quickly. [$] *Rooms from: €100* ✉ *14 rue de l'Évêché* ☎ *06–03–03–21–42* 🌐 *eveche.free.fr* 🛏 *5 rooms* 🍴 *Free breakfast.*

Le Beffroi

$ | **HOTEL** | Perched on a clifftop in the Old Town, this gracious grouping of 16th-century mansions comes together as a fine hotel. **Pros:** beautiful views; lovely garden; saltwater pool. **Cons:** pool on the small side; very narrow street to reach the hotel; some rooms dated. [$] *Rooms from: €120* ✉ *Rue de l'Évêché* ☎ *09–77–55–04–71* 🌐 *www.le-beffroi.com* 🕒 *Closed mid-Jan.–mid-Mar.* 🛏 *22 rooms* 🍴 *No meals.*

Crestet

7 km (4½ miles) south of Vaison-la Romaine.

Another irresistible, souvenir-free aerie perched on a hilltop at the feet of the Dentelles de Montmirail cliffs and of Mont Ventoux, Crestet has it all: tinkling fountains, shuttered 15th-century houses, an arcaded *place* at the village's center, and a 12th-century castle crowning the lot. Views from its château terrace take in the concentric rings of tiled rooftops below, then the forest greenery and cultivated valleys below that.

GETTING HERE AND AROUND

You can take the bus to nearby Vaison-la-Romaine, but the best way to get here is by car.

Sights

★ Chêne Bleu

WINERY/DISTILLERY | A wine destination par excellence, this extraordinary domaine benefits from an ideal setting in the Mont Ventoux UNESCO Biosphere Reserve, with sweeping views of the Rhône Valley, the Dentelles de Montmirail, Mount Ventoux, and the medieval village of Crestet. The overarching principle here is to respect the land while benefiting from its incline and altitude to make handcrafted, fully organic wines of the highest quality. Visitors are graciously received for a comprehensive tour of the winemaking facilities and estate, with a free tasting included, and a visit to the boutique where wines and other local gifts can be purchased. Between mid-April and the end of October the domaine also offers several choices for lunch and refreshment, including all-organic dishes created by the in-house chef from the estate's kitchen gardens, charcuterie and cheese plates from local artisans, and, *bien sur,* a glass or two of the estate wines. Individual tastings can be custom-tailored upon request, and the estate also includes a separate house, where up to 14 people can stay for a week in total luxury, including a private chef, a valet, and every imaginable comfort. Prices are through the roof, but the experience is assuredly one-of-a-kind. ✉ *Domaine de la Verrière* 🌐 *www.visit.chenebleu.com* 🎫 *Free.*

Le Barroux

16 km (10 miles) south of Vaison-la-Romaine.

Of all the marvelous hilltop villages stretching across the South of France, this tiny ziggurat of a town has a special charm. Le Barroux has more than a whiff of fairy tale in the air, lording over a patchwork landscape as finely drawn as a medieval illumination, as bright as an illustration in a children's book. This aerie has just one small church, a post office, and one tiny old *épicerie* (small grocery store) selling canned goods, yellowed postcards, and today's *La Provence.* You are forced, therefore, to look around you and listen to the trickle of the ancient fountains at every labyrinthine turn. Houses, cereal-box slim, seem to grow out of the bedrock, closing in around your suddenly unwieldy car.

GETTING HERE AND AROUND

There is no direct bus service to Le Barroux. The only way to get here is by car or the Malaucene (K) bus line from Carpentras.

Sights

Château du Barroux

CASTLE/PALACE | With grand vaulted rooms and a chapel dating to the 12th century, this château is Le Barroux's main draw. Some of its halls serve as venues for contemporary art exhibits, and the perfect condition of all the rooms reflects a complete restoration after a World War II fire. ✉ *Le Barroux* 🌐 *www.chateau-du-barroux.com* 🎟 *€5* 🕒 *Closed Nov.–Mar.*

Crillon-le-Brave

21 km (13 miles) southeast of Vaison-la-Romaine.

The main reason to come to this minuscule hamlet, named after France's most notable soldier hero of the 16th century, is to stay or dine at its hotel, the Hostellerie de Crillon-le-Brave. But it's also pleasant—perched on a knoll in a valley shielded by Mont Ventoux, with the craggy hills of the Dentelles in one direction and the hills of the Luberon in another. Today the village still doesn't have even a *boulangerie* (bakery), let alone a souvenir boutique. The village makes a good base camp for exploring the region if you can afford to stay at the hotel; with no other commercial establishments in the village, and little more to visit than a tiny music-box museum and an ocher quarry, you're a captive audience.

GETTING HERE AND AROUND

There is no direct bus service to Crillon-le-Brave. The only way to get here is by car.

Hotels

Hotel Crillon le Brave

$$$$ | **HOTEL** | Like the views from its interconnected hilltop houses, prices at this Relais & Châteaux property are elevated—but, in return, you get a rarefied stage-set of medieval luxury. **Pros:** outdoor pool and spa; rooms are large, beautiful, and bright; most rooms have views. **Cons:** lots of stairs; restaurant is not what it used to be; very expensive. [$] *Rooms from: €420* ✉ *Pl. de l'Église* ☎ *04–90–65–61–61* 🌐 *www.crillonle-brave.com* 🕒 *Closed Dec.–Feb.* 🛏 *32 rooms* 🍴 *No meals.*

Mont Ventoux

29 km (18 miles) west of La Barroux.

The tallest mountain in the region, Mont Ventoux has a majestic presence that dominates the sweeping vistas and landscapes of northwestern Provence. The mountain's limestone peaks—often mistaken for snow cover—reach nearly 6,000 feet and harbor a unique wind-buffeted ecosystem recognized by UNESCO and strictly protected by France. Perhaps best known for its foreboding role in the Tour de France bike race, if you can summit the "Beast of Provence" you'll be amply rewarded with some truly breathtaking views.

GETTING HERE AND AROUND

The mountain is a favorite spot for hikers and cyclists (bike rentals are plentiful in Bédoin and Sault), but unless you're in tip-top shape, you'll need a car to explore the mountain.

Sights

Mont Ventoux

MOUNTAIN—SIGHT | In addition to all the beautiful views *of* Mont Ventoux, there are equally spectacular views *from* Mont Ventoux. From Malaucène or any of the surrounding hill towns you can take an inspiring circle drive along the base and over the crest of the mountain, following the D974. This road winds through the extraordinarily lush south-facing greenery that Mont Ventoux protects from vicious mistral winds. Abundant orchards and olive groves peppered with stone farmhouses make this one of Provence's loveliest landscapes. Stop for a drink in busy **Bédoin,** with its 18th-century Jesuit church at the top of the Old Town maze.

Mont Ventoux was the site of the first recorded attempt at *l'escalade* (mountain climbing), when Italian poet-philosopher Petrarch grunted his way up in 1336. Although people had climbed mountains before, this was the first "do it because it's there" feat. Reaching the summit itself (at 6,263 feet) requires a bit of legwork. From either Chalet Reynard or the tiny ski center Mont Serein you can leave your car and hike up to the peak's tall observatory tower. The climb is not overly taxing, and when you reach the top you are rewarded with gorgeous panoramic views of the Alps. And to the south, barring the possibility of high-summer haze, you'll take in views of the Rhône Valley, the Luberon, and even Marseille. Hiking maps are available at *maisons de la presse* (newsstands) and tourist offices. Town-to-town treks are also a great way to explore the area; one of the most beautiful trails is from Malaucène to Séguret. In the off-season, lonely Mont Ventoux is plagued with an ungodly reputation due to destructive winds; attempts at saving its soul are evident from the chapels lining its slopes. Whether it's possessed by the devil or not, don't attempt to climb it in inclement weather; from late fall to early spring, in fact, the summit is closed by snow.

Restaurants

Le Chalet Reynard

$ | **FRENCH** | Opened in 1927, this is the spot for lunch and a bask in the sun on your way up the eastern slope of Mont Ventoux. The food is far beyond the merely acceptable, from simple dishes such as omelets (with truffles in season) to the traditional hearty *tartiflette* (baked dish of potatoes, cheese, and bacon from the Savoie region) or even spit-roasted pig for groups of 15 or more. **Known for:** basic French comfort food; hiker-friendly atmosphere; reasonable prices. [$] *Average main: €17* ✉ *Crillon-le-Brave* ✣ *At easternmost elbow of D974* ☎ *04–90–61–84–55* 🌐 *www.chalet-reynard.fr* 🕒 *Closed Nov. No dinner.*

Hotels

★ La Bastide de Brurangère

$$ | B&B/INN | Set among 12 acres of sun-drenched vineyards in view of Mont Ventoux, this little slice of heaven offers all the luxuries of a grand hotel along with the charm and privacy of a country hideaway—yet it is a good base for many local attractions (if you can tear yourself away from the relaxing options here). **Pros:** some rooms can accommodate more than four people; rustic elegance, including two pools; stay six nights and your seventh is free. **Cons:** closed for three months of the year; books up fast; breakfast a bit underwhelming. [$] *Rooms from: €220* ✉ *137 ch. des Rols, Crillon-le-Brave* ☎ *06–75–24–59–29* 🌐 *www.labastidedebrurangere.com* 🕒 *Closed Dec.–Mar.* 🛏 *5 rooms* 🍴 *Free breakfast* ☞ *No children under 10.*

Sault

43 km (27 miles) southeast of Le Barroux; 41 km (25½ miles) northeast of Carpentras.

Though at the hub of no fewer than six main roads, Sault remains an utterly isolated market town floating on a stony hilltop in a valley of lavender. Accessed only by circuitous country roads, it remains virtually untouched by tourism. The landscape is traditional Provence at its best: oak-forested hills and long, deep valleys purpled with the curving arcs of lavender. In the town itself, old painted storefronts exude the scent of honey and lavender. The damp church, Église Notre Dame de la Tour, dates to the 12th century; the long, lovely barrel nave was doubled in size in 1450.

From Sault all routes are scenic. You may head eastward into Haute-Provence, visiting (via D950) tiny **Banon,** source of the famed goat cheese. Wind up D942 to see pretty hilltop Aurel or down D30 to reach perched **Simiane-la-Rotonde.** Or head back toward Carpentras through the spectacular **Gorges de la Nesque,** snaking along narrow cliffside roads through dramatic canyons carpeted with wild boxwood and pine. If you're exploring the Lavender Route, head eastward some 48 km (30 miles) to discover the epicenter of Haute-Provence's fabled lavender in the sleepy, dusty town of **Forcalquier.**

GETTING HERE AND AROUND

There is no direct bus service to Sault. The only way to get here is by car.

FESTIVALS

Fête de la Lavande

FESTIVAL | This day-long festival, usually held around August 15, is entirely dedicated to lavender. Village folk dress in traditional Provençal garb and parade on bicycles; horses leap over barrels of fragrant bundles of hay; and local producers display their wares at the market—all of which culminates in a countryside lunch served with lavender-based products. ⊠ *Hippodrome le Defends, Along D950* ⊕ *www.fetedelalavande.fr.*

VISITOR INFORMATION

CONTACTS Ventoux-Sud Sault Tourist Office. ⊠ *Av. de la Promenade* ☎ *04–90–64–01–21* ⊕ *www.ventoux-sud.com.*

Forcalquier

53 km (33 miles) east of Sault; 41 km (25½ miles) northeast of Carpentras.

As a local center of lavender production, this small town has a lively Monday morning market—and an organic market on Thursday—with many lavender-based products. A wander through the picturesque old town also reveals the town's Bohemian side; many artists fled urban centers to draw inspiration from the bucolic surroundings and the town is dotted with artist ateliers. Forcalquier is also a great departure point for walks, bike rides, horse rides, or drives into the lavender world that surrounds the town. In the 12th century, Forcalquier was known as the capital city of Haute-Provence and was called the Cité des Quatre Reines (City of the Four Queens) since the four daughters of the ruler of this region, Raimond Beranger V (Eleanor of Aquitaine among them), all married royals. Relics of this former glory can be glimpsed in the Vieille Ville of Forcalquier, notably its Cathdédrale Notre-Dame and the Couvent des Cordeliers. However, everyone heads here to marvel at the lavender fields outside town; pick up a brochure and map of the lavender route at the tourist office. To explore on two wheels, get saddled up on a bicycle for a trip into the countryside at Cycles Bachelas.

GETTING HERE AND AROUND

There is no direct bus service to Forcalquier. The only way to get here is by car.

CONTACTS Forcalquier Office du Tourisme.
✉ 13 pl. Bourguet ☎ 04–92–75–10–02
⊕ www.haute-provence-tourisme.com.

 Sights

⭐ **Jardins de Salagon and Priory**
GARDEN | On a site occupied since the
Gallo-Roman period, this picturesque
11th- to 12th-century priory—a rich
archaeological site classed as a Historic Monument by the French Ministry
of Culture—presides over 10 acres of
themed gardens. The restored priory, with well-preserved Gothic and
Romanesque flourishes, now houses an
ethnological museum, a testament to
the various cultures and peoples of this
part of Provence. The garden functions
as both a visual delight and a preserve
for 2,500 species of plants and flowers native to the region, from ancient
times to the present, organized into five
themes—like "simple gardens and village
plants," which includes field and cultivated plants that were both consumed
and used medicinally. There's also a
medieval garden, a fragrant garden with
benches under the roses and honeysuck-
le for maximum sensory effect, and a
modern "exotic" garden that crosses five
continents. ✉ Prieuré de Salagon, Mane
☎ 04–92–75–70–50 ⊕ www.musee-de-
salagon.com 🎫 €8 🕐 Closed Tues.

L'Occitane
FACTORY | Nine kilometers (15 miles)
south of Forcalquier is Manosque, home
to the famed L'Occitane factory, a leading
purveyor of lavender magic. Manosque
is certainly not a draw on its own, but
a trip here is worth it for a visit to the
cosmetics and skin-care company that is
now the town's main employer. Once you
make a reservation, you can take a two-
hour tour of the production site, view a
documentary film, visit the museum and
gardens, then stock up on L'Occitane
products at the company shop. ✉ Z.I.

chemin St-Maurice, Manosque ☎ 04–92–
70–32–08 ⊕ fr.loccitane.com.

 Hotels

Le Couvent des Minimes
$$$ | HOTEL | It makes sense that L'Oc-
citane, the global Provence-based cosmetics and fragrance giant, would have
an overnight spa in the heart of lavender
country; this is where the company's
roots are, and they've made it a point of
honor to offer their guests an experience
worthy of the pedigree. **Pros:** two gastronomic restaurants and a wine bar; one of
the regoin's most famous spas; interesting building in a former convent. **Cons:**
spa treatments are expensive in addition
to the room price; lackluster service and
friendliness; restaurant pricey. 💲 Rooms
from: €275 ✉ Ch. des Jeux de Maï, Mane
☎ 04–92–74–77–77 ⊕ www.couventde-
sminimes-hotelspa.com 🛏 46 rooms
🍽 No meals.

 Activities

Cycles Bachelas
BICYCLING | A reliable and well-equipped
outfitter for all of your biking needs,
including mountain and electric bikes
(which come in handy in this countryside,
part of the Tour de France circuit). The
shop is about 500 feet from Place du
Bourguet, the town's main square. ✉ 5
av. de la République ⊕ www.bachelas-
bikeshop.com.

France Montgolfière
BALLOONING | The blue-and-purple patch-
work of the Luberon's famous lavender
fields have never been seen to better
effect than while floating freely at 1,500
feet in the air. Adventurous travelers can
take in the whole vista of mountains,
perched villages, and sprawling lavender
fields on an hour-long flight at either
dawn or dusk, when air currents are
calm. For the three-hour event, the company picks you up in the village, gives you
breakfast (or a snack), takes you up for an

hour flight, and brings you to home base. After the balloon is packed away, your courage will be honored with a *flûte de champagne* and the traditional "*toast des aéronautes.*" ⊠ *Pl. du Village* ☎ *03–80–97–38–61* ⊕ *www.franceballoons.com* ☎ *€200 per person.*

👜 Shopping

★ Biscuiterie de Forcalquier

FOOD/CANDY | Within walking distance from the town center and tourist office, this traditional bakery for the boat-shape *navette*, an emblematic cookie of Marseille and Provence, was revived by the founder of the Provence-based cosmetics giant L'Occitane. Delicately perfumed with orange flower water, the oblong cookie is said to represent the boat that brought saints Mary Magdalene and Martha to the coast near Marseille. Other traditional biscuits, flavored with lemon, almond, anis, or orange flower (including calissons d'Aix and macarons made from local almonds) are baked here by hand in gourmet versions updated by Paris superstar pâtissier Pierre Hermé. Though you'll also find them in gastronomic shops, all of the biscuits made here—easily transportable in tins—are sold in the Biscuiterie store at a 10% discount. ⊠ *28 av. St-Promasse* ☎ *09–67–22–66–36* ⊕ *www.biscuiterie-forcalquier.com.*

L'Isle-sur-la-Sorgue

30 km (19 miles) east of Avignon.

Crisscrossed with lazy canals and still alive with waterwheels that once drove its silk, wool, and paper mills, this charming valley town retains its gentle appeal—except on Sunday. Then this easygoing old town transforms itself into a Marrakech of marketeers, "the most charming flea market in the world," its streets crammed with antiques and brocantes, its cafés swelling with crowds of chic bargain browsers making a day of it. After London's Portobello district and the flea market at St-Ouen outside Paris, L'Isle-sur-la-Sorgue is reputedly Europe's third-largest antiques market. It ratchets up to high speed twice a year when the town hosts a big antiques show, usually four days around Easter and another in mid-August, nicknamed the Grand Déballage, or the Great Unpacking (⊕ *www.foire-islesurlasorgue.com*). Prices can be high, and bargains are few, but remember that in many cases dealers expect to bargain.

On a nonmarket day, life returns to its mellow pace. Dealers and clients catch up on gossip at the Place Gambetta fountain and at the Café de France, opposite the church of Notre-Dame-des-Anges. Wander the maze inside the ring to admire a range of architectural styles, from Gothic to Renaissance.

The Provençal Venice, L'Isle is dotted with watermills and canals that once drove the wheels of silk, paper, oil, grain, and leather mills. Today, these wheels—14 of them—turn idly, adding to the charm of the winding streets. If you want to explore the vestiges of L'Isle's 18th-century heyday, stop in the tourist office and pick up a guide on the town (available in English).

GETTING HERE AND AROUND

It's a 40-minute bus ride (No. 6) from the Avignon centre train station to Place Robert Vasse in Isle-sur-la-Sorgue. It's €2 one-way or €1 if returning on the same day. By car the distance is 5 km (3 miles). The TER train line links Avignon and L'Isle-Fontaine train station in L'Isle-sur-la-Sorgue.

VISITOR INFORMATION

CONTACTS L'Isle-sur-la-Sorgue Tourist Office. ⊠ *Pl. Ferdinand Buisson* ☎ *04–90–38–04–78* ⊕ *www.oti-delasorgue.fr.*

Continued on page 150

Van Gogh may have made the sunflower into the icon of Provence, but it is another flower —one that is unprepossessing, fragrant, and tiny—that draws thousands of travelers every year to Provence. They come to journey the famous "Route de la Lavande" (the Lavender Route), a wide blue-purple swath that connects over 2,000 producers across the south of France.

THE LAVENDER ROUTE

Once described as the "soul of Haute-Provence," lavender has colored Provence's plains since the days of the ancient Romans. Today it brings prosperity, as consumers are madly buying hundreds of beauty products that use lavender essence. Nostrils flared, they are following this route every summer. To help sate their lavender lust, the following pages present a detail-rich tour of the Lavender Route.

TOURING THE LAVENDER ROUTE

❶ Have your camera ready for the beautifully preserved Cistercian simplicity of the **Abbaye Notre-Dame de Sénanque,** a perfect foil for the famous waving fields of purple around it.

❷ No shrinking violet, the hilltop village of **Gordes** is famous for its luxe hotels, restaurants, and lavender-stocked shops.

❸ Get a fascinating A to Z tour—from harvesting to distilling to production—at the **Musée de la Lavande** near Coustellet.

❹ If you want to have a peak lavender experience—literally—detour 18 km (10 miles) to the northwest and take a spectacular day's drive up the winding road to the **summit of Mont Ventoux** (follow signs from Sault to see the lavender-filled valleys below).

❺ Even if you miss the biggest blow-out of the year, the Fête de la Lavande in **Sault** (usually on August 15), take in the charming *vieille ville* boutiques or the fabulous lavender fields that surround the hillside town.

❻ The awe-inspiring lavender fields around **Forcalquier** are one step away from perfection, and the Monday morning market is a treasure trove of local products.

❼ **Distillerie "Le Coulets"** on the outskirts of Apt has been a lavender farm for generations and offers free tours and products for sale at its boutique.

Provence is threaded by the "Routes de la Lavande" (the Lavender Routes), a wide blue-purple swath that connects over 2,000 producers across the Drôme, the plateau du Vaucluse, and the Alpes-de-Haute-Provence, but our itinerary is lined with some of the prettiest sights—and smells—of the region. Whether you're shopping for artisanal bottles of the stuff (as with wine, the finest lavender carries its own Appellation d'Origine Contrôlée), spending a session at a lavender spa, or simply wearing hip-deep purple as

Forcalquier Market

Purple haze

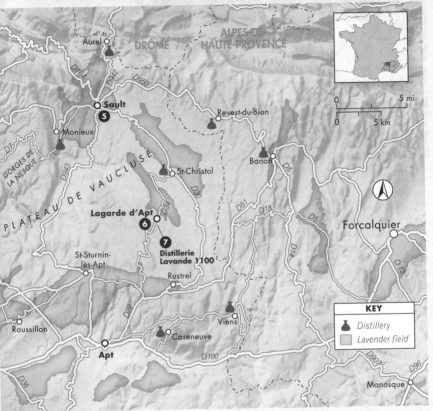

DRÔME

ALPES-DE-HAUTE-PROVENCE

Aurel

Sault
5

Monieux

Revest-du-Bion

GORGES DE LA NESQUE

Banon

St-Christol

PLATEAU DE VAUCLUSE

Lagarde d'Apt
6

7
Distillerie
Lavande 1100

St-Sturnin-lès-Apt

Rustrel

Forcalquier

Roussillon

Viens

Caseneuve

Apt

Manosque

KEY

🍶 *Distillery*

⬜ *Lavender field*

0 — 5 mi
0 — 5 km

you walk the fields, the most essential aspect on this trip is savoring a magical world of blue, one we usually only encounter on picture postcards.

To join the lavender-happy crowds, you have to go in season, which (if you're lucky) runs from June to early August. Like Holland's May tulips, the lavender of Haute-Provence is in its true glory only once a year: the last two weeks of July, when the harvesting begins—but fields bloom throughout the summer months for the most part. Below, we wind

through the most generous patches of lavender. Drive the colorful gambit southeastward (Coustellet, Gordes, Sault and Forcalquier), which will give you good visiting (and shopping) time in a number of the villages that are *fou de la lavande* (crazy for lavender).

Abbaye Notre-Dame de Sénanque

DAY 1

SÉNANQUE
A Picture-Perfect Abbey

An invisible Master of Ceremonies for the Lavender Route would surely send you first to the greatest spot for lavender worship in the world: the 12th-century Cistercian **Abbaye Notre-Dame de Sénanque**, which in July and August seems to float above a sea of lavender, a setting immortalized in a thousand travel posters. Happily, you'll find it via the D177 only 4 km (2½ miles) north of Gordes, among the most beautiful of Provence's celebrated perched villages.

An architecture student's dream of neat cubes, cylinders, and pyramids, its pure Romanesque form alone is worth contemplating in any context. But in this arid, rocky setting the gray stone building seems to have special resonance—ancient, organic, with a bit of the borie about it. Along with the abbeys of Le Thornet and Silvacane, this is one of the trio of "Three Sisters" built by the Cistercian order in this area. Sénanque's church is a model of symmetry and balance. Begun in 1150, it has no decoration but still touches the soul with its chaste beauty.

THE ESSENCE OF THE MATTER

Provence and lavender go hand in hand—but why? The flower is native to the Mediterranean, and grows so well because the pH balance in the soil is naturally perfect for it (pH 6–8). But lavender was really put on the map here when ancient Romans arrived to colonize Provence and used the flower to disinfect their baths and perfume their laundry (the word comes from Latin *lavare*, "to wash"). From a small grass-roots industry, lavender proliferated over the centuries until the first professional distillery opened in Provence in the 1880s to supply oils for southern French apothecaries. After World War I, production boomed to meet the demand of the perfumers of Grasse (the perfume center of the world). Once described as the "soul of Haute-Provence," lavender is now farmed in England, India, and the States, but the harvest in the South of France remains the world's largest.

The adjoining cloister, from the 12th century, is almost as pure, with barrel-vaulted galleries framing double rows of discreet, abstract pillars. Next door, the enormous vaulted dormitory and the refectory shelter a display on the history of Cistercian abbeys. The few remaining monks here now preside over a cultural center that presents concerts and exhibitions. The bookshop is one of the best in Provence, with a huge collection of Provençaliana (lots in English).

After spending the morning getting acquainted with the little purple flower at Sénanque, drive south along the D2 (or D177) back to **Gordes**, through a dry, rocky region mixed with deep valleys and far-reaching plains.

Wild lavender is already omnipresent, growing in large tracts as you reach the entrance of the small, unspoiled hilltop village, making for a patchwork landscape as finely drawn as a medieval illumination. A cluster of houses rises above the valley in painterly hues of honey gold, with cobbled streets winding up to the village's picturesque Renaissance château, making it one of the most beautiful towns in Provence.

Gordes has a great selection of hotels, restaurants, and B&Bs to choose from (see our listings under Gordes). Spend the

ON THE CALENDAR

If you plan to be at the Musée de la Lavande between July 1 and August 25 you can watch animations of workers swathing lavender with copper scythes.

early afternoon among tasteful shops that sell lovely Provençal crafts and produce, much of it lavender-based, and then after lunch, head out to Coustellet.

COUSTELLET
A Great Lavender Museum

Set 2 miles south of Gordes, Coustellet is noted for its **Musée de la Lavande** (take the D2 southeast to the outskirts of Coustellet). Owned by one of the original lavender families, who have cultivated and distilled the flower here for over five generations, this museum lies on the outskirts of more than 815 acres of prime lavender-cultivated land.

Not only can you visit the well-organized and interesting museum (note the impressive collection of scythes and distilling apparatus), you can buy up a storm in the boutique, which offers a great selection of lavender-based products at very reasonable prices.

There are four main species. True lavender (Lavandula angustifolia) produces the most subtle essential oil and is often used by perfume makers and laboratories. Spike lavender (Lavandula latifolia) has wide leaves and long floral stems with several flower spikes. Hybrid lavender (lavandin) is obtained from pollination of true lavender and spike lavender, making a hybrid that forms a highly developed large round cluster. French lavender (Lavendula stoechas) is wild lavender that grows throughout the region and is collected for the perfume industry. True lavender thrives in the chalky soils and hot, dry climate of higher altitudes of Provence. It was picked systematically until the end of the 19th century and used for most lavender-based products. But as the demand for this remarkable flower grew, so did the need for a larger production base. By the beginning of the 20th century, the demand for the flower was so great that producers planted fields of lavender at lower altitudes, creating the need for a tougher, more resistant plant: the hybrid lavandin.

In many towns, Provence's lavender harvest is celebrated with charming folkloric festivals.

DAY 2

LAGARDE D'APT
A Top Distillerie

On the second day of your lavender adventure, begin by enjoying the winding drive 25 km (15 miles) east to the town of **Apt**. Aside from its Provençal market, busy with all the finest food products of the Luberon and Haute Provence, Apt itself is unremarkable (even actively ugly from a distance) but is a perfect place from which to organize your visits to the lavender fields of Caseneuve, Viens, and Lagarde d'Apt.

Caseneuve (east exit from Apt onto the D900 and then northwest on the D35) and Viens (16 km/10 miles east from Apt on the D209) are small but charming places to stop for a quick bite along the magnificent drive through the rows upon rows of lavender, but if you have to choose between the three, go to the minuscule village of Lagarde d'Apt (12 km/7 miles east from Apt on the D209).

Or for a closer look, take the D22 (direction Rustrel) a few kilometres outside of Apt to **Distillerie "Les Coulets."** From mid-July to mid-August you can take a free tour of the distillery, visit the farm and browse the gift shop.

SAULT
The Biggest Festival

To enjoy a festive overnight, continue northwest from Lagarde d'Apt to the village of **Sault**, 15 km (9 miles) to the northeast. Beautifully perched on a rocky outcrop overlooking the valley that bears its name, Sault is one of the key stops along the Lavender Route.

There are any number of individual distilleries, producers, and fields to visit—to make the most of your visit, ask the Office du Tourisme (☎ *04-90-64-01-21* ⊕ *www.saultenprovence.com*) for a list of events. Make sure to pop into the Centre de Découverte de la Nature et du Patrimoine Cynégétique to see the exhibitions on the natural history of the region, including some on lavender. Aim to be in Sault for the not-to-be-missed **Fête de la Lavande**, a day-long festival entirely dedicated to lavender, the best in the region, and usually held around August 15.

Village folk dress in traditional Provençal garb and parade on bicycles, horses leap over barrels of fragrant bundles of hay, and local producers display their wares at the market—all of which culminates in a communal Provençal dinner served with lavender-based products.

DAY 3

FORCALQUIER
The Liveliest Market

On your third day, the drive from Sault over 53 km (33 miles) east to Forcalquier is truly spectacular.

As you approach the village in early July, you will see endless fields of *Lavandula vera* (true wild lavender) broken only by charming stone farmhouses or discreet distilleries.

The epicenter of Haute-Provence's lavender cultivation, **Forcalquier** boasts a lively Monday morning market with a large emphasis on lavender-based products, and it is a great departure point for walks, bike rides, horse rides, or drives into the lavender world that surrounds the town.

In the 12th century, Forcalquier was known as the capital city of Haute-Provence and was called the *Cité des Quatre Reines* (City of the Four Queens) because the four daughters (Eleanor of Aquitaine among them) of the ruler of this region, Raimond Béranger V, all married royals.

Relics of this former glory can be glimpsed in the Vieille Ville of Forcalquier, notably its Cathédrale Notre-Dame and the Couvent des Cordeliers.

MAKING SCENTS

BLOOMING

Lavender fields begin blooming in late June, depending on the area and the weather, with fields reaching their peak from the end of July to early August. The first two weeks of July are considered the best time to catch the fields in all their glory.

HARVESTING

Lavender is harvested from July to September, when the hot summer sun brings the essence up into the flower. Harvesting is becoming more and more automated; make an effort to visit some of the older fields with narrow rows—these are still picked by hand. Lavender is then dried for two to three days before being transported to the distillery.

DISTILLING

Distillation is done in a steam alembic, with the dry lavender steamed in a double boiler. Essential oils are extracted from the lavender by water vapor, which is then passed through the cooling coils of a retort.

◉ Sights

Campredon Centre d'Art
HOUSE | One of the finest of L'Isle's mansions, the 18th-century Hôtel de Campredon has been restored and reinvented as a modern-art gallery, mounting three temporary exhibitions per year. ⊠ *20 rue du Docteur Tallet* ☎ *04–90–38–17–41* ⊕ *www.campredoncentredart.com* 🖼 *€6*.

Collégiale Notre-Dame-des-Anges
RELIGIOUS SITE | L'Isle's 17th-century church is extravagantly decorated with gilt, faux marble, and sentimental frescoes. The double-colonnade facade commands the center of the Vieille Ville. Visiting hours change frequently, so check with the tourist office. ⊠ *L'Isle-sur-la-Sorgue* 🖼 *Free*.

★ Fondation Villa Datris
MUSEUM | Housed in an stately Belle Époque mansion set on the river, this vibrant center for contemporary sculpture is among the most respected arts centers in Provence. Its talented, far-sighted curators scour the European arts scene for ingenious themed shows that mix established names with up-and-coming sculptors. While the shows change only once a year, they are always revelatory, with artwork cleverly installed in every room of the house, including the old shower stalls, the pretty garden, and even from trees hanging over the canal. ⊠ *7 av. des Quartres Otages* ☎ *04–90–95–23–70* ⊕ *www.fondationvilladatris.fr* 🖼 *Free*.

★ La Filaventure Brun de Vian-Tiran
MUSEUM | Through eight generations on the same premises, the Brun de Vian-Tiran family has created France's most beautiful and luxurious woolens from fibers sourced throughout the world, including baby camel, cashmere, merino wool, alpaca, and baby llama. Housed in one of their old warehouses, the brand's state-of-the-art museum takes visitors through the process from fiber to fabric in a fun, interactive scenography that's as fun and fascinating for kids as it is for adults. Afterwards, discover what all the fuss is about in their on-site boutique, where you'll find the entire range of luxury bedding and blankets, scarves, slippers, and more, in a collection usually found only at high-end department stores in Paris. ⊠ *2 cours Victor Hugo* ☎ *04–90–38–73–31* ⊕ *www.brundeviantiran.com/en/museum-brun-de-vian-tiran*.

🍴 Restaurants

Islo
$$ | **MODERN FRENCH** | This bright, elegant-modern dining room, tucked away behind the church in the Vieille Ville, is a real find for a market-fresh gourmet meal you won't soon forget. Beautifully presented dishes include a parfait of local wild mushrooms and poached egg to start, followed by perfectly poached dorade with roasted citrus-infused fennel or succulent guinea hen with oregano polenta. **Known for:** excellent cheese plates; local wines; good value prix-fixe dinner menu. $ *Average main: €19* ⊠ *3 rue Molière* ☎ *04–90–20–18–21* ⊕ *www.islo.fr* ⊘ *Closed Sun. and Mon. No lunch.*

Le Jardin du Quai
$$ | **FRENCH** | This is where local antiques dealers come to eat, and the place feels so welcoming that it would be easy to linger for hours. Chef Daniel Hébet made his name at La Mirande in Avignon and Le Domaine des Andéols in St-Saturnin-lès-Apt before opening this bistro in his own image—young, jovial, and uncompromising when it comes to quality. **Known for:** choice of fine dining or bistro menu; charming setting and pretty terrace; well-priced wines. $ *Average main: €19* ⊠ *91 av. Julien Guigue* ☎ *04–90–20–14–98* ⊕ *www.jardinduquai.com/* ⊘ *Closed Tues., Wed., and mid-Dec.–mid-Jan.*

★ Le 17 Place aux Vins
$ | **WINE BAR** | A *cave* (wine store) by day and happening wine and tapas bar

by night, this is *the* place on the isle for sampling the best local wines and a charcuterie or artisanal cheese plate (or for a taste of the famous house-made foie gras paired with a local Beaume-de-Venise). Delighted to share their knowledge and crazy about wine, the charming staff will pour samples until you've found the perfect pairing. **Known for:** local favorite; menu of local specialties; extensive list of wines by the glass. $ *Average main: €12* ⊠ *17 pl. Rose Goudard* ⊕ *www.17placeauxvins.fr.*

★ Le Vivier

$$$ | **FRENCH** | Patrick Fischnaller returned to southern France from London and quickly won acclaim (and a Michelin star) with this dazzler just outside L'Isle-sur-la-Sorgue's center. Start off with a glass of wine (from €8) on the orange sofa in the Art Deco–style lounge before devouring some foie gras and smoked eel terrine, pigeon pie, or strawberry soup with basil and black olives from the €70 menu (or order à la carte). **Known for:** riverside views from the terrace; excellent roast beef with cherry marmalade; long, leisurely lunches. $ *Average main: €30* ⊠ *800 cours Fernande Peyre* ☎ *04–90–38–52–80* ⊕ *www.levivier-restaurant.com* ⊗ *Closed Mon. and late Feb.–mid-Mar. No lunch Tues. and Sat. No dinner Sun.*

★ Pâtisserie Jouvaud

$ | **BAKERY** | **FAMILY** | You'll never feel more like a kid in a candy shop than when you feast your eyes on the most scintillating desserts and a universe of local sweets here: candied fruits (a specialty of the Vaucluse since Roman times), chocolates, viennoiseries, and candies. At the charming café next door you can sample everything, including made-to-order sweets, tea, coffee, and a small menu of savory dishes for lunch. **Known for:** the best of French pastries; everything homemade on the premises; friendly, English-speaking service. $ *Average main: €6* ⊠ *5 av. des Quatre Otages*

☎ *04–90–26–72–94* ⊕ *www.patisse-rie-jouvaud.com.*

Hotels

★ Château La Roque

$$$ | **B&B/INN** | At this historic château, about 8 miles (13 km) from Îsle-sur-la-Sorgue in the heart of the Luberon, your gracious hosts assure the best possible experience, from your stately room to a superfresh breakfast and intimate gourmet dinner (reserve in advance). **Pros:** impeccable service; beautiful rooms and grounds; breakfast and parking included. **Cons:** must have a car; not for excitement seekers; hard to find. $ *Rooms from: €290* ⊠ *263 ch. du Château* ☎ *04–90–61–68–77* ⊕ *fr.chateaularoque.com* ⇔ *5 rooms* ⊙| *Free breakfast.*

★ Grand Hôtel Henri

$ | **HOTEL** | The refurbished Grand Hotel Henri is the best thing to happen to L'Isle-sur-la-Sorgue lodging in a while, providing a much-needed dash of high style and panache to the local hotel scene. **Pros:** nice restaurant; very reasonable prices; within easy walking distance to market and antique shops. **Cons:** no in-room coffee; lower-category rooms could use more storage space; restaurant books up quickly. $ *Rooms from: €115* ⊠ *1 Cours René Char* ☎ *04–90–38–10–52* ⊕ *www.grandhotelhenri.com* ⇔ *17 rooms* ⊙| *No meals.*

★ La Maison sur la Sorgue

$$$$ | **HOTEL** | This 17th-century home wins guests over as soon as they walk in the door, thanks to its composed elegance and authentic style rarely found in a hotel setting—innkeepers Frédéric and Marie-Claude did their architectural homework before they renovated. **Pros:** all-out treatment plus amenities (shampoos and soaps); courtyard breakfast includes morning surprises beyond basic croissant and jam fare; true elegance. **Cons:** can be hard to find, especially when driving through Sunday crowds; some handheld showers; expensive (but worth it). $ *Rooms from: €380* ✉ *6 rue Rose Goudard* ☎ *04–90–20–74–86* ⊕ *www. lamaisonsurlasorgue.com* ☯ *Closed 1st 2 wks of Nov. and 2 wks in Feb.* ⇄ *4 rooms* ⦿ *Free breakfast.*

★ La Prévôté

$$ | B&B/INN | Five beautifully decorated and freshly painted rooms, each styled with exquisite taste in soft colors and Provence chic, offer an ideal respite after a long day of antiques shopping. **Pros:** price includes breakfast; wonderful dining room; antiques-bedecked interiors. **Cons:** a little tricky to find; parking may be difficult; design in some rooms a bit kitschy. $ *Rooms from: €165* ✉ *4 bis rue Jean Jacques Rousseau* ☎ *04–90–38–57–29* ⊕ *www.la-prevote.fr* ☯ *Closed Tues. and Wed., and 2 wks late Nov. and 2 wks late Feb.* ⇄ *5 rooms* ⦿ *Free breakfast.*

Shopping

Throughout the pretty backstreets of L'Isle's Vieille Ville (especially between Place de l'Église and Avenue de la Libération), there are boutiques spilling baskets full of tempting goods onto the sidewalk to lure you inside; most concentrate on home design and Provençal goods.

Hôtel Dongier

ANTIQUES/COLLECTIBLES | A major group of *antiquaires* is found at Hôtel Dongier. ✉ *15 esplanade Robert Vasse* ☎ *04–90–38–63–63* ⊕ *www.hoteldongierantiquites.fr* ☯ *Closed Tues.–Thurs.*

La Cour aux Saveurs - Florian Courreau

FOOD/CANDY | You might just be lucky enough to arrive at this artisanal chocolaterie, set on a charming street in the old town, on a day when the chocolates are being made by hand, a process visible from the fragrant boutique. Specialties include a large assortment of fresh, delicately perfumed ganache-filled chocolates, plus local specialties like calissons, chocolate bars laden with dried fruit and

nuts, and many other regional delights. ✉ *4 rue Louis Lopez.*

L'Ile aux Brocantes

ANTIQUES/COLLECTIBLES | Of the dozens of antiques shops in L'Isle, this one conglomerate (also known as Passage du Pont) concentrates some 40 dealers under the same roof. ✉ *7 av. des Quatre Otages* ☎ *06–20–10–58–15* ⊕ *www. lileauxbrocantes.com.*

Sous un Olivier

FOOD/CANDY | This food boutique is crammed to the ceiling with bottles and jars of tapenade, fancy mustards, candies shaped like olives, and the house olive oil. ✉ *16 rue de la République* ☎ *04–90–20–68–90* ⊕ *www.sousunolivier.com.*

Un Jour

HOUSEHOLD ITEMS/FURNITURE | For more than 200 years, Brun de Vian-Tiran has been making wool blankets, cozy quilts, and other bed accessories. You can find its signature throws here among other home-style names like Nina Ricci, Cire Trudon, Yves Delorme, and Le Jacquard Français. ✉ *8 pl. Ferdinand Buisson* ☎ *04–90–38–50–19* ⊕ *www.unjour-lingedemaison.fr.*

Xavier Nicod

ANTIQUES/COLLECTIBLES | Higher-end antiques are in plentiful supply at Xavier Nicod, which "pays tribute to eclecticism" in art and architecture. ✉ *9 av. des Quatre Otages* ☎ *06–07–85–54–59* ⊕ *www.xaviernicod.com.*

Fontaine-de-Vaucluse

7 km (4½ miles) east of L'Isle-sur-la-Sorgue; 30 km (19 miles) east of Avignon.

Like the natural attraction for which it is named, this village has welled up and spilled over as a Niagara Falls–type tourist center; the rustic, pretty, and slightly tacky riverside town is full of shops, cafés, and restaurants, all built to serve the pilgrims who flock to its namesake. And neither town nor fountain should be missed if you're either a connoisseur of rushing water or a fan of foreign kitsch.

GETTING HERE AND AROUND

You can take Bus No. 6 (running eight times daily, twice on Sunday) from Avignon TGV station (€2; 1 hour). Otherwise arriving by car is your best option.

VISITOR INFORMATION

CONTACTS Fontaine-de-Vaucluse Tourist Office. ✉ *Résidence Robert Garcin* ☎ *04–90–20–32–22* ⊕ *www.oti-delasorgue.fr.*

Sights

Château

CASTLE/PALACE | Fontaine has its own ruined château, perched romantically on a forested hilltop over the town and illuminated at night. First built around the year 1000 and embellished in the 14th century by the bishops of Cavaillon, the castle was destroyed in the 15th century and forms little more than a sawtooth silhouette against the sky. ✉ *Fontaine-de-Vaucluse.*

Fontaine-de-Vaucluse

BODY OF WATER | There's no exaggerating the magnificence of the Fontaine de Vaucluse, a mysterious spring that gushes from a deep underground source that has been explored to a depth of 1,010 feet—so far. Framed by towering cliffs, a broad, pure pool wells up and spews dramatically over massive rocks down a gorge to the village, where its roar soothes and cools the visitors who crowd the riverfront cafés.

You must pay to park, then run a gauntlet of souvenir shops and tourist traps on your way to the top. But even if you plan to make a beeline past the kitsch, do stop in at the legitimate and informative **Moulin Vallis-Clausa.** A working paper mill, it demonstrates a reconstruction of a 15th-century waterwheel that drives timber crankshafts to mix rag pulp,

while artisans roll and dry thick paper *à l'ancienne* (in the old manner). The process is fascinating and free to watch (the guided tour lasts half an hour and must be arranged in advance; minimum 10 people), though it's almost impossible to resist buying note cards, posters, even lamp shades fashioned from the pretty stuff. Fontaine was once a great industrial mill center, but its seven factories were closed by strikes in 1968 and never recovered. All the better for you today, since now you can enjoy this marvelous natural spot in peace. ✉ *Rue des Bourgades* ☎ *04–90–38–04–78* ⊕ *www. moulin-vallisclausa.com.*

Le Musée-Bibliothèque F. Pétrarque

MUSEUM | The great Renaissance poet Petrarch, driven mad with unrequited love for a beautiful married woman named Laura, retreated to this valley to nurse his passion in a cabin with "one dog and only two servants." He had met the woman in the heady social scene at the papal court in Avignon, where she was to die years later of the plague. Sixteen years in this wild isolation didn't ease the pain, but the serene environment inspired him to poetry, and the lyrics of his *Canzoniere* were dedicated to Laura's memory. The small museum, built on the site of his residence, displays prints and engravings of the virtuous lovers, both in Avignon and Fontaine de Vaucluse. ✉ *On left bank, direction Gordes* ☎ *04–90–20–37–20* ⊕ *www. oti-delasorgue.fr/bouger/culture/les-musees/371734-musee-bibliotheque-francois-petrarque* ☞ *€5* ⊗ *Closed Tues. and Wed.*

Restaurants

Restaurant Philip

$$ | FRENCH | If you want a truly regional experience, take a seat on the shaded terrace of Restaurant Philip, opened in 1926 by Philip's uncle. Enjoy the river views and dig in to some *cuisses de grenouille* (frog's legs) or trout from the

Sorgue cooked in white butter sauce. **Known for:** closest dining to the river; regional wine; good value fixed-price menus. [$] *Average main: €19* ✉ *Chemin de la Fontaine* ☎ *04–90–20–31–81* 🕓 *Closed Oct.–Mar. No dinner Apr.–June and Sept.*

Hotels

Hotel du Poete

$$$ | **HOTEL** | "A river runs through it" is no exaggeration at this amiable hotel with breakfast room, pool, terrace, gardens, Jacuzzi, terrace bar, and several guest rooms overlooking (and in some cases atop) the melodious streams that meander from the famous Sorgue source, a kilometer away. **Pros:** a short walk from Fontaine de Vaucluse and restaurants; beautiful setting on the river; great for families. **Cons:** some ground floor rooms lack views; decor a bit dated; sounds from the nearby river might bother some. [$] *Rooms from: €240* ✉ *Le Village* ☎ *04–90–20–34–05* 🌐 *www.hoteldupoete.com* 🛏 *24 rooms* 🍴 *No meals.*

Gordes

10 km (6 miles) east of Fontaine-de-Vaucluse; 39 km (24 miles) east of Avignon.

The famous *village perché* (hilltop village) of Gordes is only a short distance from Fontaine-de-Vaucluse, but you need to wend your way south, east, and then north on D100A, D100, D2, and D15 to skirt the impassable hillside. It's a lovely drive through dry, rocky country covered with wild lavender and scrub oak, and it may tempt you to a picnic or a walk. How surprising, then, to leave such wildness behind and enter resort country. Once a summer retreat favored by modern artists such as André Lhôte, Marc Chagall, and Victor Vasarely, Gordes is now surrounded by luxury vacation homes, modern hotels, restaurants, and B&Bs, much patronized by chic Parisians. No matter: the ancient stone village still rises above the valley in painterly hues of honey gold, and its mosaiclike cobbled streets—lined with boutiques, galleries, and real-estate offices—still wind steep and narrow to its Renaissance château. Gordes's year-round farmers' market (Tuesday 8–1) is a grand event, offering more upscale wares than some of its neighbors—truffle-infused olive oil, charcuterie, locally made foie gras, and pretty Provençal linens.

GETTING HERE AND AROUND

There's no bus service to Gordes, so you'll need a car or taxi: a taxi ride from Avignon is about €75 or from Fontaine-de-Vaucluse, €40.

VISITOR INFORMATION

CONTACTS Gordes Tourist Office. ✉ *Le Château* ☎ *04–90–72–02–75* 🌐 *www.gordes-village.com.*

Sights

★ **Abbaye de Sénanque**

RELIGIOUS SITE | If you've fantasized about Provence's famed lavender fields, head to the wild valley some 4 km (2½ miles) north of Gordes (via D177), where this photogenic 12th-century Romanesque abbey seemingly floats above a redolent sea of lavender (in full bloom late June through August). Begun in 1150 and completed at the dawn of the 13th century, the **church** and adjoining **cloister** are without decoration but still touch the soul with their chaste beauty. Along with the abbeys of Le Thornet and Silvacane, this is one of a trio of "Three Sisters" built by the Cistercian Order in this area. Next door, the enormous vaulted **dormitory** contains an exhibition on Abbaye de Sénanque's construction, and the **refectory** shelters a display on the history of Cistercian abbeys. The few remaining monks here now preside over a cultural center presenting concerts and exhibitions. The bookshop has a huge collection of books about Provence (lots in English). ✉ *Gordes* ☎ *04–90–72–05–72* 🌐 *www.senanque.fr* 🎟 *€8.*

Belvédère

VIEWPOINT | From this spot you can overlook the miniature fields and farms below. From this height all those modern vacation homes blend in with the ancient mas—except for the aqua-blue pools. Belvédère is just downhill from the château; look for the signs. ✉ *Gordes.*

Château de Gordes

CASTLE/PALACE | The only way you can get into this château is by paying to see a collection of photo paintings by pop artist Pol Mara, who lived in Gordes. It's worth the price of admission, though, just to look at the fabulously decorated stone fireplace, created in 1541. Unfortunately, hours change without warning (afternoon visits are your best bet). ✉ *Pl. Genty Pantaly* ☎ *04–90–72–02–75* 🎟 *€4.*

Église St-Firmin

RELIGIOUS SITE | The interior of the village's Église St-Fermin is overblown rococo—all pink and gold. ✉ *Rue du Belvédère.*

Musée de la Lavande

MUSEUM | Owned by one of the original lavender families, who have cultivated and distilled the flower here for more than five generations, this museum lies on the outskirts of around 80 acres of prime lavender fields. Not only can you visit the chic, well-organized museum (note the impressive collection of scythes and distilling apparatus), see a fascinating movie, and play with their interactive screens, but you can also participate in a variety of fun workshops around lavender for adults and kids alike. Less energetic travelers can head straight to the boutique, which offers a top-notch selection of sophisticated lavender-based cosmetics and essential oils. The museum is about 3 km (2 miles) outside of Gordes (take the D2 southeast to the outskirts of Coustellet). ✉ *276 rte. de Gordes, Cabrières-d'Avignon* ☎ *04–90–76–91–23* 🌐 *www.museedelalavande.com* 🎟 *€8.*

Village des Bories

ARCHAEOLOGICAL SITE | Just outside Gordes, on a lane heading north from D2, are signs for this village. The bizarre and fascinating little stone hovels called *bories* are found throughout this region of Provence, and in this village they are concentrated some 20 strong in an ancient community. Their origins are provocatively vague—built as shepherds' shelters with tight-fitting, mortarless stone in a hivelike form, they may date to the Celts, the Ligurians, or even the Iron Age—and they were inhabited or used for sheep through the 18th century. A photo exhibition shows other structures, similar to bories, in countries around the world. ✉ *Gordes* ☎ *04–90–72–03–48* 🌐 *levillagedesbories.com* 🎟 *€6.*

🍴 Restaurants

Les Cuisines du Château

$$ | **FRENCH** | This tiny (only 26 seats) but deluxe bistro across from the château may look like a tourist trap, but it has wonderful home cooking like roast Luberon lamb, beef with truffle sauce, and the like, and the service is friendly. The '30s-style bistro tables and architectural lines are a relief from Gordes's ubiquitous rustic-chic, and there is a revolving array of paintings by local artists, many of which are for sale. **Known for:** responsive to dietary requests; good value fixed-price dinner menu; accommodating service. [$] *Average main: €22* ✉ *Pl. Genty Pantaly* ☎ *04–90–72–01–31* 🌐 *www.lescuisinesduchateau.com* 🕒 *Closed Sat. yr-round and Mon. Mar.–June and Sept.–Nov.. No dinner Sun. July and Aug.*

Restaurant l'Estellan

$$ | **FRENCH** | A little way outside of town at Les Imberts, this restaurant is worth the journey thanks to such delights as the sea bream with cherry tomatoes and flax seed, the trilogy of goat and ewe cheese with black olive jam, or the pike perch roasted with risotto—plus from here you get spectacular village views. The bistro-Provençal interior is equally as delicious in detail and the perfect setting for a long, leisurely lunch (whether inside or on the terrace) that any visit to Gordes commands. **Known for:** generous portions; lovely garden dining in warm weather; meticulous presentation. ⓢ *Average main: €19* ✉ *Montée de Gordes, about 5 km (3 miles) southwest of Gordes via D15 and D2* ☎ *04–90–72–04–90* ⊕ *www.mas-de-la-senancole.com.*

Hotels

Domaine de l'Enclos
$$ | B&B/INN | Though this cluster of private stone cottages has had a modernizing face-lift, the antique tiles and faux patinas keep it looking fashionably rustic. **Pros:** ideal for families; stunning views from the terraces and some rooms; free parking. **Cons:** breakfasts could be bigger; narrow roads to the hotel; not all rooms have separate showers. ⓢ *Rooms from: €195* ✉ *Rte. de Sénanque* ☎ *06–83–67–89–13* ⊕ *www.domainedelenclos.com* ⇨ *11 rooms, 3 suites* ⊚ *Free breakfast.*

★ La Bastide de Gordes
$$$$ | HOTEL | Spectacularly perched on Gordes's hilltop, the 16th-century 10-level Bastide has undergone a lengthy renovation that has melded its old-world charm with old-world elegance and promptly earned the hotel Palace status, the only one in Provence outside the Riviera. **Pros:** views are unmatched in the area; impeccable service; excellent dining. **Cons:** €35 for breakfast; expensive; street-side rooms disappointing considering the views opposite. ⓢ *Rooms from: €650* ✉ *Le Village, Rue de la Combe* ☎ *04–90–72–12–12* ⊕ *www.grandluxuryhotels.com/hotel/bastide-de-gordes* ⊙ *Closed Jan. and Feb.* ⇨ *41 rooms* ⊚ *No meals.*

Le Phébus & Spa
$$$ | HOTEL | This country hotel's beautiful setting, luxurious pool, and extensive gardens, full-service Carita spa, and Michelin-starred restaurant, and every modern convenience assure pampering of a high level. **Pros:** stupendous scenery; some rooms have terraces; glass of champagne offered upon arrival. **Cons:** very expensive; some rooms lack character; out-of-the-way location. ⓢ *Rooms from: €306* ✉ *220 rte. de Murs* ✛ *Take D2 northeast of Gordes for about 7 km (4½ miles), then D102 into Joucas* ☎ *04–90–05–78–83* ⊕ *www.lephebus.com* ⇨ *24 rooms* ⊚ *No meals.*

Shopping

Le Jardin
GIFTS/SOUVENIRS | If you're shopping for a gift or souvenirs, you'll find tasteful Provençal tableware at Le Jardin, which also has a charming tearoom in its leafy courtyard garden. ✉ *Rte. de Murs* ☎ *04–90–72–12–34.*

Roussillon

14 km (9 miles) southeast of Gordes; 43 km (27 miles) southeast of Avignon.

A rich vein of ocher runs through the earth of Roussillon, occasionally breaking the surface in Technicolor displays of russet, deep rose, garnet, and flaming orange. Roussillon is a mineral showcase, perched above a pocket of red-rock canyonlands that are magically reflected in the stuccoes applied on every building in town, where the hilltop cluster of houses blends into the red-ocher cliffs from which their stones were first quarried. The ensemble of buildings and jagged, hand-cut slopes are equally dramatic, and views from the top look over a landscape of artfully eroded bluffs that Georgia O'Keeffe would have loved.

Did You Know?

Ocher is quarried from Roussillon's fabled painted-desert cliffs, then applied directly to many houses of the town, creating a luminous harmony between natural and manmade beauty.

Unlike neighboring hill villages, there's little of historic architectural detail here; the pleasure of a visit lies in the richly varied colors that change with the light of day, and in the views of the contrasting countryside, where dense-shadowed greenery sets off the red stone with Cézannesque severity. There are pleasant *placettes* (tiny squares) to linger on nonetheless, and a Renaissance fortress tower crowned with a clock from the 19th century; just past it, you can take in expansive panoramas of forest and ocher cliffs.

GETTING HERE AND AROUND

There is no direct bus service to Roussillon. The only way to get here is by car from the D4.

VISITOR INFORMATION

CONTACTS Tourist Office. ✉ *19 rue de la Poste* ☎ *04–90–05–60–25* 🌐 *www.paysapt-luberon.fr.*

Sights

Sentier des Ocres (*Ocher Trail*)
TRAIL | This popular trail starts out from the town cemetery and allows you to wend your way through a magical, multicolor palette *de pierres* (of rocks) replete with eroded red cliffs and chestnut groves; the circuit takes about 45 minutes. Hours are complicated, so plan in advance. ✉ *Roussillon* 🌐 *otroussillon.pagesperso-orange.fr* 🎟 *From €3.*

Usine Mathieu de Roussillon (*Roussillon's Mathieu Ocher Works*)
MINE | The area's famous vein of natural ocher, which spreads some 25 km (16 miles) along the foot of the Vaucluse plateau, has been mined for centuries, beginning with the ancient Romans, who used it for their pottery. You can visit the old Usine Mathieu de Roussillon to learn more about ocher's extraction and its modern uses. Guided tours (50 minutes) in English are on offer throughout the year. ✉ *D103* ☎ *04–90–05–66–69* 🌐 *www.okhra.com* 🎟 *From €7.*

Hotels

Hotel les Sables d'Ocre
$ | **HOTEL** | This small, picturesque hotel, set among lovely gardens with a pool, is a 10-minute walk to town but far enough from its summer crowds to offer welcome peace and quiet. **Pros:** exceptional service; lovely pool; air-conditioning. **Cons:** breakfast isn't included in price; reception closes at 8 pm sharp; decor quaint but dated. [$] *Rooms from: €110* ✉ *Quartier Les Sablières* ☎ *04–90–05–55–55* 🌐 *www.sablesdocre.com* 🛏 *22 rooms* 🍴 *No meals.*

Le Clos de la Glycine
$$$ | **HOTEL** | This centrally located hotel combines modern comforts (an elevator, air-conditioning) with Provençal tradition, and makes up for in charm what it lacks in size. **Pros:** perfect for sunrise views; easy walking distance to town; very good restaurant. **Cons:** often fully booked far in advance; not all rooms have showers; no tea or coffee in rooms. [$] *Rooms from: €230* ✉ *Pl. de la Poste* ☎ *04–90–05–60–13* 🌐 *www.leclosdelaglycine.fr* 🛏 *9 rooms* 🍴 *No meals.*

Ménerbes

27 km (17 miles) southwest of Roussillon; 30 km (19 miles) southeast of Avignon.

This picturesque fortified town isn't designated one of the "plus beaux villages du France" for nothing. Perched high on a rocky precipice, Ménerbes's narrow streets, winding passageways, and limitless views have clinched its status as one of most visited villages of the region, along with its fellow most beautiful villages Gordes and Roussillon.

GETTING HERE AND AROUND

There is no direct bus service to Ménerbes. The only way to get here is by car.

Sights

Castellet

CASTLE/PALACE | This 15th-century fortress juts out at the prow of Ménerbes. ⊠ *Ch. du Castellet.*

⭐ **Le Jardin Botanique de la Citadelle**

GARDEN | The flowering of a 25-year project, this lovely botanical garden is planted on rediscovered 18th-century terraces perched at the highest point of the La Citadelle vineyards and offers charming walks and magnificent views of Ménerbes and the Vaucluse and Ventoux mountains. Visitors will discover hundreds of medicinal and aromatic plant species used in traditional medicines for millennia along scenic paths. Afterward, enjoy a tasting at the domaine and entrance to the Musée du Tire-Bouchon. ⊠ *601 rte. de Cavaillon* ☎ *04–90–72–41–58* ⊕ *www. jardindelacitadelle.com* 🎫 *€5.*

Musée du Tire-Bouchon (*Corkscrew Museum*)

MUSEUM | Don't miss this quirky museum, which has an enormous collection of 1,200 corkscrews on display and interesting historical detail on various wine-related subjects. ⊠ *Domaine de la Citadelle, Rte. de Cavaillon* ☎ *04–90–72–41–58* ⊕ *www.museedutirebouchon.com* 🎫 *€5.*

Place de l'Horloge (*Clock Square*)

PLAZA | A campanile tops the Hôtel de Ville on pretty Place de l'Horloge, where you can admire the delicate stonework on the arched portal and mullioned windows of a Renaissance house. Just past the tower on the right is an overlook taking in views toward Gordes, Roussillon, and Mont Ventoux. ⊠ *Ménerbes.*

🍴 Restaurants

Maison de la Truffe et du Vin (*La Cantine des Gourmets*)

$$$ | **FRENCH** | Set in a stately 17th-century mansion atop Ménerbes, the restaurant at the Maison de la Truffe et du Vin is where you can sample the region's most

prized delicacy in an all-truffle lunch (€65). The Maison also hosts wine tastings of the best Provençal appellations, and the wine boutique is absolutely tops in the area and a great place to stock up (they ship). **Known for:** truffle tastings; excellent wines and wine boutique; spectacular views. **$** *Average main: €30* ⊠ *Pl. de l'horloge* ☎ *04–90–72–38–37* ⊕ *www. vin-truffe-luberon.com* ⊙ *Closed Nov. and Sun.–Wed. Dec.–Mar.*

🛏 Hotels

⭐ **La Bastide de Marie**

$$$$ | **HOTEL** | This picturesque farmstead, set on its own 57-acre vineyard and updated to accommodate every luxe 21st-century need, is a close approximation of your dream of Provence. **Pros:** beautiful breakfast terrace with views; lovely full-service spa; perfectly located for touring Ménerbes and the Luberon. **Cons:** far from nightlife; some rooms on the smaller side; a car is essential. **$** *Rooms from: €421* ⊠ *64 chemin des Peirelles* ☎ *04–90–72–30–20* ⊕ *labastidedemarie.com* ⇥ *16 rooms* ⁙⁙ *No meals.*

Lacoste

7 km (4½ miles) east of Ménerbes; 37 km (23 miles) southeast of Avignon.

Like Ménerbes, gentrified hilltop Lacoste owes its fame to an infamous literary resident.

GETTING HERE AND AROUND
There is no direct bus service to Lacoste. The only way to get here is by car.

Sights

Château de Lacoste

CASTLE/PALACE | Little but jagged ruins remain of the once magnificent Château de Lacoste, where the Marquis de Sade (1740–1814) spent some 30 years of his life, mostly hiding out. Exploits both literary and real, judged obscene by various European courts, kept him in and out of prison despite a series of escapes. His mother-in-law finally turned him in to authorities, and he was locked away in the Paris Bastille, where he passed the time writing stories and plays. Written during his time in the Bastille, *120 journées de Sodome* (*120 Days of Sodom*) featured a Black Forest château suspiciously similar in form and design to his Lacoste home. The once-sumptuous château was destroyed with particular relish in the Revolution but for some years, the wealthy Paris couturier Pierre Cardin has been restoring the castle, which he owns, wall by wall. Under his generous patronage the **Festival Lacoste** takes place here the last two weeks of July. A lyric, musical, and theatrical extravaganza, events (and their dates) change yearly, ranging from outdoor poetry recitals to ballet to colorful operettas. Lacoste has a few lodging options, the oldest of which is Le Café de France. The castle is open to the public in the months of July and August. ✉ *Carrière du Château* ☎ *04–90–75–93–12* 🌐 *www.festivaldelacoste.com* 🎟 *Château €10; festival performances from €55.*

★ **La Forêt des Cèdres**

FOREST | Created in part to fortify France's supply of cedar and cyprus wood, this magnificent forest, covering hundreds of acres, also provides a cool, quiet place for hiking, picnicking, and taking in magnificent views of the surrounding villages and countryside. Information on the forest is available at all of the local tourist offices and the route to it is well marked from the village of Lacoste. The winding drive provides astounding views of the hilltop villages that dot the countryside. ✉ *Lacoste* ☎ *04–90–06–11–36* 🌐 *www.lacoste-84.com/foret-des-cedres.*

Hotels

★ **Domaine de Bonne Terre**

$$ | **B&B/INN** | Though only a two-minute walk from Lacoste, a more captivating country setting would be hard to find, complete with extensive gardens and olive groves, a wooded park with picturesque stone walls, a pool, and breathtaking views from every angle of the property, not to mention your room. **Pros:** freshly prepared breakfast included in price; short walk to Lacoste; very nice pool. **Cons:** closed in late fall and winter; rooms are lovely but basic; not for those seeking chic design. [$] *Rooms from: €125* ✉ *Rte. de Sainte Veran* ☎ *04–90–75–85–53* 🌐 *www.luberon-lacoste.com* 🕒 *Closed Nov.–Mar.* 🛏 *5 rooms* 🍴 *Free breakfast* 💳 *No credit cards.*

Bonnieux

5 km (3 miles) southeast of Lacoste; 42 km (26 miles) southeast of Avignon.

The most impressive of the Luberon's hilltop villages, Bonnieux (pronounced "bun- *yuh*") rises out of the arid hills in a jumble of honey-color cubes that change color subtly as the day progresses. Strewn along D36, the village is wrapped in crumbling ramparts and dug into bedrock and cliff. Most of its sharply raked streets take in wide-angle valley views, though you'll get the best view from the pine-shaded grounds of the 12th-century Église Vieille du Haut, reached by stone steps that wend past tiny niche houses. Shops, galleries, cafés, and fashionable restaurants abound here, but they don't dominate. It's possible to lose yourself in a back *ruelle* (small street) most of the year. If you have a car, you're in luck: to every point of the compass, there are lovely drives from Bonnieux threading out through Le Petit Luberon. Of the four, the best is the eastward course, along the D943 and D113, which leads to the Romanesque ruins of the Prieuré de St-Symphorien. If you have a car, follow the road above Bonnieux toward Loumarin to the lofty Forêt des Cèdres. Perched on a mountaintop, the unparalleled 360-degree views and cool breezes make it a popular spot for a picnic or hike among majestic century-old cedars.

GETTING HERE AND AROUND

The TransVaucluse (Avignon–Apt) bus line services Bonnieux. There are seven buses a day Monday–Saturday, three on Sunday, departing from Avignon's Gare Routière (€2, 1 hour 15 minutes). The only other way to get here is by car. With a car, you can explore the nearby ruins and other worthwhile sites.

VISITOR INFORMATION

CONTACTS Bonnieux Tourist Office. ✉ 7 *pl. Carnot* ☎ *04–90–75–91–90* 🌐 *www.luberon-apt.fr.*

🍴 Restaurants

★ Le Carillon

$$$ | FRENCH | Hungry travelers willing to travel 10 minutes to the tiny perched village of Goult, will be rewarded with a top-notch, thoroughly French menu in an atmosphere elegant enough for a celebratory dinner, yet casual enough for a gourmet lunch on the go. Sea-crab soup with fricassé of cuttlefish and homemade aïoli makes a nice prelude to saddle of rabbit with local girolle mushrooms stewed with kale (a rarity in France). **Known for:** classic French dishes with a certain amount of elegance; homemade sorbet for dessert; outdoor terrace overlooking the town square. [$] *Average main: €25* ✉ *Av. du Luberon, 8.4 km (5 miles) from Bonnieux, Goult* 🌐 *www.restaurant-goult.com* 🕒 *Closed Sun.*

Le Fournil

$$$ | FRENCH | In an old bakery in a natural grotto deep in stone, lighted by candles and arty torchères, this restaurant would be memorable even without its stylishly presented Provençal cuisine. For more than 20 years chef Jean-Christophe Leche has been producing adventurous dishes, available à la carte or as a fixed menu. **Known for:** beautiful terrace in the center of town; attentive service; focus on local wines. [$] *Average main: €25* ✉ *5 pl. Carnot* ☎ *04–90–75–83–62* 🌐 *www.lefournil-bonnieux.com* 🕒 *Closed Mon. and Tues.*

🛏 Hotels

Le Clos du Buis

$$ | B&B/INN | At this Gîtes de France B&B, whitewash and quarry tiles, lovely tiled baths, and carefully juxtaposed antiques create a regional look in the guest rooms. **Pros:** full access to kitchen to cook or keep supplies in fridge; plenty of restaurants within easy walking distance; guests can use washer and dryer, a rarity anywhere. **Cons:** parking is difficult; if "homey" isn't your thing, it may not be for you; not all rooms have separate showers. [$] *Rooms from: €160* ✉ *Rue Victor Hugo* ☎ *04–90–75–88–48* 🌐 *www.leclosdubuis.com* 🕒 *Closed mid-Nov.–mid-Mar.* 🛏 *8 rooms* 🍽 *Free breakfast.*

Buoux

8 km (5 miles) northeast of Bonnieux; 9 km (5½ miles) south of Apt.

To really get into backcountry Luberon, crawl along serpentine single-lane roads below Apt, past orchards and lavender fields. Deeply ensconced in the countryside, the tiny hamlet of Buoux (pronounced "bu- *ooks*") offers little more than a hotel and a café, sheltered by white brush-carpeted cliffs. If you squint, you can just make out the dozens of rock-climbers dangling, spiderlike, from slender cables along the cliff face.

GETTING HERE AND AROUND

There is no direct bus service to Buoux. The only way to get here is by car.

Sights

Fort de Buoux

HISTORIC SITE | This site contains the ruins of an ancient village and a fortification that for years defended the valley, in both Ligurian and Roman times. Several houses and an entire staircase were chiseled directly into the stone; it's uncertain whether they're prehistoric or medieval. Louis XIV dismantled the ancient fortifications in the 17th century, leaving Turneresque ruins to become overgrown with wild box and ivy. It is a hike up, and it's not kid-friendly due to the drop-offs above the ravines. ✉ *D113* ☎ *04–90–74–25–75* 🌐 *www.lefortdebuouux.e-monsite.com* 🎫 *€5.*

Saignon

15 km (9 miles) northeast of Buoux; 5 km (3 miles) southeast of Apt.

Set on the Plateau de Claparèdes and draped just below the crest of an arid hillside covered with olive groves, lavender, and stone farms, Saignon is an appealing hill town anchored by a heavyset Romanesque church. Neat cobbled streets wend between flower-festooned stone houses and surround a central *placette* (small square) with a burbling fountain. Yes, it's been gentrified with a few boutiques and restaurants, but the escapist feel hasn't been erased.

GETTING HERE AND AROUND

There is no direct bus service to Saignon. The only way to get here is by car.

Hotels

★ **Le Parfum des Collines**

$$$ | **B&B/INN** | The "haute" is emphasized in this serene and sophisticated *maison d'hôte* (bed-and-breakfast) nestled in the picturesque Luberon countryside—an elegant-modern retreat with all the amenities of an upscale auberge. **Pros:** near the village perché; excellent hiking from the grounds; dining options are a treat: breakfasts are plentiful, and gourmet lunches and dinners are available. **Cons:** pricier than the usual maison d'hôte; not for those who can't bear total quiet; adorable friendly dogs could bother some guests. [$] *Rooms from: €230* ✉ *Rte. de Saignon, D48, Auribeau* ☎ *04–32–52–93–46* 🌐 *www.parfum-collines.com* 🛏 *5 rooms* 🍴 *Free breakfast.*

Apt

40 km (25 miles) east of Avignon.

Actively ugly from a distance, with a rash of modern apartment blocks and industrial buildings, Apt doesn't attract the tourism it deserves. Its central Vieille Ville, with tight, narrow streets shaded with noble stone houses and strings of fluttering laundry, seethes with activity. The best time to visit is Saturday, when the town buzzes with a vibrant Provençal market, selling crafts, clothing, carpets, jewelry, and—not incidentally—all the finest food products of the Luberon and Haute-Provence.

GETTING HERE AND AROUND

You can reach Apt by the TransVaucluse Bus No. 15.1 from Avignon. There are seven buses a day (only three on Sunday) departing from Avignon's Gare Routière (€2, 1½ hours). The only other way to get here is by car.

Sights

Distillerie les Agnels

WINERY/DISTILLERY | Since 1895, this important local distiller has been producing not only lavender, but also essential oils of lavendin and other aromatic plants. Tour the distillery while you learn about cultivating lavender and the distillation process. Guided visits are offered from May through August. Take your time to browse among the all-natural products that line the shelves of the shop, where you can stock up on lavender as well as the many organic essential oils, floral waters, soaps, sachets, and plant-based cosmetics. ✉ *Route de Buoux* ☎ *04–90–04–77–00* 🌐 *www.lesagnels.com* 🎟 *€5* 🕐 *Closed Oct.–Mar.*

★ **La Maison du Fruit Confit**

LOCAL INTEREST | **FAMILY** | Known for its lush orchards, Apt still excels at a technique for preserving fresh fruit that dates back to Roman times and was prized by everyone from the French popes to Madame Sévigné. At this local cooperative, founded in 1962, the old techniques were updated to 20th-century standards. These colorful local fruits preserved in all their sun-ripened glory are a sight to behold, and visitors are allowed to taste for free before buying. Bigarreau cherries from the Luberon are an absolute favorite, but you'll also find Cavaillon watermelons and melons, Provence apricots, figs, plums, pears, and Corsican clementines, as well as kiwi, pineapple, and, of course, candied ginger. ✉ *538 Quartier Salignan* ☎ *04–90–76–31–66* 🌐 *www.lesfleurons-apt.com* 🕐 *Closed Sun.*

Hotels

★ **Domaine des Andéols**

$$$$ | **RESORT** | In a complete departure from traditional Provençal chic, this collection of cubic houses immerses guests in a contemporary environment—each of 11 individually decorated houses contain works by top designers and artists, private terraces, and some even have small private pools. **Pros:** lovely setting; superb dining choices, using the domaine's own olive oil, wine, and vegetables; total privacy and tranquillity, even in high season. **Cons:** breakfast expensive; rooms not available until 4 pm; must have a car to get here. [$] *Rooms from: €350* ✉ *Rte. de Roussillon Les Andéols, St-Saturnin-lès-Apt* ☎ *04–90–75–50–63* 🌐 *www.andeols.com* 🛏 *19 houses* 🍴 *No meals.*

★ **La Coquillade**

$$$ | **HOTEL** | Set among gentle rolling hills, elegant gardens, and 90 sun-drenched acres of vineyards (from which the Aureto estate wine is produced), this fabulous upscale hideaway is made up of several historic country houses restored to designer perfection and offering every modern luxury—just as terrific for a relaxing spa getaway as an active weekend of swimming, hiking through the many vineyards, biking on one of the hotel's Swiss-made mountain bikes, and, of course, wine tasting. **Pros:** total pampering; close to the Luberon's best sites; huge private terraces. **Cons:** some rooms have better views than others; expensive; some staff members could be friendlier. [$] *Rooms from: €350* ✉ *Domaine de la Coquillade, Gargas* ☎ *04–90–74–71–71* 🌐 *www.coquillade.fr* 🛏 *63 rooms* 🍴 *No meals.*

Lourmarin

12 km (7 miles) southeast of Bonnieux; 54 km (33 miles) southeast of Avignon.

The highly gentrified village of Lourmarin lies low-slung in the hollow of the Luberon's south face, a sprawl of manicured green. Albert Camus loved this place from the moment he discovered it in the 1930s. After he won his Nobel Prize in 1957 he bought a house here and lived in it until his death in 1960 (he is buried in the village cemetery). Now the village, still lovely despite being a haven of French and European holiday homes, is well worth a wander.

GETTING HERE AND AROUND

There is no direct bus service to Lourmarin. The only way to get here is by car.

VISITOR INFORMATION

CONTACTS Lourmarin Tourist Office. ✉ *Pl. H. Barthélémy* ☎ *04–90–68–10–77* 🌐 *www.lourmarin.com.*

👁 Sights

⭐ Château de Lourmarin

CASTLE/PALACE | FAMILY | Loumarin's Renaissance-era château, which was privately restored in the 1920s to appealing near-perfection, is the town's main draw. The "new" wing (begun in 1526 and completed in 1540) is the prettiest, with a broad art collection, rare old furniture, and ornate stone fireplaces—including two with exotic *vases canopes* (ancient Aztec figure vases). The château also hosts several exhibitions of contemporary art throughout the year and lots of fun activities for kids. In summer, the château hosts a series of highly regarded concerts (check the website for scheduling) on their vast terrace with pretty views of the village. ✉ *24 av. Laurent Vibert* ☎ *04–90–68–15–23* ⊕ *www.chateau-de-lourmarin.com* 🎫 *€7.*

🍽 Restaurants

⭐ Auberge La Fenière

$$$$ | FRENCH | Nadia Sammut, the third-generation of female chefs in her family and the second to hold a Michelin star, crafts a cuisine of such sensuality, refinement, and soul here that her dedicated fan base stretches well beyond France. Sammut's passion for fresh, local, and "living" foods extends to the notion that each ingredient expresses itself differently, and the flavor pairings she creates highlight and harmonize those flavors. **Known for:** completely gluten and dairy free kitchen; personable chef who works closely with local producers for her ingredients; natural wines. $ *Average main: €40* ✉ *Rte. de Lourmarin* ☎ *04–90–68–11–79* ⊕ *www.aubergelafeniere.com.*

🛏 Hotels

⭐ Domaine de Fontenille

$$ | HOTEL | Settling into this gracious retreat under the dappled shade of tall trees deep in the Provençal countryside is the easist thing you'll ever do. **Pros:** gorgeous grounds; impossible not to relax; fine dining and wine tastings. **Cons:** breakfast expensive; rooms vary drastically in size; service can be spotty. $ *Rooms from: €200* ✉ *Route de Roquefraiche* ☎ *04–13–98–00–00* ⊕ *www.domainedefontenille.com* 🛏 *19 rooms* ⏧ *No meals.*

⭐ Le Pavillon de Galon

$$$ | B&B/INN | Romantic doesn't begin to describe this beautiful eco-friendly B&B set in an 18th-century hunting lodge, where every detail is rendered with taste and refinement without an ounce of snobbery. **Pros:** magnificent setting close to the Luberon's best villages; breakfast included in price; intimate setting. **Cons:** only three rooms; minimum stay two nights, maximum four nights in high season; young children not allowed. $ *Rooms from: €250* ✉ *Chemin de Galon, Cucuron* ☎ *06–13–39–17–31* ⊕ *www.pavillondegalon.com* 🛏 *3 rooms* ⏧ *Free breakfast.*

AIX, MARSEILLE, AND THE CENTRAL COAST

Updated by
Jennifer Ladonne

 Sights
★★★★☆

 Restaurants
★★★★☆

 Hotels
★★★☆☆

 Shopping
★★★☆☆

 Nightlife
★★★☆☆

WELCOME TO AIX, MARSEILLE, AND THE CENTRAL COAST

TOP REASONS TO GO

★ **Cours Mirabeau in Aix:** The Champs-Elysées of posh Aix-en-Provence, this boulevard is lined with lovely cafés like Les Deux Garçons, where the interior looks pretty much as it did when it opened in 1792.

★ **Bouillabaisse in Marseille:** Order ahead at Chez Fonfon and indulge in classic bouillabaisse—this version will practically make your taste buds stand up and sing "La Marseillaise."

★ **The Calanques:** Near Cassis, these picturesque coves make you feel like you've stumbled onto a movie set.

★ **Paul Cézanne:** Tour Cézanne Country in the area around Montaigne Ste-Victoire, outside the artist's hometown of Aix-en-Provence.

★ **Îles d'Hyères:** In season the tourists arrive en masse but the sense of pure escape can still be enjoyed on these forested islands.

Rough-hewn and fiercely beautiful, this is the sculpted land of Cézanne and Pagnol: from a coastline of lonely pine-studded cliffs and enchanting calanques to neat rows of touristy striped sun beds and seafood platters served with a saucy comment in the local patois. Sophisticated and posh Aix-en-Provence stands carefully aloof from Marseille, tough, vibrant, and larger-than-life. Yet the backcountry between them ambles along at a 19th-century pace with boules, pastis, and country markets.

1 Aix-en-Provence. The main hub of Provence and one of its cultural capitals.

2 Marseille. A vibrant port city that combines seediness with fashion and metropolitan feistiness with classical grace.

3 Aubagne. A low-key market town once home to filmmaker Marcel Pagnol.

4 Cassis. The prettiest coastal town in Provence.

5 Bandol. A seaside resort town that once rivaled the glitziness of the French Riviera.

6 Toulon. A bustling seaside city best known for its naval role in World War II.

7 Îles d'Hyrés. A collection of verdant islands once known as a haven for pirates.

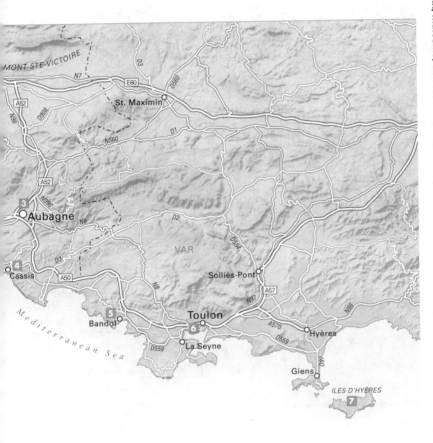

PROVENCE'S WINES

As the world has now discovered, there is a wine that is neither red nor white: rosé, a versatile wine you can drink with almost anything. Delightfully, light rosés are the perfect summer wines—and, happily, Provence turns out to be the rosé capital of France.

The Mediterranean embodies a long tradition of making fruity, dry rosés, and Provence has several appellations counting rosé as up to three-quarters of their production. Demand for it has grown greater since people have discovered that rosés are not just for summer. Still, it came as shocking news to learn the French consume more rosé than white wine. How could the most educated drinkers in the world prefer *pink* wine over a buttery white Burgundy? Fingers pointed directly to three main regions that have developed an amazingly sophisticated rosé wine culture: the Côtes du Rhône, Côtes de Provence, and Côteaux d'Aix-en-Provence.

LA VIE EN ROSÉ

One sip and you'll agree: rosé wines taste wonderful along the Riviera. Some experts even claim that the sea air enhances the aroma (perhaps why a Côtes de Provence rosé loses some of its magic at home). Rosés are usually drunk well-chilled, whether to quench arid thirsts or to hide a less-than-rounded finish. Typically regarded as a less serious wine than their red and white companions, rosés have made enormous strides in the last five years. Try a top-rated Bandol at least once.

The vast region of **Côtes de Provence** stretches across the Var toward Marseille to the west and Grasse to the east. Château Minuty (⊠ *Rte. de Ramatuelle* ☎ 04–94–56–12–09 ⊕ *www.chateauminuty.com*), near St-Tropez, is found on almost every wine list in the area in dry white, fruity rosé and medium-bodied red. Another top vineyard is Château Sainte-Marguerite (⊠ *Le Haut Pansard, La Londe les Maures* ☎ 04–94–00–44–44 ⊕ *www. chateausaintemarguerite.com*), which produces full-bodied reds, lively rosés, and tasty whites.

Côteaux d'Aix-en-Provence spreads out from the Rhône River to the St-Victoire mountain. Rosés from this area are often described as "zingy" or "fruity," while reds and whites range from solid to reasonable. Two names to look for are the stellar rosés of Domaine Sainte Lucie (⊠ *Av. Paul Cézanne, C* ☎ 06–81–43–94–62 ⊕ *www.mip-provence. com*) and the Château Lafoux (⊠ *RN7, near St-Maxime* ☎ 04–94–78–77–86 ⊕ *www.chateaulafoux.com*).

Bandol rivals Châteauneuf-du-Pape as the region's reigning red. Domaine Tempier (⊠ *Le Plan de Castellet* ☎ 04–94–98–70–21 ⊕ *www.domaine-tempier.com*) is renowned for its distinctive reds and stunning rosés.

In **Côtes du Rhône,** you'll find some of France's most drinkable AOC wines along the Rhône delta. Top choices are La Bastide Saint Dominique (⊠ *1358 Chemin St-Dominique La Bastide, Domazan* ☎ 04–90–70–85–32 ⊕ *www. domaine-pastouret.com*) and the Château de Campuget (⊠ *Mas du Campuget, Manduel* ☎ 04–66–20–20–15).

Châteauneuf-du-Pape is fondly regarded as the king of reds in Provence. Noted names include Domaine Chante Cigale (⊠ *Av. Louis Pasteur* ☎ 04–90–83–702–57 ⊕ *www.chantecigale.com*) and Château Rayas (⊠ *Rte. De Courthezon* ☎ 04–90–83–73–09 ⊕ *www.chateau-rayas.fr*).

Beaumes de Venise is an appellation that is world-renowned for its muscat dessert wine, made since the 14th century. The pale-gold wines are sweet and fruity with a high alcohol content (more than 15%) and pair well with foie gras.

Just above Vacqueyras and Beaumes de Venise, Gigondas reds are gaining ground as the region's most interesting and pairable wines. For an excellent selection of mostly organic or biodynamic wines of the region, the Rhonéa Cooperative is an absolute must (⊠ *228 Rte. de Carpentras* ☎ 04–90–12–41–00 ⊕ *www.rhonea.fr*).

When you cross the imaginary border into Provence for the first time, you may experience a niggling sense of déjà vu. The sun-drenched angular red rooftops, the dagger-narrow cypresses, the picture-perfect port towns, and the brooding massifs fire the imagination in a deep, soul-stirring way. And it's no wonder: some of the world's greatest artists were inspired by the unforgettable landscapes found here.

Cézanne colored his canvases in daubs of russet and black-green, the rough-cut structure of bluff and twisted pine inspiring a building-block approach to painting that for others gelled into Cubism. Marcel Pagnol painted pictures with words: the smells of thyme and rosemary crunching underfoot, the sounds of thunder rumbling behind rain-starved hills, the quiet joy of opening shutters at dawn to a chorus of blackbirds in the olive grove. Both Cézanne and Pagnol were native sons of this region east of the Rhône, who were inspired to eloquence by the primordial landscape and its echoes of antiquity. And yet, like most who visit the region, they were equally fascinated with the modern Provençal world and its complex melding of the ancient with the new.

A visit to this region can encompass the best of urban culture, seaside, and arid backcountry. Aix is a small, manageable city with a leisurely pace, studded with stunning architecture and a lively concentration of arts, due in part to its active university life. Marseille offers the yang to Aix's yin. Its brash style, bold monuments, and spectacular sun-washed waterfront center are reminiscent of those of Naples or modern Athens; it is often maligned for its crime rate and big-city energy, and often unfairly neglected by visitors. Up in the dry inland hills, Pagnol's hometown of Aubagne gives a glimpse of local life, with a big farmers' market in the plane tree–lined town center and makers of *santons* (terra-cotta figurines) at every turn. Both the lovely port villages of Cassis and Sanary-sur-Mer and the busy beach town of Bandol allow time to watch the tides come and go, though for the ultimate retreat, take the boat that leaves for the almost tropical Îles d'Hyères. Like most of this region, these islands are a true idyll, but even more so for being car-free.

MAJOR REGIONS

Aix-en-Provence. For one day, join all those fashionable folks for whom café-squatting, people-watching, and boutique-hopping are a way of life in

Aix-en-Provence, then track the spirit of its most famous native son, Paul Cézanne. Head into the countryside to visit the Jas de Bouffan, his family estate, and Montagne Sainte-Victoire, the main "motif" for this giant of modern art.

Marseille. France's second-largest city, Marseille is the place to enjoy the colorful sights and smells of a Mediterranean melting pot, where far-flung cultures have mingled ever since the Greeks invaded around 600 BC. Tour its cathedrals and museums, visit its spiffed-up Vieux Port's fabulous new architectural gems, then head east to Aubagne to walk its Circuit Pagnol.

The Central Coast. Stretching along the eastern coastline from Marseille, the famously beautiful calanques form a sapphire chain of jagged fjordlike coves interspersed with rugged cliffs and lovely harbor towns that conjure up the St-Tropez of the 1940s. Just inland, in the dry white hills, lies the peaceful market town of Aubagne; climb to the top of its outlying hills and you can see the ocean sparkling below. Cassis is the jewel of this region, a harbor protected by the formidable Cap Canaille, 1,300 feet high. Between Cassis and Marseille stretch the extraordinary Calanques, a series of rocky fjords that probe deep into the coastline, punctuated with pretty seaside towns and the sun-drenched vineyards of picture-perfect Bandol. The hub of the region is Toulon, an enormous naval base and a tough big city with long, sandy beaches and a charming, up-and-coming Old Town; just east of the city is Hyères, an elegant Belle Époque–era town, where you catch the ferry to Porquerolles, the best of the wild and beautiful Îles d'Hyères.

Planning

When to Go

High season falls between Easter and October, but if you come in winter you may be pampered with warm sun and cool breezes. When the mistral attacks (and it can happen in any season), it channels all its forces down the Rhône Valley and blasts into Aix and Marseille like a hurricane. But, happily, the assault may last only one day. (This is not the day, however, to opt for a boat ride from Cassis or Porquerolles; aim instead for the sheltered streets of Aix.)

Planning Your Time

To make the most of your time in this region, plan to divide your days between big-city culture, backcountry tours, and waterfront leisure. You can "do" Marseille in an impressive day or weekend trip, but its backstreets and tiny ports reward a more leisurely approach. Aix is as much a way of life as a city charged with tourist must-sees; allow time to hang out in a Cours Mirabeau café and shop the side streets. Aubagne must be seen on a market day (Tuesday, Thursday, Saturday, or Sunday) to make the most of its charms. Cassis merits at least a whole day if you want to explore the Calanques and enjoy a seaside lunch; Bandol is less appealing unless you're committed to beach time. The complete seaside experience can be found on the island of Porquerolles, one of the Îles d'Hyères.

This is an area that moves a little faster than traditional Provence, since the main hubs of Marseille, Aix-en-Provence, and Toulon are large cities, but the average day still includes a two-hour lunch. Take the time to enjoy an afternoon stroll, a long lunch, a little siesta—because this is, fundamentally, what makes living in Provence so charmingly worthwhile.

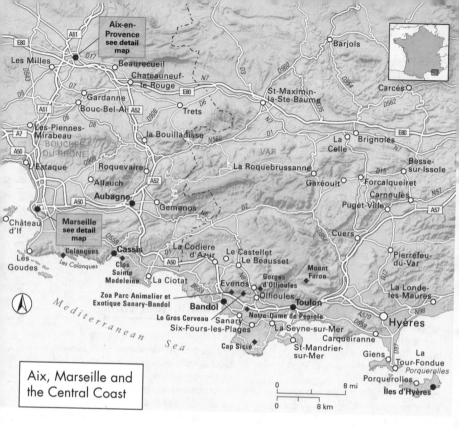

And even if the cities are, well, cities, you'll note that much of general life comes to a halt between midday and two and everything is closed on Sunday (except the markets, open until about 1 or 1:30; many shops are also closed on Monday, so plan accordingly. Keep your sense of humor intact and learn the Gallic shrug (a typical shoulder movement that can mean anything from "I don't know" to "I really don't care") when you are politely refused service because you are late (or too early). It's a different mentality, one focused on the quality of life for everyone and emphasizing the value of taking the time to dwell on the important things.

To really take advantage of the area, start your trip in a large and vibrant city center like Marseille. From here you can spiral out to Aix, Aubagne, and the coast with ease via train, car, or bus. If you want a stylish and delightful mix of urban chic and country-town beauty, though, Aix-en-Provence can't be beat for a kick-off point.

Getting Here and Around

Public transportation in Marseille, Aix, and the Central Coast is well organized, with most areas accessible by plane, train, bus, or boat.

Flying in is a good option, as Marseille has one of the largest airports in France and regular flights come in from Paris and London. The Toulon-Hyères airport is smaller but also has frequent flights.

If you prefer the more scenic route, note that the high-speed TGV trains go directly to Marseille, Aix-en-Provence, and Toulon from Paris in about the same time as a flight, and a big selection of local and regional trains will take you to the towns along the Central Coast. Another advantage is that train stations tend to be central and more easily accessible than airports.

There is a moderately good network of buses run by a large number of independent bus companies, but check with the local tourism offices for the one you need since the "who's who" in the bus world here is confusing.

If driving, get a good map, and make sure you familiarize yourself with the towns and cities along your route first, since those are the signs you'll follow. Don't count on your rental car having GPS.

AIR

Marseille has one of the largest airports in France, the Aéroport de Marseille Provence in Marignane, about 20 km (12 miles) northwest of the city center. Regular flights come in daily from Paris and London. Delta Airlines flies direct from New York to Nice (about 190 km [118 miles] from Marseille and about 150 km [93 miles] from Toulon). Airport shuttle buses to Marseille center leave every 20 minutes 4:30 am–12:10 am daily (€10); shuttles to Aix leave hourly 8 am–11:10 pm (€10).

AIRPORT INFORMATION Marseille Provence airport. (*Marignane*) ☎ *08–20– 81–14–14* ⊕ *www.marseille-aeroport.fr.*

BOAT

If you find yourself without a yacht on this lovely coastline, it's easy to jump on a tourist cruiser, whether you putter from calanque to calanque between Marseille and Cassis or commute to the car-free Îles d'Hyères. Many boats have glass bottoms for underwater viewing, and most allow you to climb onto the top deck and face the wind as the cruiser bucks the waves.

BUS

A good network of private bus services (confusingly called *cars*) strikes out from Marseille's *gare routière* (bus station), adjacent to the Metro Gare St-Charles train station, and carries you to points not served by train. Tickets costs €1.70 and multiple-ticket *carnets* are available.

From Marseille, buses link many destinations, including Aix-en-Provence (€6, 1 hour, leaving every 20 minutes), Nice (€33.50, 3 hours, serviced by Phocéens Cars, five buses daily), Cassis (€6.30, 1½ hours, every 20 minutes), Carpentras (€20, 2 hours, three buses daily), and Cavaillon (€14.70, 1 hour, three buses daily).

As for Aix-en-Provence, it has a dense network of bus excursions from its station. To/from destinations include Marseille (€6, 1 hour, every 20 minutes), Arles (€10, 1½ hours, two- to five daily), and Avignon (€18, 1½ hours, two- to four daily). Aix-en-Provence has a municipal bus that services the entire town and outlying suburbs (such as Jas de Bouffon). A ticket costs €1.20.

A *navette* (shuttle bus) connects La Rotonde/Cours Mirabeau with the bus and train station, and one heads out to the TGV station (departing from bus station), which is some 13 km (8 miles) west of town and the Marseille-Provence airport.

BUS INFORMATION Aix-en-Bus. ⊠ *300 av. Guiseppe Verdi* ☎ *09–70–80–90–13* ⊕ *www.aixenbus.fr.* **Aix-en-Provence gare routière.** ⊠ *Av. de la Europe* ☎ *08–09–40–04–15.* **Lepilote/Cartreize.** ☎ *08–00–71–31–37* ⊕ *www.lepilote. com.* **Marseille gare routière.** ⊠ *3 pl. Victor Hugo, St-Charles* ☎ *04–91–08–16–40.* **Phocéens Cars.** ☎ *04–93–85–62–15* ⊕ *www.phoceens-cars.com.*

CAR

The A6/A7 toll expressway (*péage*) channels all traffic from Paris toward the south. At Orange, A7 splits to the

Paul Cézanne, Superstar

Matisse called him "the father of us all." He helped catapult Picasso into Cubism. And nearly every artist working today owes a huge debt to the man who finally kicked over the traces of traditional art—Paul Cézanne (1839–1906), Aix-en-Provence's most famous native son. His images of Mont Ste-Victoire and his timeless still lifes are the founding icons of 20th-century painting. With them, he not only invented a new pictorial language but immortalized his Provençal homeland.

Great Cézannes may hang in museums, but you can't really understand the artist without experiencing his Provence firsthand. As it turns out, he is everywhere: Aix even has a Cézanne Trail (⊕ www.cezanne-en-provence.com). The route through the town is marked with copper "C" studs.

The two most moving locales, however, are just outside the city. Jas de Bouffan, Cézanne's cherished family home, signaled his father's rise to prominence from hatmaker to banker and was a lifetime source of inspiration for the artist, who moved there at the age of 20. Four large decorative panels painted directly on the walls bear the ironic signature "Ingres"—the young artist's rebellious jab at his father, who preferred a more prosaic career for his son. Cézanne remained here until his mother's death, in 1897, left him too broken-hearted to remain and the house was sold. One mile north of Aix's center is "Les Lauves," the studio the artist built in 1901, set in a magically overgrown olive grove. The high point here lies a mile along the Chemin de la Marguerite: the belvedere spot from which the artist painted his last views of Mont Ste-Victoire (indeed, he died shortly after being caught in a storm here).

When he abandoned Aix's art academy for the dramatic landscapes of the surrounding hills, he became smitten with the stark, high-noon light of Provence, rejecting the sugar-almond hues of Impressionism. Instead of mixing colors to create shadows like Monet, he simply used black. Instead of using translucent haze to create an effect of distance, he focused on ruler-straight Provençal streets (laid out by ancient Romans) to hurtle the eye from foreground to background.

In the end, Cézanne wanted to impose himself on the landscape, not vice versa. So why not do the same? With brochures from the Aix tourist office, head out into Cézanne Country—the roads leading to Le Tholonet and Mont Ste-Victoire. Walk these shady trails and you'll learn just how Cézanne became the trailblazer of modern art.

southeast and leads directly to Aix. From there A51 leads to Marseille. Also at Aix, you can take A52 south via Aubagne to Cassis and A50, the coastal autoroute tollway. The Aix–Marseille–Toulon triangle is well served by a network of autoroutes with a confusing profusion of segmented number-names (A50, A51, A52, A55). Hang on to your map and follow the direction signs. As with any major metropolis, it pays to think twice before driving into Marseille: if you want to visit only the port neighborhoods, it may be easier to make a day trip by train.

However, you'll need to drive to visit the smaller ports and bays outside the center. To approach downtown Marseille, try to aim for the A51 that dovetails down from Aix; it plops you conveniently near the Vieux Port, while A55 crawls through industrial dockside traffic. The autoroute system collapses inconveniently just at Toulon, forcing you to drive right through jammed downtown traffic. When mapping out your itinerary, remember that all the coastal towns hereabouts line up for easy access between Marseille and Toulon, so you can wind up cruising along A50, which follows the coastline, and take in all the sights. Although Marseille is one of the biggest cities in France, it's only a matter of minutes before you're lost in deep backcountry on winding, picturesque roads that lead to Cassis or Aubagne and beyond. Beautiful back roads between Aix, Marseille, and Aubagne carry you through Cézanne and Pagnol country; the N96 between Aix and Aubagne is worth skipping the freeway for. The D559 follows the coast, more or less scenically, from Marseille through Cassis to Hyères.

TRAIN

The high-speed TGV *Méditerranée* line ushered in a new era in Trains à Grande Vitesse (Trains at Great Speed) travel in France; the route means that you can travel from Paris's Gare de Lyon to Marseille in a mere three hours. Not only is the idea of Provence as a day trip now possible (though, of course, not advisable), you can even whisk yourself there directly upon arrival at Paris's Charles de Gaulle airport.

After the main line of the TGV divides at Avignon, the southeast-bound link takes in Aix-en-Provence, Marseille, Toulon, Hyères, and the Côte d'Azur city of Nice. There's also frequent service by daily local trains to other towns in the region from these main TGV stops. With high-speed service now connecting Aix, Nîmes, Avignon, and Marseille, travelers without cars will find a Provence itinerary much easier to pull off. For full information on the TGV *Méditerranée*, log onto the SNCF website (handily in English); you can purchase tickets on this website or through RailEurope, and you

should always buy your TGV tickets well in advance for the most savings (tickets are cheapest two or more months before a trip, but are sometimes reduced around 11 pm the night before in the off-season). From Marseille it's a brief jaunt up to Aix. The main rail line also continues from Marseille to Toulon.

Aix has train routes to Marseille (€8.30, 30 minutes, 44 trains daily), Nice (€39, 5½ hours, eight trains daily), and Cannes (€35, 5½ hours, eight trains daily), along with other destinations. Marseille has train routes to Aix-en-Provence (€8.30, 30 minutes, 44 trains daily), Avignon (€17, 1 hour, leaves hourly), Nîmes (€30, 1½ hours), Arles (€16, 1 hour), and Orange (€23, 1½ hours). Once in Marseille, you can link up with the coastal train route for connections to all the resort towns lining the coast eastward to Monaco and Menton. You can also catch trains to Cassis, Bandol, Aubagne, and Toulon. One website that provides in-depth info on train travel is ⊕ *www.beyond.fr*; another is ⊕ *www.voyages-sncf.com*.

Marseille boasts a fine metro system. Most of the two metro lines service the suburbs, but several stops in the city center can help you get around quickly, including the main stop at Gare St-Charles, Colbert, Vieux Port, and Notre-Dame. A ticket costs €1.70, with multiple carnet tickets available.

TRAIN INFORMATION Aix-en-Provence Gare SNCF. ⊠ *Av. Victor Hugo* ☎ *08–92–35–35–35.* **Marseille Gare St-Charles.** ☎ *08–00–11–40–23.* **SNCF.** ☎ *3635* ⊕ *www.sncf.com.*

Restaurants

One eats late in Provence: rarely before 1 pm for lunch (and you may find yourself still at the table at 4 pm) and 8 or 9 pm for dinner. Be prepared for somewhat disdainful looks ("Tourists!") and slow responses if you try to come any earlier.

One look at the flower-filled fields of the Bouches du Rhône region and you'll quickly understand why Van Gogh, Gauguin, and Monet loved Provence.

Most restaurants close between lunch and dinner, even in summer, and no matter how much you are willing to spend or how well dressed you are, you will be firmly turned away. If you are craving an afternoon glass of rosé *bien frais* and a light snack, head to one of the smaller beach or roadside sandwich kiosks, or the local *boulangerie* (bakery), which usually has a selection of fresh bread and treats. In town, cafés serve all day long.

The more intrepid sort can try a slice of Provençal life and brave one of the smoky, lottery-playing, coffee-and-pastis-drinking *tabacs* that line every main street in the south. You'll find they also often have basic fare for a reasonable price.

aim to provide outdoor space at its loveliest, from gardens where breakfast is served to parasol pine–shaded pools. The bigger cities will always have somewhere to stay, but the good and reputable hotels book up quickly at certain times of the year. June, July, and August are considered to be high season, so reserve ahead of time. In the larger cities, particularly Marseille, be careful to note where your hotel is located because, even if the hotel is deluxe, there are unsavory neighborhoods that can make for an unpleasant, if not downright scary, stay (especially at night).

Restaurant and hotel reviews have been shortened. For full information, visit Fodors.com.

Hotels

Accommodations in the area range from luxury villas to modest city-center hotels. This is no longer just converted *mas* (farmhouse) country. Nonetheless, hotels in this region favor Provençal flavor and

What it Costs in Euros			
$	**$$**	**$$$**	**$$$$**
RESTAURANTS			
under €18	€18–€24	€25–€32	over €32
HOTELS			
under €125	€125–€225	€226–€350	over €350

Visitor Information

The regional tourist offices—the Comité Départemental du Tourisme du Var, the Comité Départemental du Tourisme des Bouches-du-Rhône, and Comité Regional du Tourisme de Provence-Alpes-Côte d'Azur—have extensive documentation on lodging, restaurants, rentals, hikes, and attractions.

CONTACTS Comité Départemental du Tourisme des Bouches-du-Rhône. ⊠ *13 rue de Brignoles, Marseille* ☎ *04–91–13–84–13* ⊕ *www.myprovence.fr.* **Comité Départemental du Tourisme du Var.** ⊠ *1 bd. de Strasbourg, Toulon* ⊕ *www.visitvar.fr.* **Comité Regional du Tourisme de Provence-Alpes-Côte d'Azur.** ⊠ *12 pl. Joliette, Marseille* ☎ *04–91–56–47–00* ⊕ *www. provence-alpes-cotedazur.com.*

Aix-en-Provence

32 km (20 miles) north of Marseille; 64 km (40 miles) northwest of Toulon.

Longtime rival of edgier, more exotic Marseille, the lovely town of Aix-en-Provence (pronounced "*ex*") is gracious, cultivated, and made all the more cosmopolitan by the presence of some 40,000 university students. In keeping with its aristocratic heritage, Aix quietly exudes well-bred suavity and elegance—indeed, it is now one of the 10 richest townships in France. The influence and power it once had as the old capital of Provence—fine art, noble architecture, and graceful

urban design—remain equally important to the city today. And, although it is true that Aix owns up to a few modern-day eyesores, the overall impression is one of beautifully preserved stone monuments, quietly sophisticated nightlife, leafy plane trees, and gently splashing fountains. With its thriving market, vibrant café life, spectacularly chic shops, and superlative music festival, it's one Provence town that really should not be missed.

Aix's artistic roots go back to the 15th century, when the town became a center of Renaissance arts and letters. A poet himself and patron of the arts, the king encouraged a veritable army of artists to flourish here. At the height of its political, judicial, and ecclesiastical power in the 17th and 18th centuries, Aix profited from a surge of private building, each *grand hôtel particulier* meant to outdo its neighbor. It was into this exalted elegance that artist Paul Cézanne (1839–1906) was born, though he drew much of his inspiration not from the city itself but from the raw countryside around it, often painting scenes of Montagne Ste-Victoire. A schoolmate of Cézanne's made equal inroads on modern society: the journalist and novelist Émile Zola (1840–1902) attended the Collège Bourbon with Cézanne and described their friendship as well as Aix itself in several of his works. You can sense something of the vibrancy that nurtured these two geniuses in the streets of modern Aix. The city's famous Festival d'Aix (International Opera Festival) has imported and created world-class opera productions as well as related concerts and recitals since 1948. Most of the performances take place in elegant, old Aix settings, and during this time the cafés, restaurants, and hotels spill over with the *beau monde* who've come to Aix especially for the July event.

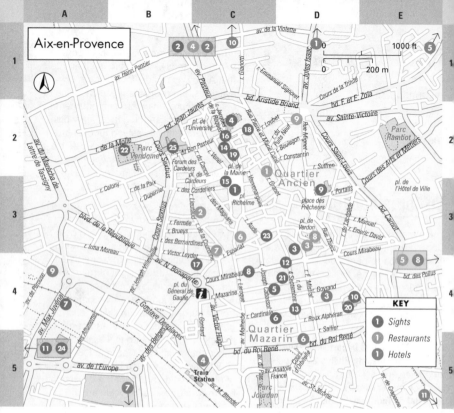

Aix-en-Provence

0 ———— 1000 ft
0 ———— 200 m

GETTING HERE AND AROUND

Aix lies at a major crossroads of autoroutes: one coming in from Bordeaux and Toulouse, then leading up into the Alps toward Grenoble; the other a direct line from Lyons and Paris, and it's a quick half hour from Marseille. The Aix-en-Provence TGV station is 10 km (6 miles) west of the city and is served by regular shuttle buses. The old Aix train station is on the slow Marseille–Sisteron line, with trains arriving roughly every hour from Marseille St-Charles. The center of Aix is best explored by foot, but there is a municipal bus service that serves the entire town and the outlying suburbs. Most leave from La Rotonde in front of the tourism office.

TOURS

Tourist Office tours

WALKING TOURS | Two-hour walking tours in English are organized by the Aix tourist office; tours of the Old Town leave at 10 on Tuesday, Friday, and Saturday. A tour of Cézanne landmarks leaves from the tourist office at 10 on Thursday; it follows the bronze plaques in the city sidewalks. Reserve ahead with the tourist office. ✉ *Aix-en-Provence* 🖆 *From €10.*

VISITOR INFORMATION

CONTACTS Aix-en-Provence Tourist Office. ✉ *Les allées provençales, 300 av. Giuseppe Verdi* ☎ *04–42–16–11–61* ⊕ *www.aixenprovencetourism.com.*

⊙ Sights

The famous Cours Mirabeau, a broad, shady avenue that stretches from one grand fountain to another, bisects old Aix into two distinct neighborhoods. Below the cours, the carefully planned Quartier Mazarin is lined with fine 17th- and 18th-century mansions. Above, the Old Town twists and turns from square to fountain square, each turn leading to another row of urban boutiques and another buzzing cluster of café tables. If you turn a blind eye to these enticing distractions, you can see the sights of Aix in a day's tour—but you'll be missing the point. The music of the fountains, the theater of the café crowds, and the painterly shade of the plane trees are what Aix is all about.

Ancienne Halle aux Grains (*Old Grain Market*)

ARCHAEOLOGICAL SITE | Built in 1761, this former grain market serves as a post office today—a rather spectacular building for a prosaic service. The frieze, portraying an allegory of the Rhône and Durance rivers, is the work of Aix sculptor Jean Chaste (1726–93); he also created the fountain out in front. That's a real Roman column at the fountain's top. ✉ *Pl. Richelme.*

Atelier Cézanne (*Cézanne's Studio*)

MUSEUM | Just north of the Vieille Ville loop you'll find Cézanne's studio. After the death of his mother forced the sale of the painter's beloved country retreat, Jas de Bouffan, he had this atelier built and some of his finest works, including *Les Grandes Baigneuses* (*The Large Bathers*), were created in the upstairs workspace. But what is most striking is the collection of simple objects that once featured prominently in his portraits and still lifes—redingote, bowler hat, ginger jar—all displayed as if awaiting his return. The atelier is behind an obscure garden gate on the left as you climb Avenue Paul-Cézanne. ✉ *9 av. Paul-Cézanne* ☎ *04–42–21–06–53* ⊕ *www. atelier-cezanne.com* 🖆 *€7* ⊙ *Closed Jan., Sun. and Mon. Feb., and Sun. Dec.*

Café-Brasserie les Deux Garçons

RESTAURANT—SIGHT | Cézanne enjoyed his coffee and papers here, as have generations of *beau monde,* intellectuals, and neighborhood *habitués*—Churchill, Sartre, Picasso, Delon, Belmondo, and Cocteau among them—since its founding in 1792. Nowadays neither the food nor the coffee are memorable, but 365 days a year you can savor the linen-decked sidewalk tables that look out to the Cours

The museums and churches in Aix-en-Provence are overshadowed by the city itself, with its beautiful fountains, elegant mansions, and charming set pieces like the Place de l'Hôtel-de-Ville.

Mirabeau, where the locals often prefer to take a table, considering it to be *the* place to see and be seen. But if you want to travel back in time to the *époque consulaire*, sit inside: the gold-ivory interior remains exactly as it was when the café opened. ✉ *53 cours Mirabeau* ☎ *04–42–26–00–51* ⊕ *www.les2garcons.fr.*

Cathédrale St-Sauveur

RELIGIOUS SITE | Many eras of architectural history are clearly delineated and preserved here. The cathedral has a double nave—Romanesque and Gothic side by side—and a Merovingian (5th-century) **baptistery,** its colonnade mostly recovered from Roman temples built to honor pagan deities. The deep bath on the floor is a remnant of the total-immersion baptisms that used to occur here, marking the forsaking of one's old life (going down into the water) for a new life in Christ (rising up from the water). Shutters hide the ornate 16th-century carvings on the **portals,** opened by a guide on request. The guide can also lead you into the

tranquil Romanesque **cloister** next door, with carved pillars and slender columns.

The extraordinary 15th-century *Triptyque du Buisson Ardent* (*Mary and the Burning Bush*) was painted by Nicolas Froment in the heat of inspiration following his travels in Italy and Flanders, and depicts the generous art patrons King René and Queen Jeanne kneeling on either side of the Virgin, who is poised above a burning bush. To avoid light damage, it's rarely opened for viewing; check with the tourist office beforehand. ✉ *Pl. des Martyrs de la Résistance* ☎ *04–42–23–45–65* ⊕ *www.cathedrale-aix.net.*

★ Caumont Centre d'Art

MUSEUM | Part of the Culturespaces network of museums and monuments, this arts center is a jewel in the organization's impressively laden crown and is one of Aix's top cultural attractions. Given that the center is housed in the glorious Hôtel de Caumont, one of the city's most spectacular 18th-century mansions, it's no wonder that its period rooms are a joy to behold. It hosts two world-class art exhibitions per year in beautiful-ly conceived exhibition spaces (the inaugural show was devoted to Venetian master Canaletto), and there are daily screenings of the film *Cézanne in the Aix Region* and a series of jazz and classical performances. The elegant gardens have been painstakingly restored to their original 18th-century layout, and visitors can enjoy a drink, light lunch, or dessert in the garden restaurant. The indoor Café Caumont is easily Aix's most elegant. ⊠ *3 rue Joseph Cabassol* ☎ *04–42–20–70–01* ⊕ *www.caumont-centredart.com* ⊠ *From €7.*

Collège Mignet

COLLEGE | It's within these walls that Cézanne and his schoolmate Emile Zola discussed their ideas. Cézanne received his *baccalauréat* cum laude here in 1858 and went on to attend a year of law school to please his father. ⊠ *Rue Cardinale at Rue Joseph-Cabassol.*

Conservatoire de Musique Darius-Milhaud

ARTS VENUE | In a striking modern edifice designed by architect Kengo Kuma in the Forum Culturel (which includes the Pavillon Noir dance center), the Darius Milhaud Music Conservatory celebrates the music of Marseille's native composer, who spent several years of his childhood in Aix and returned here to die. Milhaud (1892–1974), a member of the group of French composers known as Les Six, created fine-boned, transparent works influenced by jazz and Hebrew chant. Aix has yet to make a museum of his memorabilia, but you can visit during its eclectic concert series for student performances, jazz and classical concerts, and dance recitals. ⊠ *380 av. Wolfgang Amadeus Mozart* ☎ *04–88–71–84–20.*

Cours Mirabeau

NEIGHBORHOOD | Shaded by a double row of tall plane trees, the Cours Mirabeau is one of the most beautiful avenues anywhere, designed so its width and length would be in perfect proportion with the height of the dignified 18th-century

hôtels particuliers lining it. You can view this lovely assemblage from one of the dozen or so cafés that spill onto the pavement. ⊠ *Aix-en-Provence.*

Église de la Madeleine

RELIGIOUS SITE | Though the facade now bears 19th-century touches, this small 17th-century church still contains the center panel of the fine 15th-century *Annunciation Triptych,* attributed to the father of Jan Van Eyck, the greatest painter of the Early Netherlandish school. Some say the massive painting on the left side of the transept is a Rubens. The church is used regularly for classical concerts. ⊠ *Pl. des Prêcheurs.*

Église St-Jean-de-Malte

RELIGIOUS SITE | This 12th-century church served as a chapel of the Knights of Malta, a medieval order of friars devoted to hospital care. The church was Aix's first attempt at the Gothic style, and it was here that the counts of Provence were buried throughout the 18th century; their tombs (in the upper left) were attacked during the revolution and have been only partially repaired. ⊠ *Rue Cardinale and rue d'Italie.*

★ Fondation Vasarely

MUSEUM | After three decades of neglect, the Centre Pompidou's splendid 2019 retrospective of the father of "op-art" placed Victor Vasarely in his rightful place among the great artists of the later 20th century. Whether a fan of the genre or not, a visit to this exhilarating museum, a short drive or bus ride (lines 2 and 20) from Aix center, will delight art fans of all ages. The building itself is an architectural wonder, composed of 16 hexagonal galleries each housing six of the artist's monumental tapestries, mosaics, paintings, or sculptures. Upstairs, a detailed timeline of Vasarely's life and work reveals the versatility and genius of an artist both of and ahead of his time. ⊠ *1 av. Marcel Pagnol* ☎ *04–42–20–01–09* ⊕ *www.fondationvasarely.org* ⊠ *€12.*

Did You Know?

Aix's *centre ville* (downtown) is a maze of narrow, commercial streets, and it's difficult to keep your sense of direction. Most sights are within central Aix, where walking is the best and most delightful way to get around.

Pronunciation in Provence

Especially among a people who cut their teeth on the Academie Française, that holy arbiter of the French language, there are variations allowed when speaking French in Provence. The rule of thumb here is to pronounce everything, even letters that aren't there. *Pain* becomes "peng" in the south. *Vin* becomes "veng," *enfin* "on feng," and so forth. One of the words caught in the crossfire is *mas*. This old Provençal word for farmhouse is a "mahss" in the south,

but Parisians hold out for a more refined Frenchification: "ma." Cassis is another booby trap. Parisians refer to the blackcurrant liqueur made in Burgundy as "cass-*eess*" but southern French locals refer to the wine from the coastal country east of Marseille as "cass-*ee*." If that weren't confusing enough, Parisians also call the town of Cassis "cass-*eess*," much to the ire of the locals, who insist they live in "cass-*ee*."

Fontaine d'Eau Chaude (*Hot Water Fountain*)
FOUNTAIN | Deliciously thick with dripping moss, this 18th-century fountain is fed by Sextius's own thermal source. It seems representative of Aix at its artfully negligent best. In sunny Provence, Aix was famous for its shade and its fountains; apropos, James Pope-Hennessy, in his *Aspects of Provence,* compares living in Aix to being at the bottom of an aquarium, thanks to all the fountains' bubbling waters and the city's shady streets and boulevards. ⊠ *Cours Mirabeau.*

Fontaine des Quatre Dauphins (*Four Dolphins Fountain*)
FOUNTAIN | Within a tiny square at a symmetrical crossroads in the Quartier Mazarin, this lovely 17th-century fountain has four graceful dolphins at the foot of a pinecone-topped obelisk. Under the shade of a chestnut tree and framed by broad, shuttered mansions, it makes an elegant ensemble worth contemplating from the park bench. ⊠ *Pl. des Quatre Dauphins.*

Hôtel de Châteaurenard
GOVERNMENT BUILDING | Across from a commercial gallery that calls itself the

Petit Musée Cézanne (actually more of a tourist trap), this 17th-century mansion once hosted Louis XIV—and now houses government offices. This means that during business hours you can slip in and peek at the fabulous 18th-century stairwell, decorated in flamboyant trompe-l'oeil. Pseudo-stone putti and caryatids pop into three dimensions—as does the false balustrade that mirrors the real one in stone. ⊠ *19 rue Gaston de Saporta.*

Hôtel de Ville (*City Hall*)
GOVERNMENT BUILDING | Built between 1655 and 1678 by Pierre Pavillon, the Hôtel de Ville is fronted by a pebble-encrusted courtyard set off by a wrought-iron gateway. At the back, a double stairway leads to the Salle des Etats de Provences, the old regional assembly room (where taxes were voted on), hung with interesting portraits and pictures of mythological characters. From the window, look for the unmistakable 16th-century clock tower with an open ironwork belfry. The tree-lined square in front—where cafés set up tables right into the center of the space—is a popular gathering place. ⊠ *Pl. de L'Hôtel-de-Ville* ☎ *04–42–91–90–00.*

Hôtel Maynier d'Oppède

ARTS VENUE | This ornately decorated mansion houses the **Institut d'Études Françaises** (Institute of French Studies), where foreign students take French classes. During the Festival d'Aix in July, the hotel's courtyard is used for a series of classical concerts. ✉ *23 rue Gaston de Saporta* ☎ *04–42–21–70–92.*

La Rotonde

FOUNTAIN | If you've just arrived in Aix's center, this sculpture-fountain is a spectacular introduction to the town's rare mix of elegance and urban bustle. It's a towering mass of 19th-century attitude. That's Agriculture yearning toward Marseille, Art leaning toward Avignon, and Justice looking down on Cours Mirabeau. But don't study it too intently—you'll likely be sideswiped by a speeding Vespa. ✉ *Pl. de Gaulle.*

Musée des Tapisseries

MUSEUM | In the 17th-century **Palais de l'Archevêché** (Archbishop's Palace), this museum showcases a sumptuous collection of tapestries that once decorated the bishops' quarters. There are 17 magnificent hangings from Beauvais and a series on the life of Don Quixote from Compiègne. Temporary exhibitions highlight contemporary textile art. The main opera productions of the Festival d'Aix take place in the broad courtyard. ✉ *28 pl. des Martyrs de la Resistance* ☎ *04–42–23–09–91* ⊕ *Closed Tues.* 🎟 *€4.*

Musée Estienne de Saint-Jean (*Museum of Old Aix*)

MUSEUM | You'll find an eclectic assortment of local treasures inside this 17th-century mansion, from faïence to *santons* (terra-cotta figurines) to ornately painted furniture. The building is lovely, too. ✉ *17 rue Gaston de Saporta* ☎ *04–42–16–11–61* 🎟 *€4* ⊕ *Closed Tues.*

★ Musée Granet

MUSEUM | Once the École de Dessin (Art School) that granted Cézanne a second-place prize in 1856, the former priory of the Église St-Jean-de-Malte now showcases eight of Cézanne's paintings, as well as a nice collection of his watercolors and drawings. Also hanging in the galleries are 300 works by Bonnard, Picasso, Klee, Rubens, David, and Giacometti. ✉ *Pl. St-Jean-de-Malte* ☎ *04–42–52–88–32* ⊕ *www.museegranet-et-aixenprovence.fr* 🎟 *From €6* ⊕ *Closed Mon.*

Musée Paul Arbaud

MUSEUM | A rich and varied collection of Provençal faïence is displayed in this grand mansion in the Mazarin quarter. It also contains a library full of books on Provençal culture. ✉ *2 rue du 4-Septembre* ☎ *04–42–38–38–95* ⊕ *www.aixenprovence.fr/Musee-Arbaud* 🎟 *€5* ⊕ *Closed Sun.–Tues.*

★ Pavillon de Vendôme

HOUSE | This extravagant Baroque villa was built in 1665 as a country house for the Duke of Vendôme; its position just outside the city's inner circle allowed the duke to commute discreetly from his official home on Cours Mirabeau to this retreat, where his mistress, La Belle du Canet, was comfortably installed. The villa was expanded and heightened in the 18th century to draw attention to the classical orders—Ionic, Doric, and Corinthian—on parade in the row of neo-Grecian columns. Inside the cool, broad chambers you can find a collection of Provençal furniture and artwork. Note the curious two giant Atlantes that hold up the interior balcony. ✉ *32 rue Celony* ☎ *04–42–91–88–75* ⊕ *www.aixenprovence.fr* 🎟 *€4* ⊕ *Closed Tues.*

Place d'Albertas

PLAZA | Of all the elegant squares in Aix, this one is the most evocative and otherworldly. Set back from the city's fashionable shopping streets, it forms a horseshoe of shuttered mansions, with cobbles radiating from a simple turn-of-the-20th-century fountain. It makes a fine setting for the chamber music concerts that are held here in summer.

It's easy to understand why Cézanne painted so many *nature morte* (still life) paintings once you see the delectable delights on sale in many of the town squares.

✉ *Intersection of rue Espariat and rue Aude.*

Site-Mémorial du Camp des Milles

HISTORIC SITE | This museum and memorial is France's only still-intact deportation camp, where 10,000 men, women, and children of 38 nationalities (2,000 of whom were eventually transferred to Auschwitz) were detained over a period of three years, before the structure was repurposed as an armaments factory. Direct contact with internment areas, including sleeping and dining quarters and hiding places, makes for a rare immediacy. Traces of the many artists and intellectuals who were detained here, including Surrealist artists Max Ernst and Hans Bellmer and novelist Lion Feuchtwanger, can be found in the many artworks displayed (all made here) and the graffiti still vibrantly intact on the walls. At the conclusion of the visit, museumgoers retrace the deportees' path to a railroad wagon parked near the main building, a sobering reminder of a terrible chapter in French history. ✉ *40 ch. de la Badesse* ☎ *04–42–39–17–11* ⊕ *www.campdesmilles.org* 🎫 *€10.*

Thermes Sextius (*Thermal Baths of Sextius*)

HOT SPRINGS | Warm natural springs first discovered under the leadership of Sextius, the Thermes now house the glass walls of an ultramodern health spa. The small fountain in the interior marks the warm spring of the original 18th-century establishment; today the facility's offerings include a great gym, pressure showers, mud treatments, and underwater massages. ✉ *55 av. des Thermes* ☎ *04–42–22–81–82* ⊕ *www.thermes-sextius.com.*

🍴 Restaurants

★ Au Verre Levé

$$ | **WINE BAR** | Aix can be a bit buttoned-up, but at this convivial wine bar, the vino flows and everyone's having fun around delicious plates both hot and cold: melting burrata with roasted cherry tomatoes, dorade carpaccio, beet hummus and baby veggies, and Iberian ham with Spanish manchego. With small plates starting at €10 and a selection of 70 wines starting at €5 by the glass, this is an excellent spot for a quick light meal or an apéro on the go. **Known for:** regional wines by the glass; open at 4 pm for an apéro (not always easy to find in Provence outside a café); pop-up tastings and winemaker visits. $ *Average main: €20* ⊠ *15 rue Granet* ☎ *04–86–31–08–15* ⊕ *auverreleve.com* ☺ *Closed Sun. and Mon.*

★ Il Était une Fois

$$ | FRENCH | One of Aix's best "bistronomic" (gastronomic bistro) eateries, a stone's throw from the Cours Mirabeau, diners swoon for the small but delicious and beautifully presented selection of upscale French classics—crusted lobster with feta and coriander, squash samosas and homemade goose pâté, or roasted veal giblets with gouda-cauliflower and black truffle. Don't be alarmed by the small à la carte menu; it means you're only served what's market fresh that day. **Known for:** rigorous chef who loves to innovate; delicious dishes featuring both meat (especially organ meats) and fish; great value set menus. $ *Average main: €21* ⊠ *4 rue Lieutaud* ☎ *04–42–58–78–56* ⊕ *www.iletaitunefois-aix.fr* ☺ *Closed Tues. and Wed. No dinner Sun.*

La Fromagerie du Passage

$$ | FRENCH | You can't sample all of France's 600 types of cheese at La Fromagerie du Passage, but there's a decadent selection of 20 or so, all *fait maison* by Laurent and Hervé Mons, who won the prestigious Meilleurs Ouvriers (Best Craftsman of France) award for outstanding cheese maker. The waiters lyrically—and patiently—explain the region or texture of each cheese, and suggest a wine with the right composition to bring out the subtle (and not so subtle) flavors. **Known for:** quality handcrafted cheeses; copious cheese and charcuterie plates; delicious sandwiches to stay or go.

$ *Average main: €19* ⊠ *Passage Agard, 55 cours Mirabeau* ☎ *04–42–22–90–00* ⊕ *www.lafromageriedupassage.com.*

★ Le Mas Bottero

$$$$ | FRENCH | If you're headed from Aix to the Vaucluse or any point north of the city, do what the local gourmands do and get thee to this gastronomic restaurant 23 k (14 miles) northwest of Aix on France's famous Nationale 7 (D7). A veteran of top kitchens from London to Switzerland, Nicolas Bottero struck out on his own in 2017, creating cuisine of utmost refinement but without a trace of fussiness and following the seasons and the local producers. **Known for:** knowledgeable sommelier helps pair wines by the glass or bottle; all-vegetarian menus; bright, modern dining room. $ *Average main: €41* ⊠ *2340 rte. d'Aix RN7, Saint-Cannat* ☎ *04–42–67–19–18* ⊕ *www.lemasbottero.com.*

★ Le Saint Estève

$$$$ | MODERN FRENCH | A short drive from Aix over scenic Route Cézanne, this elegant restaurant on the grounds of Les Lodges hotel has a spiffed-up menu showing new inspiration—and who wouldn't be inspired with these breathtaking views of Cézanne's beloved mountain? Michelin-starred chef Julien Le Goff doesn't have far to look for the locally sourced products he favors, such as wild trompette de la mort mushrooms for a luscious dish of langoustines, mussels, and lemon-infused bouillon or line-caught bar with French caviar, crispy potatoes, and a champagne emulsion. **Known for:** stupendous views of Cezanne's Mont Sainte-Victoire; mind-boggling fixed-price menus; lovely terrace. $ *Average main: €70* ⊠ *2500 rte. Cézanne, Le Tholonet* ☎ *04–42–27–10–14* ⊕ *www.leslodgessaintevictoire.com* ☺ *Closed Mon. Jan.–Mar.*

★ Les Caves Henri IV

$$ | FRENCH | Take in the classic decor and polished clientele here (and the high prices) and get ready to embark on

an adventure in fine dining. It takes an expert in traditional techniques to tweak the classics just so to bring a contemporary edge, and chef Jean-Lux Le Formal is more than up to the task with dishes that are beautiful, delicious, and expressive without veering off course. **Known for:** atmosphere conducive to settling in for a long meal; top-notch service; exceptional wine list. $ *Average main: €22* ⊠ *32 rue Espariat* ☎ *04–42–27–08–31* ⊕ *www.restaurant-lescaveshen-ri4-byleformal.com.*

★ **Les Vieilles Canailles**

$$ | **WINE BAR** | Most recently the chef at Alain Ducasse's Monaco palace, the thirtysomething chef at the helm of this cozy wine bar is passionate about tracking down the best local ingredients, whether it's the juicy tomatoes with your roasted octopus salad or the Camargue rice with your succulent lamb. And he's no less scrupulous about wines, with a penchant for small natural and biodynamic producers from every region of France. **Known for:** chalkboard menu of daily specials; unbeatable prices for fixed menus; small space that fills up quick so reserve in advance. $ *Average main: €19* ⊠ *7 rue Isolette* ☎ *04–42–91–41–75* ⊕ *www.vieilles-canailles.fr* ⊘ *Closed Sun. and Mon.*

★ **Mickaël Féval**

$$$ | **MODERN FRENCH** | This is the kind of place where young cooks dream of working to learn the ropes, and Féval, quite young himself, has trained many a Michelin chef. After earning his fame in Paris, Favel opened this casual-elegant dining room, tucked away on a typically picturesque Aix side street, with a menu of dishes so masterful and flavorful that the restaurant soon became a local benchmark. **Known for:** gorgeous presentation; market-fresh dishes that change frequently; impeccable service. $ *Average main: €29* ⊠ *11 Petite rue St-Jean* ☎ *04–42–93–29–60* ⊕ *www.mickaelfeval.fr* ⊘ *Closed Sun. and Mon.*

★ **Vintrépide**

$$ | **FRENCH** | This sleek little wine bar and its understated decor belies a splendid cuisine that easily stands up to some of Aix's more pricy gastronomic tables, but with much less fuss. In keeping with the wine bar ethos, plates are small—all the better to pair with wines by the glass—but beautifully conceived and sometimes thrilling: think fois gras with apricot confit, sea bream and wild mushrooms, or zucchini flowers stuffed with ricotta and mint. **Known for:** zero snob appeal; delicious desserts; under the tourist radar. $ *Average main: €19* ⊠ *48 rue du Puits Neuf* ☎ *04–28–31–16–41* ⊕ *www.vintrepide.com* ⊘ *Closed Sun. and Mon.*

 Hotels

Château de Fonscolombe

$$ | **HOTEL** | This gracious 18th-century country château and wine estate combines a deeply Provençal setting with chic yet comfy rooms and suites in either the historic château or a more modern wing. **Pros:** extensive grounds and wooded walking paths; activities around food and wine; luxurious spa and pool. **Cons:** pool is on the small side; expensive restaurant; not close to the action of Aix-en-Provence. $ *Rooms from: €220* ⊠ *Rte. de Saint-Canadet, Le Puy-Sainte-Réparde* ☎ *04–42–21–13–13* ⊕ *www.fonscolombe.fr* ⇆ *50 rooms* ⊚ *No meals.*

Château La Coste

$$$$ | **HOTEL** | There is no actual château on this vast wine estate and sculpture park 14 miles north of Aix-en-Provence, just 28 ultracontemporary "villas" in pristine white with touches of wood, concrete, marble, and glass for maximum luminosity private terraces and pools are optional). **Pros:** incredible grounds and art free to visit for nonguests (10–5); gorgeous setting and views ; palace level luxury, including spa and restaurants. **Cons:** ridiculously expensive; snobby atmosphere not for everyone; not easy to find. $ *Rooms from: €800* ⊠ *2750*

Rte. De La Cride, Le Puy-Sainte-Réparde ☎ 04–42–61–92–92 🌐 www.chateau-la-coste.com 🛏 28 rooms and villas 🍴 No meals.

Hôtel Cardinal

$ | **HOTEL** | In a graceful 18th-century house in the Quartier Mazarin, this eccentric and slightly threadbare inn is the antithesis of slick, which, coupled with the location, makes it a favorite among writers, artists, and musicians at festival time. **Pros:** the price for the location is excellent; rooms are clean and bright; central location. **Cons:** rooms can be noisy and hot in summer; bathroom decor is a throwback to the 1970s; some rooms have only handheld showers. [$] *Rooms from: €80 ✉ 24 rue Cardinale ☎ 04–42–38–32–30 🌐 www.hotel-cardinal-aix.com 🛏 35 rooms 🍴 No meals.*

Hôtel Cézanne

$$ | **HOTEL** | **FAMILY** | Three blocks from Cours Mirabeau and the train station, this smart, spiffy, and cozily stylish hotel is a very handy option. **Pros:** spacious rooms; Clarins bath products; location in the heart of things. **Cons:** some rooms get street noise; no pool; breakfast room gets crowded. [$] *Rooms from: €145 ✉ 40 av. Victor-Hugo ☎ 04–42–91–11–11 🌐 www.hotelaix.com 🛏 55 rooms 🍴 No meals.*

★ **Hôtel Sainte Victoire Vauvenargues**

$$$ | **HOTEL** | If your heart is set on staying in Aix center, this snazzy hotel in the countryside 16 km (10 miles) outside of Aix will make you think again: set in a classic Provençal landscape at the foothills of Cezanne's Mont Sainte-Victoire, with eye-popping views of the mountain and Picasso's Chateau Vauvenargues (where he is buried), this sleek, contemporary hotel was designed to capitalize on transparency and light. **Pros:** beautiful walking trails; spacious terraces; great on-site pool and restaurant. **Cons:** outside the city center; no nightlife apart from luxurious dining; on the expensive side. [$] *Rooms from: €290 ✉ 33 av. des Maquisards ☎ 04–42–54–01–01 🌐 www.hotelsaintevictoire.com 🛏 17 rooms 🍴 No meals.*

La Maison d'Aix

$$$$ | **HOTEL** | Ancient and modern blend harmoniously in this elegant 18th-century boutique hotel set in a mansion once inhabited by a French woman named Henriette, to whom four spacious, beautifully decorated rooms pay homage. **Pros:** lovely pool; romantic vibe; terraces with great views. **Cons:** no elevator; pricey; some baths lack privacy. [$] *Rooms from: €400 ✉ 25 rue du 4 Septembre ☎ 04–42–53–78–95 🌐 www.lamaisondaix.com 🛏 4 suites 🍴 No meals.*

★ **Le Pigonnet**

$$$ | **HOTEL** | **FAMILY** | Cézanne painted Ste-Victoire from what is now the large flower-filled terrace of this enchanting abode, and you can easily imagine former guests Princess Caroline, Iggy Pop, and Clint Eastwood swanning their way through the magnificent, pool-adorned, topiary-accented garden or relaxing in the spacious, light-filled guest rooms. **Pros:** stunning garden setting; beautiful spa; in the center of the city. **Cons:** not all rooms have balconies; some bathrooms on the small side; breakfast not included in room price. [$] *Rooms from: €280 ✉ 5 av. du Pigonnet ☎ 04–42–59–02–90 🌐 www.hotelpigonnet.com 🛏 44 rooms 🍴 No meals.*

★ **Les Lodges Sainte-Victoire**

$$$$ | **HOTEL** | Set on a picture-perfect 10 acres of woods, olive groves, and vineyards, just outside Aix, with Cézanne-immortalized Mont Ste-Victoire as a backdrop, this hotel with a Michelin-starred restaurant raises the bar for lodging in the region. **Pros:** has one of the city's best restaurants; four swanky private villas; beautiful grounds and views of Mont Ste-Victoire from the infinity pool. **Cons:** outside the city center; some first-floor rooms lack views; decor a little dark on cloudy days. [$] *Rooms*

from: €370 ✉ *2250 rte. Cézanne, Le Tholonet* ☎ *04–42–24–80–40* 🌐 *www.leslodgessaintevictoire.com* 🛏 *35 rooms* 🍴 *No meals.*

★ **Renaissance Aix en Provence Hotel**
$$ | HOTEL | FAMILY | After all of Aix's old-world charm, this five-star hotel with all modern conveniences makes a nice contrast. **Pros:** plentiful buffet breakfasts; excellent location; great restaurant and fitness room. **Cons:** parking not included in the price; breakfast very good but expensive; very contemporary if you're looking for old-world charm. [$] *Rooms from: €221* ✉ *320 av. Wolfgang Amadeus Mozart* ☎ *04–86–91–55–00* 🌐 *www.marriott.com/hotels/travel/mrsbr-renaissance-aix-en-provence-hotel* 🛏 *133 rooms* 🍴 *No meals.*

Villa Gallici
$$$$ | HOTEL | Bathed in the lavenders, blues, ochers, and oranges of Aix, rooms here are adorned in the most gorgeous Souleiado and Rubelli fabrics, conjuring up the swank 19th-century Provence colonized by Parisian barons and dukes. **Pros:** rich fabrics and dashing interiors; beautiful garden spot; 15-minute walk to town and shops. **Cons:** meals are pricey; no elevator; some rooms could use some modernization. [$] *Rooms from: €500* ✉ *Av. de la Violette* ☎ *04–42–23–29–23* 🌐 *www.villagallici.com* ⏲ *Closed Jan.* 🛏 *22 rooms* 🍴 *No meals.*

Villa Saint-Ange
$$$ | HOTEL | Aix-en-Provence finally has a lodging as elegant as the city itself in the form of this glittering hotel whose sumptuous rooms are spread between five 18th-century country cottages. **Pros:** gorgeous grounds with a heated pool; ground-floor rooms have lovely garden terraces; a few minutes from the Cours Mirabeau. **Cons:** larger rooms are expensive; still working out service kinks; could use more shelf space in some bathrooms. [$] *Rooms from: €320* ✉ *7 traverse St Pierre* ☎ *04–42–95–10–10* 🌐 *www.villasaintange.com* 🛏 *34 rooms* 🍴 *No meals.*

Nightlife

To find out what's going on in town, pick up a copy of the events calendar, *Le Mois à Aix,* or the bilingual city guide *Aix la Vivante* at the tourist office.

★ **Celeste**
BARS/PUBS | Very late to the craft cocktail scene, Aix finally has a bar that stands up to its sophisticated cousins in Marseille or even Paris. While there are ten refreshing and original choices on the cocktail menu, the bartender is happy to customize a drink to your taste, offering helpful tips on rare or unusual spirits (there is no beer or wine served here). The cozy room, complete with comfy chairs and sofas, has a friendly vibe and the outdoor tables are lovey on hot Provence nights. ✉ *44 rue Mignet* ☎ *06–89–70–59–62.*

Pasino Grand
CASINOS | In between bouts at the roulette tables and slot machines of the Casino Aix-en-Provence, you can grab a bite at one of five restaurants or take in a floor show. ✉ *21 av. de l'Europe* ☎ *04–42–59–69–00* 🌐 *www.casinoaix.com.*

Performing Arts

Festival d'Aix
FESTIVALS | In late June and July, opera and music lovers descend on Aix for the internationally acclaimed Festival d'Aix to see world-class opera productions in the courtyard of the Palais de l'Archevêché and more of the city's most beautiful venues. The repertoire is varied and often offbeat, featuring works like Britten's *Curlew River* and Bartók's *Bluebeard's Castle* as well as the usual Mozart, Puccini, and Verdi. Most of the singers, however, are not celebrities, but rather an elite group of students who spend the summer with the Academie Européenne de Musique,

training and performing under the tutelage of stars like Robert Tear and Yo-Yo Ma. ⊠ *Aix-en-Provence* ☎ *04–34–08–02–17* ⊕ *www.festival-aix.com.*

Grand Théâtre de Provence

ARTS CENTERS | Jessye Norman inaugurated this contemporary 1,350-seat concert hall in 2007 and it has since matured into the city's primary venue for a world-class series of musical performances of all kinds and for all audiences, including classical, baroque, opera, recitals, jazz, and world music. It is also a major host of the Festival d'Aix. The extensive year-round program can be found on the website. ⊠ *380 av. Max Juvénal* ☎ *04–42–91–69–70* ⊕ *www.lestheatres.net.*

Le Ballet Preljocaj

DANCE | Angelin Preljocaj has created original ballets for the New York City Ballet and the Paris Opera Ballet, and his modern-dance troupe, Ballet Preljocaj, is based at the monolithic Pavillon Noir, designed by architect Rudy Ricciotti. The Pavillon hosts an annual series of contemporary ballet and modern dance performances featuring an international roster. The season runs September through May. There are also 6 pm rehearsals, free for the public. ⊠ *530 av. Wolfgang Amadeus Mozart* ☎ *04–42–93–48–00* ⊕ *www.preljocaj.org.*

Renoir

FILM | These movie theaters both show some films in *v.o.* (*version originale*, i.e., not dubbed). ⊠ *24 cours Mirabeau* ☎ *08–36–68–72–70.*

Activities

Because it's there, in part, and because it looms in striking isolation above the plain east of Aix, its heights catching the sun long after the valley lies in shadow, Cézanne's beloved **Montagne Ste-Victoire** inspires climbers to conquest. The Grande Randonée stretches along its long, rocky crest from the village of Le Tholonet at its western end all the way

east to Puyloubier. Along the way you'll traverse Beaurecueil (with splendid views of the mountain), St-Antonin-sur-Bayon's woods and fields, the vineyards of Puyloubier and Pourrières, and the green valley of Vauvenargues. An alternate route climbs the milder north slope from Les Cabassols. Along the way it peaks at 3,316 feet at Pic des Mouches, from where the view stretches around the compass. Pick up detailed maps at the tourist office or check Aix-en-Provence tourism website (⊕ *www.aixenprovence-tourism.com*).

Shopping

Aix is a snazzy market town, and unlike the straightforward country-fair atmosphere of nearby Aubagne, a trip to the market here is filled with rarefied, high-end delicacies shoulder to shoulder with garlic braids. You can find fine olive oils from the Pays d'Aix (Aix region), barrels glistening with olives of every hue and blend, and vats of tapenade (crushed olive, caper, and anchovy paste). Melons, asparagus, and mesclun salad are piled high, and dried sausages bristling with Provençal herbs hang from stands. A food and produce market takes place every morning on **Place Richelme**; just up the street on **Place Verdun** is a good, high-end *brocante* (collectibles) market Tuesday, Thursday, and Saturday mornings.

In addition to its old-style markets and jewel-box candy shops, Aix is a dazzlingly sophisticated modern shopping town—perhaps the best in Provence. The winding streets of the Vieille Ville above Cours Mirabeau—focused around **rues Clémenceau, Marius Reinaud, Espariat, Aude, Fabrot,** and **Maréchal Foch**—have a plethora of goods, including high-end designer clothes.

BOOKS

Book in Bar

BOOKS/STATIONERY | This cozy English bookshop near Cours Mirabeau is not only a great place to buy and read English-language books, but also to meet other English speakers. ✉ *4 rue Joseph Cabassol* ☎ *04–42–26–60–07* ⊕ *www.bookinbar.com* ◷ *Closed Sun.*

CANDY

One great Aixois delicacy is the *calisson*. A blend of almond paste and glazed melon, they are cut into geometric almond shapes and stacked high in *confiserie* windows.

Béchard

FOOD/CANDY | The most picturesque shop specializing in calissons is the venerable bakery Béchard, founded in 1870. ✉ *12 cours Mirabeau.*

Leonard Parli

FOOD/CANDY | Near the train station, Leonard Parli offers a lovely selection of calissons. ✉ *35 av. Victor Hugo* ⊕ *www.leonard-parli.com.*

★ **Le Roy René**

FOOD/CANDY | Aix's most famous purveyor of calissons, with their signature diamond-shape box, has kept up with the times, offering an assortment of the delicate almond pastries in gourmet flavors and enticing colors along with the white-frosted classic. Within the shop, you'll also find fruit syrups, biscuits, cakes, nougats, and a variety of other beautifully packaged candies that are perfect for gifts. The Rue Gaston de Saporta location is the flagship, but their wonderful museum just outside the city center (5380 Route d'Avignon) delves into the history and making of this historic sweet and is well worth a visit. ✉ *11 rue Gaston de Saporta* ☎ *04–42–26–67–86* ⊕ *www.calisson.com.*

Weibel

FOOD/CANDY | An Aix institution since 1954, Maison Weibel is chock-full of sweets that look good enough to immortalize in a still life, let alone eat. Their version of the iconic Provençal calisson is hands down the best around. The shop also makes sublime gifts, packaged in lovely lavender boxes. ✉ *2 rue Chabrier* ☎ *04–42–23–33–21* ⊕ *www.maisonweibel.com.*

CLOTHING

Blow Up

CLOTHING | This vintage store has everything from funky fashions to cool cameras. ✉ *26 rue Boulegon* ☎ *04–42–58–36–62* ⊕ *www.blow-up-vintage-store.fr.*

Catimini

CLOTHING | The French chain Catimini offers an imaginative, jazzy stock of kids' sweaters, jackets, and dresses. ✉ *9 rue des Chapeliers* ☎ *04–42–27–51–14* ⊕ *www.catimini.com.*

Gago

CLOTHING | Particularly noteworthy on the fashion front is Gago, a leader with stylish designer wear for women including Céline, Balanciaga, and Comme des Garçons. ✉ *20–24 rue Fabrot* ☎ *04–42–27–60–19.*

Gérard Darel

CLOTHING | Contemporary fashions with an emphasis on classic French tailoring, Gérard Darel is known for chic day-to-evening dresses and sleek trench coats; accessories are available, too. ✉ *13 rue Fabrot* ☎ *04–42–26–38–45* ⊕ *www.gerarddarel.com.*

HOUSEHOLD ITEMS/FURNITURE

Santons Fouque

HOUSEHOLD ITEMS/FURNITURE | Aix's most celebrated *santon* (miniature statue) maker was established in 1936. ✉ *65 cours Gambetta* ☎ *04–42–26–33–38* ⊕ *www.santons-fouque.com.*

Marseille

32 km (20 miles) south of Aix; 66 km (41 miles) northwest of Toulon.

Popular myths and a fishy reputation have led Marseille to be unfairly maligned as grungy urban sprawl plagued with impoverished neighborhoods and louche politics. It is often given wide berth by travelers in search of a Provençal idyll. A huge mistake. Marseille, even its earliest history, has maintained its contradictions with a kind of fierce and independent pride. Yes, there are sketchy neighborhoods, some modern eyesores—even a high crime rate—but there is also tremendous beauty and culture. Cubist jumbles of white stone rise up over a picture-book seaport, bathed in light of blinding clarity, crowned by larger-than-life neo-Byzantine churches, and framed by massive fortifications; neighborhoods teem with immigrant-friendly life; souk-like African markets smell deliciously of spices and coffees; and the labyrinthine Old Town radiates pastel shades of saffron, marigold, and robin's-egg blue.

Called Massalia, this was the most important Continental shipping port in antiquity. The port flourished for some 500 years as a typical Greek city, enjoying the full flush of classical culture, its gods, its democratic political system, its sports and theater, and its naval prowess. Caesar changed all that, besieging the city in 49 BC and seizing most of its colonies. In 1214 Marseille was seized again, this time by Charles d'Anjou, and was later annexed to France by Henri IV in 1481, but it was not until Louis XIV took the throne that the biggest transformations of the port began: he pulled down the city walls in 1666 and expanded the port to the Rive Neuve (New Riverbank). The city was devastated by plague in 1720, losing more than half its population. By the time of the Revolution, Marseille was on the rebound once again, with industries of soap manufacturing and oil processing flourishing, encouraging a wave of immigration from Provence and Italy. With the opening of the Suez Canal in 1869, Marseille became the greatest boomtown in 19th-century Europe. With a large influx of immigrants from areas as exotic as Tangiers, the city quickly acquired the multicultural population it maintains to this day.

GETTING HERE AND AROUND

The main train station is Gare St-Charles on the TGV line, with frequent trains from Paris, the main coast route (Nice/Italy), and Arles. The gare routière is on Place Victor Hugo. Here you can find Cartreize buses into the Bouches du Rhône and Eurolines coaches between Marseille, Avignon, and Nice via Aix-en-Provence.

Marseille has a very good local bus, tram, and métro system (€1.70 for 90 minutes of use), and the César ferry boat (immortalized in Pagnol's 1931 film *Marius*) crosses the Vieux Port every few minutes and is free of charge. Itineraries for wherever you want to go in the Bouches-du-Rhone can be found on ⊕ *www.lepilote.com*. Le Vélo is Marseille's citywide bicycle network. Grab a bike, take it to your destination, and then pick up another when you're ready to move on. The first 30 minutes are free and a seven-day pass (⊕ *en.levelo-mpm. fr/how-it-works*) costs only €1.

CONTACTS RTM. ⊠ *6 rue des Fabres* ☎ *04–91–91–92–10 for bus and tram timetables* ⊕ *www.rtm.fr/en.*

TOURS

★ Culinary Backstreets Marseille

SPECIAL-INTEREST | There's no better way to discover Marseille's vast culinary riches (and Marseille itself) than on foot with bilingual journalist and unabashed food lover Alexis Steinman. Her small, five- to six-hour tours and tailor-made itineraries explore all the hidden culinary corners of a city ripe for discovery—with tasting and sampling all along the way. ⊠ *Marseille* ⊕ *www.culinarybackstreets.com/culinary-walks/marseille* 🚶 *From €120.*

Icard Maritime

BOAT TOURS | Boats make round-trips several times a day to the Calanques de Cassis from Marseille's Quai de la Fraternité (Quai des Belges). This company offers 2½-hour to 3½-hour round-trips.

The heart of Marseille is its Vieux Port (Old Port), with its small boats and portside cafés, while the city's soul is hilltop Notre-Dame-de-la-Garde.

⊠ *1 quai Marcel Pagnol* ☎ *04–91–33–36–79* ⊕ *www.visite-des-calanques.com* 🎫 *From €24.*

Tourist Office Walking Tours

WALKING TOURS | A variety of walking tours are offered, including the Old Town and port, the Cours Julien and street art, Marseille by night, and many more; they take place several times a week. Tours can be requested in English. Tickets and schedules are available at the tourist office. ⊠ *Marseille* 🎫 *From €10.*

VISITOR INFORMATION

CONTACTS Marseille Tourist Office. ⊠ *11 la Canebière, La Canebière* ☎ *08–26–50–05–00 (€0.15 per min)* ⊕ *www.marseille-tourisme.com* Ⓜ *Vieux Port.*

Sights

Although Marseille is the second-largest city in France, it functions as a conglomerate of distinct neighborhoods—almost little villages. One of these microcosms is the Neapolitan-style maze of picturesque lanes, cafés, artist ateliers, and chic boutiques called Le Panier. Site of the first Greek settlements and the oldest neighborhood in France, it merits intimate exploration. Don't miss the striking museum complex of the Vieille Charité. The recently transformed Vieux Port is the most scenic walk in town: from the port's old fish market to the astonishing Musée des Civilisations de l'Europe et de la Méditerranée (MuCEM), the Villa Méditerranée, and the Musée Regards du Provence.

If in your exploration of Le Panier and the Quai du Port you examined Marseille's history in miniature via myriad museums, a walk among the Quai de Rive Nueve gives you the big picture. Either from the crow's-nest perspective of Notre-Dame-de-la-Garde or from the vast green Jardin du Pharo, you'll take in spectacular Cinemascope views of this great city and its ports and monuments. Wear good walking shoes and bring your wide-angle lens.

A direct line east from the Vieux Port, La Canebière used to serve as the dividing line between those Marseillais who had money and those who did not. In the last hundred years it has lost much of its former glory, and is now dominated by shopping malls and fast-food restaurants. Its architecture and 19th-century wedding-cake facades still make for an interesting walk, and it's a great place from which to make forays through the North African neighborhood along Rue Longue-des-Capucins, to the lively cafés and boutiques of bohemian Cours Julien via Rue d'Aubagne, and on to the Palais Longchamp and its fine-arts and natural-history museums.

Along the coastline east of Marseille's center, a series of pretty little *anses* (ports) leads to the more famous and far-flung Calanques. These miniature inlets are really tiny villages, with pretty, balconied, boxy houses (called *cabanons*) clustered around bright-painted fishing boats. Don't even think about buying a cabanon of your own, however; they are part of the fishing community's heritage and are protected from gentrification by the outside world.

Abbaye St-Victor

RELIGIOUS SITE | Founded in the 4th century by St-Cassien, who sailed into Marseille full of fresh ideas on monasticism that he acquired in Palestine and Egypt, this church grew to formidable proportions. With a Romanesque design, the structure would be as much at home in the Middle East as its founder was. The **crypt**, St-Cassien's original, is preserved beneath the medieval church, and in the evocative nooks and crannies you can find the 5th-century sarcophagus that allegedly holds the martyr's remains. Upstairs, a reliquary contains what's left of St-Victor, who was ground to death between millstones, probably by Romans. There's also a passage into tiny **catacombs** where early Christians worshipped St-Lazarus and Mary Magdalene, said to have washed ashore at Stes-Maries-de-la-Mer, in the Camargue. ⊠ *3 rue*

Marseille City Pass

If you plan on visiting many of the museums in Marseille, buy a **City Pass** (€27 for 24 hours, €37 for 48 hours, €43 for 72 hours) at the tourism office or online. It covers the entry fee for all the museums in Marseille as well as public transit, a ride on the petit train, and free guided tour of the city.

de l'Abbaye, Rive Neuve ☎ *04–96–11–22–60* ⊕ *www.saintvictor.net* Ⓜ *Vieux Port or Estrangin Préfecture.*

Bar de la Marine

RESTAURANT—SIGHT | Even if you've never read or seen Marcel Pagnol's trilogy of plays and films *Marius, Fanny,* and *César* (think of it as a three-part French *Casablanca*), you can still get a sense of its earthy, Old Marseille feeling at the bar in which it was set. The walls are blanketed with murals and comfortable café chairs fill the place, all in an effort to faithfully reproduce the bar as it was in the days when the bartender César, his son Marius, and Fanny, the shellfish girl, lived out their salty drama of love, honor, and the call of the sea. ⊠ *15 quai de Rive Neuve, Vieux Port* ☎ *04–91–54–95–42* Ⓜ *Vieux Port.*

Cathédrale de la Nouvelle Major

RELIGIOUS SITE | This gargantuan, neo-Byzantine 19th-century fantasy was built under Napoléon III—but not before he'd ordered the partial destruction of the lovely 11th-century original, once a perfect example of the Provençal Romanesque style. You can view the flashy interior (think marble and rich red porphyry inlay) of the newer of the two churches; the medieval one is being restored. ⊠ *Pl. de la Major, Le Panier* Ⓜ *Joliette.*

Château d'If

CASTLE/PALACE | In the 16th century, François I recognized the strategic advantage of an island fortress surveying the mouth of Marseille's vast harbor and built this imposing edifice. Its effect as a deterrent was so successful that the fortress never saw combat, and was eventually converted into a prison. It was here that Alexandre Dumas locked up his most famous character, the Count of Monte Cristo. Though the count was fictional, the hole through which Dumas had him escape is real enough, on display in the cells. On the other hand, the real-life Man in the Iron Mask, whose cell is also erroneously on display, was not imprisoned here. The Frioul If Express boat ride (from Quai des Belges, €10.80; for information call *04–96–11–03–50* or see ⊕ *frioul-if-express.com*) and the views from the broad terrace are worth the trip. ⊠ *Marseille* ☎ *08–26–50–05–00* ⊕ *www.chateau-if.fr* ⋑ *€6.*

Cours Julien

PLAZA | A center of bohemian *flânerie* (hanging out), this is a lovely place to relax by the fountain, in the shade of plane trees, or under a café umbrella. Its low-key and painterly tableau is framed by graceful 18th-century buildings, and the warrenlike streets surrounding the cours are full of young fashion designers, vintage shops, and hip boutiques. ⊠ *La Canebière* Ⓜ *Notre Dame du Mont or Noailles.*

Jardin du Pharo (*Pharo Garden*)

GARDEN | The Pharo, another larger-than-life edifice built to Napoléon III's epic tastes, was a gift to his wife, Eugénie. It's a conference center now, but its green park has become a magnet for city strollers who want to take in panoramic views of the ports and fortifications. ⊠ *Above Bd. Charles-Livon, Pharo* ⋑ *Free* Ⓜ *Vieux Port.*

La Canebière

NEIGHBORHOOD | This wide avenue leading from the port, known affectionately as the "Can o' Beer" by American sailors, was once crammed with cafés, theaters, bars, and tempting stores full of zoot suits and swell hats, and figured in popular songs and operettas. It's noisy but dull today, yet you may take pleasure in studying its grand old 19th-century mansions. ⊠ *La Canebière* Ⓜ *Vieux Port, Noailles, or Réformés Canebière.*

La Vieille Charité (*Center of the Old Charity*)

ARCHAEOLOGICAL SITE | At the top of the Panier district lies this superb ensemble of 17th- and 18th-century architecture designed as a hospice for the homeless by Marseillais artist-architects Pierre and Jean Puget. Even if you don't enter the museums, walk around the inner court, studying the retreating perspective of triple arcades and admiring the Baroque chapel with its novel egg-peaked dome. Of the complex's two museums, the larger is the **Musée d'Archéologie Méditerranéenne** (Museum of Mediterranean Archaeology), with a sizable collection of pottery and statuary from classical Mediterranean civilization, elementally labeled (for example, "pot"). There's also a display on the mysterious Celt-like Ligurians who first peopled the coast, cryptically presented with emphasis on the digs instead of the finds themselves. The best of the lot is the evocatively mounted Egyptian collection—the second-largest in France after the Louvre's. There are mummies, hieroglyphs, and gorgeous sarcophagi in a tomblike setting. Upstairs, the **Musée d'Arts Africains, Océaniens, et Amérindiens** (Museum of African, Oceanic, and American Indian Art) creates a theatrical foil for the works' intrinsic drama: the spectacular masks and sculptures are mounted along a pure black wall, lighted indirectly, with labels across the aisle. ⊠ *2 rue de la Charité, Le Panier* ☎ *04–91–14–58–80* ⊕ *www.vieille-charite-marseille.com* ⋑ *Exhibitions from €7* Ⓜ *Joliette.*

Le Centre d'Art MaMo

BUILDING | Eighteen stories up, atop Le Corbusier's colossal Cité

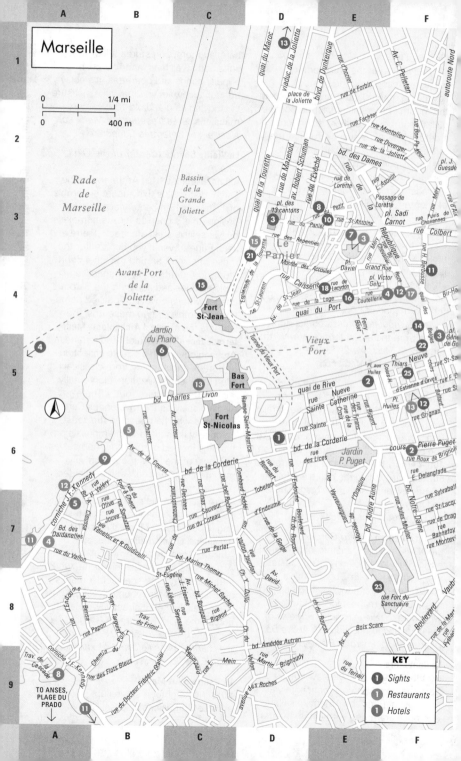

Sights ▼

1 Abbaye St-Victor **D6**
2 Bar de la Marine......... **E5**
3 Cathédrale de
la Nouvelle Major....... **D3**
4 Château d'If **A5**
5 Cours Julien............. **H5**
6 Jardin du Pharo......... **B5**
7 La Canebière **H4**
8 La Vieille Charité........ **E3**
9 Le Centre d'Art
MaMo.................... **I9**
10 Le Panier................. **E3**
11 Le Port Antique **F4**
12 Les Arcenaulx........... **F5**
13 L'Estaque................ **D1**
14 Marché aux Poissons... **F4**
15 MuCEM **C4**
16 Musée Borély **E4**
17 Musée Cantini.......... **G5**
18 Musée des
Docks Romains **E4**
19 Musée d'Histoire
de Marseille............ **G4**
20 Musée
Grobet-Labadié **I2**
21 Musée Regards
de Provence............ **D3**
22 Navette Maritime....... **F5**
23 Notre-Dame-
de-la-Garde **E8**
24 Palais de Longchamp **I2**
25 Place Thiars............. **F5**
26 Rue Longue-des-
Capucins/
Rue d'Aubagne.......... **G4**
27 Unité d'Habitation
Cité Radieuse **I9**

Restaurants ▼

1 AM by
Alexandre Mazzia **H9**
2 Balady..................... **I3**
3 Chez Etienne **E3**
4 Chez Fonfon **A7**
5 Chez Michel **B6**
6 La Boîte à Sardine **I3**
7 La Cantinetta **H4**
8 Le Capucin............... **G4**
9 La Mercerie **G4**
10 L'Épicerie Idéal.......... **G4**
11 L'Épuisette **A7**
12 Le Restaurant Peron ... **A6**
13 Les Arcenaulx........... **F5**
14 Mina Kouk **I3**
15 Regards Café........... **D3**
16 Toinou Les Fruits
de Mer **G4**
17 Une Table au Sud **F4**

Hotels ▼

1 Alex Hotel............... **G2**
2 C2 Hotel.................. **F6**
3 Grand Hotel Beauvau
Vieux Port -
MGallery Collection **F4**
4 Hermès................... **F4**
5 Hotel Peron.............. **A7**
6 Hôtel Saint Ferréol...... **G5**
7 Intercontinental Marseille
Hôtel Dieu **E3**
8 Le Petit Nice
Passedat................. **A9**
9 Les Bords de Mer....... **B6**
10 Mama Shelter............ **I6**
11 nhow Marseille **A9**
12 Residence du
Vieux Port................ **F4**
13 Sofitel Vieux-Port....... **C5**

Radieuse—undertaken in 1947–52 to house the displaced of World War II—this sun-drenched sculpture center, complete with a theater and garden, replaces an ugly gym, added in 1964, that had obscured Le Corbusier's original tiled rooftop terrace. Conceived by notorious Paris designer (and Marseille native) Ito Morabito, aka Ora-Ito, the roof of the famous building has been restored to its original glory, complete with Charlotte Perriand–designed details, and now hosts a rotating schedule of sculpture exhibitions in the summer. The building still houses an apartment complex, shops, a hotel, and a well-regarded restaurant. ⊠ *280 bd. Michelet, Prado* ☎ *01–42–46– 00–09* ⊕ *www.mamo.fr* ✉ *Free* ⊗ *Closed Tues.* Ⓜ *Rond-Point du Prado.*

Le Panier

NEIGHBORHOOD | This is the heart of old Marseille, a maze of high-shuttered houses looming over narrow cobblestone streets, *montées* (stone stairways), and tiny squares. Long decayed and neglected, the quarter is a principal focus of the city's efforts at urban renewal. In the last few years an influx of "bobos" (bourgeois-bohemians) and artists have sparked the gentrification process, bringing charming B&Bs, chic boutiques, lively cafés, and artists' ateliers. Wander this picturesque neighborhood of pastel-painted town houses, steep stairways, and narrow streets at will, making sure to stroll along Rue du Panier, the Montée des Accoules, Rue du Petit-Puits, and Rue des Muettes. ⊠ *Marseille* Ⓜ *Colbert Hôtel de Région.*

Le Port Antique

ARCHAEOLOGICAL SITE | This garden in front of the Musée d'Histoire de Marseille stands on the site of the city's classical waterfront and includes remains of the Greek fortifications and loading docks. Restored in 2013, the site, with several nearly intact boats (now exhibited in the museum), was discovered in 1967 when roadwork was being done next to the

Bourse (Stock Exchange). ⊠ *Rue Henri Barbusse, Vieux Port* ☎ *04–91–90–42–22* ✉ *€6 joint ticket, includes Musée d'Histoire de Marseille* ⊗ *Closed Mon.* Ⓜ *Vieux Port.*

Les Arcenaulx (*The Arsenal*)

STORE/MALL | In this broad, elegant stone armory, built for Louis XIV, a complex of upscale shops and restaurants has given the building—and neighborhood—new life. Its bookstore has a collection of art books and publications on Marseille, as well as gifts, perfume, clothing, and local specialties—olive oil, chocolates, nougat—with a southern accent; and a book-lined restaurant serves sophisticated cuisine. ⊠ *25 cours d'Estienne d'Orves, Vieux Port* ☎ *04–91–59–80–30* ⊕ *www. les-arcenaulx.com* Ⓜ *Vieux Port.*

L'Estaque

TOWN | At this famous village north of Marseille, Cézanne led an influx of artists eager to capture its clifftop views over the harbor. Braque, Derain, and Renoir all put its red rooftops, rugged cliffs, and factory smokestacks on canvas. Pick up the English-language itinerary "L'Estaque and the Painters" from the Marseille tourist office and hunt down the sites and views they immortalized. It's a little seedy these days, but there are cafés and a few fish shops making the most of the nearby Criée (fishermen's auction). This is where the real wholesale auction moved from Marseille's Quai de Rive Neuve. A novel way to see Cézanne's famous scenery is to take a standard SNCF train trip from the Gare St-Charles to Martigue; it follows the L'Estaque waterfront and (apart from a few tunnels) offers magnificent views.

Marché aux Poissons (*Fish Market*)

MARKET | Up and going by 8 am every day, this market—immortalized in Marcel Pagnot's *Fanny* (and Joshua Logan's sublime 1961 film adaptation)—puts on a vivid and aromatic show of waving fists, jostling chefs, and heaps of still-twitching fish from the night's catch. Hear the

Feisty Marseille flaunts its love of the sea at its famous harbor fish market.

thick soup of the Marseillais accent as blue-clad fishermen and silk-clad matrons bicker over prices, and marvel at the rainbow of Mediterranean creatures swimming in plastic vats before you, each uglier than the last: the spiny-headed *rascasse* (scorpion fish), dog-nosed *grondin* (red gurnet), the monstrous *baudroie* or *lotte* (monkfish), and the eel-like *congre*. "Bouillabaisse" as sold here is a mix of fish too tiny to sell otherwise; the only problem with coming for the early morning show is that you have to wait so long for your bouillabaisse lunch. ⊠ *Quai de la Fraternité, Vieux Port* Ⓜ *Vieux Port.*

MuCEM

MUSEUM | Made up of three sites designed by Rudy Ricciotti, MuCEM (Museum of European and Mediterranean Civilizations) is all about new perspectives on Mediterranean cultures. Themes like "the invention of gods," "treasures of the spice route," or "at the bazaar of gender" are explored here. ▮**TIP**→ **The museum's popular café, bistro, and restaurant (reservations required),**

overseen by star chef Gérald Passédat, are all great for meals and for taking in the views. You can access the 12th-century Fort St-Jean, built by Louis XIV with guns pointing *toward* the city, in order to keep the feisty, rebellious Marseillais under his thumb. If you're not the queasy type, take a walk across the suspended footbridge over the sea; it provides spectacular photo ops and unique panoramas. On the other side, you can visit a Mediterranean garden and a folk-art collection. A third building—the Center for Conservation and Resources, near the St-Charles train station—holds the museum's permanent collection of paintings, prints, drawings, photographs, and objects. ⊠ *7 promenade Robert Laffont, Vieux Port* ☎ *04–84–35–13–13* ⊕ *www.mucem.org* ☒ *From €10* ⊙ *Closed Tues.* Ⓜ *Joliette.*

Musée Borély

MUSEUM | After a top-to-bottom renovation for the city's turn as European Capital of Culture 2013, the gracious 18th-century Château Borély became home to the collections of three major museums: Musée des Arts Décoratif (Museum of Decorative Arts), Musée de la Mode (Fashion Museum), and the Musée de la Faïence (Museum of Faïence Ceramics). The bright exhibition rooms feature brilliant lacquered ceilings and installations by French artists and designers, all the better to show off a gorgeous collection of Marseille faïence pottery dating to the early 17th century, tapestries, 18th-century hand-painted murals, furniture, and fashions from the 15th to 21st century. The château's large park and café lend themselves to a pleasant afternoon in this lovely part of the city. ☒ *Château Borély, 132 av. Clot Bey, Prado* ☎ *04–91–55–33–60* ⊕ *culture. marseille.fr/musees/le-musee-borely* ✉ *€6* ⊗ *Closed Mon.* Ⓜ *Rond-Point du Prado, then Bus No. 19, 44, or 83.*

Musée Cantini

MUSEUM | Set in a beautifully restored 17th-century house, this lovely little museum is a must for fans of Fauve and Surrealist art. There are paintings by Signac, Dufy, Léger, Ernst, Arp, and Bacon, as well as Kandinsky and Dubuffet. This is one of the foremost collections in France of the genre. ☒ *19 rue Grignan, Préfecture* ☎ *04–91–54–77–75* ⊕ *musee-cantini.marseille.fr* ✉ *€6* ⊗ *Closed Mon.* Ⓜ *Estrangin Préfecture.*

Musée des Docks Romains (*Roman Docks Museum*)

MUSEUM | In 1943 Germans destroyed the neighborhood along the Quai du Port—some 2,000 houses—displacing 20,000 citizens, but this act of brutal urban renewal, ironically, laid the ground open for new discoveries. When Marseille began to rebuild in 1947, workers dug up remains of a Roman shipping warehouse full of the terra-cotta jars and amphorae that once lay in the bellies of low-slung ships. The Musée des Docks Romains was created around the finds and demonstrates the scale of Massalia's shipping prowess. ☒ *2 pl. de Vivaux, Vieux Port*

☎ *04–91–91–24–62* ⊕ *www.marseille.fr* ✉ *€3* ⊗ *Closed Mon.* Ⓜ *Vieux Port.*

★ Musée d'Histoire de Marseille (*Marseille History Museum*)

MUSEUM | With the Port Antique in front, this modern, open-space museum illuminates Massalia's history with a treasure trove of archaeological finds and miniature models of the city as it appeared in various stages of history. Best by far is the presentation of Marseille's Classical halcyon days. There's a recovered wreck of a Roman cargo boat, its 3rd-century wood amazingly preserved, and the hull of a Greek boat dating to the 4th century BC. The model of the Greek city should be authentic—it's based on an eyewitness description by Aristotle. ☒ *2 rue Henri Barbrusse, Vieux Port* ☎ *04–91–55–36–00* ⊕ *www. musee-histoire-marseille-voie-historique. fr* ✉ *From €6* ⊗ *Closed Mon.* Ⓜ *Vieux-Port or Noailles.*

Musée Grobet-Labadié

MUSEUM | This lovely and intimate museum houses the private art collection of the wealthy 19th-century couple of the same name. Their 1873 mansion, beautifully renovated, offers an intriguing glimpse into the cultivated art tastes of the time, ranging from 15th- and 16th-century Italian and Flemish paintings to Fragonard and Millet. ☒ *140 bd. Longchamp, La Canebière* ☎ *04–91–62–21–82* ⊕ *musee-grobet-labadie.marseille.fr* ✉ *€6* ⊗ *Closed Mon.*

Musée Regards de Provence

MUSEUM | This beautifully renovated 1948 architectural gem by Fernand Pouillon was once Marseille's *station sanitaire,* where every immigrant entering France was systematically "disinfected" to guard against epidemic. An absorbing 45-minute film (in English) and the intact machinery tell a fascinating story of Marseille as "gateway to the East." The museum's light-filled second-floor exhibition spaces house a permanent collection of 18th- to 20th-century paintings depicting Provence and the Mediterranean Sea, as well as a revolving series of temporary exhibitions by contemporary painters. There's also a lovely boutique. ■TIP→ **The museum café (open until 7) has some of the best views of the redeveloped new port and is a great place for a gourmet lunch, a light snack on the terrace, or a restorative beverage.** ⊠ *Av. Vaudoyer, Rive Neuve* ☎ *04–96–17–40–40* ⊕ *www. museeregardsdeprovence.com* ⊠ *€7* ⊘ *Closed Mon.* Ⓜ *Joliette or Vieux Port.*

★ **Navette Maritime**
TRANSPORTATION SITE (AIRPORT/BUS/FERRY/TRAIN) | In keeping with the Vieux Port's substantially spiffed-up image, the Marseille regional transportation service now offers an efficient public ferry service, with hourly departures from the eastern side to Pointe Rouge (8 am–7 pm), L'Estaque (8:30 am–7:30 pm), and Les Goudes (8:50 am–7:50 pm). The nominal ticket charge (€5, available only on board) is well worth it for the fun and convenience of crossing the port by boat. ⊠ *Pl. des Huiles on Quai de Rive Neuve side and Hôtel de Ville on Quai du Port, Vieux Port* ⊕ *www.rtm.fr* ⊠ *€5 (free with métro pass)* Ⓜ *Vieux Port.*

Notre-Dame-de-la-Garde
RELIGIOUS SITE | Towering above the city and visible for miles around, this overscaled neo-Byzantine monument was erected in 1853 by Napoléon III. The interior is a Technicolor bonanza of red-and-beige stripes and glittering mosaics, and the gargantuan *Madonna and Child* on the steeple (almost 30 feet high) is covered in real gold leaf. While the panoply of ex-votos, mostly thanking the Virgin for deathbed interventions and shipwreck survivals, is a remarkable sight, most impressive are the views of the seaside city at your feet. ⊠ *Rue Fort du Sanctuaire, off Bd. André Aune, Garde Hill* ☎ *04–91–13–40–80* ⊕ *www. notredamedelagarde.com* Ⓜ *Estrangin Préfecture.*

Palais de Longchamp
CASTLE/PALACE | This extravagant and grandiose 19th-century palace, inaugurated in 1869, was built to celebrate the completion of an 84-km (52-mile) aqueduct bringing the water of the Durance river to the open sea. The massive, classical-style building crowns a hill and is splayed with impressive symmetrical grace around a series of fountains with a triumphal arch at its center and museums in either wing. In the **Musée des Beaux-Arts** (Fine Arts Museum) are 16th- and 17th-century paintings, including several by Rubens, as well as fine marble sculptures and drawings by the Marseille architect Pierre Puget. There's a delightful group of sculptures by caricaturist Honoré Daumier, and the collection of French 19th-century paintings, including Courbet, Ingres, and David, is strong. In the right wing of the palace is the **Muséum d'Histoire Naturelle** (Natural History Museum) with a collection of prehistoric and zoological artifacts, plus a large aquarium with fish from around the world. ⊠ *Eastern end of Bd. Longchamp, La Canebière* ☎ *04–91–14–59–30, 04–91–14–59–50* ⊕ *musee-des-beaux-arts.marseille.fr* ⊠ *Musée des Beaux-Arts €6* ⊘ *Closed Mon.* Ⓜ *Longchamp.*

Place Thiars
PLAZA | An ensemble of Italianate 18th-century buildings frames this popular center of activity, bounded by Quai Neuve, Rue Fortia, Rue de la Paix Marcel-Paul, and Cours d'Estinenne d'Orves, where one sidewalk café spills into another, and every kind of bouillabaisse is yours for the asking. At night the neighborhood is a fashionable hangout for young professionals on their way to and from the theaters and clubs on Quai de Rive Neuve. ⊠ *Rive Neuve* Ⓜ *Vieux Port.*

Rue Longue-des-Capucins/Rue d'Aubagne
NEIGHBORHOOD | Stepping into this atmospheric neighborhood, you may feel you have suddenly been transported to

Did You Know?

A mock-Byzantine extravaganza with Technicolor stripes and mosaics, Marseille's Notre-Dame-de-la-Garde is a cousin to Paris's Sacré-Coeur, thanks to its hilltop perch.

a Moroccan *souk* (market). Shops that serve the needs of Marseille's large and vibrant North African community have open bins of olives, coffee beans, tea, spices, dried beans, chickpeas, couscous, peppers, and salted sardines. Tiny shoebox cafés sell African sweets, and the daily Marché de Noailles in the surrounding maze of streets is the city's most vibrant and colorful market. ✉ *La Canebière* [M] *Noailles.*

★ Unité d'Habitation Cité Radieuse

BUILDING | Considered at the time a radical experiment in collective living, Le Corbusier's masterpiece "habitat system" was completed in 1951. The mammoth building, set in the middle of a green park with unobstructed views of the sea, contains 337 apartments with 23 different floor plans that were ground-breaking in their simplicity, functionality, and practicality; each came with views, light, and on-site access to a restaurant, a bar, shops, childcare, a rooftop jogging track, a playground, and a stage. Guided tours (reservations can be made online) of the UNESCO World Heritage Site take you to a model apartment, the rooftop, and several common areas. The Cité also now houses a restaurant, bar, hotel, and the MAMO arts center, all open to the public. ✉ *280 bd. Michelet* 🌐 *www.marseille-citeradieuse.org* 🎫 *€10* 🕒 *Closed Sun.*

🍴 Restaurants

★ AM by Alexandre Mazzia

$$$$ | **FRENCH** | Architect, artist, creator—whatever you call him, one thing's for sure: you won't soon forget this master chef who was awarded a Michelin star within nine months of opening his own restaurant. With a background working in French, African, and Asian kitchens, his combinations are music to the mouth, like the charred satay tuna in tapioca speckled with bright green fish eggs, served with wasabi ice cream. **Known for:** exquisite small dishes; unusual pairings in choice of four set menus; far-flung influences. [$] *Average main: €140* ✉ *9 rue François Rocca, Prado* ☎ *04–91–24–83–63* 🌐 *www.alexandremazzia.com* 🕒 *Closed Sun. and Mon.*

★ Balady

$ | **MEDITERRANEAN** | **FAMILY** | Expressive of the melting pot that is Marseille, this bakery and lunch counter (by the same team behind the Egyptian restaurant La Cantine de Nour) presents a delicious melange of Mediterranean flavors and fragrances that extends from the Maghreb to the Middle East. Stone walls, mismatched chairs, copper pots, and a long marble counter brimming with delights create an atmosphere as irresistible as the food: tender *feetir* (spinach galette); *manaisch* bread glistening with olive oil and flecked with tomatoes, coriander, thyme, and onions; fresh salads; and a tantalizing selection of homemade breads and pastries, many hot from the oven. **Known for:** everything baked on the premises; warm, welcoming all-woman team; lots of vegetarian choices. [$] *Average main: €8* ✉ *66 rue Consolat, La Canebière* ☎ *09–80–99–21–03* [M] *Réformés Canebière.*

Chez Etienne

$$ | **PIZZA** | A well-known hole-in-the-wall, this small pizzeria is filled daily with politicos and young professionals who have patronized this institution since when the famous late-chef Stéphane Cassero presided. Brace yourself for an epic meal, starting with a large anchovy pizza from the wood-burning oven, then dig into fried squid, eggplant gratin, and a slab of rare grilled beef all served with the background of laughter and rich Marseille patois. **Known for:** stupendous pizza; lots of local flavor; huge portions. [$] *Average main: €20* ✉ *43 rue de Lorette, Le Panier* ☎ *04–91–90–65–45* 💳 *No credit cards* 🕒 *Closed Sun.* [M] *Colbert Hôtel de Région.*

Chez Fonfon

$$$$ | **SEAFOOD** | Tucked into the tiny fishing port of Vallon des Auffes, this local landmark has one of the loveliest settings in greater Marseille. A variety of fresh seafood, impeccably grilled, steamed, or roasted in salt crust, is served in two pretty dining rooms with picture windows overlooking the fishing boats that supply your dinner. **Known for:** some of the city's best bouillabaisse; fresh catch of the day; wonderful setting. $ *Average main: €50* ✉ *140 rue du Vallon des Auffes, Vallon des Auffes* ☎ *04–91– 52–14–38* ⊕ *www.chez-fonfon.com.*

Chez Michel

$$$$ | BRASSERIE | This beachside Michelin-starred brasserie near the Jardin du Pharo is considered the last word in bouillabaisse and draws a knowing local clientele willing to shell out a few extra euros (€75) for this authentic classic. Before dining, the fish are paraded by your table then ceremoniously filleted before being served with the classic accompaniments: a spicy rouille, buttery croutons. **Known for:** cozy atmosphere; small but excellent menu; bouillabaisse that's worth the splurge. $ *Average main: €70* ✉ *6 rue des Catalans, Pharo* ☎ *04–91–52–30–63* ⊕ *www.restaurant-michel-13.fr.*

★ La Boîte à Sardine

$$ | SEAFOOD | Owner Fabien Rugi's passion for seafood may come off as gruff, but that's only because he wants his customers to appreciate his Mediterranean-inflected seafood dishes as much as he does. He puts his formidable energy into serving the freshest seafood, prepared *comme il faut*. **Known for:** sea-anemone beignets; delicious local wines; convivial atmosphere. $ *Average main: €22* ✉ *2 bd. de la Libération, La Canebière* ☎ *04–91–50–95–95* ⊕ *www. laboiteasardine.com* ☽ *Closed Sun. and Mon. No dinner Tues. and Wed.* Ⓜ *Réformés Canebière.*

★ La Cantinetta

$ | ITALIAN | FAMILY | Ask any Marseille food enthusiast where they go for great Italian food and they're sure to send

you to this legendary spot near the Cours Julien. It's not just the food but the lively ambience, flowing wine, and happy camaraderie as gorgeous plates of charcuterie topped with giant Parmesan shavings and fragrant bowls of steaming risotto, pasta, or line-caught fish of the day exit the kitchen, followed by a towering *tiramisu maison*. **Known for:** friendly atmosphere; abundant dishes; excellent wine list of Mediterranean favorites. $ *Average main: €17* ✉ *24 cours Julien, Cours Julien* ☎ *04–91–48–10–48* ⊕ *www. restaurantlacantinetta.fr* ☽ *Closed Sun.* Ⓜ *Noailles.*

★ La Mercerie

$$$ | FRENCH | A stylishly high-low decor that joins distressed walls, minimalist lighting, and sleek designer chairs with a setting in Marseille's emerging Noailles neighborhood is your first clue that this neobistro and wine bar is perhaps Marseille's most impossibly hip eatery. British chef Harry Cummins, lately of Paris's gastronomic mecca Frenchie, crafts a subtle, imaginative cuisine from local seasonal products that's both highly satisfying and sensitive to vegetarians and those with food allergies. **Known for:** all the rage among young foodies; healthy dining; secluded outdoor terrace. $ *Average main: €25* ✉ *9 cours St-Louis, Noailles* ☎ *04–91–06–18–44* ⊕ *www. lamerceriemarseille.com* ☽ *Closed Mon. and Tues.* Ⓜ *Noailles, Vieux-Port-Hôtel de Ville.*

★ L'Épicerie Idéal

$ | FRENCH | For a fresh, seasonal lunch, try this chic little outpost in the marché Noailles that is part restaurant, part gourmet grocer. Imaginative Mediterranean-inflected salads and light dishes are healthy and delicious, and pair well with a gourmet soda, Marseille microbrew, or a local rosé. **Known for:** great value meals; perfect for gourmet discoveries and gifts; fresh, seasonal dishes and salads. $ *Average main: €13* ✉ *11 rue d'Aubagne, Noailles* ☎ *09–80–39–99–41* ⊕ *www.*

Continued on page 208

CUISINE OF THE SUN

Don't be surprised if colors and flavors seem more intense in Provence. It could be the hot, dry climate, which concentrates the essence of fruit and vegetables, or the sun beaming down on market tables overflowing with produce. Or maybe you're seeing the world anew through rosé-tinted wine glasses. Whatever the reason, here's how to savor Provence's incroyable flavors and culinary favorites.

Provence's rustic cuisine, based on local tomatoes, garlic, olive oil, anchovies, olives, and native wild herbs—including basil, lavender, mint, rosemary, thyme, and sage—has more in common with other Mediterranean cuisines than it does with most regional French fare. Everywhere you'll find sun-ripened fruit dripping with nectar and vegetables so flavor-packed that meat may seem like a mere accessory.

The natural bounty of the region is ample, united by climate—brilliant sunshine and fierce winds—and divided by dramatically changing landscapes. In the Vaucluse, scorched plains give way to lush, orchard-lined hills and gently sloped vineyards. The wild Calanques of Marseille, source of spiky sea urchins, ease into the tranquil waters of St-Tropez, home to gleaming bream and sea bass. Provence's pantry is overflowing with culinary treasures.

Simple preparations, like grilled vegetables with crusty bread, are best enjoyed with the region's famous rosé wine

PROVENCE'S TOP REGIONAL DISHES

Ratatouille

Fougasse

AÏOLI

The name for a deliciously pungent mayonnaise made with generous helpings of garlic, *aïoli* is a popular accompaniment for fish, meat, and vegetable dishes. The mayonnaise version shares its name with "grand aïoli," a recipe featuring salt cod, potatoes, hard-boiled eggs, and vegetables. Both types of aïoli pop up all over Provence, but they seems most beloved in Marseille. In keeping with Catholic practice, some restaurants serve grand aïoli only on Fridays. And it's a good sign if they ask you to place your order at least a day in advance. A grand aïoli is also a traditional component of the Niçois Christmas feast.

BOUILLABAISSE

Originally a humble fisherman's soup made with the part of the catch that nobody else wanted, bouillabaisse—the famous fish stew—consists of four or five kinds of fish: the villainous-looking *rascasse* (red scorpion fish), *grondin* (sea robin), *baudroie* (monkfish), *congre* (conger eel), and *rouget* (mullet). The fish are simmered in a stock of onions, tomatoes, garlic, olive oil, and saffron, which gives the dish its golden color. When presented properly, the broth is served first, with croutons and rouille, a creamy garlic sauce that you spoon in to suit your taste. The fish comes separately, and the ritual is to place pieces into the soup to enjoy after slurping up some of the broth.

BOURRIDE

This poached fish dish owes its anise kick to pastis and its garlic punch to aïoli. The name comes from the Provençal bourrido, which translates less poetically as "boiled." Monkfish—known as baudroie in Provence and lotte in the rest of France—is a must, but chefs occasionally dress up their bourride with other species and shellfish.

DAUBE DE BOEUF

To distinguish their prized beef stew from *boeuf bourguignon*, Provençal chefs make a point of not marinating the meat, instead cooking it very slowly in tannic red wine that is often flavored with orange zest. In the Camargue, daube is made with the local taureau (bull's meat), while the Avignon variation uses lamb.

Bourride

Bouillabaisse

FOUGASSE
The Provençal answer to Italian focaccia, this soft flatbread is distinguished by holes that give it the appearance of a lacy leaf. It can be made savory—flavored with olives, anchovy, bacon, cheese, or anything else the baker has on hand—or sweet, enriched with olive oil and dusted with icing sugar. When in Menton, don't miss the sugary *fougasse mentonnaise.*

LES PETITS FARCIS
The Niçois specialty called *les petits farcis* are prepared with tiny summer vegetables (usually zucchini, tomatoes, peppers, and onions) that are traditionally stuffed with veal or leftover daube (beef stew). Like so many Niçois dishes, they make great picnic food.

RATATOUILLE
At its best, *ratatouille* is a glorious thing—a riot of eggplant, zucchini, bell peppers, and onions, each sautéed separately in olive oil and then gently combined with sweet summer tomatoes. A well-made ratatouille, to which a pinch of saffron has been added to heighten its flavor, is also delicious served chilled.

SOUPE AU PISTOU
The Provençal answer to pesto, pistou consists of the simplest ingredients—garlic, olive oil, fresh basil, and Parmesan—ideally pounded together by hand in a stone mortar with an olivewood pestle. Most traditionally it delivers a potent kick to *soupe au pistou,* a kind of French minestrone made with green beans, white beans, potatoes, and zucchini.

SOCCA
You'll find socca vendors from Nice to Menton, but this chickpea pancake cooked on a giant iron platter in a wood-fired oven is really a Niçois phenomenon, born of sheer poverty at a time when wheat flour was scarce. After cooking, it is sliced into finger-lickin' portions with an oyster knife. Enjoy it with a glass of chilled rosé.

TIAN DE LÉGUMES
A *tian* is both a beautiful earthenware dish and one of many vegetable gratins that might be cooked in it. This thrifty dish makes a complete meal of seasonal vegetables, eggs, and a little cheese.

In Search of the Perfect Bouillabaisse

Marseille is a Mediterranean melting pot of people, styles, and, of course—since the city is home to some of the best bouillabaisse on the planet—fish. While some insist that the only true bouillabaisse is the one served to friends in fishermen's cabanons along the rocky coast of Marseille, many others acknowledge Marseille is the true mecca of this fish stew, one that relies on the particular mix of Mediterranean fish found off the Riviera coasts.

According to the bouillabaisse charter—designed to spare unsuspecting diners from poor imitations—this stew should contain at least four of the following once-unappreciated species: scorpionfish, tub gurnard, John Dory, monkfish, weever, and conger. Its robust flavor comes from a combination of tomato, onion, garlic, fennel, orange zest, and saffron, along with plenty of olive oil and sea salt (fishermen originally used seawater). The brick-red broth is served first, followed by the fish fillets, all of it with plenty of *rouille* (mayonnaise spiced up with garlic, chili, and saffron).

epicerielideal.com ♥ *Closed Sun. and Mon.* Ⓜ *Noailles, Vieux-Port-Hôtel de Ville.*

L'Epuisette
$$$$ | SEAFOOD | Artfully set on a rocky, fingerlike jetty surrounded by the sea, this fine seafood restaurant offers gorgeous views of crashing surf on one side and the port of Vallon des Auffes on the other. Chef Guillaume Sourrieu has acquired a big reputation (and a Michelin star) for sophisticated cooking featuring the fresh catch of the day—Atlantic turbot in citrus rind with oxtail ravioli, and slow-cooked sea bass baked in a salt-butter crust and walnut oil are some top delights—matched with a superb wine list. **Known for:** stupendous seafood; lovely setting; fixed-price menus worth the high price. Ⓢ *Average main: €55* ⊠ *158 rue du Vallon des Auffes, Pharo* ☎ *04–91–52–17–82* ⊕ *www.l-epuisette.com* ♥ *Closed Sun. and Mon., and last 2 wks in Aug.*

★ Le Capucin
$$ | FRENCH | Fresh from the kitchens of two-Michelin-star chef Lionel Levy, Sylvain Touati has swiftly shown what he can do given a kitchen of his own. The young chef's menu of brasserie classics shines in dishes that are at once hearty and satisfying as well as innovative and sophisticated—not to mention utterly delicious. **Known for:** fearless innovation in dishes that feel like instant classics; French comfort food; excellent craft cocktails. Ⓢ *Average main: €19* ⊠ *Mercure Hotel, 48 La Canebière, La Canebière* ☎ *04–65–58–56–93* ⊕ *www.brasseriele-capucin.com.*

Le Restaurant Peron
$$$$ | SEAFOOD | The stylish modern dark-wood interior and large windows overlooking the sea here are magnets for hip young professionals. The staff is efficient, and meals are well presented and tasty. **Known for:** to-die-for views; reasonable prix-fixe menus; great spot to watch the sunset. Ⓢ *Average main: €40* ⊠ *56 Corniche J.-.F- Kennedy, Endoume* ☎ *04–91–52–15–22* ⊕ *www.restaurant-peron.com.*

Les Arcenaulx
$$$ | FRENCH | At this book-lined, red-wall haven in the stylish book-and-boutique complex of a renovated arsenal, you can have a sophisticated regional lunch and read while you're waiting. If you've had your fill of fish, indulge in the grilled filet

of beef with fried artichokes and sweet onion. **Known for:** very good bouillabaisse; extensive wine list; nice setting in a lively square. $ *Average main: €26* ⊠ *25 cours d'Estienne d'Orves, Vieux Port* ☎ *04–91–59–80–30* ⊕ *www.les-arcenaulx.com* ⊙ *Closed Sun.* Ⓜ *Vieux Port.*

Mina Kouk

$ | **FRENCH** | **FAMILY** | Armed with her Algerian grandma's recipes and an artist's spirit, Mina Kouk abandoned advanced studies in chemistry to try her hand at something closer to alchemy. Now the smell of mint tea and pastries warm from the oven mingle with the exotic spices of her couscous, spiced chicken tagine, and savory lentil soup that perfume the air at this cozy, bright salon de thé. **Known for:** heartfelt North African cooking including excellent pastries; perfect for families with picky eaters; early closing time of 7 pm. $ *Average main: €10* ⊠ *21 rue Fontage, Cours Julien* ☎ *04–91–53–54–55* ⊕ *www.minakouk.com* ⊙ *Closed Sun.* Ⓜ *Notre Dame du Mont.*

Regards Café

$ | **MODERN FRENCH** | Close and yet so far from the hustle and bustle of the Vieux Port and MuCEM's crowded cafés, this luminous dining room in the Musée Regards de Provence has panoramic views over the new port and Marseille's top architectural gems (including the one you're sitting in). Happily, chef Thierry Lennon's cooking lives up to the ambience, with dishes like roasted cod with saffron risotto or tender duck breast with honeyed red cabbage. **Known for:** perfect spot for a quick coffee, lunch, or apéro; beautiful views of the boats leaving for Corsica and Sicily; reservations needed (unless you want to enjoy the buffet selection out on the terrace). $ *Average main: €15* ⊠ *Allée Regards de Provence, Rive Neuve* ☎ *04–96–17–40–45* ⊕ *www.museeregardsdeprovence.com* ⊙ *Closed Mon. No dinner* Ⓜ *Vieux Port or Joliette.*

Toinou Les Fruits de Mer

$$ | **SEAFOOD** | You can join the crowd at the outdoor stand and split a few oysters on the hoof. But it's more comfortable settling into a brasserie booth at this landmark shellfish joint where you can get heaps of Cassis urchins, cream-filled *violets* (a kind of monstrous sea slug), clams, mussels, and, of course, oysters. **Known for:** always-fresh seafood; North African hot sauce; good prices. $ *Average main: €20* ⊠ *3 cours St-Louis, Vieux Port* ☎ *04–91–33–14–94* ⊕ *www.marseille.toinou.com* Ⓜ *Noailles.*

Une Table au Sud

$$$$ | **SEAFOOD** | Chef Ludovic Turac—a candidate on TV's *Top Chef 2011* and one of the youngest Michelin-starred chefs in France—has evolved into a serious, mature, and highly appreciated local celebrity while at the helm of this now tried-and-true favorite. A Mediterranean menu changes every two months depending on what's in season. **Known for:** creamy, fishy Milkshake de Bouille-Abaisse; great views of the Vieux Port; vegetarian-friendly options. $ *Average main: €38* ⊠ *2 quai du Port, Vieux Port* ☎ *04–91–90–63–53* ⊕ *www.unetableausud.com* ⊙ *Closed Mon. No dinner Sun.* Ⓜ *Vieux Port.*

Hotels

Alex Hotel

$ | **HOTEL** | This reasonably priced boutique hotel, across from St-Charles train station, is set in a beautiful historic building. **Pros:** great prices; convenient to the train station and a 15-minute walk to the old port; lovely breakfast. **Cons:** nearby restaurants aren't great; rooms lack character; not in the city center. $ *Rooms from: €85* ⊠ *13–15 pl. des Marseillaises, St-Charles* ☎ *04–13–24–13–25* ⊕ *www.hotelalex.fr* ⇌ *21 rooms* ❑ *No meals* Ⓜ *Gare St-Charles.*

C2 Hotel

$$$ | HOTEL | Previously occupied by a prominent Marseille family, this 19th-century home now holds 20 beautifully designed accommodations. **Pros:** a few minutes from the port; impeccable service; intimate spa with steam room, Jacuzzi, and pool. **Cons:** extra charge for breakfast; some of the lighting in common areas is a bit too neon; rooms vary drastically in size. $ *Rooms from: €269* ⊠ *48 rue Roux de Brignoles, St-Charles* ☎ *04–95–05–13–13* ⊕ *www.c2-hotel.com* ⌸ *20 rooms* ⏀ *No meals* Ⓜ *Estrangin Préfecture.*

Grand Hotel Beauvau Vieux Port - MGallery Collection

$$ | HOTEL | Chopin spent the night and George Sand kept a suite in this historic hotel overlooking the Vieux Port. **Pros:** in the heart of the city; rooms are quiet; lovely views of the old port. **Cons:** some rooms quite small; service can be distracted when busy; a sea view will cost you. $ *Rooms from: €175* ⊠ *4 rue Beauvau, Vieux Port* ☎ *04–91–54–91–00* ⊕ *www.accorhotels.com* ⌸ *73 rooms* ⏀ *No meals* Ⓜ *Vieux Port.*

Hermès

$ | HOTEL | Although the rooms are rather snug, this modest city hotel is right around the corner from the Quai du Port and is a good value. **Pros:** location and price add up to excellent value; lovely staff; nice rooftop terrace. **Cons:** rooms are small and the bathrooms even smaller; no bar on rooftop; rooms a bit too no-frills. $ *Rooms from: €85* ⊠ *2 rue Bonneterie, Vieux Port* ☎ *04–96–11–63–63* ⊕ *www.hotelmarseille.com* ⌸ *29 rooms* ⏀ *No meals* Ⓜ *Vieux Port.*

Hotel Peron

$ | HOTEL | A family-run jewel, this eclectic, rather eccentric hotel features rooms with different decorative themes, from delicate, rather austere Japanese to playful Dutch to colorful Moroccan. **Pros:** price is excellent value, especially for sea views; very friendly service; fantastic location on the waterfront. **Cons:** rooms could do with a freshening up; some rooms are quite small; lots of steps and no elevator. $ *Rooms from: €90* ⊠ *119 corniche J.-F.- Kennedy, Endoume* ☎ *04–91–31–01–41* ⊕ *www.hotelperon.com* ⌸ *26 rooms* ⏀ *No meals.*

Hôtel Saint Ferréol

$ | HOTEL | Set back from the port in the heart of the shopping district, this cozy, charming little hotel offers a warm reception and a homey breakfast-room-cum-bar. **Pros:** cheerful and helpful service; center-of-town location is ideal; inexpensive. **Cons:** some rooms are small; street-facing rooms can be noisy; decor a little dated. $ *Rooms from: €105* ⊠ *19 rue Pisançon at Rue St-Ferréol, Vieux Port* ☎ *04–91–33–12–21* ⊕ *www.hotel-stferreol.com* ⌸ *19 rooms* ⏀ *No meals* Ⓜ *Vieux Port.*

★ Intercontinental Marseille Hôtel Dieu

$$$ | HOTEL | Housed in Marseille's majestic 18th-century Hôtel Dieu, a beloved landmark built according to plans by Jacques Hardouin-Mansart, architect to Louis XIV, this place has been transformed into a gleaming palace—and it's worth a stop even if you don't stay here (you can enjoy a drink on the sprawling terrace bar, with gorgeous views of the old port). **Pros:** a one-stop luxury spot including excellent pool, spa, and restaurants; splendid views from open-air bar; rates include breakfast. **Cons:** only a fifth of rooms have a terrace; such indulgence does have a price; snob appeal. $ *Rooms from: €280* ⊠ *1 pl. Daviel, Vieux Port* ☎ *04–13–42–42–42* ⊕ *www.ihg.com/intercontinental/hotels/us/en/marseille/mrsha/hoteldetail* ⌸ *195 rooms* ⏀ *Free breakfast* Ⓜ *Vieux Port.*

Le Petit Nice Passedat

$$$$ | HOTEL | On a rocky promontory overlooking the sea, this fantasy villa was bought from a countess in 1917 and converted to a sleek hotel-restaurant, where the Passédat family has been getting it right ever since, especially in the famous restaurant. **Pros:** home to Provence's only three-Michelin-star restaurant; breathtaking views; lovely pool area. **Cons:** leave your impatience at the door when you dine here; restaurant closed Sunday and Monday; not so easily accessible to city center by public transport. $ *Rooms from: €460 ⊠ 17 rue des Braves, Endoume ☎ 04–91–59–25–92 ⊕ www. passedat.fr ⇨ 16 rooms* ❐ *No meals.*

★ Les Bords de Mer

$$ | **HOTEL** | Entering this gleaming hotel is like walking straight into the surf, perched as it is right over the Marseille waterfront with every one of its rooms overlooking the turquoise-blue Mediterranean. **Pros:** eye-popping views of the sea and balconies in every room; beautiful rooftop pool; excellent location. **Cons:** breakfast not included; rooms are minuscule; no bar. $ *Rooms from: €220 ⊠ 52 Corniche Président John Fitzgerald Kennedy, Endoume ☎ 04–13–94–34–00 ⊕ www.lesbordsdemer.com/en ⇨ 19 rooms* ❐ *No meals.*

Mama Shelter

$ | **HOTEL** | Manufacturing hip is this urban chain hotel's claim to fame (no wonder: it's the brainchild of designer Philippe Starck) and it has the formula down pat: offbeat (preferably artsy) neighborhood, check; plenty of graffiti in the interior design, check; functional, minimalist rooms, check; sexy touches, check. **Pros:** buffet breakfasts can't be beat; great on-site nightlife; cool vibe. **Cons:** not always a bargain; not to everyone's taste; iffy neighborhood. $ *Rooms from: €99 ⊠ 64 rue de la Loubière, Cours Julien ☎ 04–84–35–20–00 ⊕ www.mamashelter.com ⇨ 127 rooms* ❐ *No meals* Ⓜ *Baille or Notre Dame du Mont.*

nhow Marseille

$$$ | **HOTEL** | Sleek, with stunning 360-degree views of the bay and the islands, this white-on-white modern hotel offers designs by Starck, Zanotta, and Emu. Service is prompt and unobtrusive, and the huge windows make for a light-filled reception area. **Pros:** the view out to sea is truly remarkable; rooms are large, most with balconies; saltwater pool. **Cons:** service sorely lacking; too many rooms for a personalized welcome; minimalist style not for everyone. $ *Rooms from: €270 ⊠ 200 corniche J. F. Kennedy, Endoume ☎ 04–91–16–19–00 ⊕ www.nh-hotels.com/hotel/nhow-marseille ⇨ 160 rooms* ❐ *No meals.*

★ Residence du Vieux Port

$$$ | **HOTEL** | **FAMILY** | The flat glass-and-concrete facade of this postwar structure grants all the port-facing rooms here broad views of the Vieux Port all the way to Notre-Dame-de-la-Garde. **Pros:** great price for this ideal location; superb views of the Vieux Port; cheerful decor and service. **Cons:** terrace views are partially obstructed by concrete railings; breakfast not included in price unless chosen when booking; some bathrooms on the small side. $ *Rooms from: €250 ⊠ 18 quai du Port, Vieux Port ☎ 04–91–91–91–22 ⊕ www.hotel-residence-marseille.com ⇨ 51 rooms* ❐ *No meals* Ⓜ *Vieux Port.*

★ Sofitel Vieux-Port

$$$ | **HOTEL** | **FAMILY** | Its plum location next to the beautiful Palais de Pharo and park and its legendary service already raised this five-star luxury hotel to a great deal more than standard issue, but the recent addition of a rooftop terrace with some of the city's best views puts it right up there with the top hotels in the city. **Pros:** exemplary service; stupendous views; great spa, restaurant, and bar. **Cons:** pool can be crowded in summer; some rooms on the small side; not an intimate hotel. $ *Rooms from: €350 ⊠ 36 bd. Charles Livon, Pharo ☎ 04–91–15–59–00 ⊕ www.sofitel.accorhotels.com ⇨ 137 rooms* ❐ *No meals.*

Nightlife

Marseille's vibrant multicultural mix has evolved a genre of music that fuses all the sounds of Arabic music with rhythms of Provence, Corsica, and southern Italy, and douses it with reggae and rap.

BARS AND PUBS

R2 Le Rooftop Marseille

BARS/PUBS | At the top of the Terrasses shopping center, Le Réctoire and its private second-tier rooftop terrace, Le Rooftop—together called R2—are a popular restaurant by day and a chic cocktail bar, dance club, and music venue by night. Dance on the rooftop to live music and DJ beats or sip a cocktail on the sprawling terrace while taking in spectacular views of the J4 Pier (home of MuCEM) and Marseille's big-ship port. The restaurant, bar, and dance space are all open until 2 am six days a week, a rarity in Marseille (it closes at 7 pm on Monday). ⊠ 9 quai du Lazaret ☎ 04–91–45–61–98 ⊕ www.airdemarseille.com Ⓜ La Joliette.

Red Lion

BARS/PUBS | This bar is a mecca for English speakers, who pour onto the sidewalk, beer in hand, pub style. There's live music, DJs on the weekend, and a lounge for the die-hard rugby and soccer fans who can't go without watching a game. ⊠ 231 av. Pierre Mendès France, Vieux Port ☎ 04–91–25–17–17 ⊕ www.pub-redlion.com.

MUSIC CLUBS

Au Son des Guitares

MUSIC CLUBS | A Marseille institution, the music is passionate and the crowd lively at this fashionable cabaret-bar featuring live music. ⊠ 18 rue Corneille, Vieux Port ☎ 04–91–33–11–47 Ⓜ Vieux Port.

Docks des Suds

MUSIC CLUBS | At this vast venue, host to the Fiesta des Suds each autumn, you'll find world and Latin music year-round. ⊠ 12 rue Urbain V at Bd. de Paris, Vieux Port ☎ 04–91–99–00–00 ⊕ www.dock-des-suds.org Ⓜ National.

Espace Julien

CONCERTS | Rock, pop, jazz, and reggae concerts, along with the occasional comedy and alternative theater performance, are held at Espace Julien. ⊠ 39 cours Julien, Préfecture ☎ 04–91–24–34–10 ⊕ www.espace-julien.com Ⓜ Notre Dame du Mont.

L'Affranchi

MUSIC CLUBS | For rap and techno, try L'Affranchi. ⊠ 212 bd. de St-Marcel, La Canebière ✛ Via A50 (direction Aubagne) ☎ 04–91–35–09–19 ⊕ www.l-affranchi.com Ⓜ Dromel, then Bus No. 15; or Timone, then Bus No. 40 (return on night Bus No. 540).

La Caravelle

MUSIC CLUBS | Restaurant by day, bluesy jazz club and tapas bar by night, La Caravelle hearkens back to prewar jazz clubs, but without the smoke. There are great views over the port and live jazz two nights a week. ⊠ Hotel Belle Vue, 34 quai du Port, Vieux Port ☎ 04–91–90–36–64 ⊕ www.lacaravelle-marseille.com Ⓜ Vieux Port.

🎭 Performing Arts

With a population of 859,000, Marseille is a big city by French standards, with all the nightlife that entails. Arm yourself with *Marseille L'Hebdo*, a glossy monthly events magazine; *A Nous Marseille*, a hip weekly on theater, art, film, concerts, and shopping in southern Provence; or the monthly *In Situ*, a free guide to music, theater, and galleries. They're all in French.

ARTS CENTERS

Le Silo

ARTS CENTERS | This performance space in a modern building right on the waterfront hosts an impressive series of classical and contemporary concerts, theater, and dance. ⊠ 35 quai du Lazaret, La Canebière ☎ 04–91–90–00–00 ⊕ www.cepacsilo-marseille.fr Ⓜ Désirée Clary or Joliette.

OPERA

Opéra Municipal de Marseille

CONCERTS | Operas and orchestral concerts are held at the Opéra Municipal. ⊠ 2 rue Molière, Vieux Port ☎ 04–91–55–11–10 ⊕ opera.marseille.fr Ⓜ Vieux Port.

PUPPET SHOWS

Théâtre Massalia

DANCE | FAMILY | A young audience thrills to entertainment with puppets, dance, and music—occasionally in English. It's by the Gare St-Charles. ⊠ Theatre Massalia, 41 rue Jobin, La Canebière ☎ 04–95–04–95–75 ⊕ www.theatremassalia.com Ⓜ Saint-Charles.

THEATER

Badaboum Théâtre

THEATER | FAMILY | At Badaboum, adventurous, accessible productions for children are performed. ⊠ 16 quai de Rive Neuve, Vieux Port ☎ 04–91–54–40–71 ⊕ www.badaboum-theatre.com Ⓜ Vieux Port.

Théâtre National de Marseille La Criée

THEATER | A strong repertoire of classical and contemporary works is performed here. ⊠ Quai de Rive Neuve, Vieux Port ☎ 04–91–54–70–54 ⊕ www.theatre-lacriee.com Ⓜ Vieux Port.

🏃 Activities

Marseille's waterfront position makes it easy to swim and sunbathe within the city sprawl. From the Vieux Port, Bus No. 83 or 19 takes you to the vast green spread of reclaimed land called the **Parc Balnéaire du Prado.** Its waterfront is divided into beaches, all of them public and well equipped with showers, toilets, and first-aid stations. The beach surface varies between sand and gravel. You can also find your own little beach on the tiny, rocky **Îles de Frioul**; boats leave from the Vieux Port and cost €11.10.

👜 Shopping

Although you'll want to stock up on savon (soap) de Marseille, the city has lots more to offer in the way of shopping. Offbeat designer clothing, vintage finds, and hip accessories made in Marseille abound around Cours Julien. Nearer the Vieux Port, rues Grignan, Paradis, and Saint form a high-end shopping rectangle, where pricey French designers comingle with chic fashion chains (like Marseille-based Sugar) and edgy-elegant concept stores, like Marianne Cat, where you can also relax over a glass of wine or a cup of tea.

CLOTHING

Jogging

CLOTHING | A small but choice selection of crème de la crème French and European designers for men and women in a beautifully conceived boutique, includes lingerie, shoes, hats, books, artworks, and Aesop skincare, all hand picked by the charming owner, who is also a well-known French fashion photographer. The shop's cozy courtyard café is the perfect place to recharge the shopping batteries. ⊠ 103 rue Paradis, Pharo ☎ 04–91–81–44–94 ⊕ www.joggingjogging.com Ⓜ Estrangin.

Le Jardin Montgrand

DEPARTMENT STORES | This soaring concept store, housed in a beautifully updated mansion, features an ever-changing array of chic women's clothes and accessories by local designers, stylish housewares, artisan perfumes and skincare, and revolving art shows. The leafy courtyard café is a great place to indulge in a sinful treat from one of Marseille's best pâtisseries, a cup of tea, or a glass of wine. The boutique also has a corner for the much-sought-after Provence-based candle makers, Rose et Marius, whose gorgeously scented bougies come in handmade Limoges porcelain holders. ⊠ 35 rue Montgrand, Pharo

☎ 04–91–00–35–20 ⊕ www.jardin-mont-grand.com Ⓜ Estrangin.

Marianne Cat

CLOTHING | A curated selection of sophisticated, superchic European-designed clothes, shoes, scarves, jewelry, and accessories for women is displayed in a soaring 18th-century space. ✉ 53 rue Grignan, Belsunce ☎ 04–91–55–05–25 Ⓜ Estrangin Préfecture.

Sessùn

CLOTHING | Emma François draws her inspiration from music to create subtle, timeless clothes that are both French and intercontinental. Leave room in your suitcase for at least a Sussùn scarf. ✉ 6 rue Sainte, Vieux Port ☎ 04–91–52–33–61 Ⓜ Vieux Port.

Sugar

CLOTHING | This Marseille-based chain sells reliably chic sportswear in luscious colors. Mix-and-match separates include everything from sexy pencil skirts to jaunty peacoats and those long French scarves. ✉ 16 rue Lulli, Vieux Port ☎ 04–91–33–47–52 ⊕ www.sugarproduct.com.

FOOD

Four des Navettes

FOOD/CANDY | This famous bakery, up the street from Notre-Dame-de-la-Garde, has made orange-spice, shuttle-shape navettes in the same oven since it opened in 1781. These cookies are modeled on the little boat that, it is said, carried Lazarus and the Three Marys (Mary Magdalene, Mary Salome, and Mary Jacobe) to the nearby shore. ✉ 136 rue Sainte, Pharo ☎ 04–91–33–32–12 ⊕ www.fourdesnavettes.com Ⓜ Vieux Port.

La Maison du Pastis

FOOD/CANDY | Specializing in pastis, anisette, and absinthe, this smart little shop offers a dizzying range, but to really savor these unique delights, sign up online for one of the 90-minute tastings. ✉ 108 quai du Port, Vieux Port

☎ 04–91–90–86–77 ⊕ www.lamaisondupastis.com Ⓜ Vieux Port.

Saladin Épices du Monde

FOOD/CANDY | A veritable Ali Baba's cave in the heart of the souklike Arab market, this colorful shop is stuffed to the brim with eye-popping mounds of dried fruit and nuts, exotic condiments, grains, and every spice under the sun. ✉ 10 rue Longue des Capucins, Noailles ☎ 04–91–33–22–76 ⊕ www.saladin-epicesdu-monde.fr Ⓜ Noailles.

GIFTS AND CRAFTS

★ Chez Laurette

CLOTHING | Ex-fashion designer Laure Traverso (Marc Jacobs, Paul & Joe) escaped the Paris treadmill to open her own wildly creative concept store that spotlights all things French, sustainable and ethical, design-conscious, and just plain cool. Discoveries abound—look for chic emerging fashion labels, beautiful leather and straw bags, shoes, belts, avant-garde jewelry, lingerie, handmade home furnishings, organic cosmetics made in Provence, and a grocery corner featuring such local delicacies as micro-brew beers, chocolates, and teas. ✉ 16 rue Edmond Rostand ☎ 04–88–04–31–70 ⊕ chez-laurette.com.

Fragonard

PERFUME/COSMETICS | Since 1926, the Riviera-based perfumer has been bottling the sun, sea, and all the luscious scents of Provence in colorful vials. Its popular fragrances—orange flower, rose-lavender, verveine, jasmine, vetiver, the signature Coeur du Soleil, and so many more—come in perfumes, candles, soaps, shower gels, and home fragrances. You'll also find gifts and stylish Mediterranean clothing and other fashion accessories. ✉ Boulevard Jacques Saade ☎ 04–91–45–35–25 ⊕ www.fragonard.com/fr/boutique/marseille.

★ Herboristerie Père Blaize

SPECIALTY STORES | This popular shop has been mixing herbal treatments on the same premises since 1805. At the *laboratoire* ,trained herbalists mix your personalized concoction from drawers and jars stuffed full of dried local and exotic herbs, as well as plant extracts, for whatever ails you—from sleep issues to digestive ailments. At the contemporary tearoom across the street, you can sip an infusion and purchase a range of packaged herbal teas, loose herbs, spices, coffee, honey, beauty products, books, and traditional candies. ⊠ *4–6 rue Meolan et du Père Blaize, Noailles* ☎ *04–22–67–80–11* ⊕ *www.pereblaize.fr* Ⓜ *Canabière Capucins, Vieux Port.*

★ Maison Empereur

LOCAL SPECIALTIES | If Made in France sounds good to you, this 190-year-old Marseille institution is your dream come true. A treasure trove of all things French, from housewares, linens, knives and kitchenware, tableware, and hardware to huge cotton scarves, towels, timeless French perfumes, espadrilles, classic toys, and the real Savon de Marseille. The main store is home to all of the above, but there's also a clothing shop across the street (8 rue des Recolettes) with irresistible items for women, men, and kids, including wool or sheepskin slippers, rakish straw hats, cashmere capes and caps, chunky wool sweaters, and classic French cotton work shirts. ⊠ *4 rue des Récolettes* ☎ *04–91–54–02–29* ⊕ *empereur.fr.*

Savonnerie Marseillaise Licorne

PERFUME/COSMETICS | One of Marseille's oldest traditional manufacturers sells fragrant savon in blocks, ovals, or fanciful shapes. This soap maker uses the highest olive oil content possible (72%) in the soaps, and only natural essential oils from Provence for the fragrances. Call ahead for a guided tour (in English) of this atmospheric factory—a great way to see the whole process done on traditional machines. ⊠ *34 cours Julien, Cours Julien* ☎ *04–96–12–00–91* ⊕ *www.*

savon-de-marseille-licorne.com Ⓜ *Notre Dame du Mont.*

SHOPPING CENTERS AND MALLS
Les Docks Village

SHOPPING CENTERS/MALLS | Part of a complex of three quayside shopping centers central to the restoration of Marseille's up-and-coming Joliette neighborhood, Les Docks Village comprises six massive shipping warehouses, each restored by a notable architect, to create a stylish, upbeat business and shopping hub. All one-of-a-kind, the shops range from high-end clothes and accessories to beauty, jewelry, sporting goods, housewares, and art galleries, all with a focus on great design. You'll also find picturesque cafés and restaurants, several with outdoor terraces. ⊠ *10 pl. de la Joliette* ⊕ *www. lesdocks-marseille.com* Ⓜ *Joliette.*

Les Terrasses du Port

SHOPPING CENTERS/MALLS | This is the most commercial of a trio of shopping centers along the restored harborfront in the Joliette neighborhood. A three-floor modern glass-and-steel complex, it houses 160 of the best-loved French boutique chains (Petit Bâteau, Comptoir des Cotonniers, and the Marseille-based American Vintage included) for women, men, and kids, along with jewelry, housewares, and a branch of Le Printemps department store. There's also a fine mix of cafés and a fabulous rooftop terrace with stunning views over the harbor, where you can have a drink or meal while watching the cruise ships sail off to Corsica. ⊠ *9 quai du Lazaret* ☎ *04–88–91–46–00* ⊕ *www. lesterrassesduport.com* Ⓜ *Joliette.*

Les Voutes

SHOPPING CENTERS/MALLS | Under these graceful vaulted arches, built in the 1850s as part of the Sainte Marie de la Major cathedral, you'll find some lovely shops and cafés, including the design giant Habitat; French perfumer Fragonard; and chocolatier L'Espérantine, specializing in chocolates made with olive oil. The superb Les Halles de la

Major gourmet food court has a tempting variety of foods for snacks, meals, coffee breaks or drinks, to eat indoors or on the wide outdoor terrace with superb views of the J4 Pier and the harbor. Details of the weekly program of arts events can be found on the website. ✉ *Quai de la Tourette* ⊕ *www.lesvoutesdelamajor.com* Ⓜ *Joliette.*

Aubagne

15 km (9 miles) east of Marseille; 10 km (6 miles) north of Cassis.

This easygoing, plane tree–shaded market town (pronounced "oh- *bahn-yuh*") is proud of its native son, the dramatist, filmmaker, and chronicler of all things Provençal, Marcel Pagnol, best known to Anglophones as author of *Jean de Florette, Fanny,* and *Manon des Sources* (*Manon of the Springs*). Here you can spend the morning exploring the animated market or digging through used Pagnol books and collectibles in the Old Town. Make sure you visit Aubagne on a market day (Tuesday, Thursday, Saturday, or Sunday), when the sleepy center is transformed into a tableau of Provençal life. The Tuesday market is the biggest, where you're sure to find santon figurines, as Aubagne claims the title of santon capital of Provence.

GETTING HERE AND AROUND

Trains run every 20–30 minutes between Marseille and Aubagne (€4.30, 20 minutes). By bus, Le Pilote's No. 240 runs from Marseille every 20–30 minutes (€2.40, 30 minutes). By car, take the A50 from Marseille to Exit 6 on the A501.

BUS CONTACTS Le Pilote. ☎ *08–00–71–31–37* ⊕ *www.lepilote.com.*

TOURS

If you don't want to hike the 12-km (7-mile) or 20-km (12-mile) loop through the garrigues (scrubland) above Aubagne, there's a bus tour of Marcel Pagnol

landmarks that leaves from the tourist office. It takes place in July and August on Wednesday at 3; the cost is €12. Request an English-speaking guide in advance.

VISITOR INFORMATION

CONTACTS Aubagne Tourist Office. ✉ *8 cours Barthélémy* ☎ *04–42–03–49–98* ⊕ *www.tourisme-paysdaubagne.fr.*

 Sights

Ateliers Thérèse Neveu

MUSEUM | The history of the craft of santon-making and other uses to which the local clay was put—faience and hand-painted tiles—can be studied at the Ateliers Thérèse Neveu, named for Aubagne's first master *santonière* (santon maker). Also on display are excellent temporary exhibitions about pottery. ✉ *4 cour de Clastre, at top of Old Town hill* ☎ *04–42–03–43–10* ≦ *Free* ⊗ *Closed Mon.*

Circuit Pagnol

TRAIL | Even if you haven't read Pagnol's works or seen his films, you can enjoy the Circuit Pagnol, a series of hikes (some up to 20 km [12 miles] long) in the raw-hewn, arid *garrigues* (scrublands) behind Marseille and Aubagne. Here Pagnol spent his idyllic summers, described in his *Souvenirs d'un Enfance* (*Memories of a Childhood*), crunching through the rosemary, thyme, and scrub oak at the foot of his beloved Garlaban. When he grew up to be a famous playwright and filmmaker, he shot some of his best work in these hills, casting his wife, Jacqueline, as the first Manon of the Springs. After Pagnol's death, Claude Berri came back to the Garlaban to find a location for his remake of *Manon des Sources,* but found it so altered by brush fires and power cables that he chose to shoot farther east instead, around Cuges-les-Pine and Riboux. (The lovely village and Manon's well were filmed in Mirabeau, in the Luberon.) Although the trails

Thanks to its rich soil, Aubagne is a center of master potters and santon artists, many of whom show their wares in the town's marketplace and ceramic festivals.

may no longer shelter the pine-shaded olive orchards of its past, it still gives you the chance to walk through primeval Provençal countryside and rewards you with spectacular views of Marseille and the sea. To access the marked trails by yourself, drive to La Treille northeast of Aubagne and follow the signs. For detailed maps or an accompanied tour with literary commentary, contact the Office du Tourisme. ⊠ *Aubagne.*

Farmers' Market

MARKET | Aubagne on a market day is a feast in more ways than one. Depending on the season, for sale are fresh local asparagus, vine-ripened tomatoes and melons, and mesclun scooped by the gnarled fingers of blue-aproned ladies in from the farm (Tuesday, Thursday, and weekends 8–1:30). The weekend markets make more of regional products; those labeled Pays d'Aubagne must be organically raised. You won't find the social scene you'll see in Aix, but this is a more authentic farmers' market. ⊠ *Cours Voltaire.*

Le Petit Monde de Marcel Pagnol (*The Small World of Marcel Pagnol*)

MUSEUM | You can study miniature dioramas of scenes from Pagnol stories here. The characters are all santons, including superb portraits of a humpback Gerard Départieu and Yves Montand, resplendent in moustache, fedora, and velvet vest, just as they were featured in *Jean de Florette*. ⊠ *Esplanade de Gaulle* 🎫 *Free.*

Musée de la Légion Étrangère (*Museum of the Foreign Legion*)

MILITARY SITE | Another claim to fame for Aubagne: it's the headquarters for the French Foreign Legion. The legion was created in 1831, and accepts recruits from all nations, no questions asked. The discipline and camaraderie instilled among its motley team of adventurers, criminals, and mercenaries have helped the legion forge a reputation for exceptional valor—a reputation romanticized by songs and films in which sweaty deeds of heroism are performed under the desert sun. The Musée de la

Provençal Clay Figures

They beckon from shop windows in every hill town, these miniatures called *santons*, from the dialect *santouns* for "little saints." But whatever commercial role they may play today, their roots run deep in Provence.

The Christmas crèche has been a part of Provençal tradition since the Middle Ages, when people reenacted the tableau of the birth of Christ, wise men, shepherds, and all. When the Revolution cracked down on these pastoral plays, a Marseillais artisan decided to substitute clay actors. The terra-cotta figures created a new fashion and the santon craze was on.

A Marseille tradition that eventually migrated to Aubagne in the hills above (where the clay was better), the delicate doll-like figurines spread throughout Provence, and are displayed every Christmas in church crèches that resemble a rustic backcountry hill village as much as they do Bethlehem. Against a miniature background of model stone houses, dried-moss olive groves, and glass creeks, quaint, familiar characters go about their daily tasks: the lumberjack hauling matchstick kindling, the fisherman toting a basket of waxy fish, the red-cheeked town drunk leering drolly at the pretty lavender-cutter whose basket hangs heavy with real dried sprigs. The original cast from Bethlehem gets second billing to a charming crowd of Gypsies, goatherds, and provincial passersby. And these days there are plenty of Gérard Depardieus, Carla Bruni-Sarkozys, and Yves Montands.

It's a highly competitive craft, and while artisans vie for the souvenir trade, some have raised it to an art form. Molded, dried, then scraped with sharp tools down to the finest detail—wrinkled foreheads and fingernails—the santons are baked at 1,000°C (1,832°F). Once cool, they are painted with a watchmaker's precision: eyelashes, nostrils, and gnarled knuckles. The larger ones have articulated limbs to allow for dressing; their hand-sewn costumes, Barbie-scaled, are lavished with as much fine detail as the painted features.

Many artisans maintain highly public studios, so you can shop direct. Little santons (about an inch high), without articulated limbs, run about €12; big ones (8–10 inches), dressed and painted by the best artists, cost around €50.

But the preferred format is the crèche tableau, and it's easy to get hooked on building a collection of Provençal rustics to be lovingly unwrapped and displayed every Christmas season.

Légion Étrangère does its best to polish the image by way of medals, uniforms, weapons, and photographs. ✉ *Caserne Viénot* ✥ *Coming from Marseille, take left off D2 onto D44A just before Aubagne* ☎ *04–42–18–12–41* 🎫 *Free* ⏲ *Closed Mon.*

Hotels

Hostellerie de la Source
$ | **HOTEL** | Its suburban location, 4 km (2 miles) outside of Aubagne, makes this good-value hotel a nice option for travelers with a car. **Pros:** quiet and secluded; nice pool; decent restaurant. **Cons:** caters to conferences and large groups; gets crowded; decor a bit sparse. [$] *Rooms*

from: €105 ⊠ St-Pierre-des-Aubagne 🕾 04–42–04–09–19 ⊕ www.hostelleriedelasource.e-monsite.com ⇆ 28 rooms ❑ No meals.

★ La Magdeleine – Mathias Dandine

$$ | HOTEL | FAMILY | Since the gracious Michelin-star chef Mathias Dandine opened this idyllic country hotel and gastronomic restaurant on a leafy estate 5 km (3 miles) from Aubagne, it has quickly become one of the region's most coveted addresses among connoisseurs of the good life. **Pros:** exceptional price-to-quality ratio; total Provençal tranquillity; beautiful grounds, including gardens and pool. **Cons:** no spa; ample parking space is uncovered; no nightlife apart from fine dining restaurant. $ Rooms from: €165 ⊠ 40 av. du 2ème Cuirassier 🕾 04–42–32–20–16 ⊕ relais-magdeleine.com ⇆ 28 rooms ❑ No meals.

Cassis

30 km (19 miles) southeast of Marseille; 10 km (6 miles) north of Aubagne.

Surrounded by vineyards, flanked by monumental cliffs, guarded by the ruins of a medieval castle, and nestled around a picture-perfect fishing port, Cassis is the prettiest coastal town in Provence. Best known for its delicate white wines and wild Calanques, it is a quiet fishing village out of season and inundated with sun-worshippers in the summer. The pastel houses at rakish angles framing the port and harbor attracted early 20th-century artists including Dufy and Matisse. Even the mild rash of parking-garage architecture in the outer neighborhoods can't spoil the effect of unadulterated charm.

Stylish without being too recherché, Cassis's picture-perfect harbor is in the shadow of the ruddy Cap Canaille, Europe's highest sea cliff and provides shelter to numerous pleasure-boaters. Sailors can restock their galleys at its market,

replenish their Saint James nautical duds in its boutiques, and relax with a bottle of local wine and a platter of sea urchins in one of its numerous waterfront cafés.

GETTING HERE AND AROUND

By car, leave the A50 from Marseille or Toulon and take Exit 8 for Cassis. The D559 from Marseille to Cassis is dramatically beautiful, continuing along the coast to Toulon, but it might be too curvy for motion-sickness sufferers.

Hourly trains between Marseille and Toulon stop at Cassis, but the station is about 3 km (2 miles) from the center. From the station, there is a local shuttle to the town center that runs at least once an hour. There is also the M06 Marseille–Cassis bus, which takes an hour.

TOURS

La Visite des Calanques

BOAT TOURS | This company offers several boat tours of the Calanques from the wooden kiosk at Quay St-Pierre, not far from the tourist office. A 45-minute, three-calanques tour runs every 45 minutes 10–4:30, February through April, October and November, and every 30 minutes 9:30–6, May through September. Longer explorations last from just over an hour to nearly two hours and cover up to nine scenic inlets. Tickets must be purchased (at the kiosk) at least 30 minutes in advance; larger groups of 15 or more can reserve ahead. ⊠ Quai St-Pierre 🕾 04–42–01–03–31 ⊕ www.lavisitedescalanques.com ⚓ From €16.

VISITOR INFORMATION

CONTACTS Cassis Tourist Office. ⊠ Quai des Moulins 🕾 08–92–39–01–03 ⊕ www.ot-cassis.com.

Sights

Calanques

BODY OF WATER | Touring the Calanques, whose fjordlike finger bays probe the rocky coastline, is a must. Either take a sightseeing cruise in a boat that dips into each Calanque in turn (tickets, sold at the eastern end of the port, are €16–€28, depending on how many Calanques you see) or hike across the cliff tops, clambering down the steep sides to these barely accessible retreats. One boat trip lets you swim in the turquoise waters under Cap Canaille, but that must be booked at the kiosk in the morning (four- to five departures per day, depending on the weather and water temperature). Of the Calanques closest to Cassis, **Port Miou** is the least attractive. It is also the only one fully accessible by car, but only in winter. It was a *pierre de Cassis* (Cassis stone) quarry until 1982 when the Calanques became protected sites, and now has an active leisure and fishing port. **Calanque Port Pin** is prettier, with wind-twisted pines growing at angles from white-rock cliffs. But with its tiny beach and jagged cliffs looming overhead, covered with gnarled pine and scrub and its rock spur known to climbers as the "finger of God," **Calanque En Vau**, reachable via a challenging two-hour hike both there and back (or your own private boat), is a small piece of paradise.

Château de Cassis

CASTLE/PALACE | This imposing castle has loomed over the harbor since the invasions of the Saracens in the 7th century, evolving over time into a walled enclosure crowned with stout watchtowers. It's private property today and best viewed from a sunny portside terrace. ⊠ *Cassis.*

Clos Sainte Magdeleine

WINERY/DISTILLERY | If you're a wine lover, pick up a "Through the Vineyards" brochure from the tourist office. There are 12 domaines open for tasting and buying, but the most spectacularly sited is the Clos Sainte Magdeleine set on the slopes of towering Cap Canaille. This four-generation AOC winery is noted for its delicately balanced whites and an elegant rosé. One-hour guided tours of the estate in English are offered twice a day from April to September, with a tasting at the end (€12, book through the tourist office ⊕ www.ot-cassis.com). ⊠ *Av. du Revestel* ☎ *04–42–01–70–28* ⊕ *www.clossaintemagdeleine.fr.*

🍴 Restaurants

⭐ La Villa Madie

$$$$ | FRENCH | Chef Dimitri Droisneau may profess his cuisine to be humble, but his two–Michelin star restaurant merits a change out of your beach-wear (closed-toe shoes are required). Droisneau and his wife, Marielle, run the restaurant and offer standouts like delicately grilled Mediterranean rouget with almonds and fennel and drizzled lightly with an urchin-and-saffron sauce. **Known for:** a top choice in the region; brilliant seafood dishes; huge wine list. $ *Average main: €75* ⊠ *Av. de Revestrel-anse de Corton* ☎ *04–96–18–00–00* ⊕ *www.lavillamadie.com* ⊗ *Closed Jan.–mid-Feb., Tues., and Wed.*

Le Chaudron

$$$ | BISTRO | Just off Cassis's picturesque port, locals and visitors alike flock to this off-the-beaten-tourist path and welcoming bistro and terrace serving classic Provençal meals on one of the town's charming backstreets. This being Cassis, fish is a mainstay on the menu; start with gratin of mussels followed by roasted John Dory with Provençal vegetables, or spicy fish soup, all to be savored with the local Cassis wines. **Known for:** top-notch bistro fare with a Mediterranean twist; fresh catch of the day; family-run since 1970. $ *Average main: €27* ⊠ *4 rue Adolphe Thiers* ☎ *04–42–01–74–18* ⊗ *Closed Tues. and mid-Dec.–Mar. No lunch.*

🛏 Hotels

⭐ Les Roches Blanches

$$$$ | HOTEL | Featuring views of the port and the Cap Canaille, both from the best rooms and from the panoramic dining room, this exquisite cliff-side villa has

With its enchanting harbor and cliffside setting, Cassis beautifully reminds us why so many artists have flocked to the Mediterranean.

shed its former Art Deco–style decor for a spiffy contemporary look. **Pros:** sweeping vistas are captivating; beautiful pools and spa; most rooms have balconies. **Cons:** hard to find (use your GPS); breakfast is expensive; in-room dining could be better. [$] *Rooms from: €360* ✉ *Rte. des Calanques* ☎ *04–42–01–09–30* 🌐 *www.roches-blanches-cassis.com* 🕒 *Closed Nov.–Mar.* 🛏 *24 rooms* 🍴 *No meals.*

Activities

Cassis Calanques Plongée
DIVING/SNORKELING | The Calanques offer some of the best diving in France. Weather permitting, there are spectacular cave dives daily to view brightly colored coral and abundant fish. ☎ *06–71–52–60–20* 🌐 *www.cassis-calanques-plongee.com* 🕒 *Closed mid-Nov.–mid-Mar.*

Ecoloc
BOATING | If you don't feel up to a rugged hike to the Calanques, you can hire a semi-rigid boat here for a half or full day with or without a license. ✉ *Pl. du Grand Carnot Quai J.J* ☎ *04–28–70–55–99* 🌐 *www.ecoloc-cassis.fr.*

Narval Plongée
DIVING/SNORKELING | Fabienne Henry leads divers to the Cassidaigne lighthouse, Riou archipelago, and the Calanques. Underwater photography courses are offered to individuals or groups. First-time divers and children are welcome. ✉ *11 av. de la Viguerie* ☎ *04–42–01–87–59* 🌐 *www.narval-plongee.com.*

Bandol

25 km (16 miles) southeast of Cassis; 15 km (9 miles) west of Toulon.

Although its name means wine to most of the world, Bandol is also a popular and highly developed seaside resort town. In the 1920s, the glamorous social life of the Riviera stretched this far west, and grand seaside mansions rivaled Cap d'Antibes and Juan-les-Pins for high society and literati. Today its old port is a massive gray parking lot and the Old

Touring the Calanques

To hike the Calanques, gauge your skills: the GR98 (marked with red-and-white bands) is the most scenic route, but requires ambitious scrambling to get down the sheer walls of En Vau; make sure to stay on approved paths. The alternative is to follow the red markers and approach En Vau from behind. If you're ambitious, you can hike the length of the GR98 between Marseille and Cassis, following the coastline, a distance of roughly 30 km (18 miles). Remember, access in the Calanques is restricted and can be prohibited anytime due to high winds and fire risk. To check weather conditions, call ☎ 08–11–20–13–13. Information for the next day is available by 6 pm the evening before.

To go on a boat ride to Les Calanques, get to the port around 10 am or 2 pm and look for a boat that's loading passengers. Two of the best choices are the *Notos II* and the *Moby Dick III*—they have huge windows and full commentary in English. But a slew of alternative boats won't leave you stranded. Round trips should include at least three calanques and average €21.

Town that fronts the quays is lined with seafood snack shops, generic brasseries, and palm trees. Yet westward, toward the Baie de Renecros, are some of the Belle Époque houses that once made Bandol famous. In high season the harbor is filled with yachts, and the waterfront promenade is packed with summer tourist crowds. A portside stroll up the palm-lined Allée Jean Moulin feels downright Côte d'Azur. If you're not a beach lover, pick up an itinerary from the tourist office and visit a few Bandol vineyards just outside of town. After a stroll through Bandol itself, most visitors head to the outskirts to discover several sights around the town that are worth exploring.

GETTING HERE AND AROUND

Trains run between Marseille and Bandol every 30 minutes (€10, 45 minutes). By car, take the A50 towards Toulon to Exit 12.

VISITOR INFORMATION

CONTACTS Bandol Tourist Office. ⊠ *Pavillon du Tourisme, Allée Alfred Vivien* ☎ *04–94–29–41–35* ⊕ *www.bandoltourisme.fr.*

Sights

Cap Sicié

VIEWPOINT | Head south on the D16 to the D2816 around the cap for a tremendous view across the Bay of Toulon.

Gorge d'Ollioules

NATURE SITE | Head north on D11 to Ollioules; just past the village, follow N8 (in the direction of Le Beausset) through a 5-km (3-mile) route that twists its scenic way beneath the awesome chalky rock faces of the Gorge d'Ollioules. ⊠ *Bandol.*

Île de Bendor

ISLAND | Boats leave every half hour to make the 2-km (1.2-mile) trip to Île de Bendor. The island was only a large rock until pastis magnate Paul Ricard bought it in the 1950s and tastefully transformed it into a tourist center with fine beaches, charming cottage shops, an "espace Ricard" showing Paul Ricard's lifetime works, and the Museum of Wine and Spirits. Although the island restaurants offer a surprisingly wide selection, sunny days and scenic views make for a lovely picnic. ⊠ *Bandol* ⊕ *www.lesilespaulricard.com.*

Le Castellet

TOWN | On the D559 perched high above the Bandol vineyards, the village of Le Castellet has narrow streets, 17th-century stone houses, and (alas!) touristy shops designed for beach lovers on a rainy day. ⊠ *Bandol.*

Le Gros Cerveau

SCENIC DRIVE | For some spectacular views, on the D20 take a left at Ollioules and follow the winding road along the crest of Le Gros Cerveau. You'll be rewarded first with inland mountain views, then an expansive panorama of the coastline. ⊠ *Bandol.*

Notre-Dame de Pépiole

RELIGIOUS SITE | Just east of Bandol on the D559, past the smaller resort of Sanary, as you turn left onto the D63 you'll see signs pointing to the small stone chapel of Notre-Dame de Pépiole. It's hemmed in by pines and cypresses and is one of the oldest Christian buildings in France, dating to the 6th century and modeled on early churches in the Middle East. The simple interior has survived the years in remarkably good shape, although the colorful stained glass that fills the tiny windows is modern—composed mainly of broken bottles. ⊠ *Bandol.*

Zoa Parc Animalier et Exotique Sanary-Bandol (*Sanary Bandol's Exotic Garden and Zoo*)

ZOO | **FAMILY** | Three kilometers (2 miles) north of Bandol via the D559 is this zoo and garden, where cacti and hundreds of exotic tropical plants grow to remarkable sizes. In a small zoo setting, animals such as flamingos, gibbons, and gazelles frolic in shady gardens. ⊠ *131 av. Pont d'Aran, Sanary-sur-Mer* ✛ *Exit Bandol from A8, take first right (direction Rte. de Beausset) and follow signs to zoo* ☎ *04–94–29–40–38* ⊕ *www.zoaparc.com* ☑ *€12.*

🍴 Restaurants

René & Jean-François Bérard

$$$$ | **MODERN FRENCH** | Chef Jean-François has taken the reins from his illustrious father, René (who consults on the menu), but the Mediterranean-inspired Provençal cuisine that put this restaurant on the map is as scrumptious as ever, emphasizing local seafood and fresh produce straight from the hotel-restaurant's kitchen garden. Try the ravioli stuffed with goat cheese, sorrel, and Parmesan in a lemon chicken broth; the lightly grilled red mullet wrapped in seaweed and topped with peas and fresh rosemary is another winner. **Known for:** good-value set menus; Michelin starred cuisine; lovely setting. Ⓢ *Average main: €53* ⊠ *Hostellerie Bérard, 7 rue Gabriel-Péri, La Cadière-d'Azur* ☎ *04–94–90–11–43* 🖃 *No credit cards* 🕑 *Closed Mon. and Tues. mid-Sept.–mid-July. No lunch Sat.–Tues.*

🛏 Hotels

Hostellerie Bérard

$$ | **HOTEL** | Master Chef René Bérard is as celebrated for his haute cuisine as he is for his elegant country inn with breathtaking views of the countryside and everything required for a pampered weekend on the hotel premises. **Pros:** although a little off the beaten track, the lovely welcome is refreshing; delicious food including a more casual alternative to the elegant gourmet restaurant; charming village setting. **Cons:** it's easy to get lost in the hotel's sprawling hallways; decor in common spaces outdated; breakfast expensive. Ⓢ *Rooms from: €145* ⊠ *7 rue Gabriel-Péri, 6 km (4 miles) north of Bandol, La Cadière-d'Azur* ☎ *04–94–90–11–43* ⊕ *www.hotel-berard.com* 🕑 *Closed Jan.–mid-Feb.* 🛏 *40 rooms* 🍴 *No meals.*

Hôtel Île Rousse Thalazur

$$$ | **HOTEL** | A view straight over the saltwater infinity pool to the (private) beach and sea beyond greets you at this luxury hotel-spa two steps from Bandol's port. **Pros:** excellent on-site restaurant; lovely saltwater pool; nice sea views from the rooms. **Cons:** spa closes on the early side; extras are expensive; decor lacks character. [$] *Rooms from: €250* ✉ *25 bd. Louis Lumière* ☎ *04–94–29–33–00* 🌐 *www.ile-rousse.com* 🛏 *67 rooms* 🍴 *No meals.*

Toulon

38 km (24 miles) southeast of Cassis; 67 km (42 miles) east of Marseille.

Toulon is a city of contrasts: crowded with unsightly postwar high-rises yet surprisingly beautiful with its tree-lined littoral; a place with some unappealing nightlife, and yet, by day, charming and colorful with its restaurant scene. Best known for the day in World War II when 75 French ships were deliberately sunk to avoid them falling into the hands of attacking Germans, Toulon has kept its place as France's leading naval port with a kind of dogged determination. Though Toulon looks much like any modern French city, the **Vieille Ville** (Old Town) and port area have well-kept cafés and a sunny waterfront where yachts and pleasure boats—some available for trips to the Îles d'Hyères, around the bay, or to Corsica and Sardinia—add bright splashes of color. In the heart of Toulon's Old Town, the maze of streets is packed with hip boutiques, quirkily appealing stretches of newly renovated medieval and Renaissance houses, and the beautifully restored Les Halles market, set in a chic Art Deco building jammed with local produce and delicacies. Park your car under Place de la Liberté and take Boulevard de Strasbourg, turning right onto Rue Berthelot, which leads into the heart of the pedestrian-only streets of the Vieille Ville. Wander through Place des Trois Dauphins, with its mossy and fern-lined fountain, or stop in the café-filled Place Puget; Victor Hugo lived in No. 5 when he was researching *Les Misérables.* One block east, the Cours Lafayette becomes a wonderfully animated, authentic Provençal morning market (Tuesday–Sunday), and the Hôtel de Ville has evocative baroque figures, carved by the Marseillais sculptor Pierre Puget.

When in Toulon, you have to take a trip to the Mémorial du Débarquement de Provence via a vertiginous six-minute cable car ride up Mont Faron for thrilling 360-degree views of the Riviera and Toulon Bay; you'll also get an equally riveting account of the French and Allied forces attack on the waterfront against the German occupiers on August 15, 1944.

GETTING HERE AND AROUND

Toulon is on the main TGV line from Paris (around 3 hours 50 minutes; €35–€126, depending on when you go and the type of ticket) and is served by regional and local trains from Marseille and Nice, so it is easy to navigate your way on the system.

By car, take the A50 from Marseille in the west and if you are coming from the east, the A57. The coastal D559 goes between Marseille and Toulon via Bandol.

Once in Toulon, there is a great network of inner-city buses run by the RMTT. Bus No. 23 goes to the beaches at Mourillon, No. 40 to the cable car.

BUS CONTACTS RMTT. ☎ *04–94–03–87–03* 🌐 *www.reseaumistral.com.*

VISITOR INFORMATION

CONTACTS Toulon Tourist Office. ✉ *12 pl. Louis Blanc* ☎ *04–94–18–53–00* 🌐 *www.toulontourisme.com.*

Sights

Brignoles

TOWN | Although it's known as the market center for the wines of the Var, Brignoles's largest attraction is still the Abbaye de la Celle, a 12th-century Benedictine abbey that served as a convent until the 17th century. The abbey was abandoned until Maria Fournier, owner of the Iles of Porquerolles, decided to open it as a hotel in 1945. Despite its sudden rise in status with the likes of Charles de Gaulle vacationing here, the town continued to resist change firmly. In fact, the simple Romanesque chapel housing a 14th-century Christ figure largely acclaimed as an anonymous masterpiece still serves today as the parish church. It's here in this historic spot that celebrated chef Alain Ducasse has his culinary hideaway, Hostellerie de l'Abbaye de La Celle. ⊠ 45 km (28 miles) north of Toulon, Brignoles.

★ Mémorial du Débarquement de Provence
MUSEUM | This museum is located on the site of a crucial fort perched at the summit of Mont Faron and recounts the planning and execution of World War II's Operation Dragoon, a mission meant to resecure the French ports of Marseille and Toulon and cut off German reinforcements. The story unfolds via firsthand accounts in French and English from men and women who fought for the French Resistance, descriptions of life under the occupation, a detailed timeline, and an 11-minute film showing original footage of the August 15, 1944, invasion—and its vast destruction—which was a decisive turning point in the war. ⊠ 8488 Rte. du Faron ☎ 04–94–88–08–09 ⊕ www.toulon.fr/envie-bouger/article/memorial-debarquement-de-provence.

Mont Faron
MEMORIAL | Rising 1,900 feet above the town, with panoramic views over Toulon, the surrounding countryside, and the sea, Mont Faron can be reached by the circular Route du Faron in either direction or in six minutes by cable car from Boulevard Admiral Jean-Vence. At the top, the World War II memorial commemorates the mountain fort's vital role in the Provence débarquement of August 1944 and the liberation of Toulon. There is also a zoo that acts as a breeding center for a dozen types of wild cats, including

lions, tigers, jaguars, lynxes, and pumas. ⊠ Toulon ☎ 04–94–92–68–25 for téléphérique ⊕ www.telepherique-faron.fr ⊠ Téléphérique €8 round-trip, zoo €16.

Musée d'Art
MUSEUM | The collection here includes paintings by Vernet and Fragonard as well as postwar abstract art and the cartoon-influenced Di Rosa brothers. ⊠ 113 bd. Maréchal Leclerc ☎ 04–94–36–81–01 ⊕ www.toulon.fr ⊠ Free ⊘ Closed Mon.

Musée National de la Marine (Naval Museum)
MUSEUM | Part of a network of marine museums around France, the Toulon branch of the Musée National de la Marine, lodged in the graceful 18th-century section of the Toulon arsenal, is particularly fascinating considering the rich maritime history of this part of the Mediterranean. The history comes alive through a collection of model ships, paintings, mastheads, and a pictorial history of the city's role in World War II. ⊠ Pl. Monsenergue ☎ 04–22–42–02–01 ⊕ www.musee-marine.fr/toulon ⊠ €7 ⊘ Closed Tues.

Opera de Toulon
ARTS VENUE | At Place Victor Hugo, the Opera de Toulon hosts theater, opera, and dance productions. ⊠ Bd. de Strasbourg ☎ 04–94–92–70–78 ⊕ www.operadetoulon.fr.

 Restaurants

Le Gros Ventre
$$$ | FRENCH | In a cozy and romantic space enhanced by soft lighting and tables set at discreet distances from each other, you can enjoy some of the best Provençal cooking in Toulon. Specializing in seafood and beef, the fish is caught daily by Toulon fishermen and you can taste locally farmed oysters and clams. **Known for:** views of the sea and Fort St. Louis; good value fixed-price menus; favorite with the locals. $ Average main: €28 ⊠ 297 Littoral F. Mistral

From Cassis, be sure to take an excursion boat to the Calanques, the rocky finger-coves washed by emerald and blue waters.

☎ 04–94–42–15–42 ⊕ www.legrosventre. fr ⊙ Closed Mon. No lunch Sat.

Le Lido de Toulon

$$ | **SEAFOOD** | Set right on the Mourillon beach—one of the nicest in Toulon— diners can sit at tables on the spacious wooden deck or directly on the sand, with pretty views of the bay and the old fort. This is Toulon's answer to the classic brasserie, serving copious platters of fresh seafood, an excellent fish soup, and the local catch of the day, along with more hefty French classics (Charolais beef, truffle risotto, foie gras). **Known for:** very good seafood, both raw and cooked; open seven days; beachside dining. $ Average main: €21 ✉ Corniche Frédéric Mistral, Plage du Mourillon ☎ 04–94–03– 38–18 ⊕ Corniche Frédéric Mistral, Plage du Mourillon.

Coffee and Quick Bites

Blackwood Café

$ | **CAFÉ** | Part of the Rue des Arts project to renew the Toulon Vielle Ville, this is the best place in town for a homemade snack and a great cup of coffee made by a seasoned barista. **Known for:** carefully sourced coffee; laid-back vibe; extremely reasonable prices. $ Average main: €3 ✉ 3 rue Nicolas Laugier ⊕ www. ruedesarts.fr/blackwood ⊙ Closed Sun. and Mon.

🛏 Hotels

Grand Hotel des Sablettes Plage

$$ | **HOTEL** | This historic Belle Époque hotel is set right on the sandy beach of Les Sablettes, part of the Saint-Mandrier- sur-Mer peninsula just across the harbor from Toulon. **Pros:** enormous garden terrace is great for breakfast or a drink; two very good in-hotel restaurants; beach access and an on-site pool. **Cons:** pool is small for this size hotel; restaurants book up quickly in high season; rooms vary drastically in size. $ Rooms from: €150 ✉ 575 av. Charles de Gaulle ☎ 04–94– 17–00–00 ⊕ www.ghsplage.com ⇗ 79 rooms ⊘ No meals.

★ **Hostellerie de l'Abbaye de La Celle**
$$$ | **HOTEL** | Superchef Alain Ducasse put this beautifully restored 18th-century bastide on the map when he opened a restaurant here in the early 2000s; other draws include guest rooms that mix Louis XVI and regional accents, private gardens, and vineyard views. **Pros:** Michelin-starred eats; lovely views; true Provençal experience, with all the glamour minus the glitz. **Cons:** restaurant service can be spotty; expensive; no elevator in hotel (it is a historic monument). [$] *Rooms from: €250* ✉ *10 pl. du Général-de-Gaulle, La Celle* ☎ *04–98–05–14–14* 🌐 *www.abbaye-celle.com* 🕘 *Restaurant closed Tues. and Wed. mid-Oct.–mid-Apr and Jan.* 🛏 *10 rooms* 🍴 *No meals.*

Îles d'Hyères

32 km (20 miles) off coast south of Hyères; 29 km (18 miles) southeast of Toulon to ferry departure point.

Strung across the Bay of Hyères and spanning some 32 km (20 miles) is an archipelago of islands reminiscent of a set for a pirate movie. In fact, they have been featured in several, thanks not only to their wild and rocky coastline but also their real pirate history. In the 16th century the islands were seeded with convicts meant to work the land; they promptly ran amok, ambushing and sacking passing ships heading for Toulon. Today the pirates are long gone, replaced by a thriving local population and tourists.

The islands consist of three main bodies: Levant, Port-Cros, and Porquerolles. Eight percent of **Levant** is military property and is kept strictly guarded with barbed-wire fences. The remaining area, Héliopolis, is a nudist colony, where you're welcome if you want to participate, as opposed to simply being curious. **Port-Cros** is a magnificent national park with no cars, no smoking, and no dogs. You can hike on pine-scented trails with spectacular views, or follow the underwater path, snorkeling or diving with aquatic life representative of the Mediterranean. **Porquerolles** (pronounced "pork-uh- *rohl*") is the largest and most popular escape from the modern world. The village of Porquerolles was originally used as a retirement colony for Napoleonic officers (the Fort du Petit-Langoustier and the Fort Ste-Agathe, although no longer active, still loom imposingly over the marina), which explains its remarkable resemblance to a military outpost. At the turn of the 20th century a Belgian engineer named François-Joseph Fournier made a killing in the Panama Canal, then bought Porquerolles at auction as a gift for his new bride. It was only in 1970 that France nationalized the island, leaving Fournier's widow with a quarter of her original inheritance; her granddaughter now helps run the luxurious Mas du Langoustier. Off-season it's a castaway idyll of pine forests, sandy beaches, and plunging cliffs over a rocky coastline. Inland, its preserved pine forests, vineyards, and orchards of olives and figs are crisscrossed with dirt roads to be explored on foot or, if you prefer, on bikes rented from one of the numerous rental outfits in both the port and village. In high season (April–October), day-trippers pour off the ferries, running for the beaches and soap boutiques, and T-shirt shops appear out of the woodwork to cater to vacationers' whims.

GETTING HERE AND AROUND

To get to the islands, follow the narrow Giens Peninsula to La Tour–Fondue at its tip. Ferries run from La Tour–Fondu in Giens (every 30 minutes in summer, every 60–90 minutes in winter; €19.50 round-trip) for the 20-minute trip to Porquerolles, and from Hyères at Hyères Plages to Port-Cros and Levant (€28.10–€31.50 round-trip). You can also get to all three islands from Port-de-Miramar or Le Lavandou (35- to 60-minute crossing, €31.50 round-trip).

VISITOR INFORMATION

CONTACTS Îles d'Hyères Tourist Office. ✉ *Rotonde du Park Hôtel, Av. de Belgique, Hyères* ☎ *04–94–01–84–50* 🌐 *www.hyeres-tourisme.com.*

Sights

★ Fondation Carmingnac

ART GALLERIES—ARTS | The Paris-based Carmignac Foundation has done nature-loving art lovers a great service at this stunning outpost offering a world-class art collection that would be right at home in London or New York. The foundation is housed in a meticulously renovated farmhouse, whose historic status required creating a 20,000-square-foot gallery space underground—the soaring daylit rooms are illuminated via a glass pool on the ground floor that doubles as a ceiling. Set on acres of gardens, vineyards, olive groves, and woods, visitors will discover dozens of site-specific works on a stroll through the property. Afterward, you can sip a glass of local wine at the on-site café. ✉ *Piste de la Courtade, Hyères* ☎ *04–65–65–25–50* 🌐 *www.fondationcarmignac.com.*

Hotels

Le Manoir de Port-Cros

$$ | RESORT | A mix of southern-coast bourgeois and Provençal touches adds a splash of color to the sunlit, airy rooms of this family-owned colonial-style hotel. **Pros:** a gentle touch of civilization in the isolated wilderness; lovely setting with enormous old eucalyptus trees; old-world elegance. **Cons:** some south-facing rooms are hot in summer; not open year-round; no Wi-Fi or TV in rooms. [$] *Rooms from: €220* ✉ *Île de Port-Cros, Hyères* ☎ *04–94–05–90–52* 🌐 *www.hotel-le-manoirportcros.com* 🕒 *Closed Oct.–Mar.* 🛏 *23 rooms* 🍴 *No meals.*

Mas du Langoustier

$$$$ | HOTEL | A fabled forgetaway, the Langoustier comes with a lobster-orange building, pink bougainvillea, a choice of California modern– or old Provençal–style guest rooms, and a secluded location at the westernmost point of the Ile de Porquerolles. **Pros:** a bastion of taste; one of the prettiest hotels on the island; beach nearby and on-site pool. **Cons:** a hike to get here; no rooms have a sea view; rooms could be brighter. [$] *Rooms from: €500* ✉ *Pointe du Langoustier, 3 km (2 miles) from harbor, Ile de Porquerolles* ☎ *04–94–58–30–09* 🌐 *www.langoustier.com* 🕒 *Closed Oct.–Apr.* 🛏 *49 rooms* 🍴 *All-inclusive.*

Villa Sainte Anne

$$ | HOTEL | This pleasant lodging in the heart of Porquerolles's main village, a five-minute walk from the ferry landing, offers clean, basic rooms with all the amenities. **Pros:** reasonably priced, especially in the off-season; very good on-site restaurants; nice location. **Cons:** there are no sea views; breakfasts are lackluster; rooms lack charm. [$] *Rooms from: €175* ✉ *Pl. d'Armes, Hyères* ☎ *04–98–04–63–00* 🌐 *www.sainteanne.com* 🕒 *Closed Dec.–Mar.* 🛏 *25 rooms* 🍴 *No meals.*

Activities

Centre Immersion Plongée

SCUBA DIVING | Here you can take a diving class, hire a guide, rent diving equipment, and refill scuba tanks. ✉ *Port Pothuau, 13 av. des Chalutiers, Hyères* ☎ *06–03–49–51–92* 🌐 *www.immersion-plongee.com.*

Cycle Porquerollais

BICYCLING | You can rent a mountain bike (*velo tout-terrain,* or VTT) for a day of pedaling the paths and clifftop trails of Porquerolles. ✉ *1 rue de la Ferme, Ile de Porquerolles* ☎ *04–94–58–30–32* 🌐 *www.velo-porquerolles.fr.*

Locamarine 75

BOATING | This shop rents motorboats to anyone interested, whether or not you have a license. ✉ *Port de Porquerolles, Ile de Porquerolles* ☎ *06–08–34–74–17* 🌐 *www.locamarine75.com.*

Chapter 6

THE WESTERN FRENCH RIVIERA

Updated by
Nancy Heslin

 Sights
★★★☆☆

 Restaurants
★★☆☆☆

 Hotels
★★★☆☆

 Shopping
★★☆☆☆

 Nightlife
★★☆☆☆

WELCOME TO
THE WESTERN FRENCH RIVIERA

TOP REASONS TO GO

★ **St-Tropez:** Brave the world's most outlandish fishing port in high summer and soak up the scene. Just don't forget the fake-tan lotion.

★ **Les Gorges du Verdon:** Peer down into its vertiginous green depths and you'll understand why this is one of the most dramatic natural sites in France.

★ **Moustiers-Ste-Marie:** Best known for its faience pottery, this town is also worth visiting for the sight of houses clinging to the cliffs—often with entrances on different levels.

★ **Château de la Napoule:** In Mandelieu-La-Napoule, discover the most bizarrely extravagant house of the coast—the gothic Château de la Napoule, festooned with tapestries, peacocks, and art students.

★ **The Estérel Corniche:** A mineral showcase, the Estérel coastline is sculpted of rock given to spectacular Technicolor displays of russet, garnet, and flaming orange.

1 **St-Tropez.** One of the most lively (and glitzy) stretches of the Riviera.

2 **Ramatuelle.** An ancient town with a thriving wine scene.

3 **Gassin.** A village with gorgeous views over St-Tropez's bay.

4 **Grimaud.** Home to a romantic castle.

5 **Port-Grimaud.** A modern version of a Provençal fishing village.

6 **Ste-Maxime.** One of the more affordable towns on the Riviera.

7 **Fréjus.** A rare unspoiled town.

8 **St-Raphaël.** A sprawling resort city with a rich port history.

9 **Mandelieu-La-Napoule.** Dual centers of golf and sailing in the region.

10 **Fayence.** The most touristy of the Haut Var hill towns.

11 **Seillans.** An inviting old-fashioned village.

12 **La Palud-sur-Verdon.** The central town of Gorges du Verdon, France's Grand Canyon.

13 **Moustiers-ste-Marie.** A striking cliffside village.

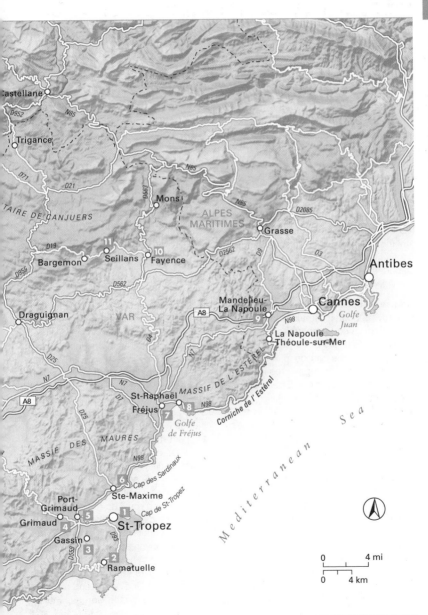

The Western Côte d'Azur can supply you with everything your heart desires (and your purse can withstand). Home to St-Tropez (or "St-Trop"—Saint Too Much—as the French call it), the region beckons to both backpackers and billionaires.

The former camp out on the stunning Estérel coast, the latter indulge in the mecca of hedonism, splashing out €1,000 a night for a room in the summer. Let's not forget the area is also home to remote hill villages colonized by artists, striking red-rock coves, and scenery gorgeous enough to steal center stage from Deborah Kerr in Hollywood's 1958 Riviera homage, *Bonjour Tristesse*.

For natural beauty the region can't be topped, although it remains less glamorous than its counterparts to the east. Above the coastline of the Var *département* (region), the horizon in all directions is dominated by the rugged red-rock heights of the Massif de l'Estérel and the green-black bulk of the Massif des Maures. Lovely azure waters lap at the foot of thriving resort towns—St-Tropez, of course, but also Fréjus, St-Raphaël, and Mandelieu-La-Napoule. But the biggest pull remains St-Tropez. The difficulty, however, is reaching this portion of the coast—the train only goes as far as St-Raphaël—so unless you're glitzy enough to arrive by helicopter, you'll have to join the crowds who crawl along in midsummer traffic jams, sweaty and miserable. You need to be a little masochistic to visit St-Tropez in August, but the town does have a few budget-friendly hotels and it sheds most of its pretension in

the off-season, becoming simply a small fishing port with very big yachts.

Neighboring resorts can't help but feel lower-key, providing stretches of sandy beach and guaranteed balmy temperatures to sun-starved northerners. Bored, sunburned, or regarding each other in mutual *snobbisme*, they then take to the hills—the glorious vineyard-lined, village-crowned hills that back the coast as the continent climbs gently toward the Alps and are home to some beautiful *villages perchés* (perched villages) and historic towns. These destinations make great day trips from the coast, though they're often dominated in high season by busloads of excursion-takers out of Cannes or St-Raphaël. But if you have a car and the time to explore, you can plunge even deeper into the backcountry, past the coastal plateau into the Haut Var. Here the harsh and beautiful countryside—raw rock, pine, and scrub oak—is lightly peppered with little hill villages that are almost boutique-free. Press on and you'll be rewarded with one of France's most spectacular natural wonders: the Gorges du Verdon, a Grand Canyon-style chasm roaring with milky-green water and edged by one of Europe's most hair-raising drives. Backpacks, hiking boots, and picnics are de rigueur around the Gorges, until you reach lovely Moustiers-Ste-Marie, an atmospheric center for faience (a type of ceramic), where you can treat yourself to a leisurely meal and take in the countryside views.

MAJOR REGIONS

St-Tropez and the Massif des Maures. Shielded from the mistral by the broad, forested mass of the Massif des Maures, this small expanse of pampered coastline is crowned by the sparkling lights of St-Tropez, itself doubly protected by the hills of the Paillas. A pretty pastel port in winter, in season it becomes glamorous "St-Trop," and *trop* in French means "too much," so you get the idea. For day trips you can escape to the simple life in the hill towns of Ramatuelle, Gassin, and Grimaud. Mere mortals—especially vacationing families on a budget—usually aim for Ste-Maxime across the bay, where the hyperdevelopment typical of the Riviera begins.

Fréjus, St-Raphaël, and the Estérel Corniche. Though the twin resorts of Fréjus and St-Raphaël have become somewhat overwhelmed by waterfront resort culture, Fréjus still harbors a small but charming enclave that evokes both the Roman and medieval periods. As you then follow the coast east, a massive red-rock wasteland, known as the Massif de l'Estérel, rears up high above the sparkling water. Formed of red volcanic rocks (porphyry) carved by the sea into dreamlike shapes, the harsh landscape is softened by patches of lavender, mimosa, scrub pine, and gorse. At the rocks' base churn azure waters, seething in and out of castaway coves, where a series of gentle resort bays punctuates the coastline. The D559 leads to one of the coast's most spectacular drives, the Corniche de l'Estérel. And if you take DN7, the mountain route to the north, you can lose yourself in the Estérel's desert landscape, far from the sea. Mandelieu and La-Napoule, the resorts that cluster at the foot of the Estérel, are densely populated pleasure ports, with an agreeable combination of

cool sea breezes and escapes into the near-desert behind.

Haut Var and the Gorges de Verdon. The hills that back the Côte d'Azur are often called the *arrière-pays*, or backcountry—a catch-all term that applies to the hills and plateaus behind Nice as well. Yet this particular wedge of backcountry—north and west of Fréjus—has a character all its own. If the territory behind Nice has a strong Latin flavor, influenced for centuries by the Grimaldi dynasty and steeped in Italian culture, these westerly hills are deeply, unselfconsciously Provençal: wild lavender and thyme sprout on dry, rocky hillsides; the earth under scrub oaks is snuffled by rooting boars; and hilltop villages are so isolated and quiet you can hear pebbles drop in their mossy fountains. The rocky swells behind Cannes and Fréjus are known as the Haut Var, the highlands of the département called Var. The untamed, beautiful, and sometimes harsh landscape beyond these hills lies over the threshold of Haute-Provence, itself loosely defined—more a climate and terrain than a region; villages like Fayence and Seillans beckon. You can also explore Moustiers-Ste-Marie, with its faience workshops, and discover the art of this brightly painted tableware. Not far away is La Palud-sur-Verdon, gateway to the spectacular Gorges du Verdon.

Planning

Getting Oriented

If it's most often associated with celeb-heavy coastal resorts—particularly St-Tropez—the Western Côte d'Azur is also a nature-lover's paradise. North of the coast, the Massif des Maures and the Massif de l'Estérel remain remarkably wild and unspoiled, while, farther up, the Gorges du Verdon draws hardcore hikers willing to forego the local rosé to keep their wits about them as they tackle France's answer to the Grand Canyon.

When to Go

Summer days are like the film *Groundhog Day*—every day seems exactly the same as the day before, with the piercing azure blue sky and sticky sunshine heat. July and August are hot, people move slower and, yes, you will sweat. As a rule of thumb, locals cite August 15 as the beginning of changing weather: clouds tend to roll in frequently and temps become noticeably cooler in the morning and evening. March to April and October to November tend to be rainier stretches and, of course, the mistral can come at any time, bringing terrible gusts and nippy drafts. To see the Gorges du Verdon in full fall color, aim for early October, though the odds of rainy days increase as autumn advances.

Planning Your Time

Unless you enjoy jacked-up prices, traffic jams, and sardine-style beach crowds, avoid the coast like the plague in July and August, especially the last week of July and first three weeks of August. Many of the better restaurants simply shut down to avoid the coconut-oil crowd. Another negative about July and August: the Estérel is closed to hikers during this flash-fire season. From Easter through October the café life is in full swing; May is mild and often lovely, but the top restaurants and hotels may be crowded with spillover from the Cannes Film Festival. Planet St-Tropez is really only open for business April–October, and during the warmer months, people-watching in the port and lunching at Pampelonne Beach's Club 55 is a must. Even at the end of the season, there's stuff going on, including regatta races and the annual sale called "La Grande Braderie" (held the last weekend of October), when

even you can afford to shop in St-Tropez (okay, so it's last season's stuff, but still). Moustiers-Ste-Marie celebrates all things lavender with the LavandEvasion festival the last week of June and first week of July. In February, La Napoule hosts its annual Mimosa festival, complete with competing float parades. Southwest, in Bormes-les-Mimosas, you can visit Fort de Brégançon, the president's former summer home now open to the public for guided tours during various weeks from July to October. On the first Sunday in September, Fréjus-St-Aygulf cracks open 15,000 eggs as it celebrates the Giant Omelette Festival. You can work all that off during a week of guided walks around hilltop villages near St-Raphaël during the Var Rambling Week (Semaine Varoise de la Randonnée Pédestre) the first week of October.

Getting Here and Around

You can visit any spot between St-Tropez and Cannes in an easy day trip, and the hilltop villages and towns on the coastal plateau are just as accessible. Thanks to the efficient A8 highway, you can whisk at high speeds to the exit nearest your destination up or down the coast; thus, even if you like leisurely exploration, you can zoom back to your home base at day's end.

Public transportation is not as good here as in other regions of the Riviera and Provence, and some itineraries may require cars, although there is no way to avoid the bumper-to-bumper traffic along the Corniche de l'Estérel or from the A8 highway into St-Tropez during the summer season. Above the autoroute things slow down considerably, and venturing farther north, say by the 314-km (195-mile) Route Napoléon, is a bigger commitment and, to be fully enjoyed, should include at least one overnight stop. Driving is the best way to village-hop in the Haut Var and take in the spectacular

Gorges du Verdon, but be prepared for some challenging bends along the way, like the Route des Crêtes (D23) from La Palud-sur-Verdon (if white knuckles are not for you, opt for the nearby D952).

If traveling by bus, remember that just because you actually found a local bus that stops at your village of choice, that doesn't mean it's going to drop you in the heart of town.

As for waterways, roughly May–September ferries to St-Tropez from Nice (2 hours 30 minutes) and Cannes (1 hour 15 minutes) offer a scenic, hassle-free route.

BOAT

Considering the congestion that buses and cars confront on the road to St-Tropez, the best way to get to that resort is by train to St-Raphaël, then hop on Les Bateaux de Saint-Raphaël. These boats, usually two per day April–October (four boats daily during July and August), leave from the Gare Maritime de St-Raphaël in the Vieux Port, take about an hour, and cost €15 one-way. Bateaux Verts offer a shuttle boat linking St-Tropez and Ste-Maxime mid-February–December; tickets are €7.70 one-way and the ride is 15 minutes. Once in St-Tropez, April–September the same company can also take you on a tour around the Calanques de l'Estérel (2–3½ hours, €24) or an hour-long tour of the Baie des Canebiers (nicknamed the Bay of Stars) to see some celebrity villas (€11–€18.60, or add an extra €1.40 for a return Ste-Maxime-St-Tropez ticket).

BOAT INFORMATION Bateaux Verts.
✉ *14 quai Léon Condroyer, Ste-Maxime* ☎ *04–94–49–29–39* ⊕ *www.bateaux-verts.com.* **Bateaux de Saint-Ralphaël.**
✉ *Gare Maritime, Quai Nomy, St-Raphaël* ☎ *04–94–95–17–46* ⊕ *www.bateauxsaintraphael.com.*

BUS

Local buses cover a network of routes along the coast and stop at many out-of-the-way places that can't be reached by train. Note that in high season, the traffic jam to St-Tropez can lead to two-plus-hour bus rides.

Timetables are available from train stations, local bus stations (*gares routières*), and tourist offices, where you can also ask for information on commercial bus excursions; there are several day-trip tours out of Fréjus and St-Raphaël into the more popular backcountry towns.

St-Tropez's Gare Routière (bus station) is on Avenue du Général de Gaulle (at 5 Quai Avancé) and has bus routes run by VarLib. This company's 248 routes linking Var municipalities include the popular No. 7601 to/from St-Raphaël (€3, 1½ hours, 13 daily), the town with the nearest train station; some buses stop in Grimaud and Port Grimaud, Ste-Maxime, and Fréjus (€3, one hour) but check the schedule to be sure. Buses link up with Ramatuelle and Gassin (€3, 35 minutes). Bus No. 7801 also connects to Toulon (€3, two hours).

From St-Raphaël's bus station, located at 100 Rue Victor Hugo next to the train station, all routes are €3 except to Nice airport (€20, 75 minutes).

The bus station in Fréjus is on Place Paul-Vernet, and there are several buses from here to St-Tropez.

BUS INFORMATION VarLib. ☎ *09–70–83–03–80* ⊕ *www.varlib.fr.*

CAR

Driving to Fréjus and Le Muy (exit for St-Tropez) from Cannes is a breeze on the A8 toll highway (€2.80–€5.20 one-way), but the D25 and D98, which connect you from the A8 to St-Tropez can move at a snail's pace in July and August. The most scenic route—although again, in the summer it's extremely slow—is the D6098 (La Corniche d'Or) between La Napoule, just east of Cannes, and Fréjus, after which point it turns into the D559. To explore the hill towns and the Gorges du Verdon, small, poky, and pretty roads lead north and west from Fréjus and Cannes, including the famous Route Napoléon.

TRAIN

The major rail crossroads from points north and west are at Fréjus's main station on Rue Martin Bidouré and St-Raphaël's Gare St-Raphaël/Valescure on Rue Waldeck Rousseau—which is the hub on the coastal TER line between Les Arcs and Nice (it's about 60 minutes from St-Raphaël to Nice; €12.80), from where the train begins its scenic crawl along the coast toward Italy, stopping in La Napoule and Cannes. In St-Raphaël, you can pick up the direct train from Marseille to Ventimiglia, Italy (there's a stopover in Nice but you stay on the train) or take the Mandelieu-La-Napoule-Ventimiglia. Either way, count on at least 70–90 minutes.

There is no rail access to St-Tropez; St-Raphaël and Fréjus are the nearest stops. The train station nearest the Haut Var and the Gorges du Verdon is at Les Arcs, below Draguignan. From there you have to rent a car or get the train to Marseille and take LER Bus No. 27 to Castellane (⊕ www.info-ler.fr).

TRAIN INFORMATION SNCF. ☎ 3635 ⊕ www.oui.sncf. **TGV.** ☎ 3635 ⊕ www.oui.sncf/tgv.

Beaches

Following upon their worldwide fame as the earth's most glamorous beaches, the real things often come as a shock to first-time visitors.

Much of the Côte d'Azur is lined with rock and pebble, and the beaches are narrow swaths backed by city streets or roaring highways. Only St-Tropez, on this stretch of the Mediterranean, has the curving bands of sandy waterfront you've come to expect from all those 1950s photographs—and even there, the 3-mile stretch of Pampelonne Beach supports

no fewer than 30 restaurants and private businesses, and can see up to 30,000 beachgoers a day.

Note that there's a range of acceptable behaviors on these beaches: some are topless while others feature full nudity. You'll be able to tell pretty quickly which is which.

Hiking

Contact local tourist offices for information on hikes in the rugged backcountry of the Massif de l'Estérel. While several *sentiers du littoral* (coastal trails) wind around the St-Tropez Peninsula, *grande randonnées* (national hiking trails) GR51, known as the Balcons de la Méditerranée, and GR49 ascend the Estérel heights. The GR49 intersects with France's most spectacular grande randonnée, the GR4, which threads the Gorges du Verdon.

Restaurants

Restaurants in the coastal resorts are expensive, particularly in St-Tropez where prices can be higher than prices in Paris, and often a risky investment, as they cater mostly to crowds *en passage*. St-Tropez is home to one of the country's finest fish markets, just off the port, but ordering it per 100g can be a costly mistake (is one *langouste* really worth 200 euros?). Do freely indulge in the *tropézienne*, a rich, pastry cream–filled brioche topped with grainy sugar. Inland, you can tap into a culture of cozy *auberges* (inns) in hilltop villages and have a better chance of finding good home cooking for your money. As a general rule, the curlier the printing on a menu the more pretensions a country auberge has; some of the best post only handwritten chalkboard menus. Your best bet is to get the daily special, which is almost always fresh and there's no surprise in the price.

Around the Gorges du Verdon, a magnet for hikers and climbers, food becomes less of a priority—expect to find mostly pizzas, salads, and simple hikers' fare.

Hotels

If you've come to this area from other regions in France you'll notice a sudden sharp hike in hotel prices, skyrocketing to dizzying heights in summer. St-Tropez's rates vie with those in Monaco. You'll also notice a difference in interior design: the look leans toward "le style Côte d'Azur," a slick, neo–Art Deco pastiche that smacks of Jazz Age glamour. If you can't disconnect while on vacation and Wi-Fi is essential, it's best to check with your accommodations beforehand about network access and signal strength.

Up in the hills you can find the charm you'd expect, both in sophisticated inns and in mom-and-pop auberges; the farther north you drive, the lower the rates.

Restaurant and hotel reviews have been shortened. For full information, visit Fodors.com.

What it Costs in Euros			
$	$$	$$$	$$$$
RESTAURANTS			
under €18	€18–€24	€25–€32	over €32
HOTELS			
under €125	€125–€225	€226–€350	over €350

Visitor Information

For information on travel within the Var region—St-Tropez to La Napoule—contact Var Tourism. For Cannes and its surroundings, look to Côte d'Azur Tourisme.

For the Haute-Provence region between Moustiers and Manosque, contact the Agence Développement Touristique des

Alpes de Haute-Provence. For the Verdon region, contact Parc Naturel Régional du Verdon.

CONTACTS Agence de Développement Touristique des Alpes de Haute-Provence. ☎ 04–92–31–57–29 ⊕ www.tourisme-alpes-haute-provence.com. **Côte d'Azur Tourisme.** ☎ 04–93–37–78–78 ⊕ www.cotedazur-tourisme.com. **Parc Naturel Régional du Verdon.** ☎ 04–92–74–68–00 ⊕ www.parcduverdon.fr. **Tourisme du Var.** ☎ 04–94–18–59–60 ⊕ www.visitvar.fr.

St-Tropez

35 km (22 miles) southwest of Fréjus; 66 km (41 miles) northeast of Toulon.

At first glance, it really doesn't look all that impressive. There's a pretty port with cafés charging €5 for a cup of coffee and a photogenic old town in sugar-almond hues, but there are many prettier in the hills nearby. There are sandy beaches, rare enough on the Riviera, and old-fashioned squares with plane trees and pétanque players, but these are a dime a dozen throughout Provence. So what made St-Tropez an internationally known locale? Two words: Brigitte Bardot. When she showed up in St-Tropez on the arm of Roger Vadim in 1956 to film *And God Created Woman,* the world started paying attention. Neither the gentle descriptions of writer Guy de Maupassant (1850–93), nor the watercolor tones of Impressionist Paul Signac (1863–1935), nor the stream of painters who followed (including Matisse and Bonnard) could focus the world's attention on this seaside hamlet as did this one fashionable, beautiful woman in a scarf, Ray-Bans, and capris.

Anything associated with the distant past seems almost absurd in St-Tropez. Still, the place has a history that predates the inventions of the string bikini and the speedo, and people have been finding reasons to come here since AD 68,

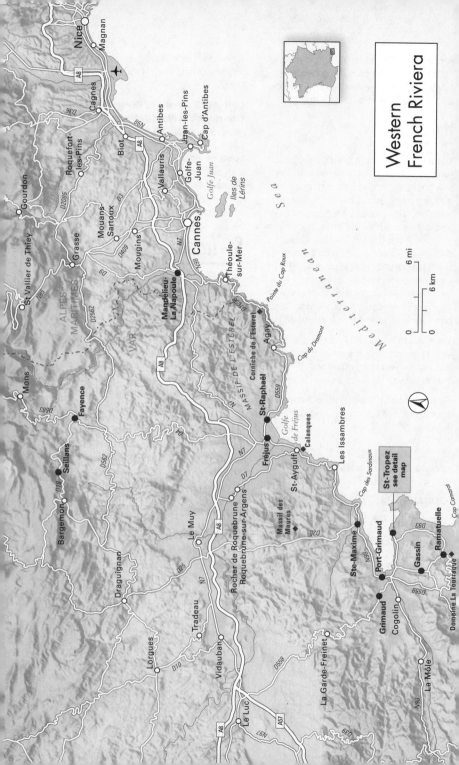

Western French Riviera

when a Roman soldier from Pisa named Torpes was beheaded for professing his Christian faith in front of Emperor Nero, transforming this spot into a place of pilgrimage. Along medieval streets lined with walled gardens and little squares set with dripping fountains, you can discover historic delights like the Chapelle de la Misericorde, topped by its wrought-iron campanile, and Rue Allard, lined with picturesque houses such as the Maison du Maure.

You'll find many accounts of the over-the-top petrodollar parties, megayachts, and paparazzi here yet you might be surprised to find that this byword for billionaires is so small and insulated. The lack of train service, casinos, and chain hotels keeps it that way. Still, in July and August, you must be carefree about the sordid matter of cash. After all, at the most Dionysian nightclub in town, a glass of tap water goes for $28 and when the mojo really gets going, billionaires think nothing of "champagne spraying" the partying crowds—think World Series celebrations but with $1,000 bottles of Roederer Cristal instead of Gatorade. Complaining about summer crowds, high prices, and poor service has become a tourist sport and yet this is what makes St-Tropez as intriguing as it is seductive.

GETTING HERE AND AROUND
Keep in mind that getting here can be hellish. Out on a limb, scorned by any train route, you can only get to St-Trop by car, bus, or boat (from nearby ports like St-Raphaël). Driving can test anyone's mettle, thanks to the crowds, the narrow roads, and the parking situation: you have the Parking du Port lot (opposite the bus station on Avenue du Général de Gaulle, with a shuttle bus into town June through September) or the Parc des Lices (beneath the Place des Lices) and Place du XVe Corps in the center of town. Street parking is to be avoided, as exceeding the maximum time limit of three hours and 24 minutes will set

you back €30. If you do decide to rent a car, take the N98 coast road, the longest route but also the prettiest, with great picnic stops along the way.

A train–bus connection can be made if you're leaving from Nice center: take the train (direction St-Raphaël) from the Gare SNCF Nice Centre-Ville station (€12.80 one-way); from St-Raphaël, there's the daily Bus No. 7601 service with VarLib (€3 one-way). Make sure you get to St-Raphaël's bus station early or you'll most likely be elbowed out of a seat and forced to stand the whole way. Travel time from St-Raphaël to St-Tropez is 1½ hours. The other option is to take a 2½-hour boat from the Nice harbor with Trans Côte d'Azur, which has daily trips June–September and costs €67 round-trip (from Cannes, it's only 75 minutes and €52 return).

VISITOR INFORMATION
Got €3 to spare? Year-round, you can rent an iPod touch with an interactive tour from the Tourist Office, which lets you explore St-Tropez at your own pace. If you're more of a people person, every Wednesday April–October guided tours (€6) depart in front of the tourist office at 10 am.

CONTACTS St-Tropez Tourist Office. ✉ *Pl. des Lices, 19 Pl. Carnot* ☎ *04–94–97–45–21* ⊕ *www.sainttropeztourisme.com/en.*

Sights

Citadelle
MILITARY SITE | Head up Rue de la Citadelle to these 16th-century ramparts, which stand in a lovely hilltop park offering a fantastic view of the town and the sea. Amid today's bathing suit–clad sun worshippers it's hard to imagine St-Tropez as a military outpost, but inside the Citadelle's dungeon the modern **Musée de l'Histoire Maritime Tropézienne** (St-Tropez Maritime Museum) resides a stirring homage to those who served the nation. ✉ *Rue de la Citadelle* ☎ *04–94–97–59–43* 🎫 *€3, includes museum entry.*

La Maison des Papillons

MUSEUM | FAMILY | A block west of Rue Clémenceau, in a pretty house at the end of a typically Tropezien lane, the butterfly museum is a delight for children (and their parents) to discover over an afternoon. Sweetly aflutter, the 35,000 specimens were a passion of late collector Dany Lartigue, the son of the famous photographer Jacques-Henri. ⊠ *17 rue Étienne Berny* ☎ *04–94–97–63–45* ✆ *€2* ☼ *Closed Nov.–Jan. and Thurs. and Fri. in Feb.–June, Sept., and Oct.*

Le Sentier du Littoral

TRAIL | To experience St-Tropez's natural beauty up close, consider walking parts of the *sentier du littoral,* or coastal path, around the peninsula and all the beaches to Cavalaire-sur-Mer. Try the 12.5-km (7-mile) route to Plage de Tahiti and its longish stretches on sand beach, which takes an average of 3½ hours. Leave from the Tour du Portalet or the Tour Vieille at the edge of the Quartier de la Ponche. Follow the footpath from Plage des Graniers along the beaches and cliffs overlooking the water, often with views toward the Estérel or out to the open sea. At Tahiti beach you can walk the 3 km (2 miles, 50 minutes) back to town or continue another 5 km (3 miles, 90 minutes) along the Plage de Pampelonne to the Bonne Terasse beach. From here it gets serious, with another 19 km (12 miles, 6 hours) to Cavalaire to complete the entire trail. But you'll need to plan ahead to catch one of the few buses back to St-Tropez. Otherwise, it's 18 km (11 miles) back to town. ⊠ *Tour du Portalet.*

Musée de l'Annonciade (*Annunciation Museum*)

MUSEUM | The legacy of the artists who loved St-Tropez—including Signac, Matisse, Braque, Dufy, Vuillard, and Rouault—has been carefully preserved in this extraordinary museum, housed in a 14th-century chapel just inland from the southwest corner of the Vieux Port.

Cutting-edge temporary exhibitions featuring local talent and up-and-coming international artists keep visitors on their toes, while works by established artists from Impressionism to Expressionism line the walls. ⊠ *2 pl. Georges Grammont* ☎ *04–94–17–84–10* ✆ *€6* ☼ *Closed Mon. Oct.–June.*

Place des Lices

PLAZA | Enjoy a time-out in the social center of the Old Town, where a symmetrical forest of plane trees provides shade to rows of cafés and restaurants, skateboarders, children, and grandfatherly pétanque players. Also called Place Carnot, the square becomes a moveable feast—for both eyes and palate—on the very affordable market days (Tuesday and Saturday), while at night, a café seat is as coveted as a quayside seat during the day. Just as Deborah Kerr and David Niven once did in *Bonjour Tristesse,* watch the boules players under the glow of hundreds of electric bulbs. Heading back to the Vieux Port area, take in the boutiques lining Rues Sibilli, Clemenceau, and Gambetta to help accessorize your evening look—you never know when that photographer from *Voici* will be snapping away at the *trendoisie.* ⊠ *Av. Foch and Bd. Vasserot.*

Quartier de la Ponche

HISTORIC SITE | Walk along Quai Suffern where the statue of the Bailli de Suffren, an 18th-century customs official, stands guard, and continue past the quayside streets lined with famous cafés to the Môle Jean Réveille, the harbor wall, where, if the wind isn't too strong, you can walk out for a good view of Ste-Maxime across the sparkling bay, the hills of Estérel, and, on a clear day, the distant Alps. Retrace your steps along the digue to the 15th-century **Tour du Portalet** and head onward to the old fishermen's quarter, the Quartier de la Ponche, just east of Quai Jean Jaurès. Here you can find the **Port des Pêcheurs** (Fishermen's Port), on whose beach Bardot did a

St-Tropez

Golfe de St-Tropez

	A	B	C	D	E

Port des Pecheurs
Plage de la Fontanette
La Glaye
Le Sentier du Littoral
r. Cavaillon
av. Antoine de St-Exupéry
Montée de la Citadelle

môle d'Estienne d'Orves

r. du Clocher

Vieux Port

q. Jean-Jaurès

r. Laugier r. de la Citadelle

r. des Remparts

av. de 11 Novembre 1918

av. de Général de Gaulle

q. de Suffren

r. François Sibilli

r. du Portail Neuf

av. Paul Signac

q. l'Épi

r. Henri Seillon

r. Gén. A. Ilard

r. Georges Clémenceau

r. Étienne Berny

r. des Charrons

r. des Tisserands

Blvd Vasserot

Place des Lices

r. Gambetta

av. du Maréchal Foch

blvd. Louis Blanc

Plaza du Quinzième Corps

Chemin Privé

av. de Général Leclerc

av. Paul Roussel

r. du Temple

Chemin des Amoureux

Chemin des Amoureux

KEY

- **1** Sights
- **1** Restaurants
- **1** Hotels

0	500 ft
0	200 m

Despite the outrageous prices, St-Tropez does prove itself to be one of the prettiest places on the French Riviera.

star turn in *And God Created Woman*. Twisting, narrow streets, designed to break the impact of the mistral, open to tiny squares with fountains. Complete with gulf-side harbor, St-Tropez's Old Town maze of backstreets and old ramparts is daubed in shades of gold, pink, ocher, and sky-blue. Trellised jasmine and wrought-iron birdcages hang from the shuttered windows, and many of the tiny streets dead-end at the sea. The main drag here, Rue de la Ponche, leads into Place l'Hôtel de Ville, landmarked by a *mairie* (town hall) marked out in typical Tropezienne hues of pink and green. Head up Rue Commandant Guichard to the Baroque **Église de St-Tropez** to pay your respects to the bust and barque of St-Torpes, every day but May 17, when they are carried aloft in the Bravade parade honoring the town's namesake saint. ⊠ *St-Tropez.*

Vieux Port

NEIGHBORHOOD | Bordered by Quai de l'Épi, Quai Bouchard, Quai Peri, Quai Suffren, and Quai Jean Jaurès, Vieux Port

is a place for strolling and looking over the shoulders of artists painting their versions of the view on easels set up along the water's edge. Meanwhile, folding director's chairs at the famous port-side cafés Café de Paris and Sénéquier—all well placed for observing the cast of St-Tropez's living theater play out their colorful roles. ⊠ *St-Tropez.*

Beaches

The *plages* (beaches) around St-Tropez are the most isolated on the Côte d'Azur, providing one of the rare stretches where your back doesn't lean up against the coastal highway. For better or worse, the beaches had remained largely unchanged for decades, until 2019. Thanks to a random French law—the 2006 Décret Plage protecting rare flora—the local town hall was able to reallocate leases from 2019 to 2030 to 30 environmentally respectful beach clubs. In came first-timers like Byblos, Hôtel de Paris, Loulou à Ramatuelle, La Serena Beach, and the Philippe Starck–designed Réserve à la Plage, and out (to the uproar of many) went institutions like Les Jumueaux and Bagatelle, owned by the world's 224th richest man, Dmitry Rybolovlev.

La Bouillabaisse Beach

BEACH—SIGHT | This sand public beach as you enter town has free showers and toilets with lifeguard surveillance mid-June–mid-September. You can rent loungers nearby. **Amenities:** lifeguards; parking (no fee); showers; toilets. **Best for:** swimming. ⊠ *Quartier La Bouillabaisse, RD98A.*

Nikki Beach

BEACH—SIGHT | Off the Route des Plages is this most notorious of all the beaches famous for A-list debauches and a regular clientele of movie megastars and wannabes. But Nikki Beach isn't actually on the beach, but rather steps from the beach with a pool and restaurant. If you want to mingle with the famous, rent an Opium bed (€100 for maximum three people), but you may want to avoid the poolside where champagne showers spare no one. There is also a VIP Bed Ponton by the Sea for up to four people; it's typically €120, but this is St-Tropez so the price may vary depending on the DJ. **Amenities:** food and drink; parking (fee and no fee); showers; toilets. **Best for:** partiers. ⊠ *Rte. de l'Épi, Ramatuelle* ☎ *04–94–79–82–04* ⊕ *saint-tropez.nikkibeach.com* ☯ *Closed mid-Sept.–mid-Apr.*

Plage des Graniers

BEACH—SIGHT | The closest beach to the town of St-Tropez, at the southern base of the Citadelle and past the cemetery, Graniers beach is easily accessible by foot (it's part of the sentier du littoral) and the most family-friendly. At the east end, you can rent loungers (€22 plus €7 for an umbrella) from the restaurant. There are no toilets or showers. **Amenities:** parking (no fee). **Best for:** swimming. ⊠ *Ch. des Graniers.*

Plage des Salins

BEACH—SIGHT | Situated between Cap des Salins and Point du Capon, this 600-meter public white sand beach is the gateway to a stretch of Pampelonne beach, although it's more exposed to the wind and the sea can quickly become rough. It's lined by huge umbrella pine trees, and you can rent loungers from the beach's private section. To the left by the coastal path is a quieter cove. **Amenities:** parking (no fee); showers; toilets. **Best for:** swimming. ⊠ *Rte. des Salins.*

Tahiti Beach

BEACH—SIGHT | Welcome to Tahiti Plage, the oldest and most famous of St-Trop's private beaches (Bardot filmed along this stretch), with its fine-sand beaches, rentable loungers close to the shoreline, restaurants, and toilets. The crowd is definitely north of 35 but as they don't act their age, there is a lot to see in terms of hardly there swimwear. **Amenities:** showers; toilets; water sports. **Best for:** swimming; walking. ⊠ *Quartier du Pinet, Ramatuelle* ☎ *04–94–97–18–02* ⊕ *www.tahiti-beach.com.*

Verde Beach by Yeeels

BEACH—SIGHT | Parisian restaurant group Yeeels are the masterminds behind this spot, the frontrunner for Ramutuelle's best new beach club. Boho loungers on Farniente Beach are available starting at 11 am, with a selection of magazines to read while you relax. Headed by Ducasse-trained Michelin-starred chef Thibault Sombardier, the on-site restaurant La Table Varoise offers Mediterranean-style oven-roasted, grilled, and marinated dishes at their most tempting (and pricey). Glasses of rosé start at €44, but the quality of service is high. After 5 pm, you can dance off that lunch with live DJs. **Amenities**: food and drink; toilets; showers. **Best for**: partiers; swimming; sunsets. ⊠ *1149 Chemin de l'Epi* ☎ *6–37–74–89–75* ⊕ *www.verde-beach.com.*

🍴 Restaurants

Basilic Burger

$ | **FRENCH** | **FAMILY** | Not every lunch in St-Tropez requires a Platinum AmEx for payment. Basilic Burger serves up tasty gourmet burgers, bagels, and copious salads at more than affordable prices. Just €15 gets you a meal and dessert; the kids' menu is only €10. **Known for:** reasonable €15 for burger or salad and dessert; veggie burgers; late hours (until 10 pm) in July and August. [$] *Average main: €15* ✉ *Pl. des Remparts* ☎ *04–94–97–29–09* 🕓 *Closed Nov.–Mar.* 💳 *No credit cards.*

Dior des Lices

$$$ | **FRENCH** | What could be more fashionable than tucking into exquisite cuisine by three–Michelin-star chef Arnaud Donckele in an enchanting sheltered garden designed by Peter Wirtz at the House of Dior? Dior des Lices elegantly serves a full menu of breakfast, lunch, dinner, and snacks, with a range of reasonable prices compared to the Vague d'Or, chef Donckele's full-time gig across town. **Known for:** huge dessert menu, including famed caramel D'Choux; comparatively reasonable prices; garden vibe. [$] *Average main: €26* ✉ *13 rue François Sibilli* ☎ *04–98–12–67–65* 🕓 *Closed mid-Oct.–May.*

Le G'envie

$$$$ | **FRENCH** | It's always a good sign when people are willing to line up for a coveted seat in a tiny joint, and G'Envie is no exception. Tucked away on an unassuming street behind the port, with views of Notre-Dame church, this is where you come for classic French food without the St. Tropez prices. **Known for:** no-reservations policy; French duck and traditional veal dishes; tiny spot on a tiny street. [$] *Average main: €39* ✉ *67 Rue Portail Neuf* ☎ *04–94–79–85–09* 🕓 *Closed Mon.*

Le Girelier

$$$$ | **SEAFOOD** | Fish, fish, and more fish—sea bass, salmon, sole, sardines, monkfish, lobster, crayfish: they're painted on the walls and they fill the boats that pull into the Old Port before finding their way onto the grill here. Grilling (with a little thyme and perhaps a whisper of olive oil and garlic) is the order of the day, with most fish sold by weight (beware the check), but this is also a stronghold for bouillabaisse. **Known for:** reasonably priced wine list; fabulous views of Vieux Port yachts; relatively affordable lunch menu. [$] *Average main: €38* ✉ *Quai Jean-Jaurès* ☎ *04–94–97–03–87* 🌐 *www.legirelier.fr* 🕓 *Closed Nov.–mid-Mar.*

Napoleon

$$$$ | **FRENCH** | This glam French eatery has instantly appealed to the A-List crowd. Built on ruins where trees eventually laid their roots to create a stone wall garden, Napolean is run by St-Tropez natives Julien and Axel, who are all about giving gourmands value for their money. **Known for:** best beef menu in town; impressive wine list; glamorous vibe in Old Town. [$] *Average main: €38* ✉ *3 rue des Tisserands* ☎ *04–94–97–59–62* 🌐 *www.napoleon-sainttropez.com* 🕓 *Closed Nov.–Apr.*

🛏 Hotels

Cheval Blanc St-Tropez

$$$$ | **HOTEL** | **FAMILY** | Perhaps the most opulent of St-Tropez's luxe hangouts, La Résidence de La Pinède—with its balustraded white villa built in 1936—recently became Cheval Blanc St-Tropez, a LVMH property. **Pros:** only St-Tropez hotel with a private waterfront; glamorous spa; excellent three-Michelin-star restaurant. **Cons:** insanely expensive; for the price, some rooms are small; not exactly a hotel for children. [$] *Rooms from: €1250* ✉ *Plage de la Bouillabaisse* ☎ *04–94–55–91–00* 🌐 *www.chevalblanc.com/en/maison/st-tropez* 🕓 *Closed Oct.–mid-May* 🛏 *30 rooms* 🍴 *Free breakfast.*

Hôtel B. Lodge

$$ | **HOTEL** | All of the small, delicately contemporary rooms of this attractively priced, four-story charmer overlook the Citadelle's green park, some from tiny balconies. **Pros:** very good value for location; breakfast and Wi-Fi included; all rooms have air-conditioning. **Cons:** four-night minimum stay in July and August; only two available parking spots; small rooms. [$] *Rooms from: €200* ✉ *12 rue de l'Aïoli* ☎ *04–94–97–06–57* 🌐 *www.hotel-b-lodge.com* 🕒 *Closed Jan. and early Feb.* 🛏 *13 rooms* 🍴 *Free breakfast.*

★ **Hôtel de Paris Saint-Tropez**

$$$$ | **HOTEL** | When you walk into the lobby of this five-star, service-friendly urban hotel, you may be too excited about the open space—a novelty for this tiny fishing port—to notice the rooftop pool suspended 15 meters in the air, with its glass floor peering down at you. **Pros:** throwback design; unique rooftop bar and pool with fabulous 360-degree views; free beach shuttle. **Cons:** some rooms are small; few poolside loungers; breakfast €35 per person. [$] *Rooms from: €450* ✉ *1 traverse de la Gendarmerie* ☎ *04–83–09–60–00* 🌐 *www.hoteldeparis-sainttropez.com* 🕒 *Closed Nov.–Feb.* 🛏 *90 rooms* 🍴 *No meals.*

Le Byblos

$$$$ | **HOTEL** | Forget five stars: this toy Mediterranean village, grouped around courtyards landscaped with palms, olive trees, and lavender has "Palace" classification and access to the exclusive Byblos Beach Ramatuellea. **Pros:** exquisite service; best buffet breakfast includes three-, four-, or five-minute hard-boiled egg; beach access with seaside restaurant. **Cons:** minimum four-night stay in July and August; some rooms can be noisy in summer; can be hard to get beach loungers. [$] *Rooms from: €955* ✉ *Av. Paul-Signac* ☎ *04–94–56–68–00* 🌐 *www.byblos.com* 🕒 *Closed late Oct.–mid-Apr.* 🛏 *90 rooms* 🍴 *No meals.*

★ **Lou Cagnard**

$$ | **HOTEL** | Set inside a lovely garden courtyard, this pretty little villa hotel is owned by an enthusiastic young couple, who have fixed it up room by room and provided amenities including satellite TV and free Wi-Fi. **Pros:** fantastic value for your money (try Room 17); walking distance to everything; free parking. **Cons:** a few of the older rooms share a bathroom, but at much reduced rates; seven-night minimum June–September; strict cancellation policy. [$] *Rooms from: €160* ✉ *18 av. Paul-Roussel* ☎ *04–94–97–04–24* 🌐 *www.hotel-lou-cagnard.com* 🕒 *Closed Nov.–Mar.* 🛏 *18 rooms* 🍴 *No meals.*

★ **Lou Pinet**

$$$$ | **HOTEL** | With this five-star hotel just steps from Place des Lices, the Pariente family gives you a chance to experience the real St-Tropez, secluded from the madness of the bling-bling crowds. **Pros:** excellent restaurant and spa; housekeeping twice a day; enormous pool (biggest in St-Tropez). **Cons:** breakfast eggs are extra; pricey in height of summer; not on the beach. [$] *Rooms from: €910* ✉ *70 Chemin du Pinet* ☎ *04–94–97–04–37* 🌐 *www.loupinet.com* 🛏 *34 rooms* 🍴 *No meals.*

🍸 Nightlife

Le Quai Saint-Tropez

WINE BARS—NIGHTLIFE | Don't be surprised to see the likes of Lindsay Lohan hanging out here with her friend, Philippe Shangti, a model-turned-contemporary-photographer who happens to manage the notorious Asian-French restaurant-lounge in the port. Friendly service makes digging into fancy appetizers more rewarding while you take in the evening's live and lively entertainment, which includes anything from break dancing to vocalists. ✉ *Quai Jean Jaurès.*

Les Caves du Roy

DANCE CLUBS | Costing the devil and often jammed to the scuppers, this kitsch disco in the Byblos Hotel is *the* place to see and be seen. When you hear the theme from *Star Wars,* take comfort while you sip your €26 glass of water that someone other than yourself has just spent €25,000 on a Methuselah of champagne. There's a horrific door policy during high season—don't worry, it's really not you. It's open every night in July and August, and weekends only the rest of the year. ⊠ *Av. Paul-Signac* ⊕ *www.lescavesduroy.com.*

VIP Room

DANCE CLUBS | So notorious is the VIP Room for drawing flashy, gilded youths with deep pockets that it spawned a VIP Room Cannes expressly for those needing a dose during the film festival before this location opens nightly from mid-June to mid-September. ⊠ *Residence du Nouveau Port.*

🎭 Performing Arts

Les Nuits du Château de la Moutte

CONCERTS | Every August, exceptional classical music concerts are given in the formidable gardens of the Château de la Moutte. You can book tickets (€60) online or by phone. ⊠ *Château de la Moutte* ☎ *04–94–96–96–94 for info* ⊕ *lesnuitsduchateaudelamoutte.com.*

🏃 Activities

Bicycles are an ideal way to get to the beaches. If you're around at the end of September, be sure to check out Les Voiles de Saint-Tropez, one of the most extraordinary regattas of modern sailboats.

Rolling Bikes

BICYCLING | Here you can rent e-bikes for riding around the city or race bikes for longer distances. Prices start at €12 for a full 24 hours. ⊠ *50 av. Général-Leclerc* ☎ *04–94–97–09–39* ⊕ *www.rolling-bikes. com.*

La Grande Braderie

La Grande Braderie (annual end-of-season sale) takes place in St-Tropez over the last weekend of October (Friday–Monday). Hit the shops from 9 to 9 with other fashion victims looking for the bargain you couldn't afford *en haute saison.* Be prepared for lots of walking and crowds, but at 50% off, who cares? ■ **TIP**→ **Trans Côte d'Azur even runs a special Nice-St-Tropez ferry just for this weekend.**

🛍 Shopping

There is something about St-Tropez that makes shopping simply irresistible—unlike Cannes, you'll be welcomed into the stores no matter what you look like or what you're wearing. Where else will you find Vilebrequin 24-carat-gold-embroidered Golden Turtle swim trunks from €8,000? **Rue Sibilli,** behind Quai Suffren, is lined with Armani, Dior, Louis Vuitton, and all kinds of trendy boutiques, many carrying those all-important sunglasses.

Caroline Dechamby

JEWELRY/ACCESSORIES | Dutch fashion and art designer Caroline Dechamby heads up this concept store focusing on art and luxury. The pop artist hand-paints the rings and leather purses for sale here and works with Swiss watchmakers for her limited edition art series, in case you can't squeeze one of the paintings into your suitcase. ⊠ *14 rue Joseph Quaranta* ☎ *04–94–96–25–80* ⊕ *www.caroline-dechamby.com.*

Fish Market

FOOD/CANDY | The picturesque little fish market occupies the Place aux Herbes, just past the tourist office, every morning. ⊠ *Pl. aux Herbes.*

La Vieille Mer

ANTIQUES/COLLECTIBLES | You probably will do more looking than buying here (unless you have a very large suitcase) but the Old Sea's owner, Walter Wolkowicz, will put you in a time machine exploring navigational tools, lamps, and antique accoutrements of nautical yesteryear at his 100% marine shop. It's open April–October, daily 10–1 and 5–midnight. ⊠ *11 pl. de l'Ormeau* ☎ *06–74–07–91–46* ⊕ *www.lavieillemer.fr.*

Le Dépot

CLOTHING | If you prefer traditional luxe, Le Dépot stocks castoffs by Chanel, Prada, Hermès, Vuitton, Gucci, and so forth. ⊠ *6 bd. Louis-Blanc* ☎ *04–94–97–80–10* ⊕ *www.ledepot-saint-tropez.com.*

Place des Lices

OUTDOOR/FLEA/GREEN MARKETS | The aorta of the village, connecting with Rue Gambetta and Rue Allard, this congregational square overflows with produce and regional foods, as well as clothing and *brocantes* (secondhand items), every Tuesday and Saturday morning. The last weekend in October is the "Grande Braderie," a four-day giant sidewalk sale across the entire town. ⊠ *St-Tropez.*

Rondini

SHOES/LUGGAGE/LEATHER GOODS | You wear those strappy flip-flops back home, but are they the real *sandales Tropeziennes*? Here's your chance to pick up the genuine, handmade article at Rodini, St-Tropez's original cobbler, launched in 1927. You can also have two or more pairs delivered within 10 days for less than €15. ⊠ *18–18 bis rue Clemenceau* ☎ *04–94–97–19–55* ⊕ *www.rondini.fr.*

Ramatuelle

12 km (7 miles) southwest of St-Tropez.

A typical hilltop whorl of red-clay roofs and dense inner streets topped with arches and lined with arcades, this ancient market town was destroyed in the Wars of Religions and rebuilt as a harmonious whole in 1620. Now its souvenir shops and galleries attract day-trippers out of St-Tropez, who enjoy the pretty drive through the vineyards as much as the village itself. During high season, traffic jams can be spectacular between the blurry line where Ramatuelle ends and St-Tropez begins, inflating what should be a short drive into a three-hour crawl. From mid-June to mid-September, a daily courtesy bus (*navette*) will take you from the parking lots to the top of the village, where you can take a free guided tour of the Moulin de Paillas, a windmill restored in the old style with a mechanism made entirely of wood (check with the tourism office for times); the site offers a panoramic view of the coastline. For music lovers, there's a jazz festival mid-August. The town cemetery is the final resting place of Gérard Philipe, an aristocratic heartthrob who died in 1959 after making his mark in such films as *Le Diable au Corps.*

GETTING HERE AND AROUND

By car from St-Tropez, take the inland D93, then the D61. By bus, there are various routes from St-Tropez provided by VarLib (€3).

 Sights

Domaine La Tourraque

WINERY/DISTILLERY | This 100-acre winery offers free wine tastings all year-round. A highly regarded domaine producing wine since 1805, they also run the Village Cellar in town from June through September. You can also reserve in advance a spot for the two-hour guided tour in English every Friday at 4 pm (€15). ⊠ *Ch. de la Bastide Blanche* ⊹ *From Ramatuelle, drive toward La Croix Valmer, then follow l'Escalet until you see signs for Domaine la Tourraque* ☎ *04–94–79–25–95* ⊕ *www. latourraque.fr* ⊠ *€15 for vineyard tour and wine tasting.*

Hotels

Villa Marie

$$$$ | HOTEL | With its circa-1930s feel, exposed beams, chic acid-toned walls, and jewel-tone upholstery, this Italian-villa-cum-hotel set in 7 acres of pine forest continues to impress. **Pros:** gorgeous views; welcome glass of rosé; each room has either terrace or balcony. **Cons:** tubs are in the middle of the rooms; €32 breakfast; might be too isolated and quiet for some. [$] *Rooms from: €450* ✉ *Ch. Val de Rian, Rte. des Plages* ☎ *04–94–97–40–22* 🌐 *en.villamarie.fr* 🕒 *Closed Oct.–mid-May* 🛏 *45 rooms* 🍴 *No meals.*

Gassin

5 km (3 miles) northwest of Ramatuelle.

Classified as one of Les Plus Beaux Villages en France (the most beautiful villages in France), this hilltop town gives you spectacular panoramic views over the Massif des Maures and St-Tropez's bay. In winter, before the summer haze drifts in and after the mistral has given the sky a good scrub, you may be able to make out a brilliant-white chain of Alps looming on the horizon. There's also less commerce here to distract you; for shops, head to Ramatuelle.

GETTING HERE AND AROUND

From Ramatuelle, follow Chemin des Moulins de Paillas 5 km (3 miles). Otherwise you can take a VarLib bus (€3).

Sights

Massif des Maures

SCENIC DRIVE | The dramatic forest scenery of D558 winding west and northwest of St-Tropez (take the D98 toward Grimaud) merits a drive even if you're not heading up to the A8. This is the Massif des Maures, named for the Moors who retreated here from the Battle of Poitiers in 732 and profited from its strong position over the sea. Covering a quarter of the 83 department, this is the largest forest area in the Var at 60 km (37 miles) long by 30 km (19 miles) wide (it reaches an altitude of 2,560 feet). It's dark with thick cork oaks, their ancient trunks girdled for cork only every 10 years or so, leaving exposed a broad band of sienna brown. Some 26 villages share the Massif's borders and between the vineyards, mushroom-shape parasol pines, unique to the Mediterranean, crowd the highway, as do cyclists in spring. Looming even darker and thicker above are the chestnut trees, cultivated for their thick, sweet nuts, which you are not allowed to gather from the forest floor, as signs from the growers' cooperative will warn. The best place to sample *châtaignes*—whether it be chestnut doughnuts, chestnut beer, or the famous *marrons glacés* (candied chestnuts)—is at the chestnut festival every October in Collobrières, aka the chestnut capital of the world.

Grimaud

10 km (6 miles) northwest of Gassin.

Once a formidable Grimaldi fiefdom and home to a massive Romanesque château, the hill-village of Grimaud is merely charming today, though the romantic castle ruins that crown its steep streets still command lordly views over the forests and the coast. The labyrinth of cobbled streets is punctuated by pretty fountains, carved doorways, and artisans' gallery-boutiques. Wander along the Gothic arcades of the Rue des Templiers to see the beautifully proportioned Romanesque Église St-Michel, built in the 11th century.

GETTING HERE AND AROUND

From Gassin follow the D61 for about 11 km (7 miles) to the D14 and take the D98 (which also takes you to St-Tropez). VarLib Buses "N" travel here from St-Tropez and Gassin (both €3).

🍴 Restaurants

Le Magnan

$$$ | **FRENCH** | Just 10 km (6 miles) west of St-Tropez and 4 km (2½ miles) south of Grimaud and the village of La Mole, this bucolic old farmhouse looms on a hillside over forests dense with cork oak and chestnuts. Whether you eat on the terrace with its views of the Massif des Maures and Gulf of St-Tropez or in the rustic dining room, the food tastes and smells of the surrounding countryside. **Known for:** roast chicken like Mamere used to make; large portions, especially for France; gorgeous views. [$] *Average main: €27* ✉ *3085 rte. de Cogolin, RN 98, Le Môle* ☎ *04–94–49–57–54* 🌐 *www.lemagnan.fr* 🕓 *Closed Tues. and Wed. May, June, Sept., and Oct. and Mon. Nov.–Apr. No lunch July and Aug.*

Port-Grimaud

6 km (10 miles) east of Grimaud.

Although much of the coast has been targeted with new construction of extraordinary ugliness, this modern architect's version of a Provençal fishing village works. A true operetta set and begun only in 1966, it has grown gracefully over the years and offers hope for the pink-concrete-scarred coastal landscape. It's worth parking and wandering along the village's Venice-like canals to admire its Old Mediterranean canal-tile roofs and pastel facades, already patinated with age. Even the church, though resolutely modern, feels Romanesque. There is, however, one modern touch some might appreciate: small electric tour boats (get them at Place du Marché, April through October) that you can rent without a license that can carry you and four others from bars to shops to waterfront restaurants throughout the complex of pretty squares and bridges (€30 for 30 minutes). Market days in the square are Thursday and Sunday.

GETTING HERE AND AROUND

From Gassin, follow the D61 for about 11 km (7 miles) to the D14 and take the D98 (which also takes you to St-Tropez). VarLib Bus No. 7760 (€3) runs between Grimaud and the port, and there are other routes. From Port Grimaud, a Bateaux Verts ferry (€7.20 one-way; 25 minutes) to St-Tropez runs April to October.

🍴 Restaurants

★ **La Table du Mareyeur**

$$$$ | **SEAFOOD** | Ewan and Caroline Scutcher haven't left Port Grimaud since they married here nearly 32 years ago and set up this waterside gem, now reputed as one of the Riviera's finest. In a fun and relaxed atmosphere, they offer the freshest fish and seafood on the coast; certainly the politicians, royalty, and film stars (think Leonardo DiCaprio) who dine portside here among the locals don't complain. **Known for:** meaty oysters perfect for slurping; summertime lunch menu that's quite a deal; celebrity-spotting. [$] *Average main: €36* ✉ *10–11 pl. des Artisans, Port Grimaud* ☎ *04–94–56–06–77* 🌐 *www.mareyeur.com* 🕓 *Closed mid-Oct.–late Mar.*

Ste-Maxime

8 km (5 miles) northeast of Port-Grimaud; 33 km (20 miles) northeast of St-Tropez.

You may be put off by its heavily built-up waterfront, bristling with parking garage–style apartments and hotels, and its position directly on the waterfront highway, but compared to overpriced St-Tropez, Ste-Maxime is an affordable family resort with fine, easily accessible, sandy beaches. It even has a sliver of a car-free Old Town (with its only one historic monument, the Tour Carrée) and a stand of majestic plane trees sheltering the central Place Victor-Hugo. Its main beach, north of town, is the wide and sandy La Nartelle.

GETTING HERE AND AROUND
Bateaux Verts ferries connect Ste-Maxime to St-Tropez in 15 minutes (€7.70). By car, if you're coming from the A8, take Exit 36 (Le Muy) and follow the D25. From Fréjus take the RD25. From Grimaud, take the RD558. SNCF trains stop at St-Raphaël where you can connect with a VarLib bus (€3).

🍴 Restaurants

La Maison Bleue
$$$ | FRENCH | Cheerful blue-and-white-checked tablecloths, massive colorful throw-cushions, and a polished wood facade give this unpretentious "blue house" on the main pedestrian street a welcoming air that matches the food. You'll find straightforward fresh pasta like tagliatelle pistou and ravioli and simple grilled meat and fish dishes, accompanied by well-chosen local wines. **Known for:** magical last dinner of any vacation; longtime friendly owner; good value €29 dinner menu. 💲 *Average main: €25* ✉ *48 rue Paul Bert* ☎ *04-94-96-51-92* 🕒 *Closed Mon. and Tues. Dec.–Feb. and Tues. Mar.–June and mid-Sept.–Nov.*

Le Bistrot de Louis
$$$ | FRENCH | This place checks all the boxes of your French bistro needs—mouthwatering classic dishes, a chalkboard menu, and a setting on a cobblestone street—with the added bonus of friendly and accommodating service. The three-course €26 menu rounds off the experience, although the selection of barbequed beef will make the meal truly unforgettable. **Known for:** menu that changes 7 days a week; barbeque steaks with truffle sauce; location on a quaint pedestrian square. 💲 *Average main: €26* ✉ *9 Pl. Colbert* ☎ *04-94-44-88-27* 🌐 *www.le-bistrot-de-louis.eatbu.com* 🕒 *Closed Jan.–Mar.*

Fréjus

37 km (23 miles) northeast of St-Tropez.

Fréjus (pronounced "fray- *zhooss*") has the honor of having some of the most important historic monuments on the coast. Founded in 49 BC by Julius Caesar himself and named Forum Julii, this quiet town was once a thriving Roman shipbuilding port with 40,000 citizens. In its heyday, Roman Fréjus had a theater, baths, and an enormous aqueduct that brought water all the way from Mons in the mountains, 45 km (28 miles) north of town. Today you can see the remains: a series of detached arches that follow the main Avenue du Quinzième Corps, leading up to the Old Town, with its maze of narrow streets lined with butcher shops, patisseries, and neighborhood stores barely touched by the cult of the lavender sachet.

In July and August, the crowds roll in for the sandy beaches by day and the seaside markets by night (daily 8 pm–midnight) as well as for fireworks (Les Nuits de Port-Fréjus) on Monday at 10:30 pm. Stick around in September for the Giant Omelette festival.

GETTING HERE AND AROUND
The direct bus to Fréjus from the Nice–Côte d'Azur airport (No. 3003) takes about an hour and costs €20. By car, you are only 35 minutes from the airport on the A8 highway (Exit 38, Fréjus/St-Raphaël). You can follow the DN7 for a more scenic drive, but it takes a lot more time, particularly with summer traffic. Train travelers will pay €13.40 for the 80-minute journey from the Nice Ville station.

VISITOR INFORMATION
CONTACTS Fréjus Tourist Office. ✉ *Le Florus II, 249 rue Jean-Jaurès* ☎ *04-94-51-83-83* 🌐 *www.frejus.fr.*

Sights

The Fréjus Pass (€6 or €9) is valid for seven days and gives you access to various historical landmarks and museums in the city, including those listed here, and can be purchased directly on-site.

Arènes

ARCHAEOLOGICAL SITE | The Arènes (often called the Amphithéâtre) is still used for concerts and bullfights, and can still seat up to 5,000. Back down on the coast, a big French naval base occupies the spot where ancient Roman galleys once set out to defeat Cleopatra and Mark Antony at the Battle of Actium. ⊠ *Rue Henri Vadon* ☎ *04–94–51–83–83* 🖾 *€3* ⊘ *Closed Mon. yr-round and Sun. Oct.–Mar.*

Chapelle Cocteau (*La Chapelle Notre-Dame de Jérusalem*)

RELIGIOUS SITE | This eccentric chapel was the last designed by Jean Cocteau as part of an artists' colony that never happened. It's an octagon built around a glass atrium and is embellished with stained glass, frescoes depicting the mythology of the first Crusades, and a tongue-in-cheek painting of the apostles above the front door that boasts the famous faces of Coco Chanel, Jean Marais, and poet Max Jacob. ⊠ *Av. Nicolaï, La Tour de la Mare* ✛ *5 km (3 miles) north of Fréjus on RN7* ☎ *04–94–53–27–06* 🖾 *€3* ⊘ *Closed Mon. yr-round and Sun. Oct.–Mar.*

Groupe Épiscopal

RELIGIOUS SITE | Fréjus is graced with one of the most impressive religious monuments in Provence: the Groupe Épiscopal is made up of an early Gothic **cathedral,** a 5th-century Roman-style **baptistery,** and an early Gothic **cloister,** its gallery painted in sepia and earth tones with a phantasmagoric assortment of animals and biblical characters. Off the entrance and gift shop is a small museum of finds from Roman Fréjus, including a complete mosaic and a sculpture of a two-headed Hermès. ⊠ *48 rue de Fleury* ☎ *04–94–51–26–30* ⊕ *www.cloitre-frejus. fr/en* 🖾 *Cathedral free; cloister, museum, and baptistery €6* ⊘ *Closed Mon.*

Théâtre Romain

ARCHAEOLOGICAL SITE | Northeast of Old Town and near the Porte de Rome is the Roman theater (circa 1st century); its remaining rows of arches are mostly intact and much of its stage, including the orchestra and substructures, are still visible at its center. Today the site is known as the Philippe Léotard Theatre and hosts Les Nuits Auréliennes every July. ⊠ *Av. du Théâtre Romain* ☎ *04–94–51–83–83* 🖾 *€3* ⊘ *Closed Mon. yr-round and Sun. Oct.–Mar.*

Beaches

The urban beaches—Capitole, République, and Sablettes—draped at the foot of Fréjus are backed by a commercial sprawl of brasseries, beach-gear shops, and realtors (for sun-struck visitors who dream of buying an apartment on the waterfront). The beaches outside the city, however, are public and wide open, with deep sandy stretches toward St-Aygulf. The calanques just south are particularly wild and pretty, with only tiny sand surfaces. During high season, *les plages* are cleaned daily, and lifeguards are on duty.

Plage de la République

BEACHES | This large, public sand beach, just east of the port and *capitainerie* is close to a restaurant where you can rent a lounger. Get here early in the summer to claim your towel space close to the sea; you'll be able to spot the tourists from the locals by the bottoms-only beach wear. **Amenities:** lifeguards; parking (fee); showers; toilets. **Best for:** sunrise; swimming. ⊠ *Bd. Alger.*

Activities

Centre International de Plongée (*International Diving Center*)

SCUBA DIVING | Contact the Centre International de Plongée for diving instruction, equipment rental, and guided outings. ⊠ *Port Fréjus* ☎ *04–94–52–34–99* ⊕ *www.cip-frejus.com.*

St-Raphaël

3 km (2 miles) east of Fréjus; 30 km (19 miles) southwest of Cannes.

Right next door to Fréjus, with almost no division between, spreads St-Raphaël, a sprawling resort city with a busy downtown anchored by a casino and a Vieille Ville that may not be the most picturesque, although you will stumble across Palladian and Belle Époque villas circa 18th and 19th centuries (the tourist office provides a map). It's also a major sailing center, has five golf courses nearby, and draws the weary and indulgent to its seawater-based thalassotherapy. Along with Fréjus, it serves as a rail crossroads, the two being the closest stops to St-Tropez. The port has a rich history: Napoléon landed at St-Raphaël on his triumphant return from Egypt in 1799; it was also from here in 1814 that he cast off in disgrace for Elba. And it was here, too, that the Allied forces landed in their August 1944 offensive against the Germans, known as the Champagne Campaign.

GETTING HERE AND AROUND

If you fly into Nice, take the airport bus No. 3003 from either terminal; it's €20 for the 75-minute journey. If you take a taxi, it'll be between €145–€192. The TGV Paris–St-Raphaël (5 hours; from €65 one-way) runs throughout the year and there are numerous trains arriving from Nice and Cannes. St-Raphaël is the western terminus of the TER line that runs along the Riviera. To get to towns farther west, you have to take a bus from just behind the train station. If you want a day trip to St-Tropez, April–October, there's a one-hour ferry ride (€15 one-way) or a taxi for at least €100. From St-Raphaël's bus station on Avenue Victor-Hugo, next to the train station, Bus No. 7601 links up with St-Tropez (via Grimaud and Ste-Maxime; €3, 1½ hours), some towns in the Haut Var, and selected stops along the coastal Corniche de l'Estérel. There are daily buses to Fréjus (€1.50), or you can take a taxi for about €20. Popular ferries leave from St-Raphaël's Vieux Port for St-Tropez, the Îles-de-Léerins, and the Calanques de l'Estérel.

VISITOR INFORMATION

CONTACTS St-Raphaël Tourist Office.
⊠ *99 quai Albert 1er* ☎ *04–94–19–52–52* ⊕ *www.saint-raphael.com.*

Sights

Casino Barrière de Saint-Raphaël

CASINO—SIGHT | Looking out over the waterfront, catering to the city's many conventioneers, the casino's 158 slot machines operate daily 9 am–3 am (4 am on Saturday), but the tables (English roulette, Black Jack, Stud Poker) don't open for play until 9 pm (4 pm on Sunday).

Mark Your Calendars

Celebrated since 1984, France's national heritage weekend allows you free access to participating museums and sites that are often closed to the public. "Les Journées du Patrimoine" is usually the third weekend in September (see ⊕ *www. journeesdupatrimoine.culture.fr*). During La Nuit des Musées (⊕ *www. nuitdesmusees.culture.fr*), usually on the third Saturday in May, hundreds of museums allow free entry, 8 pm–1 am.

Now *this* is why you came to the Riviera. St-Raphaël has one of the finest beach strands along the coast.

✉ *Sq. de Grand* ☎ *04–98–11–17–77* 🌐 *www.casinosbarriere.com.*

★ The Corniche de l'Estérel

TRAIL | FAMILY | Stay on the D559 to the D1098 and you'll find yourself careening along a stunning coastal drive, the Corniche de l'Estérel, which whips past tiny calanques and sheer rock faces that plunge down to the sea. At the dramatic Pointe de Cap Roux, an overlook allows you to pull off the narrow two-lane highway (where high-season sightseers can cause bumper-to-bumper traffic) and contemplate the spectacular view up and down the coast. Train travelers have the good fortune to snake along this cliffside for constant panoramas. It's also a hiker's haven. Some nine trails, ranging from an hour to 4½ hours, strike out from designated parking sites along the way, leading up into the jagged rock peaks for extraordinary sea views. (Don't leave valuables in the car, as the sites are littered with glass from break-ins.) You can download trail maps from the St-Raphaël tourist office website or drop by the office across from the train station. There is also a coastal path leaving from St-Raphaël port; you'll see a mix of wild, rocky criques and glamorous villas.

Église Notre-Dame-de-la-Victoire

RELIGIOUS SITE | Augmenting the Atlantic City vibe of this modern pleasure port is the gingerbread-and-gilt dome of the neo-Byzantine Église Notre-Dame-de-la-Victoire, which watches over the yachts and cruise boats sliding into the port. ✉ *Bd. Félix-Martin and 19 rue Jean Aicard.*

Église San Rafeu

RELIGIOUS SITE | Next to the Museum of Archeology in the Vieille Ville, the 12th-century Église San Rafeu (also known as St-Pierre-des-Templiers) is a miniature-scale Romanesque church. It was recently discovered that its foundations lie on top of two other churches dating back to the Carolingian era. Climb up the 129 steps of the 13th-century bell tower, the Tour San Rafeu, for its 360-degree panoramic views, and snap away. ✉ *Rue des Templiers.*

Musée Archéologique Marin (*Marine Archaeology Museum*)

MUSEUM | On the same quiet square as St-Pierre, this intimate museum offers a fascinating collection of ancient amphorae gleaned from the shoals offshore, where centuries' worth of shipwrecks have accumulated. By studying this chronological progression of jars and the accompanying sketches, you can visualize the coast as it was in its heyday as a Greek and Roman shipping center. You should also take advantage of the several temporary exhibiions held across the year. ■ TIP→ **You can use QR codes throughout the museum as a guide; iPads can be borrowed from reception too.** ✉ *Rue des Templiers* ☎ *04–94–19–25–75* ⊕ *www.musee-saintraphael.com* ✉ *Free* ☉ *Closed Sun. and Mon.*

Beaches

St-Raphaël's beaches form a snaking sliver of sand, starting just east of the port and finally petering out against the red cliffs of the Estérel, covering 8 km (5 miles) toward St-Aygulf, including one of the largest sandy beaches in the Eastern Var, surrounded by a dune. Here you'll find a nudist beach (June–September) and an area where dogs on leashes are permitted. From that point on, you can find tiny calanques and *criques* (coves and finger bays) for swimming and basking on the rocks. During high season, beaches are cleaned daily and lifeguards are on duty at Plage du Veillat, Beau-Rivage, Péguière, Plage du Débarquement, Plage d'Agay, and Plage du Lido. Flags indicate the presence of lifeguards or if the water is dangerous for swimming. ■ TIP→ **If you're looking for a different way to discover the sites along the shoreline, download the app Piste et Trésor in English and select the game "Saint-Raphaël," a cultural treasure hunt that takes about half a day.**

Plage Beau-Rivage

BEACHES | This is the second public beach in the city center, located between Veillat beach and the port of Santa Lucia. It's divided into two areas, the sandy Handiplage and a large stone pebble beach, and there is a beautiful promenade, shaded by a park with a playground for kids and minigolf. There are showers and toilets, but you can't rent a lounger here. **Amenities:** lifeguards; showers; toilets. **Best for:** sunset; swimming; walking. ✉ *120 bd. Raymond Poincaré.*

Plage du Débarquement

BEACHES | Named after the Allied landings in August 1944, this is a sand-on-top-of-red-stone beach with great views of the private Île d'Or. From town, head toward Agay until Dramont, where you'll see signs for the pebble beach. **Amenities:** lifeguards; parking (no fee); toilets. **Best for:** swimming. ✉ *1300 bd. de la 36ème Division du Texas.*

Plage du Veillat

BEACHES | This is the city's main (and its largest) sandy beach, with handicap access and lifeguard stations during the summer season, when you can also rent a mattress. There are lots of cafés around, and from the Old Port you can take a shuttle to St-Tropez. **Amenities:** lifeguards; parking (fee); showers; toilets. **Best for:** sunset; swimming; walking. ✉ *Corniche Roland Garros and Promenade René Coty.*

Restaurants

La Terrasse

$$$$ | **FRENCH** | This retro restaurant opened on-site when luxe hotel Les Roches Rouges was transformed by French hotelier Valéry Grégo, and it's already picked up one Michelin star. The dinner-only menu is dedicated to gastronomic yet inventive regional dishes, which head chef José Bailly bases on *La Cuisine Provençale de la Tradition Populaire*, a 1963 cookbook of traditional recipes by René Jouveau. **Known for:** three-course and five-course tasting menus only; spectacular seaside setting; traditional French dishes. [$] *Average main: €92* ✉ *90 bd. de la 36ème-Division-du-Texas* ☎ *04–89–81–40–60* 🌐 *www.hotellesrochesrouges.com/en* ⏲ *Closed Oct.–mid-May, Mon., and Tues.*

Les Voiles Saint-Raphael

$$ | **FRENCH** | Welcome to Les Voiles, a beach restaurant with a simple menu that's sea- and market-inspired. Order a grilled entrecôte or white cod and risotto with coconut milk à la carte or just go for the three-course prix-fixe meal for only €32, which gives you a reason to linger longer in front of the glorious azure backdrop. **Known for:** Michelin Bib Gourmand award for best table at low prices; express weekday lunch menu for €16; fabulous port views. [$] *Average main: €22* ✉ *Port Santa Lucia, 101 quai Commandant-le-Prieur* ☎ *04–94–40–39–15* ⏲ *Closed Mon., Dec., and Jan.* 💳 *No credit cards.*

Hotels

Excelsior

$$ | **HOTEL** | This urban and friendly hotel combining straightforward comforts and a waterfront position in the center of town attracts a regular clientele. **Pros:** minutes from sea; decent-size rooms; 18 sea-facing rooms offer great views. **Cons:** breakfast €13; €14/day public parking; early church bells ring from nearby. [$] *Rooms from: €185* ✉ *Promenade du René Coty* ☎ *04–94–95–02–42* 🌐 *www.excelsior-hotel.com* 🛏 *42 rooms* 🍴 *No meals.*

Hôtel Thimothée

$ | **B&B/INN** | This attractive 19th-century villa offers well-priced and comfortable rooms as well as a lovely garden, where grand palms and pines shade the walk leading to a pretty little swimming pool, making it all seem more than a two-star establishment. **Pros:** free parking and free bikes; clean rooms and modern bathrooms; sea-view rooms on top floor worth extra €30. **Cons:** beach and waterfront cafés are a 20-minute walk away; standard rooms are on the small side; breakfast costs extra. [$] *Rooms from: €90* ✉ *375 bd. Christian-Lafon* ☎ *04–94–40–49–49* 🌐 *www.hotel-thimothee.com* 💳 *No credit cards* 🛏 *12 rooms* 🍴 *No meals.*

Activities

St-Raphaël is a serious sailing and boating center, with nautical complexes at four different sites along the coast: the Vieux Port, Santa Lucia (by Fréjus-Plage), Le Dramont (at the base of a dramatic little cape below the Estérel), and within Agay's quiet harbor.

To explore the wilds of the Estérel on foot, consider a guided hike led by a qualified staffer from the tourist office.

Club Nautique St-Raphaël

BOATING | For information on boat rentals or sailing lessons, contact this club, founded in 1927. ✉ *26 pl. du Club Nautique* ☎ *04–94–95–11–66* 🌐 *www.cnsr.fr.*

Mandelieu–La Napoule

32 km (20 miles) northeast of St-Raphaël; 8 km (5 miles) southwest of Cannes.

La Napoule is the small, old-fashioned port village, Mandelieu the big-fish resort town that devoured it. Mandelieu is replete with many sporting facilities and hosts a bevy of sporting events, including sailing regattas, windsurfing contests, and golf championships (there are two major golf courses in Mandelieu right in the center of town, by the sea). A yacht-crammed harbor sits under the shadow of some high-rise resort hotels. La Napoule, on the other hand, offers the requisite quaintness, ideal for a portside stroll, casual meal, beach siesta, or visit to its peculiar castle. Unless you're here for the sun and surf, however, these twinned towns mostly serve as a home base for outings to Cannes, Antibes, and the Estérel. In fact, the easternmost beach in Mandelieu dovetails with the first and most democratic beaches of its glamorous neighbor, Cannes.

GETTING HERE AND AROUND

From Terminal 1 or 2 at Nice airport, take the A8 to Exit 40 (about 30 minutes) or the 35-minute airport bus (direction St-Raphaël, €20). The closest train station is in Cannes, and you can either take a taxi (about €30 to the city center during the day) or catch Bus No. N20 from Cannes train station, departing frequently throughout the day, for €1.50. It sets you down at "Balcon d'Azur," just past the château.

VISITOR INFORMATION

CONTACTS Mandelieu–La Napoule Tourist Office. ✉ 806 av. de Cannes, Mandelieu-la-Napoule ☎ 04–93–93–64–64 ⊕ www.ot-mandelieu.fr.

Sights

Château de la Napoule

CASTLE/PALACE | Looming over the sea at Pointe des Pendus (Hanged Man's Point), the Château de la Napoule is a spectacularly bizarre hybrid of Romanesque, Gothic, Moroccan, and Hollywood cooked up by the eccentric American sculptor Henry Clews (1876–1937). Working with his architect wife, Clews transformed the 14th-century bastion into something that suited his personal expectations and then filled the place with his own fantastical sculptures. The couple reside in their tombs in the tower crypt, its windows left slightly ajar to permit their souls to escape and allow them to "return at eventide as sprites and dance upon the windowsill." Today the château's foundation hosts visiting writers and artists, who set to work surrounded by Clews's gargoyle-ish sculptures. ✉ Av. Henry Clews, Mandelieu-la-Napoule

☎ 04–93–49–95–05 ⊕ www.chateau-lana-poule.com ✉ From €4.

Beaches

There are three private beaches nestled in between the seven public beaches, the major difference between public and private being, as it always is, a question of comfort. You can spend the extra euros for a comfortable mattress, access to shade, and the convenience of a nearby restaurant. On the public beach you have to supply your own comforts.

Le Sweet

BEACHES | A front-row lounger on the sandy beach at Le Sweet costs €20 for the day, which includes an umbrella as well as access to the locker room and shower, and in summer a lifeguard is on-site. There's beach-bar service and a restaurant that specializes in the catch of the day. **Amenities:** food and drink; lifeguards; showers; toilets. **Best for:** sunset; swimming. ✉ Av. General du Gaulle, near Av. de la Mer intersection, Mandelieu-la-Napoule ☎ 04–93–49–87–33 ⊕ www.sweetplage.com.

Sable d'Or Beach

BEACHES | Between the casino and Cannes la Bocca, this public sand beach is one of the most beautiful in Mandelieu. There are restaurants and a nautical center nearby, as well as lifeguards on duty. If the views of the Îles de Lérins grow old, head to the neighboring Robinson beach and play some volleyball. **Amenities:** food and drink; lifeguards; showers; toilets. **Best for:** views; swimming. ✉ Av. Général-de-Gaulle, Mandelieu-la-Napoule.

Restaurants

L'Oasis

$$$$ | **MODERN FRENCH** | A culinary landmark for more than 60 years, executive chef Alain Montigny has incorporated Art Deco decor that's both more intimate and more cultural, and that ties in to his high-end cuisine (so high-end in fact that the set-lunch menu starts at €65 and comes with predessert). The sea and earth options may not appeal to everyone (think pigeon, sweetbread, and red mullet) but the starters will win over the crowds. **Known for:** legendary eatery with one Michelin star; extraordinary service; scrambled eggs, caviar, and oasis truffle starter. $ *Average main: €80* ⊠ *6 rue Jean Honoré Carle, Mandelieu-la-Napoule* ☎ *04–93–49–95–52* ⊕ *www.oasisetoile-mandelieu.fr* ⊗ *Closed Sun.–Tues.*

Le Boucanier

$$$ | **SEAFOOD** | Several years ago, former French pro soccer player Wilfried Gohel teamed up with Eric Chaumier, president of the regional retailers union, and took over this waterfront favorite. They could have just banked on the wraparound views of the marina and château to bring in the dinner crowds, but instead they refined the menu to include grilled bass with smoked salt petals and salmon marinated with pure malt whisky and sautéed with matcha tea velouté sauce. **Known for:** €39 three-course menu; incredible views; vegan, pasta, and kids' options. $ *Average main: €27* ⊠ *Port de La Napoule, 273 av. Henry Clews, Mandelieu-la-Napoule* ☎ *04–93–49–80–51* ⊕ *www.boucanier.fr* ⊗ *Closed Mon. Oct.–Mar. No dinner Sun. Oct.–Mar.*

 Hotels

Pullman Cannes Mandelieu Royal Casino

$$$ | **HOTEL** | As much a resort as a hotel, this modern waterfront complex with soundproofed rooms has deluxe comforts on a grand scale, with a broad beach terrace, outdoor (unheated) pool, fit lounge, casino, restaurant, and access to the Old Course golf club next door. **Pros:** loungers on the private sand beach; Nespresso in rooms along with complimentary half bottles of water replaced daily; beautiful swimming pool. **Cons:** €30 for a taxi to La Croisette in Cannes; not

close to any shops; on-site casino open until 4 am which can mean late-night noise. $ *Rooms from: €300* ⊠ *605 av. Général-de-Gaulle, Mandelieu-la-Napoule* ☎ *04–92–97–70–00* ⊕ *www.pullman-mandelieu.com* ⟲ *213* ⦿ *No meals.*

 Activities

Classified as a *station voile* (sailing resort), Mandelieu–La Napoule is a major water-sports center.

Centre Nautique Municipal

BOATING | Small sailboats and windsurfers can be rented from Centre Nautique Municipal, next to the restaurant La Plage. It's open daily year-round. ⊠ *Av. du Général de Gaulle, Mandelieu-la-Napoule* ☎ *04–92–97–07–70* ⊕ *www.mandelieu.fr.*

Golf Club de Cannes-Mandelieu

GOLF | Grand Duke Michael of Russia founded the Riviera's first golf course in 1891, known familiarly as the Old Course, and it's been played by all of Europe's royals. Officially it's the International Golf Club Cannes-Mandelieu and has two courses, which are the most visually stunning courses in the south of France. The 18-hole course is shaded by old pine trees and features a ferry across the Slagne River from Hole 2 to 3 and again from Hole 12 to 13. ⊠ *Rte. du Golf, Mandelieu-la-Napoule* ☎ *04–92–97–32–00* ⊕ *www.golfoldcourse.com* ⛳ *18-hole course: €90 (€65 after 3 pm, €55 after 5 pm). 9-hole course: €50* ⛳ *18 holes, 6287 yards, par 71; 9 holes, 2316 yards, par 33.*

Fayence

36 km (23 miles) north of Mandelieu–La Napoule; 27 km (17 miles) west of Grasse; 30 km (19 miles) northwest of Cannes.

The most touristy of all the hill towns in the Haut Var backcountry (all of which are called Pays de Fayence), Fayence is easiest to reach from the coast and often filled with busloads of day-trippers. Nonetheless, it has a pretty Old Town at the top, magnificent wraparound views from its 18th-century church down to the Massif des Maures and the Estérel, and a plethora of artisans' galleries and boutiques. The Four du Mitan museum, where you'll see the original village oven built in 1522, is free to visit and open every day. Fayence is also home to Europe's best gliding club (you can eat at its restaurant) and Pickleball France-Pays-de-Fayence, which has some English-speaking members. Stop by on a Saturday morning near the municipal outdoor sports club and you can pay a drop-in fee and rent a paddle to get your fix.

GETTING HERE AND AROUND

There are no trains, but daily buses go from Cannes (No. 3002, 1 hour 20 minutes; €3) and Grasse (No. 3021, 1 hour 10 minutes; €3). It's an hour's drive from Nice airport—take Exit 39 (Fayence/Les Adrets) from the A8. A taxi to/from the airport will cost around €125 (count on more at night).

VISITOR INFORMATION

CONTACTS Fayence Tourist Office. ✉ *Pl. Léon-Roux* ☎ *04–94–76–20–08* 🌐 *www.paysdefayence.com.*

🍴 Restaurants

Le Temps des Cerises

$$ | **FRENCH** | You'll find your *bonheur* (happiness) in this popular and centrally located gem where Dutch owner-chef Louis Schröder has simplified his dinner menu: there's one price for entrées (€15.50), one for mains (€25.50), and one for desserts (€9.50)—or order one of each for €44.50. From shellfish and sea bass to beef tenderloin and veal kidney, the selection is classic French gastronomy (so definitely not vegan or vegetarian friendly). **Known for:** consistently high-quality meals; homemade ice cream and sorbets; lovely terrace atmosphere on a slightly noisy road. [$] *Average main: €26* ✉ *2 pl. de la République* ☎ *04–94–76–01–19* 🌐 *www.restaurantletemps-descerises.fr* ⏲ *Closed Tues. and Wed.*

🛏 Hotels

Moulin de la Camandoule

$ | **HOTEL** | On 11 acres of streamside greenery, this noble old olive mill has been turned into a lovely country inn—complete with beams, the original mill-wheel, and a *pressoir* (olive press) in the middle of the bar. **Pros:** gorgeous viney grounds and massive pool; minutes from village; excellent restaurant. **Cons:** cannot book online; three-night minimum stay June–September; 25% minimum deposit. [$] *Rooms from: €108* ✉ *159 chemin de Notre Dame* ☎ *04–94–76–00–84* 🌐 *www.camandoule.com* 🔑 *11 rooms* 🍽 *No meals.*

★ **Terre Blanche**

$$$$ | **RESORT** | **FAMILY** | Nestled in the countryside, this resort is larger than Monaco and come with an impressive roster of amenities—four pools, two world-class 18-hole golf courses, a two-story spa, and four restaurants including Michelin-starred Le Feventia. **Pros:** wine cellar with 3,000-plus different local Provençal labels; free newspapers, tea/coffee in suites, sunscreen, and driving range with unlimited balls; excellent facilities among beautiful grounds. **Cons:** need car to get here; not all rates include breakfast; visitors tend to stay in the resort and not explore the rest of the countryside. [$] *Rooms from: €820* ✉ *3100 rte. de Bagnols en Fôret, Tourrettes* ☎ *04–94–39–90–00* 🌐 *en.terre-blanche.com* 🔑 *115 rooms* 🍽 *No meals.*

Seillans

Voted one of "France's most beautiful villages" with its ruined château and ramparts, fountains, flowers, and sunny maze of steeply raked cobblestone streets that suddenly break open over valley views, this is an appealing old town that still smacks of yesteryear's Côte d'Azur. Its church, a Renaissance remake of an 11th-century structure, is the best spot from which to admire the panorama; it's worth a pause to take in the musty Latin atmosphere. There are old-style, competitive bakers here, and an active café life on a miniature scale. The French opera composer Gounod and the surrealist Max Ernst were regulars in Seillans—Ernst retired here. Year-round guided tours (€3; 60 minutes) of the town in English and French start from the tourist office Thursday at 10 but you need to reserve a few days in advance (5-person minimum per tour).

The Festival Musique Cordiale (🌐 *www.musique-cordiale.com*) takes place over the first two weeks of August at locations such as Chapelle Notre-Dame de l'Ormeau and the 11th-century Eglise St-Léger, as well as in neighboring villages.

GETTING HERE AND AROUND

From the A8 highway, take Exit 39 (Fayence) and follow the D37/Route du Lac to the D562, then follow the D19 into town. There are a few VarLib buses (€3) that can get you here from Cannes, Grasse, and even St-Raphaël.

👁 Sights

Notre-Dame-de-l'Ormeau

RELIGIOUS SITE | Just east of town on the Route de Fayence is the Romanesque chapel Notre-Dame-de-l'Ormeau, which contains a remarkable altarpiece dating to the 16th century. Sculpted portraits of the wise men and shepherds adoring the Christ child, strikingly real in emotion and gesture, contrast sharply with the simple ex-votos that pepper the walls. Guided visits (€3) take place throughout the year on Thursday at 11:15; you need to reserve with the tourist office (five-person minimum). ✉ *Maison Waldberg, Pl. du Thouron* ☎ *04–94–76–85–91.*

🍴 Restaurants

Tilleul Citron

$ | **FRENCH** | For a light meal, stop by this delightful salon du thé for a tarte salée with salad or for owner Pascale Raskin's specialty, panisse with melted goat cheese and figs compote with tomato salad. Try one of their many teas with a tasty dessert or a crêpe while you take in the local art on display in this old cork maker's shop. **Known for:** breakfast until 11:30 am; tiny covered terrace; inexpensive home cooking. [$] *Average main: €13* ✉ *La Bouchonnerie, Rue de la Capelette* ☎ *04–94–50–47–64* 💳 *No credit cards* 🕒 *Closed Tues., Jan., and Feb. No lunch Mon.*

🛏 Hotels

Hôtel des Deux Rocs

$ | **HOTEL** | This property exudes Provençal style, with its tiny square with a trickling fountain, venerable plane trees, green valley views, and two massive imposing rocks (and that's just on the outside). **Pros:** old stone house with modern quirky interiors; free Wi-Fi and parking; romantic restaurant. **Cons:** no air-conditioning; damp in wet weather; in need of some renovations. [$] *Rooms from: €80* ✉ *Pl. Font d'Amont* ☎ *04–94–76–87–32* 🌐 *www.hoteldeuxrocs.com* 🕒 *Closed mid-Nov.–mid-Mar.* 🛏 *14 rooms* 🍽 *No meals.*

La Palud-sur-Verdon

48 km (30 miles) northwest of Seillans.

Though several towns bill themselves as *the* gateway to the Gorges du Verdon, this unassuming village stands in its center, on a plateau just north of the gorge's vertiginous drop (to gain the Gorges's southern flank, enter from the

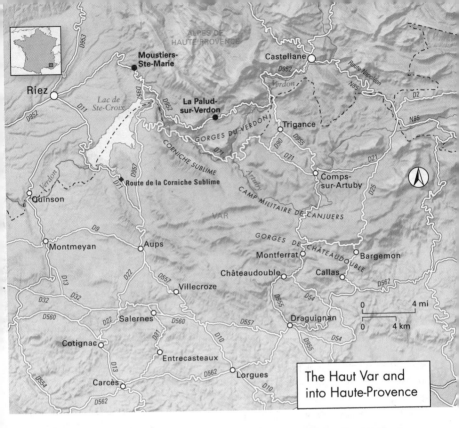

The Haut Var and into Haute-Provence

elegant village of Moustiers). It's a hikers' and climbers' town, and—as the Germans and Dutch are more *sportif* than the French—has an international feel. You'll see more beards and Volkswagen vans here than anywhere in France, and you'll probably share a café terrace with backpackers clad in boots and fleece easing off a load of ropes, picks, and cleats.

GETTING HERE AND AROUND

Coming by car (your best option) from the coast, take the A8 highway, get off at the Draguignan exit, then follow the D955 north(ish) past Comps-sur-Artuby to the D952, which you can follow west along a demanding drive—keep your eyes on the road.

VISITOR INFORMATION

CONTACTS Maison des Gorges du Verdon.
✉ *Le Château* ☎ *04–92–77–32–02*
⊕ *www.lapaludsurverdon.com.* **Maison**

des Guides du Verdon. ✉ *Rue Principale* ☎ *04–92–77–30–50* ⊕ *www.escalade-verdon.fr.*

Sights

★ Gorges du Verdon

NATURE SITE | You are here for one reason only: to explore the extraordinary Gorges du Verdon, also known as—with only slight exaggeration over another, more famous version—the Grand Canyon. Through the aeons, the jewel-green torrent of the Verdon River has chiseled away the limestone plateau and gouged a spectacular gorge lined with steep white cliffs and sloping rock falls carpeted with green forest. The jagged rock bluffs, roaring water, and dense wild boxwood create a savage world of genuinely awe-inspiring beauty, whether

The 21-km (13-mile) Gorges du Verdon was carved out of solid rock by the fast-flowing Verdon River millennia ago.

viewed from dozens of clifftop overlooks or explored from the wilderness below.

If you're driving from La Palud, follow the dramatic **Route des Crêtes** circuit (D23), a white-knuckle cliff-hanger not for the faint of heart. When you approach and leave La Palud, you'll do it via D952 between Castellane and Moustiers, with several breathtaking overlooks. The best of these is the **Point Sublime,** at the east end; leave your car by the hotel-restaurant and walk to the edge, holding tight to dogs and children—that's a 2,834-foot drop to the bottom. You can also access the famous drive along D71 called the **Route de la Corniche Sublime** from Moustiers; top lookout points here are the Horserider's Cliff, the Balcon de la Mescla, and the Pont de l'Artuby bridge.

If you want to hike, there are several trails that converge in this prime territory. The most spectacular is the branch of the GR4 that follows the bed of the canyon itself, along the **Sentier Martel.** This dramatic trail, beginning at the Chalet de la Maline and ending at the Point Sublime,

was created in the 1930s by the Touring-Club de France and named for one of the gorge's first explorers. Easier circuits leave from the Point Sublime on *sentiers de découverte* (trails with commentary) into the gorge known as Couloir Samson.

Hotels

Hotel des Gorges du Verdon

$$ | **HOTEL** | **FAMILY** | At an altitude of 3,000 feet, this four-star Châteaux & Hôtels Collection escape has breathtaking panoramas of La Palud's countryside from the breakfast table, plus plenty of activities for non-hikers. **Pros:** ping-pong table, boules, tennis, and heated pool; excellent Cinq Mondes Spa; LandArt outdoor exhibition. **Cons:** some rooms are small; meal plan option a little expensive at €37 extra, but food is delicious; expensive compared to other local accommodations. $ *Rooms from: €225* ✉ *Rte. de la Maline* ☎ *04–92–77–38–26* ⊕ *www.hotel-des-gorges-du-verdon.fr* ⊙ *Closed mid-Oct.–Easter* ⮑ *30 rooms* ⊙❙ *No meals.*

The Sentier Martel: Trial by Trail

The Main Show

Threading the Grand Canyon du Verdon is one of France's greatest hiking routes: the Sentier Martel, named in honor of the spelunker-explorer Edouard Martel (1859–1938), who first penetrated the Gorges in 1896 with a canvas canoe, an assistant, and two local trout fishermen. Despite repeated attempts, he didn't manage to negotiate the full canyon's length until 1905.

It was in the 1930s that the Touring Club blasted fire escape–style ladders and catwalks along the precarious rock walls, and drilled two tunnels through solid stone. They added occasional rope railings and steps, buttressed the trail with rock supports, and one of France's most famous hikes was born.

Martel Musts

It's best to depart from the Châlet de la Maline (the Refuge des Malines), striking out on the long descent and then working your way back up gradually to the Couloir du Samson and the Point Sublime (D952). Park your car past the Refuge and canteen, 8 km (5 miles) from La Palud-sur-Verdon, and walk 300 yards to the starting point of your descent, just left of the Refuge des Malines. Follow the white and red markings along the way (an X indicates the wrong path; an arrow indicates a change in direction).

You'll encounter all types of terrain—pebbles, stone, muddy soil—and sliding down rocks on your buttocks is not out of the question, especially when the alternative is tumbling down, down, and down. Forget about setting a world record and stop to enjoy lunch along the way to take your eyes off your feet and appreciate the magnificence of the surroundings. Once you exit the tunnels and cross a small bridge, you'll reach the Parking du Couloir Samson but even this is not the final destination. Cross the pavement and continue left to finish the final ascent to Point Sublime. Markings here are not as visible but paths are solid soil and you will eventually make it to the top, a rugged terrain where the less daring stop to simply take photos. Have the €3 ready for a nice cold beverage at the only canteen.

Words of Warning

As the Verdon is regulated by two dams, you'll often be confronted with not-so-comforting signs showing a human stick figure running for his life before a tidal wave. This is to warn you to stick to the trail and not linger on the beachlike riverbed when the water is low, as it could rise suddenly at any moment. Remember a flashlight with good batteries; you won't be able to grope your way through the tunnels without it. And be prepared for wet feet—ankle-deep puddles are unavoidable. Dial ☎ 112 if you have an emergency.

Where to Park?

A taxi pickup at Point Sublime needs to be arranged the previous night for the 14-km (9-mile) return ride, based on a rough estimate of your own abilities; or leave a car at the final destination and ask a taxi (in advance) to carry you to your takeoff point. The best taxis are **Taxi Verdun** (☎ 06–68–18–13–13) and **Taxi de l'Etoile** (☎ 06–07–37–33–78).

Le Perroquet Vert
$ | **B&B/INN** | In a restored 18th-century house on La Palud's only street, this lovely little sports store/restaurant/B&B-complex is run by charming owners. **Pros:** fine bargain prices include free Wi-Fi; free tea and coffee in common area; tasty home-cooked meals. **Cons:** no TV in rooms; free parking is more than 300 feet away in the village; early 10 am checkout. [$] *Rooms from: €60* ✉ *Rue Grande* ☎ *04–92–77–33–39* 🌐 *www.leperroquetvert.com* 🕒 *Closed mid-Nov.–mid-Mar.* 🛏 *4 rooms* 🍴 *No meals.*

Activities

If you're not up to hiking the Sentier Martel, there are other ways of embracing the Gorges.

Aboard Rafting
WHITE-WATER RAFTING | **FAMILY** | Rafting excursions in the Gorges du Verdon run from two to five-plus hours (€40–€75). You can also try canoe-rafting or canyoning, and for younger members of the family there's the Adventure Rope Course (three hours; €25). Meeting points vary, but many start from Adventure Forest near Castellane. ✉ *Rte. de Moustiers D 952, Castellane* ☎ *04–92–83–76–11* 🌐 *www.rafting-verdon.com.*

La Maison du Canyoning et de l'Escalade
CLIMBING/MOUNTAINEERING | Want to try canyoneering or climbing? Contact La Maison du Canyoning et de l'Escalade May–September for guided outings, varying from 90 minutes (€35) to full-day 5½ hour excursions (€70). Minimum age for participation is six for an introduction to climbing outing; you may be asked to bring a lunch. ✉ *1 Pl. de l'Église, Castellane* ☎ *07–85–55–15–30* 🌐 *www.maisonducanyoning.fr.*

Moustiers-Ste-Marie

10 km (7 miles) northwest of La Palud-sur-Verdon.

At the edge of all this epic wilderness, it's a bit of a shock to find this jaw-droppingly picture-perfect village of 700 residents tucked into a spectacular cleft in vertical cliffs, its bluffs laced with bridges, draped with medieval stone houses, and crowned with church steeples. The Verdon River gushes out of the rock at the village's heart, and between the two massive rocks that tower over the ensemble, a star swings suspended from a chain.

To most, the name "Moustiers" means faience, the fine, glazed earthenware that has been produced here since the 17th century, when a monk brought in the secret of enamel glazes from Faenza in Umbria. Its brilliant white finish caught the world's fancy, especially when the fashionable grotesques of Jean Berain, decorator to Louis XIV, were imitated and produced in exquisite detail. A colony of ceramists still creates Moustiers faience today, from large commercial producers to independent artisans.

More than 20,000 olive trees grow on the dry stone of Claux hill and so you'll find Moustiers olive oil at the Friday morning market, along with local delicacies like tapenade, handmade cookies, and lavender honey. The town is quite keen to promote French lavender, which is actually a hybrid called lavendin created for the perfume industry a century ago. In 2018, they launched the LavandEvasion festival, which includes tours on bike, foot, and hot-air balloon to experience lavender in bloom; you can also visit the local lavender farm overlooking Sainte-Croix Lake.

If you're in town on Wednesday from May to October, 90-minute tours in English start at 10 am and 3 pm (5 pm in

While a hot restaurant scene has made Moustiers-Ste-Marie newly fashionable, the town has been a byword for the finest in faience and pottery for centuries.

the summer), but you need to reserve in advance at the tourist office (€4).

GETTING HERE AND AROUND

There's a summer bus from Manosque that takes 90 minutes, but the bigger problem is that there is no shuttle up to the village, so a car is your best bet. From the Côte d'Azur by car take the A8 highway, exit direction "Draguignan," then "Aups, Les Salles" to Moustiers, found just off D952 (a 90-minute drive from Fréjus). There's a bus from Nice to Castellane, and a connecting bus, the LER 27, goes to Moustiers (€8.50; 90 minutes).

VISITOR INFORMATION

CONTACTS Moustiers Tourist Office. ✉ Maison de Lucie, Pl. de l'Église, Moustiers-Sainte-Marie ☎ 04-92-74-67-84 ⊕ www.moustiers.fr/en.

 Sights

Chapelle Notre-Dame-de-Beauvoir

RELIGIOUS SITE | Moustiers was founded as a monastery in the 5th century, but it was in the Middle Ages that the Chapelle Notre-Dame-de-Beauvoir (first known as d'Entreroches, or "between rocks") became an important pilgrimage site. You can still climb the steep cobbled switchbacks along with pilgrims, passing modern stations-of-the-cross panels in Moustiers faïence. From the porch of the 12th-century church, remodeled in the 16th century, you can look over the roofs of the village to the green valley, a patchwork of olive groves and red-tiled farmhouse roofs. The forefather of the star that swings in the wind over the village was first hung, it is said, by a crusader grateful for his release from Saracen prison. It takes about 20 minutes to climb the 262 steps but remember, what goes up must come down—these worn stone steps yield little traction, so be careful. ✉ Moustiers-Sainte-Marie.

Musée de la Faïence

MUSEUM | The small but excellent Musée de la Faïence has concise audiovisual explanations of the craft and displays a chronology of fine pieces. It is currently housed in a pretty 18th-century hôtel *particulier* (private mansion) with a lovely *salle de mariage* (wedding hall) lined in painted canvas. ✉ *Pl. du Tricentenaire, Rue du Seigneur de la Clue, Moustiers-Sainte-Marie* ☎ *04–92–74–61–64* 🎫 *€3* ⊘ *Closed Jan. and Tues.*

Route de la Corniche Sublime

SCENIC DRIVE | Despite its civilized airs, Moustiers is another gateway to the Gorges du Verdon, providing the best access to the southern bank and the famous drive along D71 called the Route de la Corniche Sublime. (There's also the scenic 23-km ([14-mile]) route along the northern ridge, Route des Crêtes along the D23, which starts at Castellane and has no fewer than 14 viewpoints that cut through the ridges of the canyon.) Breathtaking views over withering drop-offs punctuate this vertiginous road just wide enough for two cars if you all hold your breath. The best of the vistas is called the **Balcons de la Mescla**, with viewpoints built into the cliff face overlooking the torrential whirlpool where the Verdon and Artuby combine. ✉ *Moustiers-Sainte-Marie.*

Hotels

Hôtel les Restanques

$ | **HOTEL** | Only a 10-minute walk from the village, this motel-style building offers excellent value and has spacious, crispy clean rooms, some of which open onto a terrace and garden. **Pros:** spacious rooms; lovely view from the pool; free parking and Wi-Fi. **Cons:** rooms facing the pool can get noisy; breakfast costs extra; no minibar in room. **$** *Rooms from: €104* ✉ *Rte. des Gorges du Verdon, D952, Moustiers-Sainte-Marie* ☎ *04–92–74–93–93* ⊕ *www.hotel-les-restanques.com* ⊘ *Closed Nov. 15–Mar. 15* 🛏 *20 rooms* ⏀ *No meals.*

★ La Bastide de Moustiers

$$$$ | **HOTEL** | Gourmands from around the world flock to this lovely 17th-century bastide, transformed by Alain Ducasse into a luxury country retreat surrounded by olive and chestnut trees, lavender, and trellises filled with the blooms of rose bushes. **Pros:** excellent restaurant; peace and quiet with exceptional natural lighting; gorgeous, nature-heavy decor. **Cons:** not really walking distance of village; rooms can feel a tad cramped; set menus at restaurant start at €65. **$** *Rooms from: €295* ✉ *Chemin de Quinson, Moustiers-Sainte-Marie* ☎ *04–92–70–47–47* ⊕ *www.bastide-moustiers.com* ⊘ *Closed Nov.–mid-Mar.* 🛏 *13 rooms* ⏀ *No meals.*

Shopping

L'Atelier Soleil

CERAMICS/GLASSWARE | At this shop next to the Bastide de Moustiers, second-generation potter Franck Scherer makes custom-made plates for Alain Ducasse's auberges. You can visit the workshop and buy pieces with tiny flaws at a reduced price. ✉ *Chemin de Quinson, Moustiers-Sainte-Marie* ☎ *04–92–74–61–62* ⊕ *www.soleil-deux.com* ⊘ *Closed Sun.*

Le Souquet

CRAFTS | Stock up here on local olive oils, local food specialties and cork crafts. ✉ *Rue Marcel Provence, Moustiers-Sainte-Marie* ☎ *06–82–68–84–55* ⊘ *Closed Oct.–Mar.*

Chapter 7

NICE AND THE EASTERN FRENCH RIVIERA

Updated by
Nancy Heslin

 Sights
★★★★☆

 Restaurants
★★★★☆

 Hotels
★★★★☆

 Shopping
★★★★☆

 Nightlife
★★★☆☆

WELCOME TO NICE AND THE EASTERN FRENCH RIVIERA

TOP REASONS TO GO

★ **Picasso and Company:** As artists have long loved the Côte d'Azur, it is blessed with superb art museums, including the Fondation Maeght in St-Paul and the Musée Picasso in Antibes.

★ **Èze:** The most perfectly situated of the coast's villages perchés, Èze has some of the most breath-taking views this side of a NASA space capsule.

★ **Nice:** With its bonbon-color palaces, blue Baie des Anges, time-stained Old Town, and Musée Matisse, this is one of France's most colorful cities.

★ **Cap d'Antibes:** Bordering well-hidden mansions and zillion-dollar hotels, the Sentier Tirepoil is a spectacular foot-path along the sea.

1 Cannes.

2 Îles de Lérins.

3 Mougins.

4 Grasse.

5 Valbonne.

6 Vallauris.

7 Antibes.

8 Cap d'Antibes.

9 Juan-les-Pins.

10 Biot.

11 Villeneuve-Loubet.

12 Haut-de-Cagnes.

13 St-Paul-de-Vence.

14 Vence.

15 Nice.

16 Villefranche-Sur-Mer.

17 Beaulieu-Sur-Mer.

18 St-Jean-Cap-Ferrat.

19 Èze.

20 Roquebrune-Cap-Martin.

21 Menton.

ITALY

Menton ○ [21]

Roquebrune-
Cap-Martin
[20]

ALPES MARITIMES

La Turbie

Monte-Carlo

D2204

D2564

Èze [19]

MONACO

N7

N88

Villefranche-
sur-Mer

Beaulieu-sur-Mer

[17]

Vence ○ [14]

[16]

Golfe de St-Hospice

Nice ○ [15]

St-Jean-
Cap-Ferrat [18]

I-de-Vence ○ [13]

Haut-de-Cagnes ○ [12]

Cagnes-sur-Mer ○

euve-Loubet [11]

Baie des Anges

Biot

[10]

Mediterranean Sea

Vallauris [6]

Antibes ○ [7]

Juan-les-Pins ○ [9]

Cap d'Antibes [8]

es Golfe Juan

Iles de Lérins
[2]

0   5 mi

0   5 km

With the Alps and pre-Alps playing bodyguard against inland winds, and the sultry Mediterranean warming the sea breezes, the eastern slice of the Côte d'Azur is pampered by a nearly tropical climate that sets it apart from the rest of France's southern coast.

This is where the real glamour begins: the dreamland of azure waters and indigo sky; white villas with balustrades edging the blue horizon; evening air perfumed with jasmine and mimosa; palm trees and parasol pines silhouetted against sunsets of apricot and gold.

There has been a constant march to this renowned stretch of Mediterranean coastline, going back to the ancient Greeks, who sailed eastward from Marseille to market their goods to the indigenes. But most of the earliest inhabitants of this region were fishermen and peasants who grew wheat, olives, and grapes for wine. This was not one of those lush regions of France where the living was easy. There were no palaces or gracious châteaux, only small villages, with fortifications here and there for use when Celts, Vandals, Ostrogoths, Saracens, and pirates from Algeria's Barbary Coast were on the rampage.

It was only in the middle of the 19th century that a troupe of kings and queens (including Victoria and dozens of her relatives), Russian grand dukes seeking to escape St. Petersburg's harsh climate, princelings from obscure Balkan countries, English milords, and a rabble of nouveau-riche camp followers began making prolonged visits here. They had mansions and gardens built; luxury hotels sprang up in imitation of their palaces back home. Many have left their architectural mark: Moroccan palaces in Menton, a neo-Greek villa in Beaulieu, and a Russian Cathedral in Nice, as appealing to the eye as the works masterminded by Picasso, Matisse, and Chagall, who were attracted to the region thanks to its intoxicating light.

The rich invaders withdrew to the cooler north for the summer months. No person of quality—and above all no lady of quality—would risk getting tanned like those laboring field hands and up to that time, sea bathing was shunned by all, except as a drastic medical remedy. Then, in the 1920s and 1930s, people began to like it hot. The peasantry of the West was now pale factory and office workers, and their new badge of leisure and pleasure became the tan that their aristocratic predecessors had so assiduously avoided. Coco Chanel, the famous couturier, made *le bronzage* the chicest of fashion "accessories" in 1923 when she accidentally got scorched on a Mediterranean cruise. Toplessness, and even bottomlessness, arrived on the beaches. Meanwhile, more and more hotels, restaurants, nightclubs, and casinos were built.

The Côte remains a demi-paradise. Day-trippers seeking contrast head inland to *villages perchés* (perched villages) and historic towns—from Mougins, where Picasso spent his last years, to Grasse, with its factories that make perfume from the region's abundant flowers, to the galleries, souvenir shops, and snack stands that crowd the cobblestones of St-Paul-de-Vence. Or you could drive from Cannes to the Italian border in two hours, seeing much of the region courtesy of the swift A8 autoroute and the three parallel Corniches allow you to explore without retracing your steps too often. But like the artists and nobles who paved the way before you, you will likely be seduced to linger.

MAJOR REGIONS

Cannes. Conspicuous consumption, glamorous fanfare, and a host of wannabes characterize the celluloid city of Cannes when its May film fest turns it into a global frat party. But the Louis Vuitton set enjoy this city year-round.

The Pays Grassois. Just behind Cannes, the hills that block the mountain winds rise, sun-bleached and jungle-green. From the well-groomed Provençal village-slash-bedroom community of Mougins to the hill-city of Grasse, tiled with the greenhouses that feed the region's perfume factories, you'll find charming small towns inviting peace and relaxation. Grasse itself supports modern industry and tourist industry with aplomb, offering a dense Italian-style Old Town as well. Beyond, you can head for the hills of the *arrière-pays* on the Route Napoléon to cities like Valbonne.

Antibes and Nearby. The coastline spanning the short distance from Cannes to Antibes and Nice has a personality all its own, combining some of the most accessible waterfront resorts (Juan-les-Pins, Villeneuve, and Cagnes-sur-mer) with one of the most elite (Cap d'Antibes). This is vacationland, with a culture of commercial entertainment that smacks of the worst of Florida in the 1960s. The hot, poky N98, which goes from Antibes to Cagnes, crawls past a jungle of amusement parks, a massive beach disco and casino, and even a horse-race track. The hill towns of Vallauris and Biot cater to souvenir hunters and lunch sorties. But everyone visiting this little piece of the Côte d'Azur, whether staying in a villa or a concrete cube, is after the same experience: to sit on a balcony, to listen to the waves washing over the sand, and to watch the sun setting over the oil-painted backdrop of the Maritime Alps.

The Hill Towns: St-Paul-de-Vence and Vence. The hills that back the Côte d'Azur are often called the *arrière-pays*, or backcountry. This particular wedge of backcountry—behind the coast between Cannes and Antibes—has a character all its own: deeply, unself-consciously Provençal, with undulating fields of lavender watched over by villages perched on golden stone. Many of these villages look as if they do not belong to the last century—but they do, since they played the muse to some of modern art's most famous exemplars, notably Pablo Picasso and Henri Matisse. High in the hills these villages loom, parallel to the sea, smelling fragrantly of wild herbs and medieval history—and soap shops. So hungry have the hordes that flock to the Riviera become for a taste of Picasso that many of the hill towns have been only too happy to oblige. St-Paul-de-Vence, which once hunkered down against the onslaught of Moors, now opens its pale-blue shutters wide to surges of day-trippers. Galleries and boutiques offer everything from neo-Van Gogh sofa art to assembly-line lavender sachets, and everywhere you'll hear the gentle *breet-breet* of mechanical souvenir *cigales* (cicadas). So if you're allergic to souvenir shops, artsy-craftsy boutiques, and middle-brow art galleries, aim to visit off-season or after hours. Top sights include the famous Colombe d'Or inn and Matisse's sublime Chapelle du Rosaire.

Nice. Walking along the seaside Promenade des Anglais is one of the most iconic Riviera experiences. Add in top-notch museums, a charming old quarter open till all hours, scads of diverse restaurants, and an agenda of first-class festivals all year long, and Nice merits a visit.

The Corniches Resorts. Purists and hardcore regional historians insist that this final sunny sliver of coast—from Cap Ferrat to the Italian border—is the one and only, true Côte d'Azur. It is certainly the most dramatically endowed, backed by forested mountains and crystalline Alps, with Mediterranean breezes relieving the summer heat and radiant light soothing midwinter days. And yet it was from these cliffs that for 2,500 years castles and towers held watch over the waters, braced against the influx of new peoples—first the Greeks, then the Romans, the Saracens, trade ships from Genoa, battleships under Napoléon, Edwardian cruise ships on the Grand Tour, and the Allies in World War II. The influx continues today, of course, in the great waves of vacationers who storm the coast, spring to early fall. The sun shines most brightly on the fabled glamour ports of Villefranche-sur-Mer, Beaulieu, and St-Jean-Cap-Ferrat. Also here are Èze and Roquebrune–Cap-Martin. Then there's Menton, an enchanting Italianate resort where winters can be so mild that lemon trees bloom in January.

Planning

When to Go

Southeast France is that magical corner of France where the sun always seems to shine. It's no secret that the coast is in its prime July and August, when rain is almost unheard of, but if you're anxious to enjoy the beaches, aim for less-packed June or September. Cannes books early for the film festival in May, so unless you're determined to hover outside the Farfalla with an autograph book, aim for another month. Also, many hotels and restaurants close November–Easter, and those that do thrive year-round tend to shut down in August, at the height of the tourist season, for the traditional *fermeture annuelle.*

The region's short periods of intense rainfall, lasting half a day to a week, most likely fall October–November and March–April, but late spring can also be surprisingly wet (locals swear that it always rains on the first day of the Cannes Film Festival). If you're intent on strolling in shirtsleeves under the palms on a winter day, head for Menton, famous for having one of the mildest climates in France, and, like the rest of the eastern Côte d'Azur, protected by the Estérel from the mistral that razors through Fréjus to the west, and from northern winds by the Alps.

Planning Your Time

How you tackle this stretch of the Côte d'Azur will largely depend on the form of transportation you have chosen. With a car, you can base yourself outside a major resort and combine day trips to Nice, Cannes, and Monaco with a taste of more leisurely Provençal life. If you're dependent on public transportation, you might stay in a larger center such as Nice and even find that you don't need to leave it very often, though the great news is that trains will easily take you along the coast and whisk you to such towns as Èze and Antibes, and buses hit about every village in the backcountry, including St-Paul-de-Vence.

Should sunbathing be a priority, you might prefer the sandy beaches of Cannes to the pebbles of Nice; in the height of summer, aim for the less populated beaches of St-Jean-Cap-Ferrat, Èze, Cap d'Ail, (where you can now visit the Belle Époque Villa Les Camélias) or grab an early morning ferry to the Îles de Lérins.

Art is a super-major draw in this area, with must-see museums, such as the Matisse museum in Nice, the Fondation Maeght in St-Paul-de-Vence, the Fernand Léger museum in Biot, and the Picasso museum in Antibes.

There is plenty for music fans, too: Nice and Juan-les-Pins hold major jazz festivals in the summer and Monaco's springtime Printemps des Arts celebrates music, dance, cinema, and theater. Vence's Nuit du Sud, a world music event which started in 1997, has become so popular that festivalgoers on a flight from Paris once asked the pilot to call organizers to say they were late as they didn't want to miss the show.

Stroll through a kaleidoscopic food market—perhaps the Marché Forville in Cannes, Cours Saleya in Nice, or Menton's Marché des Halles—to see how seriously this area takes its fresh produce. Then visit a good local bistro to taste specialties such as *pissaladière* (caramelized onion tart), *soupe de poissons* (fish soup), and, of course, *salade niçoise* (which in Nice contains neither green beans nor potato).

With so much to see, it's tempting to pack too much into a visit to this area, so be sure to set aside some time for relaxing on café terraces—something that the locals have mastered.

Getting Here and Around

As home to France's second-busiest airport, Nice is a natural starting point for seeing the area. The airport's location 15 minutes from the town center is particularly convenient, and there's now a tram line that stops at both terminals and goes to the port (€1.50) so you no longer have to be wary of the high cost of taxis.

East and west of Nice, a train route connects all the main coastal towns—a magic carpet ride of convenience for travelers. Buses also spider out, but they can take a good two hours between Nice and Cannes (as opposed to 35 minutes on the train). It's a well-kept secret that the Biot train station is a five-minute walk from Marineland, a major attraction near Antibes. Trains also head up into the hills around Grasse.

Surely the biggest bargain in the South of France is the Lignes d'Azur bus ticket (€1.50), valid anywhere between Cannes and Menton. The most scenic line is No. 100, running from Nice to Menton along the Moyenne Corniche. It runs every 15 minutes but can get unpleasantly packed in high season. Buses connect Nice to Èze village (30 minutes), and St-Paul-de-Vence and Vence (at least an hour); be sure to check the schedule, because these buses are not frequent.

■ TIP→ **An excellent website to help you calculate your route—bus, tram, train, and boat—across the Riviera is** ⊕ *www.ceparou06.fr.*

AIR

The Nice–Côte d'Azur Airport, named the world's third most beautiful airport in 2019 by the annual PrivateFly poll, has frequent flights between Paris and Nice on Air France and the low-cost airline EasyJet, as well as direct flights on Delta Airlines from New York. In the off-season, or if you book well in advance, you can find a one-way trip from Paris to Nice for less than €35, which can be cheaper than the train (though baggage fees and airport transfers offset this). The flight time between Paris and Nice is about 1½ hours. A taxi from the airport into Nice center—say, the train station or the Place Masséna—is a flat-rate fare of €32, but a cheaper option is to take the Line 2 tram from either terminal, which runs daily between 4:15 am and 1:05 am (you must purchase a €1.50 ticket from the machines at the tram stop before

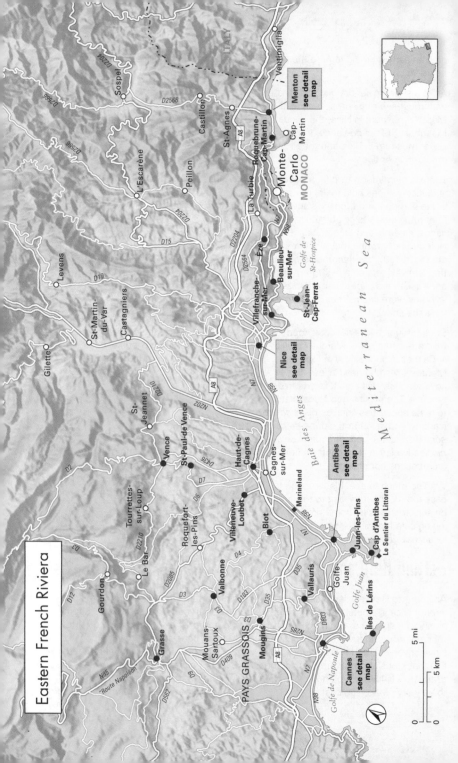

Eastern French Riviera

ITALY

Ventimiglia

Menton
see detail
map

Sospel

D2566

Castillon

St-Agnès

Roquebrune-
Cap-Martin

Cap-
Martin

D2566

D2566

D2204

D2204

Monte-
Carlo

MONACO

L'Escarène

Peillon

La Turbie

Èze

Beaulieu-
sur-Mer

Golfe de
St-Hospice

D2204

D204

D15

D2564

Levens

D19

Villefranche-
sur-Mer

St-Jean-
Cap-Ferrat

St-Martin-
du-Var

Castagniers

Mediterranean Sea

Gilette

Nice
see detail
map

A8

N7

N98

Baie des Anges

St-
Jeannet

D2210

N202

St-Paul-de-Vence

Vence

D436

Haut-de-
Cagnes

Cagnes-
sur-Mer

Marineland

D7

Tourrettes-
sur-Loup

Roquefort-
les-Pins

D6

Villeneuve-
Loubet

Biot

Antibes
see detail
map

Le Bar

D2085

D4

Juan-les-Pins

Cap d'Antibes
Le Sentier du Littoral

Gourdon

D12

D3

Valbonne

D103

D35

Vallauris

Golfe-
Juan

Golfe Juan

Îles de Lérins

Mouans-
Sartoux

D409

Mougins

A8

D35

N285

D803

Grasse

N85

PAYS GRASSOIS

N7

Cannes
see detail
map

Golfe de Napoule

D562

D60

Route Napoléon

D2

D2210

N98

5 mi

5 km

0

boarding). The airport bus No. 98 to the city center (€1.50) now only runs Monday through Thursday evenings, with five buses leaving T2 from 8:55 pm to 11:45 pm. Regular Nice AirportXpress buses also serve Cannes, Antibes, Monte Carlo, Roquebrune Cap Martin, and Menton. ⚠ **Uber with care: the French government has banned this taxi app because they consider it unfair competition. As a result, there have been disputes at the airport between cabbies and Uber drivers. It's usually best to take the tram or bus.**

AIRPORT INFORMATION Aéroport Nice– Côte d'Azur. ☎ 08–20–42–33–33 (€0.12 per min) ⊕ en.nice.aeroport.fr.

BOAT

The Côte d'Azur is one of the most beautiful coastlines in the world and there are several companies that allow you to take it all in via boat and ferry service. Riviera Lines offers routes between Golfe Juan to Cannes, Monaco and St-Tropez. Trans Côte d'Azur, with Nice and Cannes departures, has routes including the Corniche de l'Estérel, Monaco, Porquerolles, and St-Tropez, plus specialty excursions that feature nighttime dining and glass-bottom boats. Note that some routes and destinations are available June–October only.

BOAT CONTACTS Riviera Lines. ⊠ La Croisette ☎ 04–92–98–71–31 ⊕ www.riviera-lines.com. **Trans Côte d'Azur.** ⊠ 20 quai St-Pierre, Cannes ☎ 04–92–98–71–30 ⊕ www.trans-cote-azur.com.

BUS AND TRAM

If you're traveling along the coast, the train line is the quickest way to get around. However, to travel to backcountry spots not on the rail line, take a bus out of Cannes, Nice, Antibes, or Menton for a mere €1.50 per ticket (one-way). Look up schedules online either from the bus company directly or check tourist office websites. You must hail a bus to stop; don't presume the driver sees you. Drivers give change and hand you

a ticket, which you must get stamped (composté) in the ticket validator and keep as proof of payment, as inspectors often board buses to check. If you're planning on using the bus more than once, look into a multi-ride or weekly pass to save money.

Ligne d'Azur is Nice's main bus network but regional buses are operated by Zou! The Zou! No. 100 bus departs every 15 minutes (5:35 am–8:30 pm) from Nice–Port Lympia Fodéré and stops at all the villages between Nice and Menton along the Corniche Inférieure. For Villefranche, Èze, and Cap d'Ail on the Moyenne Corniche, take Bus No. 112, which departs Nice Vauban (take the Line 1 tram to get here) six times a day (no Sunday service) and ends at the casino in Monte Carlo; you can also take Bus No. 82, which goes as far as Èze via Villefranche and runs daily. Bus No. 400 goes from Nice to St-Paul-de-Vence and Vence, stopping first in St-Paul-de-Vence (about 1 hour) while Bus No. 500 takes you to Grasse (1 hour 20 minutes); both these buses now depart near the airport from Parc Pheonix, a stop on the new Line 2 tramway.

In Nice, bus stations are spread across the city: Vaubun (north and regional buses to Marseille and Aix); Gare SNCF; Station J. Bermond (the main hub); Cathédrale Vieille Ville; Alberti/Gioffredo; and Albert 1er. Lignes d'Azur also operates two modern tram lines, a fast and efficient way to get from the train station to the Old Town and to the port. Tickets (which are interchangable from bus tickets) cost €1.50 one-way and must be purchased before boarding from machines at each stop.

In Cannes, Lignes d'Azur runs routes from in front of the train station, including Bus No. 200 to Nice (1½ hours), and Zou! operates routes to Grasse (Bus Nos. 600 and 610, 45 minutes). Within Cannes, use Palm Bus, which also serves Mandelieu and Mougins (and in the summer runs Palm Night buses).

The Antibes bus station is at 1 Place Guynemer and Bus No. 200 connects with Cannes, Nice, Monaco, and Menton (€1.50, every 15–20 minutes). Cagnes-sur-Mer is one of the coastal towns served by train. From there it's an easy connection with adjacent St-Paul-de-Vence and Vence using Bus No. 400, which departs every 30-45 minutes from Cagnes Ville's bus station at Square Bourdet. Bus No. 200 (Nice–Cannes) stops at the square, too.

Transdev runs Nice Airport Xpress buses to Vallauris, Cannes, Monaco, Roquebrube Cap Martin, and Menton. Monaco's buses—Compagnie des Autobus de Monaco—help stitch together the principality's widely dispersed neighborhoods.

BUS INFORMATION Cannes Gare Routière. ⊠ *4 pl. de la Gare* ☎ *08–92–35–35–35* ⊕ *www.palmbus.fr.* **Envibus.** ☎ *04–89–87–72–00* ⊕ *www.envibus.fr.* **Lignes d'Azur.** ⊠ *3 pl. Masséna, Nice* ☎ *08–10–06–10–06* ⊕ *www.lignesdazur.com.* **Zou!.** ☎ *08–09–40–04–15* ⊕ *www.info-ler.fr.*

CAR

The A8 flows briskly from Cannes to Antibes to Nice and on to Monaco/Menton. From Paris, the main southbound artery is A6/A7, known as the Autoroute du Soleil (Highway of the Sun); it passes through Provence and joins the eastbound A8 at Aix-en-Provence.

The best way to explore the secondary sights in this region, especially the deep backcountry, is by car, allowing you the freedom to zip along A8 between the coastal resorts and to enjoy the tremendous views from the three Corniches that trace the coast from Nice to the Italian border. A car is, of course, a liability in city centers, with parking garages expensive and curbside spots virtually nonexistent.

Note: keep your car doors locked at all times, and keep any bags hidden from view. Also, this is one of the most dangerous driving regions in Europe, and the speeds and aggressive Grand Prix style of some drivers make it impossible to let your guard down. On the A8 toward Italy, tight curves, hills, tunnels, and construction keep things interesting. For traffic reports tune to 107.7 FM.

TRAIN

Nice is the major rail crossroads for trains arriving from Paris and other northern cities and from Italy, too. To get from Paris to Nice (with stops in Cannes and other resorts along the coast), you can take the TGV, though it only maintains high speeds to Valence before returning to conventional rails and rates. Night trains arrive at Nice in the morning from Paris, Metz, and Strasbourg.

You can easily move along the coastal towns between Cannes, Nice, and Ventimiglia (in Italy) by train on the slick double-decker Côte d'Azur line, a highly tourist-pleasing branch of SNCF lines, with more than 40 trains a day. Don't be shocked, though, to see a graffitied clunker pull in. The good news is that all information like departures and arrivals, and train station details, can be now easily searched by city via a one-stop website (⊕ *www.gares-sncf.com*) or Assistant SNCF. Similarly, there is only one central telephone number now (☎ *3635*) for train stations.

The Marseille–Vintimille (Ventimiglia) line heads east to Italy and Vintimille–Marseille travels west. From Nice, some main stops on this line are: Antibes (€4.80, 25 minutes), Cannes (€7.20, 40 minutes), Menton (€5.30, 30 minutes), and Monaco (€4.10, 25 minutes); stops on the Mandelieu–Vintimille line include Villefranche-sur-Mer, Beaulieu, Èze-sur-Mer, and Cap d'Ail. No trains run to the hill villages, including St-Paul-de-Vence and Vence.

A word of caution: don't be alarmed by police presence at main stations from Menton to Nice to Cannes. Security, already beefed up since the rise in migrants trying to cross the border from Italy, was increased further following the 2015 terrorist attacks in Paris. Also, hold on to your purse, wallet, and belongings when traveling by rail. There are frequent onboard recordings reminding passengers to be careful of pickpockets; it's smart to be especially vigilant while riding the train and bus.

TRAIN INFORMATION Gare Cannes Ville.
✉ 1 rue Jean-Jaurès, Cannes ☎ 3635 ⊕ www.gares-sncf.com. **Gare Nice Ville.** ✉ Av. Thiers, Nice ☎ 3635 ⊕ www.gares-sncf.com. **SNCF.** ☎ 3635 ⊕ en.oui.sncf/en. **TGV.** ☎ 3635 ⊕ en.oui.sncf/en/tgv.

Beaches

When the French Côte d'Azur starts to sizzle, it's time to beat the heat and hit the beach. Here's how—and where—to savor Provence's greatest liquid assets.

From intimate pebbly stretches to long swaths of golden sand packed with sun worshippers, from nudist beaches to family-friendly ones, the Côte d'Azur is famed for its magnificent beaches. Cagnes-sur-Mer across to Menton, however, is reviled for its notorious *galets*, round white stones that can make you feel like a fakir lying on a rounded bed of nails instead of nestling into sand. A thin foam mattress, available from the souvenir shops in close beach proximity, can make all the difference—as can a pair of €10 slip-on rubber shoes for negotiating the stones. Or consider springing for a sun-lounger. It's important to note that many beaches are privately operated, renting parasols and mattresses to anyone who pays; if you're a guest at one of the local hotels, you'll get a discount. These beaches also allow you in for free if you are drinking or eating from their menus. The good news is that public beaches (with free toilets during summer and open showers) usually alternate with private *plages*, where you'll pay on average €20 for a mattress, which usually includes a parasol. Happily, the sun is free.

◼ TIP → **If lodging inland, leave early for the beach: traffic on N98, which lines the coast, often grinds to a halt. Or head down over lunchtime when public beaches are less crowded.**

Restaurants

There is no shortage of restaurants along the Riviera, ranging from take-away Socca to three–Michelin-star establishments, nor is it a secret that the French are very attached to their food. So much so that the "Made in France" and "Nissart cuisine" movements are on the rise, protecting all that is near and dear to their stomachs as the invasion of Starbucks, Burger King, and the Hard Rock Cafe in Nice can no longer be staved off.

The best way to appreciate a meal in the region is to live like a local. Meal times are for conversation, for lingering, and many restaurants only have one seating a night—so if you're in a rush, don't bother. Order the daily special when possible, as it will be fresh and the price clearly labeled (do not try to order "without" or "on the side"); avoid ordering fish priced by the 100g, as the bill will cause you to choke on your crème brûlée. If you have young children, be prepared that some establishments may give you a less than enthusiastic welcome, and fellow diners will cast an evil eye in your direction. It's not that the French are averse to babies, but an evening out is for civilized adults. Most importantly, do not expect friendly service. Waving your platinum card won't make your waiter smile or serve you any faster, especially in the busier seasons when seating is at capacity. Accepting these guidelines will eliminate unpleasant gastronomic disappointments.

Hotels

In this golden stretch you'll see the prices rise, even beyond those of the Estérel. The atmosphere changes, too. In the coastal resorts the majority of visitors seem to value proximity to the sea over cachet, and you'll often find yourself far from the land of Provençal cottons and cozy country inns. The interior design here is a peculiar hybrid—vaguely Jazz Age, a little Hollywood—that falls into a loose category known as "Côte d'Azur style." In Cannes the grand hotels are big on prestige (waterfront position, awe-inspiring lobbies, high-price sea views) and weak on swimming pools, which are usually just big enough to dip in; their private beaches are on the other side of the busy street, and you'll have to pay for access, just as nonguests do. The glitziest hotels are in Cannes, Monaco, and the Cap d'Antibes; Nice provides a broader range of prices, while charming family-run hotels can be found around St-Paul-de-Vence and Vence.

Remember that July and August are the busiest months, but plan ahead anytime between May and October. Hotel prices skyrocket in May during the Monaco Grand Prix and the Cannes Film Festival; off-season, there are great deals to be had. Renting a rural gîte (⊕ www.gites-de-france.com) allows you to avoid overpriced breakfasts and make the most of the abundance at the markets. You'll find most hotel rates now include Wi-Fi, but much to the dismay of many travelers, signals can be weak even in the bigger towns or in upscale hotels due to aging infrastructures. Also keep in mind that five-star service is not the same in France as it is stateside. For those sensitive to sound, do your homework: check that your idyllic seaside accommodations aren't close to the train tracks or the quaint village auberge doesn't face the main square, where noise can carry on into the early hours. ■TIP→ **Don't be surprised at checkout when you see the taxe de séjour (usually around €1–€1.50 per guest per day). This city tax is never included in the price when you book online from travel websites.**

Restaurant and hotel reviews have been shortened. For full information, visit Fodors.com.

What it Costs in Euros			
$	$$	$$$	$$$$
RESTAURANTS			
under €18	€18–€24	€25–€32	over €32
HOTELS			
under €125	€125–€225	€226–€350	over €350

Cannes

6 km (4 miles) east of Mandelieu-La Napoule; 73 km (45 miles) northeast of St-Tropez; 33 km (20 miles) southwest of Nice.

Cannes is pampered with the luxurious year-round climate that has made it one of the most popular resorts in Europe. Settled first by the Ligurians and then dubbed Cannoïs by the Romans (after the cane that waved in its marshes), Cannes was an important sentinel site for the monks who established themselves on Île St-Honorat in the Middle Ages. Its bay served as nothing more than a fishing port until, in 1834, an English aristocrat, Lord Brougham, fell in love with the site during an emergency stopover with a sick daughter. He had a home built here and returned every winter for a sun cure—a ritual quickly picked up by his peers. Between the popularity of Le Train Blue transporting wealthy passengers from Calais, and the introduction in 1936 of France's first paid holidays, Cannes became the destination, a tasteful and expensive breeding ground for the upper upscale.

Cannes has been further glamorized by the ongoing success of its annual film festival, as famous as—and, in the trade, more respected than—Hollywood's Academy Awards. About the closest many of us will get to feeling like a film star is a stroll here along La Croisette, the iconic promenade that gracefully curves the wave-washed sand coastline, peppered with chic restaurants and prestigious private beaches. This is precisely the sort of place for which the French invented the verb *flâner* (to dawdle, saunter): strewn with palm trees and poseurs, its fancy boutiques and status-symbol grand hotels—including the Carlton, the legendary backdrop to Grace Kelly in *To Catch a Thief*—all vying for the custom of the Louis Vuitton set.

GETTING HERE AND AROUND

Cannes has one central train station, the completely modernized Gare SNCF. All major trains pass through here—check out the SNCF website for times and prices—but many of the trains run the Mandelieu–Ventimiglia route. You can also take the TGV directly from Paris (just over five hours). Cannes's main bus hub is in front of the l'Hôtel-de-Ville by the port and serves all coastal destinations.

Within Cannes, use Palm Bus (€1.50). For excursions out of the city, Lignes d'Azur runs routes from in front of the train station, including the 200 to Nice (€1.50, 1½ hours), which stops at every town en route. Bargain-basement ticket fares are a steal (be patient, you may not get a seat), but keep in mind that between Cannes and Nice it's much faster to take the train. The Nice Airport Xpress Shuttle No. 210 (€22, 50 minutes) also leaves from the Cannes train station.

VISITOR INFORMATION

CONTACTS Cannes Tourist Office. ⊠ *1 bd. de la Croisette* ☎ *04–92–99–84–22* ⊕ *www.cannes-destination.com.*

Sights

Allée de la Liberté Markets

MARKET | Shaded by plane trees and sheltering a sandy pétanque field, this is a little piece of Provence in a big, glitzy resort town. Every morning except Monday a flower market paints the square in vivid colors and on the weekend there's a flea market (10–6), where you can find almost any item, from moth-eaten uniforms to secondhand gravy boats. The antiques market shares the space on Saturday and the first Sunday of every month. ⊠ *Allée de la Liberté.*

Carlton InterContinental

HOTEL—SIGHT | Built in 1912, the Carlton was the first of the grand hotels to stake out the superb stretch of beach and greenery on La Croisette, and thus is the best positioned, which explains its fashionable see-and-be-seen terrace and brasserie. It is here that many of the film festival's grand banquets take place. ⊠ *58 bd. de la Croisette* ☎ *04–93–06–40–06* ⊕ *www.intercontinental-carlton-cannes. com.*

La Croisette

NEIGHBORHOOD | Head to this famous waterfront promenade—which runs for 1.6 km (1 mile) from its western terminus by the Palais des Festivals—and stroll among the palm trees and flowers and crowds of poseurs (fur coats in tropical weather, mobile phones on Rollerblades, and sunglasses at night). Continue east past the broad expanse of private beaches, glamorous shops, and luxurious hotels. In March 2020, the Croisette completed a two-year renovation, with everything from the sidewalks of the Carlton to the Palais des Festivals getting revamped, along with the addition of a bike path. ⊠ *Bd. de Croisette.*

Le Suquet

NEIGHBORHOOD | Climb up Rue St-Antoine into the picturesque Vieille Ville neighborhood known as Le Suquet, on the site of the original Roman castrum. Shops proffer Provençal goods, and the atmospheric cafés provide a place to catch your breath; the pretty pastel shutters, Gothic stonework, and narrow passageways are lovely distractions. In July, the "Nuits Musicales du Suquet" concerts mesmerize in front of Notre-Dame church, while Le Suquet des Arts provides three days of art in the streets at the end of August. ⊠ *Rue St-Antoine.*

Malmaison

MUSEUM | If you need a culture fix, check out the modern art and photography exhibitions held at the Malmaison, a 19th-century mansion that was once part of the Grand Hotel. ⊠ *47 bd. La Croisette, La Croisette* ☎ *04–97–06–44–90* ☎ *Admission varies* ⊗ *Closed weekends.*

Marché Forville (*Forville Market*)

MARKET | Opened in 1934, this market still draws the chefs, connoisseurs, and voyeurs of Cannes every morning (except Monday, when there's a flea market). You'll see showy displays of still-flipping fish from some 25 local fishing boats alongside glossy local vegetables piled high, cheeses carried down from the mountains, and sausages, olives, charcuterie, oysters, and flower stands—but the whole scene gets hosed down by 1 pm, so don't linger too long over breakfast. The nearby Cafe l'Horlage (7 rue du Marché Forville) is a good spot to recover postsampling. ⊠ *Rue du Marché Forville* ⊗ *Closed Mon.*

Musée de la Castre

MUSEUM | The hill is topped by an 11th-century château, housing the Musée de la Castre, with its mismatched collection of weaponry, ethnic artifacts, and ceramics amassed by a 19th-century aristocrat. The imposing four-sided **Tour du Suquet** (Suquet Tower) and its 109 steps were built in 1385 as a lookout against Saracen-led invasions. Guided tours in English are given Friday at 2:30 pm from June 15 to September 15, and are included in the admission price. Book your tickets in advance online at ⊕ *www.*

cannesticket.com. ⊠ *Pl. de la Castre, Le Suquet* ☎ *04–93–38–55–26* ☎ *€10* ⊗ *Closed Mon. Sept.–June.*

Palais des Festivals

ARTS VENUE | Pick up a map at the tourist office in the Palais des Festivals; the building sets the scene for the famous Cannes Film Festival. As you leave the information center, follow the Palais to your right to see the 24 red-carpeted stairs that A-listers ascend every year. Set into the surrounding pavement, the **Chemin des Étoiles** (Stars' Walk) enshrines some 150 autographed hand imprints—including those of Depardieu, Streep, and Stallone (the clay imprints are sent to a potter in—where else?—Vallauris, before being cast in metal in Rhône). From October to April, a cultural season offers music, theater, dance, and comedy at the Paiais for surprisingly reasonable prices. ⊠ *Bd. de la Croisette* ⊕ *www.palaisdes-festivals.com.*

Place Gambetta Market

MARKET | Just a couple of blocks east of the train station along rue Jean Jaurès, you can pick up fresh fruit and vegetables, as well as clothes, shoes, belts, and bags at the city's second covered market that's a little less upscale than the Marché Forville but has bargains nonetheless. While in the neighborhood you can visit the nearby Asian and kosher shops or stop in for one of the creamiest cappuccinos this side of Italy at Volupté (32 rue Hoche, closed Sunday). ⊠ *Pl. Gambetta.*

Rue d'Antibes

NEIGHBORHOOD | Two blocks behind La Croisette lies this attractive high-end shopping street. At its western end is **Rue Meynadier,** packed tight with trendy clothing boutiques and fine-food shops. Not far away is the covered **Marché Forville,** the scene of the animated morning food market. **Rue Houche,** behind Rue d'Antibes and down from Galleries Lafayette, has lots of boutiques and cafés. ⊠ *Cannes.*

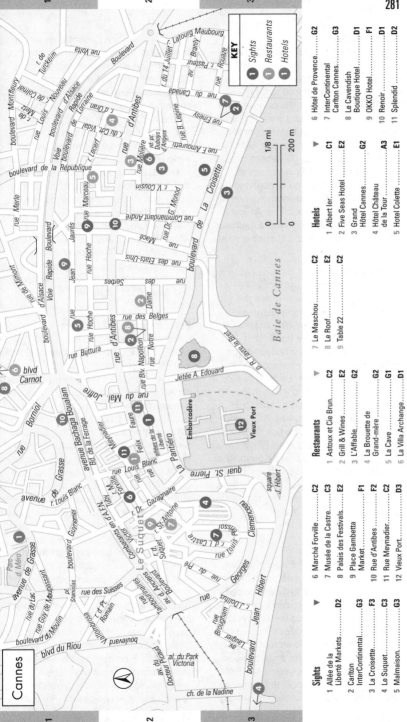

Cannes

KEY
- 1 Sights
- 1 Restaurants
- 1 Hotels

Baie de Cannes

0 ____ 1/8 mi
0 ____ 200 m

Sights ▶
1 Allée de la
 Liberté Markets...........**D2**
2 Carton
 InterContinental.........**G3**
3 La Croisette.................**F3**
4 Le Suquet...................**C3**
5 Malmaison..................**G3**
6 Marché Forville..........**C2**
7 Musée de la Castre......**C3**
8 Palais des Festivals.....**E2**
9 Place Gambetta
 Market.......................**F1**
10 Rue d'Antibes.............**F2**
11 Rue Meynadier............**C2**
12 Vieux Port..................**D3**

Restaurants ▶
1 Astoux et Cie Brun......**C2**
2 Grill & Wines..............**E2**
3 L'Affable....................**G2**
4 La Brouette de
 Grand-mère................**G2**
5 La Cave......................**G1**
6 La Villa Archange........**D1**
7 Le Maschou................**C2**
8 Le Roof......................**E2**
9 Table 22....................**C2**

Hotels ▶
1 Albert Ier...................**C1**
2 Five Seas Hotel...........**E2**
3 Grand
 Hôtel Cannes.............**G2**
4 Hôtel Château
 de la Tour.................**A3**
5 Hotel Colette..............**E1**
6 Hôtel de Provence.......**G2**
7 InterContinental
 Carlton Cannes..........**G3**
8 Le Cavendish
 Boutique Hotel...........**D1**
9 OKKO Hotel................**F1**
10 Renoir......................**D1**
11 Splendid...................**D2**

Rue Meynadier

NEIGHBORHOOD | It's hard to imagine 16th-century horse-drawn carriages being pulled down this main street of Cannes that's now home to inexpensive and trendy clothes boutiques, rare food stores, cheese and wine shops, and some of the best butchers in town. Don't miss the chic patisserie, L'Atelier Jean-Luc Pelé, at No. 36, whose delicate macaroons come in flavors such as lime-chocolate, Menton lemon, and foie gras–onion confit, and whose ganache-filled chocolates are sublime. At one end of Rue Meynadier is **Rue d'Antibes,** Cannes's main high-end shopping street. ⊠ *Rue Meynadier.*

Vieux Port (*Old Port*)

MARINA | Sparkling at the foot of Le Suquet, this narrow, well-protected port harbors a fascinating lineup of luxury yachts and slick little *bateaux de plaisance* (pleasure boats) that creak and bob beside weathered-blue fishing barques. From the east corner, off La Pantiéro at Quai Laubeuf (which is currently undergoing a €21 million renovation that will add a panoramic promenade and heliport by 2021), you can catch a cruise to the Îles de Lérins. The port, as well as Quai St-Pierre (which runs alongside it and hosts a plethora of restaurants), has emerged from its tattered and tired midlife crisis to become a smartly dressed, more energized version of its former self. ⊠ *Cannes.*

🕐 Beaches

Both Cannes and St-Tropez are known for their glorious beaches and for quite a few decades, nothing ever changed about these spreads of sand. Until now. The 2019 season brought electrifying changes to both St-Tropez's iconic beaches and to the 4-mile stretch of coastline in Cannes as part of the city's four-year, €50 million project, its largest redevelopment since 1960. In 2019 (after two years and 80,000 cubic meters of sand),

beaches along the Croisette expanded from 80 to 130 feet deep; currently the western stretch remains closed to the public, with many of the private beaches and concessions undergoing renovations to produce a more harmonized look and create demountable buildings that can withstand the intense storms that hit the region every year. These beaches, including La Môme, Cannes Beach, Le Marriott, Long Beach, and Carlton, have plans to be open by the end of summer 2020. Not to fret, nine beaches remain open: Végaluna, 3.14, L'ondine, Mandala, Rado Beach, Helen, Croisette Beach, Miramar Beach, and the beach in front of the Martinez. Also accessible are the only two public (*regie municipal*) beaches: Macé, near the Palais des Féstivals, and Zamenhoff, at the Port Canto east end.

Special anti-jellyfish nets are set-up until the end of September along Gazagnaire, Mace, and Roubine public beaches, so you can swim in peace. Most of the 30 beaches along La Croisette are owned by hotels or restaurants, though this doesn't necessarily mean the hotels or restaurants front the beach. It does mean they own a patch of beachfront bearing their name, from which they rent out chaises, mats, and umbrellas to the public and hotel guests (around €22 per day). One of the most fashionable is the Carlton Hotel's beach. Other beaches where you must pay a fee include Long Beach, Rado Plage, and Zplage, the stretch belonging to the Martinez, which is the largest in Cannes. You can easily recognize public beaches by the crowds; they're interspersed between the color-coordinated private-beach umbrellas, and offer simple open showers and basic toilets (and you can rent a lounger for only €6.70 per day). To be slightly removed from the city traffic and crowds, head west of town where the open stretches of sand run uninterrupted toward Mandelieu. There are a couple of no-smoking beaches in each sea town across the Riviera.

The Three Corniches

The lay of the land east of Nice is nearly vertical, as the coastline is one great cliff, a corniche terraced by three parallel national roads—the **Corniche Inférieure** (sometimes called the Basse Corniche and N98), the **Moyenne Corniche** (N7), and the **Grande Corniche** (D2564)—that snake along its graduated crests. The lowest (*inférieure*) is the slowest, following the coast and crawling through the main streets of resorts, including Monte Carlo. Villefranche, Cap Ferrat, and Beaulieu are some of the towns along this 20-mile-long *route nationale*. The highest (*grande*) is the fastest, but its panoramic views are blocked by villas, and there are few safe overlooks (this is the road Grace Kelly roared along in *To Catch a Thief*, and some 27 years later, crashed and died on). The middle (*moyenne*) offers views down over the shoreline and villages and passes through a few picturesque clifftop towns, including Èze.

In Cannes, Bijou Plage (also home to Handiplage) and Plage des Rochers in La Bocca are no-smoking beaches, and anyone caught lighting up is fined €11. Plage Macé, near the Palais, runs a beach library mid-June–August, 10–6. For a €10 deposit readers can sign out books for up to two days; English publications are available.

If you're not a fan of kids at the beach, lay your beach towel far away from the toy-topped poles along Cannes's seafront, which are in place to join up lost children and their parents. ■ TIP→ **If you're at the beach with your children, ask a lifeguard for a bracelet and write your child's name and mobile number on it. Explain to your children that they should go to the nearest pole if lost.**

🍴 Restaurants

Astoux et Cie Brun

$$$ | **SEAFOOD** | A beacon to all fish lovers since 1953, Astoux et Cie Brun deserves its reputation for impeccably fresh *fruits de mer*. Well-trained staff negotiate cramped quarters to lay down heaping seafood platters, shrimp casseroles, and piles of oysters shucked to order. Open 365 days a year, it is noisy, cheerful, and always busy (so don't expect rapid service). **Known for:** legendary address open 365 days a year; noisy, cheerful atmosphere; big crowds so arrive early or be prepared for long lines and slow service. [$] *Average main: €30* ✉ *27 rue Félix Faure, La Croisette* ☎ *04–93–39–21–87* 🌐 *www.chezastoux.com.*

Grill & Wines

$$$ | **FRENCH** | Could it be that Cannes finally has an eatery where good food and friendly service come together? Come for *une verre* on the terrace or a meal in one of two interior rooms, one modern and the other traditional, where the steak-house menu offers more than just grilled Argentine Black Angus steak—there is also salmon, sea bass, and chicken dishes, while dessert includes tarte citron and an exotic fruit panna cotta. **Known for:** pricey but amazing food; friendly staff who speak English; diverse wine list. [$] *Average main: €30* ✉ *5 rue Notre-Dame* ☎ *04–93–38–37–10* 🌐 *www.grillandwines.com.*

L'Affable

$$$$ | **FRENCH** | When chef Battaglia decided to set up shop in Cannes,

gastronomes were delighted—and the chef does not disappoint—so much so that it's not uncommon for tourists to eat here more than once during their stay in Cannes. The sea bass is fantastic, the roast beef succulent, and the curry prawns impossibly fragrant. **Known for:** signature Grand Marnier soufflé; open kitchen set-up; packed (and quite noisy) atmosphere so reservations essential. [$] *Average main: €44* ✉ *5 rue Lafontaine, La Croisette* ☎ *04–93–68–02–09* 🌐 *www.restaurant-laffable.fr* 🕓 *Closed Sun. and Aug. No lunch Sat.*

La Brouette de Grand-mère

$$$$ | **FRENCH** | Monsieur Bruno's charming hole-in-the-wall, complete with lace curtains, painted-wood front, fireplace, and old posters, could be a set for one of the Festival's films. Yet it's a true-blue bistro, with a €49 three-course menu that includes wine, fizzy water, a shot of vodka, and surprisingly tasty food. **Known for:** classic three-course bistro menu with just one price; wine and bottled water included; generous portions. [$] *Average main: €49* ✉ *9 rue d'Oran, Pl. Lamy* ☎ *04–93–39–12–10* 🌐 *www.labrouette-degrandmere.fr* 🕓 *Closed Jan. No lunch Mon.–Sat.*

La Cave

$$$ | **FRENCH** | With walls strewn with Niçois memorabilia, this restaurant (established 1989) is where locals go to satisfy a craving for Provençal classics. Choosing from the affordable set menu (€34), you might start with a plate of *farcis* (stuffed seasonal vegetables) before tasting an *aïoli* (cod with vegetables and garlic mayonnaise) or perhaps veal with black chanterelles. **Known for:** excellent selection of Provençal and French wines; classic Niçois dishes; reasonable prices. [$] *Average main: €30* ✉ *9 bd. de la République* ☎ *04–93–99–79–87* 🌐 *www.lacave-et-fils.com* 🕓 *Closed Sun. and Aug. No lunch Sat. or Mon.*

★ **La Villa Archange**

$$$$ | **FRENCH** | You wouldn't expect to find a restaurant with two Michelin stars set in such a residential background, 10 minutes by car from La Croisette, but Bruno Oger promises you an unforgettable evening in this très cozy spot surrounded by centennial trees and gardens. Yes, it's pricey, but concentrate on the selection, which features dishes such as No. 2 oysters with mint cucumber and Petrossian caviar or sea bass with lemongrass. **Known for:** impeccable service; wonderful pairings by sommelier; perfectly executed nine-course Inspiration Menu (€500 with wine). [$] *Average main: €100* ✉ *15 bis rue Notre-Dame des Anges, Le Cannet* ☎ *04–92–18–18–28* 🌐 *bruno-oger.com* 🕓 *Closed Sun. and Mon. No lunch Tues.–Thurs.*

Le Maschou

$$$$ | **FRENCH** | If you're tired of choosing from complicated menus, visit this long-popular restaurant in Le Suquet, where the only thing you'll have to decide is what kind of meat you want off the grill. Every dinner starts with a gigantic basket of whole raw vegetables, to be cut up and dipped in a selection of sauces, and grilled bread. **Known for:** beef, lamb, or chicken from charcoal grill menu; quaint, intimate decor; popularity during film festival. [$] *Average main: €55* ✉ *15 rue St-Antoine* ☎ *04–93–39–62–21* 🌐 *www.lemaschou.com* 🕓 *Closed Dec.–mid-Feb. No lunch.*

Le Roof

$$$$ | **FRENCH** | Occupying the fifth floor of a former post office, this trendy rooftop restaurant formerly known as Sea Sens has had an awakening, but not to worry, the fabulous views over Le Suquet are still there and so is chef Arnaud Tabarec. The whole setting oozes intimacy, with starters, desserts, and even mains ordered to share (but not the veal confit with mashed potatoes and gravy); organic eggs have their own section on the menu. **Known for:** finger foods and mains for sharing; magical rooftop; excellent brunch menu. $ *Average main: €34* ✉ *1 rue Notre-Dame* ☎ *04–63–36–05–05* ⊕ *www.fiveseashotel.com.*

Table 22

$$$$ | FRENCH | In a city where style often wins out over substance, food lovers treasure this Suquet address, run by Noël Mantel, who, among other top-notch jobs, worked with Ducasse at Louis XV in Monaco. The contemporary setting continues to harmonize with his exquisitely detailed Mediterranean cuisine you'll discover in one of the seasonal prix-fixe menus (€39, €49, or €60). **Known for:** affordable seasonal prix-fixe menus; one of city's finest restaurants; excellent and varied wine selection. $ *Average main: €39* ✉ *22 rue St-Antoine* ☎ *04–93–39–13–10* ⊕ *www.restaurantmantel.com* ⊘ *Closed Mon. and Tues. No lunch Wed.*

 Hotels

Albert Ier

$ | HOTEL | In a quiet residential area above the Forville market—a 15-minute walk uphill from La Croisette and beaches—this renovated neo–Art Deco mansion has tastefully decorated earthtone rooms that are both minimal and tidy. **Pros:** great location for price; free private parking; delicious coffee. **Cons:** need to be in reasonable shape for the walk up the hill; no room service; small rooms. $ *Rooms from: €95* ✉ *68 av. de Grasse* ☎ *04–93–39–24–04* ⊕ *www. hotel-albert1er-cannes.com* ⊶ *12 rooms* ⦿ *Free breakfast.*

Five Seas Hotel

$$$$ | HOTEL | Housed in the town's old post office, steps from the Palais des Festivals, Five Seas has a stylish interior that evokes voyages to the Far East: decent-size rooms dressed in red fabrics blend with exquisite dark-wood furniture against all-white linens and bathroom fixtures, while amenities are plentiful—a rooftop pool, personal

shoppers, jogging routes, yacht charters, and dog sitters are all at your fingertips. **Pros:** good size-rooms; free minibar for nonalcoholic drinks; rooftop restaurant with panoramic views. **Cons:** who needs a scale in the bathroom when on holiday in France?; can be tricky to find when driving; all this luxury comes with a hefty price tag. $ *Rooms from: €380* ✉ *1 rue Notre-Dame* ☎ *04–63–36–05–05* ⊕ *www. fiveseashotel.com/en* ⊶ *45 rooms* ⦿ *No meals.*

★ Grand Hotel Cannes

$$$$ | HOTEL | A two-minute walk from the Palais, this 11-story, white-brick number with an amazing hotel garden fronting the Croisette is a fun and relaxing place to stay, with rooms that are spacious, modern, and designed to have the eyes flow toward the sea view. **Pros:** location away from the road makes it quieter than other Croisette properties; lots of free tech stuff including in-room Netflix and Drigme smartphone; wonderful summer beach restaurant. **Cons:** beach gets crowded; extras can add up (€25 parking); rooms feel a little dated. $ *Rooms from: €376* ✉ *45 bd. de la Croisette* ☎ *04–93–38–15–45* ⊕ *www.grand-hotel-cannes.com* ⊘ *Closed Dec. and Jan.* ⊶ *75 rooms* ⦿ *No meals.*

Hotel Château de la Tour

$$$ | HOTEL | A stay at this 18th-century boutique hotel, 10 minutes' drive from Cannes and near a beach, feels like a miniretreat as guests relax in rooms with views of the sea, the Esterel Massif, or the garden. **Pros:** poolside reflexology at Espace Beauté spa; excellent breakfast of homemade crêpes, eggs, and bacon; parking included in price. **Cons:** breakfast is €17; uphill location, so mobility issues can arise; Wi-Fi can be spotty. $ *Rooms from: €260* ✉ *10 av. Font de Veyre, Le Cannet* ☎ *04–93–90–52–52* ⊕ *www. hotelchateaudelatour.com* ⊘ *Closed Nov.–Mar.* ⊶ *34 rooms* ⦿ *No meals.*

Celebrity-Spotting in Cannes

Remember, during the Cannes Film Festival, the film screenings are *not* open to the public and the stars themselves no longer grace cafés, beaches, or the morning market; they hide in the privacy of the Hôtel du Cap–Eden Roc on the Cap d'Antibes. Your best bets are the red carpet events at the Palais des Festivals every evening at 7:30 pm and 10:30 pm or the backstreet exits of big hotels,

like on Rue Saint Honoré behind the Majestic, where you can bump into A-listers dashing into their car en route to the Palais about an hour early. Cannes Cinéphiles (⊕ *www.cannes-cinema.com*) allows 4,000 moviegoers (including foreigners) a chance to view Official Selections, including Competition films and Special Screenings. You can apply online in February.

Hotel Colette

$$ | HOTEL | Facing the train station, this boutique hotel is suspiciously affordable considering its proximity to the beach, particularly when you book in advance for rooms in the off-season (mid-October–June). **Pros:** close to Palais des Festivals; great deals and rates if booked online; L'Occitane toiletries provided. **Cons:** €15 for breakfast; no parking at hotel; Wi-Fi reception isn't great. Ⓢ *Rooms from: €135 ⊠ 5 pl. de la Gare ☎ 04–93–39–01–17 ⊕ www.hotelcolette.com ⇌ 45 rooms* ❍❙ *No meals.*

★ Hôtel de Provence

$$ | HOTEL | This affordable choice has a fabulous location, and its very gracious owners, Julie and Jerry Duburcq (who speak English), go the extra distance to ensure guests have the service and experience of a much-higher-caliber modern hotel. **Pros:** close to Cannes city center; all-day continental breakfast for €10.80; lower rates if you prepay. **Cons:** only 10 parking places (€19 per night); smallish rooms; no spa or pool, but partners with Institut Aurélie beauty center. Ⓢ *Rooms from: €194 ⊠ 9 rue Molière ☎ 04–93–38–44–35 ⊕ www.hotel-de-provence.com* ☉ *Closed mid-Jan.–Feb. ⇌ 36 rooms* ❍❙ *No meals.*

InterContinental Carlton Cannes

$$$$ | HOTEL | Used by Hitchcock as a suitably glamorous frame for Grace Kelly in *To Catch a Thief,* this neoclassical landmark built in 1911, with its gleaming facade, staked out the best position early on, sitting right on the sidewalk of La Croisette, radiating symmetrically from its figurehead waterfront site—the better for you to be seen on the popular brasserie's terrace. **Pros:** historic spot; five-star service; legendary bar and terrace. **Cons:** rooms could use an update; breakfast €50; some rooms are lackluster so opt for sea views. Ⓢ *Rooms from: €375 ⊠ 58 bd. de la Croisette ☎ 04–93–06–40–06 ⊕ www.carlton-cannes.com ⇌ 382 rooms* ❍❙ *No meals.*

Le Cavendish Boutique Hotel

$$ | HOTEL | Lovingly restored by friendly owners Christine and Guy Welter, the giddily opulent former residence of Lord Cavendish and a listed Belle Époque building is a true delight, playing up both a contemporary style of "winter-garden" greens and "incensed" reds, and 19th-century elegance. **Pros:** close to Palais des Festival and beaches; complimentary drinks and snacks 6:30–8:30 pm; only Cannes hotel that serves breakfast until the last guest has eaten. **Cons:** located on busy street; not open year-round; valet parking €25/day. Ⓢ *Rooms* *from: €155* ✉ *11 bd. Carnot* ☎ *04–97–06–26–00* 🌐 *www.cavendish-cannes.com* 🕒 *Closed Dec.–mid-Mar.* 🛏 *34 rooms* 🍴 *Free breakfast.*

OKKO Hotel

$$ | **ALL-INCLUSIVE** | This all-inclusive four-star hotel brand now has a location in Cannes, and reception will remind you that breakfast, snacks, hot and cold drinks and a nightly aperitivo at the 24/7 rooftop bar are included in your rate, as is bottled water, Nespresso coffee, unlimited national calls (with a €10 credit for international calls), and access to the gym and kitchen facility with fridges and a large communal table. **Pros:** all-inclusive price, a rarity in Cannes; 10-minute walk to beach and 5-minutes to main shopping street; late check-out on weekends. **Cons:** small rooms; slated bathroom walls not great for nonsolo travelers; parking not included. [$] *Rooms from: €150* ✉ *6 bis pl. de la Gare* ☎ *04–92–98–30–30* 🌐 *www.okkohotels.com* 🛏 *125 rooms* 🍴 *All inclusive.*

Renoir

$$ | **HOTEL** | This graceful former mansion, now a boutique hotel, is on a residential backstreet behind the city center, within reasonable walking distance of La Croisette. **Pros:** super friendly and helpful staff; 15-minute walk to La Croisette; complimentary drinks at bar 6–8 pm. **Cons:** affiliated beach is expensive; shower separated by glass screen; small elevator and steep steps at the entrance. [$] *Rooms from: €169* ✉ *7 rue Edith Cavell* ☎ *04–92–99–62–62* 🌐 *hotel-renoir.fr* 🕒 *Closed 3 wks in Jan.* 🛏 *29 rooms* 🍴 *No meals.*

Splendid

$$ | **HOTEL** | Maintained in simple comfort, this traditional 1873 palace overlooking La Pantiéro and the Old Port offers freshly decorated rooms and up-to-date bathrooms—the modernized ones facing the sea are a good choice if you covet a waterfront position but can't afford the grand hotels on La Croisette. **Pros:** family-run with flawless service; excellent value; great public beach around the port in La Bocca. **Cons:** handheld showers in bathtub (no walk-in showers); breakfast selection limited; no on-site parking. [$] *Rooms from: €179* ✉ *Allées de la Liberté, 4–6 rue Félix-Faure* ☎ *04–97–06–22–22* 🌐 *www.splendid-hotel-cannes.fr* 🛏 *62 rooms* 🍴 *No meals.*

Nightlife

Casino Barrière

CASINOS | The famous Casino Barrière on La Croisette—open 10 am to 3 am (until 4 am on weekends and until 5 am during summer)—is said to draw more crowds to its slot machines than any other casino in France. ✉ *Palais des Festivals, 1 La Croisette* ☎ *04–92–98–78–00* 🌐 *www.lucienbarriere.com.*

Le Bâoli

DANCE CLUBS | The biggest player on the Cannes nightlife scene, Le Bâoli attracts the likes of Kim and Kanye, Channing Tatum, Jude Law, and oh, some 3,000 other revelers who pass the door selection process. It's usually packed until dawn even outside of festival time. If staying up past 10 is not your scene, head to Cloud Nine, the 360-degree panoramic rooftop bar, for sunset cocktails. ✉ *Port Canto, Bd. de la Croisette, La Croisette* ☎ *04–93–43–03–43* 🌐 *www.baolicannes.com/en.*

Zoa Sushi Bar

BARS/PUBS | Open seven days a week until 2:30 am, Zoa manages to turn a sushi eatery into the place to drink chic cocktails. Be sure to book a table in advance. ✉ *2 pl. Charles de Gaulle* ☎ *04–93–30–00–30* 🌐 *www.zoasushibar.com.*

Performing Arts

Cannes International Film Festival

FESTIVALS | The Riviera's cultural calendar is splashy and star-studded, and never more so than during the Cannes International Film Festival in May. The film screenings are not open to the public, so unless you have a pass, your stargazing will be on the streets or in restaurants (though if you hang around the back exits of the big hotels around 7 pm, you may bump into a few celebs on their way to the red carpet). *Cinéma de la Plage* shows Cannes Classics and Out of Competition films free at Macé beach at 9:30 pm. In addition, Cannes Cinéphiles (⊕ *www.cannes-cinema.com*) gives 4,000 film buffs a chance to view Official Selections; you can apply online starting in February. ⊠ *Cannes* ⊕ *www.festival-cannes.com*.

Shopping

Whether you're window-shopping or splurging on that little Maria Grazia Chiuri number in the Dior window, you'll find some of the best shopping outside Paris on the streets off La Croisette. For stores carrying designer names, try **Rond-point Duboys-d'Angers** off **Rue Amouretti, Rue des Serbes,** and **Rue des Belges,** all perpendicular to the waterfront. **Rue d'Antibes** is the town's main shopping drag, home base to every kind of clothing and shoe shop, as well as mouthwatering candy, fabric, and home-design stores. **Rue Meynadier** mixes trendy young clothes with high-end food specialties.

Activities

Cannes Stand-up Paddle
WATER SPORTS | Near Palm Beach, this is one of the first shops on the Riviera to jump (or stand) on the SUP trend, which originated in Hawaii more than 30 years ago. It's a unique way to take in coastal views, so see Jean-Marc about renting a board, starting from a half hour (€8) up to a day (€65) or even a week (€400). ⊠ *Plage du Mouré Rouge, Bd. Gazagnaire* ⊕ *www.cannesstanduppaddle.fr*.

Club Nautique de la Croisette
WATER SPORTS | With a private windsurfing base off Île Ste-Marguerite, this company organizes diving sorties and rents kayaks, windsurfers, and catamarans for 30 minutes or an hour, June–October. ⊠ *Sq. de Verdun, 19 av. du Camp Long* ☎ *04–93–45–09–40* ⊕ *www.club-nautique-croisette.fr*.

Elite Rent a Bike
BICYCLING | This outfitter rents electric, mountain, and race bikes starting at €20 per day (along with a hefty €1,000 safety deposit). For the more daring, you can rent a moped for €35 per day (plus €800 deposit) without the need of a special driver's license. It's always a good idea to read the general terms of the rental before making a reservation. ⊠ *19 av. du Maréchal Juin* ☎ *04–93–94–30–34* ⊕ *www.elite-rentabike.com*.

Rivage Croisière Catamaran
SAILING | From May to September, climb aboard a 22-meter, 3-crew catamaran, destination Lérins Islands. Swim and snorkel (kit provided) as the boat moors between the two islands, or go ashore. The full-day trip (€108) departs at 10 am every day except Monday, and returns at 5 pm; it includes lunch on board. The half-day trip (€57; three hours, no meal) departs at 2 pm. Sunset and Fireworks cruises are also on the catamaran menu. ⊠ *20 quai St-Pierre* ☎ *04–92–98–71–31* ⊕ *www.rivage-croisiere.com*.

Îles de Lérins

15–20 minutes by ferry off the coast of Cannes.

When you're glutted on glamour and tired of dodging limos and the leavings of dyed-to-match poodles, catch a boat from Cannes's Vieux Port to one of two Îles de Lérins. On one of these two lovely island getaways you can find car-free peace and lose yourself in a tropical landscape of palms, pines, and tidal pools. Ste-Marguerite Island has more in the way of attractions: a ruined prison-fortress, a museum, and a handful of restaurants. Smaller and wilder, St-Honorat Island is dominated by its active monastery and its 10th-century ruins. Allow at least a half day to enjoy either island; you can see both if you get an early start. Although Ste-Marguerite has some restaurants and snack shops, you would be wise to bring along a picnic and drinks to enjoy the designated areas, which you won't find at St-Honorat.

■ TIP→ **A mind-boggling way to experience the islands without the crowds (and earn some serious bragging rights) is the ÖTILLÖ Swimrun Cannes that happens every October. The 24-mile race starts just after sunrise from Ste-Marguerite and includes a 1 mile swim back to Cap de la Croissette on the mainland, before a run along the famous boulevard and by the red carpet at the Palais des Festivals.**

GETTING HERE AND AROUND

Buy your tickets to Île Ste-Marguerite from one of the ferry companies at the booths on Cannes's Vieux Port; look for the Horizon Company which operates year-round. It's a 15-minute ride to Îles de Lérins from Cannes (€15 round-trip; daily approximately every hour on the hour 9–4 in high season, last boat back at 6 pm; no service on Sunday). Book online for reduced rates. Boats to Île St-Honorat are run by the monks who inhabit the island and tickets must be purchased from their own company, Planaria. Île St-Honorat can be reached in 20 minutes (€16.50 round-trip) from the Vieux Port; the schedule varies depending on the month, but from April to mid-October, ferries run every hour 9–5 (to 6 in July and August) and return 9:30–5:30 (last boat back is at 6:30 pm July and August). For an extra €1.50, you can get a 15-minute tour of the vineyard and sample its wines as part of the Vineyard @ Wines Excursion.

CONTACTS Horizon Company. ⊠ *Quai Laubeuf* ☎ *04–92–98–71–36* ⊕ *www.*

horizon-lerins.com. **Planaria.** ⊠ *Vieux Port, end of parking Laubeuf, Cannes* ☎ *04–92–98–71–38* ⊕ *www.cannes-iles-delerins.com.*

 # Sights

Île St-Honorat

ISLAND | Smaller and wilder than Ste-Marguerite, Île St-Honorat is home to an active monastery and the ruins of its 11th-century predecessor. The monks are more famous in the region for their nonreligious activity: manufacturing and selling a rather strong liqueur called Lérina. Retreats at the abbey's *hôtellerie* require a two-night minimum, and you must bring your own sheets and towels and obey the rule of silence (even during mealtime). There is no cost, but a donation of €45–€55 per night per person is welcome. There is Wi-Fi, but only in a restricted area. ■ TIP→ **As of June 2019, there are no longer any garbage cans on Île St-Honorat, so be prepared to take any trash you generate back with you to Cannes.** ⊠ *Île St-Honorat* ⊕ *www.abbayedelerins. com.*

Île Ste-Marguerite

ISLAND | From the Vieux Port it's a 15-minute, €16.50 round trip to Île Ste-Marguerite. Its **Fort Royal,** built by Richelieu and improved by Vauban, offers views over the ramparts to the rocky island coast and the open sea. There are only two restaurants—L'Escale and La Guérite (both closed mid-October–spring)—on the island, but they're rather pricey and the service is not as good as the fish; you are paying for food with a view. ⊠ *Ile Sainte-Marguerite.*

Musée de la Mer (*Marine Museum*)

MUSEUM | This complex is famous for reputedly being the prison of the Man in the Iron Mask. Inside you can see his cell and hear his story; the truth of his captivity is not certain, however, it is true that many Huguenots were confined here during Louis XIV's religious scourges.

You'll also find a Roman boat dating from the 1st century BC and a collection of amphorae and pottery recovered from ancient shipwrecks. ✉ *Fort de l'Île Ste-Marguerite, Ile Sainte-Marguerite* ☎ *04–93–38–55–26* 🎫 *€6* 🕒 *Closed Mon. Oct.–May.*

🍴 Restaurants

La Tonnelle

$$$ | **FRENCH** | It's hard to believe that this tranquil island is only 20 minutes from Cannes by boat, and that it's the location of a scenic, 19th-century restaurant run by monks from the Île St-Honorat monastery alongside chef Nathan Laurent. You're here for the views, but the menu focuses on the freshest (and most expensive) grilled fish, with prices that seem aimed at the stars (literally)—and service that reflects "we're the only restaurant on the island." **Known for:** breezy luxurious atmosphere; wines and liqueurs produced by island monks; snack bar open mid-May–mid-Sept. [$] *Average main: €29* ✉ *Abbaye Notre-Dame de Lérins, Île St-Honorat* ☎ *04–92–99–54–08* 🌐 *www.tonnelle-abbayedelerins.com* 🕒 *No dinner.*

Mougins

8 km (5 miles) north of Cannes; 11 km (7 miles) northwest of Antibes; 32 km (20 miles) southwest of Nice.

Passing through Mougins, a popular residential community convenient to Cannes, Nice, and the big Sophia-Antipolis business park, you may perceive little more than sleek, upscale suburban sprawl. But in 1961 Picasso found more to admire and settled into a *mas* that became a mecca for artists and art lovers; he died there in 1973. Over the decades, others of note also colonized the town, including Cocteau, Man Ray, Léger, and Christian Dior. Despite overbuilding today, Mougins claims extraordinary (yet distant) views over the coast and an Old Town (which is a *zone piétonne*, or pedestrian zone), on a hilltop above the fray, that has retained a pretty, ultragentrified charm. You'll see a few off-duty celebrities here and any number of wealthy Parisians who have chosen to buy a Riviera pied-à-terre here. Where they go, noted chefs follow, and Mougins is now a byword in gourmet circles. If you're not coming here specifically for the food, the town also has plenty of galleries and a handful of expensive cafés with pleasant terraces.

GETTING HERE AND AROUND

Getting to Mougins by public transportation is time-consuming. Bus Nos. 600 and 630 from Cannes stop in Mougins; from there it's a 15-minute walk up the hill to the Vieux Village. Alternatively, you could get off at the Val de Mougins stop and call the on-demand 203 Palmbus to take you up to the Vieux Village (any day except Sunday). If you don't have time to burn, opt for a taxi (around €35). From Nice, the train to Cannes costs €7.20 one-way.

VISITOR INFORMATION

CONTACTS Mougins Tourist Office. ✉ *39 pl. des Patriotes* ☎ *04–92–92–14–00* 🌐 *www.mougins-tourisme.fr.*

👁 Sights

Les Étoiles de Mougins

FESTIVAL | Every other year, this festival transforms the medieval village of Mougins into a vast "open-air theater of gastronomy" as it pays tribute to Roger Vergé, one of the all-time greatest figures in contemporary French cooking. Since it first started in 2006, hundreds of the world's best chefs have converged to share their passion with demonstrations, workshops, and tastings. Now the festival hopes to increase its presence abroad in countries like Japan and Russia by taking a road tour every other year. In 2019, it kicked off in Pietra Santa, Italy, before returning to Mougins in June

2020. ✉ *Vieux Village* ☎ *04–92–92–14–00* 🌐 *www.lesetoilesdemougins.com* 🎟 *From €5.*

★ **Musée d'Art Classique de Mougins**
MUSEUM | This hidden gem "highlights the dialogue between the old and the new" with Roman, Greek, and Egyptian art rubbing shoulders with pieces by Picasso, Matisse, Cézanne, Warhol, and Dalí. Expect to come across a sarcophagus alongside a Cocteau or a Hirst sculpture next to an ancient bust. Spread over four floors, the museum also houses antique jewelry and the world's largest armory collection. ✉ *32 rue Commandeur* ☎ *04–93–90–00–91* 🌐 *www.mouginsmusee.com* 🎟 *€14.*

Musée de la Photographie
MUSEUM | Near Porte Sarrazine, the Musée de la Photographie permanently displays André Villers's portraits of his good friends—Picasso, who gave the French photographer his first camera in 1953, and Dalí, among them. Recommended as one of the world's top 10 free photography museums and attracting 25,000 visitors a year, here the iconic photographer's avant-garde images spread over three floors in a small village house. Temporary exhibits across the year pull in some big names and there's a terrific collection of old cameras. ✉ *Porte Sarrazine, 67 rue d'Église* ☎ *04–93–75–85–67* 🎟 *Free* 🕓 *Closed Mon.*

Notre-Dame-de-Vie
HOUSE | You can find Picasso's final home, where he lived for 12 years until 1973, by following the D35 south of Mougins 2 km (1 mile) to the ancient ecclesiastical site of Notre-Dame-de-Vie. From his room, he could see the 13th-century belltower and arcaded chapel, a pretty ensemble once immortalized in a painting by Winston Churchill. The **chapel,** listed as a historical monument since 1927, is said to date back to 1655. Approached through an allée of ancient cypresses, the former priory house Picasso shared with his wife, Jacqueline, overlooks the broad bowl of the countryside (now blighted with modern construction). Unfortunately, his residence was bought by a private investor and is now closed to the public. ✉ *Ch. de la Chapelle* 🎟 *Free.*

🍴 Restaurants

★ **Paloma**
$$$$ | **FRENCH** | Young Nicolas Decherchi earned his first Michelin star only one year after opening Paloma, set in the serenity of a Provençal farmhouse and complete with distant views (in this case, of the sea and the Îles de Lérins off Cannes). The service is flawless, from the valet to the sommelier, and the food combines time-honored southern cooking techniques with a hefty dollop of imagination. **Known for:** gorgeous contemporary interior; bread service with pyramids of butter; cotton candy foie gras. [$] *Average main: €80* ✉ *47 av. du Moulin de la Croix* ☎ *04–92–28–10–73* 🌐 *www.restaurant-paloma-mougins.com* 🕓 *Closed Sun. and Mon., 1 wk in Feb., and 1 wk after film festival.*

🛏 Hotels

Le Manoir de l'Etang
$$ | **B&B/INN** | Owner Camilla Richards spent 20 years in London before converting this Provençal 19th-century manor house in the Bois de Fond Merle into an upscale inn, perched over a lotus pond with a spectacular outdoor pool, and the Cannes–Mougins golf course a few minutes away. **Pros:** friendly welcome from English-speaking owner; exceptional setting; excellent restaurant. **Cons:** stone steps difficult for those with mobility issues; not all rooms equal quality; Cannes beaches 7-km (4½-mile) drive away. [$] *Rooms from: €180* ✉ *66 allée du Manoir* ☎ *04–92–28–36–00* 🌐 *www.manoir-de-letang.com* 🕓 *Closed last wk in Oct.–mid-Dec.* 🛏 *21 rooms* 🍴 *Free breakfast.*

Golfing in the French Riviera

Golf is the most-played individual sport by the French, although, according to the Fédération Française de Golf, only 0.61% of the population practices, not quite on par with the United Kingdom (8%), Sweden (5%), or the United States (8 to 10%). When France hosted the 2018 Ryder Cup at Le Golf National on the outskirts of Versailles, only the second time in the tournament's history that it took place in Europe, even the tents signs were written in English as only 45% of tickets were sold to French nationals.

Grand Duke Michael of Russia founded the Riviera's first golf course—the Old Course in Cannes-Mandelieu—in 1891. This venerated institution now hosts more than 40 competitions a year and, according to *Riviera Golfer's* Nick Kent, some 60% of the total rounds are played by English-speakers. Today there are 22 regional golf courses, from Monaco to St-Tropez, an expat club (the Riviera Expatriates Golf Society, or REGS), and a biannual tournament: the Monaco-U.S Celebrity Ryder Cup.

Le Mas Candille

$$$$ | HOTEL | Nestled in an 8-acre private park, this 19th-century *mas* (farmhouse) has been cleverly transformed into an ultraluxurious hotel with antique wallpapers, "reissued" vintage furniture, and many other high-gloss touches that make the place *Elle Decor*–worthy. **Pros:** three pools, magnificent gardens, and wonderful spa; hammocks, Zen garden, and open-air gym; Michelin-starred restaurant with 400-bottle strong wine list. **Cons:** tricky to find; need to pay extra to avoid rooms facing parking lot; food on the pricey side. $ *Rooms from: €358* ⊠ *Bd. Clément-Rebuffel* ☎ *04–92–28–43–43* ⊕ *www.lemascandille.com* ☉ *Closed most of Jan.* 🛏 *45 rooms* ❍ *No meals.*

Royal Mougins Golf Resort Hotel

$$$$ | RESORT | What it lacks in Provençal character, this plush hotel on the green makes up for in modern comforts—each suite, decorated in soothing tones of beige and gray, is an independent apartment with a separate living room and kitchenette. **Pros:** tranquil atmosphere; golf course, outdoor pool, and lovely restaurant; free two hours at spa. **Cons:** Wi-Fi can be weak; you need a car to get here; decor a bit lacking. $ *Rooms from: €380*

⊠ *424 av. du Roi* ☎ *04–92–92–49–69* ⊕ *www.royalmougins.fr* ☉ *Closed Jan. and Feb.* 🛏 *29 suites* ❍ *Free breakfast.*

🏃 Activities

Golf Club de Cannes-Mougins

GOLF | Founded in 1923 by members such as Aga Khan and Prince Pierre of Monaco, this course is a stunner. The Club has hosted the European Open of Cannes, while the PGA Senior Tour also played here. Nonmembers are welcome (if they have a maximum handicap of 28), and there's a dress code (no long-sleeve shirts or denim). ⊠ *1175 av. du Golf* ☎ *04–93–75–79–13* ⊕ *www.golfcannes-mougins.com* 💳 *From €100* 🏌 *18 holes, 6906 yards, par 72.*

Grasse

10 km (6 miles) northwest of Mougins; 17 km (11 miles) northwest of Cannes; 22 km (14 miles) northwest of Antibes; 42 km (26 miles) southwest of Nice.

Coco Chanel may have first set up shop in Cannes, but when she wanted to create her classic "No. 5" fragrance she headed to Grasse, the perfume capital of the world, with its mild microclimate, which nurtures nearly year-round shows of tropical-hue flowers: orange blossoms, pittosporum, roses, lavender, jasmine, and mimosa. In the past, Grasse's legendary perfume-makers laid blossoms facedown in a lard-smeared tray, then soaked the essence away in alcohol; nowadays the scents are condensed in vast copper stills. Only the essential oils are kept, and the water thrown away—except rosewater and orangewater, which find their way into delicately perfumed pastries. In Paris and on the outskirts of Grasse, these scents are blended by a professional *nez*, or "nose," who must distinguish some 500 distinct scents and may be able to identify 3,000. The products carry the household names of couturiers like Chanel and Dior, and perfume houses like Guerlain. The laboratories where these great blends are produced are off-limits to visitors, but to accommodate the crowds of inquisitive scent-seekers, Molinard, Fragonard, and Galimard each set up factories that create simple blends and demonstrate some of the industry's production techniques. Factory tours are free, and you pass through a boutique of house perfumes on the way out. If you're looking for a more "scent-sational" experience, create your own perfume at Galimard (you can even order refills online once back home) and be treated to VIP perks, like a glass of champagne at the end of a workshop. The annual Jasmine Festival takes place over three days at the end of July or early August with traditional floats and puppet shows.

GETTING HERE AND AROUND

The train from Nice takes just over an hour (€10.40), but it's only 25 minutes from Cannes (€4.60). Alternatively, Bus No. 500 from Nice has daily service to Grasse, and Bus No. 610 comes from Cannes; both cost €1.50. Once here, you can get around aboard Le Petit Train

de Grasse for a 35-minute circuit of the town, including Place aux Aires, Vieille Ville, and the Cathedral. It departs every day but Sunday, April–October, 11–6 from the Cours Honoré Cresp (during the summer it operates seven days a week).

VISITOR INFORMATION
CONTACTS Grasse Tourist Office. ✉ *Pl. de la Buanderie* ☎ *04–93–36–66–66* ⊕ *www.tourisme.paysdegrasse.fr/en.*

Sights

Cathédrale Notre-Dame-du-Puy

RELIGIOUS SITE | On a clifftop overlook at the Old Town's edge, the Romanesque Cathédrale Notre-Dame-du-Puy contains no fewer than three paintings by Rubens, a triptych by the famed 15th-century Provençal painter Louis Bréa, and *Lavement des Pieds* (*The Washing of the Feet*) by the young Fragonard. ✉ *Pl. du Petit Puy* 🎫 *Free.*

Fragonard

FACTORY | Built in 1782, this perfume factory is open to the public daily for free guided tours, and has the best boutique: look for the chocolate spice candle—your home will have the wonderful scent of a French *chocalatier*. Sign up for a Do-it-Yourself Perfume (DIYP) workshop for a more specialized memento of your visit. ✉ *20 bd. Fragonard* ☎ *04–93–36–44–65* ⊕ *www.fragonard.com* 🎫 *Free.*

Galimard

FACTORY | Tracing its pedigree back to 1747, Galimard is one of the world's oldest perfume houses. Today its factory is open to visitors 365 days a year, where for €53 you can create and name your own perfume in a two-hour workshop. They're held Monday through Saturday at 10, 2, and 4 in Galimard's Studio des Fragrances, around the corner at 5 route de Pegomas; for those with more time, try the Haute Parfumerie workshops with a decadent champagne break. ✉ *73 rte. de Cannes* ☎ *04–93–09–20–00* ⊕ *www.galimard.com* 🎫 *Free.*

Molinard

FACTORY | Established in 1849, Molinard offers an extensive tour that includes visits to the Soap Factory, the Distillery (witness "the nose" at work concocting new fragrances), and the Cream Room, where the packaging team hand-labels each bottle or pump. For €30—and without a reservation—you can create your perfume in a few basic steps (20 minutes). ✉ *60 bd. Victor Hugo* ☎ *04–93–36–01–62* 🌐 *www.molinard.com* 🎟 *Free.*

Musée d'Art et d'Histoire de Provence

(*Museum of the Art and History of Provence*)

MUSEUM | Just up from the Fragonard perfumery and open every day, the Musée d'Art et d'Histoire de Provence has a large collection of faïence from the region, including works from the famous pottery towns of Moustiers, Biot, and Vallauris. ✉ *2 rue Mirabeau* ☎ *04–93–36–80–20* 🌐 *www.museesdegrasse.com* 🎟 *€2.*

Musée International de la Parfumerie

(*International Museum of Perfume*)

MUSEUM | With its soaring structure of steel, glass, and teak, the MIP has long been one of the more sleekly spectacular museums along the coast. After a 2019 renovation, the new contemporary design relies on color-coding to more easily trace the 3,000-year history of perfume making (highlights include a fascinating collection of 4,000 antique perfume bottles). Artist contributions, like the "Eye Nose You" project that lets you discover details of the scented body.through a photographic lens, add a living dimension to the museum. ✉ *2 bd. du Jeu de Ballon* ☎ *04–97–05–58–00* 🌐 *www.museesdegrasse.com* 🎟 *€6.*

Place aux Aires

PLAZA | Below the central cluster of museums and perfumeries, the picturesque Place aux Aires is lined with 17th- and 18th-century houses and their arcades. Every Saturday morning there's a small market selling produce and spices (the bigger market happens Wednesday 8–1, at Place du Cours). ✉ *Grasse.*

Vieille Ville (*Old Town*)

NEIGHBORHOOD | Go down the steps to Rue Mirabeau and lose yourself in the dense labyrinth of the Vieille Ville, where steep, narrow streets, austere facades, discreet gardens, and random flights of stairs are thrown into shadow by shuttered houses five and six stories tall. ✉ *Grasse.*

Villa Musée Fragonard

MUSEUM | This museum headlines the work of Grasse's own Jean-Honoré Fragonard (1732–1806), one of the great French "chocolate-box" artists of his day (these artists were known for their maudlin style that stemmed from the type of artwork found on boxes of chocolate). The lovely villa contains a collection of Fragonard's drawings, engravings, and paintings; also on display are works by his son Alexandre-Evariste and his grandson, Théophile. ✉ *23 bd. Fragonard* ☎ *04–93–36–52–98* 🌐 *www.fragonard.com/parfums_grasse/GB/fragonard/grasse/fragonard_costa_museum.cfm* 🎟 *€2, includes entry to Museum of the Art and History of Provence* 🕒 *Closed Tues. Oct.–June.*

🍴 Restaurants

Les Delicatesses de Grasse

$$ | **DELI** | All that perfume sniffing can build an appetite and Les Delicatesses de Grasse is just the place to refuel, with its tremendous selection of cheeses, olives, charcuteries, tapenades, and chunt-neys. Open daily, you could spend hours lingering over a half bottle of wine and sampling the delicious regional selections that are part of a shared platter (three to four people) for only €30. **Known for:** quaint Provençal deli; great wine pairings; small space so gets crowded quickly. [$] *Average main: €18* ✉ *7 rue Marcel Journet* ☎ *06–16–02–44–26.*

Route Napoléon

One of the most famous and panoramic roads in France is the Route Napoléon, taken by Napoléon Bonaparte in 1815 after his escape from imprisonment on the Mediterranean island of Elba. Napoléon landed at Golfe-Juan, near Cannes, on March 1 and forged northwest to Grasse, then through dramatic, hilly countryside to Castellane, Digne, and Sisteron. Commemorative plaques bearing the imperial eagle stud the route, inspired by Napoléon's remark, "The eagle will fly from steeple to steeple until it reaches the towers of Notre-Dame." Nowadays there are some lavender-honey stands and souvenir shacks, but they are few and far between. It's the panoramic views as the road winds its way up into the Alps that make this a route worth taking. Roads are curvy but well maintained. The whole 314-km (195-mile) route from Golfe-Juan to Grenoble takes about five days, but you can just do part of it and still take in the lovely scenery. In fact, if you like scenic drives, follow the Route Napoléon to Trigance and on to the spectacular Gorges du Verdon, also called the Grand Canyon du Verdon. You can then continue on to the heart of the Var and in a mere 30 minutes be swallowed up in the beauty of the spectacular Gorges Country. See 🌐 *www.route-napoleon.com.*

Hotels

La Bastide Saint-Antoine

$$$$ | HOTEL | This ocher mansion, once the home of an industrialist who hosted the Kennedys and the Rolling Stones, is now the Relais & Chateaux domain of celebrated chef Jacques Chibois, who welcomes you with old stone walls, shaded walkways, an enormous pool, and guest rooms that glossily mix Louis Seize, Provençal, and high-tech delights. **Pros:** a bastion of culinary excellence; Malongo coffee machine and organic tea in each room; choice of Provençal or modern decor. **Cons:** restaurant is very expensive; breakfast not included; deposit of 50% of the total stay is charged at time of booking. [$] *Rooms from: €360* ✉ *48 av. Henri-Dunant* ☎ *04–93–70–94–94* 🌐 *www.jacques-chibois.com* 🕒 *Closed 3 wks in Nov.* 🛏 *16 rooms* 🍴 *No meals.*

Valbonne

18 km (11 miles) north of Cannes; 14 km (9 miles) northwest of Antibes.

This fiercely Provençal hill town has been adopted by the British and a smorgasbord of other nationalities, who work either at the nearby tech park Sophia-Antipolis (France's Silicon Valley) or commute to, say, London or Geneva during the workweek, thanks to low-cost travel from easyJet. Valbonne exudes a peculiar kind of mixed-country charm, with a plethora of tasteful restorations and restaurants (including Moroccan, Indian, and sushi). Its principal cachet is the novel layout of the Old Town, designed in a grid system in the 16th century by the monks of Lérins. A checkerboard of ruler-straight *ruelles* (little streets) lies within a sturdy rampart of wraparound houses; at the center, a grand *place* is framed by Renaissance arcades and shady elms, perfect for people-watching at one of the cafés; and at the bottom of the village is the 13th-century **Abbaye** de Valbonne. Most weekends the village hosts a festival of some type (the first Sunday of the month there's an antiques fair), and despite the not-completely French environment, there's something quite captivating about this village.

You'll find upgraded versions of typical gifts to take home at the Friday Provençal market, one of the best in the region, as is the Maison de la Presse Libris news-stand, beside the pharmacy, with its out-standing selection of international press. Memorie de Famille (18 rue Alexis Julien) have fabulous and affordable housewares that they decoratively wrap for free, while the English Reading Centre, steps from here, is owned by an American and could give Amazon a run for its money.

A few kilometers west of Valbonne is "La Pitchoune," Julia Child's former Provençal home in Plascassier. For more than 20 years, it was run by American Kathie Alex as "Cooking with Friends in France" using Julia's kitchen very much as it was in her heyday. Today Julia's legacy lives on as Le Peetch, an unconventional cooking school offering a recipe-free, all-inclusive, five-night experience.

GETTING HERE AND AROUND
There are two ways to get to Valbonne: by car (all the parking is free!) or by bus. In Cannes, in front of the train station, the daily No. 630 takes about 40 minutes (€1.50) but check that the bus continues to Valbonne after Sophia-Antipolis. And from the bus station in Antibes, Bus No. 10 accesses Valbonne via Biot (35 min-utes, €1.50) and runs seven days a week.

🍴 Restaurants

★ Daniel Desavie
$$$$ | FRENCH | Judging by the crowd of regulars flocking to his restaurant, Daniel Desavie has built quite a reputation for his classic Provençal flavors (that's hardly surprising given that he was trained for 23 years by the late Roger Vergé at the famous Moulins de Mougins).

When you're ready to order from the very refined menu, try the lobster with tabbouleh and orange-mango vinaigrette before digging into the braised lamb shoulder fricassee. **Known for:** knowl-edgeable sommelier; outstanding friend-liness and service; multicourse prixe-fixe menus. $ Average main: €37 ✉ 1360 rte. d'Antibes ✛ From Valbonne, follow Rte. de Cannes then take left at Forum roundabout along D103 ☎ 04–93–12–29–68 ⊕ www.restaurantdanieldesavie.fr ⊙ Closed Sun. and Mon.

La Table by Richard Mebkhout
$$$ | FRENCH | In the heart of the village tucked away in a small valbonnaise house, La Table has become an instant hit with both the international and local French crowds. The dishes are unpreten-tious but heartily proportioned (imagine a lobster salad loaded with lobster) and delicately presented, almost too beau-tiful to eat (we said almost). **Known for:** carefully planned menus (including kids' menu); authentic Provençal cooking; tiny rustic setting serving only 20 diners at a time. $ Average main: €30 ✉ 6 rue de la Fontaine ☎ 04–92–98–07–10 ⊙ Closed Wed. No lunch Thurs. and Sun.

Vallauris

6 km (4 miles) northeast of Cannes; 6 km (4 miles) west of Antibes.

This ancient village in the low hills above the coast, dominated by a blocky Renaissance château, owes its four-square street plan to a form of medieval urban renewal. Ravaged and eventually wiped out by waves of the plague in the 14th century, the village was rebuilt by 70 Genovese families imported by the Abbaye de Lérins in the 16th century to repopulate the abandoned site. They brought with them a taste for Roman planning—hence the grid format in the Old Town—but more importantly, a knack for pottery making. Their skills and the fine clay of Vallauris were a perfect marriage, and the village thrived as a pottery center for hundreds of years. In the late 1940s Picasso found inspiration in the malleable soil and settled here, giving the flagging industry new life. Sadly, the town has developed a more shady reputation (so keep your hands on your purse) despite Saudi's King Salman owning a 1930s villa where Churchill and Hollywood celebs stayed, running along 1 km (½ mile) of Vallauris's beachfront.

GETTING HERE AND AROUND

The SNCF Golfe–Juan train station is in Place Pierre Sémard in the center of Vallauris–Golfe–Juan. Tickets cost €5.90 one-way from Nice and €2.10 from Cannes. Bus No. 8, part of the Envibus network, runs between the Golfe–Juan train station and Vallauris about every 15 minutes (45–55 minutes on Sunday). From Place Guynemer in Antibes, Envibus No. 5 goes to Vallauris with less frequent departures. Bus No. 200, connecting Nice and Cannes (€1.50), stops in Golfe–Juan and runs about every 15 minutes. There's also the Nice AirportXpress Shuttle No. 250, a daily airport express bus (55 minutes, €11) that stops in Antibes, Juan-les-Pins with Vallauris as its final destination.

Sights

Musée National Picasso

MUSEUM | In the late 1940s Picasso settled here in a simple stone house, "le château de Vallauris"—the former priory of the Abbaye de Lérins and one of the rare Renaissance buildings in the region—creating pottery art from the malleable local clay with a single-minded passion. But he returned to painting in 1952 to create one of his masterworks in the château's Romanesque chapel, the vast multipanel oil-on-wood composition called *La Guerre et la Paix* (*War and Peace*). Today the chapel is part of the Musée National Picasso, where several of Picasso's ceramic pieces

are displayed. ⊠ *Pl. de la Libération* 📞 *04–93–64–71–83* ⊕ *www.musees-nationaux-alpesmaritimes.fr/picasso* 💶 *€6* ⊘ *Closed Tues. Sept.–June.*

Antibes

15 km (9 miles) southeast of Nice.

Named Antipolis—meaning across from (*anti*) the city (*polis*)—by the Greeks, who founded it in the 4th century BC, Antibes flourished under the Romans' aristocratic rule, with an amphitheater, aqueducts, and baths. The early Christians established their bishopric here, the site of the region's cathedral until the 13th century. It was in the Middle Ages that the kings of France began fortifying this key port town, an effort that culminated in the recognizable star-shape ramparts designed by Vauban. The young general Napoléon once headed this stronghold, living with his family in a humble house in the Old Town; his mother washed their clothes in a stream. There's still a *lavoir* (public laundry fountain) in the Old Town where locals, not unlike Signora Bonaparte, rinse their clothes and hang them like garlands over the narrow streets.

With its broad stone ramparts scalloping in and out over the waves and backed by blunt medieval towers, it's easy to understand why Antibes (pronounced "Awn- *teeb*") inspired Picasso to paint on a panoramic scale. Stroll Promenade Amiral-de-Grasse along the crest of Vauban's sea walls, and watch the sleek yachts purring out to sea. Even more intoxicating, just off the waterfront, is the souklike maze of old streets, its market filled with fresh fish and goat cheese, wild herbs, and exotic spices. This is **Vieil Antibes,** with a nearly Italianate feel, perhaps no great surprise considering that Antibes' great fort marked the border between Italy and France right up to the 19th century.

Monet fell in love with the town, and his most famous paintings show the fortified Vieil Antibes against the sea. He arrived in January 1888 and expected to stay only a few days; three months later, he had shipped off 39 canvases to be exhibited in Paris at the gallery of Vincent van Gogh's brother. To see Antibes as Monet—and Picasso, Cross, Boudin, and Harpignies—once did, head to the tourist office for a pamphlet in English on the Painters' Trail, complete with map or sign up for a guided walk along the trail.

GETTING HERE AND AROUND

Antibes has one central train station, the Gare SNCF, which is at the far end of town but still within walking distance of the Vieille Ville and only a block or so from the beach. Local trains are frequent, coming from Nice (20 minutes, €4.80), Juan-les-Pins, Biot, Cannes (10 minutes, €3.10), and almost all other coastal towns.

There are high-speed TGVs (Trains à Grand Vitesse) to Antibes. Bus service, available at Antibes' Gare Routière (*1 pl. Guynemer*) is supplied by Envibus (☎ *04–89–87–72–00* ⊕ *www.envibus. fr*). For local routes or to get to Cannes, Nice, Cagnes-sur-Mer, Juan-les-Pins, take the Lignes d'Azur No. 200 (☎ *08–10–06–10–06* ⊕ *www.lignedazur.com*), which runs every 15 minutes and costs €1.50. A new bus-tram line now serves 18 stops from Antibes via Biot to Sophia Antipolis, the tech park located near Valbonne. There are plans to extend the route to Grasse in 2023.

TOURS

Antibes Tourist Office Tours

WALKING TOURS | Several guided tours lasting 1 hour 45 minutes are offered by the tourist office. Themes range from "The Painters Trail" to "Discovering Old Antibes" (in English on Thursday at 10, March–October) to "Artists and the Mediterranean." There's also the "Gourmet Tour" (June–September), which for €16 per person (€30 per couple), enables you to taste the town by sampling at three local eateries. Tours must be reserved in advance with the Tourist Office. Or download the tourist office's Monument Tracker app and let it guide you in English through 150 local sites. ✉ *42 av. Robert Soleau* ☎ *04–22–10–60–25* ⊕ *www. antibesjuanlespins.com* 🎟 *From €7.*

VISITOR INFORMATION

CONTACTS Antibes Tourist Office. ✉ *42 av. Robert Soleau* ☎ *04–22–10–60–10* ⊕ *www.antibesjuanlespins.com.* **Gare SNCF.** ✉ *Pl. Pierre-Semard* ⊕ *www.gares-sncf.com.*

Sights

★ **Commune Libre du Safranier** (*Free Commune of Safranier*)

NEIGHBORHOOD | A few blocks south of the Château Grimaldi, aka the Picasso Museum, is the Commune Libre du Safranier, a magical little neighborhood with a character (and mayor) all its own since 1966 (it's not technically a part of Antibes). The commune even holds its own festivals throughout the year, celebrating a variety of things like chestnuts, grape harvests, and the Christmas Yule log. Not far off the seaside promenade, Rue de la Touraque is the main street to get here, and you can amble around Place du Safranier, where tiny houses hang heavy with flowers and vines, and neighbors carry on conversations from window to window across the stone-stepped Rue du Bas-Castelet. ✉ *Rue du Safranier, Rue du Bas-Castelet.*

Cours Masséna

NEIGHBORHOOD | To visit old Antibes, stroll the Cours Masséna, where every day 6–1 (except Monday September–May) a sheltered Provençal market tempts you with lemons, olives, and hand-stuffed sausages while the vendors take breaks in the shoebox cafés flanking one side. Painters, sculptors, and other artists take over at 3 pm Tuesday–Sunday in the summer, and Friday–Sunday

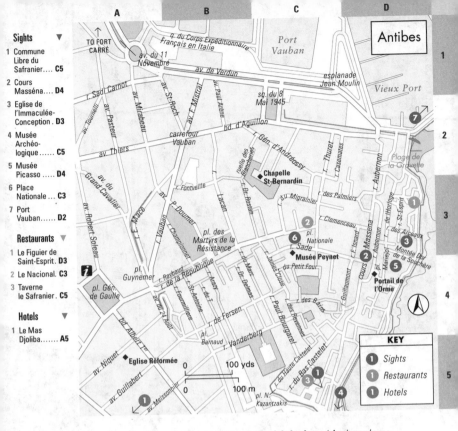

KEY

1 *Sights*

1 *Restaurants*

1 *Hotels*

September–mid-June. From Port Vauban, you'll find the cours by passing through an arched gateway beneath the ramparts and following Rue Aubernon to the old Portail de l'Orme, built of quarried Roman stone and enlarged in the Middle Ages. ⊠ *Antibes.*

Eglise de l'Immaculée-Conception
(*Cathédrale Notre-Dame*)

RELIGIOUS SITE | This sanctuary served as the region's cathedral until the bishopric was transferred to Grasse in 1244. The church's 18th-century facade, a marvelously Latin mix of classical symmetry and fantasy, has been restored in stunning shades of ocher and cream. Its stout medieval watchtower was built in the 11th century with stones "mined" from Roman structures. Inside is a Baroque altarpiece painted by the Niçois artist Louis Bréa in 1515. ⊠ *Rue du St-Esprit.*

Musée Archéologique (*Archaeology Museum*)

MUSEUM | Promenade Amiral-de-Grasse—a marvelous spot for pondering the mountains and tides—leads directly to the Bastion St-André, a squat Vauban fortress that now houses the Musée Archéologique. In its glory days this 17th-century stronghold sheltered a garrison; the bread oven is still visible in the vaulted central hall. The museum collection focuses on Antibes's classical history, displaying amphorae and sculptures found in local digs as well as in shipwrecks from the harbor. ⊠ *Bastion St-André, Av. Général-Maizières* ☎ 04–22–10–60–10 ⊠ *€3* ⊘ *Closed Sun. and Mon.*

Musée Picasso

MUSEUM | Rising high over the water, this museum is set in the stunning medieval

Did You Know?

Antibes may be famed for its Musée Picasso, but the real jewel here is the town itself, a magnificently picturesque maze of streets, cul-de-sacs, and boutique-lined promenades.

Château Grimaldi. As rulers of Monaco, the Grimaldi family lived here until the revolution; this fine old castle, however, was little more than a monument until its curator offered use of its chambers to Picasso in 1946, when that extraordinary genius was enjoying a period of intense creative energy. The result was a bounty of exhilarating paintings, ceramics, and lithographs inspired by the sea and by Greek mythology—all very Mediterranean. The château, which became the museum in 1966, houses some 245 works by the artist (but not all are on display), as well as pieces by Miró, Calder, and Léger; the first floor displays more than 100 paintings by Russian-born artist Nicholas de Staël. Even those who are not great Picasso fans should enjoy his vast paintings on wood, canvas, paper, and walls, alive with nymphs, fauns, and centaurs. ⊠ *Château Grimaldi, Pl. Marie-jol* ☎ *04–92–90–54–20* 🏛 *€8* ☽ *Closed Mon.*

Place Nationale

PLAZA | Not far from the Commune quarter, the Old Town streets invite you to explore the mix of shops, galleries, restaurants, and bakeries. Aim to wind up on Place Nationale, the site of the Roman forum. It's a pleasant place for a drink under the replanted hackberry trees, which magically provide the right amount of shade in summer and sunshine in winter. ⊠ *Antibes.*

Port Vauban

MARINA | Whether you approach the waterfront from the train station or park along the Avenue de Verdun, you'll first confront the awesome expanse of luxury yachts in Port Vauban, which has an underground parking lot and attractive esplanade from which you can admire one of Europe's oldest and largest ports home to 1,642 berths—including 19 for superyachts of up to 560 feet. It's no wonder the antiques fair and sailing show chose this spot for their events every spring. With the tableau of snowy

Alps looming in the background and the formidable medieval block towers of the **Fort Carré** (Square Fort) guarding entry to the port, it's difficult to find a more dramatic spot to anchor. This superbly symmetrical island fortress was completed in 1565 and restored in 1967, but can only be admired from afar. Across the Quai Rambaud, which juts into the harbor, a tiny crescent of sand called **La Gravette** beach offers swimmers one of the last soft spots on the coast before the famous Riviera pebble beaches begin as you head east. ⊠ *Antibes.*

🏖 Beaches

Antibes and Juan-les-Pins together claim 25 km (15½ miles) of coastline and 48 beaches (including Cap d'Antibes). In Antibes you can choose between small sandy inlets, such as La Gravette, below the port; the central Plage du Ponteil; Plage de la Salis toward the Cap; rocky escarpments around the Old Town; or the vast stretch of sand above the Fort Carré. The Plage de la Salis may be one of the prettiest beach sites on the coast, with the dark pines of the cape on one side and the old stones of Antibes on the other, all against a backdrop of Alpine white. Juan-les-Pins is one big city beach, lined by a boulevard and promenade peppered with cafés and restaurants. If you want to follow in Picasso's footsteps, head to the Plage de la Garoupe, halfway down the Cap d'Antibes peninsula and set near the cape's fabulous Sentier Tirepoil footpath: this pretty white-sand crescent is the place locals have always headed to sunbathe and celeb-spot.

🍴 Restaurants

★ **Le Figuier de Saint-Esprit**

$$$$ | FRENCH | Christian Morrisset's Michelin-starred restaurant is named after the 40-year-old fig tree that, along with a canopy of vines, gorgeously shades the private courtyard. One of the

best restaurants in the region, the haute cuisine chef is dedicated to his daily market, where he bases his wonderfully scrumptious set menus. **Known for:** the main culinary attraction of Antibes; charming courtyard; local, big labels, and organic wines. $ *Average main: €90* ✉ *14 rue Saint-Esprit* ☎ *04–93–34–50–12* ⊕ *www.christianmorisset.fr* ⊗ *Closed 1 wk in Feb., late June, 3 wks in Nov., Tues. yr-round, and Wed. Nov.–Apr. No lunch Mon. and Wed. May–Oct.*

Le Nacional

$$ | **FRENCH** | When you've had enough of the "catch of the day" and need a good old dose of red meat, this Italian restaurant in old Antibes is the place to go. The selection includes barbequed, oven-cooked Black Angus American, Australian, or Irish, beef and various cuts from rump steak to rib to sirloin XXL, all overseen by Nicolas Rondell, head chef at the Michelin-starred Pecheurs in the Cap. **Known for:** steaks priced by the gram; swanky summer terrace; providing lots of information about the meat it serves. $ *Average main: €20* ✉ *61 pl. Nationale* ☎ *04–93–61–77–30* ⊕ *www. restaurant-nacional-antibes.com* ▬ *No credit cards* ⊗ *Closed Mon.*

Taverne le Safranier

$$ | **FRENCH** | Part of a tiny Old Town enclave determined to resist the press of tourism, this casual tavern is headquarters for the tables scattered across the sunny terrace on Place Safranier. Install yourself at one, and tuck into dishes like zucchini beignet, Saint Jacques and lobster cassoulet, thick handmade ravioli, or whole *dorade,* a delicate Mediterranean fish unceremoniously split, fried, and garnished with lemon. **Known for:** pretty terrace tucked away from main streets; simple but reasonably priced dishes; laid-back vibe. $ *Average main: €23* ✉ *1 pl. Safranier* ☎ *04–93–34–80–50* ⊗ *Closed Mon. and Jan.*

Hotels

Le Mas Djoliba

$$ | **HOTEL** | **FAMILY** | Tucked into a residential neighborhood on the crest between Antibes and Juan-les-Pins, this cool, cozy inn feels like the 1920s private home it once was, surrounded by greenery and well protected from traffic noise. **Pros:** quiet neighborhood only a seven-minute walk to sandy beach; lovely swimming pool; top-floor family suite with terrace and views of Cap d'Antibes. **Cons:** breakfast costs extra; 30% deposit required; not all rooms have sea views. $ *Rooms from: €180* ✉ *29 av. de Provence* ☎ *04–93–34–02–48* ⊕ *www.hotel-djoliba.com* ⊗ *Closed Nov.–mid-Mar.* ⇌ *13 rooms* ❌ *No meals.*

Nightlife

Absinthe Bar

BARS/PUBS | It's both a museum (daily 10–7) and a time machine: take a trip back to the day of Hemingway and the Green Ferry. Taste what all that talk about hallucinating is all about, and you might just get a hat to commemorate the occasion. Open every day (10:30 to 7:30), this underground bar has a piano bar on Friday and Saturday, when it stays open until 12:30 am. ✉ *25 cours Masséna* ☎ *04–93–34–93–00.*

Blue Lady Pub

BARS/PUBS | Next to the legendary Geoffrey's British food shop, this pub is frequented by French locals and foreigners alike (and their kids and dogs). It's a great little spot to collect your thoughts over a drink after a long day, or to hear some live music. The Blue Lady has daytime appeal, too. Beginning at 7:30 am you can grab a latte, a smoothie, or even an English breakfast (there are newspapers on deck). If you stick around for lunch, you can order homemade burgers, potpies, and fresh salads (the kitchen closes at 3 pm). ✉ *La Galerie du Port, Rue Lacan* ☎ *04–93–34–41–00* ⊕ *www.blueladypub.com.*

Royal Jazz Lounge

MUSIC CLUBS | Antibes was long over-due for a classy spot that's not full of yacht-goers. At long last, here you can enjoy live jazz by the sea, and it's within walking distance of Port Vauban. From Tuesday to Saturday, starting at 6:30 pm, this club located in the Hotel Royal offers performances by local and international artists. There's also jam sessions on Tuesday and Thursday nights. ⊠ *16 bd. Maréchal Leclerc* ⊕ *www.hotel-royal-anti-bes.com/en/hotel-bar-jazz.*

 ## Shopping

In Antibes, two antiques and flea markets occur weekly, both open 7–6: one on Saturday on Place Nationale, and one on Thursday and Saturday at Place Audiberti. You'll find a stall selling the iconic Savon de Marseille in the Provençal Cours Masséna market but if you're on the hunt for a more original knickknack to take home to friends, stop by Le Comptoir des Savonniers on Rue Thuret, which sells translucent wedges of multicolor soap cut to size using a special machine and sold by weight. The shop's presenta-tion is so Modern Art you can overlook the fact that the soap is imported from Belgium.

Old Town

SHOPPING NEIGHBORHOODS | You can find plenty of eclectic little boutiques and gallery shops in the Old Town, especially along Rue Sade, Rue de la République, and Rue James Close. ⊠ *Antibes.*

Activities

Diamond Diving

DIVING/SNORKELING | Brit Alex Diamond owns this Golfe–Juan Dive Centre shop, which offers Discover Scuba courses and equipment rentals, and with his French government–recognized certification he even teaches future French diving instructors "Diving English." ⊠ *Rue des Pêcheurs, Vallauris* ☎ *06–15–30–52–23* ⊕ *www.diamonddiving.net.*

Cap d'Antibes

2 km (1 mile) south of Antibes.

For the most part extravagantly idyllic, this fabled 4-mile-long peninsula has been carved up into luxurious estates perched high above the water and shaded by thick, tall pines. Since the 19th century its wild greenery and isolation have drawn a glittering assortment of aristocrats, artists, literati, and the merely fabulously wealthy. Among those claim-ing the prestigious Cap d'Antibes address over the years are: Guy de Maupassant, Anatole France, Claude Monet, the Duke and Duchess of Windsor, the Greek ship-ping tycoon Stavros Niarchos, and the cream of the Lost Generation, including Ernest Hemingway, Dorothy Parker, Ger-trude Stein, and F. Scott Fitzgerald. Now the focal point is the famous Hotel Eden Roc, which is packed with stars during the Cannes Film Festival (not surprisingly, as movie studios always pick up the tab for their favorite celebs). Reserve a table for lunch here during the festival and be literally surrounded by celebrities to-ing and fro-ing to the pool. Just play it cool, though: keep your sunglasses on at all times and resist the urge to take photos.

GETTING HERE AND AROUND
Envibus No. 2 (€1.50) connects Cap d'An-tibes to downtown Antibes.

 ## Sights

Jardin Thuret (*Thuret Garden*)

GARDEN | To fully experience the Riviera's heady hothouse exoticism, visit the glorious Jardin Thuret, established by bot-anist Gustave Thuret in 1856 as a testing ground for subtropical plants and trees. Thuret was responsible for the introduc-tion of the palm tree, forever changing the profile of the French Riviera. On his

Continued on page 312

STROKES *of* GENIUS

Le Cantique des Cantiques (oil on canvas)
by Marc Chagall, Musée Chagall

eurs et Fruits (gouache cutout)
Henri Matisse, Musée Matisse

A kind of artistic Garden of Eden exists in the minds of many painters, a magical place painted in the vivid colors of imagination—a promised land where they can bask in warm sunshine nearly every day of the year, swim in a placid sea of incredible blue, daub flowers so colorful they would challenge even the most riotous palette, and live life as sensually as they sketch it.

This is the dream would-be Adams sought in the late 19th century when, inspired by Impressionist *plein-air* (open-air) painting, artists abandoned the airless studios of Paris for the sun-kissed towns of the South of France. By the 1920s, a virtual migration of painters and sculptors heeded the siren call of the Mediterranean muse and began to colonize the Côte d'Azur. Signac made St-Tropez the Riviera's first "Greenwich Village"; Cannes attracted Picasso and Van Dongen; Haut-de-Cagnes and St-Paul-de-Vence lured Renoir, Soutine, and Modigliani; and Matisse and Dufy settled in Nice. A veritable "museum without walls," these locales went on to nurture some of the biggest "isms" in 20th-century art. Creativity was unleashed, cares forgotten, and *le bonheur de vie*—the happiness of life—became a forceful leitmotiv.

The result was an outpouring of art whose exuberance and energy led to the paradise that exists here today: a tightly packed 100-mile stretch of coastline crammed with the houses, gardens, and towns that inspired these artists. Be content to leave their masterpieces to museums scattered around the world, and get ready to savor instead a host of virtual Matisses, 3-D Renoirs, and pop-up Picassos. This rainbow curve of a coast will prove to be an unforgettable road trip through the history of modern art.

THE MODERN ART ROAD

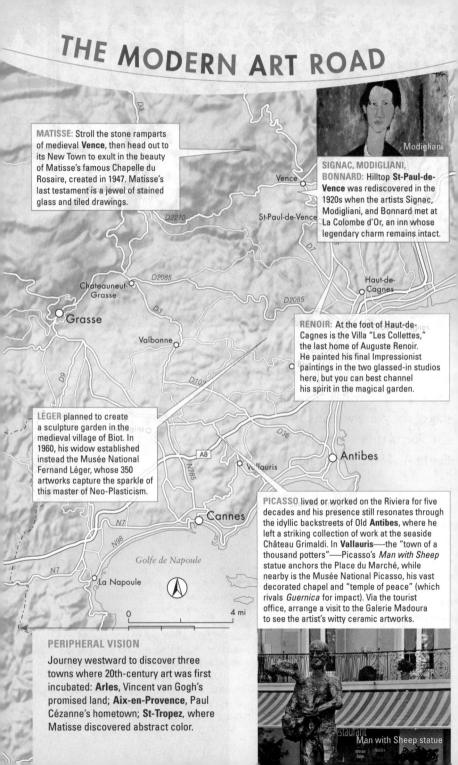

MATISSE: Stroll the stone ramparts of medieval **Vence**, then head out to its New Town to exult in the beauty of Matisse's famous Chapelle du Rosaire, created in 1947. Matisse's last testament is a jewel of stained glass and tiled drawings.

Modigliani

SIGNAC, MODIGLIANI, BONNARD: Hilltop **St-Paul-de-Vence** was rediscovered in the 1920s when the artists Signac, Modigliani, and Bonnard met at La Colombe d'Or, an inn whose legendary charm remains intact.

RENOIR: At the foot of Haut-de-Cagnes is the Villa "Les Collettes," the last home of Auguste Renoir. He painted his final Impressionist paintings in the two glassed-in studios here, but you can best channel his spirit in the magical garden.

LÉGER planned to create a sculpture garden in the medieval village of Biot. In 1960, his widow established instead the Musée National Fernand Léger, whose 350 artworks capture the sparkle of this master of Neo-Plasticism.

PICASSO lived or worked on the Riviera for five decades and his presence still resonates through the idyllic backstreets of Old **Antibes**, where he left a striking collection of work at the seaside Château Grimaldi. In **Vallauris**—the "town of a thousand potters"—Picasso's *Man with Sheep* statue anchors the Place du Marché, while nearby is the Musée National Picasso, his vast decorated chapel and "temple of peace" (which rivals *Guernica* for impact). Via the tourist office, arrange a visit to the Galerie Madoura to see the artist's witty ceramic artworks.

PERIPHERAL VISION

Journey westward to discover three towns where 20th-century art was first incubated: **Arles**, Vincent van Gogh's promised land; **Aix-en-Provence**, Paul Cézanne's hometown; **St-Tropez**, where Matisse discovered abstract color.

Man with Sheep statue

Map labels: D3, Vence, St-Paul-de-Vence, D2210, D7, Chateauneuf-Grasse, D2085, Haut-de-Cagnes, Grasse, D3, D2085, Valbonne, D9, D103, D36, A8, Biot, Antibes, N285, Vallauris, Cannes, N7, N98, Golfe de Napoule, N7, La Napoule, 0 — 4 mi

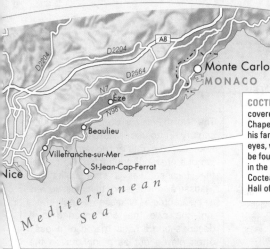

COCTEAU: "The Prince of Poets" covered **Villefranche-sur-Mer's** Chapelle Saint-Pierre in 1957 with his fanciful curlicues, angels, and eyes, while more of his work can be found up the coast in Menton in the seaside Musée Jean Cocteau and the pretty Marriage Hall of the town Hôtel de Ville.

Chagall and Matisse: A banquet of museums entices the art lover to **Nice**, including the Musée Matisse, the Musée National Marc Chagall, and the Musée d'Art Moderne, but don't forget to stroll to Matisse's favorite spots—the elegant Promenade des Anglais, Jardin Albert 1er, and enchanting Cours Saleya marketplace.

Marc Chagall Museum

"The days follow each other here with a beauty which I would describe as insolent."

—Nietzsche,
writing from Èze, near Beaulieu, 1883

St-Paul-de-Vence   Chapelle du Rosaire, Vence

Born: October 25, 1881, in Málaga, Spain.

Died: April 8, 1973, in Mougins, Côte d'Azur.

Personality Profile: Genius, philosopher-sage, egoist.

Claim to Fame: A one-man history of 20th-century art, Picasso changed styles as often as he did mistresses, but he is best known as the founder of Cubism.

Picasso Peeking: Cane fencing has been erected around Picasso's last retreat of Notre-Dame-de-Vie in Mougins by his heirs, and you are obliged to view his majestic Château de Vauvenargues (where he lies buried) through binoculars.

Picasso Peeking: The Musée Picasso in Antibes and his War and Peace Chapel in Vallauris are top spots to view his masterworks.

Best-Known Works: *Les Demoiselles d'Avignon, Guernica, Au Lapin Agile, Minotauomachy.*

Quote: "You see, I have to paint for the both of us now" (on hearing of Matisse's death).

PABLO PICASSO

The "North Pole and South Pole" of 20th-century art (to use Picasso's phrase), the two heavyweights of modernism had a famous push-pull friendship. No matter that Picasso was a structuralist and Matisse a sensualist, or that Picasso was as egocentric as Matisse was self-effacing—the two masters engaged in a decades-long artistic "game of chess," often played out as neighbors on the Côte d'Azur. It was Matisse's mesmerizingly beautiful paintings created in Nice in the 1930s that probably inspired Picasso's move to the South of France in 1946. He wound up painting in Antibes, sculpting in Vallauris, wooing in Golfe-Juan, and seducing in Mougins. But their ventriloquous dialogue began in 1906 when they first met in the Parisian salon of Gertrude Stein (who lost little time in baiting the artists against each other).

Matisse had already created a revolution in color; Picasso, 12 years younger, was about to create one in form with *Les Demoiselles d'Avignon*—the "first" 20th-century painting, whose cubistic structure was inspired by African sculpture—as it turns out, Matisse's African sculpture, since Picasso had studied his collection of Senegalese totems. When Picasso moved to the Midi in 1946, Matisse presented him with a dove, which inspired Picasso to create his famous poster in homage to France's newly won peace.

The same year, Picasso was given the keys to Antibes' Château Grimaldi, where he painted 30 canvases depicting mermaids and minotaurs, all prancing about in direct homage to Matisse's famously joyous paintings, *La Joie de Vie* and *La Danse.*

Ceramic Plate by Picasso, Galerie Madoura

HENRI MATISSE

What Tahiti was to Gauguin, Nice was to Matisse. Its flower marketplaces, palaces painted in bonbon pastels, and magnificent palm trees soothed and, together with the constantly changing show of light—so different from the relentless glare of St-Tropez (where, in 1904, he first committed chromatic mayhem with his Fauve "wild beast" masterpiece, *Luxe, Calme, et Volupté*)—inspired him.

By 1919, ailing with bronchitis, he had moved to Nice, where he started to paint images of unrivaled voluptuousness: semi-nude odalisques skimpily clad in harem pantaloons and swathed in Moroccan fabrics. Their popular success allowed Matisse to relocate, in 1921, to a rooftop apartment at 1 Place Charles Félix, which magnificently overlooked Nice's Cours Saleya flower market. To view his art, head for the city's Musée Matisse and the Monastère de Cimiez cemetery, where you'll find his grave.

But to sense his true spirit venture to nearby Vence, where he moved in 1943 when Nice was threatened by World War II. Here he created the sublime Chapelle du Rosaire, his masterpiece ("in spite of all its imperfections") of black-on-white tile drawings and exalted stained-glass windows of emerald, blue, and yellow. The intensely competitive Picasso also saw it, of course, as a challenge. So, in 1952–53 he transformed an empty Romanesque chapel in nearby Vallauris into a "temple of peace" with scenes of La Guerre (war) and La Paix (peace). Unlike Matisse, however, he designed no liturgical gear, chasubles, or altar, since Picasso remained an avowed atheist.

Born: December 31, 1869, in Le Cateau, Northern France.

Died: November 3, 1954, in Nice, Côte d'Azur.

Personality Profile: Buddha, bon vivant, hedonist.

Claim to Fame: As father of the Fauves—the phrase "wild beast" described their expressive use of shade and hue—his works simplified design and exalted color.

Meeting Matisse: Musée Matisse in Nice, Rosary Chapel in Vence.

Matisse's muse: A decade before Sister Jacques-Marie inspired Matisse's Chapelle du Rosaire, she had been a nurse and model to him.

Best-Known Works: *Luxe, Calme, et Volupté, The Dance, Jazz, The Red Studio, Pink Nude.*

Quote: "Picasso sees everything."

La danse

death the property was left to the Ministry of Agriculture, which continues to dabble in the introduction of exotic species. ⊠ *90 ch. Raymond, Antibes* ✛ *From Port Gallice, head up Chemin du Croûton, turn right on Bd. du Cap, then right again on Chemin Raymond* ☎ *04–97–21–25–00* ⊕ *www6.sophia.inra.fr/jardin_thuret* ⊠ *Free* ⊙ *Closed weekends.*

★ **Le Sentier du Littoral** (*Sentier Tire-poil*)
TRAIL | Bordering the Cap's zillion-dollar hotels and over-the-top estates runs one of the most spectacular footpaths in the world. Nicknamed the Sentier "Tire-poil" (because the wind is so strong it "ruffles the hair"), the circuit stretches about 5 km (3 miles) along the outermost tip of the peninsula, bringing it "full circle" around the gardens at Eilenroc over to l'Anse de l'Argent Faux. An educational family-fun nature walk can be booked through the tourist office, or you can tackle the path on your own. The Sentier du Littoral begins gently enough at the pretty Plage de la Garoupe (where Cole Porter and Gerald Murphy used to hang out), with a paved walkway and dazzling views over the Baie de la Garoupe and the faraway Alps. Round the far end of the cap, however, and the paved promenade soon gives way to a boulder-studded pathway that picks its way along 50-foot cliffs, dizzying switchbacks, and thundering breakers. (Signs read, "*Attention Mort*" [Beware: Death], reminding you this path can be very dangerous in stormy weather.) Continue along the newer portion of the path to the cove l'Anse de l'Argent Faux, where you can stop and catch your breath before heading up to the entrance of Eilen Roc. Then follow Avenue Beaumont until it touches the Cap's main road RD2559. On sunny days, with exhilarating winds and spectacular breakers, you'll have company, although for most stretches all signs of civilization completely disappear except for a yacht or two. The walk takes about two hours to complete, but it may prove to be two of the more unforgettable

hours of your trip (especially if you tackle it at sunset). By the way, if you come across locked gates blocking your route it's because storm warnings have been issued and you are not allowed to enter. ■ TIP→ **From the station in town take Bus No. 2 to Fontaine stop. To return, follow the Plage de la Garoupe until Boulevard de la Garoupe, where you'll make a left to reconnect with the bus.** ⊠ *Antibes.*

Phare de la Garoupe (*Garoupe Lighthouse*)
LIGHTHOUSE | You can sample a little of what draws famous people to this part of the world by walking up Chemin de Calvaire from the Plage de la Salis in Antibes—a distance of about 1 km (½ mile) via a challenging pathway—and taking in the extraordinary views from the hill surmounted by this old *phare* (lighthouse). By 2021, you'll be able to climb all 114 steps to the top. Next to it, the 16th-century double chapel of **Notre-Dame-de-la-Garoupe** contains ex-votos and statues of the Virgin, all in memory of and for the protection of sailors. ■ TIP→ **Reward your trek with a drink or a meal at the Bistrot du Curé next door.** ⊠ *Chemin de Calvaire, Antibes* ☎ *04–22–10–60–10.*

★ **Villa Eilenroc**
HOUSE | Le Sentier du Littoral passes along the beach at the Villa Eilenroc (designed by Charles Garnier, who created the Paris Opéra), commanding the tip of the peninsula from a grand and glamorous garden. Over the last decade an eco-museum was completed and a scented garden created at the entrance to the rose garden. On Wednesday, September through June, visitors are allowed to wander through the reception salons, which retain the Louis Seize-Trianon feel of the noble facade. The Winter Salon still has its *1,001 Nights* ceiling mural painted by Jean Dunand, the famed Art Deco designer; display cases are filled with memorabilia donated by Caroline Groult-Flaubert (Antibes resident and goddaughter of the great author);

A gigantic unframed painting come to life, Antibes has been immortalized by countless artists, including Monet, Renoir, and Picasso.

and the boudoir has *boiseries* (decorative wood features) from the Marquis de Sévigné's Paris mansion. As you leave, be sure to detour to La Rosaerie, the rose garden of the estate—in the distance you can spot the white portico of the Château de la Cröe, another legendary villa (now reputedly owned by a syndicate of Russian billionaires). It has a host of big names attached to it—singer Helene Beaumont built it; and King Leopold II of Belgium, King Farouk of Egypt, Aristotle Onassis, and Greta Garbo all rented here. ⚠ **Since 2017, visitors have been occasionally surprised to find the villa unexpectedly closed. Your best bet is to check the Antibes tourist office's website before you head out.** ✉ *460 av. L.D. Beaumont, at peninsula's tip, about 4 km (2½ miles) from Garoupe Bay, Antibes* ☎ *04–93–67–74–33* ⊕ *www. antibesjuanlespins.com* 🎟 *€2.*

🏖 Beaches

Plage de la Garoupe
BEACHES | Thanks to the perfect oval bay of La Garoupe, the finest, softest sand

on the Riviera, magnificent views that stretch out to Antibes, and relatively calm waters, this northeast-facing beach is a real jewel—and the first in the country to impose a "No Selfie" zone. Getting the Gucci-clad spillover from the Hotel du Cap-Eden Roc, the high-end beach clubs here open onto the sand. Partiers head to the private Joseph Plage at one end of the beach, where you can rent loungers (from €26), while the quieter folk stick to the public section at the other end, where you can now rent loungers online through the tourist office for only €11 a day. There are also two snack bars. **Amenities:** parking (no fee); showers; toilets. **Best for**: swimming. ✉ *Chemin de la Garoupe, Antibes.*

🍴 Restaurants

Les Pêcheurs
$$$$ | FRENCH | In 1954 French resistance hero Camille Rayon built a restaurant on the Cap d'Antibes between two stone fishing huts dating to the early 20th century; today it's part of the Relais &

Chateau Cap d'Antibes Beach Hotel. Although beef dishes are available at this famed Michelin-starred restaurant, fish plays a starring role in chef Nicolas Navarra's menu, backed up by vegetables and fruits from the nearby hills. **Known for:** Michelin-starred seafood; stunning "Epilogue" desserts; sunset views over the Îles de Lérins and the Esterel. [$] *Average main: €50* ✉ *10 bd. Maréchal Juin, Antibes* ☎ *04–92–93–13–30* 🌐 *www.ca-beachhotel.com* 🕓 *Closed mid-Oct.–Mar.*

Hotels

Hôtel du Cap–Eden Roc
$$$$ | **HOTEL** | **FAMILY** | Open since 1870, this extravagantly expensive hotel reminiscent of *The Great Gatsby* era continues to be the mainstay for A-Listers and those with deep pockets, and for good reason: 22 acres of immaculate gardens bordered by a rocky shoreline caters to the world's fantasy of a subtropical idyll on the French Riviera. **Pros:** hands down one of the world's best hotels; breakfast included, plus fruit and chocolate offered in-room; fascinating glimpse into 20th-century history. **Cons:** if you're not a celebrity, tip big to keep the staff interested; insanely expensive everything; formal dress required for dinner in restaurant and bars. [$] *Rooms from: €1300* ✉ *Bd. J.F. Kennedy, Antibes* ☎ *04–93–61–39–01* 🌐 *www.hotel-du-cap-eden-roc.com* 🕓 *Closed mid-Oct.–mid-Apr.* 🛏 *117 rooms* 🍴 *Free breakfast.*

Hôtel La Jabotte
$$ | **HOTEL** | At this adorable boutique hotel just steps from a sandy beach, tastefully decorated and colorful rooms surround a central courtyard, where guests relax over a gorgeous breakfast of fresh baked pastries and homemade jams. **Pros:** very warm welcome is a pleasant contrast to some of the better-known hotels; free beach umbrellas and mats; honesty bar featuring homemade snacks. **Cons:** breakfast not free; often booked-up; rooms are smallish. [$] *Rooms from: €156* ✉ *13 av. Max Maurey, Antibes* ☎ *04–93–61–45–89* 🌐 *www.jabotte.com* 💳 *No credit cards* 🕓 *Closed mid-Nov.–mid-Dec.* 🛏 *9 rooms* 🍴 *No meals.*

Activities

Supdreams
WATER SPORTS | French stand-up paddleboard champion Céline Guesdon runs a school for beginners and experienced paddleboarders on Cap d'Antibes. ✉ *Bd. du Maréchal Juin* ☎ *06–41–96–70–22* 🌐 *www.supdreamschool.com.*

Juan-les-Pins

5 km (3 miles) southwest of Antibes.

From Old Antibes you can jump on a bus over the hill to Juan-les-Pins, the jazzy younger-sister resort town that, along with Antibes, bracelets the wrist of the Cap d'Antibes. This stretch of beach was "discovered" by the Jazz Age jet set, who adopted it with a vengeance; F. Scott and Zelda Fitzgerald lived in a seaside villa here in the early 1920s, dividing their idylls between what is now the Hôtel Belle Rives and the mansions on the Cap d'Antibes. Here they experimented with the newfangled fad of water-skiing, still practiced from the docks of the Belle Rives today. Ladies with bobbed hair and beach pajamas exposed lily-white skin to the sun, browning themselves like peasants and flaunting bare, tanned arms. American industrialists had swimming pools introduced to the seaside, and the last of the leisure class, weary of stateside bathtub gin, wallowed in Europe's alcoholic delights. Nowadays, the scene along Juan's waterfront is something to behold, with thousands of international sunseekers flowing up and down the promenade or lying flank to flank on its endless stretch of sand, but the town is simply not as glamorous as its history.

GETTING HERE AND AROUND

Regional rail service connects Juan-les-Pins to Nice (30 minutes, €5.20), Cannes (€2.70), and other coastal towns; from the train station, Envibus No. 15 (€1.50) loops through town, stopping at the public beach. Juan-les-Pins can also be reached from either Nice or Cannes via Lignes d'Azur Bus No. 200 (75 minutes, €1.50).

VISITOR INFORMATION

CONTACTS Juan-les-Pins Tourist Office. ✉ *60 chemin des Sables* ☎ *04–22–10–60–01* 🌐 *www.antibesjuanlespins.com.*

Beaches

Antibes and Juan-les-Pins together claim 25 km (15½ miles) of coastline and 48 beaches (including Cap d'Antibes). The boulevard and promenade running parallel to the sea are peppered with cafés and restaurants. And Juan-les-Pins now has 10 private beaches (two of which—Estérel Plage and Plage des Iles—are open year-round) and one public beach, Richelieu, where you can rent loungers for €11 a day.

Plage d'Antibes les Pins
BEACHES | This sandy beach west of Juan-les-Pins is popular thanks to its size, and thus known as La Grande plage. You can rent a beach chair from the nearby private beaches that dominate the strip. **Amenities:** toilets; showers. **Best for:** swimming. ✉ *Bd. du Littoral.*

Port de Crouton Plage
BEACHES | **FAMILY** | Covered with fine white sand, this small public beach next to Cap d'Antibes Beach Hotel boasts shallows that slope very gently, making it ideal for kids. It's a protected bay, so there are no waves, just plenty of shallow water that's bathwater-warm in high summer. There are few English tourists, so it is a real *plage à la Française* experience. **Amenities:** parking (fee); toilets; showers. **Best for:** snorkeling; solitude. ✉ *Bd. Marechal Juin.*

Hotels

Hotel des Mimosas
$ | HOTEL | In an enclosed hilltop garden studded with tall palms, mimosas, and tropical greenery, this is the sort of place where only the quiet buzzing of cicadas interrupts silent nights. **Pros:** incredible garden and grounds with pool; easy 10-minute walk to train station; free parking. **Cons:** some rooms are small; free Wi-Fi but signal can be weak; decor feels dated. [$] *Rooms from: €100* ✉ *Rue Pauline* ☎ *04–93–61–04–16* 🌐 *www.hotelmimosas.com* 💳 *No credit cards* 🕓 *Closed Oct.–Apr.* 🛏 *34 rooms* 🍴 *No meals.*

★ **Les Belles Rives**
$$$$ | HOTEL | Lovingly restored to 1930s glamour, this fabled landmark proves that what's old is new again, as France's stylish young set make this endearingly *neoclassique* place with lovely Art Deco accommodations one of their latest favorites. **Pros:** views are quite spectacular, but ask for a room with a frontal (not lateral) sea view; lots of water sports; Michelin-starred restaurant on-site. **Cons:** everything at beach costs extra (loungers, towels, umbrella); some rooms are on the small side; thin walls. [$] *Rooms from: €315* ✉ *33 bd. Édouard Baudoin* ☎ *04–93–61–02–79* 🌐 *www.bellesrives.com* 🕓 *Closed Jan.–early Mar.* 🛏 *43 rooms* 🍴 *No meals.*

Nightlife

Eden Beach Casino (*Casino Partouche Juan-les-Pins*)
CASINOS | The glassed-in complex of the Eden Casino houses slot machines, roulette and blackjack tables, and a panoramic beach restaurant. Texas Hold 'Em Poker is played every night. The casino is open until 4 am (5 am in summer). ✉ *3 av. Guy de Maupassant* ☎ *04–92–93–71–71* 🌐 *www.casinojuanlespins.com.*

Just add water, and even an overbuilt town like Juan-les-Pins becomes a place worth scrambling for a postage-stamp portion of sun and fun.

Performing Arts

Festival International Jazz à Juan

FESTIVALS | Every July the world-renowned Jazz à Juan festival stages a stellar lineup in a romantic venue under ancient pines. Launched in 1960, this festival hosted the European debut performances of such stars as Miles Davis and Ray Charles. More recently, it spawned the fringier Jazz OFF, with 200 musicians and free street concerts, as well as the Jazz Club at Les Ambassadeurs beach, where you can enjoy a drink with live music (headliners have been known to pop in for impromptu concerts here). Book online or buy tickets directly from the tourist office in Antibes or Juan-les-Pins. ☒ *Juan-les-Pins* ☎ *04–22–10–60–01 ticket information* ⊕ *www.jazzajuan.com.*

Activities

Visiobulle

BOATING | To study underwater life while circling the cape, take one of this company's one-hour cruises in tiny, yellow glass-bottom boats. From April to September, boats leave from the Ponton Courbet in Juan-les-Pins four to seven times a day depending on the season; it's best to reserve ahead by phone in summer. ☒ *Ponton Courbet, Av. Amiral Courbet* ☎ *04–93–67–02–11* ⊕ *www.visiobulle.com* ☒ *€15.*

Biot

6 km (4 miles) northeast of Antibes; 15 km (9 miles) northeast of Cannes; 18 km (11 miles) southwest of Nice.

Rising above a stretch of commercial-industrial quarters along the coast from Antibes, the *village perché* of Biot (pronounced "Bee- otte") sits neatly on a hilltop, and, as some claim, near an ex-volcano. Threaded with cute alleyways and dotted with pretty *placettes* (small squares), the old town is so picturesque it almost demands you pick up a brush and palette—mere photographs don't do it justice, especially as it's not on the receiving end of much light. For centuries home to a pottery industry, known for its fine yellow clay that stretched into massive, solid oil jars, Biot has, in recent generations, made a name for itself as a glass-art town.

Despite the new commercialism, traces of old Provence remain in Biot, especially in the evening after the busloads of shoppers leave and the deep-shaded squares under the plane trees fall quiet. Then you can meander around the edges of the Old Town to find the stone arch gates known as the **Porte des Tines** and the **Porte des Migraniers**: they're the last of the 16th-century fortifications that once enclosed Biot. Step into the 15th-century **église**, which contains an early-16th-century altarpiece attributed to Louis Bréa and depicting the Virgin Mary shielding humanity under her cloak; the surrounding portraits are as warmly detailed as the faces and hands in the central panel. Truly photo-worthy is centuries-old **Place des Arcades,** the ancient heart of the Old Town which was first colonized by the Knights Templar and then the Hospitallers of St. John of Jerusalem. Found between the tourist office and the church, just behind Rue Barri, it has an otherworldly grace, with its Gothic arcades and tall palm trees. Picturesquely curved and shop-lined, the center of town remains **Rue Saint Sébastien.**

GETTING HERE AND AROUND
The Biot train station on the coast is 4 km (5 miles) away, but you can jump on Envibus No. 10 from outside the station and arrive in the village in less than 10 minutes (€1.50). Alternatively, you can telephone IciLa d'Envibus (☎ 04–92–19–76–33) and organize an individual pick-up by minibus—still costing only €1. It's available 6:30 am–7 pm on weekdays and 9–noon and 2–5:30 on Saturday within specified zones, which include Cap d'Antibes, Biot, St-Paul-de-Vence, and Valbonne. By car, coming up from the

D6007, take the CD4 past Marineland and you'll find signposting straight to Biot.

VISITOR INFORMATION
CONTACTS Biot Tourist Office. ⊠ *4 chemin Neuf* ☎ *04–93–65–78–00* ⊕ *www. biot-tourisme.com.*

Sights

La Verrerie de Biot (*Biot Glassworks*)
FACTORY | On the edge of town, follow the pink signs to La Verrerie de Biot, which has developed into something of a cult industry since its founding in the 1950s. Here you can observe the glassblowers at work, visit the extensive galleries of museum-quality glass art (which is of much better quality than the kitsch you find in the village shop windows), and start a collection of bubbled-glass goblets, cruets, or pitchers, just as Jackie Kennedy did when the rage first caught hold (she liked cobalt blue). Despite the extreme commercialism—there is a souvenir shop, an eco-museum, a boutique of home items, audio tours of the glassworks, a bar, and a restaurant—it's a one-of-a-kind artisanal industry, and the product is made before your eyes. ⊠ *5 chemin des Combes* ☎ *04–93–65–03–00* ⊕ *www.verreriebiot.com* 🎟 *€3, guided visit €6.*

Villeneuve-Loubet

10 km (6 miles) north of Antibes.

This tiny village, its medieval château heavily restored in the 19th century, is best known for its sprawl of overbuilt beachfront, heavily charged with concrete high-rises and with all the architectural charm of a parking ramp. However, if you're a foodie, you may want to make the pilgrimage to the eccentric Musée de l'Art Culinaire.

Sights

Musée de l'Art Culinaire (Museum of Culinary Arts)

MUSEUM | As the only museum of culinary art in France, this is a shrine to the career of the great chef Auguste Escoffier (1846–1935). The epitome of 19th-century culinary extravagance and revered by the French as much as Joan of Arc and De Gaulle, Escoffier was the founding father of the school of haute cuisine Calvin Trillin calls "stuff-stuff-with-heavy," where ingredients are stripped, simmered, stuffed, sauced, and generally intervened with, sometimes beyond recognition. His was the school of food as sculpture—the famous *pièces montées,* wedding-cake spires of spun sugar, and the world of menus of staggering length and complexity. He wowed 'em at the Ritz in Paris and the Savoy and Carlton in London and is a point of reference for every modern chef—if only as a foil for rebellion. In his birthplace you'll view illustrations of his creations and a collection of fantastical menus, including one featuring the meat of zoo animals killed in the war of 1870. ✉ *3 rue Escoffier, Villeneuve-Loubet* ☎ *04–93–20–80–51* ⊕ *www.musee-escoffier.com* 💶 *€6* 🕒 *Closed early Nov.– late Dec.*

Haut-de-Cagnes

14 km (9 miles) southwest of Nice; 10 km (6 miles) north of Antibes.

Could this be the most beautiful village in southern France? Part-time residents Renoir, Soutine, Modigliani, and Simone de Beauvoir are a few who thought so. Although from the N7 you may be tempted to give wide berth to the seaside town of Cagnes-sur-Mer—with its congested sprawl of freeway overpasses, numerous tourist-oriented stores, beachfront pizzerias, and the train station—follow the brown signs inland for the "Bourg Médiéval" and the steep road will lead you up into one of the most heavenly perched villages on the Riviera. Even Alice, of Wonderland fame, would adore this steeply cobbled Old Town, honeycombed as it is with tiny piazzas, return-to-your-starting-point-twice alleys, and winding streets that abruptly change to stairways. Many of the pretty residences are dollhouse-size (especially the hobbit houses on Rue Passebon) and most date to the 14th and 15th centuries.

GETTING HERE AND AROUND

Frequent daily trains from Nice or Cannes stop at Cagnes-sur-Mer (get off at Cros-de-Cagnes if you're heading to the beach) from where you take a navette to Haut-de-Cagnes. Bus No. 44 runs throughout the day seven days a week. The Lignes d'Azur Bus No. 200 (€1.50) also stops in Cagnes-sur Mer (which has several beachfront cafés, like Art Beach, open year-round).

By car from Paris or Provence on the A8 highway take Exit 47 (Villeneuve–Loubet/Cagnes-sur-Mer); if coming from the east (Monaco, Nice), look for Exit 48 (Cagnes-sur-Mer). Polygone Riviera in Cagnes-sur-Mer is France's first outdoor shopping and leisure center. With nearly 110 brands and open seven days a week, driving in the area can get especially congested.

VISITOR INFORMATION

CONTACTS **Cagnes-sur-Mer Tourist Office.** ✉ *6 bd. Maréchal Juin, Cagnes-sur-Mer* ☎ *04–93–20–61–64* ⊕ *www.cagnes-tourisme.com.*

Sights

Chapelle Notre-Dame-de-la-Protection

RELIGIOUS SITE | Nearly hidden in the hillside and entered by an obscure side door, the grand Chapelle Notre-Dame-de-la-Protection, with its Italianate bell tower, was first built in the 14th century after the fortress had been destroyed; as a hedge against further invasion, they placed this plea for Mary's protection at the village edge. In 1936 the *curé* (priest) discovered traces of fresco under the bubbling plaster; a full stripping revealed every inch of the apse to have been decorated in scenes of the life of the Virgin and Jesus, roughly executed late in the 16th century. From the chapel's porch are sweeping sea views. Even if it's closed when you stop by, be sure to note the trompe-l'oeil "shadows" delightfully painted on the bell tower portal. ⊠ *Rue Hippolyte Guis, Cagnes-sur-Mer* ⊙ *Closed Oct.–May and Mon.–Sat.*

Château-Museé Grimaldi

CASTLE/PALACE | Crowning Haut-de-Cagnes is the fat, crenellated Château-Museé. Built in 1310 by the Grimaldis (yes, Prince Albert of Monaco's family) and reinforced over the centuries, this imposing fortress lords over the coastline, banners flying from its square watchtower. You are welcomed inside by a grand balustraded stairway and triangular Renaissance courtyard with a triple row of classical arcades infinitely more graceful than the exterior. Beyond lie vaulted medieval chambers, a vast Renaissance fireplace, and a splendid 17th-century trompe-l'oeil fresco of the fall of Phaëton from his sun chariot. The château also contains three highly specialized museums: the **Musée de l'Olivier** (Olive Tree Museum), an introduction to the history and cultivation of this Provençal mainstay; the obscure and eccentric **Collection Suzy-Solidor,** a group of portraits of the cabaret chanteuse painted by her artist friends, including Cocteau and Dufy; and the **Musée d'Art Moderne Méditerranéen** (Mediterranean Museum of Modern Art), which contains paintings by some of the 20th-century devotees of the Côte d'Azur, including Chagall, Cocteau, and Dufy. If you've climbed this far, continue to the **tower** and look over the coastline views in the same way that the guards once watched for Saracens. ⊠ *Pl. du Château, Haut-de-Cagnes* ☎ *04–92–02–47–35* ⊕ *Closed Tues.* 🎫 *From €4.*

Musée Renoir

MUSEUM | After staying up and down the coast, Auguste Renoir (1841–1919) settled into a house in Les Collettes, just east of the Vieille Ville, which is now the Musée Renoir. He passed the last 12 years of his life here, painting the landscape around him, working in bronze, and rolling his wheelchair through the luxuriant garden tiered with roses, citrus groves, and spectacular olive trees. Today, you can view this sweet and melancholic villa as it has been preserved by Renoir's children, and admire 15 of his last paintings and 30 sculptures. Although up a steep hill, Les Collettes is a 10-minute walk from Place du Général-du-Gaulle in central Cagnes-Ville (or take the free No. 45 shuttle). ⊠ *Chemin des Collettes, Cagnes-sur-Mer* ☎ *04–93–20–61–07* 🎫 *€6* ⊙ *Closed Tues.*

Hotels

★ Château Le Cagnard

$$$ | **HOTEL** | There is no better way to experience Old Haut-de-Cagnes's grand castle views than to stay in this acclaimed 13th-century manor, perched on the ramparts of the Grimaldi fortress. **Pros:** free shuttle bus to Cagnes-sur-Mer; high-quality linens and heated bathroom floors; gorgeous setting ideal for romance. **Cons:** not much to do in village; breakfast €25; no on-site parking. 🛈 *Rooms from: €290* ⊠ *54 rue Sous Barri, Cagnes-sur-Mer* ☎ *04–93–20–73–22* ⊕ *www.lecagnard.com* ⊙ *Closed Jan.–early Feb.* 🛏 *30 rooms* ⊠ *No meals.*

Le Grimaldi

$$ | **HOTEL** | More of a bed-and-breakfast, this little hotel is smack in the middle of the Haut-de-Cagnes' liveliest square, complete with picture-perfect pétanque games. **Pros:** attentive owners speak four languages, including English; awe-inspiring views from rooms; excellent on-site restaurant. **Cons:** no elevator and steep stairs; parking difficult; some slanted ceilings a challenge for taller guests.

[$] *Rooms from: €140* ✉ *6 pl. du Château, Cagnes-sur-Mer* ☎ *04–93–20–60–24* 🌐 *www.hotelgrimaldi.com* 🛏 *5 rooms* 🍴 *Free breakfast.*

St-Paul-de-Vence

18 km (11 miles) northwest of Nice.

The medieval village of St-Paul-de-Vence can be seen from afar, standing out like its companion, Vence, against the skyline. In the Middle Ages St-Paul-de-Vence was basically a city-state, and it controlled its own political destiny for centuries. But by the early 20th century it had faded to oblivion, overshadowed by the growth of Vence and Cagnes—until it was rediscovered in the 1920s when a few penniless artists began paying for their drinks at the local auberge with paintings. Those artists turned out to be Signac, Modigliani, and Bonnard, who met at the **Auberge de la Colombe d'Or**, now a sumptuous inn, where the walls are still covered with their ink sketches and daubs.

The most commercially developed of Provence's hilltop villages, St-Paul-de-Vence is a magical place. Artists are still drawn to its light, its pure air, its wraparound views, and its honey-color stone walls, soothingly cool on a hot Provençal afternoon. Get here early in the day to get a jump on the cars and tour buses, which can clog the main D36 highway by noon, or plan on a stay-over.

It won't take you long to "do" St-Paul-de-Vence; a pedestrian circuit leads you inevitably through its Rue-Grande to the *donjon* (fortress tower) and austere Gothic church. The trick is to break away and slip into a few mosaic-cobbled backstreets, little more than alleys; door after door, window after niche spills over with potted flowers and orange trees and they usually lead to an impossibly pretty cul-de-sac. The shuttered stone houses rear up over the streets, so close you could shake hands from window to window.

From St-Paul-de-Vence, there is a scenic hiking path to Vence (next to the Chapelle Ste-Claire); the walk takes 1 hour 20 minutes.

GETTING HERE AND AROUND

It's only 15 minutes from the coast by car; take the Cagnes-sur-Mer highway to Exit 47 or 48 (depending on the direction you're coming from) and look for signs on the RD 436 to La Collle sur Loup/Vence. St-Paul-de-Vence is between the two.

There's no train station, but you can get off at Cagnes-sur-Mer and take Bus No. 400 (€1.50; 25 minutes), which departs directly from Nice or Cannes.

VISITOR INFORMATION

CONTACTS St-Paul-de-Vence Tourist Office. ✉ *2 rue Grande, St-Paul-de-Vence* ☎ *04–93–32–86–95* 🌐 *www.saint-pauldevence.com.*

👁 Sights

Café de la Place

RESTAURANT—SIGHT | On your way from the overpriced parking garages, you'll pass a Provençal scene played out with cinematic flair yet still authentic: the perpetual game of pétanque outside the Café de la Place. A sun-weathered pack of men (and it is overwhelmingly men) in caps, cardigans, and workers' blues—occasionally joined by a passing professional with tie and rolled-up sleeves—gathers under the massive plane trees and stands serene, silent, and intent to toss metal balls across the dusty square. Until his death, Yves Montand made regular appearances here, participating in this ultimate southern scenario. It's the perfect place to people-watch, but best to lower all expectations about food and friendly service. ■ **TIP→ Want to give pétanque a go? The Tourist Office rents balls for €4 per person, and you can play for as long as you want. Pay a few euros extra,**

A top pick for France's most beautiful *village perché*, Haut-de-Cagnes is an enchanting place filled with tiny piazzas, winding alleys, and staircase streets.

and you'll get your own private tutor in English. ✉ *Pl. de Gaulle, St-Paul-de-Vence* ☎ *04–93–32–80–03.*

Chapelle des Pénitents Blanc

RELIGIOUS SITE | Jean-Michel Folon had a deep affection for the town of St-Paul-de-Vence, where he befriended artists such as César, so it seems fitting that the decoration of its 17th-century Chapelle des Pénitents Blanc was one of the Belgian artist's last projects before his death in 2005. The overwhelming sensations as you enter the chapel are of peace and clarity: eight oil paintings in pastel colors by Folon collaborator Michel Lefebvre line the walls on either side and four stained-glass windows reinforce the themes of generosity and freedom. Sculptures take the place of the traditional altar and font, and the back wall is covered with a mosaic of the town made up of more than 1 million pieces. Demonstrating the versatility of this artist, the chapel reflects the town's ability to celebrate its past while keeping an eye on the future. The tourist office

can arrange for a 45-minute *visite* of the chapel in English (€7). ✉ *Pl. de l'Eglise, St-Paul-de-Vence* ☎ *04–93–32–86–95 for tourist office* ⊕ *www.saint-pauldevence. com* 🖼 *€4* ⊙ *Closed Nov.*

★ Fondation Maeght

MUSEUM | Many people come to St-Paul-de-Vence just to visit France's most important private art foundation, founded in 1964 by art dealer Aimé Maeght. High above the medieval town, the small modern art museum attracts 100,000 visitors a year. It's an extraordinary marriage of the arc-and-plane architecture of Josep Sert; the looming sculptures of Miró, Moore, and Giacometti; the mural mosaics of Chagall; and the humbling hilltop setting, complete with pines, vines, and flowing planes of water. On display is an intriguing and ever-varying parade—one of the most important in Europe—of works by modern masters, including Chagall's wise and funny late-life masterpiece *La Vie* (*Life*). On the extensive grounds, fountains and impressive vistas help to beguile even those who aren't into modern art. Café F, should you need time to reflect, is open year-round. Contact the tourist office for a private guided visit in English (€7 plus discounted admission rate of €11). ✉ *623 ch. des Gardettes, St-Paul-de-Vence* ☎ *04–93–32–81–63* 🌐 *www.fondation-maeght.com* 🎫 *€16.*

🍴 Restaurants

★ La Colombe d'Or

$$$$ | FRENCH | It might be a bit overpriced for such simple fare, but where else in the world could you dine under a Picasso, on a terrace beside a ceramic Léger mural, or next to a pool where an idyllic garden comes complete with a Calder sculpture? The quirky but unpretentious Provençal menu has hardly changed over 50 years—its famous hors d'oeuvres de la Colombe (basket of crudité and hunks of charcuterie), the salmon quenelles, the Sisteron lamb, and the Grand Marnier soufflé flambé are still as acclaimed as ever. **Known for:** dining amid priceless, museum-level artwork; lunch spot for celebs during Cannes Film Fesival; long-standing menu that hasn't missed a beat in years. [$] *Average main: €40* ✉ *Pl. Général-de-Gaulle, St-Paul-de-Vence* ☎ *04–93–32–80–02* 🌐 *www.la-colombe-dor.com* 🕓 *Closed Nov.–Christmas.*

Le Tilleul

$$$ | BISTRO | Before you plunge into the dense tangle of ruelles in old St-Paul-de-Vence, stop on the ramparts under the century-old lime tree for a meal or snack at this atmospheric outdoor café, where the breezy terrace looks onto the valley and the Alps. The kitchen makes more of an effort than you might expect, turning out colorful salads (crispy Camembert salad with peppered cider dressing) and pastas at lunch and more serious gastronomic fare in the evening. **Known for:** fairly priced traditional French dishes; daily tea menu 3–6; charming shaded terrace. [$] *Average main: €25* ✉ *Pl. du Tilleul, St-Paul-de-Vence* ☎ *04–93–32–80–36* 🌐 *www.restaurant-letilleul.com* 💳 *No credit cards.*

Le Vieux Moulin

$$$ | FRENCH | From just outside the walled village, you can see this restaurant that was once a 17th-century oil mill. Though it could be tempting to cater only to tourists, owner Frédéric Rossi brought on board the young chef Olivier Depardieu, who did his apprenticeship at the Colombe d'Or and worked at Château Saint Martin, to offer a mixture of regional dishes, like fillet of beef in rosemary gravy, *écrasé de Monalisa* and taggiasca olives, or veal in a truffle sauce and pole-fried vegetables with homemade gnocci. **Known for:** affordable Provençal dishes; hearty dinners; lots of character and lovely views. [$] *Average main: €25* ✉ *Lieu-dit-Ste-Claire, Rte. de Vence, St-Paul-de-Vence* ☎ *04–93–58–36–76* 🌐 *www.levieuxmoulin-saintpaul.fr* 🕓 *Closed mid-Nov.–Feb.*

🛏 Hotels

★ La Colombe d'Or

$$$ | B&B/INN | Often called the most beautiful inn in France, "the golden dove" occupies a rose-stone Renaissance mansion just outside the walls of St-Paul-de-Vence, and is so perfect overall that some contend you haven't really been to the French Riviera until you've stayed or dined here. **Pros:** original art, including works by Picasso and Rodin; gem of a hotel oozing charm and class in a laid-back vibe; famous guests, past and present. **Cons:** some rooms in the adjoining villa have blocked views; menu selection often outshone by the art; hard to get a reservation. [$] *Rooms from: €250* ✉ *Pl. Général-de-Gaulle, St-Paul-de-Vence* ☎ *04–93–32–80–02* 🌐 *www.la-colombe-dor.com* 🕓 *Closed Nov.–Christmas* 🛏 *25 rooms* 🍽 *Free breakfast.*

With masterworks by Miró, Picasso, Giacometti, and a roomful of Victor Vasaleys (above), the Fondation Maeght in St-Paul-de-Vence is a modern-art treasure trove.

Vence

4 km (2½ miles) north of St-Paul-de-Vence; 22 km (14 miles) north of Nice.

If you've visited St-Paul-de-Vence first, Vence will come as something of a relief. Just outside the Old Town, its morning food market, though not extensive, attracts genuine producers from the area (look for Tony and his exceptional *socca,* a pancake made with chickpea flour), and the cafés facing this square feel more down-to-earth than anything in St-Paul-de-Vence. Inside the stone walls of the Cité Historique (Historical City), the Place du Peyra invites you to linger, with its restaurant terraces, relatively tasteful shops selling tablecloths or pottery, and a pretty drinking fountain whose water comes directly from the Peyra source. Vence is slightly more conscious of its history than St-Paul-de-Vence; plaques guide you through its historic squares and *portes* (gates). Wander past the pretty Place du Peyra, with its fountains, and

Place Clémenceau, with its ocher-color Hôtel-de-Ville (Town Hall), to Place du Frêne, with its ancient ash tree planted in the 16th century, and don't miss the Rue du Marché's old-fashioned food shops, including a butcher, a baker, and a fishmonger.

GETTING HERE AND AROUND

As with St-Paul-de-Vence, take the Cagnes-sur-Mer highway to Exit 47 or 48 (depending on the direction you're coming from) and look for signs on the RD 436 to La Colle sur Loup/Vence. St-Paul-de-Vence is between the two.

There's no train station, but you can get off at Cagnes-sur-Mer and take Bus No. 400 bus (€1.50; 30 minutes), which departs directly from Nice or Cannes. You can rent an electric bike via the app Bik'Air, which geolocates the nearest available bicycle. Unlike other urban bike rentals, Bik'Air has no stations; you simple leave the bike at your destination, but the rental costs €0.15 a minute.

Inside La Colombe d'Or

In 1920, the café "Chez Robinson" was a hotspot for weekend dancing for the locals, which led to owner Paul Roux, a Provençal farmer but very much a lover of the arts, to open a small inn called La Colombe d'Or. It could only accommodate three guests but soon enough artists were exchanging paintings for a meal or night's stay with the freethinking owner, who had an instinctive eye for art.

Over the next 20 years, Paul and his wife Baptiste (known as "Tintine") developed close relationships with other "thinkers and artists" who'd moved to the south of France, and the inn started to expand with their help while still maintaining a secluded yet unpretentious atmosphere. Art was fashionable, and La Colombe d'Or was a private runway for Picasso, Matisse, and Chagall. In 1959, Tintine came downstairs one morning to find the walls bare—all the paintings had been stolen (and had never been appraised). The only masterpiece left was a Chagall, as it was apparently too large to fit through the window. This produced the famous line from Chagall "I'm a big-time artist! Why are you not stealing my paintings, too?"

Today, La Colombe d'Or is a 25-room inn and restaurant presided over by François Roux, the third-generation manager, and his wife Danièle, and

has welcomed big names from Charlie Chaplin and Winston Churchill to Elton John and Hugh Grant. The famille Roux's extraordinary sense of style would have delighted Pablo, Georges, and Henri, and their collection continues to expand, most recently with a large poolside ceramic piece by the Irish artist Sean Scully. Set under timeless fig trees, a luncheon table in the restaurant terrace is lorded over by a ceramic Léger mural of a dove under the shade of fig trees, while the pool is an idyllic garden bower, complete with a Calder stabile (if you're wondering why there are so many Calders, he was apparently in love with François's mother), and there's even a Braque by the fireplace in the bar.

While the Provençal menu hasn't changed much in decades, and its prices are as fabulous as the art collection, a meal here is a must. If you splurge for a night stay, head upstairs to your room to be bewitched by Louis XIII armoires, medieval four-posters, wood beams, Provençal borders, and painted murals; take a look out your window and you might find yourself staring at a roof of tiles painted every shade of the rainbow. While there are two annexes to the main house, all the guest rooms are flawless in taste (note that you can enjoy dinner or a drink here without being a hotel guest).

VISITOR INFORMATION

CONTACTS Vence Tourist Office. ✉ Villa Alexandrine, Pl. du Grand Jardin 📞 04–93–58–06–38 ⊕ www.vence-tourisme.com.

 Sights

Cathédrale de la Nativité de la Vierge
(*Cathedral of the Birth of the Virgin*)
RELIGIOUS SITE | In the center of the Vieille Ville, the Cathédrale de la Nativité de la Vierge was built on the Romans' military drilling field in the 11th and 12th centuries and is a hybrid of Romanesque and

Baroque styles. The cathedral has been expanded and altered many times over the centuries. Note the rostrum added in 1499—its choir stalls are carved with particularly vibrant and amusing scenes of daily life in the Middle Ages. In the baptistery is a ceramic mosaic of Moses in the bulrushes by Chagall. ⊠ *Pl. Godeau* 🕾 *Free.*

★ **Chapelle du Rosaire** (*Chapel of the Rosary*)

RELIGIOUS SITE | On the outskirts of "new" Vence, toward St-Jeannet, is the Chapelle du Rosaire, better known to the world-at-large as the Matisse Chapel. The artist decorated it with beguiling simplicity and clarity between 1947 and 1951 as his gift to nuns who had nursed him through illness. It reflects the reductivist style of the era: walls, floor, and ceiling are gleaming white, and the small stained-glass windows are cool greens and blues. "Despite its imperfections I think it is my masterpiece … the result of a lifetime devoted to the search for truth," wrote Matisse, who designed and dedicated the chapel when he was in his 80s and nearly blind. ⊠ *466 av. Henri-Matisse* ☎ *04–93–58–03–26* ⊕ *www. chapellematisse.com* 🕾 *€7* ⊘ *Closed Sun., Mon., and mid-Nov.–mid-Dec.*

 Restaurants

Les Bacchanales

$$$$ | FRENCH | Michelin-starred chef Christophe Dufau's weekly changing menu puts an inventive spin on traditional local ingredients; the suckling pig with onion, fresh walnut, and pumpkin is a must when it's available. Meals are served in a sun-filled, beautifully decorated garden villa, a mere 10 minutes by foot from Vence. **Known for:** perfect combination of innovative and French cooking; garden setting a few steps from Matisse Chapel; cheese courses. 🟪 *Average main: €75* ⊠ *247 av. de Provence* ☎ *04–93–24–19–19* ⊕ *www. lesbacchanales.com* ⊘ *Closed Tues., Wed., and Dec. No lunch Thurs.*

🛏 **Hotels**

Château du Domaine St. Martin

$$$$ | HOTEL | Occupying the site of an ancient Knights Templar fortress and set amid acres of greenery designed by Jean Mus, this hilltop domain has 180-degree panoramic views, a noteworthy restaurant, and a helicopter pad. **Pros:** spectacular views matched by flawless service; recognized biodiversity refuge that supports Bird Protection charity and provides nesting boxes; superb Michelin-starred restaurant on-site. **Cons:** steep restaurant prices; nothing really within walking distance; expensive rates. 🟪 *Rooms from: €690* ⊠ *2490 av. des Templiers* ☎ *04–93–58–02–02* ⊕ *www.chateau-st-martin.com* ⊘ *Closed mid-Oct.–Apr.* 🛏 *46 rooms* 🍽 *Free breakfast.*

L'Auberge des Seigneurs et du Lion d'Or

$ | B&B/INN | Dating to the 17th century and the only hotel set within Vence's old walls, this former stagecoach inn has an ambience *à la François Premier* and the family that has owned the place since 1919 go out of their way to make your stay memorable. **Pros:** lovely family atmosphere; excellent food; seasonal fruits and fresh flowers to welcome you. **Cons:** front rooms can be noisy in summer, quieter back rooms lack views; no air-conditioning; cancellation policy on the strict side. 🟪 *Rooms from: €90* ⊠ *Pl. du Frêne* ☎ *04–93–58–04–24* ⊕ *https:// auberge-seigneurs.fr* ⊘ *Closed mid-Dec.– mid-Jan.* 🛏 *6 rooms* 🍽 *No meals.*

🎭 **Performing Arts**

Nuits du Sud

FESTIVALS | Since 1997, world-music lovers have taken over Place du Grand Jardin in Vence in mid-July for four weeks, with up to 9,000 revelers a night gyrating to various beats. Even if you don't want to buy concert tickets, come for the atmosphere

Photographs can't do justice to the beauty of St-Paul-de-Vence—one would need to pick up brush and canvas to fully capture its bewitching ambience.

and share a picnic—the music will find you no matter where you are. ✉ *39 rue de 8 Mai 1945* ☎ *04–93–58–40–17* 🌐 *www.nuitsdusud.com.*

Nice

176 km (110 miles) east of Aix-en-Provence; 33 km (20 miles) northeast of Cannes; 20 km (12½ miles) southwest of Monaco.

United with France only since 1860, Nice has its own history and atmosphere, which dates back 230,000 years. It was on Colline du Château (now château-less) and at the Plage des Ponchettes, in front of the Old Town, that the Greeks established a market port in 350 BC and named it Nikaia, which would become Marseille's chief coastal rival. The Romans established themselves a little later on the hills of Cimiez (Cemenelum), already previously occupied by Ligurians and Celts, and quickly overshadowed the waterfront port. After falling to the Saracen invasions, Nice regained power as an independent state, becoming an important port in the early Middle Ages.

So cocksure did it become that in 1388, Nice, along with the hill towns behind, effectively seceded from the county of Provence, under Louis d'Anjou, and allied itself with Savoie. Thus began its liaison with the House of Savoy, and through it with Piedmont and Sardinia, it was the Comté de Nice (Nice County). This relationship lasted some 500 years, tinting the culture, architecture, and dialect in rich Italian hues.

By the 19th century Nice was flourishing commercially, locked in rivalry with the neighboring shipping port of Genoa. Another source of income: the dawning of tourism, as first the English, then the Russian nobility, discovered its extraordinary climate and superb waterfront position. A parade of fine stone mansions and hotels closed into a nearly solid wall of masonry, separated from the smooth, round rocks of the beach by what was originally called the Camin deis Anglés (the English Way), which, of course, is now the famous Promenade des Anglais. This magnificent crescent, which is seeking UNESCO recognition, is one of the noblest in France. Many of Nice's most delightful attractions—the Cours Saleya market, the Old Town streets, the Hotel Negresco, and the Palais Masséna—are on or close to this 10-km (6-mile) waterfront, making it the first stop for most visitors, while the redevelopment of Nice's port, around the other side of the Colline du Château, makes it easier for amblers who want to take in the Genoese architecture or peruse the antiques at the Puces de Nice, along Quai Papacino.

Nice also has the distinction of the "Family Plus" label, with free strollers, play areas, and restaurants with child-friendly activities. In addition, two LGBTQ film festivals and street parties, Pink Parade and Lou Queernaval, make the city one of France's most LGBTQ-friendly cities. If you notice local establishments displaying the *Nice irisée naturellement* logo, that means they have taken part in training provided by Nice's Convention and Visitors Bureau, a member of the International Gay and Lesbian Travel Association.

GETTING HERE AND AROUND

Nice is the main point of entry into the French Riviera region. It's home to the second-largest airport in France, which sits on a peninsula between Antibes and Nice, 6 km (4 miles) southwest of the city. From the airport, you can take a bus to almost anywhere.

In Nice, the tram is the fast way to get around the city. Lignes d'Azur operates two fast and efficient lines: T1 for Old Nice, Place Massena, and the train station, and the west-east T2, which services both airport terminals and ends at the port. Tickets (€1.50 one-way) must be purchased before boarding from automated machines at each stop, and they can be used for a bus transfer. To save

money, buy a 10-ride multivoyage ticket for €10. Line 1 runs daily 4:25 am to 1:35 am, Line 2 daily 4:15 am to 1:05 am.

Lignes d'Azur also operates Nice's buses. The fare is €1.50, or you can buy a 24-hour multipass for €5 or seven days for €15. The most popular buses are the Zou! No. 100 (Monaco–Menton), No. 200 Antibes–Cannes, and No. 400 St-Paul-de-Vence and Vence, which are cheap (€1.50) but often crowded, especially in the summer—you may find you'll have to wait for the next bus. Also, these are direct buses, which don't make frequent stops so you can't, as an example, take Bus No. 200 to the airport. Remember to wave your hand, like you would hail a cab, to indicate to the bus driver that you want to get on.

You can also hop on one of the city's blue bikes (Vélobleu) available at 175 stations across town, and over to Cagnes-sur-mer. There are designated bike paths in the city and along the Promenade as far as Antibes. It's only €1 per day or €5 per week and you can sign up with any cellphone (international numbers included) or look for the few stations that accept credit cards directly. Contact Vélobleu (☎ 04–93–72–06–06 ⊕ *www.velobleu. org*).

FESTIVALS
★ Nice Carnaval

Nice hosted its first edition of Carnaval in 1294 and today it's the world's third-largest Carnaval celebration, drawing nearly a million spectators to its free and paid events for all ages along the Promenade du Paillon, the €40 million park off Place Massena. There are 18 floats in the famed Flower Battle, a tradition that the British started, although they threw eggs, flour, and confetti plaster at each other, and now it's 5,000 tonnes of locally grown Mimosa flowers that are tossed each parade. This massive themed event is held for 15 days, culminating on Mardi Gras, with the burning of the King as the finale. ✉ *Office du Tourisme, 5 promenade des Anglais* ☎ *04–97–13–36–66* ⊕ *en.nicecarnaval.com.*

VISITOR INFORMATION

CONTACTS Nice Tourist Office. ⊠ *5 promenade des Anglais* ☎ *04–92–14–46–14* ⊕ *www.nicetourism.com.*

Sights

Framed by the "château"—really a rocky promontory—and Cours Saleya, the Old Town of Nice is its strongest drawing point and, should you only be passing through, the best place to capture the city's historic feeling. Its grid of narrow streets, darkened by houses five and six stories high with bright splashes of laundry fluttering overhead and jewel-box Baroque churches on every other corner, creates a magic that seems utterly removed from the Côte d'Azur fast lane.

For many years, all municipal museums in Nice were free, but now there's a €10 admission, unless you're a resident of Nice. However, some entries allow you access to multiple *musées,* valid for 48 hours. For example, the Museum of Archaeology and the Museum of Natural History or the Fine Arts Museum and the Museum of Naïve Art. Alternatively, for €20, you can get a seven-day pass for all municipal museums or buy a French Riviera Pass.

Nice takes on a completely different character west of Cours Saleya, with broad city blocks, vast neoclassical hotels and apartment houses, and a series of inviting parks dense with palm trees, greenery, and splashing fountains. From the Jardin Albert Ier, once the delta of the Paillon River, the famous Promenade des Anglais stretches the length of the city's waterfront.

The original promenade was the brainchild of Lewis Way, an English minister in the growing community of British refugees drawn to Nice's climate. They needed a proper walkway on which to take the sea air, and pooled resources to build a 6½-foot-wide road meandering through an alley of shade trees. Nowadays it's a wide, multilane boulevard thick with traffic—in fact, it's the last gasp of the coastal highway N98. Beside it runs its charming parallel, the wide, sun-washed pedestrian walkway with intermittent steps leading down to the smooth-rock beach; its foundation is a seawall that keeps all but the wildest storms from sloshing waves over the promenade. A daily parade of *promeneurs,* rollerbladers, joggers, moms with strollers, dog walkers, and sun-baskers vie for their piece of the pavement while looking out over the hypnotic blue expanse of the sea, often getting entangled and exchanging barbs, so beware when getting off the bus and crossing over the bike path to the sea. It used to be possible in the wee hours to enjoy the waterfront stroll as the cream of Nice's international society did, when there were nothing more than hoofbeats to compete with the roar of the waves, but these days in the early morning, you'll mostly encounter rowdy drunks, strewn garbage, and copulating couples on the beach. The promenade was also the scene of the tragic 2016 Bastille Day terrorist attack, and you'll still see machine-gun-toting military personnel partrolling the area, although this doesn't quite deter illegal goings-on.

Once the site of the powerful Roman settlement Cemenelum, the hilltop neighborhood of Cimiez—4 km (2½ miles) north of Cours Saleya—is Nice's most luxurious quarter. Villas seem in competition to outdo each other in opulence, and the combination of important art museums, Roman ruins, and a historic monastery make it worth a day's exploration. To visit Cimiez and nearby museums, you need to combine a bus pass or taxi fare with strong legs and comfortable shoes. If you brave the route by car, arm yourself with a map and a navigator. Bus No. 15 from Place Masséna or Avenue Jean-Médecin takes you to both the Chagall and Matisse museums; from the latter you can visit the ruins and monastery.

■TIP→ The French Riviera Pass is your ticket to museums, gardens, and transportation in Nice; included are guided tours, wine tasting, as well as seven attractions in nearby towns like the oceanography museum in Monaco, the exotic gardens in Èze, and the Ephrussi de Rothschild villa and garden on Saint-Jean-Cap-Ferrat. The passes are available for 24 hours (€26), 48 hours (€38), or 72 hours (€56) and can be purchased at the tourist office or online from en.frenchrivierapass.com.

Cathédrale Orthodoxe Russe St-Nicolas

RELIGIOUS SITE | This magnificent Russian Orthodox cathedral was built in 1896 to accommodate the sizable population of Russian aristocrats who had adopted Nice as their winter home. This Byzantine fantasy is the largest of its kind outside the motherland, with six gold-leaf onion domes, rich ceramic mosaics on its facade, and extraordinary icons framed in silver and jewels. The benefactor was Nicholas II himself, whose family attended the inauguration in 1912. For six years the church was challenged over ownership, but in 2013 the French courts rejected a final appeal by ACOR, a niçois religious association that managed the property for 80 years. The Russian Archpriest rejoiced: "This ruling shows that it is history that has triumphed." ⊠ Av. Nicolas II ⊹ From Promenade, hop Bus 7 up Bd. Gambetta and get off at either Thiers-Gambetta or Parc Imperial stop, or walk 15 minutes west from train station ☎ 09–81–09–53–45 ⊕ www.sobor.fr.

Cathédrale Ste-Réparate

RELIGIOUS SITE | An ensemble of columns, cupolas, and symmetrical ornaments dominates the Vieille Ville, flanked by an 18th-century bell tower and glossy ceramic-tile dome. The cathedral's interior, completely restored to a bright palette of ocher, golds, and rusts, has elaborate plasterwork and decorative frescoes on every surface. ⊠ 3 pl. Rossetti, Old Town ⊕ www.cathedrale-nice.fr ⊘ Closed Mon.

Chapelle de la Miséricorde

RELIGIOUS SITE | A superbly balanced pièce-montée (wedding cake) of half-domes and cupolas, this chapel is decorated within an inch of its life with frescoes, faux marble, gilt, and crystal chandeliers. A magnificent altarpiece by Renaissance painter Ludivico Brea crowns the ensemble. ⊠ 7 cours Saleya, Old Town ⊘ Closed Wed.–Mon., July, and Aug.

Chapelle Sainte-Rita (Église de l'Annonciation)

RELIGIOUS SITE | This 17th-century Carmelite chapel, officially known as the Église de l'Annonciation, is a classic example of pure Niçoise Baroque, from its sculpted door to its extravagant marble work and the florid symmetry of its arches and cupolas. ⊠ 1 rue de la Poissonerie, Old Town ⊕ www.sainte-rita.net.

Cimetière du Château (Cemetery)

CEMETERY | This solemn cluster of white tombs looms prominently over the city below, providing a serene or macabre detail of daily life, depending on your mood. Under Nice's blue skies, the gleaming white marble and Italian mix of melodrama and exuberance in the decorations, dedications, photo portraits, and sculptures are somehow oddly life-affirming. Founded in 1783, there are 2,800 graves here—with prominent names like Jellinek-Mercedes and Leroux—in three sections, to this day segregating Catholics, Protestants, and Jews. ⊠ Allée François-Aragon.

Colline du Château (Château Hill)

CITY PARK | FAMILY | Although nothing remains of the once-massive medieval stronghold but a few ruins left after its 1706 dismantling, the name château still applies to this high plateaulike park, from which you can take in extraordinary views of the Baie des Anges, the length of Promenade des Anglais, and the

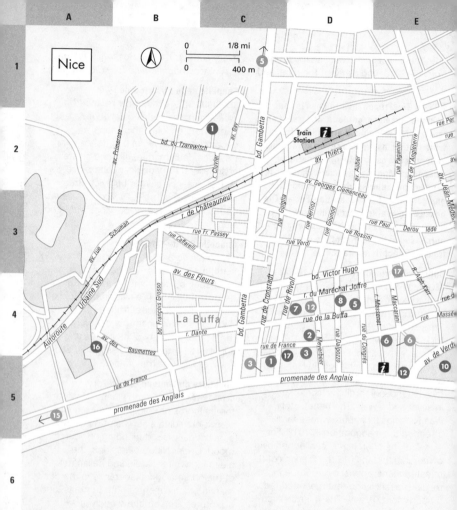

KEY	
1	Sights
1	Restaurants
1	Quick Bites
1	Hotels

Restaurants ▼

1 Attimi..................**F4**
2 Café Marché **G5**
3 Chantecler.............**C5**
4 Chez Pipo Socca........**I4**
5 Gare du Sud **C1**
6 La Femme du
   Boulanger.............**E4**
7 La Merenda............**G4**

8 La Part des Anges......**F3**
9 La Réserve de Nice ... **J6**
10 Le Bistro Gourmand....**F5**
11 Le Bistrot d'Antoine ... **G4**
12 Le Canon **D4**
13 Le Panier **G5**
14 Le Safari................**G5**
15 Lycée Hotellier
   Paul Augier **A5**

16 Restaurant Jan..........**I4**
17 Séjour Café **E3**

Quick Bites ▼

1 Glacier Fenocchio **G4**

Hotels ▼

1 Hôtel Negresco **C5**
2 Hotel Suisse **D4**

3 La Fontaine **D4**
4 La Perouse..............**H5**
5 Nice Garden Hotel.....**D4**
6 Solara...................**E4**
7 Villa Rivoli..............**D4**
8 Windsor **D4**

red-ocher roofs of the Old Town. Children can let off steam at the playground, while you enjoy a picnic with panoramic views and a bit of shade. You can also partake in a free yoga day or the Communist party's annual Fête du Chateau, both held in June. It's 213 steps to the top or you can use the free elevator next to the Hotel Suisse; alternatively, ascend the hill slower from the port side, near Place Garibaldi, which is a more gentle climb. ✉ *Promenade des Anglais, east end, Centre Ville* ⛶ *Free.*

Cours Saleya

NEIGHBORHOOD | This long pedestrian thoroughfare—half street, half square—is the nerve center of Old Nice, the heart of the Vieille Ville, and the stage set for the daily dramas of marketplace and café life in Nice. Currently in the middle of a €5 million "relooking" scheduled for completion by February 2021, shoppers come here to smell the roses (mimosas and orange blossoms) before ambling along to discover local farmers and stallholders selling produce, spices, olives, and little gift soaps in the revised single row set-up, the overflow of which will soon sprawl into a newly treed Place Pierre Gautier. Market days are Tuesday through Sunday until 2:30 pm. Arrive early, especially in summer, to avoid being at the mercy of the crowd's general movement (and a target for the rampant pickpockets). On Monday morning, antiques and *brocantes* (collectibles) draw avid vintage hounds and from June to September, there's also an artisanal craft market selling jewelry, pottery, purses, and paintings. At the east end of Cours Saleya, you'll find an imposing yellow stone building at Place Charles Félix, where Matisse lived on the third and then fourth floor from 1921 to 1938. Today, there's no plaque that bears his name, only a broken shutter of his workshop to serve as a commemoration. Its future remains uncertain, but for many Niçois, this building is a part of Nice's heritage. ✉ *Cours Saleya, Old Town.*

Eglise du Gésù

RELIGIOUS SITE | If Nice's other chapels are jewel boxes, this is a barn. Broad, open, and ringing hollow after the intense concentration of sheer matter in the Miséricorde and Ste-Rita, it seems austere by comparison. That's only because the decoration is spread over a more expansive surface. If it's possible, this 17th-century Baroque chapel is even more theatrical and over the top than its peers. Angels throng in plaster and fresco, pillars spill over with extravagantly sculpted capitals, and from the pulpit (to the right, at the front) the crucifix is supported by a disembodied arm. ✉ *Corner of Rue Droite and Rue du Jésus.*

Église St-Martin (*Église St-Augustin*)

RELIGIOUS SITE | This serene Baroque structure at the foot of the château anchors the oldest church-parish in Nice. Built in 1405, it was here that Martin Luther preached in 1510 and Garibaldi was baptized in 1807. ✉ *Rue Sincaire.*

Jardin Albert Ier (*Albert I Garden*)

GARDEN | Along Promenade des Anglais, this luxurious garden stands over the delta of the River Paillon, underground since 1882. Every kind of flower and palm tree grows here, thrown into exotic relief by night illumination. Home base for many city festivals with its Théâtre de Verdure and also Ciné Prom in the summer (screenings of box office hits at 7:30 pm), the garden is the starting point for Nice's Promenade du Paillon. ✉ *2–16 av. de Verdun, New Town* ⛶ *Free.*

La Crypte Archéologique de Nice

ARCHAEOLOGICAL SITE | Via steel walkways, explore (by tour only) this half-acre archaeological crypt beneath Place Garibaldi, holding the remains of a 14th-century tower and aqueduct that were hidden underground for centuries. When Nice's tram system was being built at the beginning of this century, excavators discovered medieval structures that had been razed by Louis XIV in 1706 and promptly forgotten. The

No wonder Matisse lived on the top floor of the golden yellow building seen here at the end of the Cours Saleya—this marketplace is one of the most colorful in France.

Centre du Patrimoine (Heritage Center) offers one-hour guided tours for up to 15 people, but you must reserve with them directly at 75 quai Etats-Unis. The meeting point—Place Jacques Toja—is just off Place Garibaldi. ■TIP→ **Bring "sensible shoes," as heels can't be worn in the crypt.** ⊠ *Pl. Jacques Toja, Old Town* ☎ *3906* ✉ *€5.*

Le Ruhl Casino Barrière Nice
CASINO—SIGHT | Renovated to the tune of €5 million, Le Ruhl now lures in the summer vacationers and the winter convention crowd with vivid colors and fiber-optic lighting. Some flock into the hushed gaming room for poker and blackjack, others try their luck at one of the 282 slot and 30 electronic English Roulette machines. ⊠ *1 promenade des Anglais, New Town* ☎ *04–97–03–12–22* ⊕ *www.casinosbarriere.com/en/nice. html.*

Monastère de Cimiez
RELIGIOUS SITE | This fully functioning monastery is worth the pilgrimage. You can find a lovely **garden,** replanted along the lines of the original 16th-century layout; the **Musée Franciscain,** a didactic museum tracing the history of the Franciscan order; and a 15th-century **church** containing three works of remarkable power and elegance by Bréa. ⊠ *Pl. du Monastère, Cimiez* ☎ *04–93–81–00–04* ✉ *Free* ☉ *Museum closed Sun.*

Musée Archéologique (*Archaeology Museum*)
MUSEUM | This museum, next to the Musée Matisse, has a dense collection of objects extracted from digs around the Roman city of Cemenelum, which flourished from the 1st to the 5th century. Among the fascinating ruins are an amphitheater, frigidarium, gymnasium, baths, and sewage trenches, some dating back to the 3rd century. ■TIP→ **It's best to avoid midday visits on warm days.** ⊠ *160 av. des Arènes-de-Cimiez, Cimiez* ☎ *04–93–81–59–57* ✉ *€6* ☉ *Closed Tues.*

Musée d'Art Moderne
MUSEUM | The assertive contemporary architecture of the Modern Art Museum makes a bold statement regarding

Nice's presence in the modern world. The collection inside focuses intently and thoroughly on works from the late 1950s onward, but pride of place is given to sculptor Nikki de St-Phalle's recent donation of more than 170 exceptional pieces. The rooftop terrace, sprinkled with minimalist sculptures, has stunning views over the city. ✉ *Promenade des Arts* ☎ *04–97–13–42–01* ⊕ *www.mamac-nice.org* 🎫 *From €10* 🕑 *Closed Mon.*

Musée des Beaux-Arts (*Jules-Chéret Fine Arts Museum*)

MUSEUM | Originally built for a member of Nice's Old Russian community, the Princess Kotschoubey, this Italianate mansion is a Belle Époque wedding cake, replete with one of the grandest staircases on the coast. After the *richissime* American James Thompson took over and the last glittering ball was held here, the villa was bought by the municipality as a museum in the 1920s. Unfortunately, many of the period features were sold; but in its place are paintings by Degas, Boudin, Monet, Sisley, Dufy, and Jules Chéret, whose posters of winking *damselles* distill all the *joie* of the Belle Époque. From the Hôtel Negresco area the museum is about a 15-minute walk up a gentle hill. ✉ *33 av. des Baumettes, New Town* ☎ *04–92–15–28–28* ⊕ *www.musee-beaux-arts-nice.org* 🎫 *€10* 🕑 *Closed Mon.*

Musée Masséna (*Masséna Palace*)

CASTLE/PALACE | This spectacular Belle Époque villa houses the **Musée d'Art et d'Histoire** (Museum of Art and History), where familiar paintings from French, Italian, and Dutch masters line the walls. A visit to the palace gardens, a park set with towering palm trees, a marble bust of the handsome General Masséna, a memorial to victims of the July 14 attacks, and backdropped by the ornate trim of the Hôtel Negresco, is a delight; this is one of Nice's most imposing oases. ✉ *65 rue de France, New Town*

☎ *04–93–91–19–10* 🎫 *€10* 🕑 *Closed Tues.*

★ **Musée Matisse**

MUSEUM | In the 1960s, the city of Nice bought this lovely, light-bathed 17th-century villa, surrounded by the ruins of Roman civilization, and restored it to house a large collection of Henri Matisse's works. Matisse settled along Nice's waterfront in 1917, seeking a sun cure after a bout with pneumonia, and remained here until his death in 1954. During his years on the French Riviera, Matisse maintained intense friendships and artistic liaisons with Renoir, who lived in Cagnes, and with Picasso, who lived in Mougins and Antibes. He eventually moved up to the rarefied isolation of Cimiez and took an apartment in the Hôtel Regina (now an apartment building, just across from the museum), where he lived out the rest of his life. Matisse walked often in the parklands around the Roman remains and was buried in an olive grove outside the Cimiez cemetery. The collection of artworks includes several pieces the artist donated to the city before his death; the rest were donated by his family. In every medium and context—paintings, gouache cutouts, engravings, and book illustrations—the collection represents the evolution of his art, from Cézanne-like still lifes to exuberant dancing paper dolls. Even the furniture and accessories speak of Matisse, from the Chinese vases to the bold-printed fabrics with which he surrounded himself. A series of black-and-white photographs captures the artist at work, revealing telling details. Note that you can't get into the museum with a backpack or travel bag. ✉ *164 av. des Arènes-de-Cimiez, Cimiez* ☎ *04–93–81–08–08* ⊕ *www.musee-matisse-nice.org* 🎫 *€10* 🕑 *Closed Tues.*

Musée National Marc Chagall (*Marc Chagall Museum of Biblical Themes*)

MUSEUM | Inaugurated in 1973, this museum has one of the finest permanent

Far from the center city, the Musée Matisse draws thousands of art lovers every month to take the long bus ride up the hill to the Cimiez suburb.

collections of Chagall's (1887–1985) late works. Superbly displayed, 17 vast canvases depict biblical themes, each in emphatic, joyous colors. Chamber music and classical concert series also take place here, though admission fees may apply. Bus No. 15 stops at the museum. ⊠ *Av. du Dr-Ménard, Cimiez* ☎ *04–93–53–87–20* ⊕ *www.musee-chagall.fr* ⊠ *€8* ⊗ *Closed Tues.*

Musée Terra Amata

ARCHAEOLOGICAL SITE | During the digging for the foundation of a building in 1966, the shovels revealed the remains of a temporary settlement once used by elephant hunters thousands of years ago. They were perhaps the oldest known inhabitants of Europe. Now the site is a museum reconstructing the ancient beach-camp known as Terra Amata ("beloved land") as it was, lodgings and all. It incorporates a real human footprint, calcified in the sand. There are recorded commentaries in English; films explain the lifestyle of these earliest Europeans. If you enjoy anthropology, it's worth a stop, but don't expect a blockbuster expo: displays are small-scale and mainly limited to tiny models. ⊠ *25 bd. Carnot* ☎ *04–93–55–59–93* ⊕ *www.musee-terra-amata.org* ⊠ *€10* ⊗ *Closed Tues.*

Palais Lascaris

CASTLE/PALACE | The aristocratic Lascaris Palace was built in 1648 for Jean-Baptiste Lascaris-Vintimille, *marechal* to the Duke of Savoy. The magnificent vaulted staircase, with its massive stone balustrade and niches filled with classical gods, is surpassed in grandeur only by the Flemish tapestries (after Rubens) and the extraordinary trompe-l'oeil fresco depicting the fall of Phaëthon. With a little luck, you'll be in time for one of the many classical concerts performed here. ⊠ *15 rue Droite, Old Town* ☎ *04–93–62–72–40* ⊠ *€10* ⊗ *Closed Tues.*

Place Garibaldi

PLAZA | Encircled by grand vaulted arcades stuccoed in rich yellow, the broad pentagon of this square could have been airlifted out of Turin. In the center, the shrinelike fountain sculpture of Garibaldi seems to be surveying you as you stroll under the very attractive arcades and lounge in the surrounding cafés. The Les Artisanales market for local crafts (jewelry, ceramics, leather goods, clothes, accessories, and food) sets up the first Sunday of the month (9–7) and an antiques market takes over the square on the third Saturday of every month (8–5). ⊠ Old Town.

Place Masséna

PLAZA | As Cours Saleya is the heart of the Vieille Ville, so this impressive and broad square is the heart of the entire city. It's framed by early-17th-century, Italian-style arcaded buildings, their facades stuccoed in rich red ocher. This enticing space hosts an event at least once a month, from Carnaval to the Christmas market; Promenade du Paillon runs through it. ⊠ Pl. Masséna, Centre Ville.

Port de Nice

MARINA | In 1750 the Duke of Savoy ordered a port to be dug into the waterfront to shelter the approach of the city's maritime traffic, and freight ships, fishing boats, and yachts still sail into its safe harbor today. The redevelopment of Nice's port paves an easier way for amblers who want to take in the Genoese architecture in this area, or peruse the antiques at the Puces de Nice along Quai Papacino. From June to mid-October, daily 10–7, the free shuttle Lou Passagin ferries you across the port from the Charles Felix dock to Quai d'Entrecasteaux. In early September, keep an eye out for the Fête du Port—a gastronomical explosion (and one of the rare occasions when you'll witness the French walk and eat simultaneously) outmatched only by fire-eaters and fireworks. From the port, you can take Bus No. 14 to visit the 16th-century Fort du Mont-Alban, which has exceptional views of Bordighera, and Saint-Jean-Cap-Ferrat all the way over to Baie des Anges (those crazy circular buildings) and Antibes. ⊠ Old Town.

Promenade de Paillon

CITY PARK | Running parallel behind the Old Town, from the Museum of Modern Art to the Théâtre de Verdure, is Nice's emerald jewel: the Promenade de Paillon, a €40 million, 30-acre park. It serves as a playground for kids, a refuge for adults (who take advantage of the free Wi-Fi), and a venue for many of the city's annual and one-off events, like April Fool's Day (in French, Poisson d'Avril, or "Fish Day"). No matter when you arrive, there's plenty to photograph here. ⊠ Promenade de Paillon, Centre Ville.

🏖 Beaches

Nice's beaches extend all along the Baie des Anges, backed full-length by the Promenade des Anglais and a thriving and sophisticated downtown. This leads to the peculiar phenomenon of seeing power-suited executives and secretaries stripping down to a band of Lycra, tanning over the lunch hour, then suiting back up for the afternoon's work a block or two away. The absence of sand (there's nothing but those famous Riviera pebbles, les galets) helps maintain that dress-for-success look. The downside of the location: the otherwise stylish streets downtown tend to fill up with underdressed, sunburned tourists caked with salt during beach season.

Posh private beaches (which sometimes share the name of public beaches) have full restaurants and bar service, color-coordinated mattresses and beach umbrellas, and ranks of tanners with phones glued to their ears. Several of the beaches lure clients with water-skiing, parasailing, windsurfing, and Jet-Skiing; if you're looking for a particular sport, check the signs posted at the entrance with the restaurant menus. Fees for private beaches average €17–€22 for a dressing room and mattress and some charge up to €5 for a parasol. Private beaches alternate with open stretches of public frontage served by free toilets and open "showers" (a cold elevated faucet for rinsing off salt). Enterprising vendors cruise the waterfront, hawking ice cream, slabs of melon, coffee, ice-cold sodas, and beer.

From mid-June to mid-September, all private and public beaches have lifeguards on duty (9–6:30). Check the flags to see if it's safe to swim: yellow means the water quality is poor (blue is good), an orange flag means danger (from waves or jellyfish), red means no swimming. Jellyfish have an unpredictable presence so keep an ear open for the word "*méduse*" or look for it on the sign boards to know if they're around that day. One helpful website for sightings is ⊕ *meduse.acri.fr/carte/carte.php*.

Beau Rivage
BEACH—SIGHT | Across from Cours Saleya, Beau Rivage Plage—which claims to be the Riviera's largest private beach—has a split personality. On the zen side, topless sunseekers can rent a cushy lounge chair with umbrella for €25; on the scene-y Trend side, bathers can enjoy cocktails and tapas. The beach itself is stony, so water shoes are advisable. If there are jellyfish sightings, you'll see a written warning of "méduse" on a beach board; ditto for strong winds. Steps from Beau Rivage on the Prom, you'll find Nice's own Statue of Liberty (look carefully, as she's only 4½-feet tall). **Amenities:** food and drink; showers; toilets. **Best for:** sunset; swimming. ⊠ *107 quai des États-Unis* ☎ *04–92–00–46–80* ⊕ *www.plagenicebeaurivage.com*.

Castel Plage
BEACHES | At the east end of the promenade, near Hotel Suisse, there is both a large public beach and a private one, where the water is calm and clear (you can rent a lounger at the latter for about €25, with umbrella). The public beach is composed of large stones, which are more comfortable to walk on than pebbles. Jellyfish are also less of a problem in this corner due to the currents, and

lifeguards at the neighboring beach are on duty mid-June–mid-September. **Amenities:** showers. **Best for:** snorkeling; sunrise; sunset; swimming. ⊠ *8 quai des États-Unis* ⊕ *www.castelplage.com/en*.

Coco Beach
BEACHES | East of the port and past La Réserve, just a few steps down from street level, lies one of the quieter beaches in Nice with very clear water, few tourists, and hardly any jellyfish. The catch? The beach is more slabs of rock than sand—this is where locals spread their towels for the day—forming a small crest along the coastline that is exposed to wind. Many fish move about below, making this an excellent place for snorkeling. **Amenities:** food and drink; parking (street); showers. **Best for:** snorkeling; solitude; swimming. ⊠ *Av. Jean Lorrain*.

Lenval and Magnan Beaches
BEACHES | Locals come early and with umbrellas, chairs, and coolers in tow to these two sizeable public beaches around the halfway point of the Promenade. Both beaches are stone and there's the occasional jellyfish, so water shoes are best for getting in and out of the sea. Lenval is a no-smoking beach; there are pay underground hot showers, toilets, and lockers, as well as portable toilets in the summer; there are no lifeguards nor a first aid station (but these are provided next door at Magnan, which is wider and lower than street level). This area is less tourist-dense, so expect to see many (too many) bare torsos. ■TIP→ **When the winds pick up, this area can be dangerous, so watch for the wind-warning flags (and always avoid swimming for 24 hours after storms).** **Amenities:** lifeguards; showers; toilets. **Best for:** sunrise; swimming. ⊠ *Promenade des Anglais*.

Ponchettes Beach
BEACHES | Almost at the end of the Promenade and in front of the Old Town, this basic stony stretch is a popular spot in the summer with a melange of tourists and locals of all ages all day. In the

Like the Rio of France, Nice is lined with a gigantic crescent beach whose prime spot, the Promenade des Anglais, is home to many palace-hotels.

summer there are sand-beach volleyball courts. Keep an eye out for jellyfish. **Amenities:** lifeguards; toilets. **Best for:** snorkeling; sunrise; sunset; swimming. ✉ *Quai des États-Unis.*

🍴 Restaurants

Attimi

$ | **ITALIAN** | Specializing in salads, pizzas, and pastas—prepared on the spot from local produce—this place offers a refreshing, light alternative to all those heavy French dishes. But Attimi is as hot as the lasagna Bolognese it serves, so you'll need to reserve or eat early. **Known for:** thin-crust pizza; terrace seating with great people-watching; long lines that are worth the wait. [$] *Average main: €16* ✉ *10 pl. Masséna, Centre Ville* ☎ *04–93–62–00–22* 🌐 *www.attimi.fr.*

Café Marché

$ | **CAFÉ** | This quaint café, behind Cours Saleya, doesn't have views of the market, but the creamy café au lait and homemade baked goods more than compensate for its people-watching limitations. If you want more than a snack, you can order from the day's €17 menu (including vegan options). **Known for:** delicious fixed-price brunch; vegetarian options; hip atmosphere. [$] *Average main: €17* ✉ *2 rue Barillerie, Old Town* ☎ *09–81–84–92–49* 🕓 *Closed Sat. and Wed. Oct.–Apr.*

Chantecler

$$$$ | **MEDITERRANEAN** | Long a showplace for Riviera luxury, the Negresco is replete with Régence-fashion salons decked out with 18th-century wood boiserie and Aubusson carpets. Its main dining room, the two-Michelin-star Chantecler, has been playing musical chefs for the past few years and currently features Virginie Basselot and her selections of impressive haute-cuisine. **Known for:** a leader in French haute-cuisine; formal dress code; giant wine cellar. [$] *Average main: €72* ✉ *Hôtel Negresco, 37 promenade des Anglais, Promenade* ☎ *04–93–16–64–00* 🌐 *www.hotel-negresco-nice.com*

⊘ *Closed Sun., Mon., and Jan.* 🎩 *Jacket required.*

⭐ Chez Pipo Socca

$ | FRENCH | There are plenty of places where you can sample *socca* in the Old Town, but if you want to understand why so much fuss is made in Nice over this chickpea pancake, this out-of-the-way café behind the Port is the place to go. As is normal for making this recipe, a batter of chickpea flour, water, olive oil, and salt is baked in giant copper tins in a wood-fired oven, but here, the cook expertly scrapes the surface of the nearly-cooked dough with a metal spatula so that it comes out extra-crispy. **Known for:** authentic Niçois food; long lines (come at 5:30 when it opens for the shortest wait); cash-only policy. $ *Average main: €7* ✉ *13 rue Bavastro, Port Nice* ☎ *04–93–55–88–82* ⊕ *www.chezpipo.fr* ⊘ *Closed Mon. and Tues. July and Aug.*

Gare du Sud

$ | FRENCH | Located in a former 19th-century train station, this indoor food court in the Liberation district is a first in the region. With a vintage vibe and communal seating for 700, the 30 stalls are a mix of well-known local names—Café de Turin, Cave du Fromager, Superlobster, Emilie's Cookies—and newcomers like Goa Deli, Ramen Ta Faim, El Kitchen Mexican, and Mahata Japense. **Known for:** first indoor food court in Nice; wide variety of cuisine, from hot dogs and noodles to French and Mexican; super trendy atmosphere. $ *Average main: €15* ✉ *35 av. Malaussena* ☎ *04–93–17–47–71* ⊕ *www.lagaredusud.com* ⊘ *Closed Mon.*

La Femme du Boulanger

$ | FRENCH | If you're looking for breakfast, this the place to come in Nice for freshly sliced country breads, a selection of mouth-watering Ö Jardin Sucré jams (say, raspberry and violet or apple-pear with hazelnut) and organic yogurts, all made in France. Sure, you can still have your flaky croissant, but here at the Baker's Wife, the friendly (that's right: friendly) owners, Bernard and Fanfan, deliver a toaster to your table, to grill the bread exactly to your liking. **Known for:** the best breakfast (and brunch) in Nice; French countryside vibes; delicious juices and coffees. $ *Average main: €16* ✉ *3 rue Commandant Raffali, New Town* ☎ *04–89–03–43–03* ▭ *No credit cards.*

La Merenda

$$$ | FRENCH | The back-to-bistro boom climaxed here when Dominique Le Stanc retired his crown at the Negresco to take over this tiny, unpretentious landmark of Provençal cuisine. He works in the miniature open kitchen creating ultimate versions of stuffed sardines, tagliatelle with pistou, slow-simmered *daubes* (beef stews), and the quintessential stockfish (the local lutefisk), while his wife whisks the dishes into the dining room. **Known for:** typical French bistro; amazing food for the price; cash-only policy and reservations accepted only in person. $ *Average main: €32* ✉ *4 rue Raoul Bosio, Old Town* ▭ *No credit cards* ⊘ *Closed weekends and 1st 2 wks in Aug.*

La Part des Anges

$$ | FRENCH | This wine shop with some 300 labels and a few tables and chairs at the back is really about *vins naturels*—unfiltered, unsulfured wines made by small producers from hand-harvested grapes—but the often-simple food served here also happens to be excellent. Whether you choose a charcuterie or cheese plate or one of the handful of hot dishes (like spaghetti with razor clams or octopus cooked in red wine), you can expect it to be generous and fresh. **Known for:** natural and organic wines; informative staff; perfect spot to sample wine and cheese. $ *Average main: €18* ✉ *17 rue Gubernatis, New Town* ☎ *04–93–62–69–80* ⊕ *http://lapartdesanges-nice.com/* ⊘ *Closed Sun.*

La Réserve de Nice

$$$$ | FRENCH | Chef Jérome Cotta knows what it takes to earn restaurant acclaim, and his originality and detail are reflected

in his creations, like millefeuille of foie gras caramelized with maple syrup; fig marmalade flavored with port wine, cranberry, and redcurrant jelly; and the cod fillet cooked in frothy butter, shallots, and Coco beans stewed with bacon in a fine truffle bouillon. It's easy to run up a bill of more than €180 per couple with drinks here, but the panoramic views, especially upstairs, from the Art Deco building jutting over the sea cannot be faulted. **Known for:** seaside location with excellent views; stylish bar; high prices. $ *Average main: €44* ⊠ *60 bd. Frank Pilatte, Mont Boron* ☎ *04–97–08–14–80* ⊕ *www.lareservedenice.com* ⊗ *Closed Nov., Sun. yr-round, and Mon. Oct.–Mar.*

★ Le Bistrot d'Antoine

$$ | **BISTRO** | You won't find any "concept" cooking here, just pure French bistro fare at its finest—beef salad with anchovy dressing, butter risotto with truffles, sliced leg of lamb, and traditional pork casserole. Leave room for the day's dessert, such as the wonderfully warm peach-and-frangipane tart. **Known for:** excellent prices; jaw-droppingly tasty food; reservations necessary. $ *Average main: €24* ⊠ *27 rue de la Préfecture, Old Town* ☎ *04–93–85–29–57* ⊗ *Closed Sun. and Mon., 3 wks in Aug., 10 days at Christmas, and at Easter.*

Le Bistro Gourmand

$$$$ | **BISTRO** | Steps from the Hotel Beau Rivage and with an outdoor terrace, the focus here is on the preservation of French cuisine, courtesy of chef David Vaqué. The sommelier amazingly seems to know your order before you do; a decent bottle of red will set you back around €50. **Known for:** six-course Legend Menu for only €85; famous soufflé; impressive wine menu. $ *Average main: €35* ⊠ *3 rue Desboutin, Old Town* ☎ *04–92–14–55–55* ⊕ *www.lebistrogourmand.fr* ⊗ *Closed Sun. and Wed.*

★ Le Canon

$$$ | **FRENCH** | Walking into this small bistrot, you can tell that this is the French dining experience people travel to Provence for, thanks to a handwritten menu on a board, wine bottles as far as the eye can see, and a low-key assemblage of chairs and tables that look like they came out of a 1970s-era attic. Owner Sébastien Perinetti and chef Elmahdi Mobarik source the freshest hyperlocal produce to bring you a parade of taste sensations, all seductively priced. **Known for:** organic food and natural wine; changing menu influenced by local suppliers; long leisurely meals. $ *Average main: €27* ⊠ *23 rue Meyerbeer, New Town* ☎ *04–96–79–09–24* ⊕ *www.lecanon.fr* ⊗ *Closed weekends. No lunch Wed.* ▭ *No credit cards.*

★ Le Panier

$$ | **FRENCH** | Located just beind Cours Saleya, this is everything you tend to expect from a French restaurant: an intimate setting on a tiny street, a chalkboard menu, and the natural skill of Nice-born chef Gaël Passigli. There's always a choice of five starters, five main courses, and five desserts (plus a few suggestions), showing a deep commitment to market-fresh seasonal cuisine. **Known for:** uncomplicated French cooking; regularly changing menu; reservations necessary for charming outside seating. $ *Average main: €25* ⊠ *5 rue Barillerie* ☎ *04–89–97–14–37* ⊕ *www.restaurantlepanier.com* ⊗ *Closed Tues. and Wed.*

Le Safari

$$$ | **FRENCH** | The Cours Saleya's desirable terrace tables provide an excuse for many of the restaurants along this strip to get away with culinary murder, but that's not the case at Le Safari, which pays more attention than most to ingredients and presentation (even if you shouldn't expect miracles). Choose from traditional Niçois dishes—the fish soup served with croutons, spicy mayonnaise, and cheese is particularly good—and Italian-inspired fare such as creamy risotto. **Known for:** pricey Niçois dishes appreciated by locals; lively outdoor

eating; colorful dining room. $ *Average main: €28* ✉ *1 cours Saleya, Port Nice* ☎ *04–93–80–18–44* 🌐 *www.restaurantsafari.fr.*

Lycée Hotellier Paul Augier

$ | **FRENCH** | Popular with both locals and expats, the three restaurants at the Paul Augier Hospitality and Tourism School, attended by 1,200 pupils and apprentices, serve lunch weekdays and some evenings. The food is prepared by aspiring young chefs. **Known for:** three-course meals at a steal; unique way to experience local Nice; chefs who could very well become the world's best. $ *Average main: €15* ✉ *163 bd. René Cassin* ☎ *04–93–72–77–79* 🌐 *www.lycee-paul-augier.com* 💳 *No credit cards* ⏲ *Closed weekends. No dinner.*

Restaurant Jan

$$$$ | **FRENCH** | South African Jan Hendrik's resume includes a stint as food contributor to the international *ELLE* magazine and two years as the head chef on a luxury yacht in Monaco before opening this exquisite restaurant. Within two years he was awarded a Michelin star, and those hard-to-get reservations for a taste of his menu—veal cheeks, potato dauphine, potato puree, trumpet mushrooms, foie gras, and lavender mayonnaise—became next to impossible. **Known for:** inventive dishes; homemade bread and ice cream; online reservations only. $ *Average main: €104* ✉ *12 rue Lascaris, Port Nice* ☎ *04–97–19–32–23* 🌐 *www.restaurantjan.com* ⏲ *Closed Sun., Mon., and 2 wks in late Nov. No lunch Sat.–Thurs.*

★ **Séjour Café**

$$$ | **FRENCH** | Owners Renaud and Marilène Geille, who used to run Les Viviers back in the day, pack this popular eatery by offering exceptional surroundings, fabulous food, and flawless service. The fish dishes are supreme, lightly accentuated by seasonal vegetables, and the *magret carnard* seems reinvented. **Known for:** small space so reservations a must; charming service; excellent salty and sweet desserts. $ *Average main: €26* ✉ *11 rue Grimaldi, New Town* ☎ *04–93–27–37–84* 🌐 *www.lesejourcafe.fr* ⏲ *Closed Sun. and Mon.*

Coffee and Quick Bites

★ **Glacier Fenocchio**

$ | **CAFÉ** | For fresh, homemade gelato-style ice cream offered in a rainbow of 94 flavors and colors, stop at Glacier Fenocchio any day of the week 9 am–midnight, March–November. There's even a choice of locally grown citrus flavors, including orange, mandarin, and lemon—even beer! $ *Average main:* ✉ *2 pl. Rossetti, Old Town* ☎ *04–93–62–88–80* 🌐 *www.fenocchio.fr* ⏲ *Closed mid-Nov.–Carnival.*

Hotels

★ **Hôtel Negresco**

$$$ | **HOTEL** | This white-stucco slice of old-fashioned Riviera extravagance accommodates well-heeled guests in elegant, uniquely decorated (and sometimes quirky) rooms replete with swagged drapes and fine antiques (plus a few unfortunate "with it" touches like those plastic-glitter bathtubs)—everyone should experience one night here. **Pros:** with 6,000 works of art it's like staying in a museum; part of Nice's history; best bar on the Riviera. **Cons:** breakfast not amazing; some rooms have more history than comfort; decor not for everyone. $ *Rooms from: €330* ✉ *37 promenade des Anglais, Promenade* ☎ *04–93–16–64–00* 🌐 *www.hotel-negresco-nice.com* 🛏 *125 rooms* 🍽 *No meals.*

Hôtel Suisse

$$$ | **HOTEL** | Charging modest prices for a spectacular view from the top end of the seafront, where the promenade winds around to the port, the acclaimed Hôtel Suisse far outclasses most other hotels in this price range, although be prepared for a small reception area and a *très petit*

A magnificent wedding-cake extravaganza, the Hotel Negresco was the haunt of the Beatles and the Burtons, and still remains the icon of Nice.

elevator. **Pros:** balconies with breathtaking sea views; clean, modern rooms; accessible prices in low season. **Cons:** tiny elevator; pricey breakfast (€18) when you can walk to Cours Saleya; small rooms. [$] *Rooms from: €298* ✉ *15 quai Raubà Capéù, Port Nice* ☎ *04–92–17–39–00* 🌐 *www.hotel-nice-suisse.com* 🛏 *38 rooms* 🍴 *No meals.*

La Fontaine

$$ | **HOTEL** | Fifty meters from the waterfront and the Negresco, this immaculate, modern hotel on a bustling shopping street offers a friendly welcome from its house-proud owners—for a great price. **Pros:** central location; leafy courtyard; anti-allergy flooring and pillows. **Cons:** rooms overlooking the street can be noisy; expensive breakfast; Wi-Fi can be dodgy. [$] *Rooms from: €135* ✉ *49 rue de France, New Town* ☎ *04–93–88–30–38* 🌐 *www.hotel-fontaine.com* 🕒 *Closed 2 wks in Dec. and Jan.* 🛏 *29 rooms* 🍴 *No meals.*

La Perouse

$$$ | **HOTEL** | Just past the Vieille Ville, at the foot of the town's château and next to Hôtel Suisse, this secret treasure cuts into the cliff (an elevator takes you up to reception), and the best rooms—including Raoul Dufy's favorite—not only have views of the azure sea, they also look down into an intimate garden dotted with lemon trees. **Pros:** discreet elegance steps from the Old Town and the Promenade; breakfast included with online reservations; heated cliff-side pool. **Cons:** some windows face a stone wall; not good for those with mobility issues; breakfast could be better. [$] *Rooms from: €238* ✉ *11 quai Rauba Capeu, Le Château* ☎ *04–93–62–34–63* 🌐 *www.hotel-la-perouse.com* 🛏 *56 rooms* 🍴 *No meals.*

Nice Garden Hotel

$ | **HOTEL** | It's hard to believe that this little gem of a hotel, with its own courtyard garden, is smack in the middle of Nice, next to the pedestrian shopping streets and a five-minute walk from the Old Town. **Pros:** delicious breakfast with homemade jam in the garden; extremely helpful owner; short walking distance to everything. **Cons:** parking is down the street at public garage; not a modern hotel; rooms are smallish. [$] *Rooms from: €120* ✉ *11 rue du Congrès, New Town* ☎ *04–93–87–35–62* 🌐 *www.nicegardenhotel.com* 🛏 *9 rooms* 🍴 *No meals.*

Solara

$ | HOTEL | One block from the beach and two from Place Masséna, this tiny budget hotel perches on the fourth and fifth floors, high above the main shopping street. **Pros:** fabulous base near the beach; top-floor terraces overlooking pedestrian street; soundproof windows. **Cons:** rooms on the small size; tricky to find by car; public areas seem a bit run-down. [$] *Rooms from: €110* ✉ *7 rue de France, New Town* ☎ *04–93–88–09–96* 🌐 *www.hotelsolara.com* 🛏 *12 rooms* 🍴 *No meals.*

Villa Rivoli

$ | HOTEL | You'll find this Belle Époque hotel, built in 1890, in the chic Quartier des Musiciens, excellently located a couple of blocks up from the beach but with very affordable rates. **Pros:** friendly and helpful service; authentic-period French feel; great location and value. **Cons:** hotel parking €18 per day, but neighborhood parking is difficult; "Lower Ground Floor" category rooms can be musty; no elevator. [$] *Rooms from: €115* ✉ *10 rue de Rivoli, New Town* ☎ *04–93–88–80–25* 🌐 *www.villa-rivoli.com* 🛏 *26 rooms* 🍴 *No meals.*

Windsor

$$ | HOTEL | This is a memorably eccentric hotel—most of its white-on-white rooms either have frescoes of mythological themes or are works of artists' whimsy—but the real draw at this otherworldly place is its astonishing city-center garden, a tropical oasis of lemon, magnolia, and palm trees, only outdone by the excellent service—and you're still only three blocks from the beach. **Pros:** private pool and garden in heart of city; a good base to explore Nice; good dining options on-site and nearby. **Cons:** artist-inspired interior design isn't for everyone (look online before booking!); street rooms can be noisy; ultraviolet elevator is cool the first time but annoying by the end of the week. [$] *Rooms from: €144* ✉ *11 rue Dalpozzo, New Town* ☎ *04–93–88–59–35* 🌐 *www.hotelwindsornice.com* 🕒 *Restaurant closed Sun.* 🛏 *57 rooms* 🍴 *Free breakfast.*

🍸 Nightlife

BARS

The Aston Club

BARS/PUBS | Don't forget your camera when heading up to this panoramic bar on the seventh floor of the Aston La Scala Hotel. The views of old Nice and the new Promenade du Paillon across to the airport are spectacular, and drink prices are more than reasonable. In summer the bar moves to the rooftop Moon Bar, where there's a pool (for guests) and a 360-degree view. Note that there are 23 steps from the hotel lobby to the bar's elevator. ✉ *12 av. Felix Faure, Centre Ville* ☎ *04–93–17–53–00* 🌐 *www.hotel-aston.com.*

★ Bar Le Relais

BARS/PUBS | If you're all dressed up and have just won big, invest in a drink in the intimate walnut-and-velour Bar Le Relais in the iconic Hôtel Negresco. It's worth the price (€15 for a glass of local red wine, or €6 for Evian) just to get a peek at the washrooms. ✉ *37 promenade des Anglais, Promenade* ☎ *04–93–16–64–00* 🌐 *www.hotel-negresco-nice.com.*

CASINOS

Casino du Palais de la Méditerranée

CASINOS | In the 1920s, the swanky Palais de la Méditerranée drew performers like Charlie Chaplin and Edith Piaf; however, the establishment lost its glory and was demolished in 1990, save for the facade you see today. Reopened with

During the famous annual Carnaval, gargantuan sculptures and the famous grosses têtes—literally, "fat heads"—fill the streets of old Nice with fantasy.

hotel service in 2004, the contemporary version has 180 slot machines, 38 electric roulette tables, and two blackjack tables, plus two Texas Hold 'Em Poker tables. ⊠ *15 promenade des Anglais, Promenade* ☎ *04–92–14–68–00 for show reservations* ⊕ *www.casinomediterranee.com.*

DANCE CLUBS
Glam

DANCE CLUBS | The city's most colorful LGBTQ club has DJs who compel you to dance to the best mixes around. It's open to all clubbers in the know, with only one criterion: be cool. ⊠ *6 rue Eugène Emmanuel, Centre Ville* ☎ *04–93–87–29–67.*

 Performing Arts

CONCERTS
Acropolis

CONCERTS | Classical music, ballet performances, traditional French pop concerts, and even dog shows take place at Nice's convention center, the Acropolis. ⊠ *Palais des Congrès, Esplanade John F. Kennedy*

☎ *04–93–92–83–00* ⊕ *www.nice-acropolis.com.*

Conservatoire National

ARTS CENTERS | The regional conservatory in Cimiez has a mixed calendar of events, from classical concerts to dance. ⊠ *127 av. de Brancolar, Cimiez* ⊹ *Take Bus No. 15 to Cdt. Gérôme stop* ☎ *04–97–13–50–00* ⊕ *www.cnr-nice.org.*

Opéra de Nice

DANCE | A half block west of Cours Saleya stands a flamboyant Italian-style theater designed by Charles Garnier, architect of the Paris Opéra. It's home today to the Opéra de Nice, with a permanent chorus, orchestra, and ballet corps. The season runs mid-September through mid-June, and tickets are from €15. ⊠ *4 rue St-François-de-Paule, Old Town* ☎ *04–92–17–40–79* ⊕ *www.opera-nice.org.*

Théâtre de Verdure

MUSIC | Built in 1945, the Théâtre de Verdure can seat 1,850 people or provide standing room for 3,200. It's a great spot for concerts and theater. Keep an eye on the summer calendar for the Ciné Prom, when you can watch big-screen movies (€2) here. ✉ *Jardin Albert Ier, Espace Jacques Cotta* ⊕ *www.tdv-nice.org.*

FILM AND THEATER

Cinéma Rialto

FILM | Don't expect to find popcorn and concession stands here, but the Rialto has the city's biggest selection of foreign- and English-language films, with some Cannes Film Festival screenings, too. ✉ *4 rue de Rivoli, Cimiez* ⊕ *lerialto.cine. allocine.fr.*

Théâtre National de Nice

THEATER | Headed by Irina Brook, the Théâtre National de Nice plays host to 40 productions from all over Europe as part of a new initiative to become a center for innovative European theater. Tickets range from €8 (last-minute) to €45. ✉ *Promenade des Arts, Centre Ville* ☎ *04–93–13–90–90* ⊕ *www.tnn.fr.*

Shopping

Nice's main shopping street, **Avenue Jean-Médecin,** runs inland from Place Masséna; all needs and most tastes are catered to in its big department stores (Galeries Lafayette, Monoprix, and the split-level Étoile mall). Line 1 of the tramway has made this mini Champs-Elysées all the more accessible, so expect crowds on Saturday (the majority of shops are still closed on Sunday). Luxury boutiques, such as Emporio Armani and Chanel, line Rue du Paradis (Louis Vuitton is at the end of the street on Avenue de Suède), while Tiffany's and Cartier can be found along Avenue de Verdun. Rue de France and the Old Town have more affordable offerings from independent shops.

Alziari

FOOD/CANDY | Tiny Alziari sells olive oil by the gallon in the famous blue and yellow cans with old-fashioned labels. ✉ *14 rue St-François-de-Paule, Old Town* ⊕ *www. alziari.com.fr.*

Confiserie Florian du Vieux Nice

FOOD/CANDY | Open every day except Christmas, this spot is a good source for crystallized fruit (a Nice specialty). It's located on the west side of the port. ✉ *14 quai Papacino, Old Town* ⊕ *www. confiserieflorian.com.*

Fish Market

FOOD/CANDY | Seafood of all kinds is sold at the fish market every day (except Monday) 6 am–1 pm. ✉ *Pl. St-François, Old Town* ☽ *Closed Mon.*

La Promenade des 100 Antiquaires

ANTIQUES/COLLECTIBLES | France's third largest *regroupment* of antiques collectors forms a triangle from Place Garibaldi to the port (Quai Papacino) and along Rue Catherine Ségruane at the bottom of the château. Rue Antoine Gautier and Rue Emmanuel Philibert are worth discovering as is Les Puces de Nice, which has 30 stalls under one roof in Quai Lunel, and Place Garibaldi hosts a morning antiques market on the third Saturday of the month. ✉ *Old Town.*

Mademoiselle

CLOTHING | You have to hand it to the French: they even do secondhand fashion right. Steps away from the Hôtel Negresco, Mademoiselle has quickly become a must-stop shop in Nice. Chanel, Dior, Louis Vuitton, Hermès—you name it, the gang's all here, at least in vintage terms. You'll find lots of luxury-brand clothes, shoes, bags, and belts to rummage through—all of it excellently priced and gorgeously displayed by owner Sephora Louis. ✉ *41 rue de France, New Town.*

Maison Auer

FOOD/CANDY | Open Tuesday through Saturday, the venerable Henri Auer has been selling chocolate and crystallized fruit since 1820. ✉ *7 rue St-François de Paule, Old Town* ⊕ *www.maison-auer.com.*

Oliviera

FOOD/CANDY | Come here for the best selection of Provençal olive oils in town. Oliviera is run by the passionate Nadim

Beyrouti in the Old Town, who also serves Mediterranean dishes made with the finest local ingredients. ✉ *8 bis rue du Collet, Old Town* ☎ *04–93–13–06–45* ⊕ *www.oliviera.com* ⊗ *Closed Sun. and Mon.*

Star Dog Boutique

PETS | For the jet-set pet, Star Dog Boutique has iPawds (a plush toy with FaceBark, DogTube, and Bark Street Journal apps), Doggle sunglasses, and Oh My Dog! cologne to get Fido's tail wagging. ✉ *40 rue de France, New Town* ☎ *04–97–03–27–40.*

🏃 Activities

Nice is one giant outdoor arena, and the Promenade is the racetrack. From the Ironman Nice triathlon to the Rock n Roll Carnival 25-km (15½-mile) run to the 140-km (87-mile) Ultra run (not to mention the cycling, kayaking and sailing … and even skiing), there are plenty of options to work off that breakfast croissant while taking in some spectacular scenery. The tourist-office website has an extensive listing of sports and activities.

Glisse Evasion

WATER SPORTS | If the idea of parasailing seems a bit terrifying, note that these guys get nothing but smiles from satisfied customers. Prices range from €60 to €100. You'll find them nearly across from the Negresco Hotel. ✉ *29 promenade des Anglais, Promenade* ☎ *06–10–27–03–91* ⊕ *www.glisse-evasion.com.*

Villefranche-sur-Mer

10 km (6 miles) east of Nice.

Nestled discreetly along the deep scoop of harbor between Nice and Cap Ferrat, this pretty watercolor of a fishing port seems surreal, flanked as it is by the big city of Nice and the assertive wealth of Monaco. The town is a stage set of brightly colored houses—the sort of place where Pagnol's *Fanny* could have been filmed. Genuine fishermen skim up to the docks here in weathered-blue *barques,* and the streets of the Vieille Ville flow directly to the waterfront, much as they did in the 13th century. Some of the prettiest spots in town are around Place de la Paix, Rue du Poilu, and Place du Conseil, which looks out over the water. The deep harbor, in the caldera of a volcano, was once preferred by the likes of Onassis and Niarchos and the royals on their yachts. But the character of the place was subtly shaped by the artists and authors who gathered at the **Hôtel Welcome**—Diaghilev and Stravinsky, taking a break from the Ballet Russe in Monaco; Somerset Maugham and Evelyn Waugh; and, above all, Jean Cocteau, who came here to recover from the excesses of Paris life. Nowadays, its population consists mainly of wealthy retired people, though families do head here to enjoy its sandy (well, gravelly) beach and jellyfish-free zones. The only fly in the ointment is Villefranche's popularity: between the endless stream of cruise ships sending their passengers ashore in very, very large numbers and a flood of new construction so villas now virtually elbow each other out of the way up the hillsides, the town's physical beauty has become more challenging to appreciate peacefully. Still and all, quaint alleyways and the heavenly panoramas of the town from on high nicely remind you why everyone headed here in the first place and the natural light will always captivate. A piece of advice: wear sensible shoes as cobblestone is no friend to thinly soled footwear (and there are lots of steps).

GETTING HERE AND AROUND

Villefranche is a major stop on the Marseille–Ventimiglia coastal train route, with more than 40 arrivals every day from Nice (6 minutes). Buses connect with Nice and Monaco via Zou! No. 100 or from Nice, Nos. 80, 81, or 84 (€1.50). Most public parking is paid during the

347

day, 9–7 (from €1.80 per hour), and can be tricky to find.

VISITOR INFORMATION
CONTACTS Villefranche-sur-Mer Tourist Office. ⊠ Jardin François Binon ☎ 04–93–01–73–68 ⊕ www.tourisme-villefranche-sur-mer.com.

Sights

Chapelle St-Pierre
RELIGIOUS SITE | So enamored was Jean Cocteau of this painterly fishing port that he decorated the 14th-century Chapelle St-Pierre with images from the life of St. Peter and dedicated it to the village's fishermen. ⊠ Quai de l'Amiral Courbet ☎ 04–93–76–90–70 ☎ €3 ⊗ Closed Mon., Tues., and mid-Nov.–mid. Dec.

Citadelle St-Elme
MILITARY SITE | Restored to perfect condition, the stalwart 16th-century Citadelle St-Elme anchors the harbor with its broad, sloping stone walls. Beyond its drawbridge lie the city's administrative offices and a group of minor gallery-museums, with a scattering of works by Picasso and Miró. Whether you stop into these private collections (all free of charge), you're welcome to stroll around the inner grounds and circle the imposing exterior. ⊠ Harbor ☎ Free.

Église St-Michel
RELIGIOUS SITE | This modest Baroque church, above Rue Obscure, contains a movingly realistic sculpture of Christ carved in fig wood by an anonymous 17th-century convict. ⊠ Pl. Poullan.

Rue Obscure
NEIGHBORHOOD | Running parallel to the waterfront, the extraordinary 14th-century Rue Obscure ("Dark Street") is entirely covered by vaulted arcades; it sheltered the people of Villefranche when the Germans fired their parting shots—an artillery bombardment—near the end of World War II. ⊠ Villefranche-sur-Mer.

Beaches

Plage des Marinières
BEACHES | To the east of the port, southwest facing Plage des Marinères is the biggest beach you'll find in Villefranche, but it's only about 1 km (½ mile) long. Popular because the shoreline is protected from winds, this beach has coarse sand and lifeguards in the summer. Note that the SNCF train line runs parallel, so the noise factor is a consideration. There are no loungers, but there are jellyfish nets. **Amenities:** lifeguards; showers; toilets. **Best for:** snorkeling; sunrise; swimming. ⊠ Promenade des Marinières.

Restaurants

Cosmo Bar
$$ | MEDITERRANEAN | Facing the Cocteau chapel with an enviable view of the sea from its terrace, this modern brasserie could easily get away with being merely mediocre. Instead, it serves fresh, colorful Mediterranean dishes ranging from an addictive anchoïade—crudités with anchovy dip—to omelettes. **Known for:** fantastic views; casual yet memorable French Riviera dining; terrace seating (call ahead to make sure you nab a spot). $ Average main: €18 ⊠ 11 pl. Amélie Pollonnais ☎ 04–93–01–84–05 ⊕ www.restaurant-lecosmo.fr ⊗ Closed 3 wks in Jan.

La Mère Germaine
$$$$ | FRENCH | This is a place to linger over warm lobster salad or sole meunière in butter with almonds while watching the world go by; the food is tasty, but the fabulous setting of this veritable institution is reflected in the prices (and service can fall on the rude side). The seaside restaurant opened in 1938, and proprietor Germaine Halap soon became a second mother to American naval officers and sailors who came into port. **Known for:** legendary local eatery for lovers of fresh seafood; setting right next to the sea; place in U.S. Navy history. $ Average

7

Nice and the Eastern French Riviera VILLEFRANCHE-SUR-MER

Did You Know?

The colorful harbor of Villefranche-sur-Mer surrounds one of the deepest and most beautiful bays on the Riviera.

main: €55 ✉ Quai Corbert ☎ 04–93–01–71–39 🌐 www.meregermaine.com ⏲ Closed late Nov.–Christmas.

★ Le Serre

$ | FRENCH | It might look like just another pizzeria, but Le Serre is a family-run restaurant where everything from the pizzas to the local specialties is prepared with care. The warm welcome ensures that the restaurant attracts plenty of locals who have learned to tread carefully around tourist traps. **Known for:** excellent Daube Provençal beef-and-wine stew; lively atmosphere; local hangout on a tiny street. [$] *Average main: €17* ✉ *16 rue de May* ☎ *04–93–76–79–91* ⏲ *Closed mid-Nov.–Dec.*

Hotels

Hôtel de la Darse

$ | HOTEL | Who needs luxury fittings and fabrics when you have a view like this one overlooking thĕ old harbor of Villefranche, and at such a highly affordable price? The most desirable rooms at this simple yet welcoming 1950s hotel even have balconies with sweeping panoramas. **Pros:** great views over the Old Port; away from the crowds of town; a good deal for Villefranche. **Cons:** no elevator; a walk to the center of town; early morning delivery noise. [$] *Rooms from: €90* ✉ *32 av. Général de Gaulle* ☎ *04–93–01–72–54* 🌐 *www.hoteldeladarse.com* 💳 *No credit cards* ⏲ *Closed mid-Dec.–early Jan.* 🛏 *21 rooms* 🍴 *No meals.*

Hôtel Provençal

$ | HOTEL | Within walking distance of the port, this inexpensive hotel run by four generations may not look like much from the outside but is friendly and accommodating. **Pros:** balconies with sea view (ask for this when booking); high quality breakfast served on the terrace; delicious Provençal-style restaurant. **Cons:** modest decor; village-facing rooms may have street noise; bit of a hike up to hotel from beach. [$] *Rooms from: €95* ✉ *4 av. Maréchal Joffre* ☎ *04–93–76–53–53* 🌐 *www.hotelleprovencal.fr* ⏲ *Closed Nov.–Feb.* 🛏 *43 rooms* 🍴 *No meals.*

★ Hôtel Welcome

$$$ | HOTEL | Somerset Maugham holed up in one of the tiny crow's-nest rooms at the top, Jean Cocteau lived here while writing *Orphée*, and Elizabeth Taylor and Richard Burton used to tie one on in the bar (now nicely renovated) at this waterfront landmark—which remains a formidable and flawless retreat. **Pros:** excellent English-speaking service; artistic heritage makes for a nostalgic trip into the Roaring '20s; paddleboard and kayak rentals. **Cons:** style, especially on the top floor, is overtly nautical in flavor; some rooms are oddly shaped—narrow and long—so they feel smaller; expensive parking in summer. [$] *Rooms from: €235* ✉ *3 quai Amiral Courbet* ☎ *04–93–76–27–62* 🌐 *www.welcomehotel.com* ⏲ *Closed mid-Nov.–Christmas* 🛏 *35 rooms* 🍴 *Free breakfast.*

Beaulieu-sur-Mer

4 km (2½ miles) east of Villefranche; 14 km (9 miles) east of Nice.

With its back pressed hard against the cliffs of the corniche and sheltered between the peninsulas of Cap Ferrat and Cap Roux, this once-grand resort basks in a tropical microclimate that earned its central neighborhood the name "Petite Afrique." The town was the pet of 19th-century society, and its grand hotels welcomed Empress Eugénie, the Prince of Wales, and Russian nobles.

GETTING HERE AND AROUND

With frequent arrivals and departures, Beaulieu is a main stop on the Marseille–Ventimiglia coastal train line. From Beaulieu's train station the hourly Bus No. 81 (€1.50) connects with neighboring St-Jean-Cap-Ferrat. Bus No. 100 takes you to/from Nice/Monaco, while No. 84 goes to Nice via Villefranche.

VISITOR INFORMATION

CONTACTS Beaulieu Tourist Office. ✉ *Pl. Georges Clemenceau* ☎ *04–93–01–02–21* 🌐 *www.otbeaulieusurmer.com.*

Sights

Promenade Maurice-Rouvier

PROMENADE | Today Beaulieu is usually spoken of in the past tense and has taken on a rather stuffy character, though its small beach attracts families with children, but on the Promenade Maurice-Rouvier, a paved pedestrian path that begins not far from the Villa Kerylos, you can stroll the waterfront, past grand villas and their tropical gardens, all the way to St-Jean-Cap-Ferrat. The 30-minute walk winds seaside along the Baie des Fourmis (Bay of Ants), whose name alludes to the black rocks "crawling" up from the sea. The name doesn't quite fit, but the walk will give you great views of the sparkling Mediterranean and surrounding mountains. ✉ *Beaulieu-sur-Mer.*

★ **Villa Kerylos**

HOUSE | One manifestation of Beaulieu's Belle Époque excess is the eye-popping Villa Kerylos, a 1902 mansion built in the style of classical Greece (to be exact, of the villas that existed on the island of Delos in the 2nd century BC). It was the dream house of amateur archaeologist Théodore Reinach, who hailed from a wealthy German family, helped the French in their excavations at Delphi, and became an authority on ancient Greek music. He commissioned an Italian architect from Nice, Emmanuel Pontremoli, to surround him with Grecian delights: cool Carrara marble, rare fruitwoods, and a dining salon where guests reclined to eat *à la grecque*. It's one of the most unusual houses in the south of France. ✉ *Impasse Gustave-Eiffel* ☎ *04–93–01–01–44* 🌐 *www.villakerylos.fr/en* 🎫 *€12.*

Restaurants

La Reserve

$$$$ | **MEDITERRANEAN** | This Michelin-starred restaurant is a marvel of light and color, and has been a crown jewel of the Mediterranean since it opened in 1880. Chef Julien Roucheteau has replaced Yannick Franque, but continues to create original recipes from fresh Mediterranean products, like the iconc Langoustine tails roasted in hazelnut butter. **Known for:** perfect wine pairings; seaside location with gorgeous views; fabulous desserts. [$] *Average main: €85* ✉ *5 bd. General Leclerc* ☎ *04–93–01–00–01* 🌐 *www.reservebeaulieu.com* 🕓 *Closed Nov.–mid-Dec. No lunch May–Oct.*

St-Jean-Cap-Ferrat

2 km (1 mile) south of Beaulieu on D25.

One of the most exclusive addresses in the world, the peninsula of Cap Ferrat is moored by the luxuriously sited pleasure port of St-Jean; from its portside walkways and crescent of beach you can look over the sparkling blue harbor to the graceful green bulk of the corniches. Yachts purr in and out of port, and their passengers scuttle into cafés for take-out drinks to enjoy on their private decks. On shore, the billionaires come and go, and trade gossip (like who purchased the world's most expensive house, the 14-bedroom Villa Les Cedres) while residents of Cap Ferrat fiercely protect it from curious tourists; its grand old villas are hidden for the most part in the depths of tropical gardens. You can nonetheless try to catch peeks of them from the **Coastline Promenade**.

GETTING HERE AND AROUND

The humor is not lost that a bus fare of €1.50 brings you to one of the most exclusive pieces of land on the planet; Bus No. 81 accesses the cape from Nice.

VISITOR INFORMATION

CONTACTS St-Jean-Cap-Ferrat Tourist Office. ⊠ *5 and 59 av. Denis Semeria* ☎ *04–93–76–08–90* ⊕ *www.saintjeancap-ferrat-tourisme.fr.*

 Sights

Coastline Promenade

PROMENADE | While Cap Ferrat's villas are sequestered for the most part in the depths of tropical gardens, you can nonetheless walk its entire coastline promenade if you strike out from the port; from the restaurant Capitaine Cook, cut right up Avenue des Fossés, turn right on Avenue Vignon, and follow Chemin de la Carrière. The 11-km (7-mile) walk passes through rich tropical flora and, on the west side, follows white cliffs buffeted by waves. When you've traced the full outline of the peninsula, veer up Chemin du Roy past the fabulous gardens of the **Villa des Cèdres,** owned by King Leopold II of Belgium at the turn of the last century. The king owned several opulent estates along the French Riviera, undoubtedly paid for by his enslavement of the Belgian Congo. Past the gardens, you can reach the **Plage de Passable,** from which you cut back across the peninsula's wrist. A shorter loop takes you from town out to the **Pointe de St-Hospice,** much of the walk shaded by wind-twisted pines. From the port, climb Avenue Jean Mermoz to Place Paloma and follow the path closest to the waterfront. At the point are an 18th-century prison tower, a 19th-century chapel, and unobstructed views of Cap Martin. Two other footpath maps can be found at the Tourist Office at 59 avenue Denis-Séméria; the shorter loop takes you from town out to the Pointe de St-Hospice, much of the walk shaded by wind-twisted pines. From the port, climb Avenue Jean Mermoz to Place Paloma and follow the path closest to the waterfront or the Promenade Maurice Rouvier, which runs along the eastern edge of the peninsula. You'll stumble on reasonably priced cafés, pizzerias, and ice-cream parlors on the promenade of the Plage de St-Jean. The best swimming in the region is a bit farther south, past the port, at Plage Paloma. Keep trekking around the wooded area, where a beautiful path (*sentier pédestre*) leads along the outermost edge of Cap Ferrat. Other than the occasional yacht, all traces of civilization disappear, and the water is a dizzying blue. ⊠ *St-Jean-Cap-Ferrat.*

Villa Ephrussi de Rothschild

HOUSE | Between the port and the mainland, the floridly beautiful Villa Ephrussi de Rothschild bears witness to the wealth and worldly flair of the baroness who had it built. Constructed in 1905 in neo-Venetian style (its flamingo-pink facade was thought not to be in the best of taste by the local gentry), the house was baptized "Île-de-France" in homage to the Baroness Béatrice de Rothschild's favorite ocean liner. In keeping with that theme, her staff used to wear sailing costumes and her ship travel kit is on view in her bedroom. Precious artworks, tapestries, and furniture adorn the salons—in typical Rothschildian fashion, each is given over to a different 18th-century "époque." Upstairs are the private apartments of Madame la Baronne, which can only be seen on a guided tour offered around noon. The grounds are landscaped with no fewer than seven gardens and topped off with a Temple of Diana. Be sure to allow yourself time to wander here, as this is one of the few places on the coast where you'll be allowed to experience the lavish pleasures characteristic of the Belle Époque Côte d'Azur. Tea and light lunches, served in a glassed-in porch overlooking the grounds and spectacular coastline, encourage you to linger. ⊠ *Av. Ephrussi* ☎ *04–93–01–33–09* ⊕ *www.villa-ephrussi.com* 🎫 *€15.*

Beaches

Paloma Plage

BEACHES | Ideally located on one of Europe's most expensive pieces of real estate, this lovely shade-dappled stretch of sand is at the bottom of a steep hill only five minutes away on foot from the glamorous village of Saint-Jean. It's also in the heart of a battle for survival as the French government begins to enforce a new law that all beach structures must be dismountable. In 1973, Saint-Jean, with its shallow bay, soft sand, and some of the Riviera's clearest waters, was given a special "natural and remarkable site" status, which included the construction of its jetty, which currently can't be dismounted. If the mayor tears it down, nothing can be rebuilt in its place. The public beach remains open, but the private Paloma Beach is currently fighting for its life. **Amenities:** lifeguards; showers; toilets; water sports. **Best for:** snorkeling; sunrise; swimming. ✉ *Av. Jean Mermoz.*

Restaurants

Le Pancha du Sloop

$$ | **SEAFOOD** | Catering to the yachting crowd, this established port-side restaurant has outdoor tables surrounding a tiny "garden" of potted palms. The focus remains fish, of course: *soupe de poisson* (fish soup), St-Pierre (John Dory) steamed with asparagus, and roasted whole sea bass. **Known for:** long-running port-side eatery; terrace views of yachts; good value for Cap Ferrat. [$] *Average main: €23* ✉ *Port de St-Jean-Cap-Ferrat* ☎ *04–93–01–48–63* 🕓 *Closed Wed.*

Hotels

Brise Marine

$$ | **HOTEL** | With a Provençal-yellow facade, blue shutters, a balustraded sea terrace, and pretty pastel guest rooms, Brise Marine fulfills most desires for that perfect, picturesque Cap Ferrat hotel. **Pros:** views, views, views; excellent value for location; close to Paloma Beach. **Cons:** some rooms are small; parking €16; no restaurant on-site. [$] *Rooms from: €206* ✉ *58 av. Jean Mermoz* ☎ *04–93–76–04–36* 🌐 *www.hotel-brisemarine.com* 🕓 *Closed Nov.–Feb.* 🛏 *16 rooms* 🍴 *No meals.*

★ Grand-Hôtel du Cap-Ferrat, A Four Seasons Hotel

$$$$ | **HOTEL** | **FAMILY** | Just this side of paradise, this extravagantly expensive hotel has always been the exclusive playground for Hollywood's elite; now, managed by Four Seasons, it is *the* standard for discreet Cap-Ferrat moneyed luxury looking for personalized experiences. **Pros:** every detail is well-thought-out and promptly attended to; world's finest haute couture spa; Michelin-starred restaurant featuring 600 French wines. **Cons:** forget it if you're on a budget (breakfast alone is €50); this level of luxury can be overwhelming; can feel snooty. [$] *Rooms from: €320* ✉ *71 bd. du Charles du Gaulle* ☎ *04–93–76–50–50* 🌐 *www.fourseasons.com/capferrat* 🕓 *Closed Dec.–Feb.* 🛏 *74 rooms* 🍴 *No meals.*

Royal Riviera

$$$$ | **HOTEL** | Parisian designer guru Grace Leo Andrieu revamped this former *residence hôtelière* for British aristocrats that now invites visitors on an intimate voyage into neo-Hellenic style, complete with an admiring wink at the nearby Villa Kerylos. **Pros:** excellent service and concierge; gorgeous property with gym and spa; heated outdoor pool and private beach. **Cons:** some small rooms facing railroad; €38 breakfast; pricey rates. [$] *Rooms from: €395* ✉ *3 av. Jean Monnet* ☎ *04–93–76–31–00* 🌐 *www.royal-riviera.com/en* 🕓 *Closed mid-Nov.–Jan.* 🛏 *94 rooms* 🍴 *No meals.*

Baroness Ephrussi de Rothschild spared no expense—a garden full of roses, a house full of Renaissance treasures—in creating her dream house above the sea in St-Jean-Cap-Ferrat.

Èze

2 km (1 mile) east of Beaulieu; 12 km (7 miles) east of Nice; 7 km (4½ miles) west of Monte Carlo.

Medieval and magnificent, towering like an eagle's nest above the coast and crowned with ramparts and the ruins of a medieval château, Èze (pronounced "*ehz*") is unfortunately the most accessible of all the perched villages. So even during off-season its streets flood with tourists, some not-so-fresh from the beach, and it was one of the first towns to post pictorial warnings that say, in effect, "No Shoes, No Shirt, No Service." It is, nonetheless, the most spectacularly sited; its streets are steep and, in places, only for the flamboyantly fit; its time-stained stone houses huddle together in storybook fashion. No wonder U2 frontman Bono and guitarist The Edge have beachside villas here.

Colonized millennia ago by the Romans (who may have built a temple here to the Egyptian goddess, Isis—hence the town name), the mountain peak aerie that is Èze was much coveted by locals fleeing from pirating Saracens. By the 19th century, only peasants were left, but when the Riviera became fashionable, Èze's splendid views up and down the coast became one of the draws that lured fabled visitors—lots of crowned heads, Georges Sand, Friedrich Nietzsche, and Consuelo Vanderbilt, who, when she was tired of being Duchess of Marlborough, traded in Blenheim Palace for a custom-built house in Èze. Remember that if you choose to stay here, it gets very quiet at night, even in high season.

GETTING HERE AND AROUND

By car, you should arrive using the Moyenne Corniche, which deposits you near the gateway to Èze Village; Bus Nos. 112 and 82 from Nice also use this road, but No. 100 (to Monaco) goes by the sea while No. 116 heads up the Grande Corniche from Nice (€1.50 each). By train, you'll arrive at the station in Èze-sur-Mer, where a daily navette shuttle bus (€1.50) takes you up to hilltop Èze, a trip that, with its 1,001 switchbacks up the steep mountainside, takes a full 15 minutes (keep this in mind if you're hiring a taxi to "rush" you down to the train station). Or you could walk from the train station up the Nietzsche Path to the village (90 minutes at least): high heels are not allowed, and the trek isn't advised in the dark.

VISITOR INFORMATION
CONTACTS Èze Tourist Office. ✉ *Pl. du Général de Gaulle* ☎ *04–93–41–26–00* ⊕ *www.eze-tourisme.com.*

Sights

Jardin Exotique
GARDEN | Set 1,310 feet above sea level, the Jardin Exotique is one of the Riviera's most visited sites. Full of rare succulents and Jean-Philippe Richard sculptures, the botanical garden is also blessed with superlative views: from this crest-top locale you can pan all the way from Italy to St-Tropez (on a clear day, you can even see Corsica). Just a few feet from the entrance, take a time-out lunch at the Nid d'Aigle, an inexpensive eatery featuring focaccias and salads, quaintly set on stone levels rising up around a tall tree. ✉ *20 rue du Château* ☎ *04–93–41–10–30* ⊕ *www.jardinexotique-eze.fr* 🎟 *€6.*

 Restaurants

Cap Estel–La Table de Patrick Raingeard
$$$$ | **FRENCH** | For over 50 years celebs have holidayed and dined at Cap Estel along Èze's *bord de mer*, enjoying its private 5-acre peninsula with all-encompassing views of the Mediterranean. Chef Patrick Raingeard's Michelin-star cuisine is worthy of the setting. **Known for:** great brunch; paradisical views; produce from the hotel's garden. 💲 *Average main: €62* ✉ *1312 av. Raymond-Poincaré, Charbonnières-les-Bains* ☎ *04–93–76–29– 29* ⊕ *www.capestel.com* 🕙 *Closed Jan.–Mar.*

Hotels

★ Château de la Chèvre d'Or
$$$$ | **HOTEL** | The "Château of the Golden Goat" is actually an entire stretch of the village, streets and all, bordered by gardens that hang from the mountainside in nearly Babylonian style; in addition to divine accommodations, it delivers some of the most breathtaking Mediterranean views—at a price. **Pros:** insane views; fabulous infinity pool; four excellent restaurants on-site. **Cons:** rooms need some TLC; no elevator; cobblestone walking involved to reach hotel. 💲 *Rooms from: €430* ✉ *Rue du Barri* ☎ *04–92–10–66–66* ⊕ *www.chevredor.com* 🕙 *Closed Nov.– Feb.* 🛏 *40 rooms* 🍽 *No meals.*

Roquebrune–Cap-Martin

5 km (3 miles) east of Monaco.

Amid the frenzy of overbuilding that defines this last gasp of the coast before Italy, two twinned havens have survived, each in its own way: the perched Vieille Ville of Roquebrune, which gives its name to the greater area, and Cap-Martin—luxurious, isolated, exclusive, and the once-favored retreat of the Empress Eugénie and Winston Churchill. With its lovely tumble of raked tile roofs and twisting streets, fountains, archways, and quiet squares, Roquebrune retains many of the charms of a hilltop village, although it has become heavily gentrified and commercialized. Rue Moncollet is lined with arcaded passageways and a number of medieval houses. Somerset Maugham—who once memorably described these environs as a "sunny place for shady people"—resided in the town's famous Villa Mauresque (still private) for many years.

Famously, Irish poet W.B. Yeats died at the Hôtel Idéal Séjour in Roquebrune-Cap-Martin in 1939. He was buried at the nearby St. Pancras graveyard, as

The "eagle's nest" village of the Riviera, Èze perches 1,300 feet above the sea; travelers never fail to marvel at the dramatic setting.

he had instructed his wife, "If I die, bury me up there and then in a year's time when the newspapers have forgotten me, dig me up and plant me in Sligo." The war prevented his body's repatriation, but it was then discovered that the poet had been disinterred in 1946, and his bones mixed with others in the ossuary. His "remains" were finally transferred and reburied in County Sligo, Ireland in 1947.

GETTING HERE AND AROUND

Despite its small size, there are two train stations here: Roquebrune–Cap-Martin, which gives access to the isolated beach and the Monte-Carlo Country Club during the Rolex Masters tennis tournament, and Carnolès, a stop closer to Menton and steps from several beaches along the promenade. Regional trains run direct between Nice or Cannes (70 minutes; €10.60 and €10.90 respectively), but not all stop at Cap Martin. From the Carnolès train station, the Zestbus No. 21 (€1.50) has 6 buses a day heading into town or from the Roquebrune–Cap-Martin train

station; otherwise, it's a one-hour hike up with lots of stairs and benches for resting. The Nice–Menton Bus No. 100, which runs from the bus station in Nice every 15 minutes (€1.50), also stops in the lower part of Roquebrune.

■ TIP→ **From Carnolès train station, you can access the scenic four-mile Corbusier foot trail (an easy-to-follow stone path with lots of steps both up and down) that traces the tip of Cap Martin and back to the Roquebrune–Cap-Martin train station before continuing on to Monaco. For more on Roquebrune's four circuit trails, see the tourism website.**

VISITOR INFORMATION

CONTACTS Roquebrune-Cap-Martin Tourist Office. ✉ *218 av. Aristide Briand, Roquebrune-Cap-Martin* ☎ *04–93–35–62–87* ⊕ *www.roquebrune-cap-martin.com.*

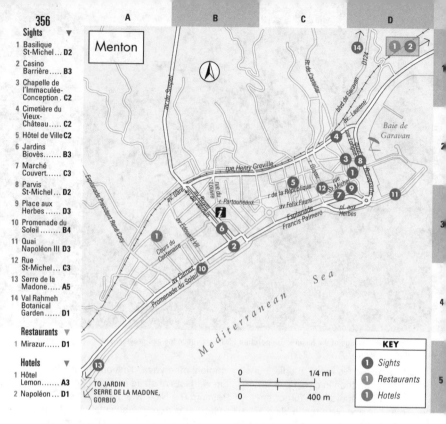

TO JARDIN SERRE DE LA MADONE, GORBIO

Beaches

Plage de la Buse

BEACHES | FAMILY | The entirely public Plage de la Buse is a wonderfully small, fine-pebble beach, with zero star-chasers and strutting high heels, and it's great for novice swimmers. Also known as Cabbé Beach, it's lovely to be protected from the elements by the curved south-facing wall of a huge villa (whose gardens add a lovely tropical feel). Access is just down a few steps from the Cap-Martin train station (where there is some parking) or Le Corbusier trail, but it's completely BYO: towel, umbrella, and water/drinks. There's no bathroom, but the tiny Le Cabanon restaurant serves lunch and dinner. **Amenities:** showers. **Best for:** solitude; swimming. ⊠ *Sentier du Corbusier, Roquebrune-Cap-Martin.*

Menton

1 km (½ mile) east of Roquebrune; 9 km (5½ miles) east of Monaco.

The most Mediterranean of the French resort towns, Menton rubs shoulders with the Italian border and owes some of its balmy climate to the protective curve of the Ligurian shore. Its Cubist skew of terra-cotta roofs and yellow-ocher houses, Baroque arabesques capping the church facades, and ceramic tiles glistening on their steeples, all evoke the villages of the Italian coast. Yet there's a whiff of influence from Spain, too, in its fantastical villas, exotic gardens, and whimsical patches of ceramic color, and a soupçon of Morocco, Corsica, and Greece. It is, in fact, the best of all Mediterranean worlds—and humble to boot: Menton is the least pretentious of the Côte d'Azur resorts, and all the more alluring for its modesty (though it can be quite a sleepy place compared to Nice, Antibes, or Cannes).

Its near-tropical climate and 316 days of sunshine a year nurture orange and lemon trees that hang heavy with fruit in winter. There's another Florida parallel: the warmth attracts flocks of seniors who warm their bones far from northern fog and ice, happy to leave the noisy city life behind. Thus a large population of older visitors basks on its waterfront benches after their morning dips and browses its downtown shops. But Menton has a livelier, younger side, too (there's even a tango festival every July), and the farther you penetrate toward the east, the more intriguing and colorful it becomes.

GETTING HERE AND AROUND

Trains run all day from Nice and Monaco. There are a couple of bus options: Zou! No. 100 from Menton to Nice ($1.50; 1 hour) or the No. 110 airport express (stopping at Monte-Carlo Casino) is an hour and costs €22 one-way. To get to Monaco via Roquebrune it's Zest Ligne No. 21, or if passing through Beausoleil, take Bus No. 18 (also €1.50), which goes along the seaside to the border.

FESTIVALS

Festival de Musique (*Chamber Music Festival*)

FESTIVALS | During the first two weeks of August, the Festival de Musique classical concerts take place at four locations around town, including the stone-paved plaza outside the church of St-Michel. Last minute tickets can be purchased for €15 at the venue just before the show. ⊠ *Menton* ☎ *04–92–41–76–76* ⊕ *www. festival-musique-menton.fr.*

Fête du Citron (*Lemon Festival*)

FESTIVALS | The Fête du Citron, running from mid-February through the first week of March, is a full-blown lemon love-in: citrus floats made of real fruit glide through town and musicians are on hand

with entertainment. Think of it as France's answer to the Rose Bowl Parade, minus the football. ⊠ *Menton* ☎ *04–92–41–76–95* ⊕ *www.fete-du-citron.com.*

TOURS

Heritage Tours

WALKING TOURS | Menton acquaints you with its rich architectural heritage by offering regular *visites due patrimoine* (heritage tours) to its gardens, cemetery, museums, and villas. Details about each tour (including points and time of departure) can be found at the Menton tourist office or the **Maison du Patrimonie.** ⊠ *Le Palais de l'Europe, 8 av. Boyer* ☎ *04–92–41–76–76* ⊕ *www.menton.fr* 🎫 *From: €6.*

VISITOR INFORMATION

CONTACTS Menton Tourist Office. ⊠ *Le Palais de l'Europe, 8 av. Boyer* ☎ *04–92–41–76–76* ⊕ *www.menton.fr.*

◉ Sights

Basilique St-Michel

RELIGIOUS SITE | This majestic basilica dominates the skyline of Menton. Beyond the beautifully proportioned facade—a 19th-century addition—the richly frescoed nave and chapels contain several works by Genovese artists plus a splendid 17th-century organ. Volunteers man the doors here, so you may have to wait for the church to open before visiting. The parvis plays host to concerts during the Menton music festival every August. ⊠ *Parvis St-Michel, 22 rue St-Michel* 🕐 *Closed weekends.*

Casino Barrière

CASINO—SIGHT | Relaunched as a modern downtown recreation complex, the huge bay windows with sea views may distract you from the slot machines. Celebrate your winnings by dancing the night away at the casion's nightclub, Le Brummell. ⊠ *2 av. Félix-Faure* ☎ *04–93–10–16–16* ⊕ *www.lucienbarriere.com.*

Chapelle de l'Immaculée-Conception

RELIGIOUS SITE | Just above the main church, the smaller Chapelle de l'Immaculée-Conception (aka Pénitents Blancs) answers St-Michel's grand gesture with its own pure Baroque beauty. The sanctuary, dating to 1687, is typically closed to the public; however, you can try and slip in to see the graceful trompe l'oeil over the altar and the ornate gilt lanterns early penitents carried in processions. ⊠ Pl. de la Conception.

Cimetière du Vieux-Château (Old Château Cemetery)

CEMETERY | High above the Parvis St-Michel, the Cimetière du Vieux-Château lies on the terraced plateau where once stood a medieval castle. The Victorian graves here are arranged by nationality, with an entire section dedicated to Russian royalty. The birth and death dates often attest to the ugly truth: even Menton's balmy climate couldn't reverse the ravages of tuberculosis. ⊠ Ch. du Trabuquet.

Hôtel de Ville

GOVERNMENT BUILDING | The 19th-century Italianate Hôtel de Ville conceals a treasure by painter Jean Cocteau: he decorated the **Salle des Mariages** (Marriage Room) with vibrant allegorical scenes; today it is used for civil marriages. ⊠ 17 av. de la République 🖭 €2 ⊙ Closed weekends.

Jardins Biovès (Biovès Gardens)

GARDEN | Directly in front of the tourist office, the broad tropical Jardins Biovès stretches 800 meters (2,600 feet) across the breadth of the center, sandwiched between two avenues. Its symmetrical flower beds, exotic trees, sculptures, and fountains representing the spiritual heart of town are free to visit, except during the Fête du Citron, when they display giant sculptures constructed out of 15 tons of citrus fruit, and also at Christmas, when it has a more festive feel. ⊠ 8 av. Boyer.

Marché Couvert (Covered Market)

MARKET | Between the lively pedestrian Rue St-Michel and the waterfront, the marvelous Marché Couvert (Les Halles) is considered one of the best food markets in France. With its Belle Époque facade decorated in jewel-tone ceramics, it's equally appealing inside, with some 30 merchants selling homemade bread and mountains of cheese, oils, fruit, and Italian delicacies daily (on Saturday, clothing is also sold). Be sure to try barbbajuans, the local dish of fried vegetables and rice. ⊠ Quai de Monléon.

Parvis St-Michel

PLAZA | Up a set of grand tiered stairs that lead from the Quai Bonaparte, the Parvis St-Michel is a broad plaza paved in some 250,000 round white and gray stones patterned in the coat of arms of the Grimaldi family. The plaza was created in the 17th century by Prince Honoré II; the letter H is mingled into the design as a kind of signature at the base of his great gift to the city. ⊠ Menton.

Place aux Herbes

PLAZA | Right by the market, the pretty little Place aux Herbes is a picturesque spot for a pause on a park bench, a drink, or a meal in the deep shade of the plane trees. ⊠ Menton.

Promenade du Soleil

PROMENADE | Stroll the length of Menton's famous beachfront along the Promenade du Soleil: broad, white, and studded with palm trees. ⊠ Menton.

Quai Napoléon III

MARINA | To get a feel for the territory, start your exploration at the far east end of the Vieille Ville and walk out to the end of the Quai Napoléon III, jutting far out into the water. Above the masts of pleasure boats, all of Menton spreads over the hills, and the mountains of Italy loom behind. ⊠ Menton.

Not far from the Italian border, Menton enjoys one of the sunniest climates in France and is home to an amazing array of fabulous gardens open to the public.

Rue St-Michel

NEIGHBORHOOD | Serving as the main commercial artery of the Vieille Ville, Rue St-Michel is lined with shops, cafés, and orange trees. ⊠ *Menton.*

Serre de la Madone

GARDEN | With a temperate microclimate created by its southeastern and sunny exposure, Menton attracted a great share of wealthy horticultural hobbyists, including Major Lawrence Johnston, a gentleman gardener best known for his Cotswolds wonderland, Hidcote Manor. He wound up buying a choice estate in Gorbio—one of the loveliest of all perched seaside villages, 10 km (6 miles) west of Menton—and spent the 1920s and 1930s making the Serre de la Madone a masterpiece. Johnston brought back exotica from his many trips to South Africa, Mexico, and China, and planted them in a series of terraces, accented by little pools, vistas, and stone steps. While most of his creeping plumbago, pink belladona, and night-flowering cacti are now gone, his garden has

been reopened by the municipality. If you don't have a car, you can reach it from Menton via Bus No. 7. ⊠ *74 rte. de Gorbio* ☎ *04–93–57–73–90* 🖃 *€8* ⊘ *Closed Mon., Nov., and Dec.*

Val Rahmeh Botanical Garden

GARDEN | Green-thumbers will want to visit Menton's Val Rahmeh Botanical Garden—especially in the fall when the hibiscus and brugmansias are in bloom. Planted by Maybud Campbell in the 1910s and much prized by connoisseurs, it's bursting with rare ornamentals and subtropical plants, and adorned with water-lily pools and fountains. The tourist office can also give you directions to other gorgeous gardens around Menton, including the Fontana Rosa, the Villa Maria Serena, and the Villa Les Colombières. ⊠ *Av. St-Jacques* ☎ *04–92–10–97–10* 🖃 *€7* ⊘ *Closed Tues.*

🍴 Restaurants

★ Mirazur
$$$$ | **MODERN FRENCH** | Argentine chef Mauro Colagreco learned his craft in Latin America before acquiring a solid French base with the likes of Bernard Loiseau in Burgundy and both Alain Passard and Alain Ducasse in Paris, and now is at the helm at Mirazur, an innovative restaurant on the border of France and Italy that's earned three Michelin stars and is frequently cited as the best restaurant in the entire world. He is a perfect example of the wave of young chefs whose style has been dubbed *la jeune cuisine*; for Colagreco, the plate is a palette, and each ingredient (many gathered from the massive on-site vegetable garden) has its precise place and significance. **Known for:** avant-garde French cuisine by Argentinian-Italian chef; sensational views of the coast; requiring reservations at least six months in advance. [$] *Average main: €160* ✉ *30 av. Aristide Briand* ☎ *04–92–41–86–86* 🌐 *www.mirazur.fr* 🕒 *Closed Mon., Tues., early Jan., and 2 wks mid-Nov. No lunch Wed.*

🛏 Hotels

Hôtel Lemon
$$ | **HOTEL** | Subtropical gardens and 19th-century architecture are two of Menton's main attractions, and this budget hotel a few minutes' walk from the train station gives you a taste of both and at prices rarely seen along the Riviera. **Pros:** plenty of charm at rock-bottom prices; five minutes to the sea; rooms are basic but tasteful. **Cons:** parking can be difficult; street often noisy; no air-conditioning. [$] *Rooms from: €64* ✉ *10 rue Albert 1er* ☎ *04–93–28–63–63* 🌐 *www.hotel-lemon.com* 💳 *No credit cards* 🛏 *18 rooms* 🍴 *No meals.*

Napoléon
$$$ | **HOTEL** | This elegantly modern hotel in Garavan—east of the town center next to Italy—is hard to beat when it comes to value, especially with the attentive service, a solar-heated swimming pool with a fitness room overlooking it, and contemporary furnishings that make it feel like a luxury hotel even though it's not. **Pros:** fantastically warm service; sea and mountain views from upper floors; very accessible with grab bars, shower stools, and elevator. **Cons:** bit of a walk from the town center; parking can be difficult; no restaurant on-site. [$] *Rooms from: €272* ✉ *29 porte de France* ☎ *04–93–35–89–50* 🌐 *www.napoleon-menton.com* 🛏 *46 rooms* 🍴 *No meals.*

Chapter 8

MONACO

Updated by
Nancy Heslin

8

● Sights	⊕ Restaurants	⊟ Hotels	⊜ Shopping	▼ Nightlife
★★★☆☆	★★★☆☆	★★★☆☆	★★★★☆	★★★☆☆

WELCOME TO MONACO

TOP REASONS TO GO

★ **Monte Carlo:** Even if you aren't a gambler, the gold leaf and over-the-top rococo in the casino are definitely worth a long look.

★ **Grace Kelly:** Follow in Grace Kelly's footsteps with a visit to the Pálais Princier, the official residence of the "royal" family, including the actress's grandson, heir apparent Prince Jacques.

★ **Parks:** Yes, Virginia, you can afford to visit Monte Carlo—that is, if you head to its magnificent Jardin Exotique de Monaco.

★ **Museums:** One of the world's best oceanography museums, the Musée Océanographique is an architectural master-piece in its own right.

★ **Beaches:** Monaco's chic waterfront is well-known for its private clubs and people-watching.

Monaco covers just 473 acres and would fit comfortably inside New York's Central Park. (That said, it also reaches a height of 528 feet, so bring some walking shoes.) Despite its compact nature, everybody drives here, whether from the Palais Princier perched on the Rock down to the port or up to Casino Gardens at the eastern tip.

1 Monaco. The principal-ity's sensational position on a broad peninsula that bulges into the Mediterra-nean seduces billionaires and A-listers, as well as those who just want to see how the 1% live. One out of every three people is a millionaire here, with the microstate boasting the world's most expen-sive property to buy ($1 million per 16 square miles) and to rent (up to $220,000 a month).

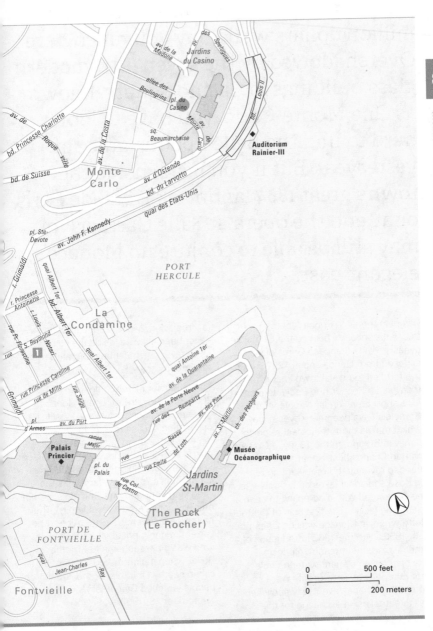

des Spélugues

av. de la Madone

Jardins du Casino

bd. Louis II

allee des Boulingrins

pl. du Casino

av. de la Costa

av. de Monte Carlo

Auditorium Rainier-III

av. de

bd. Princesse Charlotte

Roque- ville

sq. Beaumarchaise

bd. de Suisse

Monte Carlo

av. d'Ostende

bd. du Larvotto

quai des Etats-Unis

pl. Ste-Devote

av. John F. Kennedy

r. Grimaldi

PORT HERCULE

quai Albert 1er

r. Princesse Antoinette

bd. Albert 1er

La Condamine

rue Pr. Florestine

rue S. Reymond Notari

rue Louis

quai Albert 1er

quai Antoine 1er

av. de la Quarantaine

rue Princesse Caroline

rue de Millo

rue Saige

av. de la Porte Neuve

av. des Remparts

av. des Pins

rue des

ch. des Pêcheurs

Grimaldi

pl. d'Armes

av. du Port

rampe Major

Basse

de Loth

av. St-Martin

Musée Océanographique

Palais Princier

rue

pl. du Palais

rue Emile

Jardins St-Martin

rue Col. de Castro

The Rock (Le Rocher)

PORT DE FONTVIEILLE

quai

Jean-Charles

Ray

Fontvieille

0   500 feet

0   200 meters

This compact fairy-tale Mediterranean destination is one of the most sought-after addresses in the world—but even a million dollars won't buy you much here. Overshadowed by the seven ultramodern glass buildings in Casino Square, known as One Monte-Carlo, you have to look hard to find the Belle Époque grace of yesteryear. But if you head inside the town's great 1864 landmark Hôtel de Paris or attend the opera at Salle Garnier, you may still be able to conjure up Monaco's elegant past.

Reigning monarch Prince Albert II traces his ancestry back to the Grimaldi dynasty, when Franceso Grimaldi was expelled from Genoa and in 1297 seized the fortified medieval town known today as Le Rocher (the Rock). Except for a short break under Napoléon, the Grimaldis have been here ever since, which makes them the oldest reigning family in Europe. In the 1850s, a Grimaldi named Charles III saw that the Rock needed revenue, but not wanting to impose additional taxes on his subjects, he contracted with a company to open a gambling facility. The first spin of the roulette wheel in Monaco was on December 14, 1856. With the 1868 introduction of the railroad, the threadbare principality became an elegant watering hole for European society. Profits were so great that Charles eventually abolished all direct taxes; in exchange for this tax-free living, Monégasque citizens have never been allowed inside the casino, as all revenues must be generated from foreigners.

Prince Rainier III, who reigned 1949–2005, worked hard to regain Monaco's glitz and glamour post–World War II occupation and is credited for developing tourism and the financial sector. He married 26-year-old Hollywood star Grace Kelly in 1956, helping to introduce America to Monaco's "royal" family (as there is no king or queen, the Grimaldis are not officially considered a royal family). They had three children: Caroline, Albert (the current reigning price), and Stephanie, who was a passenger in her mother's Rover when it plummeted 120 feet off a cliff in nearby La Turbie. Some 100 million people watched Grace Kelly's funeral on September 18, 1982.

The principality is divided into eight quarters. To the west, bordering Cap d'Ail, is the newest area, Fontvieille, with its rose garden, soccer stadium, and tempting marina-side restaurants. Look up from here and you can see old Monaco-Ville (or Le Rocher), a medieval town perched on the Rock, topped by the palace, the government's national council, the world-class Oceanographic Museum, and the cathedral where Grace Kelly is buried. On the other side is the port-facing La Condamine, which offers a smorgasbord of eateries and pedestrian shopping streets, and connects the Rock to Monte-Carlo, home to Casino Square, the Metropole shopping center, and the illustrious Hotel de Paris.

To the east, Larvotto is all about the beach, restaurants, and bars—including places where you can spend €28 for a glass of water. Currently, Larvotto is also where Monaco's €2 billion land reclamation is underway, and to create the 6-hectare neighborhood by 2026, the government has closed the beach for two years starting September 2019. The Exotic Garden district, behind Fontvieille, includes the magical gardens, Villa Paloma art museum, the Museum of Prehistoric Anthropology, and Princess Antoinette Park, where you can play outdoor badminton and minigolf. La Rousse and Les Moneghetti are Monaco's other, more residential neighborhoods.

As you might expect, even the most modest hotels cost more here than in nearby Nice or Menton, and dining is expensive. For the frugal, Monaco is the ultimate day trip by train and you can find ways to not totally break the bank while here. The Princess Grace Rose Garden in Fontvieille and the Monte-Carlo Japanese Garden are free to stroll around from sunrise to sunset. Pick up some fresh edibles at La Condamine daily market at the Place d'Armes to enjoy while browsing the gardens or look for the daily happy hour at Stars 'n' Bars in the port.

You don't have to be a member of the Yacht Club to eat portside at the Société Nautique, Monaco's rowing club, where the food is as impressive as the views. Art lovers can visit the luminous Opera Galery, next to the Hermitage, for free. At the very least, make use of the free public toilets everywhere.

If lunch is not in the budget, splurge at one of the trendy local cafés to catch a glimpse of the working class (yes, really). With a population of 38,000, every day 55,000 employees make the commute to Monaco.

Planning

When to Go

Even Monégasques escape the swelter of July and August, and the beaches are at their best in June or September. To avoid the shiploads of travelers during high season, visit in the fall or winter. The temperatures may not be as sizzling, but you'll still get color from reflecting diamonds.

FESTIVALS

Monte-Carlo Sporting Summer Festival

MUSIC | Where else but Monaco can you see Lady Gaga and Tony Bennett, Elton John, Rod Stewart, or Duran Duran at a sit-down dinner venue for 700 people? Since 1974, the Monte-Carlo Sporting Summer Festival has been held at Le Sporting, a summer-only entertainment complex on the waterfront with a roof that opens up to the stars, perhaps justifying the €200 ticket (or the €1,000 Red Cross Gala)—although the celebrities are also part of the draw. ☎ 377/98–06–41–59 ⊕ en.sportingsummerfestival.com.

Printemps des Arts

FESTIVALS | Monte Carlo's monthlong spring arts festival, Printemps des Arts, brings together the world's top ballet, operatic, symphonic, and chamber-music performers at venues across Monaco—the Opéra de Monte-Carlo, Oceanographic Museum, Grimaldi Forum, St-Charles Church, and Auditorium Rainier III. ☎ 377/98–06–28–28 ⊕ www.printemps-desarts.com.

Getting Here and Around

If you're flying into the Nice airport, a taxi to Monaco costs a flat fee of €90 (there's no Uber in Monaco). Or you can save time with Monancair's seven-minute helicopter transfer, starting from around €140 one-way (includes door-to-door shuttle service and luggage check—you can even select MCM as your final destination with some airlines). A less glamorous but more affordable option is the Nice AirportXpress to Menton, the 110 bus, which stops in Monaco (45 minutes, €22 one-way).

From Nice, Monaco is serviced by regular trains along the Cannes–Ventimiglia line; from Nice Ville, the main station, the journey costs €4.10 one way and takes 25 minutes. By bus, the Lignes d'Azur Bus No. 100 departs from the Port in Nice, but can be very crowded in high season. You can pay the €1.50 fare on board.

Monaco is a relatively easy place to navigate on foot, especially if you take advantage of its 78 public elevators, 35 escalators, and 8 travelators. But if you're looking for an insider's view, native Jean-Marc Ferrié at Monaco Rando (⊕ www.monaco-rando.com) gives guided walking tours in English, from the secrets of the Rock and the Grand Prix Circuit to the four-hour Via Alpina with stunning overviews of the principality. Prices run €15–€50 per person.

BUS

Compagnie des Autobus de Monaco operates a bus line that threads the avenues of Monaco. Purchase your ticket on board for €2, or save €0.50 a ticket by buying in advance from a ticket machine or online (a 24-hour ticket costs €5.50). The company also operates both the Bateaux Bus, a solar electric boat from Quai des États-Unis to the casino (it runs daily 8–8 and costs €1.50) and the electric MonaBike, where you can rent one of 105 electric bikes for €1 with a valid credit card.

BUS INFORMATION Compagnie des Autobus de Monaco. ☎ 377/97–70–22–22 ⊕ www.cam.mc.

Restaurants

With nine Michelin stars, there is no shortage of lavish dining in the principality, so wear something presentable and don't forget your wallet.

Hotels

Hotel prices skyrocket during the Monaco Grand Prix, so reserve as far ahead as possible. That goes for festivals like the Printemps des Arts as well. No matter the time, however, hotels cost more here than in nearby Nice or Menton. For the cost-conscious, Monaco is the ultimate day trip by train.

Restaurant and hotel reviews have been shortened. For full information, visit Fodors.com.

What it Costs in Euros			
$	$$	$$$	$$$$
RESTAURANTS			
under €18	€18–€24	€25–€32	over €32
HOTELS			
under €125	€125–€225	€226–€350	over €350

Visitor Information

CONTACTS Monaco Tourist Office. ✉ *2 bd. des Moulins, Monte Carlo* ☎ *377/92–16–61–66* ⊕ *www.visitmonaco.com.*

Sights

Casino Monte-Carlo

CASINO—SIGHT | Place du Casino is the center of Monte Carlo and a must-see, even if you don't like to bet. Into the gold-leaf splendor of the 1863 casino, the hopeful descend from tour buses to tempt fate beneath the gilt-edge rococo ceiling—and some spend much more than planned here, as did the French actress Sarah Bernhardt, who once lost 100,000 francs. Jackets are required after 8 pm in the private back rooms, which open at 4 pm. Bring your passport (under-18s not admitted) and note the €17 admission to get into any of the period gaming rooms (open from 2 pm). For €17, you can also visit the casino in the off-hours (daily 10–1) for access to all rooms. ✉ *Pl. du Casino, Monte Carlo* ☎ *377/98–06–21–21* ⊕ *www.casinomontecarlo.com.*

Collection des Voitures Anciennes (*Collection of Vintage Cars*)

MUSEUM | FAMILY | The car collection of the Prince of Monaco is an impressive assemblage of vintage cars, with everything from a De Dion Bouton to a Lamborghini Countach. All were owned by Prince Rainier, with a few models courtesy of his son, Prince Albert, including the Lexus from the princely wedding in 2011. ✉ *5 Terrasses de Fontvieille* ☎ *377/92–05–28–56* ✎ *From €8.*

Jardin Exotique de Monaco (*Tropical Garden*)

GARDEN | More than a thousand varieties of cacti and succulents cling to a sheer rock face at Monaco's magnificent Tropical Garden, a brisk half-hour walk west from the palace. The garden traces its roots to days when Monaco's near-tropical climate nurtured unheard-of exotica, amazing visitors from the northlands as much as any zoo. The plants are of less interest today, especially to Americans familiar with southwestern flora. The views over the Rock and coastline, however, are spectacular. Also on the grounds, or actually under them by descending 300 steps, are the **Grottes de l'Observatoire**—spectacular grottoes and caves adrip with stalagmites and spotlit with fairy lights. The **Musée d'Anthropologie** showcases two rooms: "Albert I" covers general prehistory, while "Ranier III" unearths regional Paleolithic discoveries. And a rarity for Monaco, all three attractions are included in one ticket. ✉ *62 bd. du Jardin Exotique* ⊕ *www.jardin-exotique.mc* ✎ *€8.*

★ Le Tigre Yoga Club and Spa

SPA—SIGHT | Most visitors to Monaco don't know the Monte Carlo Beach Club exists—because it's located so far east it's technically in France. Built in 1929, it features an eye-popping, Olympic-size heated seawater pool overlooking a private beach—and now the ultraluxurious setting is also home to the Parisian concept Le Tigre Yoga Club and Spa, open seven days a week and, most importantly, open to nonclub members. Amid the salty sea and pine trees (and Michelin-star organic restaurant Elsa), daily outdoor group yoga, meditation, and Pilates classes take place on the pontoon. Inside, three exquisitely designed cabanas make up the 80-square-meter Le Tigre Spa, where its deep-tissue signature massage combines Ayurvedic, lomi-lomi, yogic, and Californian techniques to produce a surprisingly energizing yet overall relaxing result (60 minutes; €185). Parking is free (otherwise, take the No. 5 or 6 Larvotto bus and walk 10 minutes) and, if you're lucky, renting a lounger at the Beach Club may round off your well-being experience like a true jet-setter. ✉ *Monte Carlo Beach Club, Av. Princess Grace* ☎ *377/98–06–51–05* ⊕ *www.tigre-yoga.com/en/*

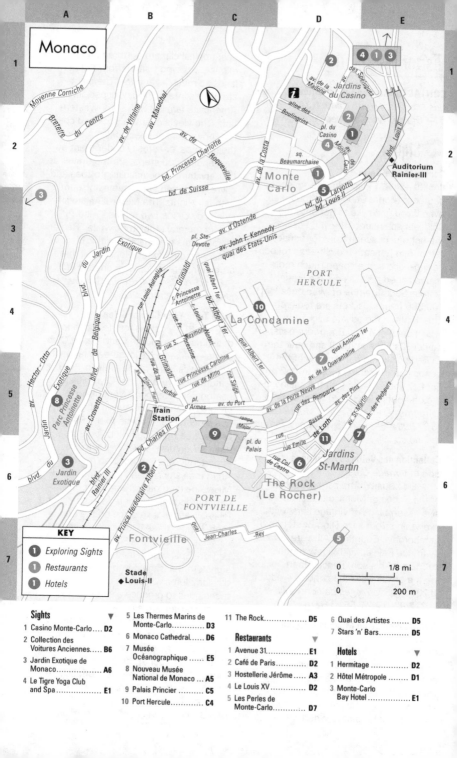

Monaco

KEY

- ● Exploring Sights
- ● Restaurants
- ● Hotels

Sights ▼

1 Casino Monte-Carlo.... **D2**
2 Collection des
   Voitures Anciennes..... **B6**
3 Jardin Exotique de
   Monaco.................. **A6**
4 Le Tigre Yoga Club
   and Spa **E1**

5 Les Thermes Marins de
   Monte-Carlo............ **D3**
6 Monaco Cathedral...... **D6**
7 Musée
   Océanographique **E5**
8 Nouveau Musée
   National de Monaco.... **A5**
9 Palais Princier **C5**
10 Port Hercule............ **C4**

11 The Rock............... **D5**

Restaurants ▼

1 Avenue 31................ **E1**
2 Café de Paris............ **D2**
3 Hostellerie Jérôme **A3**
4 Le Louis XV.............. **D2**
5 Les Perles de
   Monte-Carlo............ **D7**

6 Quai des Artistes **D5**
7 Stars 'n' Bars............ **D5**

Hotels ▼

1 Hermitage **D2**
2 Hôtel Métropole **D1**
3 Monte-Carlo
   Bay Hotel **E1**

capsule/le-tigre-monte-carlo ⊙ *Closed mid-Nov.–mid-Mar.*

Les Thermes Marins de Monte-Carlo (*Sea Baths of Monte-Carlo*)

HOT SPRINGS | Added to the city in the 1990s, this seawater-therapy treatment center stretches along the port's upper side between the landmark Hôtel de Paris and its sister, the Hermitage, and can be accessed directly from either hotel. Within its sleek, 6,600-square-meter multilevel complex, you can pursue every creature comfort, from underwater massage and seaweed body wraps to a 90-minute Prairie Platinum Ultimate Youth Treatment for €330. This is also the only spot in Europe offering cryotherapy, a treatment where you spend a couple of minutes in two cold chambers at -60°C and then-110°C, which is said to help with jet lag, sleep disorders, and antiaging. You'll definitely want to indulge in the outdoor hot tub afterward and enjoy an elegant spa lunch at L'Hirondelle as you thaw. ⊠ *2 av. de Monte-Carlo* ☎ *377/98–06–69–00* ⊕ *www.thermesmarinsmontecarlo.com.*

Monaco Cathedral

RELIGIOUS SITE | Follow the crowds down the last remaining streets of medieval Monaco to the 19th-century Cathédrale de l'Immaculée-Conception, which contains the tomb of Princess Grace and Prince Rainier III, as well as a magnificent altarpiece, painted in 1500 by Louis Bréa. From September to June, the Monaco's Boys Choir (Les Petits Chanteurs) provide the music for Sunday mass at 10:30 am. ⊠ *Av. St-Martin* ☎ *377/93–30–87–70* ⊕ *www.cathedrale.mc.*

★ Musée Océanographique (*Oceanography Museum*)

MUSEUM | FAMILY | Perched dramatically on a cliff, this museum is a splendid Edwardian structure, built under Prince Albert I to house specimens collected on amateur explorations, including Jacques Cousteau–led missions from 1957 to 1988. The main floor exhibits

the Whale Room, with skeletons and taxidermy of enormous sea creatures, early submarines and diving gear dating to the Middle Ages, and a few interactive science displays. The main draw is the blockbuster **aquarium,** a vast complex of backlighted tanks containing more than 6,000 species of fish, crab, and sharks in pools running 100–450,000 liters. ⊠ *Av. St-Martin* ☎ *377/93–15–36–00* ⊕ *www.oceano.mc/en* 🎟 *From €14.*

Nouveau Musée National de Monaco

MUSEUM | Monaco's national museum is actually divided into two separate buildings at opposite ends of town. One of the surviving buildings from the Belle Époque, Villa Sauber, with its rose garden, is in the Larvotto Beach area (take the elevator down from Place des Moulins). The Villa Paloma (next door to the Jardin Exotique) was recently restored with fabulous stained-glass windows. The museums are open to the public only during exhibitions so check the website for more information. ⊠ *Villa Sauber, 17 av. Princesse Grace* ☎ *377/98–98–91–26* ⊕ *www.nmnm.mc* 🎟 *€6.*

Palais Princier

CASTLE/PALACE | The famous Rock, crowned by the palace where the royal family resides, stands west of Monte Carlo. An audio guide leading you through this sumptuous chunk of history, first built in the 13th century and expanded and enhanced over the centuries, reveals an extravagance of 16th- and 17th-century frescoes, as well as tapestries, gilt furniture, and paintings on a grand scale. Note that the **Relève de la Garde** (Changing of the Guard) is held outside the front entrance of the palace most days promptly at 11:55 am. Les Grands Appartements are open to the public from early April through October, and you can buy a joint ticket with the Musée Océanographique. Beginning in mid-July, a summer concert series can be enjoyed at 9:30 pm in the palace's esteemed courtyard. Tickets can be purchased

Monaco's Belle Époque opulence is epitomized by its famed Casino Monte-Carlo, which is just as visually stunning at night.

through the Orchestre Philharmonique de Monte-Carlo (⊕ *www.opmc.com*). ✉ *Pl. du Palais* ☎ *377/93–25–18–31* ⊕ *www.palais.mc* ✉ *From €8* ⊙ *Closed mid-Oct.–Apr.*

Port Hercule

MARINA | It's a blissful hike down from Monte Carlo to the port along Boulevard Albert Ier, where pleasure boats of every shape flash white and blue. You can catch a glimpse of the spectacular yachting club, one of the world's most prestigious and a staple in the local social circuit, where performers like Elton John and Duran Duran have played. It's along here that they erect the stands for fans of the Grand Prix, while the far corner of the port is where the Institut Océanographique launches research boats to study aquatic life in the Mediterranean, as its late director Jacques Cousteau did for some 30 years. You can also access the seawall from here, and get some great shots of the Rock.

The Rock

NEIGHBORHOOD | On the broad plateau known as Le Rocher, or the Rock, the majority of Monaco's touristic sights are concentrated with tidy, self-conscious charm. This is the medieval heart of Monaco, and where its cathedral, palace, and Musée Océanographique can be found, along with the delightful St- Martin Gardens, the country's first public garden (opened since 1816). Only vehicles with Monaco license plates can drive through the gate, so you can either climb up the 42 long steps of the Rampe Majeur from Place d'Armes, behind the right corner of the port, or approach it by elevator from the seafront at the port's farthest end.

Beaches

Larvotto Beach

BEACHES | FAMILY | The pebbly Larvotto Beach just off Avenue Princess Grace, said to be one of the world's most costly streets to live on, is the only free public beach in Monaco, and it has the added bonus of being protected by jellyfish nets. Note that extensive renovations of the beach are currently in the works; it closed completely in October 2019, with plans to reopen July and August 2020. It will be closed again from September 2020 to June 2021. The complete reopening of the beach, with a new promenade and shops, is scheduled for summer 2021. Since construction plans can change, it's always best to confirm if the beach is open before you go. **Amenities:** lifeguards; showers; toilets; water sports. **Best for:** sunrise; sunset. ⊠ *Av. Princesse Grace.*

Plage Mala

BEACHES | This lovely stretch of sandy, shaded land is easily one of the most stylish of the Riviera beaches, and despite its proximity to Monaco—half an hour by foot—Plage Mala's public area never gets crowded. Another upside is that the coves under the impressive cliffs produce the best area for snorkeling along the coast. Nearby are private beach restaurants where you can rent loungers. The 3.5-km (2.2-mile) Mala footpath that stretches to Plage Marquet in Fontvieille in Monaco is relatively easy to walk, with the most challenging leg being the access to Mala beach itself with more than 100 steps. Walking to Monte Carlo generally takes less than an hour; however, avoid the path during stormy conditions. **Amenities:** lifeguard; showers. **Best for:** snorkeling; swimming; walking. ⊠ *Av. Raymond Gramaglia, Cap-d'Ail.*

Restaurants

Avenue 31

$$$ | ITALIAN | Away from the glossy crowds of Monte Carlo but still on one of the world's most expensive streets, you could walk past this unassuming restaurant near Larvotto Beach and not have a clue that its four eating areas are packed with locals loyal to chef Andréa Lanzillotta. Food is reasonably priced (for Monaco), but what's tremendous about 31 is that the simple, locally sourced dishes—salads, pastas, pizzas, grilled beef, and a wealth of fish choices—won't leave you feeling heavy like some Michelin-star meals. **Known for:** tucked away hotspot for locals; gluten-free pizzas and desserts; organic kale salad for vegans. $ *Average main: €28* ⊠ *31 av. Princesse Grace* ☎ *377/97–70–31–31* ⊕ *www. avenue31.mc.*

Café de Paris

$$$$ | BRASSERIE | The landmark Belle Époque "Brasserie 1900"—better known as Café de Paris—offers the usual classics (shellfish, steak tartare, matchstick frites, and fish boned tableside). Supercilious, superpro waiters fawn gracefully over titled preeners, jet-setters, and tourists alike. **Known for:** ultimate spot for people-watching while you eat; Sunday lunch menu; late hours until 2 am. $ *Average main: €36* ⊠ *Pl. du Casino* ☎ *377/98–06–76–23* ⊕ *www.casinocafedeparis.com.*

Hostellerie Jérôme

$$$$ | FRENCH | Prince Albert's country home, Roc Angel, is about 10 km (6 miles) behind Monaco in La Turbie, so it's no wonder a top-notch dinner restaurant (read: expensive, expensive, expensive) with a 30,000-bottle wine cave that picked up France's Best Wine List Award in a gastronomic restaurant is situated here as well. Chef Bruno Cirino's scampi Mediterranean in an almond crust with dates or roasted local white figs, sugared black olives, and buffalo milk sherbet have become signature dishes for a reason. **Known for:** outstanding French wine selection; exquisite dishes; experience of two-Michelin-star dining. $ *Average main: €55* ⊠ *20 rte. Comte de Cessole* ☎ *04–92–41–51–51* ⊗ *Closed Sun., Mon., and mid-Nov.–mid-Feb. No lunch.*

★ Le Louis XV

$$$$ | FRENCH | In Monaco, cosmetic surgery extends even to buildings, and no better example can be seen than at Alain Ducasse's flagship restaurant, the three-Michelin-star Le Louis XV at the Hôtel de Paris. Opulence is all part of the Ducasse experience, which goes beyond his overhauled menu—a return to the Riviera's art de vivre and simplicity, like the Provence garden vegetables cooked with black truffle or baked locally caught fish, tomatoes, and olives from Nice. **Known for:** meal of a lifetime from a celebrity chef; selection of 350,000 bottles of wine; gorgeous decor. [$] *Average main: €100* ✉ *Hôtel de Paris, Pl. du Casino* ☎ *377/98–06–88–64* 🌐 *www.alain-ducasse.com* 🕓 *No lunch Wed. and Thurs. No dinner Wed. Sept.–June* 👔 *Jacket required.*

Les Perles de Monte-Carlo

$$$ | **SEAFOOD** | Tucked away at the far end of the Fontvieille Port, with spectacular views of the Monaco Cathedral and oceanography museum suspended on the Rock above, Clooney and Pitt have been rumored to come here for a *dégustation* (tasting) at the few unpretentious wooden tables and chairs. Whether they were dining next to a prince, a model, or an ordinary local—it wouldn't matter to the owners, two marine biologists who grew up in Brittany—to them, everyone is made to eat the freshest of shellfish, crustaceans, and fish. **Known for:** hands down best seafood (and most affordable meal) in Monaco; unique location akin to eating on a yacht; small space so reservations necessary. [$] *Average main: €25* ✉ *47 Quai Jean Charles Rey* ☎ *377/97–77–84–31* 🌐 *www.perlesdemontecarlo.com* 🕓 *Closed Sun. No dinner Sat., Mon., and Tues.* 💳 *No credit cards.*

Quai des Artistes

$$$ | **FRENCH** | Packing well-heeled diners shoulder to shoulder at banquettes lined up for maximum people-watching, this warehouse-scale neo–Art Deco bistro on the port packs in the chicest of chic Monégasque residents. Rich brasserie classics (lamb shank on the bone, potato puree with rosemary, and spicy gravy) are counterbalanced with high-flavor international experiments (salmon served sushi-rare with warm potatoes, pickled ginger, and wasabi sauce). **Known for:** boisterous ambience; palatial views from the terrace; French brasserie classics with a twist. [$] *Average main: €32* ✉ *4 quai Antoine Ier* ☎ *377/97–97–97–77* 🌐 *www.quaidesartistes.com.*

★ **Stars'n'Bars**

$$ | **AMERICAN** | **FAMILY** | This American-style port-side bar–restaurant–entertainment center is almost like the Monégasque version of the Hard Rock Café, but super eco-friendly and owned by a childhood friend of the prince (the singer Prince, coincidentally, once played a secret concert here). Sports memorabilia and photos hang on the wall, while fat and juicy burgers, barbecue baby back ribs, vegan nachos, pecan pie, real iced tea in thick glasses, and (gasp!) pitchers of ice water make it the heart of Monaco's expat community. **Known for:** no-waste policy: option to order without sides, fries, or buns and pay less; vegan, gluten-free, and allergy friendly; delicious American cuisine. [$] *Average main: €20* ✉ *6 quai Antoine Ier* 🌐 *www.starsnbars.com.*

🛏 Hotels

Hermitage

$$$$ | **HOTEL** | **FAMILY** | They've all been here—kings, queens, Pavarotti in jeans—among the riot of frescoes and plaster flourishes embellished with gleaming brass in this landmark yet relatively low-profile 1900 hotel set back a block from the casino scene. **Pros:** unrivaled meals and views in Michelin-starred Vistamar; best lobby bar in Monaco; free access to Thermes Marins wellness center. **Cons:** expensive, of course; can be noisy; easy to get lost. [$] *Rooms from: €676* ✉ *Sq. Beaumarchais* ☎ *377/98–06–86–83* 🌐 *www.hotelhermitagemontecarlo.com* 🛏 *278 rooms* 🍴 *No meals.*

★ Hôtel Métropole

$$$$ | HOTEL | This Belle Époque hotel, set on land that once belonged to Pope Leon XIII, has pulled out all the stops in its decor—famed Paris designer Jacques Garcia has given the rooms his signature hyper-aristocratic look, and the late Karl Lagerfeld was the architect behind the Odyssey pool and lounge; it also has the unique distinction of housing two Michelin-starred restaurants. **Pros:** flawless and attentive service; free newspapers and Hermès products; one of the best spas in Europe. **Cons:** expensive; parking extra; check-in from 3 pm only. **$** *Rooms from: €587* ✉ *4 av. de la Madone* ☎ *377/93–15–15–15* ⊕ *www.metropole.com* ⇆ *190 rooms* ⦿ *Free breakfast.*

Monte-Carlo Bay Hotel

$$$$ | HOTEL | Perched on a 10-acre peninsula, with 75% of its rooms offering sea views, this highly acclaimed luxury resort—which immodestly bills itself as "a natural Eden reinvented"—seeks to evoke the Côte d'Azur's 1920s heyday with its neoclassical columns and arches, exotic gardens, lagoon swimming pool, casino, and concert hall. **Pros:** one of two proper beach resorts in Monaco; close to nightlife and restaurants; free access to Monte Carlo Casino. **Cons:** breakfast extra; free Wi-Fi only for maximum two devices; might seem a little too over-the-top, even for Monaco. **$** *Rooms from: €575* ✉ *40 av. Princesse Grace* ☎ *377/98–06–20–00* ⊕ *www.montecarlobay.com* ⇆ *356 rooms* ⦿ *No meals.*

Nightlife

CASINOS

Casino de Monte-Carlo

CASINOS | The bastion and landmark of Monte Carlo gambling is, of course, the gorgeously ornate Casino de Monte-Carlo. The main gambling hall is the Salle Européene (European Room), where you can play roulette and Texas Hold 'Em, while the slot machines stand apart in the Salle des Amériques, which all

open at 2 pm and have a €17 admission fee. Bring your passport, as you have to be at least 18 to enter. ✉ *Pl. du Casino* ☎ *377/98–06–23–00* ⊕ *www.casinomontecarlo.com.*

Sun Casino

CASINOS | Described as the "most American" of all the casinos in the principality thanks to a more extensive range of gaming tables, the Sun Casino is part of the Fairmont Monte-Carlo. While you can't hit the tables until 5 pm (4 pm on weekends), slot machines open daily at 2 pm and entry is free (you must be over 18 and snappily dressed). Don't be surprised to cross paths with women's poker champion Isabelle Mercier, a true fan of Sun Casino. ✉ *12 av. des Spélugues* ☎ *377/98–06–12–12* ⊕ *www.montecarlosuncasino.com.*

DANCE CLUBS

Jimmyz

DANCE CLUBS | Dominating the club scene, Jimmyz boasts an edgy reputation that reaches far beyond Monaco. This legendary disco at Sporting Monte-Carlo is not for lightweights: the year-round partying is as serious as the need to be seen, so if surgically enhanced faces and body parts or paying €28 for a water upset you, then stay at your hotel. Note that the club doesn't even open until 11:30 pm. ✉ *Sporting Monte-Carlo, Av. Princesse Grace* ☎ *377/98–06–70–68* ⊕ *fr.jimmyzmontecarlo.com.*

Performing Arts

OPERA

Opéra de Monte-Carlo

ARTS VENUE | In the true spirit of the town, it seems that the Salle Garnier Opera House, with its 18-ton gilt-bronze chandelier and extravagant frescoes, is part of the casino complex. The designer, Charles Garnier, also built the Paris Opéra, and American-born Princess Alice, married to Prince Albert I, is also credited with making the opera a cultural destination. On display are some of the coast's most significant performances of dance, opera, and orchestral music. ✉ *Pl. du Casino* ☎ *377/98–06–28–28* ⊕ *www. opera.mc.*

Shopping

Shopping in Monaco will be pricey, but it can also be a lot of fun. The Promenade Princess Charlene, located behind Casino Square in the One Monte-Carlo complex, is the heart of the most high-end shopping street in all the Riviera. Four of the biggest fashion houses are here side-by-side—Cartier, Louis Vuitton (over three floors), Chanel and Fendi—among new labels including Ralph & Russo and Harry Winston. By the end of 2020, 60 street-level luxury shops will be open along Avenue des Beaux-Arts, including Prada Femmes, Bulgari, Alexander McQueen, and Piaget. You can find the same haute couture at the very casual secondhand shop Queen's Bee at Place de la Crémaillère, run by stylist Katie Holmes (no, not of Tom Cruise fame).

The only couture made in Monaco is by fashion designer Isabell Kristensen, who was Princess Charlene's maid of honor and designed her bridal gown. Isabell's ultrafeminine gowns and cocktail dresses can be seen in her boutique on the Rock (18 rue Princesse Marie de Lorraine). Pick up a bottle of her Monaco perfume (€65), a celestial scent made for Albert and Charlene's wedding.

Another made-in-Monaco product can be found at the atelier l'Orangerie (9 rue de la Turbie). The delicious orange liqueur—a perfect cocktail when mixed with prosecco—was created by Irish-Italian Philip Culazzo who discovered a way to use the bitter oranges produced by Monaco's 600 trees.

Activities

AUTO RACING
Grand Prix de Monaco

AUTO RACING | When the film stars depart, the auto racing begins: the Grand Prix de Monaco takes place the last Sunday of the Cannes Film Festival in May. To watch live, it's €10,000 per person to stand on a balcony overlooking the course. If that's more than you want to spend but you still want to watch action on the same track, pick up tickets for the Thursday practice and qualifying rounds (€80 for Place du Casino seats) or drive the course for free when it opens that same night at 7:30 pm. Tickets for the Historic Grand Prix of Monaco, which takes place two weeks earlier on the same track every other year, run €25–€65. On alternate years, you can see the Formula E, the electric-car racing series. ☎ *377/93–25–47–78* ⊕ *www.formula1.com.*

Index

Photo Credits

Notes